Ideal Embodiment

T0369691

Ideal Embodiment

KANT'S THEORY OF
SENSIBILITY

ANGELICA NUZZO

Indiana University Press
Bloomington and Indianapolis

Publication of this book is made possible in part
with the assistance of a Challenge Grant from
the National Endowment for the Humanities,
a federal agency that supports research, education,
and public programming in the humanities.

This book is a publication of

Indiana University Press
601 North Morton Street
Bloomington, IN 47404-3797 USA

http://iupress.indiana.edu

Telephone orders   800-842-6796
Fax orders   812-855-7931
Orders by e-mail   iuporder@indiana.edu

The paper used in this publication meets the
minimum requirements of American National
Standard for Information Sciences—Permanence
of Paper for Printed Library Materials,
ANSI Z39.48-1984.

Manufactured in the United States of America

Library of Congress Cataloging-in-Publication Data

Nuzzo, Angelica, date
  Ideal embodiment : Kant's theory of sensibility /
Angelica Nuzzo.
      p. cm. — (Studies in continental thought)
  Includes bibliographical references and index.
  ISBN 978-0-253-35229-3 (cloth : alk. paper) — ISBN
978-0-253-22015-8 (pbk. : alk. paper) 1. Kant, Immanuel,
1724–1804. 2. Kant, Immanuel, 1724–1804. Kritik der
praktischen Vernunft. 3. Kant, Immanuel, 1724–1804.
Kritik der reinen Vernunft. 4. Kant, Immanuel, 1724–
1804. Kritik der Urteilskraft. 5. Sensitivity (Personality
trait) I. Title.
  B2798.N89 2008
  193—dc22
                                        2008012205

  1 2 3 4 5 13 12 11 10 09 08

Contents

Preface

IN WHICHEVER WAY THE READER WILL JUDGE THIS BOOK, and whether or not it will challenge or stimulate, the ideas presented here have changed my way of looking at Kant's philosophy and at the historical transition from the early modern period to Kant and, successively, to German Idealism. Furthermore, they have disclosed the possibility of considering classical philosophical problems in a fresh perspective, and offered the opportunity to engage with contemporary philosophical discussions from a new angle.

In writing this preface I find myself thinking more about the exciting future projects to which the work for this book has been leading me, than about the process of writing it. Thus, instead of presenting this volume by telling the story of where it has come from, I shall briefly outline the directions in which Kant's transcendental philosophy—as it emerges from the reconstruction in this book—is bringing me. In other words, I shall tentatively look at the future rather than the past. With this I also express the desire that the work be judged not only for what it directly contributes to Kant scholarship and interpretation, but also for what it brings—indirectly, to be sure, and by way of suggestion—to the endeavor to think with Kant on some important philosophical issues of the present.

I consider this book to be the first part of a larger investigation on the idea of "sensibility" (*Sinnlichkeit*) in Kant's philosophy. While I here advance the interpretive concept of "transcendental embodiment" as key for a new reading of the three *Critiques,* this same concept is now leading me to the further question of the relationship between Kant's "critical" philosophy and his "applied" philosophy. What role does "transcendental embodiment" play in this transition? In particular, how shall the *Anthropology,* the *Metaphysics of Morals,* and even the *Opus Postumum* be read in light of the interpretation of sensibility given in this book?

As mentioned above, thinking of the three *Critiques* in terms of "transcendental embodiment" has led me to view many of the current philosophical proposals—in both the "analytic" and "Continental" camps—in a new perspective. In particular, I have started to notice the presence of Kant's "ghost" in places where contemporary authors claim to be farthest from what they consider to be the flaws of Kantian transcendentalism. By contrast, it also seems to me that what they propose is not so distant from what, I suggest, Kant himself has offered in the *Critiques.* What can we make, then, of this curious predicament: Kant anticipating, unnoticed, his own overcoming in twentieth- and twenty-first-century philosophy?

Finally, the reflection on the idea of "transcendental embodiment" has re-oriented my own interpretation of the immediate post-Kantian debate that leads to Hegel. Here a methodological issue or alternative arises: transcendental philosophy or dialectic? What is the philosophical approach that allows us to come closer to an understanding of the human body? How does Kant's own critical solution of the soul-body problem influence Fichte, Schelling, and Hegel? And how are Herder and Schiller, for example, positioned in this debate?

I am grateful to the many friends and colleagues who have nourished this work over the years. I would like to single out Manfred Baum, Dan Breazeale, George Di Giovanni, Hans Friedrich Fulda, Gianna Gigliotti, David Kolb, David F. Krell, Adriaan Peperzak, and Tom Rockmore for thanks—first for the ongoing discussions, comments, and criticisms that have challenged and stimulated my work, and then for the precious lessons they have taught me with their own work. I am particularly grateful to Tom Rockmore and David F. Krell for having believed in this project over the years and supported it through all its phases; and to John Sallis for accepting the book in the Studies in Continental Thought series. Dee Mortensen has been a wonderful editor—patient, generous, and always helpful.

The support of various institutions has allowed me to concentrate on the research for this book and on its writing. I have benefited from: a grant of the CUNY Research Foundation (2003–2004), a Giles Whiting Foundation Fellowship at Brooklyn College (2004), an Alexander von Humboldt Fellowship (2004–2005), and release time from Brooklyn College (2007).

I hope this will be yet another surprise for Aurora. To her this book is dedicated. She has made my reflection on time and space "real." But her music and her art have convinced me of the importance of the "ideal."

Key to Kant Works Cited

The following abbreviations and editions of Kant's works have been used throughout in the notes. Unless specified, translations are always mine.

AA — *Kants gesammelte Schriften,* Herausgegeben von der Preußischen Akademie der Wissenschaften zu Berlin, Berlin: De Gruyter, 1910ff.—cited as AA followed by volume number (Roman cipher) and page number.

Dissertatio — *De mundi sensibilis atque intelligibilis forma et principiis*—cited according to the Akademie edition (AA II).

EE — *Erste Einleitung in die Kritik der Urteilskraft*—cited according to the Akademie edition (AA XX, 193–251).

KpV — *Kritik der praktischen Vernunft*—cited both according to the original edition: KpV A (Riga: Hartknoch, 1788) followed by page number, and the Akademie edition (AA V).

KrV — *Kritik der reinen Vernunft*—cited according to its two editions: KrV A (Riga: Hartknoch, 1781) and B (Riga: Hartknoch, 1787) followed by page number. The text of the two editions is reprinted in AA III (1787) and IV (1781).

KU — *Kritik der Urtheilskraft*—cited according to the original edition: KU (Berlin/Libau: Lagarde und Friedrich, 1890): the section number (§) is followed by the page number; in longer passages, the additional reference to the page of the Akademie edition is provided (AA V); when the line number of the Akademie edition is also specified, this follows the page number of AA V.

MAT — *Metaphysische anfangsgründe der Tugendlehre*—the second part of the *Metaphysik der Sitten*, cited according to the Akademie edition (AA VI).

MS — *Metaphysik der Sitten*—cited according to the Akademie edition (AA VI).

Prolegomena — *Prolegomena zu einer jeden kunftigen Metaphysik, die als Wissenschaft wird auftreten können*—cited both according to the original edition: *Prolegomena* A (Riga: Hartknoch, 1783) followed by page number, and the Akademie edition (AA IV).

Reflexionen   *Reflexionen* are cited according to the progressive numeration of the Akademie edition of Kant's *Handschriftlicher Nachlass* (AA XIV–XXIII); when longer *Reflexionen* are cited, their number is followed by volume and page.

Religion   *Religion innerhalb der Grenzen der bloßen Vernunft*—cited according to AA VI.

Träume   *Träume eines Geistersehers, erläutert durch Träume der Metaphysik*—cited according to the Akademie edition (AA II).

Ideal Embodiment

Introduction
Transcendental Embodiment

THE HISTORY OF WESTERN PHILOSOPHY FROM THE NINETEENTH century to the present has accustomed us to consider Kant to be the champion of an idea of rationality which each successive philosophical enterprise cannot avoid measuring itself by. In the cognitive and practical sphere, Kant's "Copernican Revolution"[1] aims at isolating an idea of "reason" in its utter *purity*. The pure dimension of rationality constitutes the knowing subject of Kant's epistemology, the rational agent of his ethics, and the evaluating subject of his aesthetics. The aim of isolating a pure, i.e., non-empirical dimension of human rationality is instrumental to the *transcendental* framework of Kant's investigation. In this perspective, what is at stake is not a direct analysis of human experience but the discovery of the a priori conditions of its possibility. However, from early on in the reception and interpretation of Kant's philosophy the notion of rational "purity," coupled with that of reason's "formality," has been often misunderstood and repeatedly brought under attack. The attempt to establish reason's purity—or the transcendental move from experience to its constitutive conditions—has been read as a forceful gesture that sanctions reason's radical independence of, separation from, and superiority to sensibility—both with regard to the empirical sources of knowledge (such as sensation and perception) and to the empirical affections of the will (such as desires, emotions, and feelings). While the idea of transcendental philosophy overcomes the opposition between rationality and sensibility by proposing a new way of conceiving their reciprocal interaction, Kant's project has often been accused of disregarding (or repressing) the "right" of sensibility for the sake of reason's formal purity.

One way to rectify such misconstructions is to assess the meaning of Kant's transcendental turn in philosophy by examining the notion of sensibility it establishes. This is the task that I undertake in the present study. Instead of drawing Kant's idea of rationality to the center, I follow the less traveled path of investigating the idea of sensibility in relation to which Kantian *Vernunft* gains its more or less rightly deserved reputation of purity and formality.

In the framework of Kant's transcendental philosophy, the idea of rationality is complemented and supported by a notion of "sensibility" (*Sinnlichkeit*) that stands largely unprecedented in the history of philosophy. For Kant, sensibility covers a complex territory broadly construed to include different functions such as intuition, sensation, feeling, imagination, desires, affects, emotions, which both the empiricist and rationalist traditions had usually and variously conflated. Human reason is shaped in relation to human sensibility. A common reading of Kant's doctrine puts this general claim as follows: pure rationality, as understanding, must collaborate with sensibility in order for knowledge (i.e., the pure synthesis of cognition) to be possible; yet, as practical reason, it must avoid sensibility for the sake of moral action. My task is to ascertain the extent to which such claims are justified and supported by Kant's texts: what is the notion of sensibility at stake for pure reason and practical reason respectively? Moreover, the opposition between rationality and sensibility seems to be supported by Kant's vocabulary: while understanding and reason are characterized by their activity, indeed by their "spontaneity," Kant uses the traditional language of "receptivity" and "affection" (hence passivity) to indicate the modality proper to sensibility.

Two points need to be underscored from the outset in this regard. The first crucial and often neglected point is that for Kant the notion of sensibility is not coextensive with the sphere of the material and empirical. In his critical philosophy the sphere of sensibility claims an independence of its own—indeed, paradoxically, even a "purity" of its own. The second point concerns the possibility of viewing certain aspects of sensibility as exercising an independent type of "activity"—an activity that is different from those of understanding and reason, but that can claim a right of its own. From the fact that sensibility is somehow receptive in relation to understanding it does not follow that it may not disclose an active—even a spontaneous—aspect. One of the tasks of this book is to show that human sensibility, when viewed in the framework of Kant's critical philosophy, discloses an irreducible *active* component responsible for shaping our human experience of and in the world. Once both points are persuasively argued, we can conclude that the resulting notion of sensibility poses a fundamental challenge to the claim that attributes to reason a preeminence in our intellectual life. Pure reason will have to share that position with pure sensibility. At this juncture, the crux of the matter regards the philosophical perspective that allows us to discover or to see the pure and active dimensions of sensibility. And this leads to an investigation of the specific character of Kant's transcendental inquiry.

Another fundamental aspect of Kant's idea of rationality is that the critically investigated *Vernunft* is specifically *human* reason; just as the experience whose a priori conditions are sought is specifically *human* experience. It is within the limits of "humanity" that pure concepts and principles claim universal and necessary validity. For Kant, human rationality differs both from a divine mind and from mere animal instinct. However, from early on in the history of Kantian interpretation, it has been noticed with suspicion or at least with puzzled surprise that despite its apparent anthropological bent, despite its task of drawing the limits of human reason, the transcendental investigation programmatically rejects all (empirical as well as metaphysical) reference to an alleged "human nature." Which raises the questions: whence the specific "humanity" of Kantian pure reason? What constitutes the human character of the rational subject? Is there a tension between the project of a *transcendental* investigation of "pure" reason and the *anthropological* delimitation of its domain? And what, more generally, is the relation between these two dimensions of Kant's philosophy? These questions lead us, once again, to the issue of the specificity of Kant's transcendental philosophy. My suggestion is that within the transcendental perspective what makes the Kantian subject specifically *human* is the role that the pure a priori dimension of sensibility plays in drawing the limits of a properly human experience.

While Kant's interpreters—supporters and critics alike—have promptly recognized the revolutionary import of his idea of rationality, the novelty and the complexities of his notion of sensibility have hardly attracted specific interest.[2] At the most, only negative consideration has been paid to it, and always in relation to the notion of reason to which sensibility is seen as subservient. In the aftermath of Herder's and Hamann's early protestations against Kant's ideal of rational purity,[3] "real" human sensibility is often deemed absent from the Kantian doctrine so that the critique of an all-too-powerful rationality is often reinforced by the need to reintroduce the destabilizing "impurity" of sensibility into the picture. Kant's *Sinnlichkeit* in its various forms and functions has been judged too reason-like, too pure, too unreal—only a shadow, as it were, of the concrete materiality of senses and affects—to count as the mark of human existence. Consequently, Kant's view of human rationality has been deemed an unreal idealization—both with regard to his a-historical epistemology and with regard to his allegedly inflexible moral rigorism and formal universalism. In Herder's aftermath, the opposition between transcendental philosophy and anthropology has gained force.

More recently, however, things have begun to change in the increasingly vast Kant literature, and more attention has been given to Kant's contributions to anthropology, moral psychology, and the empirical sciences in general. This time, Kant's applied practical philosophy is at the center, namely, the doctrine of the *Metaphysics of Morals* (the *Doctrine of Virtue* in particular), the *Anthropology,* his writings on history, the lectures on *Physical Geography,* and the essay on the *Different Races of Mankind;* in addition, pre-critical works such as the *Observations on the Feeling of the Beautiful and the Sublime* have gained renewed importance. These writings show Kant's multiform interest in the empirical aspects of the human cognitive and practical activity—an interest that seems, by contrast, completely lacking in the transcendental inquiry of the three *Critiques.*[4] Yet the price that such a reevaluation of Kant's account of the sensible side of human existence pays is to sanction—or even reinforce—the methodological opposition between the transcendental investigation of the *Critiques* and Kant's applied philosophy. The realm of a triumphing "pure reason" in which the right of sensibility is utterly denied and all anthropological consideration programmatically set aside is sharply opposed to an account of human nature that is rich in empirical anthropological and historical details. This holds true as well for those recent interpretations that aim, more critically, at showing that Kant's applied philosophy (against his intentions) ultimately infiltrates the a priori framework of reason; that the alleged "purity" of reason is instead racially biased and gendered as it smuggles empirical physical features into its a priori traits.[5]

One general aim of this book is to challenge the opposition between transcendental philosophy and anthropology (or, more generally, the empirical sciences of man) from a perspective internal to Kant's critical philosophy. I will use Kant's transcendental exploration of the articulate sphere of sensibility to make my point. For if we ask what notion of sensibility arises from recent interpretations of Kant's applied philosophy, we discover that the picture has not changed much from Herder's and Hamann's vehement critiques. For Herder and Hamann as well as for those interpreters who play Kant's applied philosophy against its transcendental foundation, human sensibility seems to gain visibility and thereby a right in philosophical discourse only insofar as it displays a distinctly empirical materiality. Carrying this view over to Kant's critical inquiry, such materiality is seen as somehow (more or less programmatically and often unintentionally) affecting the purely intellectual realm of reason's concepts and ideas. Thereby, the fundamental novelty of Kant's critical and transcendental inquiry into the nature and constitution of human sensibility is missed once and for all. For on these accounts, sensibility is nothing more than the undeniable, sheer empirical fact of human receptivity and affectivity linked to our senses and our physical constitution.[6] Kant's discovery of a pure form of sensibility (for example, the a priori form of intuition) is considered a mentalist assimilation of sensibility to reason.[7]

In sum, the inability to recognize a pure, active, and independent side of sensibility in Kant's critical inquiry leads to faulty interpretations. It leads us either to construe pure reason as unreal and inhuman because severed from its vital sensible side, or to make pure reason ultimately illusory since it is always already contaminated by the materiality of the sensible.

In this book, I take a stand against reductive accounts of human sensibility in the interpretation of Kant's philosophy. Through a careful and thorough analysis of Kant's theory, the claim is made that pure reason owes the capacity of establishing itself in the realm of concrete human experience to its embodied sensible condition—and hence that it is not an empty idealization, construction, or fantasy. Transcendentally, the knowing subject of Kant's epistemology, the moral agent of his pure ethics, and the evaluating subject of his aesthetic theory of judgment is a rational embodied being. She is a "human being"—Kant suggests in an important, convoluted formulation of the *Critique of Judgment*—insofar as she is an "animal and yet rational" being; "but not just merely as rational being[s] as such (for example spirit[s]) but also as animal being[s]."[8] The human being is a rational animal that, unlike pure spirits, is constitutively embodied.

The radical novelty of Kant's idea of sensibility is disclosed by his *transcendental* investigation. In the *Prolegomena,* Kant acknowledges: "It never occurred to anyone that the senses might *also* intuit a priori."[9] There is a dimension to our sensibility beyond its merely empirical and material receptivity to external *stimuli,* another dimension to our body than its visible physical traits. On Kant's account, this is a dimension that, historically, has escaped all inquiries, and which only a transcendental questioning is able to disclose for the first time. The transcendental perspective aims at isolating the conditions of possibility of autonomous and irreducible modes of experience. Within this perspective, the human subject is first constituted— in body as well as in purely intellectual faculty—through the distinctive types of experience possible to her. The transcendental approach allows Kant not only to formulate a new conception of reason but also to propose an alternative to the views of sensibility that dominate the history of philosophy. Transcendental philosophy is set as much against materialism as against a *schwärmerisch* spiritualism that eschews the body.[10] The target of Kant's criticism is not only the metaphysical conception of reason (and the metaphysical "dreams" that arise from such reason). He also targets the view according to which *Sinnlichkeit* is only our receptivity to the given, material factuality of the empirical world, a merely passive, empirical side of the human cognitive apparatus that is eventually brought back to or coincides with the bodily senses and constitutes the material vehicle of our experiential contact with the surrounding world. On this latter view the human body is, at the most, a mere *object* of experience.

Ultimately, the aforementioned reductive consideration of sensibility— which was influential in shaping early modern views of moral agency, although cognitively devalued by early modern rationalism, and completely de-legitimized by Hume's skepticism—is the condition on which the mind- or soul-body dualism dominating the modern tradition is formulated. Set against the empirical receptivity of the body and construed in direct opposition to it is the disembodied spiritual dimension of the soul, source of all spontaneity and activity. At the beginning of his philosophical career Kant still tackles the issue of the body's separation from and interaction with the soul (*commercium*)—one of the most intricate questions of the traditional metaphysical debate arising from Descartes's dualism. In the doctrine of the critical period, however, he completely revolutionizes the terms of this

traditional question. So much so that it is hard to relocate it within his philosophy or even to articulate its "successor" in the new critical framework.
This explains why historical discussions of the mind-body problem usually
end with modern philosophy, and only very rarely extend to Kant.[11] These
considerations form the historical background addressed by this study. What
is it in Kant's critical philosophy that puts an end to the mind-body problem
of Cartesian origin? In what sense does transcendental philosophy transform the philosophical discourse concerning the human body once the
metaphysical existence of the soul is definitively abandoned? The answer
to these questions reveals itself crucial for an understanding of the successive philosophical debate in the twentieth century. The latter can indeed be
read, by and large, as an attempt to develop in a non-transcendental way the
topic brought to the fore by Kant's transcendental investigation.[12]

The thesis of this book is that Kant's transcendental doctrine puts an
end to the traditional mind-body dualism precisely by giving visibility for
the first time to a pure, a priori dimension of our sensibility (cognitive, practical, and aesthetic)—a dimension that is irreducible to purely mental activity and is necessarily embodied. Thereby, Kant proposes a new "method"
for addressing the topic of human embodiment in philosophical discourse.
Kant fights Cartesian dualism on two fronts. First, transcendental philosophy dismantles the metaphysical doctrine of a disembodied, purely spiritual
soul—the dimension of an alleged inwardness untouched by all external
sensible affection (this happens in the Paralogisms of the first *Critique*). Second, it overcomes the merely factual and material view of human sensibility
by proposing a new, transcendental notion of embodiment according to
which the *form* of the body constitutes an a priori of our judgments, thereby
gaining an unprecedented significance in our cognitive, practical, and aesthetic experience. Throughout the itinerary of transcendental philosophy
that Kant develops in the three *Critiques,* the metaphysical concept of "soul,"
with its claim of immortality and after-life, entirely loses plausibility both
in theory and practice; the "body," on the contrary, gains an unprecedented
new dimension, namely a transcendental, purely formal side that promotes
it to active *locus* of specific transcendental a priori principles.[13] These principles play a fundamental role as conditions of the possibility of human
experience. On this view, the body is no longer a mere *object* of experience
but the necessary *a priori condition* thereof. As Kant suggests in the 1786 essay
"What Does It Mean to Orient Oneself in Thinking?" the human body,
considered in its transcendental a priori form, becomes the compass for our
"orientation" in the world—the human as well as natural world.

Moreover, if it is generally accepted that the aim of Kant's transcendental inquiry is to draw the extent and limits of human reason, we need to ask: how does Kant argue for the specifically *human* form of rationality? What is it that constitutes "humanity" (*Menschheit*) for Kant? The thesis of this book is that Kant does not ground the humanity of reason in an alleged (metaphysical or empirical) concept of "human nature" but in the *transcendental* human form of its embodiment, that is, in the distinctly human experiences made possible by the a priori of the human body, i.e., by the a priori of its sensibility. Ultimately, the difference between the human being and a divine being on the one hand, and animals on the other, is neither a metaphysical nor a physical but a *transcendental* difference: it is a difference in the type of cognitive and practical experience that defines the human being as such; it is a difference that only a transcendental investigation can bring to the fore.

In the following study, I designate the new idea of the body emerging from Kant's critical inquiry as "transcendental embodiment."[14] This concept is the guiding thread of my investigation. What is the human body and what is its sensibility within the *transcendental* perspective of the three *Critiques*? Herein, both the observation of its physical features and the analysis of its anthropological traits are in principle excluded. There is a formal side to the human body that is constitutive of our experience of rational subjects—both in our knowledge of the world and in our action in it. This formal side of our embodied condition, however, is only "visible" to (and only made visible by) a transcendental investigation. On Kant's account, the transcendental perspective discloses a purely formal, a priori, and thereby active (and not simply receptive) dimension of sensibility that constitutes the hitherto (philosophically) invisible form of the human body—the complex and multifunctional form that makes our cognitive, practical, and aesthetic orientation in the world possible.

The present work is a systematic investigation of Kant's notion of sensibility in the three *Critiques,* guided by the interpretive concept of "transcendental embodiment." Unlike the great majority of recent studies, it does not concentrate on Kant's applied philosophy but on its *critical-transcendental foundation.* Following the itinerary of the transcendental project from its pre-critical inceptions in the 1766 *Dreams of a Spirit-Seer* and the 1768 essay "On the Ultimate Ground of the Differentiation of Regions in Space" to its very last results in the 1790 *Critique of Judgment,* it is the first comprehensive study on the topic. The notion of transcendental embodiment provides the unifying thread of Kant's epistemology, moral philosophy, aesthetics, and teleology of living nature. As indicated above, the crucial question that I pursue in the three parts of the book—dedicated, respectively, to the *Critique of Pure Reason* (1781/1787), the *Critique of Practical Reason* (1788), and the *Critique of Judgment* (1790)—regards the specifically *transcendental* perspective within which Kant construes the human body and its sensibility. With the concept of transcendental embodiment I defend the novelty and irreducible character of Kant's transcendental philosophy concerning the issue of the conditions of validity of our judgments, and not, on the contrary, the different issue of the production of the contents of our mental activity, or the problem of the "application" of those conditions to concrete "cases occurring in experience."[15] Transcendental embodiment indicates the philosophical methodology that Kant elaborates in the three *Critiques,* bringing to light the *formal* dimension of sensibility, namely, the only dimension that can provide a priori conditions constitutive of a universal human experience of the world. Transcendental embodiment is neither an anthropological concept nor does it disclose an anthropological view of the subject; it is rather the concept whose articulation makes anthropology ("from a pragmatic point of view") possible for the first time. Methodologically, the notion of transcendental embodiment is opposed to the empirical view of the body as "object" of experience that arises from disciplines such as physiology, psychology, anthropology, or phenomenology. The latter all rest on the assumption that the body is something given, a self-evident (indeed a trivial) unquestionable, and yet merely contingent "fact" proper to the human being—a physical fact that we might discover empirically, observe physiologically and anthropologically, describe phenomenologically, reconstruct genetically or historically, and examine in its psychological implications.[16] Within Kant's transcendental investigation, on the contrary, the body is never a physical given; it is itself the condition for something to appear to us as a fact (and to be experienced as a fact). Once again: the body is not a (more or less contingent) *object* of experience but a necessary *a priori condition* thereof. As the transcendental site of sensibility, the body displays a formal, ideal dimension essential to our experience as human beings. Such experience could not be possible if it were not rooted in the formal structure of our embodiment. Transcendentally, the body articulates, according to specific a priori principles, autonomous spheres of experience in which the worldly dimensions of human life (man as *Weltwesen,* says Kant in the third *Critique*) are taken into account and justified in their claim of universality and necessity.[17] Transcendentally, the body is the *locus* in which different functions of sensibility such as imagination, intuition, and affects are exercised. To this extent, the notion of transcendental embodiment is broader, more comprehensive, and interpretatively more fundamental than each of the functions of sensibility.[18]

Articulating in its full critical potential the notion of transcendental embodiment, this book follows the way in which the three *Critiques* construe the irreducible spheres of human experience: the cognitive, the practical, and the reflective aesthetic experience of ourselves and the world of living nature. Systematically, Kant's applied philosophy—his moral psychology, anthropology, and philosophy of history—is possible only once the transcendental dimension of human embodiment has been spelled out in its entirety. Ultimately, its possibility is disclosed by the conclusion of the critical itinerary in the *Critique of Judgment*. Thereby, this study proposes itself as the necessary tool for any further inquiry into Kant's applied philosophy. An understanding of the specific "transcendental" character of Kant's philosophy is necessary for any attempt at comprehending the relation between his applied philosophy and the critical principles, and such an understanding is deeply needed in contemporary Kant interpretation.[19]

The present volume revisits Kant's fundamental notion of experience in the independent realms of theoretical knowledge, moral action, aesthetic appreciation of beauty, and teleological evaluation of nature, showing how our human embodied predicament contributes the necessary transcendental conditions that make experience possible for the first time. Such is the condition of space—embodied in the distinction between our left and our right hand—for knowledge; such is the peculiar uneasiness (or displeasure) produced in us by the feeling of respect for the moral law with regard to our subjective experience of freedom; and such is the feeling for our own life (*Lebensgefühl*) and for other living creatures in our aesthetic and teleological experience of nature.

Incarnated in the distinction between our left and right hands, oriented space is the first cognitive form that embodiment displays if considered transcendentally. Kant's transcendental inquiry reveals in the a priori form of the body the condition that makes it possible for us to distinguish "different regions in space" such as the oriented dimensions of objects external to ourselves (that is, to our body) or the cardinal points in relation to which we orient ourselves geographically in the world. Kant's claim already in the pre-critical essay "On the Ultimate Ground of the Differentiation of Regions in Space" is that spatial orientation is not a concept but an intuition (or "feeling") that makes possible an experience of certain objects (including our own body insofar as it is considered, this time, materially) as distinctly oriented. Kant's doctrine hinges on the connection between the left *hand* and the spatial direction "left." There is a formal dimension to our bodily asymmetry that is not simply a physical fact but a necessary condition that allows for the construction of the oriented space of our experience of external objects. In other words, while having two hands which differ for the impossibility of exchanging their respective gloves is an empirical fact, the possibility of distinguishing them as oriented according to the directions left and right is the transcendental key to our cognitive organization of the external world.

In the practical sphere, if we accept that the moral agent is, as I suggest, a necessarily embodied rational agent, we need to ask: does Kant's claim that the will's freedom, in the negative sense, is its "independence" of a desired object imply an elimination of human desire as such? Or does it rather lead to a different—non-empirical, neither anthropological nor psychological but specifically transcendental—account of desire, feeling, emotion, and passion? While sensibility for Kant ought to be excluded from the foundation of moral theory, it does play an important role in showing how the intimations of practical reason can indeed become, subjectively, *Triebfeder* (drive) and play the role of actual motive in our choice. Kant argues that the moral law, though valid for all rational beings, is an imperative only for the human being, i.e., for a rational being whose *arbitrium* is *arbitrium sensitivum* (neither *brutum* as in irrational animals nor *sanctum* as in pure spirits). In the second *Critique,* the transcendental form of the body is the condition that allows us to experience, subjectively, the force of the moral law—its figure is the only a priori *produced* moral feeling, namely, the feeling of "respect for the law" (*Achtung fürs Gesetz*).[20]

Finally, the transcendental significance of our embodied condition allows us to gain a feeling for our own life, a qualified sense of *aesthetic* pleasure (or displeasure) for our being alive, and to represent ourselves as integral parts of the whole of living nature. Such are the aesthetic experience of beauty, the feeling of the sublime, and our teleological reflection on living nature. The human being, for Kant, is the result of this complex experience, the construction of this reflection. The human being (or human nature) is not the starting point but the final result of Kant's critical inquiry.

Historically, this book places Kant's philosophy at the watershed between two radically different ways of considering the human body. Thereby, it reveals yet another, hitherto unnoticed "Copernican Revolution" brought forth by Kant's philosophy.[21] On the one hand, as mentioned above, it argues that the gesture of disclosing a new a priori active (and not merely passive) dimension of human sensibility—of revealing, transcendentally, the embodied nature of human experience—dissolves the privileged status of the metaphysical soul and puts an end to the traditional mind-body dualism of Cartesian origin. On the other hand, the interpretive notion of transcendental embodiment suggests that historically Kant's discovery of an a priori dimension of human sensibility in the spheres of knowledge, ethics, and aesthetics makes possible the emphasis on the human body and its sensibility that characterizes successive philosophical (and anthropological) projects of the nineteenth century—as different as Fichte's, Hegel's, Feuerbach's, and Marx's on the one hand, Schopenhauer's and Nietzsche's on the other. And the same holds for philosophical projects of the twentieth century such as Heidegger's existential analysis of time and space, Merleau-Ponty's phenomenology of the flesh, Levinas's ethics, and Ricoeur's philosophy of the will. To be sure, in all these cases, Kant's heritage is perceived as a largely or merely negative one: the task is to offer the radical alternative to Kantian reason's "inhuman" purity. And yet, it is Kant's gesture of freeing the human body from the reductive constraints of mere empirical investigation or "observation" that places the philosophical consideration of human sensible nature on a new basis. The possibility of considering human experience as fundamentally embodied experience and of attributing to it a crucially positive significance is disclosed by the transcendental turn that rejects the objectifying view of the body as (first) datum of experience, seeing in it the chief formal condition of experience itself. Thus, while the above-mentioned philosophers see their anthropological (and historicist) commitment in direct opposition to Kant's notion of pure reason, the present study uncovers the deeper, positive Kantian heritage of post-Kantian philosophy. It shows that the "anthropological turn" is *somehow* rooted within Kant's own transcendental investigation of the conditions of the possibility of a *human* experience. The post-Kantian reflection on human finitude and on the distinctive character of human reason can be understood—historically as well as systematically—only in the aftermath of Kant's new philosophical perspective on the human body.[22] Moreover, put very generally, one can claim that Heidegger's later anthropological shift in relation to Husserl, and Merleau-Ponty's transcendental turn in relation to Sartre, only repeat Kant's own little-noticed, hardly investigated, but deeply anthropological shift at the level of transcendental philosophy to which this study is dedicated.

Ultimately, the reading of Kant's transcendental philosophy proposed by the present study sheds new light on the most current developments of Continental philosophy in the tradition of Heidegger's reading of Kant or Merleau-Ponty's reorientation of phenomenology toward the body. In this case as well, concepts such as the idea of imagination (for Sallis), the feeling of respect, the idea of "sensuality" (for Lingis), and the sublime (for Lyotard)[23]—all originally Kantian concepts—allow philosophers to reevaluate the embodied aspect of human experience and yet to do so while criticizing and correcting Kant's allegedly too pure and formal idea of rationality. It is generally taken for granted that those concepts, in Kant's transcendental philosophy, do not have the embodied, rich meaning that is now attributed to them. In this case as well, I want to uncover the positive Kantian debt of these most recent philosophical positions. In these works imagination, feeling of respect, and the commotion produced by the sublime can do the interesting work they do because, in Kant's philosophy, they are all already instances of what I call "transcendental embodiment"—that is, they are not merely empirical, passive responses to events but active ways of shaping our human embodied experience.

Part I, "The Body in Theory," investigates the role that sensibility plays in Kant's theory of knowledge. The human body, as site of sensibility, displays for Kant a priori transcendental structures. In the *Critique of Pure Reason*, Kant distinguishes two general forms of sensibility, namely "intuition" and "sensation." While sensation is always empirical, material, and therefore a posteriori, intuition may be formal and pure, and to this extent given a priori. Time and space as a priori forms of sensible intuition indicate, transcendentally, the cognitive dimension of human embodiment. The first part of the book shows how Kant's doctrine of space is the foundation of both his epistemology and moral theory (as will become clear in the second part). Taking its departure from an analysis of the pre-critical essay "On the Ultimate Ground of the Differentiation of Regions in Space," it argues that the notion of space is rooted in our own body, in the sense of orientation that allows us to intuitively distinguish our left from our right hand, to distinguish ourselves (and our "self") from the outside world. The claim is that we owe our capacity for orientation in the world, that is, the construction of a coherent experience of nature as mechanism through its universal laws, to reason's embodiment. Kant's critique of the metaphysical doctrine of the disembodied soul (already in the *Dreams of a Spirit-Seer* and then in the Paralogisms of both editions of the first *Critique*) is the direct consequence of the thesis that the subject of knowledge is necessarily an embodied being. Furthermore, Kant's idea of freedom is based on the claim that the practical determination of the will by pure practical reason must take place in a "moral space" that is utterly independent of the sensible condition of our empirical intuition (which is the ground, instead, of the determinism of natural events and of our "sensible character"). Transcendentally, it is a new form of *practical embodiment* that defines our specifically moral orientation in the world; it allows us to place the "starry skies *above*" and "the moral law *within*" ourselves,[24] and provides reason with a feeling of orientation "in the immeasurable space of the supersensible."[25]

The idea of "practical embodiment" is the focus of the second part of the book, "The Body in Practice," which draws Kant's 1788 *Critique of Practical Reason* to the center. Here the construction of moral personality is addressed with regard to the role that the body plays in the context of the second *Critique*. "Independence" from all kind of sensibility (from space and time as well as from desires and natural inclinations) defines, for Kant, the negative concept of freedom.[26] However, this definition can lead to a positive concept of freedom only if it refers to a being that may or may not be determined by sensibility (i.e., by sensible desires, passions, and emotions). The negative concept of freedom is, on the contrary, a mere tautology for a holy will whose subject, by definition, does not have sensibility at all. Accordingly, while Kant repeatedly states that the moral law is valid for every rational will as such, the moral law is an "imperative" (and properly a "law") that discloses the consciousness of freedom, proves its objective reality as a "fact," and produces a certain peculiar feeling of reverence or "respect" only for the human being, that is, for a being endowed with reason, will, *and a sensitive body*. In Kant's moral philosophy, however, the specificity of the human subject ought to emerge in a *transcendental* way. Embodiment is the condition that *transcendentally* (that is, neither physically nor metaphysically) defines the moral subject of Kantian ethics. It follows that embodiment, for Kant, is neither a matter of anthropology nor a concern of moral psychology in the first place. Rather, it defines the project of a new transcendental and critical theory of practical sensibility. The "body" of practical reason is not the physical, visible, and natural body of the individual agent. It is the *transcendental form in and through which* action is put into reality by a rational subject (a person) as a purely and genuinely moral action. The legislation of reason and the consciousness of freedom connected to it define the moral space in which reason is embodied. The embodied human being (and not an alleged "human nature") is the final result, not the starting point, of Kant's inquiry in the *Critique of Practical Reason*.

Part 2 addresses this relationship between freedom and its law and the agent's "sensible character" while bringing to the fore the way in which the body is practically construed in its purely *transcendental* form. Transcendentally, practical sensibility—or the practical form of the agent's body—is not an empirical feature given by nature (and anthropologically or psychologically observable) but something *produced* in its form by the determination of the will through the moral law. Such is the peculiar character of the unique practical feeling of pleasure and displeasure allowed by Kant in his moral theory, namely, the feeling of respect for the law—a feeling that *does not precede but necessarily follows* as a consequence from the intellectual determination of the will. Thus, the practical form of the body is the first *effect* of reason's intelligible causality. Respect for the moral law is the only occurrence of a feeling that displays an a priori origin in relation to pure practical reason. This feeling is pure, and is the object of the peculiar "aesthetic" of practical reason—an "aesthetic of morals," as Kant will call it as late as 1797.[27] The feeling of respect applies only to human beings on the basis of their embodied condition—it cannot be assumed in animals, nor in a divine or holy will from which all sensibility is in principle excluded.

The third part of the book, "The Body Reflected," is dedicated to Kant's *Critique of Judgment.* It investigates the role played by the condition of embodiment with regard to the peculiar feeling of pleasure and displeasure that defines our aesthetic appreciation of beauty, our feeling for the sublime, and that grounds our search for order, meaning, and harmony in nature considered, this time, not as a mechanism of universal laws but as the "labyrinth"[28] of its manifold particular forms. In this labyrinth we face a new problem of orientation. The concept of life, transcendentally considered, is suggested as the unifying thread of the two halves of Kant's last critical work.

The interpretive concept of transcendental embodiment allows me to follow the successive development of Kant's notion of *Sinnlichkeit* up to the doctrine of "reflective judgment"—aesthetic and teleological—in the third *Critique.* In the first *Critique,* sensibility displays a priori structures only with regard to intuition; the body plays a transcendental role only with regard to the form of space (and time). Since sensation and feeling are excluded because of their materiality, and since sensation and feeling are associated with taste, a critique of taste cannot be "aesthetics" for Kant at this time but, at the most, only the object of psychology: a "transcendental aesthetics" has, for him, a merely cognitive value. The central point of the second *Critique* is to prove that pure reason can indeed be practical, that is, can determine the will purely and immediately to action without resorting to desires and inclinations. Thereby Kant shows that practical reason is no longer simply a "faculty of desire" empirically determined by the feeling of pleasure and displeasure. Practical reason is legislative independently of desire and feeling. Against a longstanding tradition, Kant denies feeling any *practical* significance (in the strong moral sense given by the idea of freedom). Thus, the second *Critique* makes room for the specific field of inquiry proper to the *Critique of Judgment,* namely, to the region of sensibility occupied by the "pure" feeling of pleasure and displeasure. Transcendentally, feeling has neither theoretical nor practical value for Kant. Rather, it is the pivotal concept of a theory of aesthetic judgment—an aesthetics that is thoroughly independent of both theoretical and practical concerns and interests. In 1788, intuition still has an exclusively theoretical use in relation to the faculty of knowledge (whereby is entirely excluded from the practical sphere). Sensation, instead, produces empirical cognition in relation to the understanding, and contributes to the will's empirical affection in relation to the faculty of desire.[29] Accordingly, in 1788 Kant offers the practical transformation of the materiality of sensation into a peculiar form of "moral feeling," namely, the feeling of respect. In both the first and second *Critique,* Kant's "aesthetics" betrays the specific perspective of the embodied human being, that is, a being whose existence is placed in space and time, who distinguishes an inner sense and an outer world, and whose will may follow the pure determination of the moral law but may also fall prey of material desires. In 1788, however, aesthetics or the transcendental theory of sensibility is no longer limited to cognition but becomes relevant in the practical sphere as well. Finally, in the *Critique of Judgment,* Kant strengthens the connection between sensation and feeling, while allowing for a use of intuition without determinate concepts according to which the imagination connects it to the feeling of pleasure and displeasure. In this way the third *Critique* brings to the fore the far-reaching consequences of Kant's pure foundation of ethics. Precisely because the feeling of pleasure and displeasure has been excluded from the sphere of the practical as a possible motive of moral action, it can now appear as a separate and independent faculty endowed with an a priori principle of its own. This is Kant's third and final transcendental "aesthetic," which is no longer "aesthetics" but a theory of *aesthetic judgment.* Aesthetic judgment is neither cognitive nor practical nor psychological. Its aesthetic value is now a specific value of its own, grounded in a specific a priori principle, and connected a priori with the feeling of pleasure and displeasure.

Part 3 presents the concept of life as the unifying center of Kant's *Critique of Judgment.*[30] Here I follow the important shift that leads Kant from the focus on our "experience *in life*," which emerges with the rejection of the metaphysical doctrine of the soul's after-life in the Paralogisms and is further explored in the second *Critique,* to the question of our "experience *of life*"—our own life and the life of other natural beings, which is the distinctive topic of the third *Critique.* I argue, first, that life is, for Kant, a matter of a specific form of human *sensibility:* an aesthetic matter that concerns our faculty of judgment and a peculiar *feeling* connected to it. This feeling is a feeling for our own life and a sensitivity for living nature in its manifold appearances and expressions. Second, and more generally, I contend that only reflection or the activity of the reflective faculty of judgment can disclose a transcendental perspective on our experience *of life*—in ourselves and in other beings. The a priori connection between reflection and the peculiar feeling of pleasure and displeasure betrays the embodied condition of our judgment. Only because we are *embodied* beings can we gain, by means of reflection, the awareness of being alive and part of living nature. The transcendental condition that makes our experience of life possible—an experience that is neither theoretical nor practical but specifically "aesthetic"— is "reflection" as the transcendental dimension of a new form of human sensibility. Kant's presentation of this condition implies a discussion of the difference between animal and human life: for Kant, the sense for beauty is distinctively proper to human beings and to them alone.

The conclusion of the book investigates the mediating function that Kant assigns to the faculty of judgment and its peculiar new feeling of orientation that, leading us out of the chaotic labyrinth of nature, is at play between the sensible and the supersensible elements within and without ourselves. I argue that reflective judgment fulfills the function of connecting the two realms of the sensible and the supersensible because its activity is thought under the transcendental condition of human embodiment. Transcendentally, reflection lends to reason's ideas (particularly to the idea of freedom) a sensible body that can be concretely *felt,* for example, in the experience of the sublime. Kant's critique of aesthetic and teleological judgment articulates the different ways in which the supersensible is rendered sensible in the world of living nature. While ideas inevitably appear as disembodied to the cognitive efforts of speculative reason, gaining objective reality only through the legislation of practical reason—a reality, however, that has exclusively moral validity beyond experience—in the space opened up by the third *Critique* ideas gain a new sensible body *within experience.* "Aesthetic ideas" are the *pendant* of reason's ideas.[31] Not only can their reality be immediately *felt,* but the peculiar feeling produced in us by embodied ideas allows the human subject to gain a new insight into her place in the world. The teleological, regulative concept of the human being as "final purpose" of creation is the result of such reflection. In conclusion, Kant's moral theology is presented as the final result of the critical articulation of the topic of transcendental embodiment. Eventually, only the experience of ourselves as embodied living and moral beings brought forth by reflective judgment can lend (human) "value" to the results of both theoretical and practical reason's enterprises in this world.

Part 1

THE BODY IN THEORY

A traveler who has lost his way
should not ask, Where am I?
What he really wants to know
is, where are the other places?
He has his own body, but he
has lost them.

—KENNETH REXROTH,
A Prolegomenon to a Theodicy,
1925–1927

I

Bodies in Space

Rhymes and Reasons.
Mouth, south. Is the mouth south someway?
Or the south a mouth? Must be some.
South, pout, out, shout, draught.

—JAMES JOYCE, *Ulysses*

THERE IS A CURIOUS PROPERTY SHARED BY A WIDE VARIETY OF creatures, artifacts, and geometrical figures that also plays an indispensable role when we perform such common acts as observing the motion of the sun and stars, reading a geographical map, or moving from the place where we stand toward a given destination. What does a map of the sky or the earth have in common with the shell of a snail, the hop or bean that coils itself around a pole, a screw, and the geometry of the spherical triangle? The common feature observed across these different phenomena and realms did not cease to intrigue Kant throughout his philosophical career. His theory of space as an a priori form of sensible intuition—a central piece of transcendental philosophy in the critical period—arises out of a longstanding reflection on the special property displayed by such a broad range of phenomena. Kant initiates this reflection as early as 1768 in the essay "On the Ultimate Ground of the Differentiation of Regions in Space." He takes it up again in the 1770 *Dissertatio de mundi sensibilis atque intelligibilis forma et principiis,* and he presents it three other times in the later critical period: in the 1783 *Prolegomena to Any Future Metaphysics that Shall Come Forth as Science,* in the 1786 *First Metaphysi-*

cal Principles of Natural Science, and in the essay which appeared in the same year, "What Does it Mean to Orient Oneself in Thinking?"

Kant designates the peculiar property in question as spatial "incongruence" and the objects that display it as "incongruent counterparts" (*inkongruente Gegenstücke*). In more recent mathematical terminology, this is the property that defines "enantiomorph" objects. Technically, and very generally, we meet incongruence or enantiomorphism when we deal with systems of relations among objects or parts of objects in a three-dimensional oriented Euclidean space.[1] Incongruent counterparts are objects which, being identical in size, dimensions, proportions, and relative position of their parts, differ in being mirror-image reflections of each other.

Every time that Kant addresses the issue, however, he seems to favor a more intuitive, commonsense approach to the core property of incongruence. In his repeated argument, the essential asymmetry that characterizes incongruent objects is always and most clearly revealed to us by the observation of our own body. Our hands and ears, although profoundly similar, differ from each other essentially in one respect: they are necessarily a *left* hand or ear and a *right* hand or ear. The same constitutive asymmetry is at stake when we feel our heart beating *only* in the *left* side of our body. To be sure, it is not observation, in the first place, but a more original internal "feeling" of our body that discloses to us the property in question. What does the difference between our left and right hand or the property of being left- or right-oriented say about the nature of space?

Space, Sensibility, and Embodiment

Given the immediate commonsense experience that our own body offers to us, left and right hands provide Kant with a privileged entry-point into all the discussions of incongruent counterparts. After having perceived the difference between our left and right hands, we can extend our consideration to snails, hops and beans, screws, maps of the sky and the earth, and finally to complex geometrical figures or the physical problem of rotation. Moreover, since Kant uses the case of incongruent counterparts to disclose some crucial properties of space (metaphysical properties in the 1768 essay, transcendental properties in the following writings), and since the discovery of the nature of space (namely, its "transcendental ideality")[2] plays a pivotal role in Kant's theory of knowledge, we can claim that the example of the human body and its parts has a place directly at the center of his epistemology.

However, left and right hands are not just "examples"[3] of an idea of space that is either in the process of its formulation or stands as already formulated in its general terms. In the 1768 essay, the example of the left/right hand is so essential for Kant that it functions as the only viable way to pinpoint a property of space that would otherwise remain hidden. Yet our left and right hands are also not just concrete, evident *instances* of that property. Kant's more radical claim is that we need to *use* our left and right hands in order to understand how "left" and "right" work in the outside world, and ultimately to *know* of the incongruence of incongruent objects. We need to put to use a formal characteristic of our body (namely, its oriented asymmetry) if we want to know any object of the outside world. Neither our senses nor our understanding alone is sufficient to that task. For only by referring any perceived outer object to our left and right hands (or to the left/right side of our body) can we become aware of a difference that constitutes the very essence of space and that alone can provide a complete determination of outer sensible objects. An object's orientation to the left or right can neither be simply "seen" perceptually nor constructed by concepts alone. It can only be "felt" as it is set in relation to our own body.[4] It is this feeling that grounds the possibility of all sensation and the construction of geometrical orientation. From early on, Kant uses such a connection between space and embodiment to exclude both that space is a sensible property of things that can be empirically perceived and that space is an intellectual concept, whereby he already points to the notion of space as an a priori form of sensibility (and to its ideality).

Thus, given the connection between orientation and embodiment and given the role that the discovery of the peculiar character of spatial orientation has in the development of Kant's theory of knowledge, we can conclude that if such theory hinges upon the idea of space, then it ultimately hinges upon a formal a priori component displayed by the embodied condition of the knowing subject on which his theory of space rests. While the peculiar feeling for our bodily asymmetry and its use in relation to outside objects ultimately leads Kant to affirm the transcendental ideality of space, this same connection betrays the fact that there is a "transcendental" (or, I suggest, an "ideal") component to our embodied condition. Embodiment is not simply an empirically given, philosophically trivial evidence or fact. Thus, what I will henceforth call "transcendental embodiment" does not designate a merely empirical, given basis of cognition but indicates the *formal condition* that makes knowledge of outer objects possible. To put it in the language of the critical Kant: the way in which the left/right distinction is felt incarnated in our body does not constitute the body to an "object" of experience but is the condition under which outer objects can indeed be experienced; such a distinction is formal, and not merely empirical.[5]

This is the thesis that I establish in the present chapter. Its broader aim is to provide a first argument in favor of the general interpretative concept of "transcendental embodiment." The claim is that embodiment is not philosophically relevant insofar as it designates a material empirical "fact" of human existence—that is, the undeniable fact that we have material bodies which we can observe and perceive, through which we are subject to external stimuli, desires, and so forth. Embodiment becomes philosophically relevant only insofar as the body displays formal a priori structures of its own, that is, only insofar as it can be shown that embodiment is the condition (or one of the conditions) that allows for meaningful discourse and experience in realms as different as scientific knowledge, moral action, and aesthetic appreciation. This formal—indeed properly "transcendental"—significance of the body is responsible for making any approach to its empirical materiality (any further physiological or anthropological observation) possible. However, to view the body in this way a philosophical perspective is required that is able to overcome the Cartesian split of material body/immaterial soul (as well as the alternative between material empiricism and metaphysical rationalism). Thus, the general suggestion of the first three chapters of this study is that the transcendental inspiration of Kant's thought lies precisely in the attempt to overcome the modern body/mind dualism by way of a philosophical approach pursuing a twofold objective. On the one hand, to reclaim for the body a non-material dimension and function; on the other hand, to revoke the metaphysical significance of the disembodied soul and thereby relocate the study of mind within a non-transcendent dimension. Kant's transcendental philosophy is neither physiology nor mere psychology. Transcendental philosophy should rather be understood as the unified (neither empirical nor metaphysical) perspective of both a theory of embodied mind and a theory of the ideality of embodiment. The transcendental notion of subjectivity arises precisely from and in this new perspective.

At the center of this chapter, I place an analysis of the role of the human body in the 1768 essay "On the Ultimate Ground of the Differentiation of Regions in Space," i.e., in the very first stage of the development of Kant's doctrine of space. The connection between embodiment and the notion of space will serve as the key to reconstruct the argument of "incongruent counterparts" in all four of its successive occurrences. I will show that Kant remains faithful to his initial claim regarding the function of embodiment in establishing the nature of space even though he successively uses the argument to prove different features of space. At stake in this chapter is the more general issue of Kant's theory of sensibility. The claim is that Kant's search for pure a priori forms of sensibility (space and time) is neither the process of "dis-embodiment" of the subject nor a regression into a purely formal, mentalistic abstraction from all concrete connection to our physical existence. On the contrary, the discovery of an a priori of sensibility is closely related to the recognition that our body plays a privileged, irreducible role in the process of cognition; and to the recognition that there is a formal component proper to our embodied condition irreducible to the work of the mind (because it is itself necessary to this work). Neither the body as site of sensual perception nor the body as first given object of our sensory encounter with an external world is relevant to Kant—it is rather the body as "transcendental" ground for our cognition and construction of the external world that concerns him. The human body—namely, the only part of the world that I call *my* body—is the turning point that allows Kant to establish space as a pure form of sensible intuition. The transcendental form of space is directly "incarnated" in the human body as the only "faculty"[6] that makes one aware of the difference between left and right, i.e., orientation.

In the first *Critique,* Kant claims: "we can speak of space [. . .] only from the standpoint of a human being."[7] For, we have no judgment concerning "the intuition of other thinking beings."[8] It is not thinking itself that qualifies human intuition. What is it, then, that characterizes the specifically human perspective that makes spatial discourse meaningful? Already in 1768, when space, for Kant, is still a metaphysical entity and certainly not yet an a priori form of intuition, orientation is the distinguishing property of space—a peculiar property that we would not be able to represent at all were it not for the fact that we find it embodied in the difference between our left and right hand. For intellectual concepts and mere sensation both fall short of representing the internal difference of spatial incongruence.

My discussion of Kant's argument of incongruent counterparts differs radically from the numerous analyses available in the literature. I do not offer an historical comparison of its different uses in the development of Kant's theory of space but discuss the relevant—yet unnoticed—fact that all the texts converge in connecting incongruence, space, and embodiment. In the literature, Kant's argument is generally discussed exclusively with regard to the link between the example of the left/right hand and the properties of space. This example, however, is usually considered to be interchangeable with that of a screw or spherical triangle. No attention is given to the observation that

Kant's privileged example refers, for one thing, to parts of the human body and, for another, refers to the human body as the only means we have to discern a crucial property of space.[9] On the contrary, my aim is to show that the argument of incongruent counterparts can help Kant to sound and expose the inner structure of space only because incongruence is originally grounded in a peculiar formal character of the human body. The example of the human body is not just one of many possible examples. It has a methodological (transcendental) priority over all other instances of incongruence. It is precisely this connection between incongruence and embodiment that Kant repeats, unchanged, in all successive presentations of the argument.

First, I lay out Kant's critical theory of sensibility as it stands in the Transcendental Aesthetic of the *Critique of Pure Reason*—a text where no mention is made of incongruent counterparts. Then I show the connection between space and embodiment in the 1768 essay. The claim is that the argument of the first *Critique* that sees space as form of "*outer* sense" is equivalent to the idea of "transcendental embodiment" as the condition for the possibility of the very distinction between myself and the outside world. There is a formal dimension to my body that allows me to refer my sensations to something that lies "*outside* of myself," namely to something that is in another region of space from that in which I (bodily) find myself. Thus, there is a parallel between the form of my body and the transcendental character of space. For both allow me to represent my sensations not only as different from each other (and hence as an empirical "manifold") but also as in different places and external to myself. My body shares with the form of space a constitutive originality in regard to its relation with the external world of objects. What allows for the connection between body and space is the transcendental shift that Kant accomplishes by moving the body from the position of being an "object" of the senses to the position of being a condition of their givenness to the senses. This gesture displays Kant's radical rejection of Cartesian dualism. Right at the beginning of the Transcendental Aesthetic, Kant breaks the Cartesian parallelism between body and soul. The "inner sense" —he immediately warns—"provides no intuition of the soul itself as an object." The "outer sense (a property of our *Gemüt*)" on the other hand, is not explicitly related to the body; it just refers to the representation of objects "outside of ourselves."[10] The body disappears as "object" from Kant's exposition as it is relocated among the transcendental conditions that make possible a representation of what lies "outside" of me. Thereby the body, formally considered, becomes the framework that gives meaning to the typically human discourse regarding space[11]—the framework within which the Transcendental Aesthetic articulates the characters proper to the representation of space. Ultimately, my suggestion is that space (as form of "outer *sense*") is the transcendental form that the body assumes as condition for the representation of external objects.

Kant's Theory of Sensibility and the Problem of Knowledge in the *Critique of Pure Reason*

"There can be no doubt"—observes Kant in the opening of his introduction to the *Critique of Pure Reason* (1787)—"that all our knowledge begins with experience." The very first step in the cognitive process is that our senses are affected by objects. This affection produces representations. The stimulated senses awaken our faculty of knowledge to more complex tasks such as the comparison, combination, or separation of different representations arising out of the "raw material of sensible impressions." However, while all of our knowledge starts out with the raw material provided by the senses, the senses are not the ultimate source of knowledge: "though all our knowledge *begins with* experience, it does not follow that it all *arises out of* experience."[12] For Kant, "experience" is produced by the constructive interaction between sensibility's representations and understanding's concepts. Experience is "synthesis."[13] But how does the material, merely empirical contribution of the senses relate to the more elaborate presence of that material in the synthesis of experience? What is "sensibility" for Kant?

One of the most striking suggestions of the *Critique of Pure Reason* is the claim that not only reason and understanding with their concepts but also sensibility—which opens for us an access to the external world—involve activities which imply pure a priori structures. Kant's thesis stands thoroughly unprecedented. In the *Prolegomena*, Kant recognizes that "it never occurred to anyone that the senses might intuit a priori."[14] Even though Kant takes up the traditional language of "receptivity" and "affection" to indicate the specific way in which sensibility works in relation to objects, and contrasts "receptivity" to the "spontaneity" of the understanding,[15] this receptivity, insofar as it qualifies the a priori forms of sensibility, is not sheer passivity. Kant suggests that the *possibility* for sensibility to be modified or affected precedes a priori all its affections. Sensibility (or at least a peculiar element of it) comes before all knowledge of objects and is the necessary condition thereof. Thereby Kant suggests that there is an "a priori" of sensibility that precedes even the logical a priori of understanding, and is independent of it. The possibility of indicating an "active" component of sensibility hinges upon the possibility of discovering its a priori formal elements.[16]

The metaphysical tradition, which culminates in Leibniz's philosophy and Wolff's systematization, considers the difference between understanding and sensibility—concepts and intuitions or sensations—as one of degree in clarity and distinction. Concepts are clear sensations, and sensations are more or less confused concepts. Accordingly, such a difference can always be bridged by appropriate procedures of clarification. The empiricist tradition, on the other hand, locating the source and origin of our knowledge in the senses, falls directly into Hume's skepticism regarding a posteriori, merely empirical cognition. Kant's notion of the "a priori" is the decisive answer both to the empty speculations of metaphysics and to Hume's skeptical objection against the empiricist attempts to a foundation of science. Kant concludes the introduction to the first *Critique* with a claim that radically breaks with both traditions. He maintains that human knowledge originates out of two "branches": "sensibility," through which objects are *"given"* to us, and "understanding," through which objects are instead *"thought."*[17] These two branches, or functions of human knowledge, are radically different in kind (not just in degree) so that the possibility of a transition from one to the other is impossible. Only because they are fundamentally heterogeneous can they produce a "synthesis" by working together.

Sensibility refers to given objects. The empiricist tradition considers this claim as stating that objects must first be given to us, and only then can they be taken up by our senses, which are thereby "affected."[18] Kant's radical revolution with regard to this tradition consists in the claim that objects are given to us only on the basis of the structure of our sensibility, i.e., only because of our original capacity for being affected by them. In an important way, for Kant, our sensibility is responsible for the fact that we are able to confront the reality of given objects—of being "affected," as it were, by them. Objects are given to us only because of the receptive nature of our sensibility.[19]

Kant defines *Sinnlichkeit* as the capacity of producing representations through the way in which our senses are affected by objects. Sensibility is a modality of our immediate relation to objects. Thinking never relates to objects immediately but only through the mediation of sensibility and its representations. Kant recognizes two general forms of this relation, namely "intuition" and "sensation." In §1 of the first *Critique,* Kant offers a first analysis of sensibility. His purpose is to discern its different elements in order to "isolate"[20] its specific a priori components. "Intuition" is *immediate* relation to objects; it is also *singular* and concrete representation as opposed to the generality and abstractness of the concept. For intuition to occur, the determinate affection of the *Gemüt* is required. Through sensibility, objects are given from which empirical intuitions arise; intuitions are "means" that allow thinking to relate to objects and to determine them as "objects" (as opposed to blurred clusters of sense data). "Sensation" is the other modality of sensibility. It is the effect of an object on our faculty of representation. More precisely, however, sensation always expresses the *empirical* and *material* aspect of sensibility. Intuition, on the contrary, can be either *empirical* or *pure*.

The object given to sensibility and affecting the *Gemüt* is "appearance." It is the object as it appears to our empirical intuition or sensation, which thereby constitutes their content. With regard to appearance, Kant distinguishes between "matter," which is empirically given in sensation, and "form," i.e., the structure of order in which different sensations are organized according to certain relations. Kant's further distinction regards "empirical" and "pure" representations. It is at this point that the difference between sensation and intuition starts to reveal its force and *raison d'être*. A representation is called "pure" when it does not contain anything that belongs to sensation. From this definition it follows that sensation can never be pure. In the Transcendental Aesthetic, Kant always equates sensation with the empirical and material moment of sensibility, whereas in intuition he discovers a formal and pure component of sensibility. Thus, from intuition as one of the forms of sensibility, Kant goes back to the "pure form of sensible intuitions in general" to be found a priori at the very heart of the *Gemüt*. It is *in* this pure form that all acts of intuition of objects take place. "This pure form of sensibility is itself called *pure intuition*."[21] It should be stressed, however, that with regard to the *human* faculty of knowledge, pure intuition does not cease to always be "*sensible* intuition," i.e., intuition which belongs to the general faculty of sensibility. Yet, for Kant, not all intuition need be sensible intuition.[22] We can very well think of a form of "intellectual intuition," even though human intuition will never even approximate it.

Kant's discovery of pure a priori forms of sensible intuition allows him to develop a specific "science of all the a priori principles of sensibility." This science, under the title of Transcendental Aesthetic, constitutes the first section of the *Critique of Pure Reason*. "Aesthetics," observes Kant in a footnote commenting on the title,[23] is the name that the German language uses to indicate what is generally called "critique of taste." Aesthetics indicates a theory of sensation or sensibility. In 1781 and again in 1787, albeit now in a somehow more hesitant tone,[24] Kant is clearly convinced of the impossibility of following Baumgarten in trying to develop a critique of taste in scientific

form, namely according to a priori principles. Taste's rules can only be empirical and therefore can never serve as "a priori laws" (or as "*determinate* a priori
laws" as Kant significantly specifies in the 1787 edition)[25] for the use of our
judgment. Thus, what is left is only the possibility of understanding aesthetics
according to the ancient division of knowledge in αισθητα and νοητα (the
sensible and the intelligible), and of developing a scientific "transcendental"
theory of the a priori forms of sensibility—specifically of intuition—as the
first part of a theory of knowledge. Kant now views any other attempt to
talk about sensibility as one destined to be empirical, material, and therefore
merely psychological. Consequently, a transcendental theory (or critique) of
taste is for Kant thoroughly impossible.

In the Transcendental Aesthetic, Kant presents two pure a priori forms
of sensible intuition—or formal intuitions—i.e., space and time. Space is the
necessary condition of all relations in which I intuit objects as *outside of myself;*
time is the necessary condition of my intuition of myself and of *my inner state.*
Throughout four arguments on space which precede five parallel arguments
on time, Kant discusses the specific nature of space and time as objects (as
mere forms hypostatized to objects) or formal intuitions, and concludes with
the claim that space and time are pure forms of intuition. The arguments
on space and time are crucial for establishing the general and formal features
of a priori sensible intuition. The first argument presents the *non-empirical*
character of space and time, maintaining that space is the a priori condition
of the possibility of outer experience, while time is the a priori condition of
the possibility of inner experience. The second argument proves that space
is an *a priori* intuition and as such is the necessary condition of the objects of
outer experience, i.e., of the appearances of outer sense. We cannot intuit
objects of outer sense without intuiting them in space. Time is an a priori
intuition that refers to objects of inner experience and the inner sense as
their necessary condition. In the third argument, Kant shows that space is
one and *individual* and that it is a *totum* and not a *compositum* (in it the whole
precedes its parts and is the condition of their possibility and not vice versa).
Correspondingly, time is one as well, as it has only one dimension (different times are not contemporary but successive; different spaces are not one
after another but at the same time). It follows that space and time cannot be
discursive concepts but are necessarily pure forms of sensible intuition. This
is the conclusion of the fourth argument that discusses the incompatibility
of the infinite character of space (as *quantum* of an infinite number of parts)
and time[26] with the intension of a concept which, on the contrary, can never
be infinite.

From the third and fourth arguments Kant's conclusion follows that space and time can neither be properties of things in themselves nor express relations of things in themselves. Space is rather the "form of all *appearance* of outer sense" while time is the "formal condition of *all appearance in general.*"[27] If space and time were determinations of things in themselves they would be concepts, since things in themselves are *Gedankendinge* (objects that are thought by the understanding and cannot be given in sensibility), which accordingly should be known only through concepts by the understanding. Thus, since space and time are pure forms of intuition, they cannot be determinations of things in themselves and their relations, but only forms of appearances, i.e., forms of things as they are given to our sensibility. Hence Kant's thesis of the "transcendental ideality" of space and time: space and time do not exist outside of the subjective conditions of our sensible intuition. In other words, they do not have "absolute reality" but only "empirical reality" as conditions of all experience.[28]

Kant's theory of space and time as pure forms of intuition is a milestone of the first *Critique* and its theory of knowledge. However, with regard to cognition, Kant's theory of sensibility is not yet completed by the Transcendental Aesthetic. Another important step is carried through by the Analytic of Principles. There, Kant sets out to show in what sense and in which ways sensibility works together with understanding in order to produce knowledge of objects—and in particular, in order to produce the scientific knowledge of nature proper to mathematics and physics.[29] This is the context of the doctrine of the "schematism." In *Prolegomena* §36, while asking the question "How is nature itself possible?" Kant refers back to the Transcendental Aesthetic as the place where he provided an answer concerning "nature in its material sense, namely according to intuition, as the complex of appearance." There, the question regarded the general possibility of space, time, and that which "fills up both, namely the object of experience."[30] The theory of the a priori forms of intuition—space and time—represents Kant's first answer to the problem. But what about the reference to "that which fills up both"? For what fills up space and time is nothing but sensation, which constitutes the "matter" of appearances and which, due to its assumed exclusively *empirical* character, cannot be dealt with in a transcendental inquiry dedicated to pure a priori principles. This is precisely what is stated in §1 of the Transcendental Aesthetic. However, in the Analytic of Principles, in studying the ways in which the categories of the understanding work together with sensibility in order to produce knowledge, Kant revisits the topic of sensation. At this level, in the Anticipations of Perception he discovers an *a priori of sensation* itself, namely "degree" (*Grad*). Kant characterizes sensation in a twofold way. Sensation is, first, "*modification* of our sensibility." Second, as "modification of our sensibility," it is "the only way in which objects are given to us."[31] It expresses the "reality" or material element of something existing, and as "perception" (i.e., as that which has in itself the modification or sensation), represents the "only character of reality."[32] Thus, it is precisely in creating a synthesis with the category of "reality" that sensation reveals a peculiar a priori structure. This structure could not be detected in the isolation in which it was taken at the level of the Transcendental Aesthetic.

In sum, sensibility is the faculty through which we are affected and put in immediate relation to given objects. Sensibility consists for Kant in a *form* that is intuition and has its a priori modes in space and time, and a *content* that is sensation and is instead a posteriori. Sensation, however, when taken in connection with understanding, displays, in turn, an a priori aspect. This a priori of sensation is that which can be "anticipated" in all experience. When sensation is synthesized with the category of "reality," it reveals an a priori moment that is the "degree" or the "intensive magnitude" that belongs to all reality.[33] Kant's formulation of the Axioms of Intuition states that all appearances in their *form* or *intuition* have a magnitude that can be expressed in space and time. The Anticipations of Perception, on the other hand, state that all appearances in their *material content* or *sensation* have a magnitude that cannot be expressed in space and time but by its "degree." Kant's purpose is to show that all appearances—according to both form and content—can be constructed by mathematics. The second principle is crucial for physics since without sensation no object could be given in its *reality,* no reality would *exist,* and nature "in its material sense" would have no meaning at all.[34]

Now I shall turn to the relation between Kant's view of sensibility, to which space belongs, and the role of the human body. For if space is the "form of outer sense in general," the outer sense, observes Kant in the *Anthropology,* is the limit "where the human body is affected by physical things."[35]

Bodies in Space: Making Space for the Body

In his 1768 essay "On the Ultimate Ground of the Differentiation of Regions in Space," Kant sets out to demonstrate a thesis that he will abandon only two years later in the *Dissertatio,* namely, the objective reality of absolute space. Thereby he follows Newton and radically opposes Leibniz's and Wolff's theory of space.[36] The same argument of incongruent counterparts that in

1768 seems to aim at proving this metaphysical thesis is used again in 1770 to show that space is not an intellectual concept but a form of pure sensible intuition. In 1783 and 1786 it also supports the related claim that space is not a property or relation of things in themselves but only the subjective form of our sensible intuition of things as appearances. Despite these different demonstrative aims, Kant's employment of the argument is consistent in calling attention to the necessity of referring our perception of outer objects to our own body and its left/right asymmetry in order to become aware of the same essential property of space to which he then refers the different demonstrative aims of those texts.

In the 1768 essay, Kant sets out to prove two claims that he will maintain throughout his philosophical career up to the *Opus Postumum*. (1) Space makes all sensation possible, and (2) it makes the order and composition of matter possible. Space is independent of both sensation and composition of matter, and is rather the ultimate and original condition of all outer sensation and composition of matter. This is evident, Kant contends, in those objects that show the property of being incongruent counterparts—and in this case alone. For space is the condition of the incongruence of those objects. Incongruent counterparts are called those objects or geometrical figures that are utterly identical in their physical shape, position, dimensions, as well as in the relations of their parts, and yet cannot be put one in the place of the other by way of a rigid motion, i.e., they cannot be enclosed by one and the same surface. The glove that fits the right hand cannot fit the left hand.[37] As with the left and right hands, all incongruent counterparts are mirror-image reflections of each other. This peculiar feature reveals something crucial about the structure of space, namely its independence of both sensation and the reciprocal relations of the parts of matter. We cannot become aware of the essential property that makes two objects into incongruent counterparts (or that makes one object be *either* a left *or* a right hand) unless we refer them immediately to the asymmetry that we find in our own body.[38] Moreover, Kant comes to his conclusion not through a metaphysical or rational inference but through "intuitive judgments of extension" such as those of geometry.

At stake is the problem of the "complete determination"[39] of an "extended thing" or body. Kant re-proposes at this point a central Leibnizian issue: complete determination is necessary to attain the individuality of a thing, and this, in turn, is necessary in order to differentiate it numerically from all other things. Kant starts out by distinguishing the "position" (*Lage*) of a thing or its parts in relation to one another from the "region" (*Gegend*) in which a thing or its parts are placed and oriented. Kant claims that the position of the parts presupposes the region in which they are placed and ordered according to their relations. In opposition to Leibniz, he suggests that "order" is not identical with the region of space. In every object, the position of the parts can be inferred analytically from their relations, and thereby sufficiently accounted for. On the contrary, the region to which the order of parts is directed, "refers to the space outside" of the region itself, and more precisely "to the universal space as a unity of which each extension must be regarded as a part."[40] One and the same order or set of relations of parts can be disposed in one way or another, i.e., can be oriented differently so that two things displaying the same order or position of parts can still be different from each other (and hence not be sufficiently determined) with regard to the region in which they are placed. It follows that the reference to the region by which the order is framed constitutes an additional, non-analytical relation that must be accounted for when looking for the complete determination of an object. Whether a left and a right hand could be made to coincide does not depend on their internal analytical description, but on the space or region in which the relations among their parts receive an orientation. The region implies a relation to universal space as a unity (and not to space as the complex of parts in external relations): "region," explains Kant, is the relation of the "system" of all positions to the "absolute cosmic space."[41] Thus, Kant's view is that the "principle of the complete determination of a bodily figure" is not an analytic but a synthetic principle. It does not lie only in the internal relation and position of an object's parts but, in addition, rests on the external relation to the universal absolute space.[42] This is precisely the demonstrative aim of Kant's argument: the determinations of space are the condition of all sensation and reciprocal position of the parts of matter, not the consequence of the order of these parts.[43]

Since all figures and bodies are oriented, for Kant, in a three-dimensional Euclidean space, they are completely determined only in relation to the universal absolute space outside of them. However, since this relation to absolute space as a unity "cannot be immediately perceived" by us, the question arises of how this relation can ever be established. Clearly, this is another way to ask not only the metaphysical question of the objective reality of absolute space but also the question of how space can be assessed as the "ground"[44] of the differences among extended objects.

Although Kant's explicit task in this early essay is to provide a proof for the metaphysical thesis of the reality of absolute space, he ends without having offered much more than an unsupported and problematic claim. To show that space is the principle of the possibility of all sensation and composition of matter still does not quite prove that this principle has "reality" (whatever "reality" may mean for Kant at this time).[45] Thus, concluding the essay, Kant confesses the numerous "difficulties" that this task poses to a comprehension through rational ideas, even though the reality of space (this time, however, not absolute space but the space in which our hands are determined as left or right hands) has intuitive evidence for our "inner sense."[46] Almost anticipating those inescapable difficulties Kant's argument takes, from the outset, a quasi-transcendental route and ends, as it were, with the proof of a different thesis. Kant replaces absolute space with our body. By drawing the necessary relation between space and embodiment to the center, he establishes space's originality and priority over all sensation and order of matter. If we cannot gain a direct relation to absolute space, thereby completely determining the object in question, Kant suggests that we still have another, much more intuitive way of establishing an *external* relation with regard to which the orientation of a figure can be detected and the object completely determined. Instead of relating a given object to cosmic space—a procedure that cannot be supported by any direct perception or experience—Kant maintains that we must relate it to our own body. This shift from the relation to absolute space to the relation to our own body is the decisive turning point of Kant's argument. It shows that, in point of fact—and indeed against his own initial expectations—Kant is not able to use the incongruent counterparts to prove the "reality" of absolute space. The argument serves, instead, to prove a different thesis regarding the relation between space and an aspect of our "sensibility" that is not only separated from understanding but is also not entirely reducible to "external sense perception."[47] In other words, the argument leads Kant to the discovery of a non-empirical ingredient of our sensibility, whose function in cognition is clearly expressed by the use that we make of the relation to our own body. While the metaphysical notion of a cosmic space offered no escape from the traditional alternative between empirical perception and rational concept, our body displays a function that seems to precede, as "condition of possibility," both sensory perception and conceptual intellectual construction.[48]

Hence, since the incongruent counterparts do not prove that absolute space is "real," we can conclude that there is no contradiction between the use of the argument in the pre-critical essay (where Kant still holds, with Newton, to the reality of absolute space) and its repetition in the *Dissertatio* and the critical period (where this thesis, which has never been proved, is then completely abandoned).[49] In all their occurrences, the incongruent counterparts serve Kant to establish a thesis about the nature of human sensibility, and more precisely a direct identification between a formal non-empirical aspect of our sensibility and the role of the human body in cognition. In this perspective, the body is not the site of the material senses but the reference point of our formal sense for spatial orientation.

The Body and Its Sensibility

Kant formulates his demonstrative task halfway through the 1768 essay. With the initial aim of proving the reality of absolute space in view, once the distinction between the "position" and "region" in which a thing is placed has been laid out, Kant makes a lengthy "premise." Thereby the argument of the incongruent counterparts is connected with three crucial claims.[50]

(1) Kant first maintains that since the objects of our knowledge, as objects of outer sense, are all placed in an oriented three-dimensional space, knowledge of outer objects in their complete determination must include knowledge of their orientation, i.e., of the region in which they are placed with regard to dimensions such as "up" and "down," "left" and "right." "Since through the senses we know everything that is outside of ourselves only insofar as it stands in relation to ourselves, it is no wonder that we take the first ground to generate the concept of the regions in space" from the relation of the three planes of space "with our body."[51] Empirical knowledge of objects through our senses is not the ultimate instance for Kant. Such knowledge must be referred back to a more original condition which is the relation to our own body. The reason for this move lies precisely in the spatial character of external objects. In order to be functional to the argument, however, the reference to our body as condition for our cognition of objects through the senses must be assumed as not being in turn a merely empirical one. An object of outer sense is "in relation to ourselves" when it is in relation "to our body" with respect to the region in which its figure is oriented. For the three planes of space intersect each other at a right angle at the very center of the human body. The vertical plane of the spine divides the body (and consequently space) into a left and right "region," while the horizontal plane divides the body (and consequently space) into "up" and "down." Thus, the human body appears as the first generative principle or ground for our notion of regions in space—a notion that is necessary to our cognition of objects (i.e., to their complete determination).[52]

The point that Kant thereby makes differs entirely from the empiricist claim that we are affected by an outer object when this affects our five senses.

The body, here, is not introduced as the seat of the senses. Rather, it is the "faculty" of a special kind of "feeling" (*Gefühl*) that is neither intellectual nor empirically sensuous although it is strictly connected with the sensory impression left by the object.[53] If the words on a written page were to change their disposition according to left and right, we would be unable to read them, even though the order of the words, their figures, and reciprocal relations on the page remained exactly the same. In order to meaningfully "see," we need to know how and in which direction we must turn our eyes.

In the 1786 essay, "What Does it Mean to Orient Oneself in Thinking?" Kant makes the same point by distinguishing the sense of sight from the bodily "feeling" of orientation.[54] The latter is able to reveal a difference that neither the senses nor our concepts can discern. If one day, as a kind of miracle, all stars and celestial bodies were to change their orientation so that what once was in the east is now in the west, and yet still maintains exactly the same figure and relative position, then on a clear night "*no human eye would notice the smallest change, and even the astronomer would inevitably be disoriented if he holds to what he sees and not, at the same time, to what he feels*"[55] in his own body with the help of the left and the right hand.

(2) The second point of Kant's "premise" in the 1768 essay is another experiment in generating an outer world of oriented objects in space's regions, which is opposed to the Leibnizian (or Euclidean)[56] flat, indeterminate world in which objects are described only in terms of their reciprocal positions, without reference to our sensibility. Kant thereby shows what it concretely means—and why it is so indispensable—for us to refer all outer objects to our body as criterion for discerning space's regions or orientation. Kant suggests that all our judgments on the external world depend upon the general concept of "regions" insofar as they are "determined in relation to the sides of our body."[57] If I did not relate whatever I perceive in the sky and on earth to my own body, I would know *only* the reciprocal "position" of the objects; I would know the order of the parts of the horizon or the reciprocal position of the stars, but I would still not be able to discern the direction of this order. In other words, I would be completely *dis-oriented*. Not even the most detailed and sophisticated map of the sky or earth would help me in the task of finding the east, were I not referring what I see to my left or right hand in order to generate from those bodily sides the east and the west, the north and the south. In order to gain cognition by relating the map to the real territory, the mediation of my physical body is required as condition for making sense of space's property of orientation. In achieving this mediation my physical body betrays the formal (transcendental) dimen-

sion of our sensibility: such dimension defines the body as subject and not object of cognition.

Kant presents a wide variety of oriented objects that range from celestial bodies to maps of the earth, from natural creatures to artifacts, and ends with examples taken from parts of the human body—examples that enjoy a special evidence for everybody. Geometrical figures have not yet appeared. Kant's point is immediately clear: we would not be able to recognize these objects in their different orientations and hence for what they determinately are, were they not referred to the original orientation that we find incarnated in our own body. Without the relation to the sides of the body, all the stars, spirals, creatures, maps, and tools would be meaningless and useless: we would neither be able to classify creatures that differ only in the direction in which their shell is twisted in a spiral, nor could we screw in a screw. To be sure, all these celestial and terrestrial maps with their stars and their places revolve around the center represented by the human body—a center which is both physical and ideal, both material and formal. All these spirals and natural products become meaningful only if viewed from the point of intersection between the three planes of space that we find inscribed in our flesh. Those objects constitute the world "outside of ourselves." Now the meaning of Kant's claim, that we can know this world only insofar as we relate it "to ourselves," becomes clear to us.[58]

This construction of the external world by reference to our body, i.e., to a peculiar function of our sensibility, is the preliminary condition that allows Kant to move on to the construction of incongruent counterparts in a purely geometrical space, making abstraction, this time, from our sensibility.[59] However, it is significant that even in this space, what Kant ends up constructing is not a spherical triangle but a human hand. And even in this process, he discovers that "reason" is unable to grasp the nature of the constructed space without referring it to sensibility and the "judgments of intuition."

We can ascertain orientation in the outside world only because our own body is a living instrument in which this orientation receives its most concrete figure.[60] Thereby the body discloses the duplicity of its being: it is both the condition of the experience of external oriented objects and is itself one of these oriented objects of experience. Our body is the thin line where the formality of a transcendental consideration and the materiality of its concrete observation seem to merge. Through our body, we have a direct and immediate experience of orientation in a region of space: the difference between the left and right hand or the left and right ear, the hair on top of the head that is twisted from left to right, the heart that beats on the left side of the body. Our body's immediate presence to ourselves allows us to extend our knowledge of reality from the two-dimensionality of an unknowable "absolute position" (without relation to our sensibility), in which no complete determination is possible (it is impossible to distinguish a left from a right hand, and hence to determine a hand completely as either left or right), to the three-dimensional space in which bodies are oriented and ordered in their reciprocal positions, and can be known as completely determined for what they are.[61] Thus, by means of the incongruent counterparts, Kant provides an argument for the thesis that the determinations of space are the condition of all sensation and composition of matter. This argument is not yet a proof that absolute space has "reality." However, if Kant does not manage to prove that these determinations do have "reality," he nonetheless shows that they are embodied as the original condition of our sensibility. The reference to our body is as original and constitutive as the reference to absolute space.

(3) The "feeling" of orientation that we discover in our body is so essential as the ground on which we formulate our judgments on the regions of space—and hence as the turning point of Kant's entire argument[62]—that he elaborates at length on the *internal* asymmetry between left and right. This asymmetry seems to be inscribed in our body and its mechanical functions by a providential nature that has thereby endowed us with an indispensable instrument for cognition. Despite their external similarity, the right side of the body displays its own peculiar quality over against the left side. The right side (and in particular, the right hand) is stronger and more skillful, and our movement is generally facilitated when originating on the right side (here exceptions confirm the rule, argues Kant): this is the case, for example, when we mount a horse or jump over a ditch. The left side, however, is far more sensitive. The left eye or ear is sharper and more sensitive than the right eye or ear, Kant maintains (following his sources, Borelli and Bonnet). Empirical, anthropological observations are called in support of the mere formal point that Kant has made by isolating the human body as criterion and measure for the observation of all other external objects (including the body itself as object). Evidently, Kant's discussion of the issue of embodiment oscillates here between a transcendental and formal approach, and empirical and material observation.[63]

The relation between orientation and embodiment established by means of these three premises provides the intuitive support for Kant's main issue in this essay. This concerns the epistemological question of the complete determination of a bodily figure. Against Leibniz, Kant shows that the reciprocal position of the parts of an object is a necessary but not sufficient condition to completely determine the object. In addition, a reference is required to the "region" in which the order of parts receives its orientation. This reference implies the relation to another dimension, i.e., to a unitary space "outside" of the parts of the object. Kant's argument revolves around those objects—namely "incongruent counterparts"—which clearly display orientation as a determination that cannot be analytically inferred from the mere position and order of their parts. While examples of incongruent counterparts have been presented in the long "premise" as concretely *given in and through* the asymmetry of our own body, Kant now offers for them an additional genetic definition. Incongruent counterparts can also be geometrically constructed. By providing a genetic definition of incongruence, the procedure of geometry shows its very "possibility."[64] Through the process of construction of the "incongruent counterpart" of a given "human hand" in a geometrical space, Kant shows that the geometrical description of the property at stake corresponds exactly to the experience or "feeling" that we have embedded in our own body. In both cases the quasi-transcendental question of what makes spatial orientation possible is at stake. The crucial point, however, is that the geometrical construction of an incongruent counterpart ultimately *presupposes,* as its condition, an embodied sense for orientation.[65]

What are the "philosophical consequences" or "philosophical applications" of these claims? Paradoxically, "incongruence" is an "internal difference"[66] or property that can be captured only through the "external" (i.e., synthetic) relation to another dimension. Kant provides two possibilities for this external relation: the absolute universal (or cosmic) space and our own body. Because of the impossibility of a direct access to absolute space by way of sensibility, and because of the "difficulties" involved in its consideration through rational concepts, Kant rules out any reference to it—or at least problematically suspends it, and eventually reserves it, with all its difficulties, to the "ideas of reason." Thereby the privileged and original relation to our body comes to the fore. It is with regard to our body that objects are called "outside" objects and the world becomes an "outside" world. Space, Kant claims in the critical period, is the a priori form of "outer sense." This conclusion allows me to establish the following point: I shall consider the argument of the pre-critical essay as presupposed by the opening of the Transcendental Aesthetic. For it is the formal dimension of our body as condition for the possibility of speaking of an external world and external objects that is examined by Kant under the notion of space at this later date.

In 1768, the internal property of incongruence signals, for Kant, that space and order are not the same. The original relation to our body makes clear that

space is not a consequence of the order of material parts but rather the condition of this order. An important anti-Leibnizian consequence follows: matter
does not have an intrinsic, internal order of its own which is independent
of space. "The absolute inwardness of matter (*das schlechthin* [. . .] *Innerliche
der Materie*), as it would have to be conceived by the understanding, is nothing but a phantom (*Grille*)." For, "that which inwardly belongs to [matter],
I seek in all parts of the space which it occupies, and in all effects which it
exercises, though admittedly these can only be appearances of outer sense."[67]
The *Innerliches* of matter is only an appearance of the outer sense. This is the
thesis that Kant presents in the Amphiboly of the Concepts of Reflection—
his appendix to the Analytic of Principles of the first *Critique,* which contains
a thorough confrontation with Leibniz. Although at this later time Kant's
doctrine of space differs radically from the one presented in the 1768 essay,
the anti-Leibnizian consequence is exactly the same in the two texts.[68] Its
ground, in both cases, is the relation between space and human sensibility.

Left Hands, Right Hands, and Disoriented Bodies: Concepts, Sensations, and A Priori Intuitions

In the critical doctrine that considers space to be an a priori form of sensible
intuition, the relation between space and embodiment is maintained. The
way in which the argument of incongruent counterparts—and in particular
the reference to the left/right hand—is taken up again reveals that the "transcendental ideality" of space is concretely manifested, for Kant, in the "transcendental" role that the human body plays in the cognitive process. This role
remains unchanged, even terminologically, from 1768 to the later texts.

In the 1770 *Dissertatio,* Kant definitively abandons the view that absolute
space has objective "reality." Space is now a subjective form. However, it is
not a discursive concept but a "pure intuition" (*intuitus purus*).[69] We have seen
that in 1768 the incongruent counterparts could not prove space's reality,
which remained an open problem for Kant at the end of the essay. Instead,
the reference to the left/right hand allowed him to place space, and with
it the human body, in a sort of intermediary position between intellectual
concepts and empirical sensations. The *Dissertatio* draws the final consequence
out of this earlier insight: space is now clearly a pure intuition, not an intellectual concept.

The same point is made again in 1786, in the *First Metaphysical Principles
of Natural Science.* In the critical period, the claim that space is a subjective a

priori form of intuition implies that space cannot be a property or relation of things in themselves. The latter claim could be seen as a modification of the earlier metaphysical thesis of the reality of absolute space.[70] In the *First Metaphysical Principles of Natural Science*, the issue is the definition of the "direction" of movement with regard to a body that moves itself in a circle. The real question is: how do we ascertain the direction of a circular movement, i.e., the "side" toward which movement is oriented? For in this case, despite the fact that the direction changes continuously, we still claim that the body always moves itself in the same direction. Kant points out that this problem *"has an affinity* with the question: where does the internal difference of those snails rest, that are similar and even identical in all other respects, and yet one species is wound toward the left and the other toward the right?"[71] The crucial point, for Kant, is that the "internal difference" that constitutes the incongruence of incongruent counterparts is "given" in intuition but cannot be brought to clear concepts—*dari non intelligi*[72]—even though it can be constructed mathematically. The "affinity" between the initial problem of detecting the direction of a circular movement and the claim that incongruence shows the subjective and intuitive nature of space can be understood, once again, only through the embodiment of that pure intuition in the left and right side of our own body. For as we learned from the essay "On the Ultimate Ground of the Differentiation of Regions in Space," our left and right hands are, at the same time, *examples* of incongruence and *instruments* for detecting spatial orientation. Kant's reference to the latter point, although hidden in the 1786 text, constitutes an integral part of it. One of the examples provided regards an "exception." Kant refers to those "rare" dead bodies that, once dissected, show an order of the internal organs that perfectly corresponds to all the "physiological rules" verified in other human bodies, and yet "all the organs present an inversion of left and right which is contrary to the usual order."[73]

In the essay "What Does it Mean to Orient Oneself in Thinking?" which appears in the same year as the *First Metaphysical Principles of Natural Science*, we find a strong case for the relation between orientation and the incongruence that we "feel" in our own body. In this text, Kant is not so much concerned with the properties of space as with the notion of "orientation."[74] As in the *First Metaphysical Principles*, Kant discusses an exception: the "miracle," previously mentioned, of the sky in which all the stars suddenly change their orientation, or the "trick" that someone could play on us by changing the position of all the objects in a dark room well known to us, which would maintain the same reciprocal order and yet be inverted according to left and right. The interesting question with all these exceptional occurrences is as follows: what is it in those rare dissected corpses, the inverted starry sky, or our transfigured dark room that allows us to recognize an exception? Or: what is it that makes us feel disoriented? Here, both our sense of sight and our conceptual apparatus fall short of the task. The answer (or the compass for our orientation) lies instead in the embodiment of the subject and in the "feeling" for direction that we gain because of our embodied state. The peculiar status that Kant attributes to our body is clearly expressed in its functioning as a peculiar subjective "capacity for distinguishing" things through internal differences that can neither be sensibly seen nor conceptually grasped. The body is not simply the seat of the senses whose activity or sensitivity can always be suspended, as in the total obscurity of the dark room in his example. Our bodily feeling for orientation is a natural capacity that still requires exercise and training. This capacity is epitomized in the function of our left and right hand.[75]

In §13 of the *Prolegomena,* Kant uses the "paradox"[76] of incongruent counterparts to show that space is not a property of things in themselves but a subjective form of our sensible intuition. His argument displays in detail all the elements that appear in 1768. Most importantly, it draws the connection between incongruence and embodiment to the center. The issue is, once again, the complete description or determination of two incongruent objects. Geometrical examples here come first in order to show that no understanding could ever provide the "internal difference" that explains why two spherical triangles, which share the basis and differ only in their orientation with regard to it, could never be put in the place of each other. Such a difference "reveals itself only through the external relation in space." It is precisely to elucidate this crucial point, that Kant turns to "more usual cases, which can be taken from everyday life."[77] The example is the type of similarity or identity between my hand or ear and its reflected image in a mirror. While understanding alone cannot form a concept of the difference between my left hand and its mirror-image, this difference is immediately evident to the senses (although this is so in a peculiar way, since such difference is not itself sensual or empirical—is not, in other words, a matter of sensation but of intuition). For the distinction between left and right hands rests, in its very possibility, on the relation between things and our sensibility. From this claim, which we already found in 1768, Kant now draws the conclusion that space is not a property that defines things as they are in themselves. Since space is the "form of outer intuition,"[78] it follows that we know things in their complete determination only as appearances, i.e., as they are in relation to ourselves.

As was the case in the 1768 essay, Kant contends that the "*internal* determination" of an object is revealed only "through the determination of the *external* relation to the entire space."[79] Kant presents two kinds of relation: one to "ourselves" and one to the "entire space." Such a distinction echoes the twofold determination of the "region" in 1768, which was set once in external relation to absolute cosmic space and once in relation to ourselves (to our body). The crucial point is that in the *Prolegomena* the two relations explicitly converge in a relation to our body, i.e., to the difference between left and right hand that is immediately a matter of intuition.[80] Like earlier absolute space, our body is a unitary space in relation to which we position the difference of outer objects and the constitution of the external world.[81] An object is set in relation to ourselves when it is set in relation to our body. Thereby, the clue underlying Kant's use of incongruent counterparts in all these texts comes to the fore: our left and right hands are, at the same time, concrete instances of incongruent counterparts and the condition of the possibility of detecting incongruence as a feature of the external world; they are, at the same time, examples of incongruence and the criterion for ascertaining incongruence. Theoretically, the second feature obviously precedes the first. Our body is the representative of the form of outer sense, i.e., space. To this extent it displays a non-empirical dimension that I designate as "transcendental" or indeed as "ideal." For Kant, the body (and its sensibility) becomes a topic of philosophical inquiry—rather than physiological or anthropological observation—only insofar as it displays a dimension that is neither material and sensual nor merely intellectual and conceptual. In this regard, however, the body is not primarily an object of our experience but the (transcendental) condition thereof. Thus, I understand the "ideality" of the body in the way suggested by Kant's definition of the "transcendental ideality" and "empirical reality" of space in the first *Critique:* such a formal dimension of the body—namely its being the condition for our cognitive orientation in the world—disappears (becomes indeed "nothing")[82] as soon as we lose sight of its function within possible human experience in general.

2

Bodies and Souls

Banquo. The earth hath bubbles, as the water has,
And these are of them. Whither are they vanish'd?
Macbeth. Into the air; and what seem'd corporal melted
As breath into the wind. Would they had stay'd!
—SHAKESPEARE, *Macbeth*

What is a ghost? Stephen said with tingling energy.
One who has faded into impalpability through death,
through absence, through changes of matter.
—JAMES JOYCE, *Ulysses*

Soul and ghost are certainly *something.*
—HOMER, *Iliad*

IN THE TRADITION OF METAPHYSICS WITH WHICH KANT
comes to terms early on in his philosophical career, to address issues concerning the body as *res extensa* means to confront the intricate question of its separation from and interaction with the soul (*commercium*), the mind, or the *res cogitans.* In the critical period, Kant completely revolutionized the terms of this traditional question—so much so that it is hard to relocate it within his philosophy or even articulate its 'successor' in the new critical framework. This explains why historical discussions of the mind-body problem usually end with modern philosophy, and only rarely extend to Kant.[1] The point at issue, however, already occupies Kant in the pre-critical period. Early on, he participates in the heated debate between Leibnizians and Wolffians on the issue of the soul-body relation. He takes position in favor of the *influxus physicus,* which tries to explain the possibility of the

reciprocal influence between soul and body against the doctrine of the pre-established harmony. Such doctrine, denying the possibility of reciprocal action between soul and body, resorts instead to God's arrangement. In these early years Kant's confrontation with metaphysics takes the turn that leads him to re-think the relation between mind and body in a thoroughly new perspective.

Kant's early reflections on the nature of space are central for his turn to critical philosophy and for his "transcendental" or "critical" idealism. His pre-critical investigations lead him to release space from its metaphysical connection to the soul, and to establish instead a necessary link between space and embodiment which testifies to a deeper interest in the nature of experience. The relation between space and embodiment, in turn, trans-forms the philosophical approach to the body by disclosing a hitherto un-accountable pure or formal dimension of sensibility. This complex shift is responsible for the radical transformation of the traditional mind-body problem within critical philosophy. (1) If space is the form of "outer sense," the condition of the possibility of our relating to an outside world, and (2) if this character of space is concretely experienced by us in the special role that our body plays in the cognitive process, we have to ask what, for Kant, fills the place that the soul or mind occupies in the traditional mind-body problem. What is the relation between outer and inner sense? How does the embodied subject gain its proper inner dimension and what constitutes this inner dimension? While his pre-critical reflections on the nature of space and outer sense lead Kant to connect it with the form of our body, at the very beginning of the Transcendental Aesthetic he contends that the "inner sense provides no intuition of the soul itself as an object."[2] Is a cognitive access to the inner self possible for Kant, and what role does the body play in self-cognition? Can the purely logical self by itself yield self-cognition? Since Kant's doctrine of space is pivotal to his turn to transcendental phi-losophy, to answer these questions implies a confrontation of transcendental philosophy with traditional metaphysics in general and rational psychology in particular—i.e., with that part of metaphysics (*metaphysica specialis*) that investigates the nature of the soul. While transcendental philosophy, in ad-dressing the issue of the conditions of possibility of experience, proposes a new, non-empirical way of dealing with the body and thereby brings to the fore its purely formal side, we need to ask how it approaches the traditional issue of the soul and its allegedly privileged place in self-cognition.

The viability of the idea of a Kantian "transcendental psychology"—which was much debated and ultimately abandoned by Kant interpretation in the first decades of the twentieth century, but has recently gained momentum in the Anglo-American literature—must be tested against this complex constellation of problems. What can be the "object" of such a discipline?[3] Can Kant's doctrine of the transcendental unity of apperception with its logical account of the pure self be regarded as transcendental psychology, or does this discipline rather attend only to the empirical self? Can a purely logical account of the self provide self-cognition as "experience" of the self? Or does self-cognition require the (synthetic) intervention of the transcendental form of the body?[4]

In both editions of the first *Critique*, Kant employs the expression "transcendental psychology" (*transzendentale Seelenlehre* or *transzendentale Psychologie*) as synonymous with *psychologia rationalis* (or *rationale Psychologie*). The latter term indicates a discipline of traditional metaphysics next to cosmology and theology.[5] In his later work *On the Progress of Metaphysics since Leibniz and Wolff,* Kant claims that "psychology for our human insight is nothing more—and can also be nothing more—than anthropology, i.e., knowledge of the human being with the limiting condition that he knows himself as object of the inner sense."[6] In the *Critique of Judgment,* Kant has already reached the conclusion that if psychology wants to avoid the Scylla and Charybdis of pneumatology and materialism, it should be considered a mere "anthropology of inner sense, i.e., a cognition of our thinking self *in life*."[7] Thus, to gain insight into what psychology is for Kant, beyond the scholastic division of rational and empirical psychology, we must understand how the traditional concepts of soul and its *pendant,* namely, the body are conceived and reframed within his transcendental investigation. For this connection is crucial to the possibility of self-knowledge. At this point we will be able to justify the claim that Kant's transcendental philosophy is not a psychology but rather a *unified* transcendental theory of the a priori conditions under which the mind *and* the body (the logical functions of judgment and the a priori forms of sensibility)—or an embodied mind transcendentally considered—construct the synthesis of experience or ground the possibility of true knowledge. Clearly, psychology cannot provide the answer to the question of how knowledge as true judgment is possible, by simply appealing to the empirical process or fact of cognition that occurs in a thinking subject. It is only by bringing to light the formal a priori conditions of this process that the problem can be solved. Significantly, in the framework of Kant's system, the only critical successor of psychology can be anthropology, i.e., an applied empirical discipline in which self-knowledge is rooted in the conditions of our human life. At stake, more broadly, are the questions of how Kantian transcendental subjectivity arises out of the dissolution of the body-soul split dominating modern philosophy, of what constitutes such human subjectivity, and of what philosophical discipline should attend to it.[8]

The present chapter provides the first step in the exploration of this complex constellation of problems. Yet only the discussion of the entire development of Kant's theory of sensibility throughout the three *Critiques* will allow us to gain a final insight into his position. The focus on Kant's development of the notion and structures of sensibility determines the itinerary of this chapter, which follows the *interaction* of sensibility with the forms of understanding in the first *Critique*. I show, first, that Kant's rejection of Wolff's metaphysics is closely related to his reflection on space and embodiment. To this aim, I discuss the important connection between the 1766 *Dreams of a Spirit-Seer, Elucidated by the Dreams of Metaphysics* and the 1768 "On the Ultimate Ground of the Differentiation of Regions in Space." Second, I examine the role that embodiment plays in Kant's later rejection of empirical or material "idealism," i.e., of the doctrine that denies the existence of objects outside ourselves. Our body, to which the "transcendental ideality" of space is related, is the basis for Kant's proof of the necessary existence of the external world. The key to Kant's Refutation of Idealism in the *Critique of Pure Reason* is the asymmetry between outer and inner sense, space and time. The claim that inner experience presupposes outer experience requires both the subject's embodiment and the rejection of the spiritual, disembodied dimension that rational psychology attributed to it. Thus the conclusion of this chapter intimates that, while the knowing subject of Kant's theoretical philosophy is transcendentally (and not just empirically) an embodied subject, it lacks any psychological or spiritual dimension of a metaphysical sort. Kant's subject (as unity of a purely logical and an empirical self), in its cognitive endeavor, does indeed have a body, but not a soul.[9] Transcendentally, for the purpose of self-cognition as well as for cognition of the external world (in the mathematical and physical construction of its universal laws), the subject needs a body but not a soul. Moreover, the purely logical unity of apperception by itself does not yield self-cognition. Both self-cognition and cognition of outer objects are *empirical*.

The Transcendental Aesthetic is the key to understanding Kant's definitive farewell to rational psychology. While a transcendental theory of the body does indeed find its place within the critical project, no *doctrinal* psychology in the critical perspective but only a transcendental logic is possible for Kant.[10] Transcendental philosophy is a theory of the a priori conditions under which cognitive "experience" is possible for us. On Kant's view, such a theory refers to a subject of experience who is neither body nor mind alone but is rather a unified "embodied mind"—hence a human subject. Neither materialism nor pneumatology, neither physiology nor (traditional) psychology, but only transcendental philosophy can provide an account of human experience. Can we conclude that a first critical successor of the traditional body-mind dualism emerges in the transcendental and formal transfiguration of outer and inner sense in the Transcendental Aesthetic? Does the distinction between empirical and transcendental unity of apperception in the Transcendental Deduction further develop such a transformation?[11] However this may be, the knowing subject for Kant is transcendentally (not empirically) only the synthesis of these aspects—as subject of experience it is embodied mind and ideal body in one. Transcendentally, these aspects constitute the *human* subject of cognitive experience. From the standpoint of this subject, mathematical and physical sciences construct nature in its universal laws (Analytic of Principles). The transcendental character of Kant's inquiry is, briefly put, expressed in the following objective: in order for experience to be possible (experience of oneself as well as objects in general) the two dimensions of sensibility and understanding must be taken into account as necessary and universal conditions. In the Refutation of Idealism Kant contends that only an embodied subject can have experience of her inner self through the experience of the outer world that her body channels. Psychology as science of the mind in abstraction from the body is impossible. If psychology embraces the transcendental condition of embodiment it becomes transcendental philosophy. Eventually, for Kant, the empirical, applied investigation of the "subject"—transcendentally unifying body and soul—becomes the task of anthropology.[12]

The Soul's Presence in the World:
Is the Soul in Space?

In his 1768 essay "On the Ultimate Ground of the Differentiation of Regions in Space," the difficult issues concerning the reality of absolute space revolve around the question of what "reality" Kant claims for space at that time. Clearly, it can be neither God's absolutely necessary reality nor the reality of spirits or souls—which allegedly exist separate from all matter— nor the reality of matter itself, which rather presupposes space. Only geometrical figures along with the "data" furnished by experience seem to provide Kant with a reliable notion of reality. However, at the end of the essay, Kant arrives at the important conclusion that space does not coincide analytically with the reality of geometrical figures. Absolute space is not identical with the real space of experience.[13] Logically, and supposedly also ontologically, space belongs to a higher order than that of geometrical figures. Elaborating on the gap between absolute space and geometrical figures, this essay shows in what sense space has reality in relation to our sensibility, i.e., in a dimension that is certainly not absolute but always and necessarily embodied. It is also relevant that in addition to presenting our bodily experience of incongruence, Kant makes use of the geometrical procedure of *constructing* a human hand once its incongruent counterpart is given. Geometry's construction serves him to prove the "possibility"[14] of incongruent counterparts by providing their genetic definition. Thereby, he demonstrates the "possibility" of a fundamental property of space whose "data" are given in the common experience of embodiment. Besides the *reality* of incongruence given by experience and its *possibility* offered by geometry, Kant still looks for a reality comprehended through rational concepts alone—a task that the 1768 essay leaves unsettled and that the 1770 *Dissertatio* eventually abandons.

Now we have to work our way backward, and address the philosophical debate that frames Kant's early reflection on space. The problem of space that the 1768 essay nearly brings to a solution is part of the broader issue which Kant is struggling with in 1766—in the *Dreams of a Spirit-Seer, Elucidated by the Dreams of Metaphysics.* There, Kant tackles the fundamental problem of the relation between metaphysics and experience. He seeks a way to connect the two "ends by which all knowledge can be caught"— namely, the a priori and the a posteriori.[15] At the center is one of the most-discussed metaphysical problems of the time: the nature of the soul and its relation to the body.

In the *Dreams,* the issue of the "reality" of the "soul" or "spirit" and its influence on the body takes the same methodological form that the issue of the reality of space assumes two years later: in order for a problem to be capable of solution, "data" from experience are required; the "possibility" of the hypothesis assumed must be shown; and no inference is allowed from mere a priori rational concepts. For rational concepts alone prove neither the possibility nor the impossibility of a given assumption. In light of these methodological premises, it is clear that for Kant the question of space could lead to a solution both on the basis of its formal relation to our sensibility (provided by the experience of embodiment), and on the basis of the geometrical proof of the possibility of incongruence (provided by the construction of a human hand). The case of the soul, however, is different. When the independent reality of the soul is at issue, analogous data as well as a proof of the possibility of the concept are entirely lacking. This situation motivates Kant's radical rejection of rational psychology or "pneumatology" in 1766.[16] To understand the import of Kant's work in these years, it is crucial to recognize the connection between the issue of space and the metaphysical problem of the soul.[17] The metaphysical thesis regarding the soul that Kant refutes in 1766 presupposes the same Wolffian notion of space that he openly criticizes in 1768. Hence we can conclude that it is precisely the failure of rational psychology in 1766 that turns Kant to the new idea of space reached in 1768: the failure to prove the metaphysical reality of the soul leads to the emergence of the (quasi-)transcendental reality of the body. Conversely, we can suggest that for Kant the problem of space can be solved in a non-metaphysical way, whereas the problem of the soul cannot, only because the body is necessarily involved in the former case and eliminated in the latter. This connection reveals the experience of embodiment as pivotal for Kant's fundamental turn to transcendental philosophy.

At the end of the *Dreams,* Kant argues that the "pneumatic" thesis of the existence of the soul independently of the body is a thesis of impossible solution. Metaphysics, in this regard, wastes its time on questions that allow for no answer. For no "data" from experience will ever support such a thesis. Experience is possible only in and through the body, and what pneumatology claims is precisely the possibility of an existence independent of bodily conditions. In this case, the "data" to the problem "are to be found in a world other than the one" in which we exist as embodied, sentient, and conscious beings—i.e., the data, even assuming that there are any, are thoroughly inaccessible to us.[18] It follows that the existence of the soul without the body will never be more than a dream or a fiction. Moreover, the thesis in question cannot claim the status that "hypotheses" have in natural science. For in science the *"possibility"* of hypotheses "must at all times be capable of proof."[19] Without the support of experience, however, merely "rational grounds" can confirm neither the possibility nor the impossibility of the given hypothesis, and hence these grounds can provide neither proof nor refutation. Thus, lacking both the evidence of empirical "data" and the means to show its very "possibility," the thesis of pneumatology must be discarded.[20]

"I know, of course, that thinking and willing move my body, but I can never reduce this phenomenon, as a simple experience, to another phenomenon by means of analysis." Hence, "I can recognize (*erkennen*)" the phenomenon since cognition implies my experiencing the event, but "I cannot understand it (*einsehen*)" from merely rational grounds. "That my will moves my arm is no more intelligible than someone's claiming that my will could halt the moon in its orbit. The only difference between the two cases is this: I experience the former, whereas my senses have never encountered the latter."[21] In other words, from the experiential data of the influence of my will and thought on my body I am not allowed to infer the existence of an immaterial soul that exists and acts independently of the body. My body enjoys a privileged status in the material world. It is the condition for self-consciousness: I am aware of the presence of a 'spiritual' dimension only as long as this 'inner' dimension is embodied. Embodiment draws the limits of our possible knowledge and hence ultimately decides the legitimacy of the metaphysical questions of the immortality of the soul and the communion or *commercium* between soul and body. The "limits of human reason"[22] and human self-knowledge are set by the indisputable conditions of an embodied consciousness. In the conclusion of the *Dreams*, the experience of embodiment plays a quasi-"critical" role.

In his letter to Moses Mendelssohn of 8 April 1766, Kant formulates the central issue of *Dreams* as the problem posed by the embodiment of consciousness. Endorsing a metaphysical perspective, Kant reveals his disappointment with the way metaphysics attempts to solve the problem. "In my opinion," explains Kant, "everything hinges upon this point: to find the data for the problem: How is the soul present in the world?"—namely, how is it present both "in material nature and in other entities closer to its own kind?" How can we know the presence of the soul in *Weltraum*—i.e., in "cosmic space"? In Kant's formulation, the metaphysical problem of the soul is that of its action in the world of space, time, bodies, and matter. The soul is, from the very outset, projected onto an external world. With this claim, Kant follows the Wolffian tradition that closely—and problematically—links the nature of the soul to the definition of space. Accordingly, what needs to be found is the "force of external efficacy and receptivity to being affected from without in a substance," namely the soul "of which its unification with the human body is only a particular kind." However, no experience is available to us "through which we could identify such a substance from the various relations which only and alone are able to reveal its external force or capacity."[23] The soul can be known only through its external relations to other substances. Yet, as Kant claimed in the *Dreams*, experience only makes us aware that our thinking or will (as *modi cogitandi*) somehow relate to our body; but this is certainly not the experience of an external efficacy of the soul itself or a relation of cause and effect such as that ascertained between bodies. Since no experience can support the claim of the existence of such a spiritual substance, the question remains whether it is possible "to prove a priori these forces of spiritual substances through a priori rational judgments." The metaphysical way is as impracticable as the empiricist one. Kant contends that no rational inference can ever lead us to the assumption of a "primitive force" of the soul as a first original relation of cause and effect.[24] Hence his conclusion: the central issue of "how the soul is present in the world"—and more precisely in *Weltraum*—cannot be solved since all data for the problem are lacking. In the face of the impossibility of solving the problem by way of either empirical or metaphysical knowledge, Swedenborg proposes a merely invented notion of spirit that does not even allow for a proof of its "possibility," and therefore must be rejected as sheer illusion.[25]

What is the doctrine of space that underlies the argument of the *Dreams* and how does the 'skeptical' conclusion of this text relate to that doctrine? It may seem surprising that while the conclusion of this work approaches a quasi-critical position, and Kant had already begun to criticize Wolff's concept of space in 1763,[26] the notion of space that he proposes in this work is entirely Wolffian and represents a position that Kant himself endorsed as early as 1747. Why is Kant attacking Wolff's metaphysics of the soul and, at the same time, maintaining his theory of space? The clue to this problem consists in recognizing the astute instrumental use that Kant now makes of the notion of space. The internal connection between the idea of space and the definition of the soul is at stake. Kant is clearly aware of this connection as he draws it to the center of his polemic attacks on rational psychology. His aim is to fight Wolff with his own weapons.

In his rational psychology, Wolff backs up the definition of the soul by means of the abstract rational concept of space. Unlike Leibniz, who assigned consciousness to all monads, Wolff distinguishes between material elements and conscious souls.[27] Since the soul is defined through its "force," and since force always implies "external" efficacy, spatial determination is contained, from the outset, in the concept of the soul. Space is that which supports the determination of the soul as a force that has external efficacy, while precisely through this external efficacy the soul establishes a relation to other substances. While Leibniz denies that space is a determination of substance, for Wolff there is no contradiction in claiming that the soul, though immaterial, is in space. Wolff's definition of space is functional to the issue of the reciprocal relation of substances and, in particular, to the problem of the body-soul relation: *spatium enim resultat ex possibilitate coexistendi*.[28] Space is the field of reciprocal action of substances; it is the order of coexistence. This definition directly "results" (*resultat*) from the problem posed by the interaction of substances.

The development of the doctrine of space in Wolff's school centers on the body-soul relation. In his revision of Leibniz's doctrine, Wolff restricts the validity of the pre-established harmony. This theory allowed Leibniz to think of the accordance between soul and body without having to assume any direct influence of one over the other. The harmony was delegated to God's action. The doctrine was radically opposed by the followers of the *influxus physicus* theory. Among them was Kant's influential teacher Martin Knutzen. Knutzen endorses Wolff's definition of space. In his view, substances exercise efficacy in the one all-encompassing space; the position (*Ort, Lage*) in space belongs to their determinations: the monad is *omnimode determinata* also with regard to its position in space.[29] The soul is localized in space even though it is not extended. Extension is produced and conditioned by the interaction of substances. Conceived in this way, space allows for an explanation of the physical interaction between the soul and the body.

In his early work *Thoughts on the True Extimation of the Living Forces* (1747), Kant defends Knutzen's theory of the *influxus physicus* and endorses the underlying Wolffian notion of space. Following the Leibnizians, Kant defines the essence of a body through its "force." The spatial position of the body is a condition of the efficacy of its force. At this point the two metaphysical problems arise of how the human body can produce representations in the human soul, and how the soul can put the material body into motion.[30] Kant's aim is to show that the difficulties of the theory of the *influxus physicus* can be resolved through the following proposition: "The soul must have external *efficacy because it occupies a place*."[31] In other words, space is precisely that which grounds and explains the *influxus physicus,* i.e., the soul's capacity for exercising a force outside of itself so as to produce modifications in external substances. However, if we consider the definition of space at stake in this solution, we find the same circularity that affected Wolff's definition of space. Kant explains that "place" defines "the efficacy of the substances on one another."[32] Hence: the soul occupies space (or is in a place) in order to exercise its external efficacy; but the soul exercises an external efficacy because it is in space (or is in a place). Similarly, Kant explains the body's efficacy on the soul (i.e., its capacity for producing representations) through its being in space with the soul; space is the ground of the body-soul's coexistence. Spatial relation is the condition of the possibility of reciprocal influence. Circularity, however, is again inevitable: there would be no space if substances did not have the force of acting outside of themselves.[33] Space depends on the soul's external efficacy, which, in order to be defined as 'external,' presupposes its being in space.

In the *Dreams,* Kant finds the metaphysical doctrine of the physical influence between body and soul no longer plausible. In order to show the illusory character of this metaphysical speculation, he uses Wolff's own concept of space. He thereby exposes the flawed nature of the link between the abstract notion of space as the sphere of coexistence and reciprocal action of substances, and the definition of the soul as a fundamental force that has *external* efficacy. Kant's starting point is an attempt to understand the obscure notion of "spirit." The crucial issue is whether spirit is a mere "fiction of the brain or something real."[34] Matter is that which fills up space and has the property of impenetrability. To define spirit as a simple substance endowed with reason is not enough to differentiate it from matter, since a simple being having the inner property of reason may still outwardly act like matter. The only way to preserve the notion of spirit is to define it as something that is present in space without filling it, hence without displaying the properties of impenetrability and solidity that characterize matter. Spirits are therefore "rational beings who can be present even in a space filled with matter, thus beings who do not possess the quality of impenetrability, and who never constitute a solid whole, no matter how many you unite."[35] Can this concept of spirit, asks Kant, lead to the claim that spirits are "real" or even "possible"? Whereas the concept of matter's impenetrability and solidity is an empirical concept, the idea of something that has efficacy in space and yet does not fill space is not an empirical concept. Spirit, thus defined, is something that cannot be present to my senses, i.e., cannot be experienced and hence cannot be conceived as real. On the contrary, it is a notion that brings with itself a certain "unthinkability." To be sure, both the possibility and the impossibility of such a being is unthinkable.[36] And yet assuming, with Wolff, that space is the field of reciprocal action and coexistence of substances, and assuming that a purely spiritual substance is one that outwardly acts upon a material body (or another spiritual substance), then the notion of its immediate presence in space can very well be conceived. For, given that definition of space, nothing contradicts this conclusion, even though such a notion cannot be known *in concreto.* Spirits "take up" space by being immediately active in it, even without filling it, i.e., without offering resistance.[37] Yet, the lack of contradiction is still not enough to prove the positive reality of the assumed spiritual substance. In other words, Wolff's metaphysical notion of space opens up the realm of the empty speculations of rational psychology by providing an illusory reality that is only a consequence of the assumed—abstract and ambiguous—definition of space. Wolff's concept of space is the basis of the a priori possibility of something that, according to Kant's principle of the "limits of human reason" based upon experience, cannot be claimed as a priori possible.[38] Thereby the metaphysical trick is exposed: defined as a merely metaphysical entity with no relation to our sensibility, space is used to support the plausibility of the notion of spirit because it ambiguously carries with itself a reference to the reality (efficacy) of that which exists in space.

Thus, the *Dreams* is construed as a *reductio ad absurdum* of Wolff's rational psychology on the basis of Wolff's own concept of space. The result of Kant's argument is twofold. The absurd conclusion to which the metaphysical claim is thereby brought leads Kant to reject the doctrine of the soul and, at the same time, to seek a new foundation for his theory of space. Space is no longer related to the presence of the soul in the world but rather to the presence of our body in the world.[39] Space is connected to human sensibility and bodily awareness. Thereby the transition from the 1766 *Dreams* to the 1768 "Regions in Space" is accomplished. From 1768 on space, for Kant, is the transcendental dimension of an embodied consciousness.

Daydreaming and Ghost-Seeing: Embodiment and the Inner/Outer Distinction

In the "Regions in Space," the connection between space and embodiment brings to the fore the spatial distinctions of left/right, up/down, etc.—distinctions that can be "felt" only through the body's own spatial orientation. In the *Dreams,* Kant uses the ghost- or spirit-seer Swedenborg to address the crucial inner/outer distinction. As in the case of spatial orientation, our body is the only 'sense' that allows us to maintain the 'normal' state in which objects *outside* ourselves are consciously kept separate from the dreams, images, or visions that take place *inside* ourselves. What happens when this distinction is erased? Kant discusses the difference between the daydreaming activity of philosophic fantasies and Swedenborg's ghost-seeing efforts. The daydreamer is someone who is so immersed in the figments and chimaeras of his mind as to lose contact with his sensory perceptions. However, the walking dreamer knows that he dreams: he represents his fictions "as being *in himself*, whereas other objects, which he senses, he represents as *outside* himself. As a consequence, he counts the former as the product of his own activity, while he regards the latter as something that he receives from outside and by which he is affected." In this case, Kant observes, "everything depends on the relation in which these objects are thought as standing *relatively to himself as a human being, and, thus, relatively to his body.*"[40] Even in daydreaming, our body serves us as criterion for assessing the objectivity of our representations. For it is only with regard to our body and in relation to its receptivity that we are able to discriminate between what we ourselves produce and what affects us externally. Because of this ongoing feeling for and presence in his body, the daydreamer is not deceived by his fantasies. For no matter how much those images occupy him, "the real sensation of his body creates, by means of the outer senses, a contrast or distinction with respect to those chimaeras."[41] It is the body that guarantees immediate self-awareness and a sense of self. Our sense of identity and presence in space is reached only through the self-perception of our own body. To have a body is to occupy a "region in space,"[42] and to be present in *Weltraum*. To the metaphysical question, where is the place of the human soul in the bodily world? Kant's answer is clear: "the body, whose alterations are *my* alterations—this body is *my* body; and the place of that body is, at the same time, *my place*." He pushes the question further by asking: "where then is *your* place (that of the soul) in this body?" And Kant's anti-Cartesian answer[43] refers to the most ordinary experience:

> Where I feel, it is there that *I am*. I am as immediately in my finger-tip as I am in my head. It is I myself whose heel hurts, and whose heart beats with emotion. And when my corn aches, I do not feel the painful impression in some nerve located in my brain; I feel it at the end of my toe.

While the self or soul may be separated from the body, awareness of the self is only embodied self-awareness, i.e., awareness of one's position in the world. Thus, the body is experienced as indispensable to the definition of the self even in the situation of the walking dreamer.[44]

Herein lies the difference between the walking dreamer and the ghost-seer. It is, Kant warns, a difference in kind and not in degree. The ghost-seer loses all contact with his body and consequently all discrimination between internal fantasies and external objects. He projects the inner figments of his brain outside himself, thereby using his own body to fundamentally misplace those visions. The inner figment of the imagination becomes for him a real outer object. Ghost-seeing is based upon a spatial displacement of representations, as these take an "outer place among the objects which present themselves to sensation." Kant explains this phenomenon of illusory projection from the inside to the outside in analogy with the optic notion of the *focus imaginarius*—the point of convergence and divergence of the rays of light that emanate from a point as they meet the eye.[45]

The metaphysical concept of the soul or spirit is precisely one of these figments produced by the ghost-seer. Since the property of "being present in space but not impenetrable" is meant to be spirit's distinguishing mark, it is not difficult to see how this notion is "true to its origin" as it has been generated by the illusion of an outward projection of something that is a mere inner fiction of the brain.[46] Thus ghost-seeing is, according to Kant, the "mental disturbance" whereby a victim "places mere objects of his own imagination outside himself, taking them to be things which are actually present before him."[47] Such a phenomenon is caused by a distortion and disturbance of the balance proper to the nerves and organs of the brain, a balance which is responsible for representing outside what has its place only inside the brain. Since this illness directly affects the fantastic sense-perception of the visionary, sense-perception by itself is not able to cure the illusion. However, since it does not affect his understanding but involves a deception of the senses that precedes all judgment, neither can reason alone banish the illusion. Having ruled out sense-perception and reason (i.e., the empiricist and rationalist ways), the only criterion of reality remains, for Kant, the integral bodily awareness that allows us to draw the distinction between external and internal. Such awareness is not identical with immediate sense-perception but is the organ responsible for the 'true' location of our perceptions.

Moreover, Swedenborg's ghost-seeing eliminates the objective physical space of outer things by converting it into an imaginary space in which things subsist only as symbolic representations of the inner world of spirits. In this world "corporeal beings have no substance of their own; they only exist by virtue of the spirit-world."[48] Swedenborg's "most internal interior"—jokes Kant—"has opened up" to disclose a position that a "future interpreter" would rightly call "idealist."[49] For he denies that the matter of this world has an independent subsistence of its own. The paradox to which Kant's argument ultimately leads is the following: the world of spirits that is based upon a Wolffian, abstract notion of space as field of interaction and co-existence of substances, ends up eliminating the real space of outer objects.

The outer dimension of real things is converted into the inner dimension of their alleged spiritual value.

Outer Space and Inner Time:
Embodiment and the Refutation of Idealism

In the *Dreams,* Kant comes to a twofold conclusion. On the one hand, he diagnoses the definitive failure of rational psychology as a metaphysical discipline. From now on, a doctrine of the soul is no longer possible for Kant. On the other hand, having broken completely with the Wolffian idea of space, he sees the possibility (and indeed the necessity) of working out a new concept of space. While all "data" from experience are lacking for the problem posed by the soul, for the issue of space Kant does indeed find data available. Accordingly, the problem of space promises a positive solution. The connection that leads Kant from the skeptical conclusions of *Dreams* to the positive results of "Regions in Space" shows a remarkable discrepancy between the data of inner and outer sense. The latter rest on the concrete experience of embodiment that is henceforth drawn to the center of Kant's reflections on the notion of experience. The former, on the contrary, are marked by a vacuum whose metaphysical dimension of interiority Kant attacks in all its resurgent shapes until he reduces it to a pure "form" of human sensibility (namely, time).

At the end of the "Regions in Space," Kant plays the new concept of space directly against Wolff and the Leibnizian tradition. Space is now determined as that which makes possible all sensation and composition of matter. Since space does not result from the reciprocal position of parts of matter but is the condition of matter's order, it follows that matter cannot have an intrinsic, inner order proper to it independent of space. With this thesis, the conclusion of the 1768 essay complements the conclusion of the 1766 *Dreams.* As Kant will repeat in the Amphiboly of the Concepts of Reflection in the first *Critique,* there is no metaphysical "inner" dimension of things. The new concept of space leads Kant to a positive elimination of the visionary fiction of an "internal" dimension of reality—be it Swedenborg's or Leibniz's version. Once the metaphysical reality of the soul has been removed, the human body remains as the only dividing line between inner and outer, internal and external. Thus, time is the form of inner intuition or inner sense, whereas space is the form of outer intuition or outer sense. As time is the form of our intuition of ourselves and our inner states, so space is the condition for our experience of the outer world and of outer objects.[50] Our body is the hinge that connects inner and outer sense, the experience of our inner self and the experience of the outer world. What we may call the "experience of ourselves" results from the connection of these two dimensions. The unity of embodied consciousness maintains the inner and outer dimensions of experience as distinct and immune to visionary displacement. Thus, Kant's Transcendental Aesthetic (i.e., the transcendental doctrine of space and time) is the first critical successor of traditional rational psychology.

The *Critique of Pure Reason* follows the involvement of the human body in the cognitive process along an itinerary of complex transfiguration that prepares embodied consciousness to serve as a concrete and positive response to the empty claims of "material idealism." After the Transcendental Aesthetic, the stages of this itinerary are represented by the Analogies of Experience and the Postulates of Empirical Thinking in General.[51]

According to the doctrine of the first *Critique,* the structure of the "physical object" requires, for its determination, the following constitutive elements: extension in space and time, presence of the categories (substance, causality, reciprocity—according to the Analogies of Experience), and finally sensation (with its specific quantity or degree—according to the Postulates of Empirical Thinking in General). If one of these conditions fails to occur, the physical object, i.e., appearance, vanishes and becomes unknowable.[52] The empirical presence of the physical object thereby constituted is characteristic of Kant's "transcendental" or "critical" idealism. More specifically, the question therein is: what is the role that space and time play in the constitution of the reality of the physical object as the outer object that affects us, is present to our body, and produces sensation? This is the issue at the center of Kant's longstanding opposition to empirical or material idealism.

From the *Dissertatio* (1770) up to the second edition of the *Critique of Pure Reason* (1787), Kant elaborates on the reciprocal relation between space and time as forms of sensible intuition. Given the discrepancy between the two that marks their pre-critical origin, does one form have priority over the other, and how is their imbalance manifested?[53] In the *Dissertatio,* Kant recognizes time's primacy over space as he considers it closer to a "universal rational concept" than space (despite its being a pure intuition and not a concept!).[54] In the first edition of the *Critique of Pure Reason* this imbalance, though attenuated, is maintained by the fact that time is the form of both inner and outer sense. Time "is a condition a priori of *all ap-*

pearance in general. It is the *immediate* condition of *inner appearance (our souls),* and thereby also the *mediate* condition of *outer appearances.*"[55] In the second edition of the *Critique of Pure Reason,* with the Refutation of Idealism, the balance between space and time is restored. Here Kant brings to the fore the privileged connection that space has with our body (as time has a privileged connection with the transfigured interiority of the "soul" of rational psychology). Such a link had already been established in the definition of space given in the Transcendental Aesthetic. Transcendentally, the body is space incarnated. If space is defined as the form of the "*receptivity* of the subject," i.e., as "its capacity for being *affected* by objects," this is precisely because space has its organ in the human body. Space is the form of the human body's own receptivity. The formal character of space incorporates the character of sensitivity inherited from the body. Space is not just the body's receptivity but is (transcendentally) the "form" or the formal condition for all (empirical) bodily receptivity and affection. This form necessarily precedes a priori all intuitions of objects, i.e., all actual affection through objects.[56] Thus, already at the level of the Transcendental Aesthetic, Kant defines space and time with an elliptic, and yet essential, reference to the body and soul respectively.[57] This reference plays a pivotal role in the Refutation of Idealism.

In the Analogies of Experience of the *Critique of Pure Reason,* space and time serve to develop Kant's critical solution to the metaphysical problem that the *Dreams* had brought to its most absurd and untenable consequences. The categories of relation (substance, causality, and reciprocal action), once schematized with the forms of space and time (i.e., once concretely presented in a corresponding sensible intuition), provide the synthetic a priori principles through which the understanding constructs our mathematical and physical knowledge of the world of nature as the world of appearances. In order for the concepts of the understanding to be applied to objects so as to provide knowledge, these concepts need to be realized or "schematized" through sensible intuition. The insuperable condition of space and time as forms of our sensibility is Kant's answer to the metaphysical riddles of the pre-critical period. In its "schema," the category of substance determines that which is "permanent" (*das Beharrliche*) in our spatial and temporal intuition. Substance is the object of possible experience (not thing-in-itself). Since we have no intuition of our "soul" in space and time, and since our inner perception does not offer anything permanent that would allow for the use of the category of substance, the soul is never given to us and experienced by us as substance.

Causality, as the schematized relation of cause and effect, is the order of what is given in intuition according to the unitary principle of thinking. In its sensible schematization, causality applies only to appearances, not to things in themselves.[58] As Kant contends in the *Dreams:*

> If the fundamental concepts of things as causes [. . .] are not derived from experience, then they are wholly arbitrary, and they admit of neither proof nor refutation. I know, of course, that thinking and willing move my body, but I can never reduce this phenomenon, as a simple experience, to another phenomenon by means of analysis.[59]

In other words, I cannot infer analytically from experience that the soul is the "cause" of the bodily movement that I directly experience.

Finally, the schema of the category of reciprocal action or "community"—*Gemeinschaft,* which here means both *communio* or spatial community and *commercium* or dynamical community—provides the principle of coexistence. "All substances, insofar as they can be perceived to coexist in space, are in thoroughgoing reciprocity."[60] Dynamic community is the condition of the coexistence of two objects in a possible experience. Without this principle, our perceptions of different objects (in space) would be radically separated from one another and could never yield a thoroughgoing interconnected experience. Against Leibniz's pre-established harmony, Kant claims that we can understand the possibility of community of substances only if we represent them in the outer intuition of space, i.e., as appearances. Reciprocal action is possible only as a category that is schematized with sensible intuition, i.e., space and time. Significantly, in discussing dynamic community, Kant brings to the fore the role played by our own body: by our eye that is set in "mediate community" with celestial bodies by the light playing between them, and, once again, by the peculiar experience of finding—and perceiving—the "place" (*Ort*) and "position" (*Stelle*) that we occupy in dynamic community with other objects.[61]

The next important step in the process through which Kant integrates the bodily dimension of human sensibility into his account of our knowledge of reality as appearance, takes place in the Postulates of Empirical Thinking in General. At stake is the relation between perception or sensation and the actuality of the object. Kant's goal is to show how the human body, once transcendentally involved in the cognitive process, exceeds the physical limits of the senses as it takes on a formal dimension by its functioning together with the understanding. While space accounts for the *immediate* presence of the object to embodied consciousness, perception points to the *mediation* that the body receives from the understanding with its analogies of experience. Kant argues that the "postulate" regarding our knowledge of the "actuality" of things (the second postulate) demands "perception, and hence sensation, of which we are conscious not immediately from the object whose existence is to be known." For if our consciousness of the object were immediate we would merely have formal intuition of the object, and not sensation. What is required, in addition, is the object's "connection with some actual perception in accordance to the analogies of experience, which define all real connection in an experience in general." The givenness of the object in intuition (i.e., in space) makes it possible for it to be perceived as actual. "Perception," explains Kant, is the material side of our sensibility (its formal side is intuition). Perception is "the only character of actuality."[62] While our body is *formally* represented by space as a priori intuition, it is *materially* active in the cognitive process through sensation. The materiality of sensation involves but is not reduced to the participation of the bodily organs. Since the perceptual activity of the body is predicated upon the work of the understanding—for only through it does perception gain the crucial connection with the category of actuality—the body emerges, once again, as transcendentally transfigured. The analogies of experience allow us to make the transition from our actual perception to a real thing by proceeding through the series of possible perceptions. Thereby perception extends beyond the limitation of our bodily organs. Our body somehow gains "more refined" senses.

> From the perception of attracted iron filings we know of the existence of a magnetic matter pervading all bodies, *although the constitution of our organs cuts us off from all immediate perception of this medium.* For, in accordance with the laws of sensibility and the context of our perceptions, we should, were our senses more refined, come also in an experience upon the immediate empirical intuition of it.

Through the mediation of the analogies of experience, our sensation extends from what is immediately perceived to the "context of our perceptions"— i.e., to all possible as well as actual perception. Significantly, in the face of the apparent obstacle represented by the "grossness of our senses," Kant does not suggest abstraction from the materiality of sensibility. Rather, he claims that we must refine our senses through the mediation of the understanding by placing our perception in the "context" of the cognitive process as a whole. Embodied sense-perception (both actual and possible) is indispensable to this process as the only mark of the actuality of the object. "Our

knowledge of the existence of things reaches [. . .] only so far as perception and its advance according to empirical laws can extend."[63] The crucial
objection to this doctrine is raised by empirical "idealism."

In the second edition of the *Critique of Pure Reason* the discussion of the
second of the Postulates of Empirical Thinking in General, the postulate
of actuality, is immediately followed by a "Refutation of Idealism." Since
the 1755 *Nova Dilucidatio,* Kant had repeatedly attempted to refute empirical
idealism.[64] The pre-critical antecedents of the Refutation of Idealism are
the conclusion of "Regions in Space" on the one hand, and the cathartic
itinerary of *Dreams* on the other. Kant needed both steps in order to refute
the idealist's denial of the reality of the outer world. In the *Dreams,* Kant
encountered the fantasies of the "idealist" Swedenborg against which only
the experience of embodiment (neither sheer sense-perception nor reason
alone) seemed able to restore a reliable sense of reality. In 1766, however,
Kant did not yet have a positive argument to counter the idealist's claim.
Kant's point in the Refutation is to put forward his complex conception
of the physical object as definitive proof against the idealist's denial of the
reality of the outer world. By showing the different ways in which the body
is present in the cognitive process—from the Transcendental Aesthetic to
the Analytic of Principles—Kant has provided the ultimate foundation for
the experience of embodiment already underlying the *Dreams.* The Refutation of Idealism is based upon a general premise that has its birthplace in
the joint reflections carried through in those two pre-critical texts, namely:
(1) there are things that can only be intuited and not conceptually thought
(incongruent counterparts, whereby space is defined as formal intuition),
and (2) there are things that can only be thought and not intuited (the soul,
things as they are in themselves).[65] Kant's critical argument will always
maintain the twofold connection with the topic of space and the issue of
psychology. The refutation of empirical idealism plays itself out in the gap
between the transcendental ideality of the body and the absence of a metaphysical soul.[66]

Kant's argument refutes the claim of "material" idealism in its two historical manifestations, i.e., Descartes's "problematic" (or "psychological")[67]
idealism and Berkeley's "dogmatic" idealism. He identifies the central claim
of idealism in its attack on the proposition that establishes the "existence
of objects in space outside ourselves." While problematic idealism considers this existence doubtful and indemonstrable, dogmatic idealism simply
rejects it as false and impossible. Evidently, with this thesis, idealism undermines the milestones of Kant's construction, namely the claim (1) that the

objects of which we have knowledge are "real" things (not mere fictitious entities), (2) that they are in space (as appearances), and (3) that they are "outside" ourselves (present to our bodily perception).[68] Descartes holds on to the merely empirical certainty of the "I think," whereas Berkeley declares things in space to be "mere imaginary entities."[69] Thereby both the alleged superiority of an interior spiritual dimension over the outside world and the ghost of imaginary fictions reappear as targets of Kant's proof. Kant easily dismisses the claim of Berkeley's dogmatic idealism by referring back to the Transcendental Aesthetic and its proof of the transcendental ideality and empirical reality of space as a priori form of intuition. For space and the existence of things in space become a fiction (*Unding*) only if space is considered a property of things in themselves, i.e., of things taken apart from any reference to our sensibility.[70] The claim of problematic idealism is more difficult to tackle since it does not engage directly with the issue of space, but simply denies the possibility of proving by "immediate experience" any existence *except our own* and any existence *outside our own*.[71] Thereby, problematic idealism suspends the reality of the world outside us and demands a positive proof for it. In the face of this version of idealism, Kant probably felt that both the merely negative conclusion of the *Dreams* and the solution of the Transcendental Aesthetic, as well as the refutation that in 1781 was integrated into the fourth Paralogism of the Transcendental Dialectic, were insufficient to positively restore the suspended reality of the outside world. A definitive refutation[72] was needed even before getting into the Paralogisms of the Dialectic. After all, material idealism is a direct attack on the "rule" expressed by the second postulate. The weapons at Kant's disposal are now the results of the Aesthetic as well as the whole development of the Analytic of Principles.[73] This explains the addition of the separate Refutation in the 1787 edition of the first *Critique* at the very end of the Postulates of Empirical Thinking.

Descartes's objection shapes the aim of Kant's proof: what needs to be demonstrated is that we do indeed have "experience" of outer things, i.e., that we experience and not only imagine, fancy, or dream of things in space outside ourselves. This aim is achieved by showing, against the empirical certainty of Descartes's *cogito,* that "even our inner experience [. . .] is possible only on the assumption of outer experience."[74] Thereby Kant is not directly responding to Descartes's intention in soliciting a proof of the reality of external things. What is at stake, for Kant, is not a supposed "inference" from inner consciousness to outer experience: this inference is impossible.[75] More radically, Kant's move consists in overturning the very assumption of Descartes's idealism. He contends that the inner dimension of consciousness presupposes and requires outer experience. In other words, Kant intimates that only an embodied subject can have experience of her inner self through the experience of the outer world that her body channels. Descartes's *cogito* cannot be a disembodied subject. But if the subject is necessarily embodied, then the existence of outer objects is the first condition of all inner experience. Thereby, the priority of space over time comes to the fore. Thus, Kant's thesis is the following: self-consciousness is always and necessarily embodied consciousness; "the mere, but empirically determined, consciousness of my own existence"[76] proves the existence of objects in space outside myself. His proof is accompanied by three remarks.

Kant articulates the proof as follows. I am conscious of my own existence only through my empirical determination in time. Self-consciousness, for Kant, is not an abstract, empty certainty but a state always and necessarily determined by an empirical content apprehended in time. Kant establishes two connected points: the ground for the determination of my existence in time is not "in me" (nor is it effected by me) but "outside me"; this determination is not a representation but a real thing. According to the first analogy of experience, determination in time presupposes "something permanent" or enduring (*Beharrliches*) in perception. Substance and its permanence are neither the interiority of a soul or spirit nor an "intuition in myself." For all ground of determination of my existence that can be found *in me* is only representation, and representations determine my existence in time through their change; however, in order for their change to serve as determination of my inner state, something permanent is required in relation to which change can be determined and hence can serve as determination of my inner state. Hence, this something permanent must be *outside* me. In addition, the permanent must also be an existing *thing,* not a representation. If "*perception*" of the permanent is needed for my inner determination, then, for the second postulate of empirical thinking, this permanent can only be perceived through a real *thing* that exists outside me, not through a mere *representation* of a thing outside me. Moreover, as Kant clarifies in the 1787 preface, "the representation of something *persisting* in existence is not the same as a *persisting* representation."[77] By referring to perception, Kant underlines the *material* side of our cognition of appearances. As established by the postulate of actuality, it is only from the existence of things outside ourselves that "we derive the whole material for cognition, *even for our inner sense.*"[78] Thereby, the Refutation of Idealism carries the second postulate a step further and shows that we need perception not only to know real objects of the external world but even to get the kind of inner "certainty" of our own existence that Descartes rescued from his radical doubt.

Kant's conclusion follows: "the determination of my existence in time is possible only through the existence of actual things (*Existenz wirklicher Dinge*) that I perceive outside me." Now, self-consciousness is precisely consciousness of my time-determination; time-determination presupposes and requires perception; perception, revealing the presence of the body in the cognitive process, implies the form of space in which the existence of things is perceived as outside me. Hence, inner experience presupposes outer experience, i.e., perception of a real world intuited in space outside me. The existence of outer things is the necessary "condition of time-determination" because consciousness is necessarily embodied. "Consciousness of my own existence is *at the same time* an *immediate* consciousness of the existence of other things outside me."[79] Thereby, Kant proves that if time is the mediate condition of all outer appearances,[80] the *immediacy* of outer experience is the "condition of the possibility"[81] of all inner experience. Consciousness of my existence in time and consciousness of the existence of outer things occur "at the same time" (*zugleich*).[82] Consciousness of my existence is the immediate consciousness both of my being in space, i.e., of my having a body (that is *my* body), and of my being in time, i.e., of the inner dimension within which my outer experience is ordered and apprehended through time-determination. With the failure of rational psychology to prove the existence of a soul, the inner sense finds itself necessarily projected onto the "outside." Inner experience is utterly dependent upon the body's immediate relation to objects. The inner world does not have "sense" (or determination) independently of the outer world. On the contrary, the outer sense, on the ground of its formal relation to the body, enjoys the immediacy of contact with objects (receptivity). Thus, while inner sense is constitutively "mediated," outer sense is constitutively "immediate." This conclusion goes against the fundamental claim of Descartes's psychological idealism, i.e., the immediate certainty of the *cogito*. To be sure, however, Kant's thesis not only overturns Descartes's problem; rather, it radically changes its structure. Only through the mediation of outer experience, which is properly immediate, is inner experience possible. However, "inner experience" is not "consciousness of our own existence," but rather consciousness of the determination of our existence in time. The formal representative of our subjectivity, the "I think," yields neither "knowledge" of ourselves nor "experience" of ourselves. For inner experience to take place, intuition is always needed in addition to the simple thought of the "I think."[83]

To be conscious of my existence in time is indeed "*more* than simply being conscious of my representations." Yet, to be conscious of my existence in time is "*one with* the empirical consciousness of my existence." Such "empirical consciousness of my existence," which first appears in the enunciation of Kant's theorem, is based upon the consciousness of my existence in space, i.e., of my being present in a body. As Kant restates his polemic against Swedenborg, embodiment is the necessary condition of "experience" as opposed to "invention," and of "sense" as opposed to the non-sense of empty imaginations, "dreams and delusions."[84] It is only through my body, as formal representative of my existence in space (of my occupying a place in the outer world), that the relation to something real, permanent, external to me and yet "connected to my existence" is first established. This relation is necessary in order to have inner experience of my existence in time. The body (as sense and not imagination) is the hinge that "inseparably joins" the outside world with my inner sense.[85] Significantly, in the second remark to the Refutation's proof, the reference to our perception of the "motion of the sun relatively to objects on earth" reappears. Our perception of time-determination depends on the capacity of detecting "change in outer relations (motion) relatively to the permanent in space."[86] As Kant had argued in the *First Metaphysical Principles of Natural Science* with explicit reference to the incongruent counterparts, our capacity of detecting such motion (in particular, a body's circular motion) requires our physical presence in the world, i.e., the capacity of assessing the direction of the motion. In this case, the "permanent in space" is immediately represented by our own body.[87]

After the Refutation, in the General Remark to the System of Principles, the notion of consciousness' necessary embodiment is raised to a fundamental fact—indeed a "noteworthy" one—for the objective employment of the concepts of understanding. "In order to understand the possibility of things in accordance with the categories, and thus to demonstrate the *objective reality* of the latter, we do not need merely intuitions, but even always *outer intuitions.*"[88] This is the ultimate consequence which the Transcendental Aesthetic is brought to, through the Refutation of Idealism, at the end the Analytic of Principles.

3

Disembodied Ideas

My soul walks with me, form of forms.
—JAMES JOYCE, *Ulysses*

La nostra mente fa corporeo anche il nulla
—EUGENIO MONTALE

IN HIS 1770 *DISSERTATIO,* KANT MENTIONS PLATO FOR THE first time.[1] The reference to Plato has a twofold function there: on the one hand, it gives the theoretical frame of reference for Kant's introduction of the term "idea" and for his own use of it; on the other hand, it allows him to place the theory of the *Dissertatio* and the notion of metaphysics proposed therein into the historical context of a criticism of both British empiricism and Leibnizian-Wolffian rationalism. Moreover, Kant's reference to Plato's idea is explicitly accompanied by an historical comment that discloses the lines along which Kant's theory develops. What Plato used to call "idea"—observes Kant—is "nowadays called Ideal." However, the *Critique of Pure Reason* will teach that "idea" and "ideal" are two different notions and not just different names for the same thing. What is already at stake in 1770, with this terminological specification, is the fundamental issue of the distinction between theology and moral philosophy in Kant's view of metaphysics. Given the way in which the ancient—i.e., Platonic—theory of ideas has been corrupted by the British empiricists (who were preceded by Epicurus) in relation to practical philosophy, and by Wolff in the sphere

of theoretical or speculative philosophy, Kant wishes to regain the true
Platonic significance of the concept. This becomes possible, however, only
through the necessary specification of the use of the term in theology and
moral philosophy. What Kant is not yet clear about in his philosophical program, in 1770, is the fact that there is a specific faculty of ideas different and
separate from the faculty of concepts—i.e., that the function and domain of
the "intellect" need to be specified not only in relation to "sensibility" but
also in relation to "reason." Intellect and reason—in the *Dissertatio* both are
subsumed under the term *intelligentia*—each make use of a different type
of concepts, and have two different spheres of application. The analysis of
Kant's conception of ideas in the *Dissertatio* reveals that, if he senses the
crucial difference separating the "concept" of substance from the "idea" of
moral perfection, he is not able yet to draw a corresponding distinction in
the respective faculties that generate and use concepts and ideas.

The aim of this chapter is to broaden the perspective within which embodiment has been thematized so far in Kant's philosophy. Up to this point
I have shown how the body, displaying a purely transcendental form, plays
a crucial role in the development of Kant's notion of sensibility, and how,
precisely through the body, sensibility is radically distinguished from—and
yet also necessarily related to—understanding and its concepts. Analyzing
some crucial moments of the doctrine of schematism of the first *Critique,* I
have shown in what sense the cognitive experience proper to the mathematical and physical construction of nature as well as empirical self-cognition
result from the synthetic interaction of sensibility's pure forms and understanding's concepts. I now draw to the center of the discussion a "region"
of our cognitive faculty that, on Kant's account, is constitutively separated
from sensibility—a region, that is, whose interaction with sensibility is in
principle excluded as it yields no knowledge of objects. This is the realm
of reason's "ideas." Continuing the inquiry begun in the previous two
chapters, I start with the analysis of a pre-critical text. I show how the 1770
Dissertatio gains the concept of "idea" by thinking through the distinction
between sensibility and understanding (or intellect).

By means of the notion of "idea" Kant is able to give a new transcendental status to the 'absence' that characterizes the disappearance of the
metaphysical soul proper to rational psychology.[2] We have seen that while
the body, transcendentally transfigured in its pure form, finds its legitimate
place in the theory of the Transcendental Aesthetic, the soul as metaphysical entity is completely eliminated from Kant's critical inquiry. Facing the
traditional opposition between the physical materiality of the body and

the metaphysical immateriality of the soul, Kant's investigation brings to the fore the fundamental asymmetry between the two. On Kant's account, the obvious and trivial empirical givenness of our physical body cannot be eliminated (Descartes's psychological idealism or material idealism in general is false). It can (and should) instead be referred back to the transcendental conditions which, inscribed in the body (as constitutive of the subject's empirical self), make an empirical investigation or observation of the body (as object) possible. Transcendentally, the body provides the condition of space as form of outer sense—a form with which (along with time) understanding's categories are schematized in order to yield knowledge of objects. The metaphysical existence of the soul, on the contrary, cannot be maintained and must be entirely rejected. Its critical transformation implies the gesture of a radical replacement. For, if accepted, the claim of rational psychology leads to metaphysical solipsism and to the outright elimination of all sensibility. Accordingly, Kant develops an articulated and complex theory in order to account for the counterpart of the body in his critical philosophy. The place of the soul is taken, first, by the notion of "inner experience" or "inner sense" which is based upon outer experience or outer sense (Refutation of Idealism). Second, Kant points to the merely logical or "intellectual" representation of the thinking subject (the I or "I think"), whose existence, however, cannot be experienced.[3] The "idea" of the soul—or the soul taken as idea of reason—is Kant's final answer to the theoretical problem of finding the body's counterpart in the critical philosophy. The discussion of this idea leads us to one of the main issues of Kant's practical philosophy. For while the idea of the soul is, according to Kant, the example of a thoroughly dis-embodied (and hence empty) concept, his practical philosophy shows that ideas gain reality in the realm of freedom as concretely "embodied ideas." According to this program, the task of the Transcendental Dialectic of the *Critique of Pure Reason* is twofold. Kant completely empties out the concept of the soul, and yet, by giving to it the peculiar status of an "idea," he opens up the possibility of its practical enactment and actual embodiment in a realm that is no longer determined by the conditions of space and time. Thereby he discloses the possibility of a new transcendental meaning of embodiment. To be sure, in the Appendix to the Transcendental Dialectic, Kant seems to envision another, "regulative" function for reason's ideas in our pursuit of science. However, we will have to wait for the third *Critique* in order for this regulative value to be transcendentally sanctioned by an independent a priori principle—i.e., to be no longer the topic of a mere appendix but that of a new critical inquiry. At this later point in Kant's itinerary, reason's ideas will find a new 'body' within our reflective experience of ourselves and of living nature. The connection between the notion of idea and that of "world" (in their common reference to the notion of "system"), explored by the first *Critique,* will prove itself crucial for this further development of Kant's critical philosophy.

In addition to the necessary reference to the soul as counterpart of the body, the discussion of Kant's notion of idea allows us to discover another important element in the general issue of embodiment. This is the idea of the "world," taken as the "place" that articulates the reality of the body and our cognition of reality. The body hints, at the same time, at the inner dimension of a soul, a self, or inner experience, and to the outer world. I have shown how, according to Kant, we come to define experience and perceive the world as being "outside" ourselves. Now I ask the different question: what does philosophy indicate by the term "world"? On the basis of the difference between "idea" and "ideal" provided by the chapter on the Ideal of Pure Reason of the first *Critique,* I suggest that in the *Dissertatio* the notion of idea is crucial to Kant because of its fundamental relation to the notion of "world" (*mundus*). This holds true not only on the basis of the distinction between the sensible and intelligible world, but also because the notion of *mundus* is thought of in terms of *totality*—as *totum* and *universitas.* At this early date, the world is already presented by Kant as the "cosmological idea" of the world. Since ideas display the structure of a totality, their comprehension represents an eternal "cross" (*crux)* for the philosopher— indeed a thoroughly *spinosa quaestio,* observes Kant. Thereby, the *Dissertatio* already announces the critical notion of the "antinomy" of pure reason.[4]

In this chapter, I examine Kant's notions of "idea" and "ideal" in the *Dissertatio* using Kant's reference to Plato to examine the different meanings and uses that this crucial term presents from now on in transcendental philosophy. I relate the discussion of Kant's conception of idea in 1770 to two different issues raised in the general argument of the *Dissertatio.*[5] I suggest, first, that even if Kant does not provide an explicitly formulated theory of ideas by 1770, the term plays an essential role for him in setting up the major theses of this work. Accordingly, Kant's brief remark on Plato's ideas in §9 is not a marginal addition to the general argument that separates sensibility and understanding; rather, it represents a fundamental development in Kant's conception of metaphysics by the time of the *Dissertatio.* Idea and ideal play a crucial role in the distinction that Kant draws between *cognitio sensitiva* and *cognitio intellectualis.* Such a distinction, in turn, is related both to the separation between *Phaenomenon* and *Noumenon* and between *mundus sensibilis* and *mundus intelligibilis*. Second, I show in what sense the reference to Plato's notion of idea is essential to Kant in creating the historical presuppositions for his own critical philosophy. Viewed in the light of some of his contemporary *Reflections,* the position of the *Dissertatio* points to the relation between a dogmatic and a critical conception (or "stage") of metaphysics. In his attempt to produce an historical "need" for his philosophical claims, Kant's position in 1770 is close to that of the *Critique of Pure Reason* both in 1781 and 1787.[6] The reference to Plato allows Kant to overcome both the metaphysical and dogmatic positions of Christian Wolff, and the empiricism of Shaftesbury's moral philosophy. I conclude the chapter with a brief discussion of the Paralogisms of Pure Reason in the first *Critique,* where Kant repeats his longstanding polemic against rational psychology. Swedenborg's illusions, Plato's mysticism, and Leibniz's and Wolff's metaphysical psychology now share the fate of reason and its ideas. It is in this section that the 1781 *Critique* places the argument in refutation of material idealism. Even though the *Dissertatio* established the necessarily *disembodied* nature of ideas, in the Transcendental Dialectic Kant intimates that ideas do exhibit a reality of their own. What is this disembodied reality of ideas? It is neither the illusory reality of fictions nor the disembodied abstract being of the soul. Kant's solution opens up a different perspective: it is the reality in a 'body' placed outside the conditions of space and time, namely, in a body that lives and acts in the practical realm of freedom.

Sensible and Intelligible World, Phenomena and Noumena, Sensible Knowledge and Intellectual Knowledge

One could easily be tempted to locate the first apparent and most obvious reference to Plato already in the title of Kant's *Dissertatio inauguralis: De mundi sensibilis atque intelligibilis forma et principiis,* as this title seems to point to a metaphysical opposition between two orders of reality that are clearly of Platonic derivation. However, this same separation between intelligible reality and the realm of sensible experience can be found in a tradition well known to Kant and closer to him.[7] Alexander Gottlieb Baumgarten, for example, in his *Metaphysica* §869 writes: "insofar as the world is sensibly represented, it is the sensible world [. . .], insofar as it is known in a distinct way, it is the intelligible world."[8] The world is twofold according to the type of knowledge or representation that we have of it: what makes the difference is whether the world is object of sensible representation or of clear and distinct cognition. In the *Dissertatio*, referring to this way of presenting the question, Kant criticizes the traditional argument for what is called "sensible" in the sensible cognition of the world, and for what is called "intellectual" in its intellectual cognition. Kant's notion of idea is placed precisely in the space that divides these two types of knowledge. Idea is not their mediation but rather the sign that all mediation is impossible.

In the *Dreams of a Spirit-Seer* (1766), Kant uses the Latin phrase *mundus intelligibilis* to describe the "immaterial world"[9] constituted by the totality of all immaterial, i.e., spiritual substances and their mutual relations. To this world belong also the constitutive principles of organic nature and organic life. Kant's problem—both in 1766 and in 1770—concerns the foundation of this immaterial or intelligible world as a "*totality* that subsists for itself and whose parts are in reciprocal connection with each other and subsist together even without the mediation of material things."[10] In this case, what is relevant in Kant's use of the expression *mundus intelligibilis* is the modality according to which the *totality* of the world is constituted as a realm of immaterial substances. That the issue raised by the concept of *mundus* is the logical and metaphysical problem of the notion of totality as *totum*, is a basic claim of traditional metaphysics. Kant's significant transformation of the problem consists, as it were, in its reformulation or reconstruction in terms of human knowledge and its possibilities.

Whereas the title of Kant's *Dissertatio* cannot be viewed as entailing a specifically Platonic reference, in discussing the distinction between sensible and intelligible Kant recuperates an explicitly Greek and Platonic terminology—namely, that of *Phaenomena* and *Noumena*. On the basis of these concepts (first introduced in §§2–3) Kant frames, retrospectively, the problem of the sensible and intelligible worlds. In other words, on Kant's account, the distinction between *mundus sensibilis* and *mundus intelligibilis* can be gained only through a threefold progression that (1) starts with the description of the faculties of the subject, (2) proceeds with the description of their specific objects, and (3) finally draws the distinction between the kind of cognition proper to the different faculties and to their related objects.

(1) Both *sensualitas* and *intelligentia* display, for Kant, a representational character:

> Sensibility (*sensualitas*) is the receptivity of the subject through which it is possible that its representative state should be affected in a certain manner by the presence of some object. Intelligence (*intelligentia*) (rationality) is the *faculty of*

the subject through which it is able to represent things that cannot by their own nature come before the senses of that subject.[11]

The first denotes a passive attitude of the subject (*receptivitas*) toward immediately present objects (i.e., objects of the senses); whereas the second is an active *facultas* that by itself, on the basis of its own innate laws, represents those objects whose givenness to the senses is utterly impossible, and thereby replaces their sensible and physical presence with a purely intellectual one.

(2) The definition of two different types of objects follows immediately from the foregoing analysis: "The object of sensibility is the sensible (*objectum sensualitatis est sensibile*); that which contains nothing but what *must be known* through intelligence is the intelligible."[12] Significantly, Kant chooses to name these two classes of objects of knowledge after the vocabulary of "the ancient schools": the first type of objects has been called *Phaenomenon,* the second *Noumenon.* In a later *Reflection,* Kant further develops the historical dimension of this thought, and suggests the way in which the notion of idea relates to the phenomena/noumena distinction: "History of the difference between *sensitivis* and *intellectualibus.* Pythagoras. Heraclitus (Eleatics). Plato (*ideae innatae*) and Pythagoras made the *intellectualia* into particular objects of possible intuition."[13] Systematically, in the light of the *Critique of Pure Reason,* the distinction between *Phaenomena* and *Noumena* represents the true introduction to Kant's theory of transcendental ideas.[14]

(3) Since from the very outset *Phaenomena* and *Noumena* do not describe for Kant a reality independent of the constitution of the subject and his/her cognition—which is the reason why for him, in agreement with the Greeks and against scholastic metaphysics, sensible and intelligible worlds can be understood only on the basis of this distinction—their further characterization is provided in relation to the two types of *knowledge* that we respectively have of them. In a formulation that runs parallel to what Kant has argued so far, he explains: "Knowledge, so far as it is subject to the laws of sensibility, is sensuous (*cognitio sensitiva*); so far as it is subject to the laws of intelligence, is intellectual or rational (*intellectualis seu rationalis*)."[15] Because of the nature of *sensualitas* and *intelligentia,* Kant can claim that "representations of things as they appear are sensitively thought (*sensitive cogitata*), while intellectual concepts (*intellectualia*) are representations of things as they are."[16] Thereby, both *Phaenomena* and *Noumena* gain an essentially representational character. However, making use of Lambert's distinction between matter and form—already at play at the very beginning of the *Dissertatio* (§2)—Kant's analysis of the two types of cognition aims at specifying the nature of their

representational character. What is represented, in both cases, is not the object as such (the way in which it *is* or the way in which it *appears*), but the relation between the object and the mind on the basis of the activity or passivity (receptivity) of the mind itself. Thus, Kant contends that in sensible knowledge the "*form* of the representation [. . .] *is not properly an outline or schema (adumbratio aut schema) of the object but only a certain law inborn in the mind.*" With this suggestion, he sets up the epistemological position of the *Dissertatio* against all "idealism" in the theory of knowledge.

Moreover, if phenomena are not *adumbrationes* of things they are, he says, *rerum species, non Ideae.*[17] In other words, Kant places them between two extremes—namely, between the position that views them as representations of the external contour of the object (*schema* or *adumbratio*), and the position that makes of them the expression of the internal and absolute essence of things (*idea*). And yet, in relation to this second point and against both idealism and skepticism, Kant contends that phenomena do provide *cognitio verissima*[18]—a perfectly genuine and true knowledge—as they still bear witness to the presence of the object. Thereby, Kant sets up his concept of phenomena both against the empiricist theory of representation (such as Locke's notion of idea and Hume's skeptical radicalization), and against Plato's idea as model and exemplar of things. The latter is a meaning that he needs to save for employment in the realm of noumena. On Kant's view, both positions eventually deny the true validity—or the objective reality—of the phenomena.

But how can phenomena fulfill a true cognitive function if they are neither immediate representations of things nor their original idea or model? Because of the *formal* aspect of sensible cognition, phenomena are said to be *rerum species*. It is precisely in relation to this element of *species*[19] or *form* that Kant declares a priori knowledge possible: "In order that the various representations of objects which affect the senses coalesce *into some whole of representation,* there is required an internal principle of the mind through which these *various* representations may take on a certain configuration (*speciem*) according to stable and innate laws."[20] The form of the sensible world, the form that first institutes the "whole" of a manifold of representations of things considered as phenomena, is provided by the two subjective conditions of space and time. Kant dedicates §3 of the *Dissertatio* to the exposition of these subjective conditions of human knowledge of phenomena.

This concept of phenomenon allows Kant to develop a crucial argument against Leibniz and the metaphysical tradition. Sensible and intellectual cognition represent two radically different types of knowledge and not a continuous progress of perception that ranges from vagueness to distinctness through a mere difference of degree. "It is not a good explanation of the sensitive to present it as that which is *more confusedly* known (*per confusius cognitum*) and of the intellectual as that of which our knowledge is *distinct* (*cognitio distincta*)."[21] Geometry represents, for Kant, a perfect example of very distinct and yet sensible knowledge, while metaphysics provides a case of extremely confused and yet purely rational knowledge. This argument becomes the touchstone for the further development of Kant's critical philosophy.

Embodied Concepts and Disembodied Ideas: The Domain of Metaphysics and Plato's Notion of Idea

Kant places intellectual cognition in opposition to sensible cognition. In relation to *cognitio intellectualis,* he distinguishes a twofold "use" of the intellect—a "real use" (*usus realis*) and a "logical use" (*usus logicus*).[22] In the first case, the intellect *gives* or produces the concepts of the objects and their relations from its own nature and from its own laws, whereas in the second case, it works on already given concepts only by performing on them the various logical operations (subordination, coordination, classification, comparison of intension and extension of the spheres of the concepts, etc.). Even though sensible cognition may be indebted to the logical use of the intellect, it does not cease to be of sensible nature (an example is provided by geometry).[23] This confirms that phenomena are not immediately sensible objects; rather, they are the more complex constructions formed by senses and intellect on the basis of experience. The logical use of the intellect is shared by all sciences. By contrast, its real use is confined to metaphysics only. According to Kant, since the intellect does play a role in the construction or cognition of phenomena, metaphysics cannot be sufficiently determined as intellectual knowledge; rather, it should be further qualified as the intellectual cognition that reason (*intelligentia* or *rationalitas*)[24] pursues in its *real* use. Although the distinction between phenomena and noumena reached in §3 is indeed necessary for Kant to gain a determination of the specific nature of metaphysics, it is not yet sufficient for this determination. The most revealing sign of this insufficiency is Kant's urge to overcome Wolff's position—namely, a position that recognizes the distinction between phenomena and noumena, and yet immediately annuls it by assuming its merely "logical" nature.

In a later *Reflection,* Kant supplements the foregoing argument with an historical claim:

> Already before Plato, we encounter the distinction between intellectual and empirical knowledge; the latter was called sensible knowledge, and even a distinction between intelligible and sensible things was drawn. All a priori knowledge was considered to be intellectual [. . .]. *But in order for this distinction to become really important,* a specific need of reason (*Bedürfnis der Vernunft*) was necessary—the need to go beyond the empirical since this is always conditioned and therefore cannot be a thing-in-itself, which requires, on each occasion, its complete conditions.[25]

In the theory of the *Dissertatio,* the distinction between real and logical use of the intellect is crucial to understand, on the one hand, *how* the intellect thinks and knows in metaphysics, and, on the other hand, *what type* of difference separates the sensible and the intelligible, phenomena and noumena. It is precisely in taking this further step that the reference to Plato's ideas becomes important for Kant.

Going back to the real use of the intellect, we now need to ask: what does it mean for concepts to be *given* by the very nature of the intellect? Kant writes, of all the concepts that the intellect uses in its real function, *"conceptus tales dantur per ipsam naturam intellectus."* These concepts are *purely* intellectual—are *Ideae purae*—because their *origin* is in the pure nature of the intellect.[26] They are neither abstracted from the activity of the senses (and thus are "ideas") nor do they entail any form of sensible knowledge (and thus they are "pure"). For this reason, observes Kant, they should be called "abstracting" (*abstrahens*) rather than "abstract" (*abstractus*) concepts. "An intellectual concept *is not abstracted from* the sensitive, but *abstracts from* all that is sensitive."[27] The syntactical structure of this claim, as well as the demonstrative intention that underlies it, parallels the famous opening statement of the Introduction to the 1787 edition of the *Critique of Pure Reason:* "Though all our knowledge *begins with* experience, it does not follow that it all *arises out* of experience."[28] Despite the differences in these texts, in both cases Kant is in search of the a priori conditions of knowledge and experience.

If the concepts in question cannot be said in any way to have empirical origin, they are nevertheless not simply *innate notions*—i.e., concepts that are "connate" (*conceptus connati*) to the intellect on the sole ground of its specific nature.[29] Kant contends that since they are produced by an activity of the intellect and arise from its laws on the occasion given by experience, they should be called "acquired" concepts (*conceptus acquisiti*).[30] As examples of these notions Kant mentions the modal categories (possibility, existence, and necessity) as well as the categories of relation (substance and cause); he then leaves the list open ("etc."). However, these are not the only instances Kant has in mind when thinking about this type of concepts. In setting up his argument against the traditional view of the distinction between phenomena and noumena as one that concerns the degree of clarity and distinctness in our cognitions, Kant offers another crucial example of what these purely intellectual concepts—or now, significantly, these "pure *ideas*"—may be. He claims that "moral concepts"—as typically metaphysical concepts—"are known not by experience but by the pure intellect itself."[31] Here, for the very first time, Kant declares moral concepts to be utterly a priori concepts.

Thus, we can conclude that in the *Dissertatio* Kant associates the use of the intellect in metaphysics with two very different types of concepts, both of which are opposed to sensibility: categories of the understanding and ideas of reason, to use the later terminology of the *Critique*. In 1770, not having a clearly formulated theory of the two independent faculties of understanding and reason, Kant seems to reach a decisive argument for the difference between *conceptus* and *idea* only with the help of Plato.

Kant defines metaphysics as that "part of philosophy that contains the first principles"[32] of the real use of the pure intellect. The *Dissertatio* intends to provide a necessary "propaedeutic" to this science. According to the two-fold partition of the objects of metaphysics already presented in the *Dreams*,[33] the "pure ideas" that the intellect generates in its real use have, in turn, a twofold function. The first is a *negative* and *critical* function (*usus elenchticus*) meant to keep sensible concepts from being applied to noumena. This function is fulfilled by the *propaedeutica* to metaphysics that grounds the difference between phenomena and noumena, sensible and intelligible cognition, thereby deriving the principles of the true method of metaphysics. The second function is a *dogmatic* one (*usus dogmaticus*) according to which "the general principles of the pure intellect [. . .] *issue in some exemplar* conceivable only by the pure intellect, and *in a common measure of all other things with regard to reality.*"[34] Metaphysics (explicitly ontology and rational psychology) is the science that makes a *dogmatic* use of the principles of the pure intellect. According to this use, such principles are meant to institute the positive—and even constitutive—"exemplar" and "common measure" for the intelligibility and even for the reality of things. These principles are ideas.

Kant sets up this complex definition of metaphysics and its aims against two philosophical traditions. On the one hand, he attacks Wolff's speculative metaphysics that is held responsible for great detriment to the development of philosophy, in destroying "the noble enterprise of the ancients," i.e., the determination of the true "nature of phenomena and noumena."[36] On Wolff's view the distinction between phenomena and noumena—a distinction first established by the ancients (Plato) and now taken up again with full historical consciousness by Kant—is only a *logical* one. On the other hand, Kant criticizes Epicurus' and Shaftesbury's empiricist ethics for being unable to recognize the a priori character of moral concepts and for confusing moral ideas with moral sentiments. Thereby such ethics makes impossible what for Kant is already the idea of a metaphysics of morals:

> Moral philosophy, so far as it supplies the first principles of moral judgment, is known only through the pure intellect and belongs to pure philosophy. Epicurus, who reduced the criteria of morals to the feeling of pleasure or displeasure, is therefore rightly condemned, along with certain moderns who, like Shaftesbury and his school, follow him in a much less thorough manner.[36]

This twofold polemic corresponds to Kant's need to develop a new metaphysics: both a *theoretical* and a *practical* one.

Aiming against Wolff on the one hand and Shaftesbury on the other, Kant coherently brings the distinction between phenomena and noumena back to Plato's notion of idea. We have already seen how in describing the dogmatic use of the intellect's pure concepts Kant refers them to an "exemplar" valid as "common measure" of all things with regard to their reality. Kant thereby reaches the concept of *perfectio noumenon*[37] through which he further clarifies the different functions of ideas in metaphysics. The idea is not a copy (*Abbild*) but a model (*Urbild*) of the reality of things. This is true both in the *theoretical* sense (ontology), according to which we attend only to what pertains to the existence of things or to how things *are* in their constitution, and in the *practical* sense (moral philosophy), according to which we consider what ought to belong to things "through freedom"[38]—or how things *ought to be*. Accordingly, *perfectio noumenon* gives rise to two different concepts: to the idea of God as the highest being (*ens summum*) and to the idea of moral perfection (*perfectio moralis*). Traditionally, the idea of perfection (*perfectio* or *Vollkommenheit*) implies both *completeness* of the determination of a concept and *axiological value*.[39] Thus, the notion of perfection leads to the idea of a "maximum." "In every kind of thing in which quantity is variable," the maximum provides, ontologically, the "common measure" of things and, epistemologically, the principle of their cognition. It is at this point that Kant inserts his reference to Plato and to his ideas: *Maximum perfectionis vocatur nunc temporis Ideale, Platoni Idea (quemadmodum ipsius idea reipublicae)*. In a contemporary *Reflection*, Kant observes: "Plato rightly provides the origin of the concepts of perfection (*Vollkommenheit*). But not that of the *notionum*."[40]

The idea functions, for Kant, as a principle for all objects that are contained in the general concept of a certain perfection "insofar as lesser degrees are supposed not to be determinable save *by limiting the maximum*."[41] As he will later show in the *Critique of Pure Reason,* in the "Ideal" of pure reason, the notion of idea leads to a totality whose parts do not precede the whole but can only be generated through immanent "limitation" (*limitando, Einschränkung*) of the whole.[42] Accordingly, the ideal is the idea not only *in concreto* but *in individuo* as it expresses the nature of the whole as completely determined individuality. This structure clearly suggests that for Kant the logic of the notions of idea and ideal is the logic of *intuition.* The idea presents the same rational structure that characterizes space as a pure form of intuition—the logic that Kant discusses in the four arguments of space in the Transcendental Aesthetic.[43]

Ideas display the logical and epistemological structure of intuition and yet, since no intuition in space and time is available for them—i.e., no direct reference to our body is possible—ideas remain necessarily disembodied. Kant's revolutionary project of radically breaking with the traditional, hierarchical continuity between concepts and intuitions, namely, his attack on the claim that concepts and intuitions are separated only by degrees of clarity and distinctness, culminates in a gesture that establishes a twofold kind of intuition. On the one hand, he recognizes the independent status of an intuition that is always and necessarily embodied, i.e., *sensible* intuition as space and time; on the other hand, however, he points to a sort of 'improper' intuition that seems to be structurally dis-embodied, i.e., the idea and the ideal. No *human* intuition, warns Kant, is able to grasp the individual and concrete whole of the idea because no reference to the sensibility of one's body is possible in this case. Since the human intellect works only through universal concepts *in abstracto* and never through individual ideas *in concreto,* it is capable only of discursive cognition or—as Kant says, taking on a Leibnizian thought—only of "symbolic knowledge."[44] Human intuition is only *sensible* intuition since it is always and necessarily informed by space and time. To this extent, it can never become intellectual.

In the Introduction to the *Critique of Pure Reason,* Kant shows the inconsistency of Plato's illusory fantasy of a disembodied mind that is able to produce cognition even without a body, only by working with pure ideas. Opposing Plato's position, Kant maintains that the boundaries of our experience are set by sensibility, i.e., by what we can construct by means of our bodily approach to the world combined with abstract concepts. "The light dove, cleaving the air in her free flight, and feeling its resistance, might imagine that her flight would be still easier in empty space." Deceived by the same fantasy, Plato

> left the world of the senses, as setting too narrow limits to the understanding, and ventured out beyond it, in empty space. He did not observe that with all his efforts he made no advance—meeting no resistance that might serve as support upon which he could take a stand, to which he could apply his powers, and so set his understanding in motion.[45]

The illusion by which we are constantly tempted—as are the light dove and Plato—the illusion of being better off without the resistance of our body and sensibility, can only be cured by the critical separation between sensibility, concepts, and ideas. Only then will we learn what it means to be free *in* our own body and to cognitively relate to the outer world *by means* of our body. Thereby will we be able to abandon all illusion of abstract freedom and disembodied knowledge.

In Kant's view, Plato's notion of idea as disembodied intuition is source of a pernicious position with regard both to the theory of knowledge and to moral philosophy. It is the position that he repeatedly stigmatizes as *Schwärmerei*, i.e., as the deranged "enthusiasm" and fanaticism of the visionary. To the extent that they share the same illusion of disembodiment, Plato has something in common with Swedenborg and the visions that Kant criticized in the *Dreams of a Spirit-Seer.* Against the enthusiasts of disembodied ideas, Kant holds on to the importance of a way of thinking anchored in embodied intuition which, alone, can provide us with an indispensable sense of orientation—an orientation in space, but also an orientation "in thinking."[46] Without addressing the issue of orientation no justified use of ideas is possible in Kant's view.

The *Dissertatio* provides an example of "pure intellectual intuition" (*intuitus purum intellectualem*) completely exempt from the laws of the senses and relation to the body, as it brings in a further reference to Plato's notion of idea: the name that Plato has for this "divine" intuition is "idea."[47] In a contemporary *Reflection* we read: "All pure ideas of reason are ideas of reflection (*discursivae* and not *intuitus* as Plato claimed). Hence, through them, we do not represent objects but only the laws by means of which we compare the concepts given to us by the senses."[48] In this *Reflection,* Kant offers an explanation for the lack of separation between understanding or intellect and reason in the *Dissertatio.* Given Plato's identification of idea and pure intellectual intuition, since Kant accepts the claim that ideas are given to us and nonetheless denies the possibility that they function in the same way as intellectual intuition, his conclusion is that ideas can be used only in the reflective and discursive way of the understanding. This is why, at this time, Kant feels no need for assuming that reason is a specific faculty of ideas opposed to understanding.

In the *Critique of Pure Reason,* Kant's discussion of the notions of idea and ideal repeatedly goes back to Plato. In one crucial passage, repeating almost literally the formulations of §9 and §25 of the *Dissertatio,* Kant states: "What for us is an Ideal, was in Plato's view an *idea of the divine understanding,* an individual object of its pure intuition, the most perfect of every kind of possible being."[49] Kant's Plato is here clearly not the historical Plato but rather the image of Plato developed by the later Roman authors. According to this tradition, Plato's ideas are the divine intellect itself taken in its full creative power. The critical Kant positions his own doctrine of ideas precisely against this conception by claiming that "human reason contains not only ideas, but also ideals, which, *although they do not have, like the Platonic ideas, creative power,* yet have practical power."[50] The *Dissertatio* reaches an analogous conclusion as it shifts its attention to the role played by ideas in the realm of the practical.

In relation to the second part of metaphysics, Kant presents the notion of *perfectio moralis* as the practical side of the *perfectio noumenon.* This is the domain of moral ideas, in which metaphysics takes the form of a "*pure* moral philosophy." The importance of ideas for Kant's project of a "metaphysics of morals" by 1770[51] lies in the fact that ideas—as Plato teaches—can never be given in experience. To this extent, the *Critique of Pure Reason* simply restates the suggestion of the *Dissertatio:* "Plato found the chief instances of his ideas in the field of the practical." The idea of the "Platonic republic" has become the most significant example of this type of perfection.[52] Ideas belong exclusively to the noumenon, and for Kant—even if not for the historical Plato—they cannot be said to properly *exist.* Or, at least, they cannot be said to exist in the same sense in which God—as idea of an *ens summum*—can be said to exist. "God, however, while as ideal of perfection is the principle of knowledge (*principium cognoscendi*), is at the same time, *as really existing,* the principle of the coming into existence (*principium fiendi*) of all perfection whatsoever."[53] This remark further explains what Kant means by stating: *"we now entitle ideal* the maximum of perfection that Plato calls idea." With this claim, Kant specifically endorses Cicero's understanding of Plato's ideas. Ideal is the criterion both for moral perfection and for our judgment of moral perfection. We can approximate this ideal in our actions but we can never fully and completely find it realized in reality.

In some marginal notes to Baumgarten's *Initia philosophiae practicae primae* which were written at the same time as the *Dissertatio,* we find the entire spectrum of mediations through which Kant refers to Plato's ideas in the realm of the practical. As Reich aptly put it, it is "Plato seen through Cicero's spectacles with Rousseau's eyes."[54] Kant notes:

> The concept, the idea, the ideal [. . .]. With regard to virtue, only a judgment according to concepts and therefore a priori, is possible. Empirical observation according to intuitions in images *(Bildern)* or according to experience does not provide us with any law, but only with examples *(Beyspiele)* that do not require any judgment according to concepts.

This argument repeats Kant's presentation of moral concepts as pure a priori concepts—or properly ideas—that we analyzed in the *Dissertatio.* Kant then comes to a more detailed discussion of the notion of idea:

> Idea is the a priori cognition (of the intellect) through which the object becomes possible. The idea relates to the objective practical sphere as a principle. It contains the highest perfection *(größte Vollkommenheit)* in a certain perspective [. . .]. It lies only in the intellect, and, in man, in concepts. The sensible is only an image *(Bild)* [. . .]. All morality is grounded on ideas and their image in man is always imperfect. In the divine intellect, ideas are intuitions of itself, and therefore original models *(Urbilder)*.

Besides Plato, Rousseau is the only modern author through which Kant can hope, in the doctrine of ideas, "to improve the ancients."[55]

The Soul as Disembodied "Idea": Against Rational Psychology and Toward an Idealized Body

In the *Critique of Pure Reason,* the specific issue raised by reason's own concepts or ideas is concerned with the type of "reality" that can be legitimately ascribed to them. From the beginning of the Transcendental Dialectic, Kant insists that even though ideas are placed beyond all possible experience, they do have a reality that is not purely fictitious. The visionary dreams of Swedenborg have been left behind once and for all. As we know from the

Dissertatio and its references to Plato, it is in the realm of the practical that ideas display positive reality. Since ideas have no relation to the necessary conditions of our sensibility, i.e., space and time, the object that corresponds to the idea cannot be known through understanding and its categories. Hence, we can form only a "problematic concept"[56] of it. Thus, the issue of "transcendental deduction" arises at this point. Reason's legitimate use of its ideas in cognition requires justification. However, under the conditions dictated by the disembodied nature of speculative reason, a deduction similar to the one provided for the concepts of the understanding is excluded from the outset.[57]

The conclusion of Kant's argument in the Transcendental Dialectic is that ideas of reason never allow for any "constitutive employment" with regard to objects of experience. When considered in this mistaken way, they generate the deceitful illusion in which reason remains inevitably entangled—namely, the illusion of generating (or constituting) a new type of knowable objects. Kant concedes, however, that reason's ideas do have an "indispensably necessary regulative employment"[58] in relation to the understanding. Although ideas are not embodied in experience they serve to direct the understanding toward its immanent goal within experience. The regulative function of ideas is the sign that reason's concepts *if used in a certain way*[59] may gain a different kind of embodiment than that proper to understanding's schematized concepts and different also from the fictitious one of speculative metaphysics. Ideas become forms of order and purposeful, systematic organization of knowledge.

Significantly, in presenting the regulative function of ideas Kant takes up again the image that he once used, in the *Dreams of a Spirit-Seer,* to describe the visionary fantasies of the ghost-seer. The ghost-seer, in losing contact with his own body and hence the possibility of distinguishing internal and external, invents fantasies and real objects, and projects the figments of his brain outside of himself, hypostatizing them as alleged real objects. Once the presence of the ghost-seer's body is suspended his mind's representations become disembodied figments as well. Kant suggests that ghost-seeing is based upon a spatial displacement of representations as these take an "outer place among the objects which present themselves to sensation."[60] This illusory projection from the inside to the outside is explained in analogy with the optic notion of the *focus imaginarius.*[61] The notion designates the point of convergence and divergence of the rays of light that emanate from a point as they meet the eye. The issue is whether the point of emanation is a real object, in which case the *focus* establishes the necessary connection between our perceptual organs and the real object yielding cognitive experience of it (as it happens in the Third Analogy of Experience); or it is a merely "imaginary" one, a point, that is, that under no condition can be made real (i.e., a perceivable object in space). This is precisely the case with the imaginary visions of the ghost-seer. In the Appendix to the Transcendental Dialectic, Kant presents yet another case—a case that stands between the former two. The image of the *focus imaginarius* is now rescued from the exclusively negative significance it had in the earlier work. Accompanied by a fundamental precautionary warning, the image serves Kant to suggest for reason's concepts a form of "ideal" embodiment—a (mirror-)reflection, as it were, of the real objective one; a form of embodiment which, although it cannot be known and experienced, may nonetheless have a positive employment with regard to the organization of experience. To be sure, the issue of embodiment plays itself out on two different—yet connected—levels. On Kant's transcendental account, the possibility for concepts to gain objective validity—to be embodied (or schematized) so as to produce a cognitive experience—is brought back to the transcendental significance of our own embodied condition, namely, to the forms of pure sensible intuition and to our perception of objects with which we are in "dynamic communion." Sensibility is the limiting condition of human experience. This, at the same time, is a transcendentally subjective and an empirically objective condition: it is the condition that makes it possible for us to perceive objects in space and time, and it is the objective condition on which objects thought under the categories are indeed real perceivable objects. However, in the case of reason's ideas (as in the case of the ghost-seer and more generally of *Schwärmern* of all kinds) the correspondence between the subject's embodiment and the objective validity of the concepts is interrupted, whereby the risk of "subreption"—the projective, visionary confusion between subjective and objective—immediately arises.[62] In the first *Critique* Kant concedes that if we recognize the error of the ghost-seer—that is, if we maintain the necessary contact with our own body and sensibility and resist the temptation of abstracting from it—the *focus imaginarius* no longer indicates a purely unreal and fictitious entity but an "ideal" one. The objectivity of ideas does not belong to the realm of objects of experience but to the rational order of the understanding's organization. Under the condition of embodiment—i.e., if kept within the bounds of experience—the *focus imaginarius* can serve as regulative principle for the organization of understanding's cognition. Ideas do not provide knowledge of objects; they are the structures that organize our knowledge of objects as aiming at an ideal, complete, and interconnected "system" of experience. The crucial point of Kant's suggestion is precisely the condition of maintaining our own body as the reference (or orientation) point of our cognitive enterprise. Kant warns that we have to use reason's ideas in the constant awareness that our aim is trying to see with their instrumental help—as if in a mirror—not objects that "lie before our eyes" but objects that "lie at a distance *behind our back*."[63] The fundamental distinction between objects that we directly see and objects that we cannot see (as they lie behind our backs or beyond the limits of experience) is drawn in relation to the watershed of our bodily oriented constitution, thereby determining Kant's distinction between constitutive and regulative use of ideas. In the first *Critique,* however, the discussion of the systematic regulative function of ideas is relegated to an appendix. We will have to wait for the *Critique of Judgment* for that function to gain an independent transcendental status. In the third *Critique,* the relation between the embodied subject and a possible embodiment of ideas in a reality other than the practical—and functional to our scientific investigation of nature—will be revisited. "Aesthetic ideas" on the one hand, and living organisms (our own and that of other beings outside of us) on the other will provide Kant's final answer to the problem of ideas' embodiment—a problem that only surfaces at the end of the Transcendental Dialectic.

At the beginning of the Transcendental Dialectic Kant refuses to resolve the problem of the objective validity of reason's concepts and procedures following Plato's shortcut of a "mystical deduction,"[64] i.e., by hypostatizing ideas into metaphysical entities. The deduction of ideas needs to take a more complex course. If ideas are to have reality, they must receive a 'body' different from the sensible one that provides us with outer experience and orientation in space. The Transcendental Dialectic sets the stage for the emergence of a different form of embodiment that will take us to the realm of Kant's practical philosophy. The transcendental deduction of the understanding's categories followed a juridical model according to which an appointed "judge" had to decide on the right and the legitimacy of a certain possession and use, on this ground declaring the victory of one party (skepticism or pure understanding) over the other. As a result, the deduction established the conditions for the "truth" of knowledge seen as its "objective validity." The deduction of reason's ideas imposes a change of model that complies with the image of a "legislation" of reason rather than with that of the "judge," and with the "certainty" and "interest" of reason in its proper knowledge rather than with its logical truth.[65]

The first step of Kant's argument takes place in the Paralogisms chapter of the Transcendental Dialectic, and establishes that ideas are unique "possession"[66] of reason, for no synthetic judgment of the understanding can ever be successful in their realm. Kant's awareness of the importance of this step is well expressed in his suggestion that "a huge, actually the only stumbling block (*Stein des Anstosses*) against our critique would be the possibility of demonstrating a priori that all thinking beings are in themselves simple substances."[67] If the propositions of rational psychology could be established by the understanding as synthetic a priori propositions, then this faculty would have no limits, and consequently reason would have neither a specific use nor a proper realm of its own. In this case, the world of the senses would dissolve in its embodied, sensible specificity; both ideas (as reason's unique possession) and the empirical givenness of our body would indeed be nothing but fictitious entities; and practical philosophy (and the idea of freedom) would lose its ground.

The second step of Kant's deduction is undertaken in the Antinomies and draws the cosmological idea of the "world" to its center. The third antinomy in particular shows that the "pure transcendental idea of freedom"[68] can have a *practical reality* since this claim does not contradict the necessity that reigns in the world of nature and appearances (the highest good is *possible*). This is precisely the first objective of Kant's deduction of ideas. At this level, however, Kant has not yet proved that reason can be practical (or that reason can make a practical use of the idea of freedom). This conclusion will result from Kant's argument in the Ideal of Pure Reason. In formulating the notion of "moral theology," Kant shows that reason can be practical (or can make a practical use of its ideas) within the sphere of religion.[69] The idea of God is therefore presented as a "postulate" which is necessary if reason has to be practical (the highest good is *necessary*).

In the four Paralogisms, Kant revisits his longstanding polemic against rational psychology. At stake is the function of the pure "I think" as the means of distinguishing two kinds of objects. "'I', as thinking, am the object of inner sense, and am called 'soul'. That which is an object of the outer sense is called 'body'."[70] Significantly, in this formulation, the metaphysician identifies the perspective of the 'subject' (or the first person)[71] with the soul, not with the body. This position defines the aim of rational psychology, which attempts to know the "I think" as soul independently of any empirical or experiential determination. The "I" is soul, not body. In the previous chapters, we have seen how Kant, in the pre-critical writings and the Refutation of Idealism, reverses this claim: an *experience* of myself, as

inner experience, is possible only through outer experience, i.e., by reference to the body as *my* body. I am an embodied being placed in the outer
world of space and time (a claim further reinforced by the third Analogy
of Experience).[72] To be sure, as shown in the fourth Paralogism, the very
possibility of distinguishing "my own existence as that of a thinking being,
from other things outside me—among them my body" is already predicated
upon my existence in a body and follows analytically from it.[73]

While the Refutation of Idealism aims at showing the implications of
the *empirical* proposition "I think"—namely, the dependence of inner sense
from outer sense—the Paralogisms show the fallacy of confusing the *empirical* representation of the thinking subject with the merely *logical* function
"I think." Thus, in the first chapter of the Transcendental Dialectic, Kant
directly addresses the more radical undertaking of rational psychology, i.e.,
the assumption of the possibility of knowing the nature of the "I think"
not only independently of the body but, more generally, independently of
any kind of determinate experience. To this extent, rational psychology
does not even need to assume the (empirical) certainty of existence that
Descartes attached to his *cogito, ergo sum.*[74] Kant claims that the formality of
the logical "I think" is the "one and only text of rational psychology." The
extent to which inferences can be drawn from that one and only source
defines the precarious dividing line between rational and empirical psychology. Since the I is taken as a disembodied thinking being, it is represented
as a "thing-in-itself."[75] We are back to the doctrine criticized in the *Dreams
of a Spirit-Seer.* In the Paralogisms, Swedenborg, Plato, Leibniz, and Wolff
all share the natural destiny of reason and the illusion of disembodied ideas
that will always try to affirm their alleged validity and existence among real
bodies. Ultimately, Kant shows that rational psychology is necessarily committed to "idealism" (at least to "problematic idealism"). Insofar as it claims
to prove the "existence" of the soul independently of all external things,
simply drawing inferences from that initial proposition, it eliminates all
necessity to refer to the external world as source of inner determination.[76]
The solipsism of the soul is thereby perfectly justified.

Kant directs the critical eye toward the flawed enterprise of transforming analytic inferences into synthetic propositions. With that sole text as
its source, rational psychology constructs its claim: the soul is immaterial,
incorruptible, has personality, and is in *commercium* with bodies in space. To
be sure, not even rational psychology can ignore the relation to the body.
Such relation, however, is overturned, as it is analytically derived from the
concept of the soul. The soul, as *anima,* is viewed as "principle of life in mat-

ter" and ground of "animality" (*Animalität*). Animality spiritualized leads to the notion of the soul's immortality.[77]

Kant's discussion of the Paralogisms of rational psychology shows that this metaphysical discipline illegitimately converts merely analytic propositions regarding an empty "thinking being in general" into synthetic propositions regarding the existence of the soul. The root of the illegitimacy lies in the fact that the synthetic step can be undertaken only by means of sensible intuition, i.e., through the experience of myself, which always implies the presence of my body (outer experience). The idea of the soul, on the contrary, by its very definition, is the idea of a disembodied subject (and, accordingly, is a notion that regards every thinking being in general). Thus, the illusion of rational psychology arises from the confusion of an "idea of reason (the idea of a pure intelligence) with the completely undetermined concept of a thinking being in general." The possibility of making abstraction from my empirically determined existence cannot be confused with the alleged consciousness of a possible existence of my thinking self separate from my body. The merely "*logical* function" "I think" should not be confused with the *empirical* proposition "I think or I exist thinking."[78]

This conclusion brings Kant a step further with regard to his previous critique of rational psychology. For now he grants to the notion of a pure intelligence the status of an "idea of reason." In the light of the Paralogisms, the issue of the reality of ideas is immediately linked to the issue of reason's *use* of them. If all constitutive use is banned by the exposure of the transcendental illusion in the cognitive realm, Kant still allows for a regulative and problematic use of reason's ideas and, more importantly, for their "practical use."[79] The possibility of a practical employment of ideas discloses the possibility (or, at least, the non-contradictory character) of their practical "existence." Thereby, the potentialities of the "idea" of a "pure intelligence"—or an alleged *noumenal* reality of the subject as pure spontaneity—is reserved for further developments in the practical sphere. Only in this sphere can the issue of the soul's immortality—with regard to which both "materialism" and "spiritualism" failed in their proof[80]—again be taken up, this time successfully.

Significantly, at the end of the Paralogisms, Kant links the idea of a pure intelligence to the idea of an "intelligible world." He suggests that the rational idea of the subject may become "determinable" with regard to an (as yet) unspecified "inner faculty"[81] as being related to "an intelligible world (which can only be thought)." As was the case in the *Dissertatio,* where Kant introduced ideas in order to complicate the opposition between sensibility's intuitions and understanding's concepts, in the Paralogisms he shows that reason is in possession of rational concepts of its own whose employment must be radically distinguished from the logic of understanding and its syntheses. In other words, the flawed use of the concept of the soul displayed by rational psychology is confined to *only one* possible employment of reason's ideas and does not rule out that a legitimate use may indeed be found for them.

> Should it be granted that we may in due course discover, not in experience but in certain laws of the pure employment of reason—laws which are not merely logical rules, but which while holding a priori *also concern our existence*—ground for regarding ourselves as *legislating* completely a priori *with regard to our own existence,* and *as determining this existence,* there would thereby be revealed a spontaneity through which our reality would be determinable, independently of the conditions of empirical intuition.[82]

We begin to see the far-reaching consequences of Kant's argument against rational psychology. In the speculative sphere he allows for no successor of the metaphysical soul in transcendental philosophy: herein the body is the only orientation point for self-knowledge, whereby our "experience" is significantly limited to our existence "in the present life"[83] and in the sensible world. In this sphere, psychology is necessarily confined to empirical psychology. Rational psychology, for Kant, cannot claim the status of a "doctrine" but only of a "discipline" that sets limits to speculative reason's employment of its ideas—against both materialism and spiritualism. The merely negative value of psychology is meant to "divert our self-knowledge from fruitless and extravagant speculations to its fruitful practical employment."[84] For it is in the practical sphere that the metaphysical issues raised by the soul as idea of reason eventually find their legitimate justification. Herein the soul receives practical *existence* while the body is "idealized" in a dimension that is not conditioned by space and time, i.e., by the limited experience of this present life but is somehow constituted, along with its peculiar feeling, as an "effect" by practical reason.[85] At the end of the Paralogisms, in sketching out the transition from rational psychology to cosmology, Kant suggests the possibility of a new way of confronting human *existence* or the existence of the subject—an existence that is no longer merely empirical and yet is not the disembodied non-existence of the metaphysical soul. The key to Kant's suggestion is in the *kind of existence* that the first *Critique,* at this point of its development, allows us to think of for the human subject.

To be sure, the insistence on the *Dasein* and *Existenz* of the subject has been Kant's crucial concern in the entire development of the Paralogisms. Kant has shown that, with regard to our *cognitive* access to ourselves (to our empirical existence as thinking beings) embodiment cannot be escaped. Embodiment, which comprehends the functions of intuition, sensation, and perception,[86] is rather the very first condition of our *existence* in the world of nature: inner experience (time) is necessary to our empirical determination as subjects, and inner experience rests, in turn, on outer experience (space), namely, on the discriminating function of our body that allows us to distinguish ourselves from *other* objects and from the *external* world. However, since the "I think"—besides its empirical use in self-cognition—is also a merely logical function that indicates the place of the subject in judgment, the illusion arises of the possibility of a fictitious self-cognition that would determine our existence independently of the inescapable transcendental conditions of embodiment, i.e., space and time. This is the origin of the fiction of a disembodied necessary existence (and hence immortality) claimed by rational psychology for all thinking beings. However, since in the doctrine of the first *Critique* Kant grants to the notion of a "pure intelligence" the status of an "idea" of reason (it is neither a merely empirical representation nor a pure category of the understanding), the possibility of thinking of a form of existence (or of a form of "objective reality" for reason's idea) that is not determined by the sensible conditions of space and time but by the self-legislation proper to reason itself, must be allowed (i.e., it is not a self-contradictory assumption). Since the Refutation of Idealism along with the Paralogisms have shown that existence is necessarily embodied existence, the solution of the dialectic illusion opens up the possibility of a form of embodiment dependent upon reason and not upon sensibility. In this case, however, our access to this existence will not be a *cognitive* access but a *practical* one. With this suggestion, Kant points to a crucial transformation of the body and the world in which the subject places its embodied existence (this time, a noumenal instead of a phenomenal existence). To this transformation, I now direct my analysis.

Part 2

THE BODY IN PRACTICE

On ne voit pas les coeurs

—MOLIÈRE,
Le Misanthrope

4

Bodies in Action

A Cat fell in love with a handsome young man, and begged the
goddess Venus to change her into a woman. Venus was very gracious
about it, and changed her at once into a beautiful maiden, whom the
young man fell in love with at first sight and shortly afterwards married.
One day Venus thought she would like to see whether the Cat had
changed her habits as well as her form; so she let a mouse run loose
in the room where they were. Forgetting everything, the young woman
had no sooner seen the mouse than up she jumped and was after it
like a shot: at which the goddess was so disgusted that
she changed her back again into a Cat.

—AESOP, *Fables*

KANT ENDS THE *DREAMS OF A SPIRIT-SEER* WITH A "PRACTICAL
conclusion," in which he draws attention to the pernicious consequences
of the metaphysical doctrine of the soul on moral life. He protests against
the common claim that the spiritual nature of the soul is necessary to the
conviction that there is life after death, and that this conviction, in turn, is
necessary for leading a virtuous life. For Kant, the argument runs exactly
in the opposite direction. In order to safeguard the idea of morality in its
"purity," the expectation of a future world must be based on the "noble
constitution of the soul" and its conduct, rather than virtuous conduct being based on the belief in another world. This argument is crucial to Kant's
notion of "moral faith,"[1] which already surfaces in this early text and sig-

nals the ultimate direction taken by his attack on rational psychology. By reversing the relationship between the metaphysical claim regarding the existence of the soul and its practical consequences—thereby establishing the independency of moral life from the soul's immortality—Kant suggests that the only predicates that can be attributed to the empty notion of soul are practical ones. The starting point is the "noble" constitution of the soul, not the demonstration of its separate existence in an after-life. The conclusion is that only practical philosophy—not pneumatology—has the right to take the soul as object of its investigation.

Because of the inescapable condition of human embodiment, cognitive access to an after-life or to an alleged world of pure spirits is, in principle, forbidden. Accordingly, Kant offers a double conclusion. On the one hand, he ironically responds to those who desire *to know* of a future life with "this simple but very natural advice: that it would probably be best if they had the good grace to wait with patience until they arrived there." On the other hand, Kant suggests that once we have resigned ourselves to cohabitation with our body and have learned to reject all inferences that are not based on data from experience, we must recognize that what is left is to live a good life in this world. Thus, Kant seals his 1766 essay with Voltaire's well-known advice in *Candide:* "Let us attend to our happiness, go into the garden, and work."[2] However, while pointing in the direction of practical philosophy, this conclusion leaves open a fundamental question. What happens to the metaphysical notion of the soul once it becomes the topic of practical philosophy, that is, once embodiment is no longer disputed but accepted, and is considered, this time, as the starting point of human agency in the world? How shall the soul be transformed in order to describe the human being as embodied *agent*? And what are the consequences of declaring moral philosophy independent of the notion of the soul's immortality?

These questions emerging from the conclusion of Kant's pre-critical *Dreams* constitute the guiding thread for my analysis of the "transition" (*Übergang*) from the Paralogisms to the Antinomies of pure reason in the Transcendental Dialectic of the first *Critique.* Interpretations of these chapters generally regard Kant's attack on rational psychology and the antinomies of cosmology as radically separate issues. Historical analyses of the genesis and sources of Kant's third antinomy, on the other hand, point to the displacement of the problem of freedom from empirical psychology to cosmology, but leave the crucial reasons for this Kantian shift unanswered.[3] Moreover, discussions of the definition of freedom as "absolute spontaneity" overlook the important fact that Kant already attributes spontaneity to understanding in opposition to sensibility—an opposition that runs throughout the Transcendental Aesthetic and the Analytic.[4] Unlike these interpretations, I read Kant's solution of the third antinomy in the framework provided by the Paralogisms. What is at stake in the formulation of the concept of "transcendental freedom" as "absolute spontaneity" is precisely the redefinition of the human subject as a possible moral agent in the world of nature. Ultimately, the "key" to the solution of the antinomies and the condition for the possibility of transcendental freedom lies in the same thesis of the transcendental ideality of space and time that allows Kant to refute material idealism and to reject the possibility of a cognitive determination of the soul independent of experience. The claim is that the nature of human sensibility and its a priori constitution—the condition of "transcendental embodiment"—represents, for Kant, the unifying basis for the solution of two crucial problems of metaphysics.

The present chapter deals with the transition from speculative reason to practical reason. Its aim is to show the intimate connection between speculative and practical reason. Thereby, it introduces the topic of this second part of the book, dedicated to embodiment in Kant's practical philosophy. The concept of "transcendental embodiment"—that is, the possibility of indicating an a priori formal component proper to our human existential situation as the condition for morality itself—allows for a new approach to the main issues of Kant's critical project. I argue that Kant needs to deny the possibility of knowing the metaphysical soul independent of the experience of embodiment if he wants to claim (1) that human reason is endowed with transcendental freedom, and (2) that freedom in the "cosmological" sense grounds freedom in the "practical" sense. The starting point of Kant's practical philosophy, i.e., the notion that transcendental freedom is possible within the world of nature (or at least is non-contradictory with regard to nature's laws), is offered precisely by the conclusion of the Paralogisms: there is no self-knowledge of an abstract, disembodied human self. The possibility of making abstraction from my empirically conditioned existence by no means authorizes the conclusion that I can exist independently from my experience (of myself and the world). The subject of speculative reason or the 'I think' that knows the world of nature, constructs the world of natural science, and knows itself as object among objects is always and necessarily an embodied sensible being. Transcendentally, embodiment is one of the conditions that make empirical self-cognition possible. At this point, Kant's further task is to show that *this same subject* can also be a free moral agent within the realm of a possible experience—precisely 'in this life'—thereby acquiring true subjectivity defined as moral agency. Thus, I argue that the notion of transcendental freedom—introduced as the solution of the third antinomy—is predicated upon the result of Kant's critique of rational psychology since it ultimately follows from the impossibility of attributing freedom as spontaneity to the metaphysical soul. Freedom defines, for Kant, the transcendental, intelligible 'character' of the embodied human agent; even though it is fundamentally distinct from the sensible character, freedom is not the property of a disembodied soul.

This chapter is dedicated to the analysis of a twofold transition. First, it shows how Kant moves from the issue of human *self-knowledge* taking place by means of the body and its a priori forms of space and time, to *free action* which, being the manifestation of practical reason in the world of nature is always action taking place (and lived) in and through the human body. While self-knowledge is empirical knowledge determined by outer and inner sense, free action requires intelligible causality acting through the physical body, though this causality is never determined by it. Second, I present Kant's move from the spontaneity of thinking to the spontaneity of freedom. Interestingly, in this transition Kant uses in a cosmological sense the notion of spontaneity that the German scholastic tradition usually discusses in the context of empirical psychology. I argue that Kant can define "transcendental freedom" as "absolute spontaneity" only because, in the aftermath of the critique of the Paralogisms, the subject of spontaneity is no longer the metaphysical substance or soul that it still was for Leibniz, Wolff, or Crusius, but an embodied being endowed with *both* sensibility and reason. While for these authors spontaneity is an empirical concept based on the metaphysical constitution of the soul, Kant's critique of the concept of soul allows him to disengage freedom from its metaphysical substrate and to recognize the a priori validity of the notion of spontaneity as freedom. As a concept of transcendental philosophy, spontaneity can find no place in a psychology but only in a (pure) practical philosophy. In this framework, I discuss the way in which sensibility and its receptivity are modified in order to serve as counterparts of the spontaneity of freedom for the purpose of action, instead of being counterparts of the spontaneity of thinking for the purpose of knowledge. Thereby, I open the investigation on the transcendental, non-empirical but formal and a priori function that human embodiment plays in Kant's foundation of a pure practical philosophy. This is the topic of the following three chapters.

Searching for the 'Subject'—From Rational Psychology to Cosmology

The inner connection between the problem of the soul and that of the world—or between psychology and cosmology—is already suggested in Kant's letter to Moses Mendelssohn of 8 April 1766.[5] In this letter, Kant formulates the central issue that occupies him in the *Dreams* with the following question: "How is the soul present in the world?" Since for Kant the soul is placed, from the outset, in relation to the external world, an account should be given of the soul's action in the world of space, time, bodies, and matter. This fundamental connection is taken up again and further elaborated in the 1770 *Dissertatio,* in which the status of the notion of *mundus* as "idea" and the distinction between sensible and intelligible world already point in the direction of the antinomies of pure reason. In the *Dissertatio,* Kant connects the problem of the totality of the world with that of the simplicity of the monad or of immaterial substances. In both cases at issue is the *spinosa quaestio* of the notion of "totality" (*totum*) and the specific logic of this concept.[6]

At the end of the Paralogisms-chapter of the *Critique of Pure Reason,* the embodied subject, triumphant over the metaphysical disembodied soul, is projected onto a transfigured world. Surprisingly, what appears to the subject that empirically knows itself through the affection of the body's sensibility (and hence knows itself in its phenomenal existence and not as a purely logical 'I think'), is not the mechanism of nature but a world thought *in analogy* with it. For a moment, reason's "order of purposes" takes the place of the "order of nature" established by the understanding, and is immediately identified with it.[7] Thereby Kant makes clear that he is referring to one and the same realm of experience, not to a metaphysical distinction between a sensible and an intelligible world. While the claim of a "future life" is an illegitimate assumption of speculative reason, it is a necessary postulate in the practical employment of this faculty. In its practical use, however, the idea of a future life only serves the purpose of defining the way in which we ought to live the *present* life, and produces no advance in the aims of rational psychology.[8] If the theoretical use of reason is defined, transcendentally, by the limits of the body's sensibility, in its practical use, reason re-locates the embodied subject in the "peculiar domain" (*Gebiet*) of the order of ends. Within this new "domain" a curious transfiguration takes place. At stake is the possibility, which now appears entirely justified, of extending the order of ends—and with it "our own existence—beyond the limits of experience and life."[9] Thereby, practical reason accomplishes the objective that rational psychology tried in vain to achieve. Kant's suggestion regards precisely the possibility of a different type of "experience" of the world and a different "life" and "existence" in it. This new form of experience will eventually change, transcendentally, the constitution of the world itself: it will transform the world of nature's mechanism into the practical realm of freedom (and eventually into the world of living organisms and natural purposes within which human beings occupy a peculiar position).

Kant's argument carries out an "analogy with the nature of living beings in this world." According to this analogy, the simple presence of the moral law in us allows us to infer the idea of a "citizenship" in a world that we value as "better" than the world of nature. Thus, the conclusion of the Paralogisms points to the discovery of a different "domain" in which a different way of judging the "world" (namely, through moral values rather than through the understanding's categories)[10] discloses an alternative way of thinking and living in it. We are not only parts of this world but we can claim a right of "citizenship" in it. This world, underlines Kant, is a world "in the idea."[11] The new *Gebiet* of transcendental philosophy now takes the place of both the improbable after-life claimed by rational psychology, and also of the "intelligible world" of the 1770 *Dissertatio*, which was still the object of pure theoretical knowledge.[12] In the *Critique*, Kant suggests that since no after-life can be cognitively justified, we have to explore the possibility of living the present life in a different way, that is, by following a different (or additional) set of principles, maxims, and laws than those legislating the mechanism of nature. Such conclusion, this time devoid of any ironic tone, parallels the "practical conclusion" of the *Dreams*. Instead of renouncing sensibility for the illusion of a disembodied existence in an after-life, the human embodied subject must try to define itself in relation to an intelligible world in which *this* present life *ought to* be lived. To be sure, at this point, Kant's argument aims at proving not so much the independent existence of the sphere of practical reason but its intimate connection with the world of speculative reason.[13]

In the "transition"[14] from the Paralogisms of rational psychology to the Antinomies of cosmology, Kant moves from the problem of representing the 'I think' as *object* of thought and cognition, to the possibility of thinking of it as genuine *subject* of action. In this transition, the relation to the practical sphere is established for the first time. The subject is presented, henceforth, as "*acting* subject (*handelndes Subjekt*)" or "*active* being (*tätiges Wesen*),"[15] whereby it receives a characterization that the 'I think' of speculative reason could never attain. At stake is the general issue of representing the 'I think' no longer as an object among objects in the world of nature, but as a subject that lives and acts within this world.[16] Its status as subject is defined by additional principles that somehow extend the validity of the transcendental principles which describe it instead as part of the natural world. The possibility for pure reason to have a practical employment is predicated upon the possibility of representing the subject as subject of a distinctive form of causality within the world of nature, so that this causality is compatible or non-contradictory with the framework laid out by the Analytic of the first *Critique*. Thus, in the transition from rational psychology to cosmology, Kant sets the conditions for the fundamental connection between speculative reason and practical reason, nature and freedom.

The central point regards the determination of the subject's "existence." Through the notion of soul, rational psychology offers a first—yet failed—attempt to think of the subject as irreducible subject in opposition to material objects. In the transition to cosmology, concluding his critique of psychology, Kant suggests that in order to claim a privileged place in the world of nature and material bodies we do not need to leave the body behind and dogmatically assume an immaterial, immortal soul. On the contrary, all we need to do is to qualify the embodied subject through a different 'character' than the merely empirical one, and through a different type of causality than the causality of mechanism. Ultimately, what is needed is not an argument that rejects sensibility *tout court* but a way of overturning (or re-formulating) the relationship between spontaneity and receptivity.

The transcendental construction of the world of nature presented in the Analytic is based upon the claim that the "I think" is "merely the logical function of thinking" that needs the determination of an empirical intuition in order to yield *knowledge* of objects. To this extent, there is no difference between our knowledge of given outer objects and our knowledge of ourselves in our determinate existence.[17] The Refutation of Idealism makes clear that determinate self-knowledge has to run through the bodily constitution of the subject, i.e., that inner sense ultimately depends upon outer sense. The embodied subject is nothing but the first object (in space) to which the 'I think' relates. To rational psychology's protest that, in this way, the "soul is completely transformed into appearance," Kant responds with the notion of the merely logical function of "thinking" that, in opposition to knowing, makes abstraction from the "mode of intuition, whether it be sensible or intellectual." If I do not aim at *knowing* myself in my determinate empirical existence but only at *thinking* of myself regardless of any intuition, then, indeed, I do not represent myself as mere appearance. However, with this merely logical thought of myself, not much is gained. And certainly the existence of an immaterial soul is not proved. In addition—and this is Kant's crucial point—in the purely logical thought of myself I am still "object" to myself; the subject of consciousness is still regarded as I regard "any object in general from whose mode of intuition I abstract."[18] While in the first instance I know myself as determinate object (as appearance) with regard to my existence, in the second case I am a mere indeterminate object of thinking in general. In the latter case, no progress is made in the direction wished by rational psychology. For, even though I represent myself as the "subject of thoughts" or as the "ground of thinking," I cannot say what this subject is, since I am not allowed to say that it is "substance" or "cause" attributing to these concepts the same meaning that they have when employed as categories.[19] In other words, nothing allows me to qualify the subject as "subject" since this is nothing more to me than an entirely empty object in general of which no knowledge is possible.

However, while in the Paralogisms Kant stresses the importance of recognizing the phenomenal nature of the existing subject against the empty speculations of metaphysics, in the "transition" to cosmology he opens up a new possibility of representing the subject as subject. He thus goes beyond the alternatives of representing the subject as empirical object of knowledge, indeterminate object of thinking, or metaphysical disembodied soul. According to the new—albeit still merely hypothetical—perspective that Kant now attempts to disclose, the subject is still described by (and yet not known through) the category of cause. However, its causality, manifested in the world of nature and in accordance with its laws, follows from a radically different principle than the one that rules natural phenomena. The concept of cause, Kant suggests, will have, in this case, a meaning that is only "analogical" to the one displayed in its theoretical use.[20] The crucial issue leading Kant to the practical extension of the conceptual framework that rules the world of nature is the problem of the determination of the existence of the subject. The alternative between empirical determination and logical indeterminateness, ultimately responsible for the failure of rational psychology, can be overcome only if we can find a form of determination of our existence that does not require the empirical intuition of space and time but takes place completely a priori. It is immediately clear that this determination cannot be theoretical or cognitive. However, Kant advances a hypothetical thought:

should it be granted that we may in due course discover, not in experience but in certain laws of the pure employment of reason—laws which are not merely logical rules, but which while holding a priori *also concern our existence (Existenz)*—a ground for regarding ourselves as *legislating completely a priori with regard to our own existence (Dasein)*, and *as determining this existence (Existenz)*, there would thereby be revealed a *spontaneity* through which our *reality (Wirklichkeit)* would be *determinable,* independently of the conditions of empirical intuition. And herein we would become aware that in the consciousness of our existence (*Dasein*) there is contained something a priori, which can serve *to determine our existence (Existenz)*—the *complete determination* of which is possible only in sensible terms—as being in relation, with respect to a certain inner faculty, to an intelligible world (albeit a world of which we can only think of).[21]

Kant's insistence on the issue of the determinability and determination of our existence—*Existenz* and *Wirklichkeit*—could not be stronger. Throughout the Analytic, Kant always conjoins the spontaneity through which thinking determines its objects with the determinability of the receptivity proper to the senses. To produce knowledge, the spontaneity of thinking must determine its object with regard to empirical intuition so that the determined object of cognition is necessarily appearance in space and time. Kant's suggestion, at this point, addresses a new possibility: can we think without contradiction of a form of spontaneity that would not require the conditions of sensible intuition and yet would still determine the existence of the subject entirely a priori (i.e., would not abstract from this existence)? This type of spontaneity, necessarily different from the spontaneity of thinking, would still entail a kind of "legislation." Yet, unlike the spontaneity that intervenes in cognition, it would indeed be "absolute" or "unconditioned" in the sense of not being constitutively dependent upon the sensible conditions of embodiment. In addition, since this new form of spontaneity would not determine my existence cognitively—i.e., would not offer a modality of self-knowledge independent from the experience of my body and its affection—this type of spontaneity would not pursue the same aim as rational psychology and hence would not be a psychological concept. It would then have to be placed in another problematic realm. The issue raised by this new kind of spontaneity regards, in fact, the sphere of cosmology to which the transition is thereby effected. This is the first step that allows Kant to shift the traditional problem of spontaneity from psychology to cosmology and from the sphere of theoretical reason to the realm of its practical employment.[22]

The new form of spontaneity would determine my existence in relation to an "intelligible world," not in respect to space and time but "in respect (*in*

Ansehung) to a certain inner faculty"—indeed, a "marvelous faculty." The "principle" of determination followed by this spontaneity would be "purely intellectual," and yet would still be a principle immanently determining "my existence"[23]—not simply representing it as abstract subject (or object) in general. On the other hand, the practical use of the predicates designating my existence (cause, substance, etc.) would still "be directed to objects of experience," albeit in a merely analogical way. It follows that this spontaneity would have to be described in terms of a peculiar form of causality, which would be somehow intelligible and unconditioned or absolute. With the introduction of the concept of causality, the transition from psychology to cosmology—namely from the notion of soul to the issue of the subject's causality in the world—is completed.

Thus, while cognitively the subject's existence in the world of nature is ultimately determined by the physical presence of the body and its transcendental structures, practically, the subject's concrete existence in the intelligible world is entirely determined with regard to the rational faculty. This claim has far-reaching consequences. From it follows a confirmation that, with regard to cognition, the receptivity proper to sensibility is not sheer passivity: transcendentally, sensibility possesses a power of determination of its own; sensibility is able to *determine* our knowledge of objects. It also follows that, with regard to practical determination, a specific receptivity is required that could be "receptive" for an absolute and unconditioned spontaneity[24]: this is the case of a receptivity that would not function as condition for spontaneity (but would rather follow from it). Framing Kant's problem in this way, we can easily see that it contains *in nuce* both the task of the *Critique of Practical Reason* (namely, to prove that pure reason can be practical) and the main issue raised by the *Critique of Judgment* (namely, the idea of the purposive constitution of nature with regard to the actualization of freedom and the moral law; or the idea of a possible purposive coordination or harmony between the sensibly conditioned realm of nature and its supersensible "substrate").

What is relevant to my present argument in Kant's suggestion is the assumption of a peculiar determinability of our existence or reality (*Wirklichkeit*) through the new type of spontaneity. To be sure, this suggestion immediately displays two related sides. At stake is not only the problem of determining this new form of spontaneity, but also the issue of bringing to the fore the new receptivity to which such spontaneity refers. What is it that absolute spontaneity can determine completely a priori, so that it does not fall under the conditions of space and time? In other words: what is the "determinable" that now takes the place that the body's sensibility occupies, both in our knowledge of objects outside of ourselves and in our knowledge of ourselves through the determination of inner sense? Throughout, Kant's argument is firm in making no concession to rational psychology. By insisting that absolute spontaneity would still determine our existence and reality—our very life and experience in this world (and not an abstract self in general or in an after-life), Kant reveals that the body, which defines the subject's existence in space and time, has not disappeared. Rather, the body remains—albeit transfigured in its transcendental function—as that reality which is "determinable" in the subject. How does this determination take place in the sphere of the practical and what constitutes our "determinable reality"?

Spontaneity of Thinking and
Spontaneity of Freedom

In the German tradition that goes back to Leibniz and is continued by Wolff, the concept of *spontaneitas* belongs to empirical psychology, and is considered accordingly as an empirical concept predicated of the metaphysical soul.[25] Wolff discusses it in his *Deutsche Metaphysik* (1719) and *Psychologia empirica* (1732, 1738). By translating the Latin *spontaneitas* with the German *Willkür*, Wolff ultimately identifies the two terms: spontaneity is identical with the faculty of will. Many authors immediately endorsed Wolff's translation, as well as the philosophical thesis contained therein.[26] For Wolff and the Wolffians spontaneity is the activity of determining oneself to action through an internal ground or inner principle. Herein, Wolff repeats Leibniz's influential thesis according to which "an action is spontaneous when its ground is contained in the agent."[27] Moreover, Wolff maintains that to the extent to which the soul has in itself the ground determining its actions, the soul has a will.[28] Freedom is spontaneity because it implies the will's capacity of choice. "Freedom of the soul is the capacity of choosing spontaneously [or voluntarily, *sponte*], among many possibilities, the one that we like, without being determined in ourselves to any of them." Wolff's discussion of *spontaneitas* points primarily to the general issue raised by the principle of determining or sufficient reason and refers to the problem of freedom only by means of this principle.[29]

Baumgarten, on whose *Metaphysica* (1739) Kant lectures from the summer semester of 1756 until the end of his life, reacts against Wolff's identification of spontaneity and will, and proposes a definition of *arbitrium* or *Willkür* as an independent faculty of the soul distinct from spontaneity. In this gesture, he probably follows the analogous distinction drawn by the theologian Friedrich Wagner. According to Baumgarten, *actio spontanea* (which he translates as *selbstthaetige Handlung*) is an "action that depends upon a sufficient ground internal to the agent."[30] This, however, does not by itself indicate possession of will. Crucial for the connection between spontaneity and freedom is Crusius's rejection of Wolff's definition of *spontaneitas* as based upon the principle of determining reason. For Crusius, freedom is an "active fundamental force (*thätige Grundkraft*)"[31] that acts with no antecedent determination—external or internal. With this claim, Crusius refutes the universal validity of the principle of sufficient or determining reason. This principle, on his view, grounds a universal determinism in which freedom is utterly impossible. Since freedom is the capacity to start a series of events with no determination, Crusius defines it as unconditioned force or causality. Finally, with regard to Kant's appropriation of the term spontaneity, Tetens's work is important. His use of the term is not confined to the problem of freedom but extends to a description of the cognitive faculty as such. Spontaneity is the *Selbstthätigkeit* by which the cognitive faculty produces representations, connects them, and separates them.[32] This meaning is clearly relevant for Kant's own definition of the activity of understanding or thinking as spontaneity. In addition, for Tetens, spontaneity in the sense of freedom does not designate the capacity of choice (will) but points instead to the general problem of causality.

In the cosmological framework of the Antinomies, the traditional concept of spontaneity lends itself to Kant's critical diagnosis. The soul as substance endowed with an original activity (*vis activa primitiva*) to which spontaneity belongs—both in its Leibnizian and Wolffian meaning—cannot be saved from universal determinism. To this extent, although Kant seems to endorse Crusius's shift from spontaneity as internal determination to freedom as original causality,[33] his critical argument affects Crusius's position as well, insofar as he still works within the metaphysical tradition criticized in the Paralogisms. In other words, for Kant spontaneity can no longer be a character—however conceived, as inner determination or original force—proper to the soul. What, then, is the "subject" of spontaneity according to Kant, and what is the "determinable" reality on which spontaneity operates its determination?

The problem of spontaneity is, for Kant, a problem of "determination." This general concern explains its occurrence both with regard to understanding or thinking as theoretical faculty and with regard to the practical faculty of reason. In the *Nova Dilucidatio* (1755), Kant follows Leibniz's and Wolff's definition of *spontaneitas* by means of the principle of sufficient reason—which Kant, in Crusius's aftermath, renames as the principle of "determining reason." "Since to determine"—Kant explains—"is to posit something so as to exclude every opposite, it denotes that which is certainly sufficient for conceiving something in one way and in no other."[34] Accordingly, *spontaneitas* as "action proceeding from an *internal principle*" is always and necessarily determined action. Repeating Leibniz and Wolff, Kant defines freedom as that which "is determined in conformity with the representation of the good."[35]

In the *Critique of Pure Reason,* while the meanings of both determination and spontaneity have changed for Kant, he still considers the two notions as parts of the same issue. To determine now means "to judge synthetically,"[36] whereby the problem of determination is brought directly to bear on the central question raised by transcendental philosophy, i.e., the possibility of a priori synthetic judgments. In this connection, spontaneity defines the essential character that distinguishes understanding from sensibility and sets it apart as a radically separate branch of our cognitive faculty. The "spontaneity" of understanding (i.e., concepts) is opposed to the "receptivity" of sensibility (i.e., sense impressions). While the latter indicates the capacity of our *Gemüt* for receiving representations as a consequence of being *affected* in a certain way, the former indicates the faculty of *producing* representations by and from itself. Through sensibility and its receptivity, an object is *given* to us; through the understanding and its spontaneity, an object is *thought.*[37] Spontaneity defines the productive character of thinking and, from the outset, gains its specific meaning by being contrasted with receptivity. In describing the constitution of *knowledge,* i.e., of determination or synthesis, the spontaneity of concepts must always and necessarily be referred to the receptivity of sensibility. In other words, due to its very nature, understanding's spontaneity is neither an independent process nor an autonomous function of cognition. It is only one constituent thereof—indeed, a necessary but not a sufficient one. It follows that what is really crucial to Kant's connotation of the activity of understanding with spontaneity is not so much that representations are self-produced; the essential point regards instead the "function" of spontaneity in the determination of thought for cognition, that is, its role in the broader process of synthesis. In other words, the central issue consists in the actual "exercise" (*Ausübung*) of spontaneity by thinking.[38] But to be exercised and produce cognition, spontaneity must meet with receptivity. The interdependence that binds spontaneity and receptivity complicates the task of describing their respective contributions to the process of determination or synthesis. Thus, the issue at stake here is: what kind of activity is the activity of understanding?

Kant defines "synthesis, in its most general sense," as the "act" or "operation" (*Handlung*) "of putting different representations together and grasping what is manifold in them in one cognition."[39] Here, with *Handlung,* he translates the Latin *actus* (or *operatio*). The term is used by Baumgarten in *Metaphysica* §210 to describe change of state (*mutatio status*) and, more generally, to indicate the fact that the accident is given in the substance *per vim ipsius* and not *per vim alienam. Actus* is thereby opposed to *passio.* In this connection, however, "act" does not designate causal activity; rather, it refers to the coexistence of the ground with what is grounded. Kant comments on Baumgarten's text as follows: "To act (*Handeln*) means: to contain the sufficient ground of the accident. The possibility of action is the capacity [or faculty, *Vermögen*]. The inner sufficient ground of action is force (*Kraft*)."[40]

Following the radical separation between understanding and sensibility, Kant seems to have an easy job in neatly assigning the part that spontaneity and receptivity respectively play in the synthesis of cognition: spontaneity is "*bestimmend*" (determining), while sensibility is "*bloß bestimmbar*" (merely determinable).[41] Spontaneity is *Actus,*[42] while sensibility as receptivity seems to be there to simply and passively receive. However, in the exercise of the determination that proves itself essential to cognition, the act of spontaneity is made so dependent upon receptivity that sensible intuition becomes that which ultimately (and actively) determines the generality of the concept. For sensibility provides the external condition that qualifies the determinability under which alone actual determination can occur. The claim that determination is not possible through the act of understanding alone is the same as the claim that the transcendental condition for all knowledge (including self-knowledge) is the subject's embodiment. In the cognitive sphere, transcendental embodiment is the limit of the exercise of understanding's spontaneity. In its determining activity spontaneity is, in turn, always and necessarily determined by an external, sensible condition, i.e., by the peculiar nature of that which serves as determinable. In the cognitive sphere, absolute spontaneity is impossible. It would coincide with the thought of an intuitive understanding or an intellectual intuition—a notion that Kant views as radical alternative to his transcendental philosophy. Ultimately, the very act (*Handlung*) of synthesis shows, on the one hand, that the separation between spontaneity and receptivity is not adequately described (or exhausted) by the opposition between activity and passivity; on the other hand, the act of synthesis underscores that the opposition between activity and passivity is not absolute. To put it differently, understanding's spontaneity is the activity of a *Vermögen,* not the activity of a *Kraft,* i.e., is only the *"possibility* of the activity."[43] The *actual* exercise of that faculty to produce determination (*Ausübung*) requires the additional condition of sensibility; sensibility becomes the other active constituent in the process of cognition.

The "determination of my existence can take place only in conformity with the form of the inner sense, according to the particular way in which the manifold which I combine is given in inner intuition."[44] The 'I think' as spontaneity "expresses the act of determining my existence." However, in this determination, I cannot determine myself as *selbstätiges Wesen* because my existence, as that which is "determinable," is nothing but my given sensible receptivity. That is, my existence is not itself a product of spontaneity; it is rather presupposed by the exercise of spontaneity as its condition.[45] Precisely to the extent that the spontaneous 'I think' cannot determine its own existence as spontaneous or as the existence of a "self-active being," the subject is still object of cognition—it is either an object in general or an empirical object (determined as substance, cause, etc.). Moreover, in order to transform the mere thinking of an "object in general" into the determinate cognition either of myself or of "an object distinct from myself," what is needed besides the understanding's category is an intuition *"through which I determine* that general concept."[46] Here it is intuition (i.e., receptivity) that is called upon to actively *determine* the general concept (i.e., the product of spontaneity). Thus, just as understanding's spontaneity encounters its limit in the condition of sensibility (whereby it is not absolute or unconditioned spontaneity), so sensibility is endowed with a determinative function of its own. The receptivity that belongs to sensibility is, in its own peculiar way, somehow "active" or "spontaneous" as well.[47] For it is only through the forms of space and time—"conditions for the receptivity of our *Gemüt*"— that representations of objects can be received. To produce knowledge, these representations *"must always affect (jederzeit affizieren)* the concepts"[48] of the objects that we perceive. Sensibility, for Kant, is a capacity of being affected that, in turn, actively affects the exercise of understanding's spontaneity by determining its general concepts. Furthermore, Kant suggests that the possibility for sensibility to be modified precedes (a priori) all its affections. The representation "I think" is defined as an "act of spontaneity" that as such can by no means belong to sensibility.[49] And yet, without an empirical representation provided by receptivity the "act, I think, would not take place at all." Thinking would still be spontaneous (i.e., representations would still be self-produced) but no *actual exercise* of thinking with regard to a particular content or matter would take place. Ultimately (and transcendentally), embodiment is the "condition of the *application* or the *use* of the pure intellectual faculty."[50] For a disembodied "intelligence,"[51] spontaneity would be of no use at all as it would yield no knowledge at all.

What happens to the notion of spontaneity and to its correlate, the transcendental form of the body or its active receptivity, when Kant, in the transition from the Paralogisms to the Antinomies, shifts from the conditioned spontaneity of thinking to the absolute spontaneity of freedom? How is sensibility and its receptivity transformed in this transition?

In the proof of the thesis of the third antinomy, discussing the peculiar character of the causality of nature's causes, Kant introduces the notion of "absolute spontaneity" to describe an alternative way in which causality may operate. Such is the "causality through (*durch*) freedom." In the proof of the thesis, absolute spontaneity is intended to break the ascending series of natural causes that always find their determining ground in an antecedent cause. Accordingly, "transcendental freedom" is defined as the "absolute spontaneity of a cause, whereby a series of appearances, which proceeds in accordance with laws of nature, begins *of itself.*"[52] Absolute spontaneity is the unconditioned beginning of a series of events, a determination not previously determined. The proof of the antithesis insists on the character of absolute beginning and on the lack of determination that would belong to "freedom in the transcendental sense."[53] It does so to the point that, in the perspective voiced by the antithesis, freedom appears as lack of lawfulness and sheer contingency. From the outset, the spontaneity proper to freedom, unlike the spontaneity of thinking, is not just productivity: in opposition to the causality of nature's efficient causes (in the claim of the antithesis), it is causality that operates without being determined or conditioned ("unconditioned causality").[54]

Kant indicates the "key to the solution"[55] of the cosmological dialectic in transcendental idealism. Taking up the argument presented in the Refutation of Idealism and formulated again in response to rational psychology, Kant distinguishes the thesis of the ideality of space and time from "material idealism" and its denial of—or doubt toward—the existence of external things.[56] The thesis that our knowledge of objects and natural events is necessarily limited by the transcendental condition of embodiment, i.e., by space and time as a priori forms of intuition, becomes the turning-point that allows Kant to introduce the possibility of (1) a different type of causality and (2) a type of spontaneity that is independent of that condition. If, on the contrary, we were to free our knowledge from the condition of embodiment—i.e., from the constitutive and determinative reference to our sensibility and receptivity[57] whereby we know things as they appear to us within the context of experience—then the possibility of a different kind of spontaneity would have to be entirely ruled out. The result would be universal determinism with no appeal. Spontaneity of thinking and spontaneity of freedom would not be distinguishable. Spontaneity would only designate the way in which, for Aristotle (in Wolff's own rendition) the fire's flames move upwards spontaneously (i.e., not being determined by an external cause).[58] The "idealist"—suggests Kant in an early reflection on Baumgarten's *Metaphysica* (probably written in 1769)—"sees all his external (actual) representations as spontaneous."[59] For the idealist, the denial of the existence of external things is one with the rejection of receptivity (and of a transcendental character of sensibility). Since the idealist does not recognize the transcendental role that sensibility plays in determining representations of objects as *external* to oneself, i.e., as real, all representations are, for him, internally produced (or self-produced) hence "spontaneous." For Kant, however, internal self-production is not freedom.

In presenting transcendental idealism as the key to the solution of the cosmological antinomies, Kant extends the discussion of the argument first established by the Transcendental Aesthetic to include an account of the notion of cause. The transition from the spontaneity of thinking to the absolute spontaneity of freedom runs through the shift from the "transcendental object" to the "transcendental subject" raised as complement of sensibility's receptivity. Kant repeats that the sensible "faculty of intuition is properly only a receptivity," a capacity of being affected in a certain way by representations that can be called "objects" (*Gegenstände*) to the extent that they lend themselves to synthesis in a possible experience. Since receptivity is defined as the capacity for being affected, the question arises: what is the *cause* of affection? Kant's answer is unequivocal: since the "non-sensible cause" of the representations that affect our senses remains for us "entirely unknown," we cannot intuit this cause "as object" (*Objekt*). For, being non-sensible, it would be an object that does not respond to the conditions of space and time—conditions outside of which no intuition is possible for us.[60] And yet, Kant proposes to call this "transcendental object (*Objekt*)" the "intelligible" (and not simply "non-sensible") cause of appearances in general—just in order "to have something corresponding to sensibility as receptivity."[61] Significantly, it is a reflection on the nature of sensibility as the capacity for being affected (and not an "analogy" with the understanding's spontaneity) that allows Kant to infer the possibility of a non-sensible cause. Even though throughout the Analytic understanding's spontaneity has always been defined in opposition to sensibility as complementing its function in producing knowledge, at this crucial juncture it is not this spontaneity that Kant sees as corresponding to sensibility's receptivity, or as the intelligible cause of representations. In fact, as we have seen above, against the idealist's claim, in Kant's transcendental idealism representations with cognitive value (or indeed "meaning")[62] are not entirely self-produced by understanding's spontaneity—for they are not self-produced with regard to their external empirical determination. Empirical determination can be gained only in reference to the body's formal receptivity or capacity for being affected. However, due to the condition of embodiment that allows us to determine as existing only that which falls within the context of our actual perception or a series of possible perceptions, the transcendental object as cause of affection has no sense for us. It can gain meaning only if we think of it as "transcendental subject" endowed with a peculiar kind of causality, namely "causality from (aus) freedom."[63]

Freedom as Absolute Spontaneity:
From Disembodied Soul to Embodied Will

In the solution of the third antinomy, Kant connects the idea of absolute spontaneity, i.e., "freedom in the cosmological sense," with the issue of defining the subject of that spontaneity as a human agent. The crucial relation between transcendental freedom and practical freedom is at stake. Transcendental freedom is "the capacity (Vermögen) for beginning a state out of itself (von selbst)," i.e., spontaneously, by breaking the linear succession of time-determination. It is the pure idea of a "spontaneity which can begin to act of itself (von selbst), without needing to be determined to action by an antecedent cause in accordance with the law of causality"[64]—i.e., the law that is valid without exception within nature. Kant suggests that the transcendental idea of freedom "grounds" the idea of freedom in the practical sense, and constitutes the core of the peculiar difficulty encountered in dealing with the concept of practical freedom. By underscoring this crucial connection, he insists on its indeed "remarkable" character. The denial of transcendental freedom would immediately make practical freedom impossible.[65] For the claim that appearances are things in themselves, i.e., that space and time are not forms of our sensible intuition but properties of things in themselves, would hand the world over to universal determinism in which freedom could no longer be saved.

In discussing the problem raised by reason's antinomy, the reflection upon the nature of human sensibility and its function in cognition (the thesis of transcendental idealism) led Kant to the hypothetical inference of a type of causality affecting sensibility and yet located outside the determination of phenomena in time and space. Clearly, for Kant, this "cause" of affection (as "transcendental object") can be neither a proper object of cognition nor a subject in the sense claimed by rational psychology for the metaphysical soul. Only the cosmological idea of transcendental freedom allows Kant to introduce a notion of absolute spontaneity that can account for the different—"ideal"—type of causality implied by the problem of the cause of sensibility's affection. Absolute spontaneity as causality from/through freedom is the spontaneity of an action independent of the conditions of sensibility. The question, at this point, is the following: what kind of receptivity corresponds to freedom's spontaneity? What does spontaneity, in turn, determine or whereupon does it act? It is only once the concept of spontaneity is complemented by a specific practical form of sensibility that the subject of action—or the acting subject—will emerge. Thereby the realm of practical reason will be introduced in its connection with speculative reason and its dialectic. Kant's conclusive thesis is that *practical freedom is transcendental freedom embodied in and enacted by the human sensible will.* Practical freedom arises from the "application" of the idea of transcendental freedom to the condition of embodiment that the critique of the paralogism of rational psychology has established as belonging, inescapably, to the human subject in the natural world. Practical freedom is the actual "exercise" of transcendental freedom by the human agent.[66] Hence, by way of reference to human embodiment, Kant introduces a new notion of sensibility and a new concept of affection, which, this time, bear directly on the issue of a possible spontaneous determination of our existence in relation to an intelligible world. Such a determination, denied in the sphere of speculative reason, becomes a real possibility (though not yet a reality)[67] in the practical realm disclosed by the solution of the third antinomy.

Once Kant has suggested the close connection between transcendental and practical freedom, he proceeds to the definition of the latter as "the will's (*Willkür*) independence of coercion through the impulses of sensibility." Thereby, sensibility and affection are introduced as functions of the will and its determination. From the outset, Kant's argument aims at defining the specificity of the *human* will. The will is called "sensible" (*sinnlich*) when it is "pathologically affected," i.e., when sensibility functions as cause or motive of its action. However, since sensibility and affection may or may not determine the will, they do not necessitate it. Kant maintains that human *arbitrium*, despite its being *arbitrium sensitivum,* is not *arbitrium brutum* but *arbitrium liberum.*[68] In the practical sphere, the role played by *arbitrium brutum* (animal will) in animals exactly corresponds to the deterministic role that sensibility plays in our cognition of objects as a necessary ingredient for synthesis. For in the case of *arbitrium brutum,* sensible affection necessitates the will (animal will is "pathologically necessitated"): no action is possible without a sensuous motive as its determining ground just as no empirical cognition is possible without the a priori forms of space and time.[69] The spontaneity of the dog's action of coming to greet its master when it hears his voice is the type of spontaneity accepted by Wolff—who provides this specific example—but certainly not by Kant.[70] Kant contends that with regard to the human will, sensibility does not necessitate the will, for sensibility is only one of the possible motives of its determination. To this extent, the human *arbitrium sensitivum* differs radically from the *arbitrium brutum,* just as the practical determination of my human existence differs from the way in which I can cognitively determine my existence only in reference to the conditions of sensible intuition. Now, to the affective and sensible character of the human will corresponds a form of spontaneity that, no longer cosmologically but practically defined, is identified with the faculty or capacity (*Vermögen*) that the human being has for "*determining itself out of itself (von selbst),* independently of the coercion of sensible impulses."[71] This is practical freedom. This definition of practical freedom translates the cosmological idea of absolute spontaneity with regard to the human being and her sensibility. In the practical sphere, sensibility gains its specific (transcendental) meaning and function in relation to the will and its determination. Once again, for Kant, the issue of spontaneity is an issue of determination. This time, however, the "determinable" to which spontaneity applies in its determination is the human sensible will.

Kant's complex itinerary up to the present point can be summarized as follows. Separating spontaneity from the will (against Wolff and following Baumgarten), Kant shows that the subject of absolute spontaneity can be neither the knowing subject (whether the logical or empirical 'I think') nor the immaterial soul of rational psychology. Spontaneity is not a concept belonging to rational or empirical psychology, but a concept of transcendental philosophy—it is a "pure transcendental idea."[72] Kant's critical argument against rational psychology, repeated yet again as the "key" to the solution of the antinomies of cosmology, shows that spontaneity must be compatible with the condition of human embodiment since this condition cannot be eliminated. Yet, in contrast to the cognitive situation that defines the complementary functions of understanding's spontaneity and sensibility's receptivity, the idea of transcendental freedom leads us to think of a form of spontaneity that is "absolute," i.e., not conditioned by sensibility. In other words, sensibility must be present (the human being is not a disembodied soul), but it may not necessitate the human will (which is not *arbitrium brutum* but *arbitrium sensitivum*). This is precisely the situation that allows transcendental freedom to be the ground for practical freedom.[73]

   In relation to the cosmological idea of a capacity for beginning to act entirely from oneself, sensibility receives a twofold re-definition. On the one hand, as sensible inclination or affection, it is one of the possible motives of the will insofar as this is *arbitrium sensitivum*. On the other hand, it characterizes the human will in its *determinability* (or indeterminacy) as *arbitrium sensitivum* and yet *liberum* (as opposed to *brutum*), thereby pointing to the fact that the will's embodiment is a necessary, yet not a sufficient condition for its practical determination. The human will can choose to be determined or not to be determined by sensible motives only because it may be *determinable* by them. This determinability (and, to this extent, indeterminacy) constitutes precisely its sensible character. Such character (as possibility or *Vermögen*) places the human will between the animal will, which is exclusively determined by sensible motives, and the divine will, which is exclusively determined by intellectual principles. Accordingly, human freedom is defined as *libertas hybrida*.[74] Thus, in its practical function, sensibility is no longer transcendentally represented by space and time as pure forms of intuition. Rather, it is either the sensible affection of the will—namely its actual determination through pathological motives—or its mere determinability compatible with practical freedom. Transcendentally, the will is the first practical transfiguration of the human body: the will's determinability takes the place of the body's receptivity. This practical determinability, however, is open to a twofold possibility—that is, a merely empirical and a purely intellectual determination. The will is free when it acts "free from all influence of sensibility and from all determination through appearance,"[75] i.e., when it acts "out of itself." Thereby Kant undertakes a fundamental step toward the definition of the subject of action as a human subject.

Practical freedom defines a type of causal determination that, taking place in the world of nature and appearances, determines events that respond to empirical laws according to time-order but determines them so that the causality of the cause is spontaneous in the sense of being able to "begin a series of events *entirely of itself* (*ganz von selbst*),"[76] independently of natural causes. Thereby, practical freedom enacts transcendental freedom (as pure idea) and brings it to manifestation within the world of nature. Kant takes up again the suggestion of an "intelligible cause" as that whose determination does not lie within the series of natural causes although its effects do appear in the world of nature and, accordingly, can be determined through other appearances. Now he qualifies this cause as free. The effect produced by the non-sensible cause, however, is both "free" with regard to its intelligible cause, and necessitated in accordance with nature's laws. While the intelligible cause remains entirely unknown to us, to the point that it can never be an "object"[77] for us, we are now in the position of saying that the intelligible cause constitutes the subject as a "subject" of free action.

At this point of his argument Kant has all the elements at hand to present the cosmological—and eventually practical—metamorphosis of the embodied human subject that a longstanding tradition, culminating in rational psychology, has in vain attempted to dismember by separating an immortal, immaterial soul from a merely passive, receptive body. Kant re-defines the terms of the problem in the following way: "*intelligible*" is now "whatever *in an object of the senses* is not itself appearance," while "*character*" is that certain "law" of causality without which a cause would not be cause at all.[78] The split between sensibility and understanding is thus complicated: now a sensible or "empirical character" and an "intelligible character" define one and the same subject. According to its definition, "intelligible" is a property displayed by (certain) sensible objects that can behave like subjects. It is neither a metaphysical nor a cognitive feature defining the soul apart from the body; it is, on the contrary, the peculiar additional "character" (or "law") that qualifies a sensible embodied being in the different perspective disclosed by its "action" in the world of nature. This "intelligible" is not a property of the subject taken in abstraction from its sensible existence, but rather the particular way in which a sensible embodied being can be the cause that produces effects in the realm of appearances without being itself a phenomenally determined or conditioned cause. More precisely, Kant designates as intelligible a capacity or faculty (*Vermögen*) that can be the "cause of appearances" without being itself appearance—i.e., without being an object of intuition (and hence of knowledge)—even though its

effects are manifested as appearances. This faculty is indeed, as Kant puts
it elsewhere, a "marvelous faculty"[79]—it is practical reason. Accordingly,
the causality of such a subject or faculty with regard to one and the same
effect is viewed from two different sides: on the one hand, it is an "intelligible" (*intelligibel*) causality of "action" (*Handlung*), while on the other, it
is a "sensible" (*sensibel*) causality that produces "effects" (*Wirkungen*).[80] The
two sides belong, as it were, to the same subject as well as to the same effect.
To this extent, the sensible and the intelligible ultimately coexist to define
the human being as a possible free agent in the world. The "transcendental
object," previously introduced with the modest justification of fulfilling the
need for "something corresponding to sensibility as receptivity,"[81] has now
clearly become a "transcendental *subject*" as "acting subject" (*handelndes
Subjekt*).[82] In its intelligible character, the transcendental subject cannot be
"*immediately* known."[83] And yet, the effects of its intelligible causality do
appear in the sensible world even though this causality itself is not determined by the natural order but is, instead, absolutely and unconditionally
spontaneous or free.

If the idea of transcendental freedom is to ground the possibility of the
will's practical freedom, then it must be possible to describe the causality
of certain sensible beings in the world according to two different sides, as
displaying two different "characters"—namely, an "empirical" and an "intelligible" character.[84] However, intelligible and sensible character do not
run parallel to each other but meet in both the effect produced by the agent
within the world of nature and in the agent itself as an embodied free being.
While the transcendental description of the subject as knowing subject (or
object of self-knowledge) plays itself out exclusively within the dimension
of its phenomenal nature and its a priori structures, the practical problem of
free agency (or practical causality) requires the two dimensions (or characters) of the intelligible and the sensible. Kant has argued that, in the cognitive sphere, the notion of a pure "intelligence" is not sufficient to determine
the 'I think' in its empirical existence (nor is it sufficient to determine the
nature of the soul). The "intelligible character," on the contrary, sufficiently
explains a peculiar type of causality in the world of nature, namely, the
causality of a free agent who begins a series of events "entirely of itself."[85]
Moreover, a pure, disembodied intelligence has, for Kant, no causality or
agency at all: neither the soul's *commercium* with bodies nor a community
of disembodied spirits is possible for such intelligence. On the contrary,
precisely because the subject is always and necessarily embodied—i.e., is
itself "a part of the sensible world"[86] in which every effect responds to the

conditions of space and time—an intelligible causality can be assumed in the subject without contradicting nature's laws. "Intelligible" is, for Kant, the character of sensible objects or of a subject acting in the sensible world, not the character of a pure mind projected into the after-life of another world.[87] In other words, while *transcendental* freedom can be thought only under the condition of having abandoned the perspective of the disembodied soul (or of rational psychology), the cosmological idea of absolute spontaneity must be embodied in a sensible agent in order to function as *practical* freedom. For even though a disembodied subject can indeed be thought as pure intelligence, its spontaneity still does not allow one to define it as a "self-active being" (*selbstätiges Wesen*).[88] Only as an embodied being endowed with intelligible causality is the subject a truly "active being" (*tätiges Wesen*), whose activity is spontaneous in the sense of being "independent and free" from all natural necessity. Only an embodied being is an agent in the proper sense.

Thus, "we may quite correctly say that the active being begins *of itself* (*von selbst*) its effects in the sensible world, without any action beginning *in* this active being itself (*in ihm*)." Thereby Kant opposes his dynamic definition of spontaneity to a static one.[89] He maintains that the acting subject is not the place of an absolute beginning of action. Thereby two points are made. On the one hand, freedom cannot be defined through the 'place' in which an action begins (namely, as beginning in the acting subject itself as opposed to outside of it). On the other hand, the free subject cannot be described in terms of what "happens" (also psychologically) *in it*, i.e., of what action or passion takes place "in it."[90] The acting subject is still part of the sensible world and hence is a phenomenal cause among other causes. No action begins "in it" simply because everything in the sensible world—to which intelligible causality belongs—is determined by an antecedent cause, so that there is no first beginning of action or no first term of a causal series but only a continuation of the series.[91] Nature is precisely the thoroughgoing interconnectedness of the series of causes and effects. By contrast, Kant defines the absolute spontaneity of the intelligible cause as the capacity for beginning "of itself" a series of events. The reason why the will can be said to be free is not that action simply begins in it. Insofar as the will is inescapably part of the sensible world, no action can be said to begin *in it* because each of its actions is determined by an antecedent cause, i.e., refers backwards to a cause outside of itself. Thereby, Kant overcomes the traditional definition of freedom that takes the exclusively internal (as opposed to the external) determination of the will as a sufficient condition of freedom. Within the world of appearance, to which the embodied free will still belongs, there is no absolute internal determination to action. Relevant to Kant's notion of spontaneity is not the fact that an action begins *in* the cause, but rather the way in which causality is exercised. Since the intelligible cause is never an object for us, no effect can actually arise *in it*. Intelligible causality is revealed instead by the way in which it is exercised, namely "out of itself" or through itself—*von* and *aus selbst*. Accordingly, Kant maintains that reason's intelligible causality "*does not arise* or begin at a certain time"—which would make of reason a sensible cause. Reason is the "faculty *through* which the sensible condition of an empirical series of effects first begins."[92]

Kant's argument pursues two aims. First, he shows the way in which no "direct contradiction"[93] separates the two types of causality, namely, empirical causality and intelligible causality. The different way in which causality is exercised in the two cases allows Kant to make his point. Second, he implies that if it is possible to consider one and the same event both according to the laws of empirical causality and as the effect of a non-empirical, intelligible cause, then the relation between the two types of causality needs to be more rigorously explained. From both conclusions it follows that freedom is possible in the world of nature and that the problem must be addressed: What is the relation between empirical and intelligible character? Kant sets out to answer this question by calling attention to its application to experience.[94] Thereby, the former question is re-formulated as follows: *who* is that being in which the two types of causality can coexist without contradiction? And how can we recognize this being among other natural beings, given that the understanding "sees nothing but nature"?[95] While intelligible causality *per se* remains entirely unknown to us, if considered in its *application* to experience, i.e., in the concrete case of those peculiar "natural causes" that display a "faculty that is only intelligible,"[96] then something more precise can be said regarding the relation of the two types of causality. Now the class of natural causes or beings to which the two characters apply is *Mensch*—the "human being."[97] The transcendental subject as "active being" and "acting subject" is now clearly the embodied human being as possible free agent in the world of nature. Thereby Kant pursues the transition from speculative reason to practical reason. His strategy is to describe transcendental freedom *indirectly*,[98] taking a sort of anthropological detour through the way in which freedom is embodied in the action of a peculiar sensible agent endowed with an intelligible character. Sensible character now becomes the transfigured "body" or the material "sign" of reason's most proper freedom. At this point, however, anthropology and its observation as well as any kind of "physiological" account of causality are left behind for a purely moral insight into the nature of human agency.[99]

Due to its necessary embodiment, the human being is "one of the appearances of the sensible world" that exercises causality in the mode of all other natural causes. Its empirical character is expressed by its action in the sensible world as well as by its sensible faculties. However, in opposition to both "lifeless nature" and mere "animal nature," a reconsideration of the human cognitive faculty allows Kant to find a first trace of the intelligible character in the human being.[100] Kant's argument works, at this point, only in force of a sort of homonymous—and implicit—use of the notion of spontaneity. A radical distinction is drawn between knowledge of outer objects (which is always sensible) and self-knowledge. In the latter case the necessary reference to "mere apperception" betrays the presence of faculties that cannot be understood as falling within the receptivity of sensibility (and hence must be understood as spontaneous). Understanding and reason are those non-sensible, intelligible (or allegedly intelligible) faculties that the human being is conscious of possessing.[101] Kant's exclusion of lifeless nature and animal nature from the realm of beings endowed with intelligible character is due exclusively to the fact that this inference is based upon our (reflective) experience of self-knowledge. We can draw this inference in the case of the human being because we are human beings ourselves. But for this reason we can draw the inference *only* for the human being. At this point, Kant capitalizes on the occurrence of speculative reason's natural dialectic. Even though speculative reason cannot *know* itself as pure intelligence (for the understanding's spontaneity cannot determine itself as spontaneous), the attempt to do so (indeed its natural, unavoidable tendency to do so), which leads to the illusion of rational psychology, seems to qualify it for the attribute of 'non-sensible' or 'non-empirically conditioned'. As faculty of ideas, reason is indeed a non-sensible faculty. This feature, in turn, applied to the way in which reason exercises causality, lends to it an intelligible character. Kant's suggestion is that "ideas of reason" may prove able to exercise "real causality" with regard to human action in nature.[102] It will be the task of the second *Critique* to unravel this intricate situation.

The crucial issue lies in the claim that "this reason does indeed have causality."[103] This is the core question of the *Critique of Practical Reason*. In the present connection, however, Kant is extremely cautious in presenting it.[104] Instead of constructing an argument, he resorts to evidence. He calls upon reason's notion of a *Sollen,* the imperative that expresses the peculiar necessity of actions determined by mere concepts and not by the causality of phenomena. In executing the voice of this *Sollen,* reason does not follow the order of nature and appearances "but frames for itself *with perfect sponta-neity* an order of its own according to ideas, to which it adapts the empirical conditions, and according to which it declares actions to be necessary."[105] As practical reason or intelligible cause acting out of absolute spontaneity, reason constructs a world of its own distinct from the natural world. And yet, the effects of reason's causality must inevitably appear in the world of nature. Kant's own marginal remark to the initial claim "that reason does indeed have causality" reads: "this causality is called the will."[106] The hu-man will has an empirical character that is cause of all its actions. Although reason is not empirically determined, it is, nonetheless, necessarily embod-ied (in *arbitrium sensitivum*) and as such "it *must,* despite its being reason, ex-hibit an empirical character."[107] On this premise, Kant concludes that "the will of every human being has an empirical character, which is nothing but a certain causality of his reason" insofar as this causality exhibits a rule or principle that can be viewed as the subjective ground of the will's action. Thus, the empirical character of the human will is the concrete embodi-ment and sensible representative of the intelligible character of reason in the sensible world. However, no empirical observation—anthropological or psychological—is able to discern freedom at work in and through the empirical character. A "physiology" of the human will would yield only natural necessity.[108] For in this perspective, all actions of the human will are necessitated by antecedent conditions within the natural order. On the other hand, no "pneumatic" explanation of the soul's activity can discover the spontaneity of reason's causality. It is only with reference to the *practical* use of reason that the connection between empirical and intelligible char-acter can finally emerge.

In the practical perspective we can establish the following propositions. We can claim (1) that the empirical character is a "mere appearance of the intelligible"; (2) that the intelligible character is the "transcendental cause" of the empirical; (3) that the empirical character is the "sensible sign" (*das sinnliche Zeichen*) of the intelligible so that, even though we cannot directly know the intelligible character itself, we can "indicate" or "mark out" (*be-zeichnen*) its nature by means of appearances; and finally (4) that the sensible character is the "sensible schema" of the intelligible.[109]

We can conclude that in the practical sphere, the will in its empirical character takes the place that the body occupies in the cognitive sphere by way of the a priori forms of its sensibility. The will is that which is receptive and *immediately* determinable by freedom, and which, in turn, determines through its empirical character a series of events in the sensible world. As was the case in cognition with the transcendental form of the body—the dividing line between inner and outer sense—in the practical sphere the will is the line that separates empirical and intelligible character, sensible affection and rational motive, and eventually, as *arbitrium sensitivum* and *liberum,* participates in both. As human knowledge is always dependent upon the transcendental condition of embodiment, so human action is possible only through the causality of the embodied will in the sensible world. In this case, however, it is freedom's unconditioned causality that constitutes the *immediate* condition under which alone the will can be *arbitrium liberum.* To the extent to which the will—as *arbitrium sensitivum* and yet *liberum*—is conditioned by a non-sensible, intelligible cause, the will expresses the figure that transcendental embodiment displays in the practical sphere. Transcendentally the will is the practically transfigured "body" through which reason performs its intelligible causality in the order of nature. While understanding's concepts need a schematism in order to produce cognition, freedom's spontaneity is always schematized through the will's empirical character. In the world of appearance, the will is embodied in the human agent.

5

Pure Practical Reason and the Reason of Human Desire

E li uomini in universali iudicano più alli occhi che alle mani; perché tocca a vedere a ognuno, a sentire a pochi. Ognuno vede
quello che tu pari, pochi sentono quello che tu se'

—NICCOLÒ MACHIAVELLI, *Il Principe*

Plotinus was ashamed to be in a body

—PORPHYRY, *Life of Plotinus*

IT IS KANT'S CONTENTION THAT THE CONCEPT OF FREEDOM
constitutes the "keystone (*Schlußstein*) of the whole architecture of the system of pure reason"—even of speculative reason.[1] The concept of freedom
is proved by the apodictic law of practical reason, i.e., by the imperative of
moral legislation and by the consciousness of freedom that arises from it.
However, the solution of the third antinomy of the *Critique of Pure Reason*
is still unable to provide this positive proof. There, Kant goes only as far
as securing the possibility that freedom be *thought* without contradiction
within the framework of natural causality. Nonetheless, this is still a highly
relevant result; not only because it establishes the systematic starting point
of Kant's inquiry in the second *Critique,* namely, the transformation of
a merely possible "thought" into the peculiar practical "fact"[2] of reason.
Kant's need to guarantee the compatibility of the concept of freedom with
nature's mechanism, i.e., ultimately, with the specific constitution of the

human being's cognitive faculty, necessarily affects the structure of the purely moral enterprise of the second *Critique*. The *Critique* of speculative reason shows that freedom is possible (thinkable) only under the transcendental assumption of the ideality of space and time, i.e., only under the necessary limitation of human knowledge to appearances through the condition of embodiment. Freedom cannot be an object of cognition or (cognitive) experience because all experience falls under the inescapable condition of time-succession in which mechanistic causality is ordered. However, time is not a property of things in themselves but the transcendental form of human sensibility. Moreover, because of the connection between the third antinomy and the critique of rational psychology in the Paralogisms, the concept of transcendental freedom also implies that only an embodied being can be a transcendentally and practically free being—a "subject" or agent. On Kant's account, a purely rational, disembodied soul would not be free but would be determined in all its actions by the law of causality (as is Spinoza's substance). For in this case, space and time would not be mere forms of sensible intuition (the transcendental form of the body) but objective properties of this being's existence. Consequently, such a "soul" could never be a properly moral agent or subject. Thus, in presenting speculative reason's dialectic, the first *Critique* establishes both that freedom discloses a noumenal or purely intelligible—although unknowable—dimension of human existence, and that this purely intelligible dimension, despite its preeminence over the phenomenal one, is still only one aspect of the entire reality of reason. This aspect is, in Kant's words, "character": neither a metaphysical essence nor a defining feature of "human nature," but the peculiar "law of its causality."[3] It follows that while, for the sake of analysis and of philosophical exposition, the transcendental concept of freedom certainly requires an independent development, with regard to its practical application or exercise it is intrinsically connected with the world of appearances. The *Critique of Practical Reason* is built upon this twofold character that the transcendental concept of freedom inherits from the Dialectic of the first *Critique*. Eventually, the same connection will emerge as one of the crucial topics of the *Critique of Judgment*.

Unlike most reconstructions of Kant's moral philosophy, the present chapter examines the way in which the second *Critique* develops the abovementioned implications of Kant's transcendental idealism (the thesis of the Transcendental Aesthetic). "Independence"[4] from all sensibility—from space and time, the necessity of natural inclinations and the matter of the law as a desired object—constitutes, for Kant, the first, negative concept of freedom. However, this definition is not tautological and can effectively lead to a positive concept of freedom only if it refers to a being that may or may not be determined by sensibility. It is, on the contrary, a mere tautology for a holy will, whose subject by definition entirely lacks sensibility. Accordingly, while Kant repeatedly states that the moral law is valid for every rational will as such, the moral law is an "imperative" (and properly a "law") that discloses the consciousness of freedom, proves its objective reality as a fact, and produces a certain peculiar feeling in the *Gemüt* only for the human being, i.e., for a being endowed with reason, will, *and sensibility.*

The second issue addressed in this chapter immediately follows from the one just presented. It regards the specific way in which Kant's practical philosophy takes up the topic of human embodiment in a critical and transcendental perspective. Kant's 1788 work is a critique of "practical reason" and not of "pure practical reason" since it is concerned with the possibility of reason being either empirically conditioned or unconditionally practical—and hence is not concerned with a holy will. Still, Kant declares at the outset that this work provides "only the principles of the possibility of duty, of its extent, and limits, *without particular reference to human nature,*" i.e., to the way in which duties are specifically "human duties" (*Menschenpflichten*).[5] Otherwise knowledge of man—of man's "actual" nature—would be required. Kant's pure moral philosophy radically rejects all anthropological reference or presupposition—let alone foundation. On the contrary, Kant suggests that the moral subject examined in the second *Critique* is never qualified as a human being by "human nature." This implies that the specifically human character of the moral agent is derived through a purely transcendental (not empirical or anthropological) argument. The subject of the second *Critique* is a being that as thinking being displays an "empirical" consciousness as mere "appearance," whereas as moral agent it is endowed with an intelligible character and a "pure" consciousness. This claim, which Kant does not hesitate to recognize as "strange and yet incontrovertible," defines the subject as *Mensch.*[6] However, it is obviously neither a metaphysical, anthropological, or psychological assertion for it does not define human nature but the *transcendental* structure of the faculty of reason in its practical use.[7]

In the *Groundwork of the Metaphysics of Morals* (1785), when Kant's project of moral philosophy still envisions a "critique of pure practical reason," he presents a similar claim in opposition to Wolff's *philosophia practica universalis.* Unlike Wolff's universal practical philosophy, the task of a "metaphysics of morals" is "to investigate the idea and principles of a possible pure will, and not the activities and conditions of human willing as such, *which are drawn for the most part from psychology.*" Moreover, with regard to the task of finding out the highest principle of morality, Kant issues the crucial warning that we should "not dream for a moment of trying to derive the reality of this principle from the *special characteristic of human nature.*"[8] Kant's ethics makes no reference to an alleged human nature or soul. It breaks with the tradition of moral philosophy precisely because it radically rejects the (empirical as well as metaphysical) presuppositions of both anthropology and psychology. His moral philosophy makes the "paradoxical"[9] claim that practical freedom is a human reality and yet is radically independent of human nature. In Kant's perspective, it is the nature of practical freedom that first defines our human reality; it is not an alleged human nature that determines what human freedom is.

Thus, if Kant's moral philosophy refers, as it were, to a specific class of subjects, this specificity ought to emerge in a *transcendental* way. In the practical sphere, the transcendental notion of embodiment—the practical figure of "transcendental embodiment"—is construed precisely as the solution of the paradox of freedom. This chapter suggests that *embodiment* is the condition that transcendentally defines the moral subject of Kantian ethics (as it transcendentally defines the knowing subject as well as the known object of his epistemology). It follows that embodiment, for Kant, is neither a matter for anthropology nor a concern of moral psychology in the first place.[10] Rather, it defines the project of a new transcendental and critical theory of practical sensibility. The "body" of practical reason is not the physical, visible, and natural body of the individual agent.[11] It is the *transcendental form in and through which* action becomes real for an acting rational subject (a person) as purely and genuinely moral action. The legislation of reason and the consciousness of freedom connected to it (and one with it) as "fact" define the "moral space" in which reason is embodied. The body of practical reason is not that through which reason *is known* as acting, but that through which reason *does act* as free. While this space is indeed *purely* moral and rational, it defines a subject that is necessarily endowed with sensibility—this time with a *practical* form of sensibility. The human being as embodied being (not an alleged human nature) is the final result, not the starting point of Kant's inquiry. Hence, it is only *after* the critical foundation of a pure moral philosophy has shown what the transcendental practical form of the human body is—and only on this basis—that we can turn to the study of Kant's anthropology, moral psychology, and generally to his "applied" practical philosophy.

The present chapter shows the fundamental function that embodiment reveals in Kant's practical philosophy. It discusses a twofold connection: on the one hand, it addresses the way in which freedom and its law refer to the subject's "sensible character"; on the other hand, it brings to the fore the way in which the body is practically construed as a pure *transcendental* form. My analysis follows the development of the *Critique of Practical Reason* and offers a general account of the transformation of the notion of sensibility in the practical sphere. If the moral agent is, as I suggest, *transcendentally* a necessarily embodied rational agent, we need to ask the following: what does it mean that freedom's causality is independent of space and time, i.e., of sensible intuition, and yet appears in the world of nature? Does Kant's claim that the will's freedom, in the negative sense, is its "independence" of a desired object imply an elimination of human desire as such? Or does it rather lead to a different—non-empirical, neither anthropological nor psychological but specifically transcendental—account of desire, feeling, emotion, and passion?[12] And what could such a *transcendental* account of moral feeling be?

Moral Space

The enterprise of the first *Critique* runs contrary to the tendency of common sense to assume a fixed and given truth in things that the human mind would have to capture with its concepts in order to produce knowledge. But it also comes up against the dialectical illusions of speculative reason which it holds responsible for constructing a metaphysical world that can claim no other reality than that of an inevitable—indeed "natural"—error. Kant's project of a "pure" ethics, on the contrary, sees in common sense an ally that confirms, with its certainty and with the example of its activity, the insight of the critical philosopher. In Kant's view, only "philosophers" with their empty speculations can mix up these matters and cast doubts on what for common sense is simple and straightforward.[13] This holds true for Kant in both the *Groundwork* (1785) and the *Critique of Practical Reason* (1788). He conceives the "method" of the former as proceeding analytically from the "common knowledge" of morality to its supreme principle, and then as going back, synthetically, from the philosophical examination and proof of this principle to the common knowledge in which the moral imperative finds its application.[14] Thereby, common sense and philosophical insight are interwoven and reciprocally refer to one another. In the division of the

Critique of Practical Reason, Kant clarifies that the "methodology" of pure practical reason does not concern the theoretical and scientific knowledge of the principles of morality. Its task is rather to secure the law of pure reason with an *"access (Eingang)* to the human *Gemüt"* and, accordingly, with an "influence" on its maxims so that a subjective application of the objective principle of reason can take place.[15] While the project of "pure" ethics represents, in the history of moral philosophy, a revolution of no less importance than the one carried out in the theory of knowledge, Kant recognizes that the former is hardly a novelty for common sense.

> If one asks [. . .] what *pure* morality *(reine Sittlichkeit)* properly is, by which, as the touchstone *(Probemetall),* the moral import of each action must be tested, I must confess that only philosophers can put the decision on this question in doubt. For by common human reason it is long since decided, not by abstract general formulas but rather by habitual use, *like the difference between the right and the left hand.*[16]

Thereby, Kant suggests that the central topic of the second *Critique*—namely the issue of a "pure" morality, independent of empirical motives and not grounded on material desire—is a matter immediately decided by a sort of "feeling" or certainty or consciousness that exactly parallels the physical feeling of an internal difference within our own body such as the difference between left and right hand. Within the project of a pure morality, however, Kant distinguishes between the common sense evidence of the morality of actions and the evidence of the *principle* of morality as "fact" of reason. Given the longstanding history of the recurring spatial distinction between left and right (hands) in Kant's theoretical philosophy, its occurrence in the context of his practical philosophy is relevant for understanding the way in which the "moral space" of reason's domain is defined.

From early on in the development of Kant's philosophy, the capacity of distinguishing between left and right betrays a crucial transcendental and a priori feature of human sensibility. In an important way, the capacity for distinguishing true virtue and pure motives from empirical desires and pathological inclinations is precisely the criterion that, in the Analytic of the second *Critique,* allows Kant to find the *pure* principle of morality in the *form* of moral legislation and to identify it with the positive concept of freedom.[17] If read in the light of the methodological conclusion of the 1788 work, Kant's famous thesis of the "fact of reason" receives an unexpected new meaning. Freedom is embodied *(factum)* in the actual exercise of practical reason (*facere*)—not only objectively (in the moral imperative) but also subjectively (in subjective maxims). The exercise of reason takes place as the will's capacity for being purely determined by the moral law: objectively as the *capacity for recognizing pure morality and acting accordingly;* subjectively in examples, education, and judging others' actions. Thereby, the extent of the purely "moral space" of Kant's practical philosophy—the space within which the distinction between pure motives and pathological affection can be transcendentally drawn—is defined as the concrete space of an unconditioned action. Since pure morality (or free causality) does not itself appear in space and time (only its effects do), the capacity for recognizing freedom cannot be the cognitive capacity for reading out appearances. The moral space is unconditioned, i.e., completely independent of sensibility; its extension cannot be seized by knowledge and is not offered in intuition. Moral space is itself the condition for distinguishing true virtue and truly moral action since only within this "space" is such a distinction (the noumenon) meaningful for us. Freedom is unknowable to us, but as consciousness of the moral law it has the reality of a *factum* (not a *datum*) that precedes even our consciousness of it.[18] Kant suggests that as embodied human beings we do have a "sense" for this moral space, whereby access to it is available to us and orientation in the moral world provided. Such a sense differs radically from our sense for physical space, namely, from the a priori conditions of our knowledge of objects—in other words, it is not intuition. Kant argues that the consciousness of the moral law as the only "fact of reason" cannot be obtained by sophistical pseudo-rational arguments drawn from antecedent data of reason (not even from the consciousness of freedom itself, which is not a *datum*). Rather, it "*forces itself upon us* as a synthetic a priori proposition that is based on no intuition—neither pure nor empirical."[19] Similarly, albeit on a different level, common sense does not need the abstract formulas of the philosophers to define pure morality; it suffices to point to its "habitual use, *like the difference between the right and the left hand.*"[20] The *factum* of reason has for us the urgency and immediate force of evidence that defies intuition because it speaks to our sense for a *moral* space—one that is alternative to the space in which natural phenomena appear and are known by us as objects. The moral space identified by—and embodied in—the "fact of reason" is the transcendental condition of what one *does,* not the condition of what one *sees* and *perceives;* this space is the transcendental condition of *subjectivity* and *personality,* not of *objectivity.*[21]

Thus the pure character of the concept of morality and, consequently, the formalism of Kant's ethics, do not refer to an abstract intellectual dimension placed beyond any concrete example or reality. Consciousness of the moral law identifies the form of a moral space whose extent Kant's second *Critique* is in charge of exploring. The peculiar "sense" for this moral space is the consciousness of freedom that is "forced upon us"[22] with the same immediacy with which the sense for spatial orientation is inscribed in our physical body as its transcendental form. Transcendentally, this sense is the practical substitute for intuition, is the condition on which hinges the possibility of a critical moral distinction. Because of its transcendental constitution, this sense offers Kant's radical alternative to and critique of moral intuitionism. On Kant's account, the purity and formality of the moral law is embodied in the action (*facere*) of practical reason, namely, in that through which practical reason is not only possible, but also actual. Thereby, it discloses the consciousness of freedom and allows us to recognize and distinguish true virtue and pure motives of action. In the same way, the sense that we have for the distinction between right and left hand is embodied in our sensibility and reveals its purely a priori component, namely, the *pure formality* of space as a priori sensible intuition.

In the Transcendental Dialectic of the first *Critique,* Kant establishes that no intuition can provide knowledge of freedom as object, and that moral action, in its absolute spontaneity, cannot take place in space and time, which define the world of nature and the mechanical causality of all natural events. In other words, freedom is possible (thinkable) only if its causality identifies a domain irreducible to the conditions of space and time, i.e., only if speculative reason's pretension of knowledge is abandoned in favor of a different, non-cognitive access to freedom. In addition to this claim, however, we have seen that the Transcendental Dialectic makes two additional points. First, it establishes the impossibility for freedom to be attributed to a merely spiritual, disembodied being as the soul of rational psychology; second, it suggests that reason, in the regulative use of its ideas, constructs an "order" of ends alternative—and yet analogous—to the order of natural causality. Such order is reason's most proper domain (*eigentümliches Gebiet*).[23] Accordingly, the first *Critique* does not exclude the possibility that freedom is embodied in a dimension other than the one provided by sensible intuition in the world of nature; rather, it does require an alternative embodiment that could give an account of the specifically *oriented* structure of reason's "order." This is the "paradoxical demand"[24] from which the second *Critique* begins: in her empirical consciousness, the human subject must think of herself as phenomenon—i.e., as natural embodied being; whereas in her moral agency, she must regard herself as subject of freedom—i.e., as noumenon, endowed with an intelligible character and a free will.

Thus, both the Transcendental Dialectic of the *Critique of Pure Reason* and the Methodology of the *Critique of Practical Reason* allow us to recognize that the specific problem of Kant's practical philosophy, namely, the question of the possibility of pure reason being practical or the problem of "pure morality," is framed from the beginning to the end by the issue of defining the "moral space" within which the practical *orientation* of reason's action, the construction of its intelligible *order,* and the very *distinction* between "pure" and "empirical" (or spontaneous-autonomous and pathological-heteronomous) motives can take place. For, as the "methodology" of practical reason suggests, these distinctions are not a matter of theoretical knowledge; rather, they become meaningful only within the space of reason's own action (the *factum* of reason as connected to—and identical with—reason's own *facere*). In other words, practical reason, on the basis of its pure determination, is not placed in the world of space and time (nature) and recognizes no necessitating condition in the human body and its transcendental cognitive form (pure intuition). However, neither is practical reason placed in an abstract metaphysical void. On the contrary, on the basis of its original *factum,* reason creates its own space, or *Gebiet,* within which a sense of orientation is required for action to take place, for an ordered world of ends to be possible, and for the very distinction between formal and pathological motive to be significant. Thereby, a different type of embodiment than the one explored in the first *Critique* comes to the fore. It is the embodiment of practical reason, which now constitutes the point of "access" (*Eingang*) whereby freedom is present in the human *Gemüt* and the extension of its consciousness is ultimately disclosed. Moral space is not the condition for knowledge of morality but is the condition for reason's action according to its law—both objectively and subjectively. Such moral space is the transcendental form of practical reason's embodiment in subjective action, just as the space of intuition is the transcendental form of embodiment necessary for our knowledge of objects.

In Kant's 1786 essay "What Does it Mean to Orient Oneself in Thinking?" we find another explicit connection between the problem of orientation in the sensible world, which resorts to the bodily feeling for a difference between the left and right hands, and the issue of reason's orientation in the immeasurable "space of the supersensible."[25] The former is geographical and mathematical orientation in space; the latter is orientation "in thinking."[26] The context of Kant's argument in this essay is Mendelssohn's discus-

sion with Jacobi, and is aimed at defending reason against *Schwärmerei,* i.e.,
against the pretensions of an alleged supersensible, transcendent intuition
(*überschwengliche Anschauung*) that under the name of "faith" threatens to
remove reason from its "throne."[27] Kant argues that orientation in thinking is obtained by extension of the general procedure of "self-orientation,"
whose first application is geographical and takes place in the natural world.
Kant contends that this general procedure is based upon a "feeling" (*Gefühl*)
that functions as an indispensable *Unterscheidungsvermögen*[28]—a faculty that
draws distinctions and provides awareness thereof. Such a feeling is the
only means that we have for drawing differences that cannot be empirically ascertained—seen or perceived—but can only be internally felt or
discovered a priori. Indeed if we did not have a special "sense" for these
differences, knowledge of reality would be impossible for us: we would
stand completely disoriented in a world with no reference points—not even
a horizon. Such a world, to be sure, would not have any order for us—
properly, would not even be a "world."[29] Kant's argument proceeds through
a progression of examples: how do we orient ourselves geographically in the
night of a starry sky; how do we manage to orient ourselves mathematically in a dark room or a dark street at night; and finally, how can reason
orient itself "in the immeasurable space of the supersensible, which, for us,
is enveloped in an impenetrable night?"[30] Common to all these situations
is the fact that we are plunged into the darkness of a night that makes our
physical senses useless in trying to understand where we are on the ground
of external evidence alone. To this extent, Kant suggests that orientation in
the sensible and in the supersensible world display similar features: in both
cases the construction of a space (or order) is at stake, in which oriented
movement and action is possible even in the darkness of the night, even
when all external visible clues are lacking. To solve the problem of orientation is indeed an Enlightenment task.[31] We know that Kant's answer to the
problem of orientation in the sensible world—namely, geographical and
mathematical orientation—is the discovery of the transcendental form of
the human body, i.e., a priori character of space (and time) as form of
sensible intuition. But what is orientation in thinking, and what kind of
problem does Kant thereby raise?

　　The connection—which is properly an "analogy"—between geograph-
ical/mathematical orientation and "logical" orientation is relevant here.
Since the question of self-orientation in thinking arises as soon as intuition
can no longer assist us, it is evident, Kant argues, that this is a matter of no
other faculty but of "pure reason." The problem arises when reason ven-

tures in a territory where it finds "no object of intuition, *but mere space for it.*"[32] Since space is a transcendental form that makes objects first possible for us—not an objective property of things—with this claim Kant hints at reason's need to construct a different type of "space" than that of sensible intuition—a space, however, that works in analogy with the space of sensible intuition. If we consider the kind of objects that Kant places in this realm (God, the highest good, the idea of morality, freedom), it soon becomes clear that what is at stake is the definition of reason's "moral space" from which all intuition (since it is always cognitive) is banned. In this realm, reason does not determine objects for cognition but determines itself for action. Hence, reason's orientation is *self*-orientation in the most proper sense (as self-determination). At this point, Kant needs to provide a new solution for the problem of orientation. He needs to introduce a different type of feeling capable of offering to reason subjective "grounds for distinction" (*Unterscheidungsgründe*),[33] and thereby for orientation, in the nightly regions of the supersensible. In the case of geographical orientation we find in ourselves, in the difference between our left and right hands, the ground for an objective distinction that we would otherwise be unable to see in things. Analogously, reason finds *in itself* a feeling that generates the otherwise invisible difference that allows reason to pronounce its judgments. This means of orientation, Kant declares, is "no other but the *feeling* of reason's own *need.*"[34] Thus, the *"need"* most proper to reason now takes the place of the bodily distinction between left and right.

On the basis of this analogy, we can suggest that reason's need reveals the transcendental form of its practical embodiment, i.e., the transcendental structure that makes the "space of the supersensible"—or moral space—meaningful and "sensible" for us. On Kant's account, both the distinction between left and right and the peculiar feeling of reason's need reveal a form of "incongruence" that can be ascertained only internally and, more importantly, a priori. Moreover, in both cases, this incongruence manifests, at the same time, the presence of an active power or capacity and its internal and constitutive limitation. The distinction between left and right betrays the transcendental form of the physical body and allows Kant to present space as pure a priori form of sensible intuition, i.e., as the condition under which alone something becomes for us object of knowledge. By orienting practical motivation, the "need" of reason, on the other hand, is the necessary condition under which the supersensible space as moral space becomes a meaningful and somehow "sensible" dimension of reason's own action. "A need of pure practical reason [. . .] is based on a *duty* to make something (the highest good) the object of my will so as to promote it with all my strength."[35] Connected to reason's need, morality has, for us, the evidence of a unique "fact" that leads us to the consciousness of freedom, and furthermore to the concrete obligation (duty) of promoting the highest good in the world. In suggesting that this "need" constitutes the first transcendental form of reason's *practical embodiment,* I want to underline the crucial link between the following points: (1) to establish the consciousness of freedom is (2) to recognize the need for moral action *in the world,* i.e., the need to transform the natural world into a moral world. In addition, I want to suggest that moral action, for Kant, does not occur in a vacuum from which sensibility is in principle excluded but is placed, from the outset, in a dimension in which sensibility is required *in its purely formal character.* Kant's effort is precisely to show in what sense a *pure form of practical sensibility*—as necessary condition of a "need" and of the "feeling" for it—is constitutive of reason's orientation. In an important way, the only condition that must be respected in order to discover the pure formality of practical sensibility is to recognize that sensibility neither precedes nor grounds the principle of morality but rather *follows* from it. Reason's need *is based on* a "duty."

In the 1786 essay, Kant takes pains to spell out the nature of reason's *Bedürfnis.* This is neither a fleeting caprice based upon merely empirical desires nor an ungrounded pretension, which would only produce the empty "dreams" of metaphysics and the illusions of *Schwärmerei.*[36] It is instead a "real" need that *necessarily* affects reason and leads it to think of objects whose existence and connection with experience can by no means be proved. Moreover, it is a need that can lay claim to a peculiar "right."[37] On Kant's account, the subjective need of reason, not the assumption of a supersensible intuition, grounds reason's "right" to presuppose and assume that for which no cognition is possible (no sensible intuition is given)—namely, the concept of freedom and, more generally, reason's ideas. This need is the transcendental, subjective condition that first institutes the legitimacy of the practical use of reason's ideas and, accordingly, justifies the claim of their "objective reality."[38] In the realm of the supersensible the only orientation on which reason can count is the *internal* one provided by the feeling of its own necessary need.[39] Only this need can ground the "right" to assume supersensible objects. In the second *Critique,* Kant completes this argument by claiming that reason's need, which implies a "right," is in turn based upon a "duty" to make something the object of our moral endeavor.[40] As the transcendental form of space allows us to assume objects only as *appearances* and not as things in themselves, so reason's need provides a subjective ground—

or a maxim—for the assumption of the *practical reality* of its objects, not for their possible knowledge. Moreover, this subjective ground must be recognized as *necessary and sufficient* to institute reason's right to a moral space that is completely independent of intuition, i.e., a moral space in which freedom is possible and actual as a fact. To deny this right means, for Kant, to leave the door wide open to "all *Schwärmerei,* superstition, and even atheism." For, if we reject the claim that reason's need is indeed sufficient to ground the right to assume the reality of its objects,[41] then we have to deny that the moral space is independent of the condition of physical embodiment, namely, of the condition that defines the mechanism of nature's events. At this point, freedom can no longer be saved. Either we reject freedom and endorse universal determinism, or we appeal to a supersensible intuition that, by denying freedom's lawfulness, takes all ground of its concept away. To claim that only theoretical knowledge, in the form of intuition, can provide speculative thinking with orientation in the supersensible means for Kant to renounce reason and to embrace *Schwärmerei.*

Thus, reason's *Bedürfnis* is the only condition—a transcendental and subjective condition—for the constitution of moral agency. Such a need points to a peculiar form of practical sensibility that necessarily (and subjectively or "aesthetically," as Kant puts it)[42] accompanies the activity of practical reason as condition for its orientation in the moral space of the supersensible. More precisely, reason's peculiar need hints at a form of sensibility that *follows* from the unconditioned moral command and thereby displays the embodiment of freedom as its consequence. Against the enthusiasm of the genius and its improbable disembodied intuitions, Kant puts forth the idea of reason's embodiment. He allows for no supersensible intuition but only for reason's "need"; for no original consciousness but only for reason's "fact." This is, to be sure, a *transcendental embodiment* that, as such, does not infringe upon the unconditioned (or non-pathological) character of moral space. While speaking of "reason's *felt need,*" Kant accurately specifies:

> reason does not feel; it has an insight into its want (*Mangel*), and *produces* (*wirkt*) the feeling of the need through the impulse (*Trieb*) to cognition. It is the same as with the moral feeling, which is not cause of the moral law [. . .] but is caused or produced (*verursacht oder gewirkt*) through the moral law, and hence through reason.[43]

Similarly, in the *Critique of Practical Reason,* the objectivity of the *Vernunftbedürfnis* arising from the moral law is opposed to the empirical character of a mere "inclination," which for reason does not constitute a need.[44]

The famous conclusion of the second *Critique* shows how reason successfully orients itself in a world that includes both a sensible and a supersensible dimension. The starry sky, no longer immersed in a dark night, gives rise to a feeling that has the same name as the feeling that we prove for the moral law:

> Two things fill the *Gemüt* with ever new and increasing wonder and awe (*Bewunderung und Ehrfurcht*), the oftener and more steadily we reflect on them: the starry skies above me and the moral law within me. In both cases, I do not merely conjecture them and seek them *as though obscured in darkness or in the transcendent region outside (außer) of my horizon:* I *see* them *before me,* and I connect them *immediately* with the *consciousness of my own existence* (*Existenz*).[45]

With the help of the second *Critique,* at the end of its itinerary, we have moved from darkness into light. Initially, at the beginning of the itinerary started in the Dialectic of the first *Critique* and in the 1786 essay, Kant needed darkness to impede the senses and block the temptation of vision. Blinding the senses was necessary to discover their hidden, invisible transcendental form.[46] While neither rational psychology nor all the efforts of the spirit-seer succeed in abstracting from the body, Kant's experiment of orientation manages to replace the givenness of the physical body with its transcendental form. Darkness and night are the conditions on which this experiment is construed: the sense of sight has to be impeded so that the transcendental form of the body can emerge as something that we cannot see but which allows us to see. Kant's further step—and the first toward practical reason—still leaves us plunged in darkness. This time, however, it is because even the transcendental form of the body (i.e., pure sensible intuition) is no longer able to provide us with a means for orientation. The second *Critique* shows the only way that reason has, as practical reason, to transform the supersensible space from being a dark world in which we are inexorably disoriented and constantly tempted to look for a transcendent substitute for sensible intuition, into a bright (yet invisible) moral world that can excite the same feeling of awe that arises from our contemplation of the starry sky. At this point, when the supersensible space has been fully transformed into a moral space, vision can be restored since it is no longer deceitful: we have learned how to live in another dimension of our existence and to appreciate it with our feeling; we know that moral agents as persons are embodied beings, but we know that their "body" is an invisible one. Daylight can again be called into the picture.[47] Kant suggests that this transformation of space—this move from geographical and mathematical orientation to moral orientation—discloses a new "consciousness of my own existence."

In the *Critique of Pure Reason* Kant presents us with a dilemma: pure self-consciousness is a merely formal (logical) thought; it is not the consciousness of my concrete existence. Consciousness of my own existence, on the other hand, is empirical consciousness of myself as embodied being: it always implies my body, and never allows me to access an alleged immaterial soul or pure intelligence. In other words, there is no theoretical alternative to embodiment for Kant: the choice between transcendental philosophy, with its necessary limitation of knowledge to appearances, and the metaphysics of rational psychology is inevitable. The second *Critique* proposes a solution—the only possible solution—to this dilemma. Its condition, however, is the full acceptance of the results of transcendental idealism. For if there is no theoretical alternative to embodiment, there is an alternative *form* of embodiment, namely, a practical one. Thereby, a different form of "consciousness of my own existence" comes to the fore. Thus, Kant's practical philosophy is as much an alternative to the "materialism without soul" as to the "spiritualism without body" that dominate all dualistic ontology of body and soul.[48]

It must be clear at this point that nowhere along his itinerary does Kant renounce the condition of embodiment. His efforts are always aimed at a complete and nuanced understanding of what embodiment means as condition of our human *existence* and *life*—not merely as condition of thought or self-representation, and not simplistically as an empiricist acceptance of natural given data. Transcendental philosophy offers a real means for thinking about the body in a radically new way. The dialectic of speculative reason arises precisely because embodiment cannot be escaped; while practical reason *is* itself a "need" (and not only *has* one) precisely because the condition of embodiment designs morality as "moral space"—as an order of ends and a moral world within which orientation is a human problem (as need). While transcendentally the "body" of reason in its theoretical use is reason's first immediate condition, the "body" of reason in its practical employment is a consequence or construction that necessarily follows the pure principle of morality that must precede it. Hence the reversal of the structure of the Analytic in the two *Critiques*.

The subject that we observe contemplating in awe the wonderful things described at the end of the *Critique of Practical Reason* (Kant himself speaks to us in the first person or, more generally, as a human being that has followed the itinerary of the *Critique*) is very similar to the reconciled subject of the *Critique of Judgment*—i.e., is a being who eventually finds her orientation in the world.[49] In the final pages of the 1788 *Critique*, the physical and moral dimensions of my embodied existence are emphatically stressed by the importance given to the act of locating what I observe with regard to myself.[50] The starry heavens are "above me" while the moral law is "in me"; both are within, not "without" the horizon of my sight; both I see, as it were, "before me"—and I can indeed "see" them now, since darkness no longer obscures my vision. Since I can see them concretely, immediately before me, conjecture (and even an alleged transcendent intuition) is no longer a temptation or a need. This contemplation is both my *self-orientation in relation to* the starry heavens and the moral law, and the positioning of the starry heavens and the moral law *in relation to myself*. It is this contemplation and orientation that "*immediately*" produces a new "consciousness of my own existence." Thus, in the light of this orientation, the "paradoxical demand" that the second *Critique* inherits from the first *Critique* no longer sounds so paradoxical. As Kant announced in the preface to the second *Critique*, that demand eventually finds its "full confirmation."[51] For we now know what it means to have empirical consciousness of ourselves as phenomena and to be subjects of freedom (or moral agents) as noumena. It means that we can place the starry sky *above* ourselves, the moral law *within* ourselves, and have a peculiar feeling of awe with regard to both. This is what it means to have a *moral* consciousness of our own existence in both the natural and the moral world.

In all its different varieties, orientation creates an order, which, in turn, takes on the shape of a "world" transcendentally produced by our rational faculty. The subject who orients herself in space—both in visible and invisible space—creates a world that stands necessarily in connection to herself and has meaning only in this connection. Consciousness of our own existence is gained precisely by establishing this oriented connection in the domain of a "world."[52]

> The heavens *begin at the place I occupy in the external world of sense*, and extend the connection in which I stand into an unbounded magnitude of worlds beyond worlds and systems of systems and into the limitless times of their periodic motion, their beginning and their duration. The moral law *begins at my invisible self, at my personality*, and exhibits me in a world which has true infinity but which is comprehensible only to the understanding—a world in which *I recognize myself as existing in a universal and necessary connection* (not, as in the first case, a merely contingent one), and thereby *also in connection with all those visible worlds*.[53]

Once we abandon the cognitive pretensions of speculative reason and recognize that the heavens *begin* at the place that we physically occupy "in the
external world of the senses," reason's antinomies can be *lived* (and *felt*) in
a different way. Our perspective has changed since we now occupy a place
within those very same antinomies; we are a part of the problem that speculative reason is unable to solve; we are the generative point of the universe.
Where do the heavens begin? They begin in that compass of the universe
which is my oriented self positioned in the external world of senses. The
construction of the moral world follows the same procedure. We first ask for
the "beginning" and thereby draw the horizon of the moral world of which
we are part because we first institute it. Where does the moral law *begin?*
Kant answers: it begins in my moral personality, in the self that cannot be
sensibly seen (*unsichtbares Selbst*)[54] but is lived as something that exists in connection with a purely moral space. Indeed, the moral self is invisible because
it does not need to be sensibly "seen" in order to count as a person or agent
that is accountable for its actions. And yet, we also know now that such an
agent is not a disembodied, purely spiritual self whose life is projected in
a transcendent world with no connection to the natural world. The agent
who is able to place the moral law within herself is able, at the same time,
to contemplate and admire the starry heavens above. In the moral realm a
new connection with the sensible world is established. Kant argues that in
the view of countless "worlds" the consciousness of my existence is not just
the consciousness of my being an "animal creature." It is the consciousness
of being an animal creature who, in addition, stands *in connection with* the
infinity of worlds to which the imagination can extend my perception of
the natural world. Such consciousness conveys the feeling of being "a mere
speck in the universe"—a feeling of annihilation. Thereby, the horizon of
the first *Critique*—the empirical consciousness of myself—receives an additional non-cognitive meaning with regard to the peculiar *feeling* that I gain
of my own existence. My experience of myself is the experience of being an
animal creature endowed with a sensitivity or receptivity for a very peculiar
"feeling." Herein Kant's horizon extends to the limits of the domain of the
third *Critique*—moral feeling meets the feeling of the sublime. Similarly,
the consciousness of my existence as a person is defined *in connection with*
the moral world. It discloses my "value" as "intelligence"—that intelligence
which rational psychology was unable to meaningfully define.[55] In the moral
perspective provided by this connection I view my "life" as independent of
"all animality and even of the whole world of sense—at least insofar as it
may be inferred from the final determination of my existence (*Bestimmung*

meines Daseins)" assigned to me by the moral law.[56] This independence is our consciousness of freedom.

Ultimately, we can conclude that if transcendental philosophy refuses to take the issue of human nature directly as its topic, it does so in order to lead the subject (whoever she may be) to an independent discovery of—and reflection on—what it means to be a human being, that is, to an independent reflection on the consciousness of one's own existence in reason's moral space. The second *Critique* provides the transcendental conditions for such an experience of oneself as a human moral being.

Making Room for Reason's Practical Embodiment: Practical Reason and the Faculty of Desire

At the end of the second *Critique,* we learn that orientation in moral space implies the construction of the purposive "order" of reason's "world" and the recognition of our place within it. At the very beginning of this work, Kant brings to the fore the crucial condition on which this entire construction is built. Orientation means organization, and requires us to follows a strict "order of the concepts."[57] The methodological requirement of order plays itself out on different levels, and eventually is responsible for the peculiar structure of the second *Critique.* On the one hand, the order of concepts regards the relation between speculative and practical reason. While speculative reason seems to be the first to pose the problem of freedom in its Dialectic, it is now clear that were it not for practical reason, the concept of freedom would never be introduced in the self-sufficient world of nature's mechanism. On the other hand, more specifically, what is at stake is the relation of order between moral law and consciousness of freedom. Kant contends that "morality first reveals the consciousness of freedom to us."[58] As is the case in the last pages of the work (with the question: where does the moral law begin?), Kant here addresses a methodological question of order. He asks: "*from where* does our knowledge of the unconditionally practical *start (anhebt)*—from freedom or from the practical law"? Since freedom is neither immediately known to us nor is given to us in experience, the very first task of the *Critique of Practical Reason* is to establish the pure principle of morality as its point of departure.

It follows that if sensibility plays any substantial *transcendental* role, as I claim it does,[59] in Kant's project of pure ethics, its transcendental form can be discovered only on the basis—and as a consequence—of the articulation of the pure principle of morality—on the way toward the constitution of the (subjective) consciousness of freedom. Sensibility can be admitted in the project of a "pure" ethics, and thereby can display a somehow "pure" form of its own, if and only if sensibility is not the starting point of the investigation but its necessary consequence. The pure form of practical sensibility or reason's practical form of embodiment is the sensible *effect* (and *affect*) that the moral law has on us as rational—and yet sensible—beings. The moral law, we have just seen, *"begins at my invisible self, at my personality"* and only then extends to a connection in which the sensible world participates. Thus, the problem of order is crucial for the methodological construction of the second *Critique* and indicates the structural difference between speculative reason and practical reason. In the *Critique of Practical Reason,* "aesthetics" as theory of sensibility does not come first, as in the *Critique of Pure Reason,* but last.

I now turn to a closer analysis of the ways in which the *Critique of Practical Reason* exhibits the structures of a practical form of sensibility as an integral part of Kant's pure ethics.

Seventeenth- and eighteenth-century moral philosophy generally holds that human action cannot be motivated by reason but only by passions. Human will is moved to decision and action exclusively by the influence of inclinations, passions, and sentiments. The empirical affection of the will is considered as the only possible type of determination. The interplay of passions is represented as a mechanism whose elements are all homogeneous: the empirical affection exercised by the passions and the empirically affected will. Accordingly, the will's act (deliberation or choice) is nothing but its mechanical response to the stimulation of the passions. The way to fight a set of "bad" inclinations consists in replacing them with "good" inclinations. Consequently, the task of moral philosophy is to study how this mechanism functions and to devise different balancing strategies among the passions. It follows that, in this tradition, ethics is closely related to—if not mixed with—disciplines based upon the empirical observation of human nature such as empirical psychology, anthropology, and even physiology. Hume draws extreme consequences out of this general picture, claiming that reason is thoroughly impotent if set against the mechanism of passions and sentiments. Reason is an exclusively theoretical faculty that can by no means exercise causality over the will. Reason, according to Hume, can never be practical as it can never be "passionate." At most, it can be instrumental in relation to already set goals. Since morality is based upon a specific sentiment, namely "moral sentiment," it is an empirical discipline to be developed entirely a posteriori. In the context of the rationalist tradition on the other hand, Wolff, moving from radically different premises than Hume, reaches analogous results in denying the autonomous value of practical reason in relation to theoretical reason. Wolff's "monistic" approach to the faculties of the mind reduces morality to theoretical knowledge (or to a unitary *vis repraesentativa*) by ultimately deducing the will from the understanding.[60]

In the *Groundwork of the Metaphysics of Morals*, Kant sets out his theory against the conclusions of both empiricist and rationalist traditions. He argues that moral philosophy is possible only as *"pure"* moral philosophy, i.e., only on the basis of an a priori foundation of its first principle. This foundation, however, is feasible only under the condition that reason, opposing Hume's thesis, can really be *practical* as *pure* reason. In other words, the project of a pure moral philosophy can succeed in finding an a priori principle entirely based upon reason if and only if reason can indeed exercise immediate causality over the will. Furthermore, to prove that reason can indeed be practical means, for Kant, to claim that morality cannot be derived from or reduced to theoretical knowledge. In the *Groundwork*, however, Kant still regards the critical task of practical philosophy as parallel to that of the *Critique of Pure Reason*. The *Groundwork* provides only the preliminary step toward a comprehensive "metaphysics of morals." Its aim is to find out and to secure the first principle of morality. A "critique of *pure* practical reason"[61] would then follow. The object of criticism is, in this case as in that of theoretical reason, pure reason itself. Therefore, in 1785, "pure practical reason" seems to be both that which allows a transcendental foundation of moral philosophy by providing a first principle of morality, and that which needs to be criticized precisely in this function. Kant's distance from Wolff is not yet deep enough.

Kant opens the *Critique of Practical Reason* with a different—and indeed clearer—position. He argues that the critique now regards "the *entire* practical faculty." The question of whether pure reason can be practical at all is set directly at the heart of the inquiry and thereby gains decisive priority.[62] Kant argues that if we succeed in showing that pure reason is indeed practical, then a critique of *pure* practical reason is no longer required. What needs to be provided, instead, is a critique of the *"entire"* practical faculty, i.e., of practical reason in general or of practical reason insofar as its causality may also include the influence of sensibility and hence be empirically conditioned. Thereby, Kant makes his refutation of Hume's position even more articulate and effective. He does not simply oppose Hume's empirical moral philosophy based upon moral sentiments with an a priori foundation that, being based on reason alone, radically cuts out the influence of passions by denying their effectiveness over the will. Kant does recognize that although pure reason provides the "sufficient"[63] determination of the will, this is not the only type of determination possible. Since the influence of feeling is both undeniable and unavoidable, he needs to show the only way in which the empirical affection of the will can be *included* in the project of a *pure* moral philosophy without jeopardizing its "pure" character.

In seventeenth- and eighteenth-century moral philosophy, the issue of the role played by passions and inclinations in human action is placed in the wider context of the discussion on the relation between the body and the soul. In light of this tradition, we can reformulate the problem of Kant's moral philosophy as follows: how is the body present in the pure moral philosophy articulated by the transcendental perspective granted that, on the one hand, no disembodied soul can be the subject of action or of freedom's causality, and given that, on the other hand, pure moral philosophy cannot begin with—or be grounded on—empirical conditions? Kant argues that a criticism of the "entire" practical faculty draws, in its own right, the limits of the legitimate use of practical reason, whereby it shows, at the same time, the role played by the sensible affection of the will in the determination of action. Kant's suggestion is, first, that sensibility should never be considered motive but always matter of moral action. For the motive is always and necessarily formal. This is the crucial idea of Kant's so-called moral formalism. Only on the basis of this formalism can the transcendental transformation of the will's sensible affection take place. Feeling can be presented, this time, as proceeding from the pure principle of morality, and not from the pathological solicitation of material objects of desire. But a feeling that *follows* the pure determination of the will can never itself be the determining ground of the will. In this way, Kant's itinerary in the second *Critique* eventually overturns the empiricist's claim: the thesis that reason can be practical, i.e., can affect the will immediately and formally, discloses a feeling that can never affect the will as it rather indirectly follows from its pure determination, and therefore is itself determined a priori. Therein we have a unique feeling that is not pathologically produced but is instead bound to the transcendental a priori structure of human sensibility.

Thus, from the programmatic aim of Kant's 1788 work it is clear that the second *Critique* is not a continuation of the first.[64] The first *Critique* criticizes the *speculative* use of reason because reason is transcendent—and therefore illegitimate in its theoretical use—when it is pure, i.e., when it raises claims of knowledge beyond all possible experience. The second *Critique*, on the contrary, criticizes reason when it is *empirically* conditioned because only in this case does its practical use become illegitimate by transcending its purity and giving in to the determination of pathological affections.

With the claim that opens the *Critique of Practical Reason*—namely, that pure reason is practical—Kant suggests that reason, insofar as it is pure (i.e., taken in its complete independence from sensibility), exercises an *immediate* and *effective* causality on the will. The category of *causality* lends the first meaning to the practical use of reason. The third antinomy of the *Critique of Pure Reason* has already revealed the possibility of a specific kind of causality exercised by reason, namely "causality *through* freedom" or "causality *from* freedom." However, the notion of "transcendental freedom" that expresses reason's causality does not analytically imply that reason is effectively practical.[65] This is precisely the additional step that Kant needs to undertake in the second *Critique*. Moreover, Kant projects the importance of the thesis of the second *Critique* back onto the results of the critique of speculative reason. By significantly reversing the order of the relation between practical and theoretical reason established by the first *Critique*, Kant maintains that it is practical reason that originally poses an "unsolvable problem" for speculative reason by introducing the concept of freedom. Thereby he suggests that if reason were not practical through the moral law, then there would be no escape from the third antinomy, and the concept of freedom could never be introduced in practical philosophy.[66]

The second specification of reason's practical causality establishes the claim that reason is practical insofar as the peculiar type of causality exercised by it, namely causality through freedom, is directed not towards objects but towards the *will*.[67] Only through reason's free causality are objects produced out of their representation. The causality of reason as *pure practical* reason consists in the *immediate determination of the will*. This distinction allows Kant to separate theoretical knowledge from "practical knowledge." In the latter, knowledge itself is the ground of the existence of the object, and is thereby opposed to theoretical knowledge that presupposes the object as given.[68] Kant argues that while theoretical reason is determined by the constitution of the objects in its cognition of nature, in practical knowledge reason is concerned only with the grounds of the determination of the will. Consequently, being set only in relation to the subject, reason is self-determined in its causality.[69] Pure reason is practical as it relates to the subject's "faculty of desire" (*Begehrungsvermögen, facultas appetitiva*) in the form of the "pure will." With this claim, Kant takes up the traditional Aristotelian—

and successively Wolffian—terminology that opposes the faculty of desire to the theoretical faculty; yet he does so only in order to radically change the meaning of both the *facultas appetitiva* and its desire. Kant's suggestion is that since it is pure reason that relates to the faculty of desire, this faculty, in the form of pure will, proves itself to be a *faculty that does not (only) desire*—or a faculty whose "desire" is not simply pathological but can also be formal and pure.[70] For, if this faculty could *only* desire, then it would be, as it is in the tradition, a merely empirical faculty. On the contrary, Kant's claim that pure reason is practical implies the suggestion that there is a pure motive—which is not empirical desire but still functions as impulse or drive with subjective motivational force—through which the faculty of desire is determined to action. Once Kant has established that practical reason is a faculty that not only (empirically) desires, he can show that there are feelings connected to this faculty and following from it that display a peculiar "pure" character. In other words, sensibility is not excluded from Kant's moral philosophy. It is rather re-positioned or re-oriented in relation to practical reason and its moral space once practical reason becomes the critical substitute for the traditional, merely empirical "faculty of desire." Thereby, Kant overturns the argument of traditional moral philosophy: instead of defining practical reason on the basis of the empirical nature of sentiments and desires, he re-defines desire with regard to the pure determination of the will produced by practical reason. In this framework, sensibility is no longer immediate motive but indirect consequence. The body and its affections are not the starting point of moral determination but a consequence of it. Precisely because it follows from a pure motive, the practical construction of the body loses its empirical "visible" features and gains a formal transcendental dimension of its own. The distinction between "higher" and "lower" appetitive power becomes the distinction between ground or cause and consequence. A sense of orientation in the moral space and its regions is indeed, once again, the basis of Kant's argument in the second *Critique*.

Kant's solution of the problem posed by the traditional "faculty of desire" consists in showing that pure practical reason determines the will in an exclusively *formal* way through the moral law. However, in order to arrive at this solution, Kant needs to establish, against Wolff's distinction between a "lower" and a "higher" *facultas appetitiva*, the only sense in which practical reason can legitimately be called the "higher faculty of desire."[71] Thus, the first step in the demonstration that pure reason is practical consists in establishing what counts, on the contrary, as *empirical* determination of the will. Wolff maintained that while the lower faculty of desire is determined by merely empirical representations, i.e., by representations that have their origin in the senses, the higher faculty is determined by intellectual representations, i.e., by representations that have their origin in the understanding. In both cases, however, what moves the will is a representation conjoined with a "feeling of pleasure or displeasure." With regard to this point, Kant's argument runs parallel to the one that, at the beginning of the first *Critique,* draws a radical distinction between sensibility and understanding. Yet, in the practical sphere, Kant's claim seems to present the opposite direction than in the theoretical sphere. This is due to the above-discussed difference between the respective tasks of the two *Critiques.* In the *Critique of Pure Reason* Kant argues against the traditional view that the difference between concepts and (sensible) intuitions is only a difference *in degree* of clarity and distinctness of our representations. Accordingly, his aim is to establish a radical separation—properly, a distinction *in kind*—between the two branches of our knowledge. In the *Critique of Practical Reason* Kant maintains that the mere difference in the *origin* of our representations cannot justify the internal distinction within the faculty of desire in a higher and a lower faculty. For, if we assume that the only thing that the faculty of desire can do is to desire following a feeling of pleasure, and given that all desires and feelings of pleasure functioning as motives for action are empirical and material, then the different origin of our representations of what is desirable (i.e., of an object) would not make any real difference in the type of motive that moves this faculty. In other words, as long as the will is determined by a representation *of the object*—namely, by the representation of the pleasure or displeasure that the subject can expect from it—the determination of the faculty of desire is material and empirical, no matter what the origin of that representation (senses or understanding). In this case, Kant argues, the different origin of our representations of what is pleasurable amounts only to a difference of "degree,"[72] not to a difference in the type of force that actually moves the will. On Kant's account, the difference that justifies a real separation between higher and lower faculty of desire can be provided only by *the way in which the will is determined,* i.e., by the difference between *material* and *purely formal* determination. Hence, the possibility for pure reason to be "higher faculty of desire" is predicated upon the possibility that pure reason determines the will through a "*purely formal* law."[73] This law is a "fundamental law," namely the "moral law" or, in the terminology of the *Groundwork,* the "categorical imperative." The general issue of determination that in the first *Critique* accounts for the definition of both understanding's spontaneity and the absolute spontaneity of transcendental freedom now receives its conclusive discussion with regard to practical freedom.[74]

At this point, Kant's argument has opened up an alternative. Since the principle of one's own happiness—no matter what its origin—contains only an empirical determination of the will and hence must be ascribed to the lower faculty of desire, the clear-cut alternative that Kant presents is the following: "either no higher faculty of desire exists or *pure reason* must be in itself alone practical." That is, reason must be practical directly and immediately without presupposing any feeling or representation of what is desirable and agreeable as the matter through which it can move or determine the will. Thence the conclusion: pure reason is practical (and hence is truly the "*higher* faculty of desire") as it determines the will *immediately* through the "*mere form* of the practical rule." And this means that pure reason is practical insofar as it is "legislative" reason.[75] Moreover, the claim of Kant's conclusion, namely, that feeling or desire can never be motive or ground of moral action, opens up the possibility that feeling could still *follow from* the will's purely formal determination to action. In other words, Kant's moral philosophy does not reject feeling outright but only re-positions and re-orients it with regard to practical reason and its causality. What, transcendentally, is the structure that feeling displays in this case?

The further step in Kant's argument leads to the reciprocal relation between *pure practical reason,* i.e., the form of the moral law, and the *freedom* of a will determined by it.[76] Once the opening claim that pure reason is practical has been satisfied by the formality of the determination of the will through the moral law (free will), Kant needs to address the other formulation of the same programmatic claim, equally anticipated at the beginning of the preface. The *Critique of Practical Reason,* Kant argues in its very first page, "has simply to prove *that pure practical reason exists*"—or *that there is* practical reason.[77] Hence, what needs to be proved seems a simple "fact." However, in the same opening passage, Kant suggests that this peculiar "fact" can only be demonstrated by the very "act" of pure reason itself. *Factum* is what *factum est,* i.e., is the result of an action, of reason's own action and spontaneity. No moral psychology, no anthropological analysis of human nature, no observation of any sort, and no logical inference from an empty 'I think' or consciousness can be appealed to in order to provide its ground. For Kant, the fact of reason is not a mere given; it is a fact only in relation to the cognitive function of reason taken in its most general sense; the fact must first be "introduced" and recognized as such by the critical inquiry. Kant's doctrine of the *Faktum der Vernunft*—the *factum* of reason—is nothing but the most advanced formulation of the central issue of the second *Critique*.[78] In Kant's view, what counts as actual and real (*wirklich*) is the "fact of reason," not the reality of an alleged "human nature."[79] "If reason as pure reason is actually practical (*wirklich praktisch*), then it will prove its own reality and the reality of its concept *through action,* and all disputations to prove its impossibility will be in vain."[80] Reason's *factum* is proved by reason's own *facere*. It is precisely this additional step—or rather this specific formulation of the question of the second *Critique*—that allows Kant to overcome the *impasse* at which the *Groundwork* had left the relation between categorical imperative and freedom.

In the *Groundwork*, Kant's "deduction" moved from the freedom of the will to a justification of the categorical imperative. This procedure came up against the difficulty of reconciling the result of the deduction with the conclusions of the first *Critique*. The dialectic of speculative reason reached only the possibility of transcendental freedom—or only its compatibility (non-contradiction) with the necessity of nature's mechanism. Hence, this result allowed only for a hypothetical assumption of freedom and consequently of the moral law. In the practical sphere, however, this conclusion can hardly be satisfactory. In the second *Critique,* Kant's argument is still developed in the form of a "deduction." Here, however, deduction should not be taken in the sense of a "transcendental" deduction (that is, in the sense of the first *Critique*). Deduction means now "derivation." Kant maintains that the moral law cannot be derived from any first certainty of thought and is, accordingly, a "fact." The "fact of reason," as consciousness of the moral law, now grounds the idea of freedom. In this connection, Kant grants the moral law the status of a *factum* that does not need to be deduced since its objective reality is immediately proved through the very action of pure reason itself (an action that has always already been accomplished and exists as the *factum* of its own result). Now the deduction sets out to demonstrate the unity—or the inextricable bond—between the *factum* of reason and the consciousness of the freedom of the will.[81]

As in the first *Critique,* Kant's model for his deduction is a juridical one.[82] In the legal vocabulary of Kant's time, *factum* is the action committed by someone upon whom legal judgment is to be passed. The *factum* is, as such, the basis of the deduction. The "objective reality" of the *factum* of reason is not a sensible one, for it is not a *datum* that can be presented in a sensible intuition and known by theoretical reason.[83] The reality of the *factum* is, for Kant, the supersensible or intelligible reality of the practical—a reality that cannot be conceived through the conditions of space and time, and yet is so apodictically certain as to "be firmly established for itself."[84] The reality of the *factum* is reason's practical "embodiment": it is neither the visible body given to us by nature nor its transcendental cognitive form but the invisible body of moral personality, which, as *factum,* is practically construed by reason's own action (is not presupposed as a given means to action) and thereby constitutes the modality of our "intelligible existence" as moral agents. "When it comes to the law of our intelligible existence (the moral law) *reason recognizes no temporal distinctions, and the only thing it asks is whether the event belongs to me as an act.*"[85] This model of moral accountability is used for the first time by reason itself with regard to its own action, that is, in relation to the *factum* as the ground for a deduction of the freedom of the will. Moving from the *Faktum der Vernunft,* the deduction proves that the subject accountable for that action is pure reason itself or a pure will determined solely and immediately by the formality of the moral law. This determination is the act of freedom. Thus, Kant's doctrine of the *Faktum der Vernunft* ultimately establishes the central thesis that pure reason is indeed practical. Henceforth, this thesis is brought to bear on the account that Kant gives of the unitary dimension of human existence—of the bond between what the first *Critique* called sensible and intelligible character. Indeed, at stake is the relation between the intelligible consciousness of freedom and our *Sinnenleben,* i.e., our life as sensible beings subject to affection and feeling.[86]

Consciousness of Freedom Embodied

Kant's proof that pure reason is practical and therefore able to determine the will formally through the moral law without resorting to an object given by the feeling of pleasure or displeasure already entails a response to an objection raised against the *Groundwork.* The objection regarded, once again, a problem of order, namely, the inversion operated by Kant in presenting the highest principle of morality *before* the concept of the good, and even before the notion of a "faculty of desire" (which, Kant argues, is generally provided by psychology and simply assumed from it).[87] In confronting both the method and structure of the *Critique of Pure Reason* with those of the *Critique of Practical Reason,* Kant underlines the inversion that needs to take place in the order of the exposition of the Analytic of Practical Reason. Herein, we begin with the *principle* of morality, which provides the only guarantee for the possibility of the critical task. The principle is followed by the *concepts* of the objects of practical reason—namely, the concepts of good and evil—whereas the last part is more problematically indicated as a transition to *sensibility*.[88] The order of the first *Critique* is exactly the opposite, starting out with sensibility and its pure forms in the Transcendental Aesthetic, moving on to the concepts of understanding, and ending with an Analytic of Principles. The inversion is due precisely to the nature of pure practical reason as discussed above—namely, both to the condition for its being effectively practical and to its relation to the will and not objects. In the moral space of transcendental philosophy, the body and its sensibility are not a (naturally or transcendentally) given starting point but a construct, an effect or a result—they are the result of reason's own action. What needs to be explained now is the way in which Kant introduces sensibility in the framework of his pure ethics.

At the beginning of the first *Critique,* Kant distinguishes two branches of sensibility: "intuition" and "sensation." In the *Critique of Practical Reason,* sensible intuition still has, for Kant, an exclusively theoretical use in relation to the faculty of knowledge (understanding as faculty of concepts). Sensation, on the contrary, allows for a differentiated use in relation to different faculties of the *Gemüt*. Accordingly, Kant's discussion of sensibility in the second *Critique* shows, on the one hand, a repeated insistence on the radical exclusion of intuition (any form of intuition, i.e., both sensible and intellectual) from the realm of the practical, and presents, on the other hand, the practical transformation of the materiality of sensation into "feeling"[89]— into a peculiar form of "moral feeling." In the *Critique of Judgment,* on the basis of the results of the second *Critique,* Kant's theory of sensibility is carried a step further. Here Kant strengthens the connection between sensation and feeling, while allowing for a use of intuition without determinate concepts according to which imagination connects it to the feeling of pleasure and displeasure. Thereby, the third *Critique* brings to the fore the far-reaching consequences of Kant's pure foundation of ethics. Precisely because the feeling of pleasure and displeasure has been excluded from the sphere of the practical (*stricto sensu*) as possible motive of moral action, it can appear in the third *Critique* as a separate and independent faculty of the *Gemüt* endowed with an a priori principle of its own.

Kant refers to the methodological difference between the first and the second *Critique* as a "curious contrast," and even as the "paradox of the method of a critique of practical reason."[90] In the case of theoretical reason, a beginning is made by the first transcendental *datum* given to cognition—namely by "pure sensible intuition (space and time)."[91] In the case of pure practical reason, on the contrary, the *factum* of reason itself in the form of the principle (i.e., the law) of morality comes first. That this *factum* is not, in turn, a *datum* is due precisely to the impossibility of its being given or presented in any sensible intuition: the "body" of the moral, free agent is not a sensible, visible, and natural one. Moreover, as freedom is not the determination of the will through sensible motives, such body cannot be identified by cognition of the agent in the sensible world. The action of pure practical reason belongs to the intelligible world whose events cannot be grasped, exhibited, or given in sensible *or* intellectual intuition. On Kant's account, the claim that the activity of practical reason is determined by sensible intuition identifies the positions of determinism, fatalism, and Spinozism,[92] i.e., the sheer negation of freedom. On the other hand, the attempt to introduce intellectual intuition into the realm of the practical leads to *Schwärmerei* or "enthusiasm"—a position that Kant opposes in its many forms.

In the Critical Elucidation of the Analytic of Pure Practical Reason, Kant addresses the problem of the free causality of an agent that belongs, at the same time, to the sensible and to the intelligible world. To affirm that moral actions are affected by time (and space)—or, as Kant puts it, that time is a property of things in themselves and not simply of appearances—means to regard every action as necessarily determined by a previous occurrence in time. In this situation, freedom is utterly impossible and its concept void and self-contradictory;[93] the only possible form of causality remains the necessary causality of nature[94] which reduces actions to mechanism and agents to marionettes or automata.[95] Therefore, the only way to save "transcendental freedom" (and not just "psychological freedom")[96] is to recognize its radical independence from the empirical conditions of time and space. It is only under the condition that time determines the natural necessity of appearances but does not affect the reality of the noumena, that moral freedom and natural necessity can be thought together without implying contradiction.

To this conclusion, already reached in the first *Critique,* the Critical Elucidation adds an important, yet highly problematic dimension. In the second *Critique,* Kant needs to address the question of the "application" of the solution of the third antinomy to the case of a subject whose action manifests the unity of natural necessity and causality through freedom in one and the same occurrence. He recognizes that to consider the efficacy of practical freedom in the sensible world in the perspective of the finite agent is a problem that presents "great difficulties"—difficulties "which seem to make such unification impossible."[97] Kant's suggestion is that the subject, as part of nature, is thoroughly determined by natural necessity.

Natural necessity posits the conditions of the subject's causality (i.e., her own character as well as the whole history of her past deeds) in a past moment of time that necessarily exceeds her own powers to control and determine. This same subject, however, is also conscious of her noumenal existence and of her intelligible character. This *consciousness,* in the form of the "marvelous faculty" of the *Gewissen,*[98] allows for the possibility of regarding one's own action in a totally different perspective, namely one in which there is no time-determination and where only agency itself (as accountability) is relevant. "For reason, when it comes down to the law of our intelligible existence (the moral law), *recognizes no temporal distinctions, and the only thing it asks is whether the event belongs to me as an act.*"[99] Kant's conclusion is a further implication of the "fact" of reason, which is identical with the consciousness of the moral law. Such consciousness or conscience (*Gewissen*) now grounds, on the side of the subject, the awareness of her twofold existence as part of nature on the one hand, and as free agent on the other. In particular, it grounds the possibility of the subject considering her own existence as not affected by time and space, and therefore as an existence which lies completely in her power to shape and to determine according to the law of reason. In this perspective—i.e., with regard to the consciousness of one's noumenal existence—every action as well as every determination of inner sense and one's entire existence as a sensible being, is not a consequence of a previous determination or action in time. Every action belongs instead to a single determination of the subject's character "which he himself creates, and according to which he imputes to himself, as a cause independent of all sensibility, the causality of those same appearances."[100] As *Gewissen,* the consciousness of the moral law eventually lends a concrete meaning to our noumenal existence. Thus, moral consciousness allows for a return to the world of phenomena by addressing the problem of what it means, for one's own free causality within this world, to be independent of time and space.

Kant's argument renders the meaning of his idea of freedom as autonomy extremely concrete for the life of the particular individual subject. The agent, in her physical and natural existence, now struggles to find the space of a freedom that radically exceeds the realm of natural determinism. To be sure, Kant's ethical formalism provides a highly concrete argument in favor of a "supersensible" meaning of human existence based precisely on our own *consciousness* of freedom. Essential to Kant's concept of autonomy is the recognition that reason cannot be determined by sensibility—not only by sensation, feeling, and desire, but also by pure sensible intuition, i.e., by the conditions of space and time. This move follows precisely from Kant's suggestion that pure practical reason refers to the will and not to desired objects. For only objects can be given in space and time or produce a feeling of pleasure or displeasure, and hence desire. What needs to be determined in practical knowledge is, on the contrary, the pure form of the will itself or pure practical reason as will. The *immediacy* and *formality* of this self-determination excludes the possibility that both intuition and feeling intervene as determining grounds.

If, in the second *Critique,* Kant ultimately leaves the task of radically excluding sensible intuition from the realm of practical knowledge to the principle of the "fact of reason" and to its identity with the consciousness of freedom, the same principle also provides him with a strong argument for banishing even "intellectual intuition" from practical knowledge as such. Kant argues against the claim that only "if we were capable of an intellectual intuition" of the acting subject "we would then discover that the entire chain of appearances, with reference to that which concerns only the moral law, depends upon the spontaneity of the subject as a thing in itself." Against this claim he insists that we do not need the appeal to an unreachable intellectual intuition since we have consciousness of the moral law, which is perfectly sufficient to the task at hand.[101] In other words, we do not need to assume that human freedom can be explained only from God's perspective—or generally from a perspective that is by definition not human—since the fact of reason provides us with an immediate consciousness of freedom. Moreover, as Kant argues in "What Does it Mean to Orient Oneself in Thinking?" to claim an intellectual or "supersensible intuition" taking place in the practical realm can only lead to fanaticism and enthusiasm.[102] For such a claim cancels in one stroke the distinction between theoretical and practical reason, and ultimately makes the very existence of practical reason and its moral space impossible.

While freedom is not dependent on the condition of physical or natural embodiment—nor on the cognitive condition of transcendental embodiment—it creates by itself the condition of a practical embodiment in which and through which freedom is brought to existence in connection with the sensible world. The fact of reason is lived by the finite agent in the consciousness of her intelligible existence. In the moral space, the agent is identified by a "body" or a form of existence that is not given for and to cognition, but is consciously made for and through action: the agent's (non-physical) body gives moral visibility to the law, is itself the practical embodiment of the law. In this case, the body is not determined by the conditions of space and time and hence is not visible as appearance. It is not properly object: instead it is spontaneously—and invisibly—shaped by moral action thereby becoming part of what the subject is (or makes herself into, which is indeed the condition for the "pragmatic" standpoint of Kant's anthropology). Moreover, since it does not determine the will with its sensible desires and affections (its feelings are rather *produced* by the will's pure moral determination), the body—in its physical as well as its transcendental powers—is not a limit for moral action (as it is instead a limit for our cognition of nature). Kant's crucial gesture of displacing the body of the moral agent to the position of mere intelligibility (the noumenon) has the immediate consequence of re-defining the form that sensibility assumes in the moral space. Within this perspective sensibility belongs to the agent's "character." Thereby reason's practical embodiment gains the affective— and yet formal—dimension lent to it by a "feeling" that is a priori constituted. Arguably, this is Kant's most decisive move toward an ethics that is radically independent of both anthropological and psychological observation. Such is an ethics that does not simply deny the import of sensibility in moral life, but re-defines the function and nature of practical sensibility within a transcendental and critical perspective. Moral personality is indeed "invisible"[103] to those empirical disciplines, just as the feeling proper to the body is invisible to them (along with the form of this same body). Nonetheless, it is this "invisible" that constitutes and identifies, for Kant, the moral agent as a human being. According to the conclusions of the two *Critiques,* the moral agent is an embodied being endowed with an intelligible and a sensible character. The body of this agent, however, is not visible, i.e., is not subject to the conditions of space and time under which alone its empirical givenness can be perceived, and is not the ground or the source of the moral determination of the will. The body is not a first given through which the moral agent appears in the world. It is rather a result, constituted as a consequence of the purely formal determination of the will through the moral law. The body that identifies the moral agent with its sensations, feelings, and desires is not the condition of free action but the *consequence* of it. It is, to put it in a way akin to the line of argument pursued by the third *Critique,* a morally educated body, a body that can become morally sensitive and morally receptive.[104]

By distinguishing between intuition and sensation, the *Critique of Pure Reason* already makes clear that while the pure a priori forms of intuition have only a cognitive function, sensation may have different uses according to the different faculty of the *Gemüt* involved. In particular, and according to an established tradition, sensation in conjunction with the will produces a feeling of pleasure or displeasure whereby it leads to action. As shown above, Kant's aim in the second *Critique* is to radically separate the "faculty of desire" from the "feeling of pleasure and displeasure," pointing to the immediate and formal determination of the will through pure reason. Reason can be promoted to the role of higher faculty of desire only if it can be the immediate determining ground of the will. In this way, Kant separates the realm of the *"practical"* (*strictu sensu,* as that which belongs to freedom) from the *"pathological"* sphere that defines the realm of the empirical determination of the will. It is precisely in this latter sphere that sensation as *Gefühl* or feeling enters Kant's critique of the "entire" practical faculty as integral part of a critique of practical reason.[105]

The *immediate* determination of the will through pure reason or the moral law defines "morality." However, if the determination of the will occurs according to the moral law, and yet is not immediate but requires the *mediation* of a presupposed feeling, we have "legality." The distinction regards the *Triebfeder*—the *elater animi,* the springing motive or drive—of the will in its determination to action. Because of the general alternative that Kant opens up between pure reason and pathological feeling, from the outset the "subjective determining ground" of the will is at issue—a will that, like the human will and unlike the "holy" will, can be subject to sensuous impulses. At stake is a will that is not necessarily determined by its nature in accordance with the moral law. Human will is *arbitrium sensitivum* and yet *liberum;* it is neither *arbitrium brutum* nor *sanctum.* Accordingly, Kant's problem is twofold. First, he has to show *a priori* "the way in which the moral law becomes the drive" for the will, and then he has to show "what happens to the human faculty of desire"[106] in consequence of the effect that the moral law has on it when the law functions as drive to action. In other words, once practical reason has been proven to be the higher faculty of desire, Kant's problem regards the possibility of bringing an a priori presentation of "feeling" or the a priori determination of a "moral feeling" to bear on his project of a pure ethics. Since embodiment is a necessary condition for agency, as shown in the Dialectic of the first *Critique,* the specific form of the drive to action as well as the general structure of determinability and affectivity proper to sensibility are still transcendentally constitutive of Kant's account of the human will. However, since embodiment is not a condition of the will's moral determination, its position within the order defined by the moral space (its *topos* or "topic") can be only that of a *consequence* of moral determination. Thus, Kant suggests that whereas feeling needs to be excluded as *grounding motive* or *determining ground* (*Bestimmungsgrund*) of the will in order for "morality" to be possible, it can now be reintroduced in relation to the moral law as its very peculiar *effect or consequence*. At this point, the moral law shows its effect in the form of peculiar *affects* that it produces on practical sensibility, thereby lending a concrete content to the practical embodiment of freedom.

The first, a priori determinable effect of the moral law upon feeling is a merely negative one. By determining the will immediately, the moral law rejects and thwarts all inclinations thereby producing a *feeling of pain*. "Here we have the first, and perhaps the only case in which we can determine a priori from concepts the relation between a cognition (here a cognition of pure practical reason) and the feeling of pleasure and displeasure."[107] Since the moral law is the form of an intellectual causality, namely causality through freedom, it is in itself something "positive." As such it is, at the same time, "an object of respect" which humiliates our self-conceit. By imposing itself as object of the highest respect, the moral law is "the ground of a *positive feeling that does not have an empirical origin, and can be known a priori*." This feeling is "respect for the moral law." Moreover, "this feeling is the only one that we can know completely a priori and the necessity of which we can discern."[108] The feeling of respect is, according to Kant, the only "*moral feeling*."[109]

Such a feeling does not precede the moral law as motive or determining ground but rather follows from it as effect. This discloses a further reason for Kant's methodological inversion in the division of the second *Critique*. While in the *Critique* of theoretical knowledge sensibility comes first because of the immediacy with which it relates to objects, in the *Critique* of practical reason it is pure reason that determines the will immediately and that produces, as an effect of this determination, a specific form of "practical sensibility" which is the moral feeling of reverence for the law. Paradoxically, sensibility is not a first and immediately given moment. Rather, it is a *produced* consequence of pure practical determination. From this follows Kant's peculiar qualification of the reverence for the law as moral feeling. As opposed to all feeling, which is "pathological" (i.e., derives empirically from other feelings and inclinations), the feeling of reverence before the law (and negatively that of humiliation and its pain) is the effect of an intelligible causality and is therefore qualified as a "moral," i.e., genuinely *practical* feeling. As feeling, reverence is necessarily sensible, and therefore can never be the ground for a moral determination of the will. Yet, having its origin in pure practical reason, this "sensation [. . .] is not pathological but must be said to be *practically-produced*."[110] In other words, reverence is a feeling or sensation that is not suffered ("pathologically produced") by the subject but practically produced and experienced precisely in this active form.[111] As is the case for the pure form of sensibility in the theoretical sphere, the a priori form of practical feeling or affection of reverence also betrays the active character that human sensibility displays when taken up in the transcendental perspective. This practical form of sensibility is the figure that transcendental embodiment displays in the practical sphere.

Kant's awareness of the peculiar character of the moral feeling as feeling or sensation is revealed by his need for a careful qualification of the ways in which it works. (One may even suspect that respect for the law might be something that *functions as* feeling or in analogy to it, rather than a feeling proper.) "Respect for the law is not a drive for morality but is morality itself"[112]: it is morality taken in its subjective embodied and experienced meaning ("regarded subjectively as a drive"); it is neither a principle for judging actions nor properly a "feeling of pleasure" (or displeasure).[113] It is the "drive" through which the moral agent—this time an embodied being that has feelings and affections—assumes the moral law as maxim of her action. While no cognitive experience of freedom is possible through the physical body and its transcendental form, practical embodiment brings to the fore, for the first time, the possibility of a sensible experience of freedom. This "experience" takes place, negatively, as painful humiliation before the law, and positively, as the affect of reverence for it.

Thus, Kant views the moral law as the determining ground (*Bestimmungsgrund*) of the will on different levels. Through pure practical reason it represents a "*formal* determining ground of action." Through the notions of "good and evil" it provides the "*material* though purely *objective*" determination of the objects of action. Finally, through the moral feeling of reverence it also generates a "*subjective*" motive for the will.[114] Accordingly, the moral agent is identified in the sensible world by the peculiar form of reason's practical embodiment. Freedom's "body" is given neither by its visible empirical appearance in space and time, nor by its transcendental function of first instituting appearances in space and time for cognition, nor in its merely pathological determination. Freedom's body is never object (of cognition or self-consciousness or empirical affection) but always subject—is the moral agent itself. It is the "character" that ultimately constitutes the subject's *existence* in a moral space that stands *in connection with* the sensible world.[115] Because it institutes this connection, character is both sensible and intelligible—and it is sensible both cognitively and practically.

It is, to be sure, the unitary character of the person. For both sides of it are determined—albeit according to a different order—by reason's pure legislation over the will. In the practical perspective the sensible character identifies the body of the moral agent as the capacity for connecting a concrete (yet non-empirical) feeling to the intelligible causality of freedom. Thereby, the subject experiences a feeling of pain, humiliation, respect, and admiration—admiration and wonder for "the moral law *within me*" and for "the starry heavens *above me*."[116]

To sum up, in the transcendental perspective of Kant's moral philosophy the condition of embodiment plays itself out at different levels. First, embodiment is constitutive of the operation through which Kant institutes the sphere of practical reason as a "moral space" within which oriented action discriminating between pure and empirical motive takes place. Second, it gives a further meaning to the notion of *Faktum der Vernunft* in its unity with the consciousness of freedom. And finally, embodiment expresses the transcendental modality of a specific form of practical sensibility, i.e., moral feeling, that constitutes the moral agent's character or her peculiar receptivity to the causality of practical reason. It is only through these stages that the agent is finally defined as human being.

6

Freedom in the Body

> If the headache preceded the joys of
> intoxication instead of following them, then
> alcoholism would be a virtue, and highly
> disciplined mystics would cultivate it.
>
> —SAMUEL BUTLER

KANT'S EFFORTS IN THE SOLUTION OF THE THIRD ANTINOMY
are to suggest that reason actually and effectively (*wirklich*) "has causality
with regard to appearances,"[1] but that its form of causality is not itself appearance. The crucial thesis of the *Critique of Practical Reason* is that pure
reason is effectively (*wirklich*) practical,[2] as it is able to exercise a peculiar
form of causality and to determine the will immediately, i.e., without requiring the mediation of any empirical motive, material impulse, or desired
object. Thus, the first step of Kant's argument consists in showing that the
will can—and indeed must—be immediately determined through the form
of the moral law. In the previous chapter, I have argued that it is only *after*
having established a purely formal foundation of the moral principle that
Kant can take up his analysis of human sensibility and find a legitimate
place for it within his moral theory. Sensibility is not excluded from Kant's
doctrine. Yet, in the transcendental framework, practical sensibility—or
the practical form of the agent's body—is no longer an empirical feature
given by nature (and physiologically, anthropologically, or psychologically
observable) but something *produced* in its form by the determination of the

will through the moral law. The practical form of the "body" is the first *effect* of reason's intelligible causality. The peculiar character of the practical feeling of pleasure and displeasure for which Kant makes room in his theory consists in its connection with a cognition of pure practical reason that can be known a priori.[3] The condition for this connection is that such feeling does not precede but necessarily follows as a consequence from the intellectual and formal determination of the will. This is the case of the feeling of respect. The question of order—namely, the question of what precedes and what follows—is essential to the structure of the second *Critique*. Order is, in this case, both the logical order of foundation—which decides the type of determination proper to the will as well as the relation between freedom and the moral law[4]—and the temporal order according to which something comes first as cause and something else follows as its effect. To be sure, it is this very order that gives its proper meaning to the terms of Kant's moral theory: (1) it defines practical reason as "faculty of desire" in an anti-psychological sense that radically separates it from the tradition of Leibniz and Wolff; (2) it presents the "good" as non-empirical "object" of pure practical reason only after having established the principle of morality, thereby offering an alternative to the theories that assume the concept of the good as starting point and real criterion of moral inquiry;[5] and (3) it defines respect as a "moral feeling" that functions in a way quite different from Hume's "moral sense" and from empiricist moral sentiments in general.

However, determination and causation are not synonymous.[6] They designate two different, albeit related issues addressed by Kant's moral theory. He contends that practical reason immediately *determines* the will; that reason has an *effect* (*Wirkung*) (both negative and positive) on our feeling, which can be recognized a priori. In another formulation, he claims that reason itself *effects* or *produces* (*bewirkt*) a special feeling and, more generally, that reason has an effect on the sensible world of appearances and is the "condition" of all voluntary actions. Moreover, in its causality through freedom, reason expresses the "intelligible character" whose "immediate effect" (*unmittelbare Wirkung*) is the agent's "empirical character"[7] manifest in the world of nature. How shall we understand these formulations regarding the form of reason's *determination* on the one hand, and its (causal) *effects* on sensibility and the sensible world on the other? More specifically and concretely, what are these *effects*? To answer these questions means to fully address the issue of the transcendental construction of the moral agent or moral "person" as an embodied rational being in Kant's practical philosophy. The issue of "how the moral law becomes *Triebfeder*" and what is thereby produced or effected by it in the *Gemüt* is the topic of the last chapter of the Analytic regarding the Drives of Pure Practical Reason. Since Kant presents two distinct arguments to prove, respectively, that reason immediately *determines* the will and that reason itself becomes *Triebfeder* for the will in its *effects,* the two actions of reason—or its two ways of being "cause"—must be kept distinct as well.

A Transcendental Perspective
on Practical Embodiment

A common interpretation of Kant's moral philosophy views it as a strictly dualistic doctrine that aims at separating practical reason from empirical affections and sensible desires to the point that reason eventually finds itself emptied of all sensibility and unable to re-compose the dualism thereby assessed.[8] Against this view, I contend that once Kant has guaranteed a pure intellectual ground for the determination of the will, his crucial objective becomes to explain how practical reason manifests itself through its effects in—and on—human sensibility and the sensible world. The separation of reason from empirical affections, emotions, and desires is a required critical strategy *only* with regard to the foundation of the highest principle of morality and with regard to the idea of a "*pure* will." As explained in the previous chapter, the second *Critique* is, after all, a critique of practical reason—not of pure practical reason.[9] There is, indeed, a constitutive and essential relation that connects pure practical reason and sensibility in its practical forms, a relation that is central to Kant's transcendental philosophy. Such a connection is an integral part of the argument of the second *Critique.* It is neither a consequence to be drawn only in applied moral philosophy nor the topic of an empirical discipline such as moral psychology or anthropology. On the contrary, it is a crucial moment of Kant's critical project.[10] To this extent, the third *Critique* draws new conclusions from the results of the 1788 work. It builds on Kant's efforts to rescue the "feeling of pleasure and displeasure" from its exclusively empirical meaning by finding an a priori connection with practical cognition. The *Critique of Judgment* promotes this feeling to an independent faculty of the *Gemüt* endowed with an a priori principle of its own, accordingly re-articulating its connection to practical reason and to morality. Moreover, my discussion of the second *Critique* shows that Kant's 1790 work does not "invent" the problem of the conciliation of nature and freedom, as it is generally assumed; rather, it further elaborates on this issue, already present in the 1788 *Critique,* in the light of the newly discovered transcendental principle of the feeling of pleasure and displeasure, namely, the principle of *Zweckmäßigkeit.*

In recent years, a number of important studies have been published that aim at rehabilitating the topic of emotions in Kant's practical philosophy. The new attention to this topic can be referred to a more general interest in the subject of emotions that is confined not just to ethics but includes psychology, psychoanalysis, and anthropology. 'Emotion' is often taken to comprehend terms that Kant carefully distinguishes, such as *Gefühl* (feeling), *Leidenschaft* (passion), *Trieb* (drive), and *Affekt* (affection). Kant's collective designation for these different manifestations of affectivity is *Sinnlichkeit* (sensibility). This is the general, more traditional term that I prefer to employ. My work builds on the results of some of these recent studies.[11] However, it takes a new path in focusing on a foundational point that has never been sufficiently investigated. Unlike many interpreters, whose work is centered on the later *Doctrine of Virtue* of the *Metaphysics of Morals* or, more generally, on Kant's "applied" ethics, I concentrate my analysis on Kant's *transcendental* and *critical* efforts in the second *Critique,* and view the issue of practical sensibility—of emotions and affectivity—not as empirical or applied consequence of his pure ethics but as integral part of this transcendental theory itself. My aim is precisely to locate Kant's transcendental theory of practical sensibility within his ethics and to spell out its different components. From this perspective, one of the most relevant aspects of my inquiry follows. The emotional side of agency or the practical form of sensibility that is crucial to Kant is not constituted by the same emotions, affections, and passions that are naturally (and more or less instinctively) given to us. Philosophically, natural emotions and their bearing on morality have been widely addressed by a tradition of moral philosophy going back to Aristotle, the Stoics, Epicurus, Cicero, Augustine, and then enriched by the modern views of the Enlightenment—a tradition well known to Kant. For Kant, the sensibility that interacts with practical reason is the *transcendental form* of affectivity that is produced by reason itself; it is a pure (though sensible) *form* that, on the ground of the very activity of reason, institutes an a priori *cognitive* relation to the moral principle. Kant's claim is neither the trivial recognition that human agents have bodies which influence and serve them in making decisions and in performing actions; nor is it simply that emotions play a crucial role in the actual exercise of morality (virtue), as most studies that counter the traditional "rigoristic" reading of Kant's philosophy rightly understand him to say.[12] The fundamental point is Kant's critical discovery that there is an a priori aspect of human affectivity, an aspect that—precisely on the ground of its being produced by reason and not simply given by nature—is integral to the reality of human freedom and to the project of its critical and transcendental foundation. Kant argues for a view that runs opposite to what common sense holds: the agent's body does not exercise an influence on moral decision but is rather an effect thereof; is not a presupposed (empirical) condition but a consequence of the will's moral determination. In addition, as shown in the previous chapters, Kant's ethics does not presuppose that morality is concerned with *human* agents. This is rather the complex result of the pure foundation of the principle of morality itself. The phenomenology of natural emotions as well as their "application" to individual empirical cases and decisions *follow* precisely from the transcendental form of practical sensibility.

This thesis allows me to draw a fundamental distinction between the natural, empirical side of practical sensibility—namely, the "visible" body that feels physical pleasure and pain, natural emotions, and affects, and is the "object" of empirical cognition—and the "invisible," transcendental, practical form of the body which is the "subject" of action and practical cognition. In the first case, the body is known as appearance in space and time, has senses and feels sensations, and may be apprehended in its gendered and physiognomic features. However, for Kant, this body's capacity to act does not define a specific form of practical causality, does not indicate the agency of a subject or person but falls entirely within nature's mechanism. To this extent, it can be relevant in moral psychology, anthropology, or physiology but not in pure ethics. In the second case, by contrast, the body is a form and a construction. This body is not naturally and pathologically given but "*practically* produced" as an effect; is not the body that suffers passions but the body that wills and acts as the body of a free rational agent in the world; is not the body that betrays what a rational agent looks like or to what actions determinate feelings lead, but the body that indicates how a rational agent feels in consequence of a purely moral determination of her will. It is this second perspective that allows Kant to include an analysis of practical sensibility in the transcendental theory of the second *Critique*. This crucial distinction is nowhere to be found in the literature on Kant's practical philosophy. As Kant clarifies in the *Critique of Pure Reason,* hinting at a point that will show its relevance "in all successive considerations" (and I underscore: not only with regard to the first *Critique* but also in relation to the later developments of the third *Critique*): "not every a priori cognition must be deemed transcendental, but only that cognition through which we know that and how certain representations [. . .] can be applied or are possible exclusively a priori."[13] In this sense, I argue for the inclusion of practical sensibility in the specifically transcendental perspective of Kant's moral philosophy. The result is the "ideal" construction of the a priori form of the body of a free rational agent.

In the practical sphere, the asymmetric relation that connects reason and sensibility is pivotal to Kant's argument. On the basis of this asymmetry, Kant contends that reason is not "affected" (*affiziert*) by sensibility[14] but itself affects sensibility; as cause, reason does not exist within the series of appearances even though its effects do. The "actions of reason are also not appearances, rather, only its effects are." This relation, in its asymmetry, defines the specific conditions of the moral space of Kant's theory: "If everything were determined by reason, then everything would be necessary, but also good. If everything were determined by sensibility, then there would be nothing good or evil; in general, there would be nothing practical." The asymmetric relation that connects reason to sensibility is the condition of practical freedom, i.e., the condition for the "practical" *strictu sensu*. Such asymmetry is the distinctive character of a human will placed between holy will and animal will. It is the condition that operates on a will that is neither *arbitrium sanctum*—in which case everything would be necessarily good without deliberation or choice—nor *arbitrium brutum*—in which case moral distinctions would not hold at all. As Kant already makes clear in the solution of the third antinomy, at stake is an *arbitrium sensitivum* and *liberum*. In this case, Kant explains,

> actions are, for the most part, *induced* by sensibility, but not entirely *determined* by it; for reason must provide a complement of sufficiency. Reason progressively draws sensibility to become *habitus, stimulates* (*erregt*) drives, and thereby forms (*bildet*) a character. This character itself must be attributed to freedom, and is not sufficiently grounded in appearances.[15]

Reason is not subject to affections but—at least at a certain point in Kant's doctrine—it speaks the language of affection and is itself the cause of affection. The difference between theoretical and practical reason is that "in free actions reason does not flow through as a principle that comprehends (*begreifendes*) but as one that acts (*wirkendes*) and drives (*treibendes*)."[16] While moral determination is exclusively a matter of reason, Kant recognizes the importance of reason's work in shaping sensibility, in transforming it into moral habit, in stimulating certain drives and in becoming itself a drive. This is the complex connection that I investigate in this chapter.

In the previous chapter I discussed the first, foundational side of the relation between reason and sensibility, concerned with the will's pure and formal *determination* through the principle of reason; here, I examine the other side of this asymmetric relation, namely, the ways in which reason can be said to affect sensibility and to have actual effects in the sensible world. While the previous chapter was concerned with a problem of "deduction," in what follows I engage in a problem of "schematism." How is the relation between two heterogeneous terms such as reason and sensibility possible in the practical sphere? Kant suggests that there is indeed a necessary connection—a *Zusammenhang*—between reason and the *phenomenis,* although this connection cannot be (cognitively) understood since they are heterogeneous terms. The activity of reason takes place in the intelligible world. Kant recognizes, however, that "actions here in the world are mere schemata of the intelligible." The word *Erscheinung,* Kant observes, already means "schema"—and his concern at this point is with a practical connection and practical cognition.[17]

Thus, given that no theoretical experience of freedom is possible to us, is a practical experience of freedom possible? Provided that the agent of Kant's moral theory is a rational embodied being, what is freedom *in the body,* i.e., what is freedom not just as idea of reason but as concrete modality of the agent's existence and "life"? The concept of "life" is introduced by Kant as one of the notions that define the moral space of his philosophy. Both at the beginning of the second *Critique* and at the very beginning of the *Metaphysics of Morals,* he defines "life" as the "faculty of a being by which it acts according to the laws of the faculty of desire" or "by which it acts according to its representations."[18] Life has an essential connection both to desire and to feeling. "Feeling is the sensation (*Empfindung*) of life. The complete use of life is freedom."[19] In Kant's doctrine, the moral life of the person is structured by the intersection and interaction of reason and sensibility.[20] As is the case of the agent's body, life is neither the natural, biological life studied by natural science nor the inscrutable after-life of an immortal disembodied soul. It is instead the moral life of a free embodied being whose actions are not subject to the conditions of time and space.

In the remainder of this chapter I address two related sets of issues through which I come to a more specific definition of the embodied rational agent as "person." First, I examine the question of the effects that reason has on our feeling: how are our feelings affected, influenced, and shaped by the intimations of morality?[21] How are they transformed to constitute the invisible body of the moral agent—a body construed as effect of moral decision?

How shall *this* body feel and desire not to act morally but in consequence of moral *Gesinnung* and moral decision? These issues make up the topic of an "aesthetic" of freedom[22] as a necessary condition for Kant's doctrine of virtue. Second, I address the question of how reason appears in the world of phenomena: what are freedom's effects in the world of nature? Reason is not itself the source of moral action but the source of a principle of action determining the will to choice. And yet, Kant contends that practical reason does have "causality with regard to appearance" and is the "condition of all voluntary actions under which the human being appears."[23] I show that, for Kant, freedom appears in the world not as the occurrence of empirical action but as the process of the will's deliberation to action. While reason itself is not the beginning of an action, it is the direct intelligible cause of the (sensible) condition that initiates the process of deliberation. On Kant's account, the phenomenology of moral action is entirely internal to the moment of intention, deliberation, and motivation. To this extent, I claim that conceptually the terminological distinction between *Wille* and *Willkür*, which Kant introduces for the first time in the 1790s, is already operative in the first and second *Critiques*. Finally, the discussion of these two issues leads me to brief conclusive remarks regarding the way in which Kant's moral theory is able to address the intersubjective dimension of human action as based on the notion of "personality." What is the ground of our recognition of other moral agents as persons? How do we distinguish them from mere things and compare them to ourselves? How is the existence of other embodied rational and free beings articulated in the framework of Kant's moral philosophy? On what level does the recognition of other persons play itself out—given that intentions are inscrutable and the practical form of the agent's body is invisible or not observable? Clearly, at this point, Kant has significantly advanced beyond the illusionary visions of Swedenborg, who claimed the mysterious perception of the existence of disembodied spirits and advanced such conviction as an argument for a community of spirits.

Aesthetic of Freedom

Kant considers practical reason and speculative reason to be "similar cognitive faculties."[24] On this basis he builds their respective critiques according to the same structure, although, as we have seen, the order of the critical argument is inverted in the practical sphere. While the aesthetic constitutes the first part of the Analytic of the critique of speculative reason, it comes last in the critical examination of practical reason. To be sure, in the practical critique, Kant speaks of "aesthetic" with caution: the term, he warns, is used herein only analogically.[25] In this case, aesthetic deals with "feeling"—*Gefühl*—not with intuition and its a priori forms. However, if feeling is defined only as that which can function as the empirical "subjective ground of desiring,"[26] then the issue raised by it can be easily solved on the basis of Kant's distinction between "morality" and "legality."[27] The former is the immediate determination of the will by the moral law; the latter implies the mediation of feeling as determining ground or motive. It follows that, in transcendental philosophy, feeling cannot be admitted as what it naturally tends to be, namely, the empirical ground of desiring. Practical reason is not a faculty that "desires" in this sense. Moreover, for Kant, feeling in general is not simply "sense" (*Sinn*). It already implies "choice" (*Wahl*) and a relation to practical evaluation.[28] Kant's aim is to "isolate" an aspect of sensibility that is both formal and genuinely practical.[29] Accordingly, in the practical sphere the aesthetic presents for him yet another side. In order for an aesthetic (even a merely analogical aesthetic) to be admitted in the transcendental inquiry, it must be possible to find an a priori form proper to the type of sensibility related to its respective cognitive faculty. Otherwise, feeling remains the object of moral psychology or applied practical philosophy but cannot be a part of transcendental inquiry.[30] Thus excluded from the motives of the will, practical sensibility, as feeling, presents Kant with a twofold problem: namely, with "the relation (*Verhältnis*) of pure practical reason to sensibility and with its *necessary influences on it that can be known a priori*, i.e., with *moral feeling*."[31] This means that feeling, for Kant, is not just subjective ground of action. To establish that in morality "the moral law"—and not feeling—"immediately determines the will"[32] is not enough. A further argument is required that gives an account of the nature of the will thereby determinable, and of the consequences that this determination has on the will and on its sensible nature. It is "feeling," taken as consequence or effect, that now needs investigation. For a feeling that follows (and never precedes) the moral determination of the will discloses the a priori relation to reason that justifies its inclusion in the "aesthetic" of pure practical reason. At this juncture, Kant introduces the notion of *Triebfeder*. He offers the following definition and draws the following consequences:

> if by drive (*Triebfeder*) (*elater animi*) we understand a subjective determining ground of a will whose reason does not by its nature necessarily conform to the objective law, it follows, first, that absolutely no drives can be attributed to the divine will; and second, that the drive of the human will (and that of every created rational being) can never be anything other than the moral law.[33]

In the *Groundwork,* Kant distinguishes between *Triebfeder* and *Beweggrund,* and connects this distinction to that between subjective and objective ends: "The subjective ground of desiring is the drive (*Triebfeder*); the objective one is moving ground (*Bewegungsgrund*); hence, the difference between subjective ends, which rest on drives, and objective ends, which concern moving grounds that are valid for all rational beings."[34]

In eighteenth-century German psychology, the term *Trieb* is synonymous with instinct and is often opposed to reason.[35] Implicitly rejecting that opposition, Kant designates the moral law itself as a (special) drive. *Triebfeder* has, for Kant, the same definition as feeling: it is a "subjective determining ground of the will." This definition, however, is complemented by a condition that specifies the nature of the will determinable by it. For not every will is subject to—and needs—drives. The concept of *Triebfeder* applies only to a certain kind of will, i.e., to a will for which the distinction between subjective and objective *Bestimmungsgrund* does indeed make sense. Drive is the subjective ground that decides whether we will a subjective end or not. Consequently, the notion of *Triebfeder* does not apply to the divine will, for which no subjective maxim can be conflicting with the objective principle of morality.[36] For the divine will, as we have seen, everything is necessarily good without choice: subjective and objective grounds coincide, and decide on ends that are objective (i.e., as claimed in the cited passage of the *Groundwork*—"valid for all rational being"). In the formulation of the moral law, at the beginning of the Analytic of the second *Critique,* Kant makes clear that its validity is extended to "every rational being." This designation includes the human being, "all finite beings endowed with reason and will," and the "infinite being, as highest intelligence." However, it is only for the human being that the moral law has the force of an "imperative," implies a "constraint" (*Nötigung*) and even "compulsion/violence" (*Zwang*) (albeit an intellectual one), and gives rise to a relation of obligation and "duty." Ultimately, the reason for all these specifications of the moral law is the presence of sensibility—the human will is *arbitrium sensitivum,* i.e., a will that is "pathologically *affected,* even though not pathologically *determined,* and thus still free."[37] It is the split between affection and determination that explains the possible separation between subjective maxim and objective law in the case of the human will. For the decision of the human will (whether an end should or should not be willed) must always pass through a subjective maxim. Moral determination occurs when the subjective maxim is the objective law, is immediately one with it.

In the last chapter of the Analytic, after having established that the moral determination proper to this type of will occurs only under the

condition of being purely formal, with the exclusion of all sensible motives, Kant proceeds to attribute to the moral law itself the force of those
(sensible) drives that he had previously excluded as motives. In the case of
a will that can be *affected* by sensibility or is *pathologically determinable,* and
yet is immediately *determined* by the moral law, reason functions in the way
in which sensibility functions, namely, as a (subjective) drive. In the act of
moral determination, it is reason that actively *affects* the will; the objective
moving ground is thereby also endorsed as subjective *Triebfeder.* Hence, it is
not surprising that the consequence of this kind of (intellectual and moral)
affection is a feeling, namely, the feeling of *Achtung.* Retrospectively, we can
say that reason is already affecting the will in the foundation of the moral
principle, as it is precisely on this basis that the moral law, as imperative, can
be said (and felt) to exercise violence and coercion on the will. Thereby, the
aesthetic of practical reason accounts for the way in which practical reason
sensibly (and effectively, *wirklich*) determines—or has an influence on—the
human will. Kant's argument parallels the argument of the first part of the
Analytic. However, an important change of perspective has taken place.
Now Kant observes the will's determination through the moral law not in
the perspective of every rational being as such but in the perspective proper
to the human being insofar as this is a being endowed with a form of sensibility that is capable of a practical response, or of a "relation" (*Verhältnis*)[38]
to pure practical reason.

Kant's further point in introducing the notion of a *Triebfeder* of pure
practical reason is that the moral law, in becoming the drive that exercises
an "influence over the will," is sufficient to its full determination.[39] No
other drive needs to be assumed along with it. Thus, we discover that the
pure formal determination of the will through the moral law entirely *replaces* the sensible affection of passions and desires. Reason does not simply
set aside and radically repress sensible affection as such. This very act is, in
an important way, already an effect—the first effect—that reason has on the
agent and that can be sensibly felt by her. Kant recognizes that the capacity
of being affected or affectivity is constitutive of the will of the human being.
On this premise, his argument consists, first, in re-positioning affection,
transforming it from motive to consequence, and, second, in allowing reason to take onto itself the same structure of affectivity so as to re-orient it
on the basis of the a priori nature of reason's own principle. Reason replaces
sensible affection by functioning as *Triebfeder;* thereby sensibility is radically
transformed. "The moral law *becomes* the drive,"[40] and the issue consists in
determining "what happens to the human faculty of desire" as a consequence of this transformation. The task is to solve the problem of how the

moral law becomes *Triebfeder* by looking at "what it effects (*wirkt*) (or better must effect) on the *Gemüt*."[41] Indeed by addressing the issue of the way in which the principle of morality produces a feeling or affects the will, Kant does not add anything to the *validity* of the moral law, which has already been established. Rather, he presents an argument in favor of its *efficacy*, thereby spelling out the notion of a "causality" of reason "with regard to appearance"[42] that the first *Critique* had left indeterminate.

The first "effect of the moral law *as drive*" is merely negative. It complements the negative definition of freedom as independence from the matter of the law and the sensible determination through nature offered in Analytic §§5–6. If the will is free, i.e., *immediately* determined by the moral law, then it is also determined *exclusively* by it so that all other sensible impulses, inclinations, and drives are necessarily rejected, kept in check, and thwarted. Unlike all other natural and empirical drives, the *Triebfeder* that is the moral law "can be known a priori"[43] in its effects. The first, negative effect of the moral law *as drive* is a feeling—a feeling of pain. Because of its origin, this feeling can be known a priori as well (and hence belongs to the "aesthetic" of practical reason). Moreover, as is the case at the beginning of the Analytic with the positive concept of freedom as capacity to act on the basis of practical reason alone, the moral law as drive is itself something positive that, in its intellectual causality, produces also a "positive feeling," namely, the feeling of respect. Because of its "non-empirical origin," the feeling of respect can be known entirely a priori.

Thus, Kant's argument presents a cognitive situation in which pure practical reason is set in confrontation with or relation to sensibility so that a series of a priori statements can issue.[44] We can see (*einsehen*) a priori: (1) that the moral law is indeed *Triebfeder*, i.e., that it can exercise an effect on feeling; (2) that as such it produces as effect a specific feeling of pain; and (3) that it produces a correspondent positive feeling of respect. Kant finally contends (4) that we can know (*erkennen*) this latter, positive feeling entirely a priori and discern (*einsehen*) its internal necessity.[45] The progression of the argument is as follows: from the a priori claim that the moral law *is* *Triebfeder*, it follows that it "can" and "must"[46] *produce* a feeling in us; the feeling is then specified a priori or construed as "pain" or "humiliation" and "respect"; finally, what can be *known* a priori is, directly, the feeling of respect *itself*. Through this progression, Kant shows that the moral law is not only the "*formal Bestimmungsgrund* of action" through pure practical reason; nor is it the "*material* but only *objective Bestimmungsgrund* of the objects of action" as good and evil. It also becomes the "subjective *Bestimmungsgrund*, i.e., *Triebfeder*"[47] or subjective motive to moral action according to the first definition of this term. By transforming itself into drive and by producing a feeling of respect, the moral law unifies subjective and objective ground of determination in the case of the human *arbitrium sensitivum* as well. Since in the case of the *arbitrium sanctum* both grounds are already and necessarily one, no *Triebfeder* can be attributed to the holy will. In human beings, the moral law produces a feeling of respect precisely because the law is, positively, the formal ground of the will's determination. To formulate the same situation from the position of the human agent subject to that *Gefühl,* we can say that we feel respect for the moral law because we practically know (i.e., we recognize or discern with our moral insight or *Einsicht*) that the law can indeed function as a purely formal and yet positive ground for the determination of our will. The intellectual recognition of the fact that the moral law is *Bestimmungsgrund* is that which renders the moral law *Triebfeder,* and thereby effectively capable of exercising affection on the *Gemüt*. While feeling is still not the ground of moral determination but its consequence, it does reinforce or promote, on the subjective side, the efficacy of the law on the human will in its process of deliberation. Thus, the feeling produced by the *Triebfeder* of pure practical reason is still "pathological"[48]—as every feeling is—and yet can also be said to be "rational" and specifically "moral." In the case of the human will, the law is drive to moral action "since it has an influence on the sensibility of the subject and *effects a feeling which promotes the influence of the law on the will*." For this reason, the feeling of respect is called "moral feeling."[49] Practical cognition is, in this case, one with (the principle of) action.

The discovery of "moral feeling" is the crucial result of the aesthetic of practical reason. Its place in a *transcendental* aesthetic of practical reason (and not in moral psychology) is justified by its a priori relation to reason as well as by the peculiar character of its pathological nature. As is the case for space and time (pure a priori forms of sensible intuition and transcendental form of the body in the theoretical sphere), in the case of moral feeling (transcendental form of the human agent's embodied will) we have a type of sensibility or affection that is not suffered but actively produced by the subject. With regard to its origin, moral feeling "cannot be said to be pathologically effected; rather, it is *practically effected*." For it is not a feeling that we passively submit to but is itself *identical with* the very principle of action: "the respect for the law is not the drive to morality but is morality itself, *regarded subjectively as a drive*"[50]—namely, in the perspective of the acting human subject and her sensibly determinable will. In other words, to be *af-*

fected by reason means to act, not to suffer. This is the transcendental condition that justifies Kant's claim, in the *Doctrine of Virtue* of the *Metaphysics of Morals,* regarding the duty to cultivate our emotional, "natural (aesthetic)" capacities.[51] At this point, Kant concludes his argument by returning to its first condition: since respect is an effect on feeling exercised by reason, its occurrence rests on a condition, namely, on the sensible nature of the will and on the finitude of the subject of that will. Hence, no feeling of respect for the moral law can be assumed in a being whose will lacks sensibility.[52] In the human being the feeling of respect is not only a feeling produced *by freedom.* It is also a feeling *of freedom,* a feeling that has freedom not only as *ratio essendi* but also as object. The feeling of respect is the "consciousness of free submission (*freie Unterwerfung*) of the will to the law," and thereby it can be said to offer an *emotional experience of freedom.*[53]

At the beginning of the argument, in presenting the feeling of pain that the moral law produces in us by thwarting inclinations and desires, Kant suggests that "here we have *the first and perhaps the only case* wherein we can determine from a priori concepts the relation of a cognition [. . .] to the feeling of pleasure and displeasure."[54] Indeed, he has proved that pain is, in the order of its occurrence, the "first" effect of reason on sensibility. At this point, however, he seems uncertain as to the possibility of extending the inference to other particular feelings besides this peculiar type of pain. As the argument proceeds to show the positive effect (or the positive side of the effect) of the law on feeling in the form of respect, Kant states, in a somehow more decisive way: "this feeling" of respect for the moral law "is *the only one* that we can know entirely a priori and the necessity of which we can discern."[55] Just as the first part of the Analytic dealing with *Grundsätze* discovers the unique principle of morality in the moral law, so does the aesthetic of practical reason arrive at a unique form of practical sensibility whose origin, universality, and necessity we can discern completely a priori—namely, moral feeling.

But in what sense is this form unique; why is it the only one that occupies the last part of the Analytic?[56] I shall argue that moral feeling is unique precisely because of the way its a priori character is obtained. The a priori character of moral feeling accounts for this feeling's universality and formality, for its connection to life, and hence for its relation to other particular feelings. That a feeling can be universal, formal (that is, not related to objects but to the form of the will's determination), and necessary already makes it a unique kind of feeling. Since moral feeling is formal and universal, it pervades our emotional life in all its different particular manifestations. It is not the natural life of the senses or sensible pleasures (happiness) that is at stake, but the moral life of an embodied free agent. These characters make possible an extension of moral feeling to the entire phenomenal sphere of natural sentiments and emotions, and hence make possible its use (or application) in Kant's doctrine of virtue.

Moral feeling belongs to an aesthetic of practical reason because it is not simply "sense," i.e., does not indicate a theoretical and merely empirical capacity of perceiving and having sensations.[57] Its a priori relation to the principle of morality lends necessity and universality to it. "With regard to feeling [. . .], we do indeed feel only through the senses; and yet, we can assume the standpoint in which we set ourselves in relation to the object, in whichever way we want." Here, in the moral sphere, "we assume our standpoint in reason and feel in a universal standpoint."[58] Kant thinks that moral feeling "is no particular feeling" because it opens up to a universal standpoint. Herein lies the peculiarity and indeed uniqueness of this form of practical sensibility: moral feeling "is *no particular feeling* but a *general manner of considering something from the universal point of view.*" Admittedly, the question is: "How can morality be felt since it is an object of reason?" Being an object of reason, we would assume that it exceeds all possible experience— even a practical one through feeling. And yet, Kant argues that morality "is related *to all our actions* in accord with our pleasure and displeasure, and contains the condition for their agreement in general; through this, it is related to the feeling of pleasure according to the form."[59] The claim is not only that we can indeed take pleasure in action, and more precisely in the possibility of conducing actions according to the universal moral principle.[60] On the basis of this assumption (pleasure is consequence, not motive of moral action), Kant further maintains that according to (or from the perspective of) our pleasure and displeasure, morality is a *form* that pervades "*all* our actions" (not only the moral ones) as a criterion. We cannot escape moral (self-)evaluation in any of our deeds because we cannot escape our moral feeling. Morality pervades all of our actions as it contains the condition of the agreement of all our actions in general, i.e., their form. Since the ground of feeling is the moral principle, moral feeling relates to the universality of this form (not to a particular content or action), whereby it gains its own formality and universality manifest in the "universal point of view." This is a point of view of feeling, not of reason. Hence the answer to Kant's initial question is that morality can be felt (and we have moral feeling) when we set ourselves within the general perspective of *all* our actions—so as to relate to ourselves not just with regard to single actions in their material singularity but with regard to the universal form in which they ought to agree. This idea takes the place of the eudemonistic notion of happiness.[61]

This claim allows us to understand why in the practical sphere Kant connects feeling to the idea of life. Moral feeling is concerned with the principle of the general conduct of life, not with enjoyment and pleasure in individual objects or actions. This notion can be distinguished from the Aristotelian position only if feeling is understood in its a priori connection to freedom, and not taken in the empiricist sense of pleasure and happiness. "Feeling is the sensation (*Empfindung*) of life. The complete use of life is freedom." The "formal condition" for the relation between feeling, life, and freedom is regularity and lawfulness. Reason is the faculty that uses a priori rules to unify a manifold under principles. For Kant, not only freedom but also feeling must follow at least rules if not laws.[62] This additional point justifies the inclusion of moral feeling in a transcendental aesthetic of practical reason. Kant contends that "we do *not have particular feelings,* even though we have a different capacity of sense and sensation. There is only one principle of life and also only one *principium* of the feeling of pleasure and displeasure"—just as there is only one principle of morality. In the case of the *principle* of feeling (not just of particular feelings) of pleasure and displeasure, the relation to life is mediated by reason: pleasure and displeasure "can be enlivened also through reason (through regularity or lack of rules of freedom)." At stake is the way in which reason—and freedom—does "move" our feeling. "With regard *to our entire existence and to all our forces,* our feeling becomes active in view of accord and opposition because free use of forces and freedom in general is the most important and the noblest thing."[63] Herein, the occurrence of feeling in the moral sense comes close to the peculiar feeling of pleasure and displeasure that Kant will address in the third *Critique,* that is, in a new "aesthetics" of the faculty of judgment. Thus, the uniqueness of the moral law is paralleled by the uniqueness of the moral feeling: in both cases, their uniqueness is due to their principled formality and universality.[64]

In a *Reflection* that discusses in the same connection issues of taste and the idea of freedom, Kant draws attention to the structure and the feeling of life:

> Since life is unity, all taste has as *principio* the unity of the enlivened sensations. Freedom is the original life (*ursprüngliches Leben*) and in its connection is the condition of the accord of all life. Hence, that which facilitates the feeling of universal life [. . .] produces pleasure. [. . .] Universality renders all our feelings in accord, even though this universality is not a particular type of sensation. This is the form of *consensus*.[65]

Freedom can be felt to the extent that it is "the original life" and that its universality is criterion of the morality of all our actions. Thereby, Kant offers the transcendental determination of two general concepts "borrowed from psychology" whose definitions are given at the beginning of the Preface to the second *Critique*: "*life* is the faculty of a being by which it acts according to the laws of the faculty of desire"; "*pleasure* is the representation of the agreement of an object or action with the *subjective* conditions of life."[66] If we assume that freedom is *ursprüngliches Leben,* then we obtain the peculiar form of the feeling of life that Kant names moral feeling. This can only improperly be named a "feeling of *pleasure.*"[67] Thus, we can conclude that the feeling of respect for the law as moral feeling is the only case of a *Gefühl* whose necessity can be known entirely a priori precisely because of its pure and formal origin in practical reason. Its transcendental structure makes of this feeling the universal and formal condition of all other particular feelings manifest in the practical sphere in conjunction with freedom and moral action. Moral feeling allows one to recognize a priori that the influence of practical reason on sensibility is indeed possible.

A New Form of Affectivity

In the Critical Elucidation of the Analytic of the second *Critique,* after the discussion of moral feeling as "drive" of pure practical reason, Kant takes up again the "apparent contradiction between the mechanism of nature and freedom"[68] already addressed in the solution of the third antinomy. At stake is the problem of the "realization" of freedom—not only its appearance but also its consequences (and hence causality) in the sensible world. The issue of the *Triebfeder* of pure practical reason and the derivation of moral feeling provide the new basis on which the *Critique of Practical Reason* solves that contradiction and suggests, at the same time, the way in which we can think the influence of morality as extended through moral feeling to the entire sensible life of the moral agent in the world of appearances. Kant contends that "through pure practical reason, by means of the moral law," we experience a "great revelation (*herrliche Eröffnung*)—the revelation of an intelligible world through the realization (*Realisierung*) of the otherwise transcendent concept of freedom." However, Kant warns, this revelation or opening is possible only if we avoid the merely "psychological"[69] and empiricist concept of freedom and endorse the "transcendental" one. Kant contends that determinism is the only option left open to those who pretend to explain freedom as a psychological and empirical property of the soul. The transcendental perspective, on the contrary, allows one to conceive not only of the *possibility* of freedom but also of its *reality;* it allows not only for an insight into the intelligible world but also for a peculiar "experience" of it within the sensible world. In other words, moral psychology aims at comprehending freedom as a property of the soul and remains stuck at the empirical principles which explain it in the same terms of any other natural ability. Within this perspective, no distinction between sensible and intellectual can hold. The transcendental inquiry, on the contrary, explains freedom as a transcendental notion; by drawing a clear-cut distinction between intellectual and sensible causality, it is able to recuperate the emotional, affective side of sensibility. Thus, the transcendental perspective lends a new meaning to practical sensibility in connection with the idea of freedom. At stake at this point is the issue of freedom's reality. While the moral law can be said to directly "reveal" the intelligible world (as well as the intelligible causality of reason), our *experience* of it and the fact that freedom is thereby actually *realized* betray the intervention of a subjective, sensible condition transcendentally expressed as moral feeling.

Kant revisits the solution of the "apparent contradiction" between nature and freedom and proposes, once again, the central thesis of the Transcendental Aesthetic. Time is not a property of the subject considered as thing-in-itself but only the condition of its phenomenal existence. In the realm of nature framed by the condition of time, every action as well as every natural event is determined by the past, whereby it completely escapes the subject's power. In the perspective of the acting subject, to the *Bestimmungsgründe* of its actions "must be counted his already performed acts and his character as a phenomenon, as this is *determinable* for him in his own eyes by those acts." But this same subject, on the basis of the consciousness of freedom disclosing the noumenal dimension of its *Dasein*, "views his existence" as "not standing under temporal conditions, and himself as *determinable* only by laws which he gives to himself through reason."[70] Within this perspective, the subject's action is determinable exclusively by the moral law as nothing can be said to precede the determination of the will as its condition or motive—neither the series of its former deeds nor its susceptibility to empirical drives, passions, or desires. The ground of determination lies outside of the temporal series. The moral law is the one and only intellectual principle that, placed outside of the temporal order, can determine the will. In this perspective—and in this perspective only—the will is completely free or spontaneous while itself placed, in such determination, outside of temporal conditions; and the agent must be held accountable and responsible for all her actions—even for those that seem to be necessitated by the mechanism of the sensible world and by the sensible constitution of human nature.

At this point, we can integrate into Kant's argument the other transcendental condition that constitutes the world of appearance, namely, space. As the form of outer sense, space is the condition of the subject's sensible affection from the outside—the condition of sensation and perception of external objects that may be desired or avoided as procuring a feeling of pleasure or displeasure. That the (phenomenal) causality of the subject stands under the condition of space (in addition to time) means that the will is determinable by *externally given objects* that can be known as producing pleasure (or displeasure) and desired (or rejected) accordingly. If space were a property defining the subject's existence as thing-in-itself, then it would define the only possible manner of the subject's presence in and response to the world. The existence of external objects affecting us would be the only ground of the will's determination, which would be necessarily sensible and always material, induced only by feelings and desires. Feeling would be exclusively material and pathological as it could only be caused by externally given objects; no feeling would be produced in us by merely intellectual causes, i.e., by causes not given in the spatial world. Ultimately, all motives could be reduced to the influence of external objects, as the difference between sensible and intellectual would be entirely lost. We would be sensibly receptive only to material stimulation, not to intellectual motives. To us, other agents would be "visible" objects or things, never "invisible" subjects or "persons." Sensibility would have no *practical* employment (in Kant's strong sense of the term), that is, no pure moral feeling would be possible (no sense of respect—neither for the law nor for other persons). This position is common to all eudemonistic philosophies. Epicurus's radical reduction of all pleasures to bodily pleasures expresses the extreme consequence drawn from this standpoint.[71] Eventually, to assume that the acting subject is determined *in itself* by the condition of space means to render not only a formal component of practical sensibility but practical reason itself impossible. It means to reduce the invisible body of the free agent—the body that can only be practically recognized by its feelings (more precisely, by those feelings which offer an a priori connection to reason) but never known in its motives through its acts—to the naturally given, visible body that can always be known as an object or thing among similar natural objects.[72]

By recognizing that time and space are merely conditions of one's phenomenal existence and that reason's intelligible causality through freedom escapes the determination of *both* time and space, the subject gains a view that extends to *all* her actions in the phenomenal world, and hence can be applied to *all* manifestations of feeling and sentiment shaping her character of sensible being.

Every action and, in general, *every changing determination of [the subject's] existence in the inner sense, even the entire succession of his existence as a sensible being,* is seen in the consciousness of his intelligible existence as nothing but a *consequence* of his causality as a noumenon, not as a determining ground.[73]

The view gained by recognizing the phenomenal nature of time and space and the intelligible character of freedom is not a flight from sensibility and from our sensible nature. On the contrary, such a view allows for the "great revelation" of freedom's realization in the sensible world, i.e., allows us to live and experience in a different way our existence of sensible rational beings endowed with a free will. Kant makes two points. On the one hand, he underlines that the consciousness of freedom shapes the *entire* phenomenon of the agent's character (it does not induce the feeling of respect only); while on the other hand, he projects the effects of moral determination on our existence as *sensible* beings (not only on our intelligible *Bestimmung*). Accordingly, we are conscious of freedom's presence in *"every* action" we undertake, of its influence on *"every* changing determination" of our existence in the inner sense—i.e., on every successive internal determination and modification of our self, on every deliberation-process in which our will engages. Freedom shapes our sensible character in its wholeness. Herein, Kant's claim parallels his description of moral feeling as one that presents the structure of a unique universal principle and itself issues from a unique principle: again, moral feeling "is no particular feeling but a general manner of considering something from the universal point of view."[74]

Moreover, freedom is independent of the condition of time, and yet exercises influences and produces consequences that manifest themselves as changes in the inner sense (in time). The condition of time is now re-introduced, as it were, in our practical evaluation of ourselves, of our actions, and of the succession of our deeds that constitute our existence as agents in the sensible world. Freedom is independent of space, and yet affects us in the way in which we morally relate to the outside world as embodied beings: we direct our action, feelings, and emotions not to objects or things— external bodies recognizable by sensible properties (as color, shape, physical appearance)—but to other persons. We consider them not as means to pleasure but as ends in themselves. Persons are embodied in forms that are impenetrable to theoretical knowledge (sensible intuition) for, as persons, they are not appearances in space and time. Yet it is not inscrutable properties of metaphysical souls that constitute them as persons, but features that can be recognized only by moral insight and that affect us through moral feeling (induce respect or call for benevolence). Not only are we aware that temporal and spatial conditions are not the determining ground of our action but we also know that what appears under those conditions as change in our inner self and as appearance to our external self is in "consequence" of our own causality as noumenon—not the inexorable effect of nature's mechanism. Being conscious of our freedom, we relate differently to the world and to our own nature as sensible creatures. We become responsible for our feelings as well as for the external manifestation of our actions. On this view, freedom has the further *consequence* of shaping our entire sensible existence and affecting the way in which we feel and exist as sensible beings. This is the step that the second *Critique* undertakes beyond the first. The idea of a moral cultivation of emotions and feelings, central to Kant's later *Doctrine of Virtue* (and to the *Critique of Judgment*), is the direct corollary of this fundamental thesis of the second *Critique*.

Thus, the result of the new perspective on the relation between moral principle and moral feeling disclosed by the Elucidation is a radical change in the character of our *affectivity*. Kant makes two suggestions. First, he introduces the idea of an *intelligible determinability of our entire sensible being*. On this account, *every* manifestation of our sensible character (and not only the unique feeling of respect) may be considered as a "consequence" of the determination of the will through the moral law.[75] For example, on Kant's account, the feeling of love for other human beings cannot be commanded and perceived as a duty—it is a matter of feeling and not of willing. However, the development of this feeling can follow, as a consequence, from our acting morally towards our fellow human beings. On Kant's view, love for other human beings is not the condition for doing good to them but is a feeling that arises from our moral behavior. It is an effect of morality on our feelings that produces the education and cultivation of our sensible nature. In the case of "beneficence," Kant argues that the saying 'you ought to love your neighbor as yourself'

> does not mean that you ought *immediately* (*first*) to love him and (*afterwards*) *by means of this love* do good to him. It means rather *do good* to your fellow man, and *your beneficence will produce love of man in you* (as an aptitude of the inclination to beneficence in general).[76]

Once again, a crucial question of (causal) order is at stake. Only what is moral can come "first" (as motive), determine the will "immediately," and have the force of an imperative or duty ("do good"). Feeling follows as effect (is *bewirkt*): in this case, what follows is not (only) respect, but another "moral" feeling, namely, love of other human beings. Thus, in the practical sphere, our sensibility is the capacity of receiving moral determination, capacity of being emotionally shaped by the moral law, capacity of having feelings that do not determine us to action but are determined by moral action.

Second, Kant suggests the notion of an *intellectual receptivity of our sensible nature*—an idea that seems to play the same mediating function between two heterogeneous things such as intellectual and sensible (character/causality), which he attributes to the "schema." Already in the first *Critique,* the general feature that defines sensibility in contrast to understanding's activity and spontaneity is "receptivity."[77] Receptivity is passivity, determinability (*Bestimmbarkeit*) through externally given objects, and the capacity for being *affected* (*affiziert*)—and thereby modified[78]—by them. In the practical sphere, sensibility in general indicates the passivity of pathological affection. The capacity for being affected is susceptibility or affectivity—*Empfänglichkeit.* Affectivity is dependence on the material existence of the object from which we expect pleasure and which we consequently desire. It defines the sphere of "feeling" as opposed to "understanding." For it institutes a relation to the subject (and not to the object), and has "practical" value in relation to the faculty of desire (and not cognitive value in relation to the understanding, as sensation and intuition do).[79] The traditional, merely empirical construct of the faculty of desire (*Begehrungsvermögen*) is predicated precisely on this notion of susceptibility or affectivity. Kant makes this clear in the opening of the *Critique of Practical Reason,* where his effort is to introduce a purely *formal* principle of determination of the will—one that is not based on our empirical affectivity or susceptibility to desire. Since a principle based on our *Empfänglichkeit* can only be material, empirical, and subjective, the highest principle of morality cannot be based on this defining feature of our sensibility. If reason has to be practical, the faculty of desire must be separated from the determinability offered by our sensible affectivity (it must be defined through its spontaneity not through its receptivity). However, *Empfänglichkeit* is constitutive of the human being as sensible creature; it cannot be simply cast aside and ignored by moral inquiry. And yet, this feature can be *modified* by practical reason's causality so that it can reappear as the sensible basis on which the intelligible causality of freedom (and not the mechanical causality of material objects) is exercised. This confirms Kant's view that sensibility is not an original *datum* rooted in an allegedly eternal "human nature" that can only be accepted and observed but not modified. On Kant's account, affectivity becomes a sensible construct or effect of freedom's intelligible causality—a product of freedom. In the practical sphere, receptivity is not the condition for the will's determination through the moral principle but its consequence or effect. As such, it no longer indicates the capacity of being affected by material, visible objects (nor is it the a priori condition for our knowledge of them). It designates a peculiar "sense" for the invisible, moral property of embodied agents as noumena; it expresses our susceptibility to freedom's effects. Here we meet again the notion of moral feeling.

At the beginning of the Analytic of the second *Critique,* Kant claims that our *Empfänglichkeit* for pleasure and displeasure (1) yields affections that can, in each case, "only be *known* empirically"; (2) yields affections that are not universally valid—i.e., are not valid "in the same form for all rational beings"; (3) yields no "principle"—not even for the subject of that receptivity, because her affections lack "objective necessity, which must be known a priori"; and (4) that *Empfänglichkeit,* being susceptibility to the pleasure in the existence of objects, has material character.[80] This description must be contrasted to the way in which Kant presents moral feeling in the last part of the Analytic on the drives of pure practical reason. There he offers the transcendental transformation of affectivity by showing how, once displaced from the site of being *ground* of the will's determinability to the site of being *effect* of an intellectual determination, each one of the abovementioned characters of *Empfänglichkeit* is consequently modified. Moral feeling is empirical susceptibility or receptivity to an *intelligible* cause that, accordingly: (1) can be *known a priori* in relation to its origin, namely, to the intellectual causality of practical reason; (2) is *universally valid* for all rational and yet sensible beings, i.e., for those beings for which reason can become *Triebfeder* or subjective ground of determination; (3) is a feeling that *follows from the moral principle,* not from the affection of objects, and hence is subjectively necessary; and (4) does not depend on the *material* existence of particular objects but rests solely on the *form* of the moral law to which it owes a sort of derivative "formal" character.

The *Doctrine of Virtue* of the *Metaphysics of Morals* confirms all of these elements of Kant's theory of moral feeling. These should be read in light of the transcendental foundation that the idea of practical sensibility—or the "aesthetic" of freedom—receives in the last chapter of the *Critique of Practical Reason.* They are not elements of a moral psychology or anthropology, as they do not depend on an assumed "human nature." The introduction to the *Doctrine of Virtue* (§XII) deals with the "Aesthetic Pre-Concepts of the *Gemüt*'s Receptivity to Concepts of Duty as such."[81] Kant's presentation of "moral feeling, conscience, love of one's neighbor, and respect for oneself" and for other persons, systematically presupposes and is based on the argument of the second *Critique* reconstructed above. These "aesthetic" concepts regard our "receptivity to the concept of duty"; they concern a form of sensibility (determinability) by which we are "sensitive" to *intellectual* determination despite the fact that such sensitiveness belongs entirely to our *sensibility*. How such receptivity is possible, that is, how is it possible to be *"affected"* by the concept of duty, is explained precisely by the second *Critique*.[82] Accordingly, Kant's claim that there are "moral endowments" (*Beschaffenheiten*) that we can have no duty of acquiring and yet are an integral part of morality is a claim based on the distinction between the *"subjective* conditions of the susceptibility to the concept of duty" and the "objective conditions of morality": those endowments are merely subjective conditions. Kant qualifies all those predispositions as "aesthetic." The "aesthetic state" of the *Gemüt* as "affection (*Affizierung*) of the inner sense" can be either "pathological" or "moral"—thereby repeating the crucial result of the analysis of the Drives of Pure Practical Reason. Those dispositions are "antecedent, but natural predispositions of the *Gemüt* (*praedispositio*) for being *affected* by the concept of duty"—hence, are not simply pathological. This is the point where the natural becomes moral. The origin of this transformation is not empirical (or psychological) but "transcendental." Its further development is the specific topic of Kant's applied moral philosophy and occupies the *Doctrine of Virtue* specifically. Herein, Kant's definition of "moral feeling" brings together the second *Critique*'s derivation of the feeling of respect and the more general issue of the transformation of *Empfänglichkeit* from being empirical receptivity to material pleasure in objects, to being receptivity to the formal determination of the moral law (as imperative), and receptivity to its obligation. Thus, moral feeling is defined as *"Empfänglichkeit* to feel pleasure or displeasure merely from the consciousness that our actions are consistent with or contrary to the law of duty." Kant's specific claim in the *Doctrine of Virtue* is that there can be no duty to have or acquire moral feeling since the consciousness of moral obligation "depends upon moral feeling to make us aware of the constraint present in the thought of duty." There can only be a duty to "cultivate" and strengthen this feeling. This is Kant's step beyond the second *Critique*. In the 1788 work, Kant maintains that no feeling can be the ground of the moral principle. In the *Doctrine of Virtue,* he claims that moral feeling is the ground of our consciousness of the obligation connected to the moral law as principle of duty. On Kant's account, moral feeling is "natural" or is "originally" inscribed in the constitution of the "human being" (*Mensch*) as "moral being."[83] Susceptibility to this kind of feeling distinguishes human beings from animals (as well as from God). Obviously, however, this claim means neither that moral feeling is given to us by nature nor that feeling is the first ground of moral determination. Moral feeling, for Kant, is transcendentally the a priori form of the embodied human agent as moral person.

In the 1793 *Religion within the Limits of Reason Alone,* Kant characterizes *Empfänglichkeit* by directly referring to the concept of "personality." Susceptibility to the feeling of respect for the moral law is not only an *"Anlage"* of the human being as opposed to animals but is constitutive, more precisely, of the notion of *"Persönlichkeit"* and to its actual realization in the world of nature and history. By addressing the "Original Disposition to Good in Human Nature," Kant presents the "elements of the determination of the human being" with regard to its end in the following progression: (1) "the disposition to the *animality (Thierheit)* of the human being as a *living* being," (2) "the disposition to its *humanity (Menschheit)* as a living and, at the same time, *rational* being," and (3) "the disposition to its *personality (Persönlichkeit)* as a rational being that, at the same time, is *subject to imputability."*[84] The disposition to personality is defined as "the *Empfänglichkeit* for respect for the moral law as a *Triebfeder* of the will *(Willkür) that is in itself sufficient."* Thus, one of the crucial elements that define moral personality is the intellectual transformation of sensible affectivity that issues from Kant's purely formal foundation of the principle of morality, namely, the capacity to feel respect for the moral law. Furthermore, Kant maintains that receptivity for moral feeling is the ground for *imputability.* The capacity of feeling respect for the law becomes an end of the natural disposition of the human being insofar as this feeling is drive of the will, i.e., insofar as the moral law becomes subjective maxim of the will. Thus incorporated into the will, moral feeling gives rise to "good character." This, as any feature of the free will, is not something given but a disposition that can only be acquired *(erworben)*[85] and developed. Herein lies the difference between the claim of the second *Critique* on the one hand, and the arguments of the *Religion* and the *Doctrine of Virtue* on the other. While the 1788 work aims first at the transcendental foundation of the pure principle of morality, and only then at the construction of the human agent that enacts that principle, the latter works are concerned with the actual enactment of the principle under contingent empirical conditions (its proper application). Kant maintains that

> the idea of the moral law by itself, along with the respect that cannot be separated from it, cannot be called a disposition to personality; it is personal-

ity itself (the idea of humanity considered in a completely intellectual way). However, the fact that we take up this feeling in our maxims and make a drive of it [. . .] seems to be an addition to personality whereby it deserves the name of a disposition that favors it.[86]

These passages of the *Religion* and the *Doctrine of Virtue* testify to the far-reaching implications of the last chapter of the Analytic of the second *Critique*.

Embodied Persons and Moral Choices

The second chapter of the Analytic deals with the "concept of an object (*Gegenstand*) of pure practical reason."[87] At stake is the general question of what moral judgment or practical cognition are concerned with—what does it mean "to decide whether or not something is an object of *pure practical reason*"? Kant's answer is that the problem of the object of pure practical reason is the problem of moral decision itself, i.e., is the issue of discerning "the possibility or impossibility of *willing* the action by which a certain object would be made actual." To be sure, Kant's formulation recognizes that to discern the possibility or impossibility of the act of willing something hinges upon the evaluation of our having or not having the ability to bring it about. But this is part of the problem that can only be addressed by experience and its contingencies.[88] However, if decision rested on the latter evaluation, i.e., if in order to decide whether something can be an object of pure practical reason we *first* had to be sure of our capacity of making it actual, then the problem of moral deliberation would escape the transcendental inquiry as it would be an empirical matter (a matter of prudence and estimation of our physical force). Accordingly, to avoid this result, Kant's strategy is to show that decision is indeed dependent on the evaluation of our ability of making something happen, i.e., of our being in control of its conditions and of the means to bring it about, but only in the case that the "determining ground" of our will is, directly, the "object" itself in its existence. In this case, the determination of the will is empirical, is based upon our receptivity to material motives and desires, has neither necessity nor universality, and the will is not free. Decision is neither moral nor free. On the contrary, only if the *Bestimmungsgrund* of our will is not the material object but the a priori determining form of the moral law, then our decision is rendered completely independent of our physical ability to realize certain effects as well as independent of the conditions (time and space) of phenomenal events that fall under (or outside of) our control. The foundational gesture of Kant's moral philosophy radically changes the nature of the process of decision in which the will engages since it transforms the question of *what we decide upon* when we ask whether we ought to will something as "object" of pure practical reason. Thus, Kant contends that at stake in this question is not the evaluation of the "*physical* possibility" of the realization of the object by means of the free use of our forces, but a judgment regarding the "*moral* possibility" of the action itself, namely, whether the action must be the object of our will.[89] In other words, the physical body and its capabilities are not part of the moral decision. In a reversal that by now we can easily recognize, the opposite is rather the case: what constitutes the (transfigured) body of the agent and what it can do is a *consequence* that follows from the will's purely moral determination. It is moral decision that determines what we can do; it is not what we can physically do that determines what we ought to will. The body that performs the moral action is no longer the merely physical body—it is the body of the moral *person,* i.e., a body that is empowered by the enactment of the agent's freedom. This gives a new perspective on Kant's claim according to which *Sollen* grounds *Können*—"you ought to, then you can."

In what follows, I show that the process of deliberation, along with the formation of moral feeling, are the two places in which Kant's transcendental inquiry addresses the problem of freedom's *realization* or of its *effects* in the phenomenal world—that is, the issue of practical reason's transcendental embodiment.[90] Thereby, the structure of moral personality as embodied person is instituted at the intersection of intelligible and sensible character. I argue that in Kant's view freedom does not appear in the phenomenal world as the empirical action itself, taken in its observable consequences. Freedom's effects appear, instead, in the (theoretically) inscrutable process of deliberation that takes place in the subject's inner sense, implies a confrontation with sensible drives, unfolds under the condition of time, and, more importantly, *precedes* action (and hence cannot be one with it).[91] Thereby, the process of deliberation rescues the subject's causality from the natural causality of the mechanism and institutes her character as a person accountable and responsible for her own actions in the sensible world. The moral person, as reconciled unity of body and mind, is Kant's *practical* substitute of the metaphysical notion of personality, which, as disembodied soul, occupied rational psychology in vain.

In the solution of the third antinomy, in a group of pages that we have already analyzed, Kant's argument aims at showing that "reason's ideas really/effectively (*wirklich*)" exercise "causality with regard to human actions as appearances" insofar as these actions are determined not by empirical causes but "through grounds of reason."[92] Free action is determined "in the intelligible character" or "*Denkungsart*" which, Kant maintains, we cannot know theoretically in the way we know the cause of all natural events. However, we do "indicate" (*bezeichnen*) the intelligible character "through appearances that properly let us know immediately only the *Sinnesart*" or empirical character. In the perspective of theoretical knowledge, the "true morality of actions" remains "entirely hidden to us."[93] In this regard, there is no difference between other agents and ourselves: even the morality of our own behavior, i.e., our true intentions, escapes our cognition and self-awareness. In the *Groundwork,* Kant makes it clear that experience cannot provide any certain example of an action performed exclusively for the sake of duty. Not even the most acute introspection can help us discover the true determining ground of action:

> It often happens that in the keenest self-examination, we find absolutely nothing except basic moral duty that could have been powerful enough to move us to this or that good action [. . .]. But it cannot be ruled out with certainty that in fact some secret impulse of self-love, under the mere pretense of this idea, has been the real determining cause of the will. For this we gladly flatter ourselves by falsely appropriating a nobler motivational ground. But, in fact, even the most strenuous probing of our hidden motives yields absolutely nothing, because *when the issue is moral worth, it is not about the actions one sees but rather about their internal principles that one does not see.*[94]

It follows that, within the perspective of what we can know, the only criterion for imputability is a relation to what we can "see," namely, the empirical character, and consequently a relation to our causality insofar as it is strictly determined by the laws of nature's mechanism. Herein, however, no difference can be discerned between the "pure effect of freedom," the contribution of "mere nature," and the "defect of temperament, which is not culpable."[95] Freedom is, at this level, impossible—and along with it true morality, moral worth, and accountability. We can know directly only the agent's empirical character, only that which we can see. If this knowledge pretends to appraise the agent's freedom, it necessarily fails since it cannot provide a criterion for accountability that can distinguish between the subject's empirical "temperament," the contribution of mechanical causes, and freedom's spontaneity. This difference is indeed invisible. And yet, Kant suggests that the empirical character does have a certain relation to the intelligible since it is its "sensible schema."[96] In this function, it can offer a clue to the way in which reason does have causality with regard to appearances and to human actions as appearances.

The passage of the *Groundwork* confirms an additional crucial point. The "effects" of practical reason in the sensible world cannot be represented by something merely observable, such as empirical action. They must be effects invisible to the eye of theoretical cognition and yet discernable to our moral sense—with that same eye that, at the end of the *Critique of Practical Reason,* is able to "see" the "starry sky above me" and the "moral law within me."[97]

> Now, the action, insofar as it has to be attributed to the *Denkungsart* as its cause, does not thereby ensue from it according to empirical laws, i.e., so that the conditions of pure reason *precede* it, but only *so that their effects in the appearance of the inner sense precede* it. Pure reason, as merely intelligible faculty, is not subject to the form of time [. . .]. Reason's causality in the intelligible character does not arise or begin, in some way, at a certain time in order to produce an effect. For otherwise it would be itself subject to the natural law of appearances, insofar as this determines causal series according to time, and hence would be nature and not freedom. Thus, we could say: if reason can have causality with regard to appearances, then it is a faculty *through* (*durch*) which *the sensible condition of an empirical series of effects first begins.* For the condition that lies *in* reason is not sensible and hence does not itself begin.[98]

At stake in this central passage is the way in which reason can be said to exercise free causality (i.e., produce effects) with regard to appearances once the distinction between intelligible and sensible character has been introduced. For Kant's claim is that reason's "appearances" are the "way in which reason manifests itself (*sich zeigt*) in its effects."[99] The crucial issue of imputation is raised in this connection. Accountability and moral responsibility follow from the idea of freedom and imply the possibility for the subject to relate her own actions to laws. The issue of imputability arises in conjunction with the problem of constituting the moral subject to whom actions can be ascribed. It should be noted, however, that the second *Critique* addresses the problem of the foundation of the principle of morality— and hence the issue of the identity of the principle of morality and the idea of freedom—independently of any question concerning the "subject" of freedom. For the idea of moral personality follows from the pure foundation of the principle of morality at the beginning of the Analytic.[100]

In the passage of the first *Critique* quoted above, Kant structures the problem, once again, as a problem of order: *by what* is free action "*preceded*"?[101] Both free action and action according to natural causality follow laws and are based on determinate "conditions." In the case of empirical laws, the conditions of pure reason and the temporal series on which the intelligibility of the effect is based precede the action or the event, and allow for the possibility of its cognition as an effect. Kant thereby suggests that, in this case, there is no decision involved: when all rational conditions are given, the appearance of the event necessarily (and mechanically) follows. The effect of natural causality is identical with (is the manifestation of) the event or action itself. Such action is not voluntary. In the case of free action, on the contrary, the situation is more complex. In this case, three terms are involved: (1) pure reason's conditions or the law, (2) "their effects in the appearance of the inner sense," and (3) action itself. Action is now *preceded* by the effects that reason's conditions produce in the inner sense—i.e., is not preceded by these conditions directly. This means that action cannot be identical with those effects. Hence, the first conclusion: practical reason's effect in the world of appearance is *not* the empirical action itself. Practical reason is not the immediate cause of action in the sensible world.[102] What is it, then, that reason produces as effect? What are its effects with regard to appearance and, more precisely, "in the appearance of the inner sense"? Kant's suggestion meets here with the theses of the Analytic of the second *Critique*. He tells us *where* we should look for those effects. The claim is that the effects of reason's free causality *appear* in the agent's inner sense and thereby *come before* the action. Practical reason does not directly produce empirical action. It prompts a process of deliberation from which action first begins through the will. Hence Kant's thesis: the effect of freedom in the world of appearance is the *inner process of deliberation* that makes of the subject a moral person (as opposed to an object of cognition) and renders her action a *voluntary,* free action (as opposed to a mere natural, necessary event) so that action can rightly be imputed to her.

Kant contends that pure reason, being practical, exercises its effects "in the appearance of the inner sense," i.e., in a process that is subject to the condition of time, develops in a temporal succession, and can be the "object" of our awareness. This is the inner process of deliberation that involves the will as middle term between pure reason and the actual occurrence of the action. In the formulation of the second *Critique,* at stake is the *decision* on whether or not an action ought to be undertaken once the will is determined not by the representation of the object but by the pure form of the law. This evaluation must *precede* the action itself as its condition. The process of moral deliberation concerns the "moral possibility"—not the "physical possibility"—of the action. It affects the action by specifying its form and intentional content in accordance with the universal and necessary conditions of practical reason (the moral law). In turn, the process of deliberation is prompted not by the material desire for an object (i.e., does not fall under empirical conditions), but is effected through pure reason itself (i.e., by the will's formal determination through the law). Moral deliberation is not *determined* by the condition of time because pure reason itself, as intelligible faculty, is not subject to the form of time. Decision, however, is a process that does appear in time, i.e., takes place in the inner sense. It follows that reason itself does not decide, does not begin an action (no action begins "in" reason); it *determines* the intelligible character formally and outside of the temporal series. Thus, it is "through" reason's determination that deliberation must take place and action can first begin. Hence, Kant argues that if reason has to have causality with regard to appearances, then it must be the faculty "*through which*" (not in which)[103] "*the sensible condition of an empirical series of effects first begins.*" Practical reason intellectually determines the will to begin the process of deliberation (hence, this process begins *in* the will *through* reason). Such a process, in turn, provides the sensible condition from which a series of effects, namely action, arises and is actualized in the world. Reason is the faculty "through which" the will's deliberation first begins by finding its sensible condition. Practical reason sufficiently determines the will through the moral law. However, in order for this determination *to appear* as effect in the inner sense, and for consciousness to arise, a sensible condition (i.e., a feeling or an interest) is needed. In the case of the human will, the objective ground of determination needs to become subjective ground as well. This sensible condition specifies the content of the intentional "object" of the will, i.e., the action, in accordance with the universal form of the law (it evaluates its moral possibility). Furthermore, it provides the motivational force or the "subjective" *Triebfeder* that the will needs to incorporate into the objective ground given by the moral principle in order for action to ensue.[104] The moral law, we have seen, becomes itself *Triebfeder* for the will (whereby moral feeling arises as effect).

In a *Reflexion* on Baumgarten's *Metaphysica* concerning the notion of *arbitrium,* Kant explains the specific character of free action through the fact that reason, in this case, becomes "*wirkendes und treibendes principium*"— i.e., a force that has the power of producing effects and of moving the will as a drive, whereby it "*takes the place* of a natural cause" (*die Stelle einer Naturursache vertrete*). However, theoretical cognition cannot understand how this is possible. The question that Kant raises in this connection sheds light on the passage of the first *Critique* just analyzed. In this *Reflexion,* he addresses the issue of "how the representation of the good in general, that makes abstraction from my own condition, *can nonetheless have effect on my condition,* and how this consideration, which itself contains no affection

(*Affektion*), can be contained in the series of the appearances of nature."[105] At stake here is not the problem of the will's determination. It is rather the issue of the translation of the pure determination of the will in the realm of appearance—the translation of a formal and abstract determination into a "personal" motive to moral action (how can the general representation of the good have an effect on my own condition as moral agent?). Kant's suggestion is that freedom manifests itself not directly in action but in the appearance of the inner sense, i.e., in the process of deliberation through which the moral law becomes subjective *Triebfeder* and produces sensible effects on feelings. Thereby, Kant's argument grounds the distinction between *Wille* and *Willkür* that, terminologically, is introduced only in the 1790s.[106] In the later formulations of the *Metaphysics of Morals* (1797), *Wille* is practical reason itself as the legislative power or as "the faculty of desire considered not so much in relation to action (as *Willkür* or choice is), but rather in relation to the ground determining choice to action."[107] *Willkür*, on the contrary, is the executive power of deliberation or the faculty of choice, *arbitrium*, which relates to action itself. "Laws proceed from *Wille*, maxims from *Willkür*." The human being's *Willkür* is free, while *Wille*, which is identical with practical reason in its legislation, cannot be called either free or unfree because "it is not directed to actions but immediately to giving laws for the maxims of actions."[108]

At the end of Kant's argument in the same passage of the first *Critique,* the thesis that pure reason indeed has causality with regard to appearances reads as follows: "Thus, reason is the *permanent condition of all voluntary actions under which the human being appears.*"[109] Kant makes two distinct points here. First, he infers that since reason's effect is the process of deliberation through which the will resolves to action, practical reason is the condition of *all voluntary* actions as such—just as nature is the condition of *all* mechanistic events (in which no will or choice is involved). Whenever deliberation takes place, practical reason is present as its unitary and permanent condition.[110] Reason's effects in the world of appearance, already qualified as "human actions"[111] are now, more specifically, "*voluntary* actions." Second, Kant maintains that what "appears" or manifests itself in these voluntary actions is the human being—*Mensch*—as unity of sensible and intelligible character. Voluntary actions are the appearance of the human being as moral agent or person, i.e., as the subject to which actions can be ascribed or imputed on the basis of the deliberation process that has led to them.

In sum, reason appears in instituting the process of the will's deliberation by providing the beginning of a sensible condition (a feeling or an

interest) through which the will specifies the intentional object of its action with regard to its "moral possibility." Deliberation produces voluntary
actions; voluntary actions are actions that can be ascribed to an agent who
is morally responsible for their occurrence; they are actions that are not *exclusively* determined by the condition of time but rest on the unconditioned
causality of reason that prompts the will's (*Willkür*) decision process. Voluntary actions are not just the appearance of reason or rationality as such.
They are, more specifically, manifestations of the "human being": i.e., of
a rational being endowed with *arbitrium sensitivum* or *Willkür* which "has
an empirical character that is the (empirical) cause of all his actions,"[112] is
subject to feelings and emotions, is in need of subjective impulses or drives
to action, but is also determinable objectively and exclusively by the pure
form of the moral law. To conclude, Kant's complex argument indicates in
the human being as moral person the unified subject of an intelligible and
an empirical character. The moral person is the embodiment of transcendental freedom.

The concept of person indicates the embodied human agent to which
voluntary actions can be imputed. This notion is central both to Kant's
moral philosophy and to his philosophy of right.[113] In the *Religion,* the concept of "personality" (*Persönlichkeit*) defines a rational being to which actions
can be imputed, whereby a specifically *moral* qualification is added to the
idea of "humanity" (*Menschheit*). The idea of the moral law is "personality"
itself.[114] Similarly, in the *Metaphysics of Morals,* "moral personality" defines
the very idea of "freedom of a rational being under moral laws." Moreover,
"imputability" marks the difference between persons and things: while "a
person (*Person*) is a subject whose actions can be imputed to him," "a thing
(*Ding*) is that to which nothing can be imputed."[115] Only persons are free
agents, and only towards persons can the feeling of respect—and hence
the intelligible aspect of our affectivity—be directed. Thus, the notion of
personality defines the intersubjective dimension of Kant's moral world.[116]
We recognize other agents as persons when we relate to them as subjects
responsible for their actions on the basis of the voluntary deliberation process that has spurred them to action; we relate to persons as ends and not as
means; we feel respect towards other persons, and we act according to the
maxim of beneficence and of analogous moral feelings.

The first systematic occurrence of the notion of "personality" in the
second *Critique* is in the table of the categories of freedom. Herein, it appears under the title of the categories of relation: substance is modified
as relation to personality; cause as relation to the state of the person; and

reciprocal action is the community or reciprocity of the relation of one person to the state of other persons.[117] This table establishes that relation to personality, to the state of a person, and to the community of persons respectively is the *conceptual condition* for the recognition of an event as action and, specifically, as moral action. First, it is the relation to a person that allows one to understand an event as a possible moral action—an action is "good" for and to a person. A subject is a person insofar as it is an agent that, persisting throughout its intentions and volitions in the deliberation process (substance), decides on the intention that determines to action. Second, all action must be considered with regard to "the state of a person," i.e., must be explained as consequence or effect of the condition (physical or psychological) of a person; an action is moral when it arises out of the moral determination of the person's will. Finally, all action is set in the context of reciprocity or community with the actions of other persons. It is essential to moral action that it can be recognized by another person as an action imputable to a determinate agent and following from this agent's intentions and volition. The concept of action implies, as it were, the idea of an intersubjective community of persons.

In the second *Critique,* Kant summarizes the connection between reason and sensibility in the unitary phenomenon of personality by claiming that

> reason, when it is a question of the law of our intelligible existence (the moral law), acknowledges no temporal distinctions and *only asks whether the event belongs to me as my act,* and *then it morally connects with it always the same feeling, whether the event occurs now or is long since past.*

Thereby, imputability as defining mark of personality replaces temporal determination in Kant's description of moral agency. The response of feeling—in this case the pain of repentance—is now transformed accordingly. This response does not depend, in turn, on time conditions and its contingencies (as it does not depend on when the action was committed). Feeling, in this case, rests exclusively on the intelligible character of imputation, i.e., on whether or not the event can be attributed to me as a voluntary act, and, in this regard, is a feeling that does not itself change. As product of reason, it remains always "the same feeling" throughout—under all temporal conditions and for all agents as persons. In this way, Kant presents a new perspective from which to judge our "sensible life" or "life of the senses"—*Sinnenleben.*

> Our *Sinnenleben,* with regard to the intelligible consciousness of its existence (of freedom) has the absolute unity of a phenomenon (*absolute Einheit eines*

Phänomens) that, insofar as it contains only appearances of the moral intention (*Gesinnung*) which concerns the moral law (appearances of character), must be judged not according to natural necessity but according to the absolute spontaneity of freedom.[118]

Thus, through the idea of personality by way of which actions appear as voluntary and are claimed by a moral agent as her actions, our *entire sensible life* (or our whole life as sensible beings) is invested with a moral meaning and recognized as the appearance of character, moral disposition, and freedom. Sensible life itself (and not just the intelligible character) is now judged according to freedom.

Kant's concept of moral person is the practical solution of the paralogisms in which rational psychology remains inexorably locked up in its attempts to ground a speculative notion of personality based on the dualism of body and soul. The critique of the paralogisms leads Kant to abandon the speculative use of the notion of personality.[119] While personality cannot be predicated of the disembodied soul, in the practical sphere "person" indicates the embodied human being endowed with an intelligible and a sensible character, purely determinable by the intellectual causality of practical reason, and sensitive to moral feelings. Thereby, the human agent fully responsible for all her actions is a person that is free in and through her own body—not in abstraction from it. She is a person that does not sacrifice bodily desires, feelings, and emotions, but knows how to shape and transform her desires, feelings, and emotions according to an intellectual susceptibility or receptivity gained through and cultivated by the moral determination of her will. In this transformation, sensibility is not opposed to but is rather the indispensable ally of freedom's spontaneity.

Part 3
THE BODY REFLECTED

Les huîtres ont, dit-on, deux sens.

Les taupes, quatre. Les autres animaux,

Commes les hommes, cinq : quelques

Personnes en admettent un sixième.

—VOLTAIRE

7

Aesthetics of the Body

Enlightenment is not a place, no use rushing to get there
—ANNE CARSON, *Plainwater*

IN THE CONCLUSION OF THE *MEDITATIONES PHILOSOPHICAE de nonnullis ad poema pertinentibus* (1735) and then in his *Aesthetica* (1750/58), Baumgarten proposes the idea of a new scientific discipline that should parallel and complement logic by presenting a theory of "sensible cognition." According to Baumgarten's famous definition, "*Aesthetica (theoria liberalium artium, gnoseologia inferior, ars pulchre cogitandi, ars analogi rationis) est scientia cognitionis sensitivae.*"[1] Following the ideal of science promoted by German eighteenth-century scholasticism, "aesthetics" must be developed as "science," address the "lower faculties of the soul," function as "lower gnoseology," and thereby work as an *analogon rationis*. Within the framework of his theory of knowledge, for which Baumgarten introduces the neologism *gnoseologia*, aesthetics is the "science of sensible cognition" and parallels logic as the science of rational cognition. *Sensitivus* is the Latin translation of the Greek *aisthetikos*, out of which Baumgarten coins the Graecism *aesthetica*. The term is thereby introduced for the first time in philosophy as the title for an independent discipline. Baumgarten's aesthetics has the merit of promoting the topic of sensibility to a dignity of its own. Thereby, he rehabilitates the lowest, darkest region of the soul—the *fundus animae* or *grunt der sêle*, which after Eckhart and departing from his view came to designate the confused and inscrutable depths of the soul. In Wolff's empirical psychology, the

"kingdom of darkness (*regnum tenebrarum*)"[2] of the soul had a merely negative significance and indicated only a "defect in perception." Baumgarten
is the first to attribute to the sensible representations that populate this
realm—and remained ignored, on his account, by most philosophers[3]—the
positive meaning of Eckhart's *fundus animae*. In Eckhart's doctrine, however,
the *grunt der sêle* is neither the lowest part nor the most obscure region of
the soul. It is, on the contrary, the pure light that is immediate knowledge
of itself and of all things, the source of all the faculties of the soul and its
innermost essence, the point of utmost proximity to god, and the place of
the subject's pure self-determination. Moreover, in Eckhart's view, the *grunt*
der sêle escapes any ontological or psychological hierarchy, for hierarchiza-
tion can only concern the soul's faculties, not their uncreated source (their
grunt). Scholastic anthropology and psychology later imposed on Eckhart's
original idea the hierarchy of lower and higher (*inferior* and *superior*) faculties
of the soul that is still alive in Kant's writings.[4] Following this tradition,
Baumgarten places the *Grund der Seele* at the bottom of the hierarchy, and
yet recognizes, against Wolff, both its cognitive accessibility and its specific
and positive content. Thereby the sphere of aesthetics marks the lowest limit
of cognition and the origin of a peculiar *impetus aestheticus*.[5]

Baumgarten offers a rationalistic approach to an issue that traditionally
led either to the assimilation of sensibility to logic or to epistemological
skepticism. In the first case, since sense-apprehension and concept-forma-
tion are not distinct in kind but merge psychologically into each other, sensibility loses its autonomy with regard to the higher concept. In the second
case, the uncorrectable subjectivity and relativity of sensibility lends itself to
the skeptical doubt that undermines the truth of sensible cognition. In the
Leibnizian tradition endorsed by Baumgarten, sensible representations are
the most indistinct and confused ideas. Sensible cognition deals with ideas
or representations that can never be distinct—even though they may very
well be clear. It is precisely the clarity of indistinct representations that constitutes the "perfection" of sensible cognition.[6] Here Baumgarten takes up
Leibniz's doctrine and claims that sensible perfection is "beauty." Thereby,
the important link between sensible cognition and the idea of the beautiful
is established for the first time under the name of aesthetics.

Baumgarten's aesthetics is based upon two general assumptions rooted
in the tradition of German scholasticism. First, as a branch of "gnoseology,"
aesthetics admits sensibility in science *exclusively with regard to the cognitive*
faculty and in relation to its cognitive function. To the extent that the dark region
of the soul can be cognitively explored, it can also, at the same time, be

brought to the light of reason whereby darkness is fully dissipated. Second, despite its independence as a new discipline, *aesthetics is ultimately based upon empirical psychology as a branch of metaphysics.*[7] For aesthetics rests on the *psychological* classification of representations that builds an axiological hierarchy going from the "lower" region of sensibility to the "higher" realm of rationality. It is this classification that eventually allows Baumgarten to link sensible cognition, i.e., aesthetics, to beauty.

Baumgarten's legacy in the second half of the eighteenth century sees the development of the idea of aesthetics bound to the rejection (or to the radical reformulation) of both these assumptions. On the one hand, aesthetics aims at liberating itself from the exclusive relation to cognition (and hence from the relation to logic): sensibility will be accorded a special non-cognitive value, whereby the rehabilitation of the "lower" faculties of the soul is sanctioned. On the other hand, a new relation to psychology (or a relation to a new idea of psychology) is established: coupled with aesthetics, psychology finds an alternative to the *impasse* of traditional metaphysics, namely, out of the strictures represented by empirical and rational psychology. Since antiquity and until Baumgarten's introduction of aesthetics as a philosophical discipline, the topic of beauty—*to kalon* or *pulcher*—relates to issues of ethics and metaphysics. After Baumgarten, aesthetics as science of a peculiar form of human sensibility unifies a complex constellation of interests and fields of intellectual inquiry ranging from the theory of beauty and taste to psychology, anthropology, and physiology, from epistemology to ethics, from the investigation of the realm of organic nature to history.

Kant is the protagonist of the crucial transformation of aesthetics after Baumgarten. His transcendental and critical investigation overcomes both the psychology of traditional metaphysics and Baumgarten's rationalistic and cognitive aesthetic.[8] The confrontation with Baumgarten's theory of sensible cognition prompts Kant's new understanding of the role that sensibility plays in constituting philosophical discourse. This, in turn, leads to a new understanding of *philosophical* aesthetics or of aesthetics as science, and to a clarification of the legitimacy of the use of the term "aesthetic" in *transcendental* philosophy (as qualification of a certain type of judgments). Ultimately, Kant's critical reflection on aesthetics yields a radically new view of the relation between theoretical and practical philosophy, between logic, ethics, psychology, and anthropology. The systematic place of this new reflection is the last part of Kant's critical project, the *Critique of Judgment* (1790).

This chapter builds the transition from the first two *Critiques* to the *Critique of Judgment*. I show how the third *Critique* arises both historically and systematically out of Kant's longstanding reflection on and progressive refinement of the issue of human sensibility—*Sinnlichkeit* as realm of the *sensitivus*. With regard to Baumgarten's pioneering enterprise, the *Critique of Judgment* proposes a thoroughly different model for integrating sensibility into philosophical discourse.[9] Such is the peculiar perspective of *transcendental* philosophy, whose investigation has already led to the results of the first two *Critiques*. By opening up this perspective, Kant establishes ontological and epistemological conditions that radically break with the modern paradigm of the mind/body dualism. His aim is to overcome such metaphysical dualism by proposing not only a new concept of rationality but also a new, broadly construed notion of human sensibility that includes *Anschauung, Empfindung, Gefühl, Affekt/Affektion,* and *Einbildungskraft.* Kant's transcendental question is whether these modes of sensibility display a purely formal component that precedes (cognitive, practical, aesthetic) experience and makes this experience possible for the first time. In other words, the status that Kant is willing to recognize for sensibility (and hence, according to its etymology, for aesthetics) beyond Baumgarten—namely, its not exclusively cognitive function—is predicated on a view of the human being that is no longer the one proper to the rationalist and to the empiricist tradition. In the former, rational psychology dealt with a disembodied metaphysical soul and its properties; while the view of empirical psychology as a branch of metaphysics implied the reduction of all faculties to the theoretical one and hindered the important results of empirical research to connect with fields such as history, anthropology, and moral philosophy in a way that could positively defy materialism and skepticism. Aesthetics remains based on a rationalist account of the soul so that only its obscure ground can claim (with Baumgarten) an—albeit relative—independence. By contrast, in the empiricist tradition aesthetics is generally reduced to a physiology of our response to beauty and the sublime, and because of its empirical foundation, is ultimately unable to solve the standard problem of the rules of taste.

In the argument of the present chapter, the issue of aesthetics leads to a further discussion of the following general questions: what, for Kant, is the role of human sensibility in philosophical discourse after Baumgarten's rehabilitation of it through the discipline of aesthetics? How is aesthetics linked to a new idea of philosophy that draws the *embodied human being* to the center? In the preceding two parts of this book, we saw that in the critical period Kant's answer to these questions is provided by a transcendental perspective on aesthetics that looks for the formal a priori conditions of sensibility, i.e., for a *transcendental* and *"ideal" form* of human embodiment—in both the theoretical and the practical realms. Transfigured in its transcendental form, human sensibility is successively developed and articulated throughout an itinerary marked by the Transcendental Aesthetic of the *Critique of Pure Reason,* by the peculiar "aesthetics" of practical reason in the second *Critique,* and finally by the theory of "aesthetic judgment" of the *Critique of Judgment.* The last station of this itinerary is the focus of the third part of this book.

This chapter analyzes two issues. On the one hand, it discusses the relation between Kant's first and last aesthetic—namely, the Transcendental Aesthetic or doctrine of space and time of the first *Critique* and the theory of "aesthetic judgment" (*Urteilskraft*) of the third *Critique*. On the other hand, it shows how the crucial connection between aesthetic and morality—both in 1788 and 1790—is established by Kant on the basis of a new transcendental form of human sensibility, a pure "feeling" (of pleasure and displeasure). We have seen in the previous chapters how the idea of morality leads Kant to radically separate the way in which the moral agent is embodied as free agent, from the conditions of space and time valid in the realm of nature, and hence from the cognitive aesthetic of the *Critique of Pure Reason*. In the third *Critique,* Kant brings a new connection to the fore. Through the activity of aesthetic judgment and its peculiar principle, morality gains a new sensible (and yet symbolic) "body." This connection, which this chapter approaches and the next fully develops, sheds a new light on the problem of the "unity" of the human being—of its sensible and intelligible nature or character—a problem that Kant poses in the center of his 1790 work.

On the basis of what has been shown so far, preliminary questions need to be addressed. Since the traditional separation between soul or mind and body has already been healed within the transcendental perspective laid out in the first two *Critiques,* what is it that the new principle of reflective judgment is in charge of unifying? And since Kant's own answer to this question hints at the separation between nature and freedom, what is the relation between the (pre-transcendental) split between body and mind on the one hand, and the (transcendental) split between nature and freedom on the other? In what sense is Kant's idea of aesthetics the underlying (and implicitly unifying) theme of all those dualisms?

Transcendental Embodiment and the Possibility of Aesthetics

Against the trivial empirical evidence that human beings possess, as it were, a physical body endowed with senses to which they owe their material contact with the world, Kant's *transcendental* approach to human embodiment commits him to the claim that one of the *a priori conditions* under which the human cognitive faculties can yield true knowledge and the possibility of moral action is that they belong to an *embodied* being. Accordingly, the status of the condition of embodiment is shifted from that of mere empirical *datum to which* cognitive activity (theoretical and practical) is directed, to that of *transcendental a priori form by which* the cognitive activity is first made possible. In its transcendental form, the body is not simply "object" of cognition but is, in the proper sense, "subject" as well. In Kant's critical perspective, the pure forms of sensibility and the categories of understanding are not sorted according to an axiological hierarchy. Both are equally necessary in order for the cognitive synthesis to be possible. They are, however, distinct in kind.[10] The dividing line that Kant draws between "empirical" and "pure" is no longer meant to separate the body from the soul or the mind. As I have argued in the previous chapters, it is rather a line that separates two very different conceptions of the body—its empirical, merely physical givenness and its transcendental ideal form—as well as two very different conceptions of the soul or mind—the metaphysical soul and the transcendental subject. Transcendentally and theoretically considered, the body is not empirically given but itself has (or better, is) an a priori form that conditions any physical givenness as well as any construction in which givenness first acquires meaning. Construction, as cognitive *factum,* is made possible by the enactment of the a priori forms of sensibility along with the a priori forms of understanding. Moreover, in the practical sphere, the body is itself an ideal construction that arises out of the activity of reason. In other words, our physical senses whose seat is the physical body yield meaningful experience only because of the transcendental form of the body that constitutes the a priori condition of any actual sensible experience of the world—an experience taking place, as it were, in this world. If the body is not—as it was for the modern rationalist tradition—just a limiting material condition from which to abstract in the enterprise of building the edifice of science, but is something displaying a priori forms that contribute to the activity of reason itself, a critique of (pure) reason to be complete will have to spell out *all* the different formal components of that notion. Sensibility becomes the proper topic of a critique of reason. Against the empiricist tradition, however, Kant's interest is neither a physiology nor a phenomenology of the body and its perceptual activity, but a critical inquiry into the ways in which the body counts among the a priori conditions of human knowledge and the necessary consequences or effects of moral action. More generally, Kant's analysis aims at finding the ways in which sensibility displays different *purely formal* components. This perspective commits Kant (1) to the "isolation" of the a priori element that transcendentally constitutes the different forms of sensibility—*Anschauung, Empfindung,* and *Gefühl;* and (2) to the distinction of the specific function that those forms display when set in conjunction with the different activities of reason or, in the terminology of the third *Critique,* with the different faculties of the *Gemüt.*

In Kant's critical project the development of the a priori forms of sensibility does not follow a plan that is complete from the outset in all its details. Rather, such development is marked by progressive conquests which, in turn, lead to the successive revision of the internal partition of the critique of reason. Kant is able to complete the last part of this project, the *Critique of Judgment,* only when a heretofore irremissibly empirical and material part of sensibility, *Gefühl* as "feeling of pleasure and displeasure," is found to display a pure form whereby it is brought back to an a priori principle of its own. At this point, Kant's project of a "critique of taste" is transformed into a "critique of judgment." It is the second *Critique,* with its radical separation between practical reason and feeling, and its discovery of a peculiar feeling whose necessity follows a priori from the moral law, that first opens the way to the possibility of an aesthetic other than the cognitive one of the *Critique of Pure Reason.*

In §1 of the Transcendental Aesthetic, Kant defines *Sinnlichkeit* as the "receptivity"[11] through which we are affected and put in immediate relation to given objects. Sensibility displays a *formal side,* which is intuition (*Anschauung*) and has its a priori pure modes in space and time, and the side of a *content,* which is sensation (*Empfindung*) and is instead always empirical (a posteriori). In the cognitive context of the first *Critique,* sensation, due to its material character, has a merely subjective validity: it is a "perception that relates exclusively to the subject as the modification of its state." Herein, the subjectivity of sensation is opposed to the objectivity of both intuition and concept as elements of cognition (as "objective perception[s]" both intuition and concept are called *cognitio* and opposed to *sensatio*).[12] While sensation refers only to the subject and testifies to a modification of its state, intuition and concept refer to objects of possible cognition. Sensation, however, when taken up in connection with the understanding in the "schematism" reveals an element that can be known a priori and "anticipated" in all experience. When sensation is synthesized with the category of "reality," it shows an a priori moment which is the "degree" or the "intensive magnitude" belonging to all reality.[13] The possibility of a Transcendental Aesthetic as "science of *all* the a priori principles of sensibility"[14] taken in isolation from the understanding, hinges upon the presence in sensibility of the pure a priori forms of intuition. Sensation must be excluded from it since its a priori component emerges only at the level of the schematism, that is, in relation to and cooperation with the understanding.

In an important footnote at the end of §1 of the Transcendental Aesthetic, modified in the second edition of the *Critique of Pure Reason*,[15] Kant challenges Baumgarten's use of the term *aesthetica* to indicate a specific science of sensibility that includes "taste" and the critical appraisal of beauty. In Kant's view, Baumgarten's promotion of aesthetics to science is predicated on the assumption that it is possible to bring taste and the critical evaluation of beauty under rules or "rational principles." However, on Kant's account in 1781, Baumgarten's *scientia cognitionis sensitivae* by no means meets the requisites of a true science for no rational principle can be provided for taste.[16] Because of their "source," rules of taste can only be empirical and consequently never serve as "a priori laws" in the use of our judgment. Hence, against the typically German employment of the term aesthetics introduced by Baumgarten, Kant proposes to restore the more accurate distinction of the ancients, who divided knowledge into *aistheta* and *noeta*—the sensible and the intelligible. It follows that for Kant the only way in which sensibility can indeed be admitted into science is in a "transcendental" theory in which it appears under the title of "transcendental aesthetic." Since such a doctrine, in order to be science, can address sensibility only in its pure a priori forms, and since only intuition displays an a priori element, "transcendental aesthetic" can extend only to space and time as the two pure forms of intuition. On this account, "aesthetics" is possible only as first part of a theory of knowledge; as such, however, it must leave out the inquiry into the principles of taste. Thereby, aesthetics is returned to its etymological meaning and fully disjoined from its relation to taste. In this gesture, despite his critique of Baumgarten, Kant shares a twofold claim with him. First, he aims, as Baumgarten does, at the inclusion of sensibility into science and hence at its cognitive rehabilitation. Second, in agreement with Baumgarten, he still limits "aesthetics" to an exclusively cognitive function.[17] Precisely *because* Kant shares these two assumptions with Baumgarten, he is brought to the opposite conclusion: aesthetics cannot be a theory of taste; taste must be left out of "*transcendental* aesthetic." Thus, in 1781, aesthetic is the doctrine of space and time as pure a priori forms of sensible intuition. Taste, as well as sensation and feeling are excluded from it because of their exclusively material, a posteriori character. Kant now views any other account of sensibility as one destined to be empirical, material, and therefore not scientific. Consequently, at this stage, a transcendental theory (or critique) of taste is for Kant thoroughly impossible.

In the 1787 edition of the first *Critique,* when Kant is setting out to work on the *Critique of Judgment,* he revises his position toward Baumgarten. The claim that rules and criteria of taste, because of their sources, can only be empirical and never serve as a priori principles is now corrected by the specification that rules of taste, being of empirical nature because of their *"principal" (vornehmste)* source, can never serve as *"determinate (bestimmte)* laws a priori."* This specification leaves open the possibility for taste to have its own a priori source, even though this source has remained up until now unnoticed by Kant himself (and certainly has not appeared as a "principal" source). Moreover, Kant concedes that taste may also have its own a priori principle or law, even though not a "determinate" one (but, as it turns out, a reflective one). Furthermore, the reformulation of the remark invoking the ancient division of knowledge into sensible and intelligible, against the German use of the term "aesthetics," introduces a concession to Baumgarten that betrays Kant's own struggle with the problem of taste. For we now stand in front of an alternative that was not there before. Kant advises us *"either"* to give up the name of "aesthetics" for the doctrine of taste and shape the theory of knowledge in the aftermath of the more accurate terminology of the Greeks *"or else* to share the name with speculative philosophy, employing it partly in the transcendental and partly in the psychological sense."[18] Thereby Kant declares his willingness to share the terminology of aesthetics with Baumgarten. The term "aesthetics" is now permitted not only for a transcendental but also for a psychological inquiry. And yet, despite the apparent concession to Baumgarten, Kant here is decisively moving away from the view of aesthetics as an exclusively cognitive doctrine. In 1787 Kant's position is further removed from Baumgarten's than in 1781, even though at the earlier date his criticism of Baumgarten seems harsher. For if aesthetics has to deal exclusively with cognition, as Kant holds in 1781, then the only acceptable aesthetic is its transcendental version from which taste is in principle excluded. If, however, there is more to the sensible than mere cognition, as Kant intimates in 1787, then a psychological (and hence a merely empirical and not properly scientific) inquiry is also allowed—albeit as a discipline standing outside of science and consequently not displaying the scientific validity that Baumgarten claimed for it. It follows that this 'psychology of taste' will not be *gnoseologia* in Baumgarten's sense.[19]

In sum, in the first *Critique,* sensibility displays a priori structures only with regard to intuition. Since sensation and feeling are left out because of their materiality, and since sensation and feeling are associated with taste, a critique of taste cannot be a transcendental aesthetic but, at the most, only (empirical) psychology. At this time, feeling (*Gefühl*), as "feeling of pleasure and displeasure," is deferred to the practical sphere, i.e., to its association with the faculty of desire.

In a footnote in the Canon of Pure Reason in the Transcendental Doctrine of Method of the first *Critique,* Kant bars from the realm of transcendental philosophy all concepts that refer to objects of feeling. He maintains that these concepts insofar as they relate to "pleasure and displeasure" belong to the sphere of the practical and are merely empirical.[20] Thus, the next step in Kant's transcendental articulation of the forms of sensibility requires the separation of the feeling of pleasure and displeasure from the practical sphere *strictu sensu.* Traditionally, because of the necessarily empirical foundation of all eudemonistic moral philosophy, the feeling of pleasure and displeasure is associated with the faculty of desire (*Begehrungsvermögen, facultas appetitiva*) and with its subdivision into a "higher" and a "lower" faculty. According to Wolff, while the higher faculty of desire is determined by intellectual representations, the lower faculty is determined by sensual representations. The crucial point is that in both cases the will is moved to action only when a representation is associated with the "feeling of pleasure or displeasure." In the second *Critique,*[21] as we have seen, Kant's idea of a pure a priori foundation of morality leads him to the claim that if the pure will does relate to the faculty of desire, it can be moved by a special type of desire that is pure and formal and does not promise any pleasure or displeasure. By separating the faculty of desire from the feeling of pleasure, this claim radically transforms the faculty of desire as practical faculty and frees the sphere of feeling of practical concerns. Practical reason can move the will immediately without having recourse to empirical desire or the feeling of pleasure. Kant's suggestion is that since feeling, as motive of action, is always and inevitably material, it can never function as a ground for moral action. Opposing the entire tradition, Kant denies to the feeling of pleasure and displeasure any *practical* significance (in the strong moral sense that connects the practical to the idea of freedom). Thereby the second *Critique* makes room for the specific field of inquiry proper to the *Critique of Judgment,* that is, to the region of sensibility occupied by the feeling of pleasure and displeasure. While the first *Critique* excludes feeling from the cognitive sphere, the second *Critique* declares it practically insignificant (at least at the level of the foundation of

morality). It is only for this reason that *Gefühl* can become the crucial concept of a theory of aesthetic judgment—i.e., of an aesthetics, which, in its
very principle, is thoroughly independent of both cognitive and practical
aims and hence stands in need of its own critique.[22]

However, as I have shown in the previous chapters, Kant's transformation of the faculty of desire and its connection to feeling does not imply that
sensibility plays no role—or only a negative one—in the second *Critique*. It
is only *after* Kant has established the a priori principle of morality that he can
investigate the peculiar feeling that *follows as a consequence* and according to
a priori necessity from the determination of the will through the law. More
generally, Kant does admit that feelings always *affect* us "aesthetically," i.e.,
pathologically. Thus, in the practical sphere, the term "aesthetic" is employed in the sense of "pathological."[23] The crucial point, however, is that
pathological feelings (unlike moral feeling) do not always *determine* us.[24] As
long as it is not taken as determining ground for moral action, pathological
affection does have a place in Kant's moral theory.

In 1788 sensible intuition has, for Kant, an exclusively cognitive use
in relation to the understanding as faculty of concepts. Sensation, on the
contrary, allows for a differentiated use when enacted by different faculties
of the *Gemüt*. In relation to understanding, sensation produces empirical
(merely subjective) cognition; in relation to the faculty of desire, it contributes to the will's empirical affection.[25] Accordingly, Kant's discussion
of sensibility in the practical sphere shows, on the one hand, a repeated
insistence on the radical exclusion of intuition (both sensible and intellectual) from the realm of the practical; on the other hand, he presents the
practical transformation of the materiality of sensation into a peculiar form
of "moral feeling." Moral feeling still betrays the *subjective* character proper
to feeling and sensation in general. The feeling of respect for the law is the
only occurrence of a feeling that displays an a priori origin in relation to
pure practical reason along with a genuinely practical, and yet subjective,
significance. This feeling is pure, and it is the object of the peculiar, analogical "aesthetic" of practical reason—an *Aesthetik der Sitten* as Kant will
call it in 1797.[26]

It should be noted that the feeling of respect applies only to human
beings (endowed with *arbitrium sensitivum*) on the basis of their embodied
condition—it can be assumed neither in animals (whose *arbitrium* is *arbitrium
brutum*, not *arbitrium sensitivum*) nor in a divine or holy will (*arbitrium sanctum*)
from which all sensibility is excluded. Thus, both in the first and the second
Critique, Kant's aesthetic betrays the specific perspective of the embodied

human being, i.e., a being whose existence is placed in space and time, who is able to distinguish between an inner sense and an outer world, and whose will is subject both to the pure determination of the moral law and to the empirical, pathological affection of material desires. In 1788 "aesthetic," or the transcendental theory of sensibility, is no longer limited to theoretical cognition but displays its own relevance in the practical inquiry as well. In this case, Kant is careful to stress that the aesthetic of practical reason has nothing to do with a psychological or anthropological investigation of human nature on merely empirical grounds. Even when the realm of pathological feelings and affections is addressed, it is not addressed as the determining ground of moral action. Transcendentally, the practical form of human embodiment is not the basis but the consequence of morality, not the motive for but the response to the will's moral determination. We do not need to presuppose a body (its physical powers, its sensible affections) to act morally; and yet, by acting morally, feeling allows us to discover our body as the body of a *moral* (not merely physical) agent or "person." To this extent, feeling has no practical relevance of its own as it does not function as a *grounding* principle of morality.

Taste and Feeling

Since its first appearance in the Spanish language with the work of Baltasar Gracian[27] during the second half of the seventeenth century, the term *gusto* (taste) shows an inner connection with the empirical universality of inter-subjective agreement. In Gracian's terminology, *gusto* refers to the sphere of moral and political dispositions rather than to properly aesthetic experience. It designates the ability to make the right choice, that is, a choice that is always accompanied by universal consensus. Taste applies to man in society; it is the source of sociability, culture, and social development. Gracian's influence extends in particular to France, and through French authors his work is introduced in Germany by Christian Thomasius. Gracian's "man of taste"—the *discreto*—becomes Thomasius' *politicus:* the man who knows the rules of correct behavior in court. Yet, the practical disposition expressed by the word *taste* was so foreign to German culture that Thomasius did not dare to translate it in German, or better, to coin a new term for it. Instead, he rendered Gracian's maxims in French. In his 1687 program on the "imitation of the French people" we find a formulation that Kant repeats and comments on in his early *Reflections*. Thomasius' rendering of Gracian's sixty-seventh maxim is: "*le gout universel d'autrui* [. . .] *est la vrai méthode de choisir.*" Along the same lines, Kant considers *Geschmack* as "*Vermögen zu wählen*"—the capacity or faculty to choose not what pleases the individual in her private subjectivity but what meets general or public approval.[28]

This historical reference sheds light on the connection in which taste is placed from the beginning in Kant's thought. On the one hand, taste relates to judgment; on the other, it implies universality and intersubjectivity (and therefore communicability). One of the achievements of eighteenth-century aesthetics is the subjective (anti-Platonic) turn that brings judgments on the beautiful back to the subject's *sensibility*. Whether "sensible evaluation" (Kant speaks of *sinnliche Urtheilskraft* and *sinnliche Beurtheilung*) takes place without understanding[29]—and as its alternative—or understanding itself operates as a sensible power in this type of evaluation,[30] taste is considered a *feeling* for the beautiful. The sphere of taste is the sphere of sensibility, and this, in turn, is further specified as the realm of feeling. Moreover, feeling is directed both to the realm of the beautiful (and sublime) and to the practical sphere. Along with the "feeling for the beautiful," we also have "moral feelings." However, by establishing this important parallel or analogy between the two families of feelings—aesthetic and moral—the empiricist tradition complicates Kant's route toward an understanding of the specificity of *Gefühl*. To be able to recognize the independence of the feeling of pleasure and displeasure Kant first has to understand that morality cannot be based on feeling. Only at this point can he claim that the feeling of pleasure rests on a specific kind of a priori principles. Early on, Kant's theory of taste follows from his attempt to determine the role of feeling in relation to the other faculties of the mind. *Gefühl* is an intermediary faculty at play between the cognitive faculty and the faculty of desire.[31]

From the beginning, Kant's theory of taste plays itself out between two different issues. The *Critique of Judgment* arises only when the two issues eventually meet in the same problem. Kant firmly determines the realm of taste as the realm of *sensibility* and attributes to it *merely empirical validity*. Consequently, up until the second edition of the *Critique of Pure Reason* he strenuously opposes any attempt to base aesthetics on a priori rules. But Kant is also determined to save the entire sphere of sensibility (not only its cognitive function) from the fate to which the empiricist tradition had confined it.[32] The *Critique of Judgment* is the latest result of Kant's lifelong philosophical experimentation on the topic of sensibility. Taste and the feeling of the beautiful are the spheres in which this experimentation starts (in his 1764 *Observations on the Feeling of the Beautiful and Sublime*) and is the systematic place in which this experimentation culminates. Given that sensibility (intuition, perception, feeling, drive, etc.) permeates human existence in all its manifestations, Kant's effort is to find the a priori component of the forms of sensibility respectively implicated in the activity of the different faculties of the mind. Viewed from the late perspective of the *Critique of Judgment,* the title that Kant proposes in 1771 for his philosophical project, namely *The Limits of Sensibility and Reason,*[33] already accurately outlines the program of critical philosophy in its entirety.

Since taste relates to the subject's sensibility, the "perfection" that characterizes the beautiful is different in principle from logical perfection. In Meier's definition, which Kant comments on in a variety of ways, the notion of "perfection of cognition" implies both teleological orientation and organic constitution:

> When the manifold in cognition agrees toward an intent or entails the sufficient ground for it: therein consists *perfection of cognition (perfectio cognitionis).* Perfections of cognition are to be found in it either insofar as cognition is clear or insofar as it is unclear. The former is *logical perfection of cognition (perfectio cognitionis logica),* the latter is *its beauty (pulchritudo et perfectio aesthetica cognitionis).*[34]

Kant's early recognition[35] that sensibility has its own lawfulness (in whichever way this lawfulness might be thought) leads him to follow Baumgarten's and Meier's suggestion that attributes a particular kind of perfection to sensibility. Yet this perfection is still determined in a somehow subsidiary way in relation to understanding's cognition. Accordingly, taste is defined as the faculty that presents abstract concepts in a sensible individual intuition.[36] Taste prepares for the "clear" cognition of the understanding.

Kant's notes on Meier's quoted passage reinforce the distinction between aesthetic and logical perfection. Yet Kant insists on specifying beauty's relation to the subject, and does so by inserting a series of further oppositions relevant to the development of his theory of sensibility. Kant's gesture is an attempt to combine rationalist and empiricist traditions in order to find precisely that universality—or lawfulness—of sensibility on the basis of which alone a theory of taste could be established. "Logical perfections relate to the *object,* beauty to the *subject.*★ The *form* of cognition in relation to the *subject* is called *appearance.*" That which pleases always discloses an "agreement." If it is agreement within the subject, we have the "feeling or taste." If the agreement is objective, then it is also "universally

---

★(The *matter* of cognition in relation to the *subject* is *sensation*).

valid."[37] Aesthetic perfection is not the agreement or correspondence of the object with its concept—which would be logical "truth"[38]—but rather the agreement of the object with the law or form of sensibility, an agreement that takes place not in the materiality of sensation but in the formality of appearance and intuition. What specifies aesthetic perfection against logical perfection, for Kant, is not its lack of clarity but the *relation to the subject*. Moreover, the reference to the subject becomes the starting point for an important series of oppositions placed right within the sphere of sensibility itself. As far as cognition is concerned, because of its relation to the subject, we can distinguish "matter" and "form." Here, as later in the first *Critique*, matter is that mode of sensibility called sensation; form is instead appearance; "the feeling of the form is taste."[39]

By locating both "feeling" and "taste" in "appearance" (thereby providing the conditions for aesthetic perfection) and opposing them to "sensation," Kant further specifies the difference between "sensation" and "appearance" as follows: "Appearance is distinguished from sensation in that sensation is that element within sensibility which constitutes a part of the subject's own condition; appearance, instead, is an *effective action of the cognitive faculty* that moves toward the object and is the cause of this sensation."[40] On this view, there are two components of sensibility: a thoroughly passive and material one that reveals the status of the subject, which is sensation; and a decidedly active and formal one, which is appearance and is identified as the *cause* of sensation. Beauty is perfection in sensibility;[41] it is more exactly the "exterior side of perfection." As perfection is a form of agreement, Kant does not hesitate to relate it to the form of *Zweckmäßigkeit*—purposiveness.[42] Beauty is the "internal perfection"[43] of a thing that manifests itself in external form and thereby becomes sensible. Viewed in the light of the doctrine of the first *Critique*, Kant's early efforts to promote taste and feeling for the beautiful to objects of science go in the direction of assimilating the aesthetic components of those forms of sensibility to the universality of space and time as a priori forms of intuition, i.e., to that which constitutes the topic of the Transcendental Aesthetic.

The other issue addressed by Kant's reflection on the problem of feeling, taste, and beauty regards the possibility of rules and the type of rules that can be ascribed to taste. Kant's attack on Baumgarten in the first *Critique,* we have seen, ruled out the possibility of raising "aesthetics" as theory of taste to a science because of the necessarily empirical nature of its principles. And yet, Kant has been strenuously looking for a way of granting to taste and beauty a kind of universality and formality that, despite its merely

empirical character, could nonetheless be distinguished from the materiality of sensation. The aforementioned distinction between two elements of
sensibility was the condition thereof. If sensibility had been for Kant only
sensation, he would not have felt the need to include that note in the two
editions of the *Critique of Pure Reason*. What makes his remark so significant
and dramatic is that it applies not only to Baumgarten but to Kant's own
research during the second half of the 1760s and throughout the 1770s.

Both the idea of an intersubjective, public dimension of consensus and
the notion of taste as judgment were constitutive of the theory of taste
since the introduction of the term in the philosophical vocabulary. From
the outset, Kant places his own reflection in this context. But how can the
"universal validity" of taste and feeling be justified if taste is confined to the
subjective realm of sensibility? Kant is aware that there can be neither an "*a
priori doctrine*" of taste, a "*theory* of taste," nor a "*science* of the beautiful."[44]
Yet there can very well be a "*critique* of taste." "Our judgments of taste follow not a rule, but intuition,"[45] so that there are "aesthetic observations"[46]
but not *dogmata*. If, with the title "critique of taste," Kant explicitly follows
Home's designation,[47] he is nonetheless developing it out of a quite different
theory of sensibility. Kant attempts to specify the type of rules that belong
to taste's proper way of evaluation and judgment. The general question is
"whether taste has fixed and universal rules," to which Kant answers: "Yet
not rules to know a priori (*in abstracto*), but to know *in concreto*. [Taste] is a
sensible judgment that is valid for everyone."[48]

Thus, a critique of taste should be based upon—and account for—
the *empirical* universality of aesthetic agreement. However, given Kant's
suggestion that the empirical sphere of sensibility displays a differential
articulation—i.e., given that there are "sensible" representations, "even
more sensible" ones, and representations which are "sensible in highest
degree"[49]—the question to be raised now concerns the *particular kind of
sensibility* that belongs to judgments of taste.

> The evaluation of an object through sensation is not universally valid; the
> evaluation through true taste is valid for all human beings—both are subjec-
> tive [. . .]. If the object agrees with the feeling of the subject according to
> *matter*, is agreeable and charms as well as moves; if it agrees with the feeling
> according to *form*, it is beautiful.[50]

It is the distinction between form and matter of sensibility, between sensation and appearance, that grounds the legitimacy of the universality of taste.
For in the case of taste and feeling, universality lies in formality, intuition,
and appearance.

In a period in which Kant is developing his "aesthetic" doctrine of space and time as a priori forms of intuition, this same doctrine seems to influence his reflection on his other aesthetic concerning taste and feeling.[51] At this point, Kant seems to distinguish even three levels of sensibility (that eventually intersect with one another).

> A representation is *sensible* if in it is the form of space and time; it is *even more sensible* if is accompanied by a sensation (color); it is *sensible in the highest degree:* if it is attributed to the observer precisely as it is observed by others. Beautiful objects are those objects whose order pleases according to the laws of intuition.[52]

Hence the definition of taste as the capacity of choosing what sensibly pleases in accordance to others. However, the agreement on which the universality of taste is based cannot be grounded on *sensation* because "in sensation the agreement *is not as necessary* as it is in appearance."[53] Kant appeals not only to the criterion of universality but also to that of necessity. Since the agreement that leads to a judgment of taste is not based on sensation, it must be based in *appearance*. Now, "taste in appearance is grounded upon the relations of space and time [. . .] and upon the rules of reflection."[54] "That which in an object pleases and we regard as one of its properties must consist in what is valid for everyone. The relations of space and time are valid for everyone, whatever sensation one might have. Accordingly, in all appearance the form is valid for everyone." This form is known by the logical rule of coordination. "Hence that which is in agreement with the rule of coordination in space and time pleases *necessarily* everyone and is beautiful."[55]

Kant's attempt to justify the universal agreement of taste through the universality and necessity proper to the relations of space and time will prove, in this form, unsuccessful. For what meaning could the reference to the forms of space and time ever have for a judgment of the beautiful? However, this attempt is significant to understand both Kant's uneasiness with the empiricist notion of "universal validity" as referred to taste, and his own striving toward a more articulate definition of sensibility. Moreover, Kant's shift toward the formality of space and time establishes a crucial point of intersection between the two aesthetics, which, in its successive critical development, is ultimately responsible for Kant's so-called aesthetic formalism. Finally, the reference to the first aesthetic—or better to the forms of space and time as conditions of our perception of objects as appearances— accounts for the fact that in Kant's later theory of taste the work of art is not the only object that occasions aesthetic pleasure. For all objects given by intuition in space and time (both natural objects and objects produced by technique) can occasion aesthetic pleasure.[56]

Transcendental Embodiment:
Not an "Aesthetics of Feeling"
but an Aesthetic Faculty of Judgment

On 6 January 1788, the publisher Hartknoch writes to Kant inquiring about his "Critique of practical reason" and the "critique of beautiful taste" (*Kritik des schönen Geschmacks*). Work on the *Critique of Practical Reason* helped Kant shed light on the new direction that his critique of taste was about to take. Only after having separated feeling of pleasure and faculty of desire and freed that faculty, as practical reason, from all connections to the feeling of pleasure, only then can the peculiar sphere of *Gefühl* emerge as independent field of transcendental inquiry. A passage at the end of the second *Critique* is significant for the direction of Kant's reflection in these crucial years. At the end of the Doctrine of Method, Kant presents yet another perspective on morality, the one eventually disclosed by our judgment on moral conduct. The question here is: how shall we judge action—our own as well as that of our fellow human beings? At this final stage of the argument, Kant's answer is straightforward: we should judge according to the moral law by asking whether an action is performed *both objectively and subjectively* according to it. Once the legislative function of practical reason has been investigated and the grounds for its becoming subjective *Trieb* for moral action explored, Kant addresses the activity of "reason *in its judging* concerning the practical" (*über das Praktische urteilende(n) Vernunft*).[57] Legislative reason yields now to judgment (or to reason that pronounces judgments). And we discover that our judging with regard to the practical has a strong effect on our feeling. All pedagogical efforts in the sphere of morality must be directed precisely on this effect. It is not reason alone that produces a specific practical "interest" in the action itself (in the principle, not in the object of action, which would characterize it instead as pathological interest). Eventually, the habit of judgment in moral matters leads us to take a particular pleasure in the observation of moral action because we

> take a liking in that the observation (*Betrachtung*) of which makes us feel (*empfinden*) that our powers of knowledge are extended, and this extension is especially furthered by that wherein we find moral correctness, since reason, with its faculty of determining according to a priori principles what ought to occur, can find satisfaction only in such an order of things.

The pain and uneasiness we initially feel as reason thwarts our passions and morally determines our will eventually yields to a pleasure in the contemplation of moral action.[58] However, we immediately learn that this peculiarly pleasurable feeling arising from reason's judgments of actions is not limited to our considerations within the moral sphere. Thereby, this feeling gains a characterization of its own and a quasi-independence from the practical. Kant points to the "observer of nature" (*Naturbeobachter*) who "finally comes to like objects which first offended his senses when he discovers the great purposiveness (*Zweckmäßigkeit*) of their organization, so that reason finds nourishment in observing them (*Betrachtung*)."[59] Here as well, Kant dwells on the characterization of a second, final stage in the observation of phenomena. The feeling of violence and repugnance that at first seems to radically oppose reason to the senses in the observation of nature is eventually overcome by a feeling of their harmony and accordance. Thus, two types of observation and judgment connected to two distinct and yet analogous types of order—the moral order of reason and the purposive order of nature—generate the same pleasurable feeling. This feeling recounts a *development* in our judging attitude and is grounded on the *initial* opposition between reason and sensibility as much as in the *final* overcoming of that opposition in a purposive structure of "order."

Moreover, Kant suggests that this peculiar activity of the faculty of judgment puts us in contact with ourselves: in all those cases, judgment is as much about actions performed and natural objects observed as it is about us (who judge of those actions and objects). The feeling that arises is mainly a feeling about our inner state. Through this feeling the moral order as well as the purposive order of nature is referred back to our own activity. While our faculties are directly involved in cognition and moral action herein performing their respective functions, judgment puts us in contact with ourselves and allows us to gain a feeling for what those faculties actually do. Since our faculties transcendentally entail the conditions of the possibility of their objects, our judgment on those objects is necessarily also a judgment on the mental activity that issued them. This is precisely what Kant will later call "reflection." Reflection is a sort of meta-faculty that observes and considers—"judges," as it were—what the other faculties do (and not directly the objects with which those faculties are concerned). Kant brings to the fore a peculiar "activity of the faculty of judgment (*Urteilskraft*) that *makes us feel* (*fühlen*) our own cognitive faculties," which is not yet "interest in actions and their morality itself." Judgment simply *makes us feel ourselves*: it neither produces knowledge of objects nor action itself. Rather, this activity of judgment lends the "form of beauty" to virtue as well as to the attitude of the mind according to moral laws. This form of beauty

> is admired but not yet sought [. . .]. It is the same with everything whose contemplation produces subjectively a consciousness of the harmony of our powers of representation *by which we feel* our entire cognitive faculty (understanding and imagination) strengthened; it produces satisfaction (*Wohlgefallen*) that can be communicated to others, but the existence of its object remains indifferent to us.[60]

At this point, the moral space opens up to a new "aesthetic space." The form of beauty establishes a new kind of *subjective* order that is neither cognitive nor moral. The form of beauty is the expression that the faculty of judgment gives to the feeling of pleasure arising out of the finally perceived harmony between the sensible and the rational part of ourselves. The concept of "transcendental embodiment" expresses precisely this convergence. Our condition as embodied beings is now experienced with a sense of attained and contemplative peace and satisfaction (*Wohlgefallen*): the senses do not interfere with reason and its investigation of nature nor does pathological affection interfere with the principles of moral action. It is true, we find ourselves neither in the pathos of decision nor in the midst of action, our aim is not the pursuit of science; we are observing and judging actions and things in general; we admire, we are free of interest, and hence do not seek to attain anything—neither virtue nor knowledge. We are in a purely subjective state that offers us the "consciousness" of an inner harmony among our sensible and intellectual faculties. The *feeling* of inner satisfaction arises precisely because the two parts of ourselves are indeed working together, thereby overcoming the initially perceived conflict: observing reason is reconciled with the senses in the purposive order of nature, practical reason is reconciled with the affecting pathological desires in the moral order. In this condition the activity of judgment "makes us feel our own cognitive faculties."[61]

Kant argues that this feeling, although merely subjective, does not remain private and inarticulate. For it is a sense of satisfaction that can be communicated to others—it is, as it were, an *intersubjective* feeling (or better, a feeling of ourselves as members of a community in which that feeling can be shared).[62] The satisfaction that judgment produces in us and that we communicate to others is independent of the existence of the object to which judgment is addressed. The object is only the contingent occasion "for our becoming aware of our store of talents which are elevated (*erhabenen Anlage*) above the mere animal level (*Tierheit*)."[63] At this point, both the moral and the natural order refer us to ourselves and allow us to see that our embodied condition, of which we now are fully aware, is not the same as that of animals. On the other hand, if we did not have a body to offer resistance to the enterprise of knowledge[64] and to moral conduct—if we were pure disembodied souls—this latter reflection and its associated feeling of satisfaction would simply not occur. The realm of feeling characterizes the condition of embodied beings and is unknown to a holy, disembodied will. What makes us feel our store of talents as placed above (*erhaben*) the animal level is that we are, among other things, nonetheless still animals. And yet, now we can experience for ourselves—upon "reflection," as it were—what transcendental philosophy has been contending all along, namely, that there is a use or a sense of our embodied, sensible condition that is constitutive of the activity of reason, so that we do not need to abstract from it. To be sure, reason could not even function as *human* reason (both in theory and in practice) if it were not *embodied* reason. Thus, the feeling of satisfaction is the feeling for the discovery of a new harmony established *within our embodied human condition*.

The conclusion of the *Critique of Practical Reason* pursues this connection to its last implications. Here two distinct and yet converging feelings are mentioned: "wonder and awe" (*Bewunderung und Ehrfurcht*), which explicitly betray the "sublimity" of their object (but truly the sublimity of the faculties that relate to those objects through such feelings).[65] They both connect to my embodied condition, which alone allows me to feel admiration for the starry sky "above me" and the moral law "within me."[66] Although in the previous passage Kant underlines the disinterested nature of the feeling that arises from reason's judgment (I am not interested in the existence of that which I admire and respect), he now reveals that those feelings immediately provide me with "the consciousness of *my own existence*."[67] This is the new *reflective* space of inquiry that is left for Kant to explore. What is the embodied human being in her worldly life, in her concrete existence placed *between* the starry heavens and the moral order—an in-between existence neither exhausted by the cognitive exercise of reason nor by the demands of moral action? In this space of (self-)reflection, aesthetics is no longer a matter of (material) sensibility for Kant; it becomes, instead, a matter of judgment, of *Urteilskraft*. For it is (a peculiar kind of) judgment that refers us to a *pure* form of feeling—to a *pure* pleasure that does not arise out of sensation but out of judgment. This is the crucial turn of the third *Critique*.

We have reached a seemingly paradoxical result. If set against the general presuppositions of pre-Kantian philosophy and its view of the body, the point at which Kant's transcendental inquiry seems to promise the closest proximity to the material side of sensibility (taste, sensation, feeling) is also the point at which aesthetics becomes, for Kant, a matter not of the (physical) body but of a mental operation or faculty—judgment in its necessary and constitutive relation to a yet unexplored pure form our sensibility. The body must be transcendentally reflected to usher in a new aesthetics.

What is the last figure of transcendental embodiment that Kant's philosophy proposes by tying together aesthetics and judgment? In what sense is the aesthetic feeling of pleasure and displeasure not an immediate bodily feeling (something like the sense of taste or mere sensation) but a pure feeling connected a priori to judgment? It is precisely the peculiar character of this connection that allows Kant to construct the last form of transcendental embodiment as the reflected form of our sensible existence. Reflective judgment is the last figure of reason's transcendental embodiment.

At this point, we can approach the crucial connection between aesthetics and judgment by asking a question that brings us back, yet again, to the first *Critique*. Given that Kant expels the issue of "taste," and more precisely the currently debated topic of a "critique of taste" from the discipline of "aesthetic," what prompts this issue to eventually reappear as a theory of "aesthetic judgment"? We have seen how Baumgarten's idea of *aesthetica* as science of sensible cognition institutes for the first time the discipline that deals with taste in a scientific way. Although Kant fully acknowledges this historical result, he also expresses his reservations: since taste is a matter of merely empirical analysis, Baumgarten's aesthetics aims at the impossible task of discovering rational principles for "our critical appraisal (*Beurteilung*) of the beautiful." In other words, if aesthetics is to be taken as science of sensibility, taste should be excluded from it (or, in Kant's early experimentations on the topic, taste, reduced to space and time, actually disappears); if, on the contrary, aesthetics remains an empirical "critique of taste" (as the common German denomination has it), it cannot claim a scientific character. Kant still holds this view in 1790. Now, however, taste is no longer a troublesome gap in the critical inquiry—something that can hardly be more than the object of anthropological "observations,"[68] mixed as it is with moral feelings and moral psychology. Taste has been replaced by a specific form of the feeling of pleasure and displeasure, which is connected to a peculiar function of our faculty of judgment. Observation is no longer the empirical activity of a spectator but the self-reflective activity of judgment. For Kant at this point the title of aesthetics—*Ästhetik*—no longer indicates an independent discipline (in addition to Transcendental

Aesthetic). Its specificity and legitimacy shifts to the adjective *ästhetisch,* whose transcendental significance is expressed by a peculiar function of judgment. Passing through Baumgarten's *aesthetica,* the critique of taste is finally transformed into a *critique of aesthetic judgment.*[69] The rationalistic and still entirely psychological realm of darkness proper to the soul within which Baumgarten places the *impetus aestheticus* yields to a *reflective* form of human embodiment. It yields to a new transcendental consideration of the sphere of feeling, to the way in which human *sensible existence* is concretely lived and experienced as placed *between* the starry heavens above and the moral law within—between, as it were, the two orders that we need to consider purposive: the realm of nature and the realm of freedom.

In §VIII of the First Introduction to the *Critique of Judgment,* Kant offers a new analysis of the term *ästhetisch.* At stake is the issue of its value and function, which would justify its new employment in transcendental philosophy as the legitimate topic of a third "critique." The expression *"ästhetische(n) Vorstellungsart"*—or aesthetic mode of representing—"is quite unambiguous," observes Kant, "if we mean by it the relation of a representation to an object, as appearance, to produce cognition of that object." In this case, the adjective "aesthetic" indicates "that the form of sensibility," namely "the way in which (*wie*) the subject is affected," "attaches necessarily to the representation so that this form is inevitably transferred (*übertragen*) to the object (though to the object only as phenomenon)." In the case of cognition of objects, the adjective "aesthetic" signals an important transfer that takes place between the subject and the object, and leads, more specifically, from the way in which the subject is affected to the way in which the object of possible cognition is constituted and represented as appearance. Thereby, Kant summarizes the core conclusion of the Transcendental Aesthetic. Aesthetic refers, in this case, to the "cognitive faculty."[70]

However, on account of a longstanding use of the term that differs sensibly from his own, Kant must add a second consideration. This is prompted by the prevailing employment of the term that has brought a certain ambiguity to it and needs to be dispelled. A way of representing has been said "aesthetic, i.e., sensible" also when it means "that the representation is referred not to the cognitive faculty but to the feeling of pleasure and displeasure." The problem, Kant suggests, consists in understanding what this "feeling of pleasure and displeasure" properly is, to what it refers, and to what faculty of the mind it relates and in which function. Does this feeling belong to sensibility at all (to our capacity for being affected)? Kant acknowledges that we do indeed have the habit, due to lack of adequate terminology, of calling this feeling a "sense (*Sinn*) (a modification of our state)."[71] To this extent, the feeling of pleasure and displeasure seems to share with sensation (*Empfindung*) the same definition: sensation is a "perception that refers to the subject as the modification of its state."[72] However, if this feeling is a sense, Kant argues that it is certainly no "objective sense, whose determination we would use to *know* an object."[73] Indeed, this is the principal difference between what is aesthetic in intuition, which is used for cognition, and what is aesthetic in feeling, which yields no cognition of objects. "To intuit or otherwise to know something with pleasure (*mit Lust*) is not merely to refer the representation to the object but is a receptivity (*Empfänglichkeit*) of the subject."[74] Sensation seems to present us with a similar case. However, although sensation is certainly subjective if compared to the objectivity of both intuition and concept, feeling is even more subjective than sensation. Sensation does ultimately have a cognitive value of its own, which emerges in its interaction with the understanding in the schematism. Sensation is somehow still belonging to an "aesthetic" of the cognitive faculty. Feeling, on the contrary, even when it accompanies intuition and knowledge—as is the case when we intuit or know "with pleasure"—can claim no cognition and has no reference to objects. In these cases feeling, far from yielding cognition seems rather to qualify cognition itself or to designate the subjective modality in which cognition takes place ("with pleasure"). Kant's argument at this point seems to pass against "feeling" the same sentence that the footnote of the Transcendental Aesthetic had pronounced against "taste." "Precisely because all determinations of feeling have only subjective significance, there cannot be an *aesthetic of feeling* (*Ästhetik des Gefühls*) as science as there is, say, an *aesthetic of the cognitive faculty*"[75] (and, we should add, an analogical aesthetic of the practical faculty). However, at this stage of the development of his theory of sensibility, Kant reaches a different conclusion than in 1781 or 1787. He now suggests that "aesthetic" in the transcendental sense is not feeling but the faculty that judges with regard to that feeling. If an *Ästhetik des Gefühls* remains indeed impossible, transcendental philosophy now makes room for a critique of the aesthetic faculty of judgment.

Kant suggests that the only way to avoid the ambiguity arising from the double meaning of the adjective "aesthetic" referred once to the cognitive faculty and once to feeling, is to employ it not with regard to "intuition, let alone to representations of the understanding, but solely to the acts of the *faculty of judgment* (*Urteilskraft*)." It is only through the faculty of judgment that the adjective "aesthetic" can legitimately recuperate its reference to feeling in transcendental philosophy. This shift seems indeed paradoxical. And yet, the paradox is intended to dissipate the ambiguity of the term. The very expression "aesthetic judgment" (*Urteil*), if meant for objective determination and hence for cognition of objects, is evidently contradictory because, being a matter of the understanding, judgment can never be "aesthetic or sensible judging" (*urtheilen*).[76] It follows that, if Kant nonetheless advocates its use, the expression must be used with a different aim than the cognitive one. In other words, the cognitively contradictory expression "aesthetic judgment" stands, as it were, for its necessarily non-cognitive value. What is aesthetic or sensible judging, then, judging of if not of objects to yield knowledge?

"In calling a judgment about an object aesthetic"—explains Kant— "we indicate immediately that, while a given representation is referred to an object, by judgment here we mean not the determination of the object but the determination of the subject and his feeling." Thereby he draws the thematic of the faculty of judgment in the center of a new type of aesthetic. The novelty of this aesthetic, however, is no longer measured in relation to Baumgarten but rather to the critical itinerary of Kant's own philosophy. Since judgments in the Transcendental Aesthetic (in the aesthetic of the cognitive faculty) are all "logical," and judgments in the "schematism" all refer to the "objective" relation between understanding and imagination to produce knowledge of objects, Kant can maintain that the activity of 'judging aesthetically' does indeed claim a specificity of its own that has not yet been addressed by the previous *Critiques*. This specificity consists in the "subjective"[78] value of the relation between understanding and imagination contained in judgment. As Kant suggested at the end of the second *Critique*, judgment, in this case, deals with the subject and her feeling, i.e., with the feeling of the relation between her cognitive faculties (understanding and imagination). Subjectively, this relation, instituted in and by judgment, is relevant insofar as it "*affects* (*afficiert*) one's mental state (*Gemüthszustand*)."[78] To this extent, the relation among faculties is constitutive of judgment itself since it produces a "*modification* of our state,"[79] i.e., it is not a mere epiphenomenon accompanying a cognitive judgment (expressing, for example, that we "intuit or otherwise know something *with pleasure*").[80] Accordingly, aesthetic judgment is the faculty responsible for instituting the unique situation in which we are able to *feel* the inner relation among our own faculties. Thereby, the concept of *Sinnlichkeit* receives an important extension. Kant makes two different points here. First, he underscores that aesthetic judgment turns to the subject and her feeling and does not aim at cognition (it is neither logical nor determinative; it regards a feeling whose object is the relation among the mental faculties). Second, he further suggests that the mental state or feeling that concerns aesthetic judgment *is the product of an "affection"* grounded on judgment itself. Thereby, aesthetic judgment is "reflective" in a twofold sense: not only because in it the subject reflects on herself, but because judgment puts the subject in contact with an "effect" (*Wirkung*)[81] that judgment itself produces. Judgment is aesthetic because it *'affects'* and changes us, i.e., has a sensible, subjective effect on us. Kant makes this point even stronger by claiming that neither in its cognitive nor in its practical use does judgment possess the capacity of affecting our feeling. The "sensation" (*Empfindung*) through which the subject feels herself is certainly neither sensation of an object nor is it produced by an object. However, insofar as it is connected with judgment's procedure of "making concepts of the understanding sensible (*Versinnlichung*)" through the imagination, this sensation is essential to the way in which aesthetic judgment works. Such sensation does belong to "sensibility" since it represents the subject's own "state," namely, it expresses the way in which the subject "*is affected by an act [Actus] of that faculty*," i.e., the faculty of judgment.[82] Kant's claim is not only that judgment is aesthetic *when it concerns* the inner state of the subject, but that the state of the subject is itself the result of the subject's "affection" by an act of the faculty of judgment. It follows that judgment is aesthetic when it displays (through the manifestation of our feeling) the power of affecting the way in which we feel ourselves. It is actually only when we are affected in that way that we come to first feel ourselves. On this account, a new peculiar aspect of human sensibility is brought to the fore: our capacity of being intellectually (self-)affected by our own power of judgment. What is "sensible" and "aesthetic" in this case is not the source of affection (which is judgment and not a sensible object or a sensible faculty or receptivity), but the way in which we become aware of it, namely, through feeling. Insofar as the faculty of judgment *affects* us, it produces a peculiar feeling in which we feel ourselves and the relation of our cognitive powers.

Kant clearly construes the case of aesthetic judgment as similar to the one taking place in the practical sphere, in which the pure determination of the will through the principle of morality produces, as its effect, the pure feeling of respect for the moral law. A judgment is called sensible or aesthetic not with regard to its *Bestimmungsgrund* or determining ground (which would be, in the case of judgment, impossible) but with regard to its "subjective effect" (*Wirkung*),[83] which is a feeling. While the transcendental aesthetic of the first *Critique* shows, against the traditional dualism of body and soul, the "pure" contribution of sensibility to cognition (the effect of the body's sensibility on the mind), the notion of aesthetic judgment aims at highlighting the "sensible" contribution of the mind to the constitution of the body's own sensibility (the effect of the mind on the body's sensibility). While in the first *Critique* Kant argues that sensibility displays pure a priori forms that are necessary to the synthesis of knowledge, in the third *Critique* he reverses the situation, and contends that the intellectual faculty of judgment displays a sensible modality of action, namely an action (*Actus*) that "affects" the body and its sensibility, an action that is immediately and bodily felt by the subject (as a peculiar feeling of pleasure and displeasure). It is this complex crossing—this chiasm, as it were—between reason and sensibility, distinct in kind and yet reciprocally acting on each other, that I call "transcendental embodiment."[84]

In *Critique of Judgment* §3, Kant makes a conclusive point on the fundamental difference between "sensation" (*Empfindung*) and "feeling of pleasure and displeasure" (*Gefühl der Lust und Unlust*). The properly aesthetic character of judgment must claim its independency from both cognition and the practical. Kant draws attention to the "two meanings that the word sensation can have." The crucial link between sensation and feeling of pleasure and displeasure must be saved for the specificity of aesthetic judgment. "When a determination of the feeling of pleasure or displeasure is called sensation, this term means something quite different from what it means when I call sensation the representation of a thing (through the senses, a receptivity that belongs to the cognitive faculty)." In the latter case, sensation is properly "objective sensation" since it refers to objects, has a merely cognitive value, and has no relation to the feeling of pleasure. On the contrary, when "sensation" is exclusively referred to the subject with no cognitive aim whatsoever (not even the aim of knowing the subject itself, which amounts to consider the subject as object), sensation is a "determination of the feeling of pleasure or displeasure." In this case (and in this case only), "feeling" indicates that which "must always remain merely subjective, and cannot possibly be the representation of an object."[85] However, the link between sensation and feeling of pleasure requires the further distinction between aesthetic and practical judgment.

Kant reviews the common claim that "all liking [. . .] is itself sensation (of a pleasure)." At stake is the possibility of a critical distinction, this time between practical and aesthetic judgments. If we concede that "whatever is liked, precisely inasmuch as it is liked is agreeable (*angenehm*)," then sense impressions that determine inclination, or principles of reason that determine the will, or mere forms of intuition that we reflect on and that determine the faculty of judgment, will all be one and the same insofar as their effect (*Wirkung*) on the feeling of pleasure is concerned, since pleasure would be the agreeableness in the sensation of one's state.

If we look only at the *effects* on our feeling, the pathological determination of inclination, the purely moral determination of the will, and reflection on the forms of intuition, all yield the same result, namely a "sensation" of pleasure. The consequence is that, on this view, pathological-practical, moral-practical, and aesthetic judgments become utterly indistinguishable. What needs to be addressed instead is *what determines* the feeling of pleasure (its *Bestimmungsgrund*). Thus, to measure the fundamental distance of these types of judgment, Kant distinguishes three types of "liking" (*Wohlgefallen*) according to their reference to the notion of the "agreeable," the "good," or the "beautiful."[86] Although in the case of aesthetic judgment the "liking" presupposes only the judgment about the object (insofar as we are affected by it), in the case of the practical liking we need to presuppose an affection that comes from the object and produces a "desire" for it and an interest in its existence.[87] Only in the case of aesthetic judgment does the liking arise not from the object but from the judgment itself. Unlike the disinterested character of the beautiful, both the agreeable and the good imply an interest in their respective objects—be it a pathological or a purely practical interest. The pleasure in the beautiful is thereby isolated both from the merely empirical pleasure that arises from the "agreeable" and from the practical pleasure that arises with regard to the "good." Kant's crucial point is that only the aesthetic feeling of pleasure is somehow "pure," and produced by a mere "form." I shall return to this connection in the following chapters.

In the *Critique of Judgment*, Kant's transcendental view of human embodiment is brought to its conclusive results. Here we find the last chapter of his critical theory of sensibility. Kant strengthens the connection between sensation and the feeling of pleasure and displeasure while allowing for a use of intuition without determinate concepts according to which the imagination connects intuition to the feeling of pleasure and displeasure. Thereby, the third *Critique* brings to the fore the far-reaching consequences of Kant's pure foundation of ethics. Precisely because the feeling of pleasure and displeasure has been excluded from the sphere of the practical as a possible motive for moral action, it can now appear as a separate and independent faculty of the *Gemüt,* endowed with an a priori principle of its own. This is Kant's third and final transcendental "aesthetic," which is no longer an aesthetics but a theory of *aesthetic judgment*. As such, Kant's doctrine has taken a different route than Baumgarten's theory of taste. Aesthetic judgment is neither cognitive nor practical nor psychological. Its aesthetic value is rendered independent of other concerns, grounded in an a priori principle of its own, and connected a priori with the feeling of pleasure and displeasure. In Kant's critical itinerary, this 'third aesthetics' could come only after the name of aesthetics had been lent to the cognitive doctrine of space and time; after it had been expanded to a broader significance through the practical exploration of moral feeling and desire; and finally, after the a priori, specifically aesthetic (i.e., non-cognitive and non-practical) connection between feeling of pleasure and faculty of judgment has been established.

8

Reflections of the Body, Reflections on the Body

Era appena la Vita, qualche cosa
che tutti supponiamo senza averne le prove,
la vita di cui siamo testimoni
noi tutti, non di parte, non di accusa,
non di difesa ma che tu conosci
anche soltanto con le dita
quando sfiori un oggetto che ti dica io e te
siamo UNO

—EUGENIO MONTALE, *Diario del '71 e del '72*

IN THE FIRST *CRITIQUE*, KANT CONCENTRATES THE PRINCIPAL problems of the metaphysical doctrine of rational psychology in his exposition of the paralogisms of speculative reason. To the speculative claim of the soul's immateriality, incorruptibility, and personality, he adds the difficulties arising from its alleged *commercium*[1] with the body (with its own body and with other bodies placed outside of it in space). This issue had extensively occupied him already in the 1766 *Dreams of a Spirit-Seer*. As we have seen in the first part of this study, Kant's critical assessment of rational psychology leads to the conclusion that the only meaningful and non-tautological articulation of the concept of myself as thinking being can take place within the realm of experience and refer to my present life.[2] Thereby, the metaphysical notion of soul yields to the transcendental notion of an embodied human being whose existence is rooted in the a priori conditions of its worldly experience. I can know and experience myself as thinking being only on the basis of my being human (*Mensch*), i.e., in relation to my body and its transcendental form (the conditions of space and time).[3] It is my embodied condition, not an inscrutable disembodied principle that discloses to me what my *life* really is—to be sure, my *present* life, not an alleged existence beyond it. In the first *Critique,* my 'present life' is the theoretical space in which experience of reality alone is possible for me. Thereby Kant points to the only critical alternative to both "materialism without soul" and *schwärmerisch,* "ungrounded spiritualism."[4]

Kant's general illustration of the metaphysical doctrine of the soul entails yet another set of issues that the first *Critique* does not directly address in this connection. The idea of "spirituality," argues Kant in the Paralogisms chapter, represents the "thinking substance as the *principle of life in matter,* i.e. as soul (*anima*) and as the ground of *animality (Animalität)*; this, limited through spirituality, gives immortality."[5] At stake in this claim is not only the traditional psychological doctrine of self-knowledge and of the personal soul's attributes but also, more broadly, the problem of the relation between spirit and matter in the construction of living beings in general—a topic that lies at the center of Kant's reflection in the third *Critique.* The question can be formulated alternatively as follows: what is the principle that gives life to (or "animates") dead matter; what is a *living* being or what is the "ground of *life* in the universe"? In the *Dreams,* Kant declares it impossible "to determine with certainty how far and to which members of nature life extends, of what those degrees of life, which border on the very edge of complete lifelessness, may be."[6] Although he confesses to be "very much inclined to assert the existence of immaterial natures in the world," and to put his own soul in the class of these beings,[7] as far as the rational explanation of life is concerned, he opposes both "hylozoism," which "invests everything with life," and "materialism," which "deprives everything of life."[8] The two opposites of "materialism without soul" and enthusiastic "spiritualism" of rational psychology correspond, respectively, to a materialistic and a hylozoistic view of life in nature and in natural beings in general. While rational psychology poses the unsolvable problem of life after death, a crucial difficulty seems already entailed in the very definition of life as such.

In the *Dreams* Kant attempts a definition of life that steers the metaphysical and theoretical discussion toward the idea of practical self-determination. While the essential character of matter is the "filling of space in virtue of a necessary force which is limited by an external force operating against it," "all *life*"—Kant argues—"is based upon the inner capacity to determine oneself *voluntarily*" and consequently is a distinctive mark of those "natures which are supposed to be *spontaneously active* and to contain within themselves the ground of life in virtue of their inner force."[9] As voluntary and spontaneous action is opposed to mechanical force, voluntary action becomes the distinctive mark of life. Evidently, this is hardly a solution of the problem. Voluntary self-determination is invoked to define life but self-determination is circularly characterized against mechanical forces by its having in itself the ground of life.

Similarly, in the first *Critique,* although here within the framework of a different conception of the practical, Kant connects the idea of life to practical activity. The solution of the paralogisms gives to the problem of life a specifically moral turn, which contributes, for the moment, to putting off the general difficulty posed by the concept of life. To be sure, Kant's argument proceeds "*in analogy* with the nature of living beings in this world," whose structure shows that every organ, faculty, or tendency is purposively constituted according to "its determination in life." Following the analogy with nature, the argument moves on to the idea of the moral law as that which gives meaning to man's citizenship in this life and authorizes at the same time to practically extend the prospect of one's existence beyond the limits of experience and life.[10] Moreover, Kant suggests that in speculative reason's indiscreet questions stretching beyond the limits of our present life, we should recognize that reason itself is giving us a "hint" (*Wink*)—a hint that should encourage us to put to a fruitful "practical use" the otherwise speculatively sterile task of self-knowledge.[11] Reason's unavoidable speculative check entails the promise of its practical success.

The issue raised by the paralogisms concerns purely rational versus empirical self-knowledge. The general problem of life, however, is not limited to (knowledge of) myself. As Kant's passage in the *Dreams* makes clear, the question of the boundaries to which life extends is integral to the problem of life. What kind of things can be said to be *living* beings; and how can I say of myself that I am a living being? In addition: what defines the specific *experience of* a living being (in both senses of the genitive)? These questions, although intrinsically connected with the dialectical problem raised by the paralogisms of the first *Critique,* ultimately exceed this work's competence. In raising a problem that it cannot solve, speculative reason gives us a "hint" that points in the moral direction of practical reason—hence in the direction of the second *Critique.* There we find a practical access to the problem of our own life, which is connected, this time, to the "postulate" of a future life, but still no answer to the general issue of life in nature (in other beings and in ourselves as part of nature) is provided. In order to gain transcendental access to the latter problem, we have to follow another "hint" (*Wink*) which, this time, in a new dialectical situation, comes from nature itself. For this "hint," however, we have to wait for the third *Critique* since only at this point do we become sensitive to nature's gesture toward us and become able to understand its ciphered language.[12] In the framework of Kant's conclusive critical work, nature's *Wink* to us is accompanied and complemented by a "suspicion" (*Ahnung*) or presentiment of our reason. For reason is now learning to recognize itself as part of nature and to think in a way that is "attuned" to nature. Such a *Wink* is the suggestion that the hidden secrets of life lie neither in the constitution of matter nor in a spiritual soul (to which we have a supposedly privileged access through introspection). Rather, it lies in the new possibility of thinking the concept of *Naturzweck* by means of a reflection that conjoins our sensible and our intelligible nature. In raising the problem of life and in pointing to the critical means to articulate it, nature's *Wink* indicates to us a supersensible basis for reflecting upon our embodied condition of living rational beings. The systematic innovation that Kant's transcendental philosophy inaugurates by following nature's "hint" is signaled by the assumption, at the center of the inquiry, of a concept that is indeed a "stranger" (*Fremdling*) in natural science, namely, the concept of "natural purpose."[13]

In the *Dreams,* Kant acknowledges that the idea that the soul is the principle or ground of life goes back to the ancients (Aristotle), who distinguished three types of life: the "vegetative, the animal, and the rational."[14] In defining life as voluntary and spontaneous self-determination Kant refers in particular to rational life—and beings endowed with rationality are *Geister,* spirits. However, Kant recognizes that the "obscure" reason that leads him to pose the problem of life is neither peculiar to introspection nor proper only to rational beings. Instead, "it is a reason that applies at the same time to the sentient being of animals (*auf das empfindende Wesen in den Tieren*)." Raising the general problem of life we are necessarily brought outside of ourselves. But what then is the "ground of *animal* life" in general?[15] The quoted passage from the Paralogisms chapter alludes to the answer given by metaphysics: the soul as the "principle of life in matter" is also "the ground of *animality* (*Animalität*)."[16] In the tradition, the problem of life is (at least in part or among other things) the problem of what it means to be *animals,* or what animals distinctively are. Animal life is *sensitive* life—life defined and circumscribed by the sensitive soul or by sensibility. Sensitive life is a life of action but also of reaction, a life of activity as well as passivity and receptivity, a capacity to act but also the feeling of being acted upon. However, the concept of sensibility does not solve but only re-proposes the problem of the relation between material and spiritual elements (or between lower and higher faculties of the soul). This is signaled by Kant's presentation of the way in which rational psychology obtains the soul's "immortality," namely, by limiting animality through spirituality.[17]

This chapter presents the topic of life as the unifying center of Kant's *Critique of Judgment*.[18] I follow the important shift that leads Kant from the focus on our "experience *in life*," which emerges as the solution of the paralogisms and is further explored within the moral space of the second *Critique*, to the question of our "experience *of life*"—our own life and that of other natural beings—which is the distinctive topic of the third *Critique*. I argue, first, that life is for Kant a matter of a specific form of human *sensibility*, i.e., an "aesthetic" matter that concerns our faculty of judgment and a peculiar *feeling* connected to it. This feeling is a feeling for our own life and a sensitivity for living nature in its manifold appearances and expressions. Second, and more generally, I contend that only reflection or the activity of the reflective faculty of judgment is able to disclose a transcendental perspective on our experience *of life*—in ourselves and in other beings. The close connection (which is a necessary and a priori connection) between reflection and the peculiar feeling of pleasure and displeasure betrays the embodied condition of our judgment. Only because we are *embodied* beings can we gain, by means of reflection, the awareness of being alive and being part of living nature. The transcendental condition that makes our experience of life possible—an experience that is neither theoretical nor practical—is the idea of reflection as the "transcendental embodiment" of a new, specific form of human sensibility. Kant's presentation of this condition implies a discussion of the difference between animal and human life, whereby the ultimate, critical solution to the metaphysical problem of materialism, spiritualism, and hylozoism, as well as a new perspective on the discipline of psychology, is provided. Kant's crucial suggestion, in opposition to a longstanding metaphysical tradition, is that the specific difference between animals and humans is neither a physical difference concerning external appearances nor a difference in psychological capacities or faculties, nor a metaphysical distance due to their respective position in the "chain of being." It is, rather, a *transcendental* difference rooted in the peculiar type of *experience* possible to human beings as such.

Animal Souls and Animal Bodies

In the eighteenth-century philosophical debate on the organization of living beings all the aforementioned issues come together.[19] Historically, the discussion is placed at the intersection between two competing models of science: the one, going back to Aristotle and renewed by Diderot, according to which in order to understand natural processes it is necessary to study the organization of the living beings that populate this earth; the other, going back to Galilei and reaffirmed by Newtonian science, according to which the key to natural processes lies in the observation of the skies and in their mathematical description. At stake is the opposition between exact mechanical sciences (Galilei, Newton) and experimental "sciences of life" such as chemistry, medicine, and biology (Diderot). The latter are, more properly, "arts"; their activity is closer to artistic creation; their heuristic enterprise seeks proximity to nature (not forceful detachment from it).[20] The debate has its modern roots in Descartes's mechanicism and mind-body dualism; is fueled by Bayle's atheism and skepticism and provoked by the issue of "Spinozism"; is renewed by Leibniz's metaphysical doctrine of the pre-established harmony; and finally culminates in the naturalistic materialism of Diderot and the *Encyclopédie* and in the empiricism of Locke and Hume. The problem of defining sensibility—or *sensibilité*—is the problem of defining the experience and observation of life in/of matter. It is an issue that regards both *external appearance* and *internal organization* of determinate natural forms.[21] It is also, at the same time, the problem of tracing the origins of life and solving the mystery of generation, as well as the problem of drawing a classification of the manifold forms of natural phenomena, of constructing the system of nature. Throughout the stations of this debate, the crucial issue is that of determining the status of those living beings that are *animals,* and of marking out the place of man among them.

In an epoch of triumphal Newtonian science, Diderot draws the crucial question of the organization of living beings to the center. Significantly, he gives to the problem the rhetorical form of a "dream." This time, however, what is staged is not the dream of a visionary metaphysician as in the early Kant, but the dream that haunts the sleep of the mathematician D'Alembert and, with him, of all mechanist physicists of the time. While these scientists do not even think of the issue of life when they are awake, as no place can be found for it within their theories, the problem keeps reappearing to them in their dreams. On Diderot's account, sensibility is immediately identical with "life." His theory of generation is construed on the radical claim that extends sensibility to all beings—minerals included.[22] "Sensibility" as "the general and essential quality of matter" is the principle that replaces the metaphysical assumption of a god and an immaterial soul. From this principle it necessarily follows that "the stone feels"—even though man, in cutting it, does not hear its cry.[23] Thus, Diderot declares that "every animal is more or less human; every mineral is more or less plant; every plant is more or less animal."[24] Limits in nature are imprecise and elusive. There is no point in nature that is not endowed with sensibility and not affected by pleasure or pain. This theory suggests not only the extension of sensibility to all beings; it also urges us humans to develop a type of sensibility able to respond to that of other living things and attuned to theirs—a sensibility or sensitivity which is able to hear the stone's cry, a cry to which the senses of the mechanist physicist are instead completely deaf.

To disclose the far-reaching implications of the discussion on animal life for metaphysics, ethics, and religion once the relation between soul and body is brought into the picture it is historically useful to turn back to Bayle's provocative analyses. The article "Rorarius" in his *Dictionnaire historique et critique* (1697) can be considered a *summa* of the issues entailed in the problem of animal life from antiquity to the close of the seventeenth century, and leading to Kant.[25] Relevant for my purposes here is the systematic connection that gathers issues of psychology, biology, morality, and religion in the debate on animal versus human life. At the end of the eighteenth century, Kant's transcendental principle of *Zweckmäßigkeit* radically transformed the way in which this entire problematic constellation is addressed. In his article "Rorarius," Bayle discusses both the difficulties that arise from the mechanistic argument of Descartes and the Cartesians denying a soul to animals, and the difficulties arising from the counterargument that vindicates to animals a soul as worthy as the human one. Thereby, he sketches out the background of Kant's reflection in the third *Critique*. Bayle argues that since the soul as principle of life is equated with sensibility and the capacity for feeling and affection, to extend possession of the soul to animals is to eliminate our human metaphysical privilege over them. In Bayle's view, the difference between animals and humans as well as that between sensation and thought cannot be a substantial one but one only of degree. The psychological distinction between "higher" and "lower" faculties of the soul—a distinction that disappears under Kant's critical attacks—is rooted precisely in this debate.[26] Moreover, the argument deeply undermines the theory of the human soul's immortality. For since the material, corporeal soul of animals dies with the body, and since between animal and human soul there is only a difference of degree, no basis is left for the argument supporting the human soul's distinctive immateriality and hence immortality. Finally, by attributing a soul to animals the idea of divine justice is compromised: how, then, can the suffering of innocents be justified? In this case, as opposed to the case of children's suffering, not even the argument of original sin can be appealed to. This view ultimately opposes Descartes's dualism and its reduction of animals to machines— indeed is aimed at "destroying Descartes' machines."[27] Bayle concludes that for religion it is definitely safer to maintain the Cartesian position. But Cartesian mechanistic dualism meets no lesser difficulties, among which is the claim that Descartes's doctrine leads us to consider not only animals but also all other human beings to be machines. On the Cartesians' account, life becomes an utterly solipsistic fact rooted in self-consciousness.[28] In addition, Bayle uncovers the anti-anthropocentric aim of the argument in favor of animal souls as set against the extrinsic teleology of the claim that all natural phenomena are not only inferior to man but created for the sake of man.[29] Finally, Leibniz's philosophy proposes a third hypothesis beyond the Scholastic idea of the "*influence* of the body on the soul and the soul on the body" on the one hand, and the Cartesian idea of the "*assistance* or occasional causality" on the other. Leibniz advances the hypothesis of the "pre-established harmony,"[30] which is supported by a theory of generation as preformation and responds both to Descartes's mechanism and to Epicurus's (and in Epicurus's aftermath, Gassendi's)[31] deterministic materialism. Thereby, we have reached the immediate antecedents of the debate that frames the third *Critique*.

Reflection on Life—Life Reflected

Kant's *Critique of Judgment* is the final—critical and transcendental—answer to the problematic constellation that conjoins the issue of (animal and human) sensibility occupying both rational and empirical psychology, with the question of the definition and origin of life attempted by both metaphysics and natural science. The two parts of the *Critique of Judgment*—the critiques of aesthetic and teleological judgment—address this constellation of problems under the new unifying perspective opened up by the reflective faculty of judgment. Such a faculty is connected to an a priori principle (the principle of *Zweckmäßigkeit*, purposiveness) that discloses a peculiar form of sensibility, namely, the pure feeling of pleasure and displeasure that distinguishes human sensibility from animal sensibility as well as from the 'insensitive' rationality of disembodied spirits; while the principle of nature's *Zweck-mäßigkeit* allows us to reflect on and gain awareness of ourselves as natural living beings and, as such, parts of the whole of nature. In this way, the principle connects the moral significance of our present life (and the practical postulate of a future life) to a *reflective experience* of it. Eventually, it leads us to discover in the critical use of the concept of *Naturzweck* the solution of the dogmatic and dialectical dispute between mechanism and teleology, materialism or Spinozism (or Epicureanism) and hylozoism or theism.[32]

Accordingly, in the third *Critique,* Kant's final articulation of the idea of reason's transcendental embodiment, i.e., the recognition of an independent a priori space proper to human sensibility as condition of experience, arrives at a new systematization of two *Fremdlinge* in science and philosophy. Thereby it radically re-orients the philosophical discussion on the topic. On the one hand, it gives a place within transcendental philosophy to that "stranger" that is the concept of *Naturzweck.* This concept discloses its scientific validity only in its critical (heuristic and regulative) use, whereby it allows us to reflect on life and give a unitary meaning to our natural and moral destination. On the other hand, the idea of transcendental embodiment allows Kant to reach the final critical transformation of the discipline of psychology.

In the Methodology of the *Critique of Pure Reason,* discussing the form that metaphysics must assume in the aftermath of the critique, Kant raises a question for which, at the time, he has no satisfactory answer. It is only with the third *Critique* that Kant is able to provide this answer. In 1787, after the critique, the fate of empirical psychology and the place that it has traditionally occupied in metaphysics are at stake. At this point, so much is clear to Kant: empirical psychology belongs where "the properly (empirical) doctrine of nature" belongs, i.e., on the side of "*applied* philosophy." Hence, opposing a longstanding tradition, Kant contends that empirical psychology "must be completely banned from metaphysics."[33] And yet, immediately after this strong declaration, Kant nonetheless capitulates to the need for making a place—albeit a "little place" (*Plätzchen*)—for empirical psychology in metaphysics. The reason for Kant's systematic uneasiness toward this discipline is that although he recognizes its philosophical importance, he is unable to decide with which discipline empirical psychology has a "kinship" (*Verwandtschaft*). As neither reason nor nature gives us a "hint" (*Wink*) in this respect, Kant is left with a puzzling conclusion: empirical psychology is a "stranger" (*Fremdling*) that as yet has no place in science; and it will have to remain a stranger with no fixed abode until hosted "in a fully developed anthropology (the *pendant* to the empirical doctrine of nature)."[34] The *Critique of Judgment* provides the transcendental conditions that allow Kant to finally settle this systematic issue. In the Methodology of the critique of the teleological faculty of judgment, Kant presents the idea of "ethico-theology" as the solution of the problem posed by rational and empirical psychology. Opposing, once again, both spiritualism and mechanic materialism, and following this time nature's "hint" accompanied by our reason's "presentiment," Kant discloses the perspective of an "anthropology of the inner sense, i.e., our knowledge of our thinking self *in life*."[35] The principle of nature's *Zweckmäßigkeit* allows Kant to recognize, reflectively, the place of man as natural and moral being in the universe. And yet, it is precisely this reflection (and not a spiritual soul or possession of reason or outer appearance) that *transcendentally* distinguishes man from all other living beings in nature. Man's self-reflection in life—rooted in the fact that we are living beings—reveals the furthest point to which the transcendental condition of embodiment has led us in the enterprise of drawing the a priori conditions of our possible experience. At this point, man is finally reconciled with his animal nature. This is, to be sure, the deeper conciliation that the third *Critique* achieves as condition for the unification of nature and freedom, theoretical and practical reason.

The *Critique of Judgment* reformulates the question "What is sensibility or life?" as the question: how can we feel ourselves part of living nature? Transcendentally: what is the a priori condition that allows us (internally) to experience our own life, and (externally) to feel our life "attuned" to that of other living beings and to the universe as a systematic whole? This is, to be sure, the new problem of "orientation" that the world poses to us. Its solution follows a transcendental pattern similar to the one that guided Kant in the previous two *Critiques*.[36]

The need for a third Critique arises out of the discovery of an independent a priori principle for the faculty of judgment—a principle that regulates a judging activity that is neither purely theoretical nor purely practical, yet lays claim to a validity of its own within human experience. The first *Critique* deals with knowledge as product of the "determinant" (*bestimmende*) activity of judgment, which subsumes particulars under a "universal (the rule, the principle, the law)" *given* by the understanding. However, a new and as yet unexplored problem is posed by the act of judging of particulars when no universal concept, rule, or law is given. In this case, judgment's principal problem consists in "finding out"[37] the universal under which to subsume. In this task, judgment reveals its nature as a *searching* (or heuristic) faculty. Its search is reflection. For the faculty of judgment cannot simply take the universal as already constituted (and given) from a different source (in this case it would still be determinant). Rather, judgment has to be itself the "source"[38] of the principle, has to give the principle to itself in a reflective act of self-legislation. This is reflective judgment's peculiar "heautonomy."[39] The faculty of judgment is both the source of the principle and the faculty on whose activity the principle is legislating: judgment's principle is legislating neither on nature nor on freedom but on judgment itself, namely, on its own reflection on both realms of human experience. Thereby, reflection discloses a new and different way of relating to nature and freedom; it opens up the possibility of a mediating and unifying (or encompassing and overarching: reflection is *Über-legung*) "mental disposition" (*Denkungsart*)[40] toward the natural and the moral world.

How does the world in which reflective judgment sets out in search of its new universals and to which it addresses its principled "reflection" look like? What judgment meets in its endeavors is indeed the world of nature; but it is not the same nature that understanding and determinant judgment constructed in the first *Critique*. While the latter is the physical world of mechanism laid out by Newtonian science—a system whose *universal* laws are given in their necessity by the understanding's a priori synthetic judgments—we now face a world that appears to us as a chaotic "labyrinth"[41] of infinite and contingent *particular* laws. Between those universal laws and these particular laws an abyss lies open. For particular empirical laws cannot be deduced from the transcendental laws of nature in a merely analytical way.[42] Since there is no deductive transition from "experience in general" to a system of particular empirical laws, if we place ourselves in the perspective of the understanding a gap of legislation seems to threaten the world of nature. Understanding's a priori synthetic judgments *leave undetermined* all the infinite cases that can be counted under those universal laws. Placed in front of nature's manifold forms, the understanding, Kant confesses, becomes suddenly dumb: it is simply incapable of saying anything about them.[43] Understanding, which legislates over "nature in general," is no longer legislative in "the labyrinth of the manifold of possible particular laws."[44] And since determinant judgment by simply executing understanding's rule "is only subsumptive" it can provide no real determination for those manifold empirical forms of nature that are left, as it were, thoroughly "indeterminate."[45] The paradigm of mechanical science cannot offer knowledge of the world of living nature as a coherent, organized system. Newtonian physics construes the model of a homogeneous "system of nature" in which all bodies in the universe are seen as interacting, and movements localized in some spatially limited subsystem are given no privilege in relation to trajectories with no spatial limitation. In this world, phenomena speak a unique, universal language; it is a world in which no heterogeneity can significantly emerge. In other words, Newton's system (and the theory Kant exposes in the Analytic of the first *Critique*) is unable to attribute any sense to spatial differentiation, to the constitution of natural limits, to heterogeneity, and to the emergence of organized functions—in a word, it does not accord any specific sense to those particular processes that imply the development of a living being.[46] Consequently, if we endorse the perspective that understanding and determinant judgment establish in the first *Critique,* we feel disoriented looking at the world of particular natural processes and organized living being, as if placed in a chaotic "labyrinth" in which we need to find a way out or, at least, a "guiding thread" (*Leitfaden*)[47] that would allow us to securely proceed in our path. Alternatively, following Diderot's image of analogous inspiration, we must recognize that in sketching the view of a material world pervasively imbued with life, the mathematician D'Alembert is dreaming the disturbing "dream" of a (physically) sick person—a dream, however, that seems dangerously close to the truth. How, then, can we dissipate the dream and master the labyrinth? In either case—whether we find ourselves wandering in a labyrinth or dreaming an unsettling dream— what is needed is a principle that provides us with a sense of orientation in a reality in which the emergence of unknown details and contingent features threatens the systematicity (and thereby the truth) of our worldview. For, at this point, such features can no longer be set aside. Ultimately, our sense of ourselves depends on them.

Moreover, a second implication of mechanistic science calls for emendation and is now subject to further reflection. To be sure, Kant addresses this point already in the *Critique of Practical Reason* (and even earlier, in the solution of the third antinomy of speculative reason). Rational mechanics describes a world in which man is an *automaton* like all other "objects" of possible knowledge. In the framework of this theory, no account of the specificity of human existence *within* nature is provided. Metaphysics responds with a spiritualist dualism according to which the scientific description of mechanical nature receives its correlate in the representation of man as automaton endowed with a spiritual soul. Paradoxically, the reduction of man's "body" to natural mechanism, i.e., the gesture that makes it equal to all other natural material bodies in the universe, has the consequence of alienating man's "soul" from nature, since the soul is endowed with all the properties the body does not have. Such alienation results from metaphysics' pneumatic doctrine of the soul. But it results also (although on the basis of a different inspiration and pointing in a very different direction) from Kant's critical attack on spiritualist dualism. For Kant, after the first *Critique,* man's redemption from mechanism takes place not in nature but in the moral world of the second *Critique.* And yet, as we have seen in the second part of this study, within the moral sphere a new construction of human sensibility—and of the human body—begins. The third *Critique* offers Kant's final efforts at reconciling man's soul with his body. The task is now a reconciliation of man with nature that takes place, this time, *within* nature. Such reconciliation is based on man's reflective experience of life—within and without himself. At this point, the idea of transcendental embodiment expresses precisely this program of reconciliation.

Thus, the image of the labyrinth of nature and the need for orientation in it suggests that, in addition to the understanding, a particular faculty must be found that can effectively *determine* all the particular, empirical cases that nature offers to us as contingent. This faculty would connect general laws to particular cases, and particular cases to their general laws, thereby rescuing the world of nature from the menacing lack of legislation suggested by the idea of the labyrinth (and by the unsettling flight from reality that is proper to dreams). It is at this point that Kant introduces the specific function of the *reflective* faculty of judgment and a new set of questions: how is an *experience* of nature's labyrinth possible for us? Can we ever come to think of this labyrinth as a *systematic* and *ordered* whole, thereby gaining orientation in its manifold contingent forms? And how can we get to the point of placing ourselves within this world as one of its many forms—abandoning, for a moment, the attitude of legislators whereby we stood as if separated from nature itself? Since Kant clearly confesses that the very "concept of a system according to [. . .] (empirical) laws is thoroughly alien to the understanding,"[48] this task defines the peculiar activity of the reflective faculty of judgment and its a priori principle, and thereby provides the ground for an independent third *Critique.*

In the traditional psychology of the faculties, reflection counts as one of the higher faculties of the mind. Reflection is the encompassing act of *Überlegen, Über-denken, Über-blicken.*[49] It does not deal directly with objects but indicates the "condition" (*Zustand*) of the subject's *Gemüt.*[50] It is the activity of comparing or considering synoptically given representations together (*Zusammenhalten*, as opposed for example to successive apprehension of different representations), and thereby relating them either to one another or to one's own cognitive faculty with regard to a concept made possible by this very same faculty. Reflective judgment is also named *facultas dijudicandi*. Reflection, Kant argues, is not distinctively human; it is proper to animals as well. Animal reflection, however, is only "instinctual"[51] and may appear as an "inborn drive."[52] That reflection in animals is instinctual means that it does not aim at attaining an as yet undiscovered concept. Animals do not reflect in order to produce concepts or to find new universal rules. They reflect as moved or determined by an inclination that precedes the act of reflection.[53] In animals, reflection has a merely pragmatic or technical use: its task is to determine or give direction to natural instinct. And yet, in animals reflection still maintains its searching, heuristic function. Reflection serves the bird to find a suitable place to nest, and serves the hunting dog to find the quickest path on which to chase the prey.[54] Thus, reflection in animals expresses the way in which nature is at work—it is, in other words, already an example of nature's art or "technique." Yet in order to understand what animal reflection is (and what kind of beings animals are), we need to appeal to our *human* reflection, i.e., to reflective judgment, and draw, as it were, an "analogy" with ourselves.[55] In man, reflection is the function according to which even the meaning of animal reflection can be understood and placed within the broader context of nature's systematic organization. In other words, with Kant's suggestion we can argue that the entire discussion concerning animal versus human psychology can meaningfully take place only if addressed, transcendentally, by the heuristic means of our reflective faculty of judgment. In the third *Critique,* transcendental philosophy lays out the principles according to which understanding and experience of *living* nature and its particular *organization* are possible for us. This is Kant's radical—namely, transcendental—reformulation of the constellation of problems addressed by the tradition.[56]

In man, the reflective activity of judgment is based upon an a priori *transcendental* principle. Kant formulates this principle as that of the "formal *Zweckmäßigkeit* of nature."[57] A transcendental principle, as opposed to a metaphysical one, is a principle that represents the sole universal condition under which things can become objects of our experience and "cognition in general." The possibility of thinking nature as an ordered system (as opposed to a chaotic labyrinth) that comprehends things such as living beings and their specific processes is predicated on the possibility of the *reflective* faculty of judgment displaying a *transcendental* principle of its own. Nature's formal purposiveness is a principle that makes possible our experience of nature not as "nature in general" but, this time, as "nature determined through a manifold of particular laws."[58] Kant suggests that to represent an object as ordered according to a lawful unity that responds to the "necessary aim (a *need*) of the understanding,"[59] and yet is in itself merely *contingent,* is to represent the object according to the form of purposiveness. That which is conducive to a certain aim and is nonetheless in itself contingent, is purposive. Understanding *needs* to think that experience of nature is possible not only in its analytic but also in its synthetic unity, i.e., in the heterogeneity of its empirical forms. It is only reflection, however, that is able to fulfill this subjective need.

> The faculty of judgment *must* assume as an a priori principle for its own use that what to human insight is contingent in the particular (empirical) laws of nature, does nonetheless contain a lawful unity—unfathomable although still thinkable for us—in the connection of its manifold into an experience which is in itself possible.[60]

In the perspective of reflective judgment, the contingency of particular laws is not denied but simply ordered within the whole of experience. Such a system is in itself objectively possible and subjectively necessary. The principle of reflective judgment provides, as Kant suggests, the "lawfulness of the contingent as such."[61]

Kant recognizes that if the general problem of life remains the monopoly of determinant judgment, the issue can find no other solution than a metaphysical one. On the path of determinant judgment the labyrinth of nature leads only as far as an antinomy that cannot be decided—an antinomy that pinpoints a conflict only within reason's own legislation—because reason can find no principle determining a priori the possibility of things according to merely empirical laws. The traditional dispute between philosophical and scientific systems accounting for nature's organization and for the origin of life cannot be settled until the transcendental status of the notion of *Naturzweck* is recognized and the entire issue is taken up by the reflective faculty of judgment. In other words, in order to find a solution, the *Widerstreit* of reason's legislation must yield to the antinomy of the faculty of judgment.[62] The systems of materialism and those of hylozoism and theism treat this notion dogmatically, i.e., metaphysically. While the "dogmatic" procedure of reason is metaphysical and is followed by the determinant faculty of judgment, the "critical" procedure is transcendental and is followed by the reflective faculty of judgment. To treat a concept (even if its origin is empirical) "dogmatically" is to think of it as "contained under another concept of the object that constitutes a principle of reason" and to determine it according to this principle. This procedure "has the force of law"—is *gesetzmäßig*—for determinant judgment in all its subsumptions and leads to claims regarding the objective constitution of things. On the contrary, a concept is treated "merely *critically* if we consider it only in relation to our cognitive faculty, and hence in relation to the subjective conditions under which we think of it, without venturing to decide anything about its object."[63] The critical and transcendental procedure of reason is *gesetzmäßig* not for objects but for the reflective faculty of judgment. The concept of "natural purpose" is a concept whose objective reality cannot be proved. Therefore, no determination of objects is possible through it except in a dogmatic and metaphysical way. The concept, however, can be used by the reflective faculty of judgment to critically and transcendentally reflect upon the relation between the object and our cognitive faculties. The concept of natural purpose contains the condition under which we can meaningfully think of living nature (and of ourselves as part of it): the experience that arises is not a cognitive one, it is reflection.

The transcendental principle of nature's formal purposiveness is opposed not only to metaphysical but also to psychological principles. Since the idea of *Zweckmäßigkeit* does not regard the objective constitution of things but only the way in which we relate to them by judging them, its fundamental "subjectivity" is not a merely psychological character. Kant argues that the idea of formal purposiveness and all the maxims by which this idea is instantiated and through which it guides empirical research (such as the *lex parsimoniae,* the *lex continui in natura,* and the rule: *principia praeter necessitatem non sunt multiplicanda*) do not have a psychological origin. For these maxims do not describe what happens, i.e., according to what rule our cognitive processes take place and how we go about formulating our judgments. Rather, they prescribe how we "ought to judge" in order to make sense of the particular empirical constitution of nature.[64] As a transcendental principle, the idea of formal purposiveness sets an accord between our cognitive faculties and the infinite variety of nature's forms and empirical laws. Thereby it explains our psychological reaction when scientific endeavors are rewarded with success (hence, Kant contends, it is not psychology that justifies the transcendental principle but rather this principle that accounts for certain psychological events). It "explains why we [. . .] rejoice (actually we are relieved of a need), just as if it were a lucky chance that favors our intentions, when we meet such a systematic unity under merely empirical laws."[65] The systematic unity of experience is assumed as a regulative principle for our research. Understanding, in all its efforts, will never be able to prove this principle as objective and constitutive of nature. The sensible world meets us with particular cases of objects for which applicable general concepts are lacking. While these cases leave both understanding and determinant judgment utterly disoriented and dumb, they are viewed by the reflective faculty of judgment as extremely fortunate cases—to wit, as cases to be used as orientation marks on judgment's way out of nature's labyrinth. In reflection we judge as if the constitution of those objects were attuned to our cognitive faculties; as if those objects were meeting a need or an aim proper to our cognitive powers; as if those objects were made by an understanding like ours (although not ours) to meet the demand of a meaningful and ordered experience. The encounter with such fortunate cases is obviously merely contingent—it is, as Kant puts it, nothing more than a "lucky chance." In these occurrences we are presented with nature's formal purposiveness. A feeling of pleasure—a rejoicing—arises here for the first time. We begin to orient ourselves in the labyrinth of nature, which is thereby progressively transformed into a systematic whole. The important point in this reflective operation is that we become integral part of nature. Reflection reconciles us with the object we are judging and unifies us with it; our experience of the object is an experience of ourselves. The principle of purposiveness indicates a meeting point between nature's forms and ourselves—an *Ein-Stimmung* and *Zusammen-Stimmung,* as it were. The fact that in this encounter the condition of a *Stimmung* is established and felt, means that a *Stimme*—nature's voice, or its *Wink*—is received, heard, and somehow responded to as a meaningful language. Nature now speaks a language that our imagination understands (as opposed to understanding, which remains deaf and mute to nature): it speaks in a figurative way through its "beautiful forms."[66] Our feeling of joy—or our pleasure—is not simply an accessory consequence of our searching enterprise; it is, rather, a constitutive ingredient of it.

Thus, while the discussion on reflective judgment leads Kant to the transcendental principle of nature's purposiveness, this principle discloses the embodied dimension of our reflection. Nature's formal purposiveness is necessarily connected with our emotive responsiveness to (our reflection on) nature, i.e., with a pure feeling of pleasure or displeasure.[67] That responsiveness integrally belongs to what our human capacity for reflection is.

The "connection" (*Verbindung*)[68] between purposiveness and feeling of pleasure and displeasure is not merely psychological but has an a priori and necessary character (whence its peculiar universality). The claim that a natural object—and nature in its empirical manifestations—is in accord with our cognitive faculties poses a specifically new problem because this accordance or attunement is thoroughly contingent.[69] Kant suggests that only the intentional setup of our cognitive faculties, i.e., our explicit "endeavor" or aim to systematize nature in its empirical forms can call our attention to "nature's purposiveness for our understanding."[70] Pleasure is, in general, the result of a successful endeavor. What we feel pleasure in is, in our case, the contingent accordance, the harmony or "suitability"—the *Ein-stimmung, Überein-stimmung, Zusammen-stimmung*—between nature and those faculties of the mind that made success possible. What we feel pleasure in is the possibility of attributing meaning to the world that we experience, and thereby of responding to its manifestations in our own human way. The opposite feeling—one of displeasure—arises, on the contrary, when we find ourselves in a world that appears meaningless. Kant warns us that the search for meaning is not always and not necessarily successful,[71] and that experience of a chaotic manifold of forms with no regularity is a possibility which we may very well conceive.[72] The threat of the labyrinth with no way out is always an open chance (it is, this time, an 'unlucky' chance): such a representation of nature would indeed "cause us displeasure."[73] The "connection" between the principle of nature's purposiveness and the faculty of feeling—*Gefühl*—is a connection that always leaves open the alternative between feeling of *pleasure* and feeling of *displeasure*. The duality of feelings is constitutive of this faculty precisely because of the contingency proper to the order in which it is inscribed. While pleasure arises out of the accordance and harmony between our cognitive faculties and nature's order, displeasure is the result of a conflict[74] between nature's disorder and irreducible heterogeneity and reflective judgment's quest for meaning. The alternative possibility of meaning and lack of meaning—of pleasure and displeasure—pervades the whole development of the third *Critique* and is integral to the experience of the world that this work outlines in its transcendental principles.[75]

The connection between the principle of nature's formal purposiveness and feeling brings us back to the "orientation" problem that Kant discusses in the 1786 essay "What Does It Mean to Orient Oneself in Thinking?" Here the setting for Kant's analysis is, in the first place, geographical. According to common sense, self-orientation is the *subjective* procedure of determining the position that *we* occupy in the surrounding world of nature. The problem is rooted in a deeply felt "need" of our mental faculties; the key to its solution is a subjective feeling—*Gefühl*. This feeling is physically embodied in the irreducible distinction between our left and right hands. To be sure, the starry sky that appears as an object of admiration at the end of the second *Critique* serves us also and primarily for a fundamental purpose of orientation. Seen in this perspective, that starry sky displays a crucial connection with our own body (the left-right distinction from which the north-south orientation is derived), whereby we gain the sense of order that allows us to proceed in our movement—be it on earth or at sea. The third *Critique* shows that the feeling of "orientation" and that of "admiration"[76] are transcendentally connected and compose the two sides of one and the same experience. The peculiar feeling of pleasure and displeasure rooted in the function of reflective judgment and its principle expresses precisely this crucial connection. Such feeling has neither a theoretical origin, although it is somehow cognitive, nor is it practical since it does not relate to the lower or the higher appetitive faculty, although it presents an analogy with practical purposiveness.[77] What kind of feeling is it, then?

Kant argues that if the condition that allows us to achieve a certain aim is an a priori condition, then the feeling of pleasure that arises from the attainment of our goal is determined through an "a priori ground."[78] In our case, the a priori condition for the understanding of nature's labyrinthine order is the principle of formal purposiveness. Our cognitive quest of finding out a variety of empirical laws that are intelligible because placed within the systematic unity of experience depends upon the assumption that nature is designed as if in agreement with our faculties in their cognitive endeavor. Since this assumption is the a priori condition of our reflection upon nature, we can conclude that the feeling of pleasure which arises when our inquiry is crowned with success is a peculiar feeling that has an a priori ground.

But what does it mean for a feeling to be determined by an a priori ground? Kant's longstanding difficulties with *Gefühl*, both in relation to moral eudaimonism and in relation to taste, are due to the impossibility of attributing shared universality and necessity to the propositions built upon it. In short, the difficulties arise from the merely pathological and subjective validity of feeling. Being occasioned by the different affection of the lower faculty of desire, feeling seems condemned to be necessarily a posteriori and limited to one's individual experience. Now, on the contrary, Kant introduces for the first time a feeling that rests on an a priori condition and hence has an a priori *necessary* ground and displays *universal validity:* it is a feeling that "is valid for everyone."[79] Kant underlines the novelty of this connection between feeling and purposiveness by distinguishing it from the purposiveness that relates to the faculty of desire. In our case, the determination of feeling "takes place simply as the object is related to the *cognitive* faculty," not to the faculty of desire (as is the case for the instinctive reflection of animals). And since *nature's* purposiveness is at stake, we are certainly not dealing with a "*practical* purposiveness of nature."[80] The purposiveness that constitutes the a priori ground for feeling is not technical-practical or moral-practical purposiveness, nor is it animal instinctive reflection or the moral law. It seems 'as if' we were imposing practical purposiveness on nature but in fact we are dealing with a purposiveness of its own kind, which relates neither to understanding nor to reason, neither to the cognitive faculty (strictly defined) nor to the faculty of desire but to a faculty in the middle—the reflective faculty of judgment.

The peculiarity of such a priori grounded feeling consists in its being purely "aesthetic"—a character that Kant opposes to all feelings that are merely pathological.[81] Such feeling is the last form in which Kant's transcendental philosophy investigates our embodied human condition at the level of critique. The connection between the reflective faculty of judgment, the principle of formal purposiveness, and the feeling of pleasure is the structure that articulates the specificity of a twofold possible experience—an aesthetic and a teleological one. This is an experience of ourselves as part of living nature; it is the experience of conciliation between our natural and moral determination, between our animal and spiritual sides. The human being (or human nature), for Kant, is the result of this experience, the construction of this reflection. This makes it clear why an "anthropology of the inner sense"[82] becomes possible in philosophy only after Kant's final *Critique*.

At this point for Kant, "aesthetic" designates that aspect of a representation of an object that is merely subjective and irreducible to cognition but is "*immediately connected*"[83] to a feeling of pleasure or displeasure. The representation of an object's formal purposiveness with regard to our cognitive faculties fulfills all these requisites and transcendentally defines the space of our aesthetic experience expressed by the reflective "judgment of taste" (*Geschmacksurteil*).[84] The *only reason* why an object is called purposive—and thereby beautiful—is that its representation *immediately* produces pleasure in the subject. In this case, the representation of purposiveness is grounded upon a pleasure that is "immediate" (not mediated by concepts, practical aims or interests, material determinations of the object, etc.) and merely *subjective* since it arises only out of "mere reflection" on the form of the object.[85] Purposiveness does not express anything about the object's constitution or existence. Rather, it presents a subjective mode of apprehending the object. It voices the suitability of the object's representation to the subject's faculties whereby pleasure is immediately produced. This means that the pleasure connected to the representation of the object's purposiveness is referred to the *form* of the object because purposiveness is not a material feature of the object itself. The representation is called, in this case, "*aesthetic* representation of purposiveness" and expresses simply a "*subjective formal* purposiveness of the object.*" In this case, the feeling of pleasure voices the purposiveness of the object, the *Angemessenheit*—the "conformity" or "agreement"—of its form "to the cognitive faculties that are at play in the reflective faculty of judgment, and insofar as they are at play therein."[86] It is therefore clear that "pleasure" is another word for "purposiveness" when the relation to the subject is taken as relation to its *Gefühl* rather than to the faculty of reflective judgment. Both pleasure and purposiveness are, in this case, purely formal.

Certainly, the purposive relation between subject and object can be looked at in a reverse way as well. This time, purposiveness is not ascribed to the form of the object with regard to the subject's faculties, but to the subject itself with regard to the form—and even to "the lack of form" (*Unform*)—of the object. While the first type of relationship is inscribed within the framework of the concepts of nature where "taste" prompts aesthetic judgments of the beautiful, the second type of relationship is determined by the concept of freedom and prompts aesthetic judgments of the sublime. The latter arise "from a feeling of spirit."[87] In the case of the sublime, no purposiveness seems to be contained in the form of the object. The fact that the object displays a lack of form seems to speak against the very possibility of regarding the object as purposive. In this case, however, the representation of the object can be set in relation to a purposiveness that lies instead *in the subject*. Purposiveness speaks, this time, to the *Geistesgefühl*. This, as the "supersensible determination of the subject's *Gemütskräfte*,"[88] is also the feeling connected to *Geist* as "the principle that gives life" (*das belebende Prinzip*) to the soul.[89] Thereby Kant suggests that our receptivity and sensitivity to an aesthetic feeling is a feeling for (the principle of) life itself and for its presence within our *Gemüt*, as well as in nature outside of ourselves.

Kant argues that when the form of the object apprehended in the imagination produces a harmony among our cognitive faculties independently of (or prior to) any concept that we might have of the object, we have a "*merely subjective* ground" for representing the object's purposiveness.[90] On the other hand, we have an *"objective* ground" for a representation of purposiveness when the form of the given object is represented as in agreement with a concept that grounds the very possibility of the thing in its form. In this case, as is obvious, the concept must "precede" our reflection upon the object's form as its condition of possibility. The form of the object is not set in relation to the subject's faculties in view of "cognition *in general,"* as in the case of judgments of taste. Rather, it is set in relation to a *"determinate* cognition of the object under a given concept."[91] However, since the reflective and not the determinant faculty of judgment is at stake, we must assume that the concept is not used to determine the subject for cognition but only to reflect upon it.[92] In this case, however, the representation of purposiveness is still mediated by a concept and has nothing to do with a "feeling of pleasure *in things"* or, more precisely, "has *no immediate relation* to the feeling of pleasure and displeasure."[93] What Kant thereby denies is not all kind of relationship with the feeling of pleasure as such but only the *"immediate* relation" proper to aesthetic judgments, on the one hand, and the practical or pathological "pleasure *in things,"* on the other.

In sum, two possibilities are at hand: a reflection that *precedes all concepts* and relates the object's form to the *subject*'s faculties according to the conditions for *cognition in general;* and a reflection that *follows a concept* and relates the object's form to the concept that grounds the *object*'s own possibility in view of a *determinate cognition* of the object. The partition of the critique of the faculty of judgment into *"aesthetic* and *teleological* faculty of judgment"[94] follows from this argument. The aesthetic faculty of judgment is responsible for judgments regarding formal and subjective purposiveness, i.e., beauty of objects, pronounced by means of the feeling of pleasure and displeasure with no relation to concepts; the teleological faculty of judgment is responsible for the real and objective representation of purposiveness of natural products, i.e., for the representation of objects as natural purposes by means of understanding and reason.

A Feeling for Life

Kant establishes the notion of purposiveness of the forms of things (*Sachen*)— products of nature as well as art—with regard to the faculty of judgment and on the basis of the subject's "receptivity" (*Empfänglichkeit*) or responsiveness to a peculiar kind of pleasure and displeasure, that is, to a particular structure of sensibility. It is a transcendental condition of our sensibility to be *receptive* or *responsive* to a pleasure that is not material but formal as it arises "out of reflection (*aus Reflexion*) on the form of things."[95] Although in the first *Critique* receptivity designates the material side of sensibility (sensation) that is functional for knowledge of objects, the second *Critique* proposes its practical transformation as product of freedom's intelligible causality. Its transcendental validity within the moral sphere no longer indicates the capacity of being affected by material, visible objects but a peculiar "sense" for the invisible, moral property of agents as noumena; as "moral feeling" receptivity is our responsiveness to freedom's effects. As we have seen, however, this is only the last station of the itinerary of the *Critique of Practical Reason*. At the beginning of the Analytic, to the contrary, Kant opposes the assumption of our natural *Empfänglichkeit* for pleasure and displeasure as foundation of morality on the basis that (1) it yields affections that can "only be *known* empirically"; (2) that these affections are not universally valid, i.e., not valid "in the same form for all rational beings"; (3) that it yields no "principle" since its affections lack "objective necessity, which must be known a priori"; and (4) that *Empfänglichkeit,* being receptivity to the pleasure produced by the existence of objects, has a material character.[96] While this description holds for all feelings of pleasure and displeasure which are pathologically produced (and which serve as the basis for all eudemonistic doctrine), moral feeling is receptivity to an *intelligible* cause that, accordingly, (1) can be *known a priori* in relation to the intellectual causality of practical reason; (2) is *universally valid* for all rational and sensible beings; (3) is a feeling that *follows from the moral principle,* not from the affection of objects, and hence is subjectively necessary; and (4) does not, as moral feeling, depend on the *material* existence of particular objects but rests on the *form* of the moral law.

The third *Critique* brings the inquiry into the transcendental structures of our receptivity to pleasure and displeasure a step further. The transcendental perspective allows Kant to discover a new exception to the general description of pathological feelings. In the third *Critique,* our peculiar *Empfänglichkeit* for pleasure and displeasure is the principled starting point of a new critical inquiry.[97] Now a peculiar feeling is set at the center of the activity of reflective judgment and connected a priori and with necessity to its transcendental principle of formal purposiveness. From this connection, our receptivity to (a specific kind of) feeling of pleasure and displeasure gains (1) its a priori ground, (2) its *universal* and (3) *principled* validity, and (4) its specific *formality*. This peculiar kind of *Empfänglichkeit* is no longer passivity opposed to spontaneity. It is, rather, the function that complements the notion of purposiveness in the subject's *Gemüt;* it is the condition in us that makes possible purposive *Einstimmung* with the form of the object, or the contingent yet meaningful encounter with it. We can use the concept of purposiveness to orient ourselves in a world populated by living beings, beautiful forms, and art products only because we are transcendentally *sensitive* or *responsive* to the (neither theoretical nor practical) meaning of the form that characterizes all these things in relation to our mental faculties; only because we are receptive to a purely formal pleasure grounded a priori in reflection. Ultimately, we can make critical use of the idea of nature's formal purposiveness and thereby pronounce judgments of taste and employ the notion of natural purpose because we are, transcendentally (and not just empirically), embodied rational and living beings. Kant makes this point clear from the beginning of the third *Critique.*

What constitutes the "aesthetic" character of the judgment of taste? And how does this question lead Kant to establish the specificity of the feeling of pleasure and displeasure in which reflection finds its transcendental embodiment? *Critique of Judgment* §1 clarifies this crucial point. When we ascribe beauty to something and thereby pronounce a judgment of taste, what we do, transcendentally, is refer a representation of the object to ourselves and to our feeling of pleasure and displeasure. The standpoint of the subject is here defined by its purely aesthetic feeling of pleasure and displeasure. Since neither cognitive nor practical aims are at stake, no concept and no faculty of concepts (understanding or reason) are involved. While all forms of sensibility as such are always in some sense subjective, some of them (like intuition and sensation) can gain, on occasion, objective validity and be used as ingredients in the cognitive process. The "aesthetic" character of the judgment of taste, on the contrary, consists precisely in the fact that its "determining ground (*Bestimmungsgrund*) can be *no other than subjective.*"[98] Feeling can never become an ingredient of cognition—neither of objects nor even of the subject. Subjectivity here is an irreducible and therefore transcendentally specific feature of the feeling on which judgment is based. What is the meaning of this subjectivity?

In a judgment of taste, we express something about a peculiar feeling that defines our subjective *Gemüt*-condition in the encounter with the object. Nothing else but this feeling prompts (and determines) our judgment. To say that the feeling of pleasure and displeasure is subjective in this specific aesthetic sense means not only that it does *not* express anything (cognitive or practical) about the object. Kant's crucial *positive* claim is that this feeling voices the mode in which "the subject *feels himself* in the way

in which he is affected by the representation" of the object.[99] On this account, subjectivity is not just non-objectivity; it is, most importantly, the
indication that promotes the sphere of feeling to a transcendental validity
of its own. The new space opened up by the third *Critique* allows Kant,
yet again, to focus his critical eye on the issue of self-knowledge discussed
in the Paralogisms of speculative reason. There, Kant established that self-
knowledge is only knowledge of our empirical, embodied self and that no
cognition of a pure disembodied soul is possible. In fact, the cognitive issue is completely exhausted by this answer and no further visitation of the
problem is needed. However, at this point, Kant suggests that our reflective
relation to ourselves as embodied human beings is not only cognitive. In
other words, transcendentally, (empirical) self-knowledge does not exhaust
the possible experience that the subject can have of herself. Kant's suggestion in the third *Critique* is that a completely non-cognitive experience of
ourselves is possible that involves feeling and has a crucial transcendental
validity.[100] This experience is not just a material, pathological, and solipsistic
recounting of our individual states (in which case it would belong to empirical psychology and require no critique) but is made possible by a priori
conditions—as yet unexplored—that single out a universal human experience of ourselves as *embodied living* subjects. The task of the third *Critique*
is to bring to the fore, for the first time, the a priori conditions that make
this *aesthetic reflective* experience of ourselves possible. Feeling, which can
be formal and pure, is the transcendental *locus*[101] where this ulterior form
of experience of oneself in one's own existence takes place. In this perspective, the claim that feeling can by no means have cognitive value, far from
excluding this faculty from the realm of transcendental investigation, is the
very first step in the critical assessment of its independency within the field
of transcendental philosophy.

Kant's argument further elaborates on the peculiar—reflective—experience of "feeling oneself" taking place in the judgment of taste. First, in
the aesthetic (non-cognitive) experience we become conscious of the representation of the object (in Kant's example a regular building that appears
to us as purposive) in its connection with the "sensation of satisfaction"
(*Wohlgefallen*) that we feel. More precisely, Kant suggests that we become
conscious of the representation "*with*" (*mit*) this feeling (as opposed to apprehending the representation with the cognitive faculty). Feeling makes
us conscious of how inner processes of apprehension relate to ourselves
and indeed "affect" us. Thereby, our sensibility displays *active* features.[102]
Second, such consciousness, instead of producing (any kind of) knowledge

of the object, is more precisely the way in which we become aware of a fundamental character of our own subjectivity—a character that no cognitive determination of the self or moral determination of the will could bring to the fore, namely, that we are embodied *living* creatures. As the peculiar feeling of aesthetic satisfaction in the representation of an object makes us aware that we are *living* beings, it presents itself as a feeling for our own life. Aesthetic liking, by which we judge an object beautiful is the act through which we get in touch with that inscrutable and indefinable property in ourselves that is *life.* Kant argues that when we become conscious of the representation of an object in the feeling of satisfaction, the representation is referred "entirely" (*gänzlich*) to the subject and precisely to her *Lebensgefühl.*[103] In this aesthetic situation the subject is, *in its entirety,* immediately identical with the feeling of being alive, with the feeling of life: nothing else (aims, desires, concepts) counts. The feeling of life is an all-encompassing, completely absorbing feeling. In a *Reflection* dating back to 1776–1778, Kant claims that "pleasure and displeasure are *the only absolutes* because they are life itself."[104] Moreover, he urges that "the absolute sense is feeling."[105] In 1790, the feeling of life and the peculiar aesthetic feeling of pleasure and displeasure are, transcendentally, utterly identical. The feeling of being alive is not just an instinctive sensation (or a quasi-mechanical response to stimuli); it is a conscious reflective (and yet non-cognitive) state of the subject. The feeling of pleasure and displeasure through which we gain this awareness is the basis (*gründet*) of a special "faculty of distinction and evaluation" (*Unterscheidungs- und Beurteilungsvermögen*). It is, in the school terminology, a "higher" faculty. It is, in Kant's transcendental perspective, the act of reflective judgment through which we call the object beautiful: it is an aesthetic feeling for life. In the *Religion Within the Limits of Reason Alone* (1793), in discussing the "Original Disposition to Good in Human Nature," Kant presents the "elements of the determination of the human being" with regard to man's end in the following progression: (1) "the disposition to *animality* (*Thierheit*) of the human being as a *living* being"; (2) "the disposition to its *humanity* (*Menschheit*) as a *living* and, at the same time, *rational* being"; and (3) "the disposition to its *personality* (*Persönlichkeit*) as a rational being that, at the same time, is *subject to imputability.*"[106] Throughout its development, the third *Critique* attempts to show the unification of these human dispositions. The aim is clear from the outset: if "animality" is that aspect of ourselves by which we are alive, what needs to be explored is the transcendental condition that allows us to reach that claim. Transcendentally, we are not just living beings; we are conscious of being alive because we have a pure aesthetic feeling for this state. This is *human* reflection—and this is reflective judgment.[107] In reflective judgment (and particularly in *aesthetic* judgment), man is transcendentally reconciled with his animal side.

The "mystery" of aesthetic judgment does not lie only in the traditional difficulty of defining what beauty is. In the framework of Kant's thoroughly new perspective on aesthetics, it consists, at the same time and indeed primarily, in the difficulty of defining what makes us *living* beings. This is, transcendentally, the condition for the possibility of beauty as well as the condition for our understanding of life in other beings outside of ourselves. If self-cognition, because of its limitation to the conditions of space and time, i.e., to our empirical self, cannot grasp the intelligible property of our moral destination and freedom, this is not its only limitation. Now it is clear that it also could not grasp the specificity of our being alive—our being not just machines or automata, as all other objects in nature, but also *living* beings—that is, our being alive not only in the biological sense but as aware of being endowed with life so that this awareness becomes integral to our experience of ourselves and of other things. Herein, we find expressed the crucial problem of the deductive gap that lies open between nature's homogeneous universal laws and the particular laws that describe specific natural forms—the problem that reflective judgment is called upon to solve. The mechanistic view of nature simply sidesteps the problem. It reduces the issue of life (in ourselves) to the speculative assumption of a "soul" as the principle that gives life to matter, and to the claim of the soul's immortality after this worldly life.[108] The critique of this assumption allows mechanical science to dismiss the problem along with the dreams of pneumatology. Yet the issue of *embodied life* (not that of the disembodied soul; D'Alembert's dream, not Swedenborg's), in its neither cognitive nor moral validity, remains open for Kant until its definitive solution in the third *Critique*. It is here, in the critique of aesthetic and teleological judgment respectively, that the problem of life receives its full critical articulation. The precious and inscrutable property that makes us embodied *living* beings can neither be penetrated by the efforts of the understanding or the cognitive aims of introspection, nor accessed by practical reason—yet it cannot be left aside either. Such a mysterious property reveals itself in a peculiar form of feeling, which is the feeling of pleasure and displeasure constituting the transcendental condition of our experience of beauty. This experience, to be sure, is at the same time an experience of ourselves as living beings.

Feeling of Satisfaction:
Animals, Humans, and Pure Spirits

The aesthetic feeling of pleasure and displeasure is the basis of (and is a priori connected to) a judging faculty that allows us to draw distinctions and thus orient ourselves in the world of nature's particular forms. Just as the feeling for spatial orientation refers all outside objects to the central axis that runs through the middle of our body and thereby disposes them in different oriented regions of space (left and right, up and down, etc., in relation to ourselves), so the reflective faculty of judgment refers all our representations through the feeling of pleasure and displeasure to that very inner center (or that "absolute" inner point)[109] of ourselves that is the *Lebensgefühl*. This is the primary orientation point that allows us to distinguish beauty in things placed in relation to us. Reflection is an act that takes place "in the subject." The place of the subject is her *Lebensgefühl*. In it, the given representation of the object is contrasted to or set synoptically against (*zusammenhalten*) the "entire faculty of representation." A feeling is thereby produced, which is the internal feeling of one's own state. Through this feeling, the *Gemüt* becomes conscious of all the powers of the faculty of representation.[110] The feeling of life is, more precisely, a feeling for what our mental powers can accomplish when prompted by given representations and when completely free of cognitive or practical aims, free of "interests" as well as of the mate-riality of objects or sensations.[111] The feeling of life is a feeling of complete *mental freedom*.

As Kant claims at the end of the second *Critique*, the object that we represent as engaging the faculty of judgment is only the contingent oc-casion "for our becoming aware of our store of talents which are elevated (*erhabenen Anlage*) above the mere animal level (*Tierheit*)."[112] The situation is re-proposed at the beginning of the third *Critique*, yet this time without the moral significance of that earlier passage. The feeling of being alive is a reflected feeling rooted *in* our embodied condition and is, in turn, a feeling *for* our embodied condition. But it is not just a feeling of our being animals. Made aware of the store of talents or of the powers of our "whole faculty of representation," we are elevated above the mere animal level. This time, the operation is possible even without having recourse to practical reason (although practical reason will present itself again, within the new aesthetic experience, in the case of the sublime: the starry sky above us will again join the moral law within us). While the First Introduction underlines that even animals reflect, as it were, in their practical enterprises—albeit instinctively—the purely aesthetic reflection that sets us in contact with our *Lebensgefühl* and makes us consider objects to be beautiful is typically human. We reflect as animals do, but when in reflecting we feel the peculiar pleasure that alerts us to our inner feeling of life we have a typically human experience—an "aesthetic" experience. Yet, only the *transcendental* perspective allows Kant to disclose the field of aesthetic experience as a typically human experience of life, because it is only from the transcendental perspective that the a priori connection between the feeling of pleasure and displeasure and the faculty of reflective judgment can be brought to the fore.[113] Animals reflect and feel pleasure and desire, while pure spirits may have rationality and respond to the moral law. Yet neither for animals nor for pure spirits are a pure aesthetic feeling of pleasure and a pure appreciation of beauty possible.[114] To be sure, while the reflective faculty of judgment represents a "middle" and mediating faculty between nature and freedom, it also reveals the transcendental "place" of the human being—and of *human life*—between animals and pure rational beings or spirits, between biological life and the practical postulate of an afterlife as well as the moral duty to respect life as such.[115] At this point, we reach Kant's final solution of the metaphysical problem of life (and of the issue of animal versus human life).

Kant uses the proximity between the concepts of life, freedom, and feeling to define the sphere of the practical both at the beginning of the second *Critique* and the beginning of the *Metaphysics of Morals*. In those texts, life is respectively defined as the "faculty of a being by which it acts according to the laws of the faculty of desire," or "by which it acts according to its representations."[116] Life has an essential connection both to desire and to feeling. "Feeling is the sensation (*Empfindung*) of life," and "the complete use of life is freedom." "Freedom is the original life."[117] Moreover, whatever contributes to further or maintain our sense of life we feel as pleasant, even though its character is utterly material. Hence, the fact that this same connection between life, freedom, and feeling is crucial to the definition of the sphere of reflective judgment (and in particular aesthetic judgment) requires Kant, at the beginning of the third *Critique,* to indicate the specificity of the aesthetic value of judgments of taste as well as the peculiarity of the feeling connected to it, in contrast both to the values and drives of moral life and to the agreeable feelings of material pleasures. This demonstrative aim occupies the argument of the "first moment of the judgment of taste."[118] Kant argues that the feeling of pleasure and displeasure that "determines" (*bestimmt*) the judgment of taste is a peculiar feeling of "satisfaction" (*Wohlgefallen*).[119] In this case, however, satisfaction is not produced by the material presence or existence of an object: neither by the "interest" that we may have in it (in its existence), and which would move our faculty of desire but make us dependent upon the object, nor by the material pleasure or agreeable sensations that our senses convey when affected by it.[120] When satisfaction determines a judgment of taste, i.e., makes us declare a given object beautiful, we express total independency—and freedom—from the material existence of the object, from all interests that may be connected to it, and from all pleasant sensations that may arise from it. In judging something beautiful I indicate an "aesthetic space" within myself in which the only important thing is "what I make of the representation [of the object] within myself."[121] In this space, satisfaction or feeling of pleasure meets my *Lebensgefühl* and thereby makes me aware of the powers of my cognitive faculties. Such powers are not perceived by what the cognitive faculty actually (or determinately) does but rather by the indeterminateness of the possibilities that this aesthetic space discloses to us for the first time. In this inner space, I am free of doing whatever my *Lebensgefühl* suggests me to do with a given representation—neither an interest nor a desire takes the lead or gives the rule, no purpose is dominating.[122] The inner feeling of life gives the rule to itself and this is its (aesthetic) freedom. The aesthetic feeling of pleasure is a feeling of the freedom that I now have to do whatever I want with the representation of the object: the imagination can simply "play" with it, concerned with no further aim or purpose, guided by no determinate concept. This is Kant's concept of the "free play of the cognitive faculties."[123]

Thus, the principal difference between the good, the pleasant, and the beautiful is established. The "good" is object of reason's interest. The liking that is connected to it is "mediated" by practical reason and its concepts.[124] The "pleasant" or agreeable, which may indeed please "immediately"[125] is still (materially) connected to the faculty of desire: in this case, what pleases is the material existence of the object (not its mere representation with no further will of realization).[126] Despite their fundamental differences, both the good and the pleasant are connected to an interest in the existence of their object.[127] The pleasant, the good, and the beautiful are three fundamental and specifically different types of relations between the representation of objects and the feeling of pleasure and displeasure. Accordingly, they produce specifically different types of *Wohlgefallen*.[128] It is with regard to these types of relations that we distinguish among objects, namely, that we reflect. The satisfaction that we feel for the pleasant is "pathologically conditioned" by material sensory stimuli and impulses, while the satisfaction connected to the good is "purely practical." In both cases, however, the subject's feeling depends upon the existence of the desired object. It is only in the case of the judgment of taste, i.e., in the case of the beautiful, that the feeling is both pure and formal, and utterly "indifferent" toward the object's existence. The judgment of taste, Kant contends, is merely "contemplative," i.e., does not involve the faculty of desire. In it, the formal constitution of the object "is held up to" (*zusammenhält*) the subject's feeling of pleasure and displeasure and attuned to it. This is "contemplation."[129] It is neither a practical desire (pure or pathologically conditioned) nor a cognitive act; hence it does not involve the mediation of concepts—neither as aims to be realized nor as grounds for cognitive determination. In the judgment of taste what matters, we have seen, is not the existence of the object but only what we are left free to do with its mere representation within ourselves, i.e., the sphere of possibility and indeterminateness that puzzles (and leaves dumb) the understanding.

But what is the basis of these distinctions between the good, the pleasant, and the beautiful? That the beautiful differs in type from the pleasant and the good is neither the result of empirical observation nor psychological introspection. It is a difference that only a transcendental inquiry can bring to light. The issue is even more crucial as the separation between those three types of satisfaction is connected with different modes of existence or life and, consequently, with different modalities of possible experience. Kant's point is that if we do not recognize that this difference has a *transcendental* basis we need to appeal, with a longstanding tradition, to dogmatic metaphysical principles. Receptivity and responsiveness (*Empfänglichkeit*) to pleasure in general—the sign of a being's embodied condition—go to the very heart of what being alive is. "Ultimately, everything depends on life; what enlivens (*belebt*) (or the feeling of the furthering of life) is pleasant."[130] Responsiveness to pleasure, the capacity for feeling the furthering of life when affected by objects (by their representation or directly by their existence) is proper to animals as well as to humans. Animal instinctive reflection 'serves the purpose' (to put it in the conceptual terms of the third *Critique*) of preserving and furthering life. Kant distinguishes three types of life that parallel and complement the three distinctively different types of feeling of pleasure and displeasure or *Wohlgefallen* related, respectively, to the pleasant, the good, and the beautiful. In laying out the specific place that the experience of the beautiful occupies in contrast to the good and the pleasant, Kant's *transcendental* solution to the traditional constellation of problems discussed at the beginning of this chapter—the distinction between animals and humans, and the problem of the spiritual principle of life—finally comes to the fore.

In a *Reflection* of the years 1776–1778, taking up the practical context in which satisfaction and life are conjoined, Kant writes:

> The value of satisfaction and dissatisfaction relate to possible choice, i.e., to the will (*willkühr*), and consequently to the principium of life. What can be an object of our choice? That which brings about our welfare (*Wohl*), and consequently enhances [or amplifies, *vergrößert*] the actus of life. Hence, the feeling of the furtherance or impediment of life is satisfaction or dissatisfaction [. . .]. But we have an animal, a spiritual, and a human life. Through the first, we are capable of gratification (*Vergnügen*) and pain (feeling); through the third, we are capable of satisfaction through sensible judgment (taste); through the second, of satisfaction through reason. Epicurus says: all gratification arises only with the participation (*Mitwirkung*) of the body, even though its first cause is in spirit.[131]

The question is: which of these three kinds of life can be described by *transcendental* a priori conditions and thus be said to constitute a specific field of possible experience and the object of critique? This *Reflection* mirrors and complements the analysis of *Critique of Judgment* §5. The aim of §5 is to bring to the fore the distinctively *transcendental* character (or more precisely "quality") of the judgment of taste that §1 describes as "aesthetic." In that earlier *Reflection,* Kant endorses the inclusive perspective that regards 'us' human animals who participate in spiritual life through practical reason. Animal life is not just a life of the senses; it is the life of animals endowed with reflection and thereby with a kind of consciousness that connects material gratification with an—albeit instinctive—tendency to further one's life. Here the "states of our body measure the actus of life"; the feeling of life is one with the instinct to preserve one's (biological) life. Animal life is, for us human animals as well, a fundamental mode of existence.[132] However, the level of animal life does not constitute a realm of experience with a *transcendental* validity of its own. While its investigation belongs to the practical sphere (i.e., to the functions of the faculty of desire in its material determination), the feeling involved is pathologically conditioned. Animal satisfaction has merely material validity, has no universality, and cannot be brought back to a priori principles.[133] Kant suggests that to feel this kind of "animal" pleasure we need a body but do not need reason—and neither do we need an aesthetic sense. In this kind of satisfaction we are just *vernunftlose*

Tiere.[134] The body is involved in animal life through the mere materiality of its senses and pathological feelings. Accordingly, animal life can only be the object of physiological explanation or empirical psychology. The moral validity of the good, on the other hand, lifts us to the level of purely rational beings or pure spirits. The good is valid for all rational beings as such, no matter what their embodied appearance is: the transcendental validity of this concept lies in the a priori principle of practical reason's legislation; its formal determination is free from the body (as we have seen, it affects the body as moral feeling, but this affection does not determine the good as such).[135] The satisfaction procured by the good has nothing in common with the purely contemplative and disinterested pleasure connected to the beautiful—it has no aesthetic validity. Moral freedom and the freedom of aesthetic satisfaction[136] must be brought back to transcendentally different (although, as we will see, related) principles. The moral law cannot give an account of the purely disinterested feeling of pleasure proper to aesthetic judgment in which no concept is involved, nor can it explain the purely reflective awareness connected to the *Lebensgefühl* implied in aesthetic contemplation.

Kant places the case of taste and the value of beauty between the pleasure proper to irrational animals and the values recognized and chosen by pure rational spirits—between the life of material enjoyment and the moral life of pure practical reason. Kant's fundamental claim is that taste can indeed represent an independent sphere of experience which is, more precisely, a typically *human* mode of experience, *if and only if* we endorse the *transcendental* perspective of the third *Critique*.[137] Its specificity lies in a transcendental a priori principle, and not in a metaphysical, physiological, or psychological difference between animals, men, and pure spirits. In order to recognize the peculiar character of aesthetic judgment, it is necessary to go beyond Epicurus's hedonistic dogmatism—beyond both his materialist and mechanist worldview and his empirical anthropology—and it is also necessary to go beyond the *Critique of Practical Reason* in which hedonistic moral theory found its definitive refutation. If we want to gain a complete view of the extension of human possible experience, it is necessary to move beyond the practical legislation of the faculty of desire. Kant's argument at the beginning of the third *Critique* can be presented as a *reductio ad absurdum*. If we assume Epicurus's materialist perspective (or even the perspective of any other dogmatic philosophical system), the experience of beauty displays no independency. The specific value of beauty and the peculiar form of pleasure on which beauty is based immediately disappear: they are reduced to the same kind of pathologically conditioned sentiments or desires we find in the practical sphere or, alternatively, they are assimilated (following Baumgarten's rationalist position) to a cognitive enterprise. On the former account it follows that human life is entirely reduced to animal life and the materiality of bodily gratification. If we maintain the dogmatic standpoint, on the other hand, the only way to avoid this view is to postulate an immaterial soul (the automaton becomes a *spiritual* automaton). Accordingly, the principle of life must lie either in sensory bodily response to stimulation or in a spiritual soul. In both cases—Epicurus's materialism and speculative pneumatology—no purely *formal* feeling of pleasure and displeasure and no purely *aesthetic* access to our "feeling of life" are possible. In both cases, no account can be given of a disinterested (neither cognitive nor practical) appreciation of beauty. In other words, our embodied condition is reduced to an empirical fact that has no transcendental significance: it either occupies the entire theory ("materialism without soul") or is a transitory condition that is dualistically separated from the soul (*schwärmerisch,* "spiritualism").[138] A (dialectical) alternative opens up between animal embodied life and the life of pure disembodied spirits. Under these premises, man is a mixed, divided creature whose existence only furthers an antinomy with no solution: he is either (rational) animal or (embodied) spirit.

However, as we have seen, the critical itinerary that in the second *Critique* defeats hedonism on purely practical grounds discloses, in its conclusion, the space of a different kind of human sensibility: the space of an aesthetic form of feeling. Correspondingly, at the beginning of the third *Critique,* a third type of life (and not just a hybrid of animal and spirit) comes to the fore—a distinctive mode of life defined precisely by the irreducible conditions of aesthetic experience. These conditions are "visible" (and make sense) only within Kant's critical perspective because their distinctive character is brought back to the *transcendental* principle of the reflective faculty of judgment. "Beauty," urges Kant, "concerns only human beings" insofar as they are "animal and yet rational beings." And to leave no doubt as to which aspect needs to be underscored most heavily, he continues "but not just merely as rational beings as such (for example spirits) but also as animal beings."[139] Since rationality is here the mark of moral life, it is the difference between animal and human sensibility or feeling which grounds the specificity of taste and aesthetic pleasure. However, it is only a transcendental principle that allows us to discern and make sense of the specific difference between animal and human sensibility. For this difference is neither physiological nor psychological nor metaphysical, but transcendental. It does not lie in a specific bodily function, sense, or organ for beauty; it does not lie in an immaterial soul or rational capacity that man would have and animals would lack; and neither does it lie in the authority of an ontological principle which places man higher than other animals within the hierarchy of the "chain of being."[140] The indispensable condition for experiencing beauty is not animal sensibility, which offers only material gratification; nor is it the reflection which man still shares with animals; nor is it reason alone, which man shares with pure spirits but leads only to the good. It is rather a type of sensibility (or a *formal* character of our sensibility) that is necessarily connected to our human embodied condition since it gives us a feeling for our own life—i.e., for the animal part in ourselves—to which, however, we relate differently than animals because we find in it no material gratification. We relate to our *Lebensgefühl aesthetically,*[141] and not only practically (i.e., with regard to the faculty of desire). This crucial difference cannot be described materially but only *formally* and *transcendentally,* i.e., only on the ground of the independent a priori principle connected with the peculiar *formal* pleasure that arises in the encounter with certain objects—the principle of nature's formal purposiveness.

In sum, the sphere of "aesthetics" or the domain of beauty could not gain any independence in philosophical discourse until the traditional dispute regarding life (and in particular human life as opposed to animal life) kept searching for its source in either a metaphysical principle or a physiological property or sense. Under those conditions, taste's response to beauty was considered either under the category of animal physiological pleasure or of moral sentiment—the beautiful was reduced either to the pleasant or to the good. The problem can find a solution only in the *transcendental* perspective of Kant's philosophy. Herein, life is defined by the specific experience we can have of it. This experience, in turn, is brought back to the a priori condition that renders it possible and meaningful for us. The difference between animals and humans lies in the different experience of life that man can have. Such experience is not only practical (moral) but aesthetic. What defines aesthetic experience—and hence grounds the *transcendental difference* between animal, man, and a pure rational being or spirit—is the transcendental principle of the reflective faculty of judgment, i.e., the connection between reflective judgment, formal feeling of pleasure and displeasure, and the principle of nature's formal purposiveness. This connection defines the transcendental meaning of our human embodied condition.

Transcendental Embodiment versus Physiology

In the convoluted announcement that beauty is valid only for man in his "animal and yet rational"—rational, yet not merely rational but at the same time animal—nature, Kant places man between irrational animals, whose life is centered on the body, and purely rational disembodied beings. He seems to feel the potential and also the obscurity of this claim, when he concludes, no less enigmatically: "This is a proposition that can only be completely justified and explained in what follows."[142] Where and how does this explanation take place in the third *Critique*? The argument laid out above shows that this proposition goes to the heart of Kant's last critical enterprise. From which we may infer that its complete demonstration occupies Kant in both the critique of the aesthetic and of the teleological faculty of judgment. While aesthetic judgment, through the peculiar feeling of pleasure that connects us with the principle of life in ourselves, allows us to feel our proximity to, yet also difference from other animals, teleological judgment makes us understand the place that we occupy within the whole of living nature—again, it makes us aware of both our proximity to other animals, with which we share the common destiny of physical weakness and mortality, and of the higher moral destination that separates us from them.[143]

We have seen that from the outset the transcendental principle of aesthetic judgment concerns not only the traditional issue of taste and beauty but also the conditions of our experience of life. This problem, in turn, leads Kant to discuss the specificity of the beautiful as opposed to the pleasant and the good on the one hand, and the specificity of human sensibility and human life on the other. Kant's inquiry into the faculty of judgment is a reflection on the necessity of *transcendental* philosophy and, more generally, of the transcendental method. Since only this method can provide an answer to the above-mentioned problems, the idea of "transcendental embodiment" shall be considered as the demonstrative center of the *Critique of Judgment*. The name of Epicurus epitomizes, for Kant, an idea of human embodiment that fails precisely because it is not transcendental but merely empirical and physiological. With regard to the explanation of the beautiful and of the feeling of pleasure and displeasure connected to it, Epicurus is unable to see the formal specificity of aesthetic judgment, while with regard to the explanation of life in nature, he remains stuck in reason's unsolvable dialectic.[144] The reduction of all feelings of pleasure to material, bodily gratification, and the reduction of all natural events and processes to nature's blind mechanism are two faces (aesthetic and teleological) of one and the same philosophical methodology, which Kant names "physiology." Kant's transcendental account of life in ourselves and in other natural beings, on the contrary, is predicated upon the idea of transcendental embodiment, which completely revolutionizes the way in which philosophy frames the problem of the relation between body and mind, "animality" and humanity, nature and freedom. This connection can now be brought to light by contrasting Kant's *transcendental* exposition to Epicurus's *physiological* account of human embodiment—an opposition that Kant himself sets up by explicitly referring to Epicurus's position at crucial junctures of both parts of the third *Critique.*

One of the fundamental characters of aesthetic judgment is its *subjectivity,* whereby the relation of the object's representation to the merely subjective feeling of pleasure and displeasure is expressed. The study of reflective judgment is a *transcendental* inquiry into the irreducibly subjective, neither cognitive nor practical a priori structures of the subject's *Gemüt.* It investigates, on the one hand, the purely formal feeling of pleasure and displeasure that discloses our feeling for life in ourselves, and on the other hand, the transcendental principle of purposiveness that provides a heuristic access to the phenomenon of life in other natural beings. It is Kant's general contention that "the study of the object is either dogmatic or skeptic; that of the subject is either physiologic or critic."[145] Alternatively, he also puts the issue as follows: "The use of the understanding is either mystic or logic; the latter can be metaphysic or physiologic. Aristotle and Epicurus."[146] Among the ancients, Plato is for Kant representative of the mystical way, Aristotle of the logical; while Epicurus is the founder of the physiological method to which Kant's criticism is opposed.[147] Plato's mysticism of the soul finds its antagonist in Epicurus's reduction of every mental and physical event to the body. "Epicurus says: all gratification arises only with the participation (*Mitwirkung*) of the body, even though its first cause is in spirit."[148] There is no disembodied spiritual pleasure for Epicurus; all bodily pleasure, however, is for him utterly material. The physiological method is favored among the moderns as well: physiology is the path followed by Locke's inquiry—the true "physiologist of reason." His concern is the issue of the "origin of concepts"[149]—the same problem that occupies Kant in the deduction of the concepts of the understanding in the first *Critique.* Locke's fundamental mistake is to confuse the access that we have to concepts, namely, experience, with their "source" (hence, the *generatio aequivoca* of understanding's concepts).[150] This confusion leads Locke to the "physiological deduction" of the concepts that Kant's "transcendental deduction" directly and program-matically opposes.[151] For Kant, Locke's inquiry is ultimately a "physiology of the human understanding."[152] As the opposite of critique, physiology is characterized by its merely empirical and psychological nature, and by the confusion between the experiential context in which our concepts occur and the source of these concepts. With regard to the origin of concepts, for Epicurus's physiology as for Locke's "there is nothing a priori."[153] In the sphere of the practical, the same "physiological" muddle characterizes the operation that leads the Epicurean to contaminate the purity of the source of moral consciousness with the pleasant effects that moral conduct has on life. To which confusion Kant replies: "The venerable value of duty has nothing to do with the enjoyment of life" (*Lebensgenuß*). In opposition to Epicurus, for Kant physical and moral life must be kept apart in the prin-ciples that discipline their respective worth.[154] Just as Locke's physiological deduction of the concepts confuses the empirical context in which they occur with their empirical origin, so in the practical sphere the physiologi-cal method creates the illusion that takes moral motivation (i.e., the subjec-tive aspect of the will's pure determination through the moral law) for the pathological influence of a sensible motive. In both cases, the possibility of a pure a priori origin or determination of concepts is entirely obliterated. In the practical sphere, physiological explanations produce a deadly confusion between "eudemonia (the principle of happiness)" and "eleuteronomia (the principle of freedom of inner legislation)," a confusion that leads, as Kant puts it in the Metaphysical Principles of Virtue, to the "euthanasia [. . .] of all morals."[155]

To be sure, the line that separates physiology and transcendental phi-losophy is a thin one. For they ally in another battle: both oppose the metaphysical assumption of an objectivity that cannot be given in sensible intuition. However, since physiology does not acknowledge the a priori formality of intuition (and feeling), it reduces all sensibility to the material givenness of the body (i.e., to sensation, material feeling, and desires). In other words, since physiology does not recognize the formal transcenden-tal dimension of human embodiment, i.e., is methodologically 'blind' to form, it hypostatizes the body to an absolute (material) fact. Accordingly, physiology is unable to see the pure source of the understanding's concepts as well as the purely formal determination of the will through the moral law. Ultimately, as shown by the results of Locke's philosophy, empirical physiology meets metaphysical *Schwärmerei* and is itself a form of metaphysics.[156] And yet, to the extent that the transcendental dimension of human embodiment is brought to light, physiology can be taken up in Kant's philosophy—in the form, one could suggest, of a 'transcendental physiology' of sorts. In the *Prolegomena*, the "*logical* table of judgment" is followed by the "*transcendental* table of the concepts of the understanding" and by the "*pure physiological* table of the universal principles of natural science."[157] Within the transcendental perspective, the pure physiological character of the principles indicates the embodied dimension of the understanding's schematism. In the terminology of Kant's time, physiology is the descriptive doctrine of the nature and constitution of an object in general. Kant's transcendental perspective opposes physiology's empirical approach to its object by indicating the a priori conditions that make empirical knowledge of the constitution of the object possible.[158] In the Architectonic of Pure Reason of the first *Critique*, Kant distinguishes two parts of "metaphysics" narrowly conceived: "*transcendental philosophy* and *physiology* of pure reason." The principal difference between these two parts is that the former has only the understanding as its object, and when it takes reason into consideration it refers to "objects in general" without considering objects that *would be given*. Physiology of pure reason—as *physiologia rationalis*—on the contrary, refers to "nature" as "the sum total of *given* objects." The object's givenness implies intuition—either sensible intuition or "another type of intuition." Since reason's use therein can be either transcendent or immanent, Kant presents two corresponding kinds of physiology. Immanent physiology, which regards all objects of the senses in the way in which they are given to us, refers, in turn, to two kinds of objects: "bodily nature" given to the outer senses and "thinking nature" given to the inner sense. The part of metaphysics that includes *physica rationalis* and *psychologia rationalis* is "rational physiology" as "*Naturlehre der reinen Vernunft.*" Thus, rational physiology makes up the second main division of the entire "system of metaphysics," which consists of "1. ontology, 2. rational physiology, 3. rational cosmology, 4. rational theology."[159] Significantly, in this partition, physiology replaces traditional psychology.

In the third *Critique*, Kant's engagement with the method of physiology goes a step further. The flaw of Epicurus's physiology is now its blindness to reflection. Such blindness reduces humans to animals and living animals to machines. At the end of the General Remark on the "transcendental exposition" of aesthetic reflective judgment, Kant directly connects Epicurus's physiological views to an influential modern "physiological exposition of aesthetic judgments,"[160] that of Burke (broadly received and followed also in the German contemporary discussion). Importantly, Kant frames the contrast between transcendental and physiological exposition as a methodological one. The reference to Burke's *Enquiry* serves the purpose of showing the flaws of the merely empirical investigation into the *origin* of our concepts of the beautiful and the sublime and, by contrast, is instrumental in underscoring the peculiarity of Kant's transcendental perspective. Burke's exposition of the concepts of the beautiful and the sublime is truly an empirical description of the psychology and physiology of our response to certain objects, i.e., of the way in which our *Gemüt* and our body react to certain sensible stimulations. Kant recognizes the value of such investigation in providing "rich material" for the "favorite investigations of empirical anthropology." However, this is also the limit of Burke's enterprise. Kant maintains that in the particular case of the beautiful and the sublime, because of their connection with the feeling of pleasure and displeasure—or with "gratification" and "pain"—this physiological way may seem the most 'natural' to assume, i.e., may seem the way that goes to the very bottom of the phenomenon and its explanation. "One cannot deny," urges Kant, "that all representations in us [. . .] subjectively can be connected with gratification or pain, even though both may be imperceptible." The reason is that "they affect the feeling of life" (*Gefühl des Lebens*); none of them can be "indifferent" to the subject since they are a "modification" of her state.[161] The connection of pleasure and pain (albeit of a peculiar form of this feeling) with the "feeling of life" is, as we have seen, the starting point of Kant's analysis as well. The argument hinges on the fundamental difference between a transcendental and a merely natural or physiological connection between the feeling of pleasure and the feeling of life.

At this point, however, instead of proposing a too-simple dualistic opposition between Burke's physiology of the body and an inquiry that would seek an allegedly more 'spiritual' principle of explanation, Kant brings in Epicurus's radical physiological views and expresses his agreement with them.[162] Epicurus ultimately reduces all gratification and pain to the body and bodily sensations, whether the source of the feeling be a representation arising from the imagination or from the understanding. The reason is that

> life without the feeling of bodily organs would be the bare consciousness of its existence, but not the feeling of being well or unwell (*Gefühl des Wohl-oder Übelfindens*), i.e., of the furthering or the hindrance of the vital forces. The *Gemüt* by itself alone is life itself (the very principle of life), and hindrance and furtherance must be sought outside it and yet in the human being, consequently in connection with its body.[163]

The human body is seen here as a sort of 'in-between' that lies 'outside' of the *Gemüt* but still 'within' the human being. The feeling of life is enriched or qualified, positively or negatively, as it were, as a *determinate feeling* only by the intervention of the body, whereby the bare consciousness of one's existence becomes a concrete feeling of pleasure and displeasure (or of gratification and pain). Life, without the body, would be the unqualified, indeterminate, and merely formal consciousness of a *Gemüt* incapable of feeling. This is the reason why *aesthetic* feeling is, for Kant, always an *embodied* feeling—a feeling that man has as a rational yet also and necessarily animal embodied being. While pure rational beings (or spirits) would have a bare consciousness of their existence, they would not be able to qualify their "life" as pleasurable or painful; they would have no feeling at all for their lives. This is the reason why neither beauty nor gratification has any meaning for them.[164]

But if Kant agrees with Epicurus on the embodied nature of the connection between pleasure and life, why does he reject the physiological method in the exposition of aesthetic judgments, given that he basically agrees with the fundamental tenet of Burke's and even Epicurus's views?[165] The salient question in order to understand the crucial methodological point at stake here is a different one: what is the difference between mere gratification and aesthetic pleasure, between animal feeling and aesthetic human feeling? This is the question raised in the first moment of the judgment of taste. The point, as we have seen, is that according to Epicurus's physiology no difference can be indicated between these two types of feeling.[166] And the fact that Burke assumes the physiological method in his specific analysis of the concepts of the beautiful and the sublime is no guarantee that its results apply *exclusively* to aesthetic feelings, i.e., that they define the specific *aesthetic* nature of those feelings as differing from feelings for the merely pleasurable or the good. His analysis, to be sure, provides only a description of love, terror, and similar pathological affects but does not justify the universal validity and necessity of the judgments based on those feelings. In other words, Kant's *transcendental* perspective (and hence the need to assume aesthetic judgment as object of a third "critique"), unlike Burke's physiological inquiry, does not arise out of the conviction that the source of the beautiful and the sublime is (something like) pure spirit as opposed to the body. It arises instead out of the view that lends to the body (and the animal side in man) a formal component, a pure feeling of pleasure and displeasure that no physiological or psychological analysis will ever be able—on methodological grounds—to detect. Only this formal aspect of feeling, which is a priori connected with the transcendental principle of reflective judgment, can account for the universality and necessity proper to the judgment of taste.[167] To this extent, Kant can oppose Burke's physiology and support, at the same time, Epicurus's connection of all feeling with the body. On Kant's view, Epicurus's mistake is not the claim that all pleasure is bodily pleasure; it is rather to maintain that material bodily pleasure or pain is the only possible type of (bodily) feeling, that the difference between physical and intellectual pleasures (and hence that between animals and humans) is only a difference in degree.[168] His mistake is due to a methodological limitation, for physiology can lead only as far as detecting a difference in degree among pleasures (just as Locke's physiology of human reason made it impossible for him to recognize the difference in type between sensibility and understanding). It is only "critique" that makes that crucial, "essential difference" (*wesentlicher Unterschied*)[169] visible for the first time. The transcendental perspective allows Kant to claim that there is a pure form of pleasure and displeasure that is necessarily embodied and that in this embodied form relates to the feeling of life in ourselves. This pure form of pleasure is connected to the reflective faculty of judgment and to its a priori principle of formal purposiveness. Such aesthetic feeling of pleasure is different in kind (or differs *essentially,* i.e., transcendentally) from merely material bodily pleasure or gratification. But it is different not because it is a 'spiritual' pleasure as opposed to a mere 'bodily' animal pleasure—a position that would simply re-propose the traditional discussion on the difference between body and mind, animals and humans. Instead, it is different because it is a corporeal but at the same time purely formal feeling of pleasure and displeasure.

Now, just as the pure formal aesthetic feeling puts us in contact with the principle of life within ourselves and allows us to feel (not to know but to reflect on) what life in us is, the same principle of reflection (in teleological judgment) allows us to understand (and yet not to know) what life in other natural beings is. Epicurus's physiological blindness to the formality of aesthetic pleasure corresponds to his outright denial of a "technique of nature" and to his reduction of life to mechanism.[170] Ultimately, within the framework of physiology reflection—aesthetic or teleological—is utterly impossible.

9

Embodied Ideas

[*Precognizione,* invero, non è la parola più adatta, perché
la conoscenza ne era esclusa. Piuttosto,] la stranezza di quegli
occhi ricordava l'idiozia misteriosa degli animali, i quali non
con la mente, ma con un senso dei loro corpi vulnerabili, "sanno"
il passato e il futuro di ogni destino. Chiamerei quel senso—
che in loro è comune, e confuso negli altri sensi corporei
—il *senso del sacro:* intendendosi, da loro, per *sacro,*
il potere universale che può mangiarli e annientarli,
per la loro colpa di essere nati.

—ELSA MORANTE, *La Storia*

KANT OPENS THE INTRODUCTION OF THE *CRITIQUE OF JUDGMENT*
by sketching out a topological map portraying the inner geography of the
human mind. The aim is to provide us with orientation within the new
realm of transcendental inquiry to which the last part of the critical project
is dedicated. Thereby, he also presents a reflection on the path followed so
far by transcendental philosophy.[1] The map offers a progression that binds
together, in a more and more specific way, cognitive faculties and objects of
cognition. In Kant's topography of the human mind we find a renewed effort at differentiating regions in (mental) space that, if contrasted to the early
attempt of the 1768 essay, sanctions the final transformation of the issue of
embodiment within transcendental philosophy. Aesthetic judgment turns
out to be the vehicle for our orientation out of the labyrinth of nature.

The most extended region of this geography is the "field," which indicates the objective range of application of a priori concepts when the

question of the possibility of our cognition of objects is suspended and the cognitive faculty in relation to which the object is taken is just our "cognitive faculty in general." The "territory" (*Boden, territorium*) of the concepts and the respective faculties is that part of the field in which "knowledge is possible for us."[2] The section of the territory in which concepts exercise a right of jurisdiction due to their legislative function toward objects is the "domain" (*Gebiet, ditio*). The other part of the territory, complementary to the domain, in which concepts are not legislative and yet do provide (a certain kind of) cognition of objects is their "residence" (*Aufenthalt, domicilium*). In this geography, all regions are enclosed by limits that imply a 'within' and a 'without.'[3] Moreover, though the field encompasses the territory and this, in turn, includes both domain and *domicilium,* these lie next to each other in a relation of mutual exclusion. Kant's suggestion is that our entire cognitive faculty has two domains but only one territory. The domains are theoretical philosophy, in which concepts of nature are a priori legislative, and practical philosophy as domain of freedom's a priori legislation. Applying these topological distinctions to the idea of philosophy, Kant argues that the territory on which philosophy establishes its twofold domain can only be constituted by "the complex (*Inbegriff*) of the objects of all possible experience" taken as mere appearances.[4] Experience is the realm within which all appearances are ultimately located. This important limitation is imposed on our cognitive faculty by the nature of the understanding, which can legislate a priori only if placed on the territory of experience. Moreover, since the territory on which our cognitive faculty operates can only be one (for the "subject" of that faculty is one),[5] it is on the territory of experience that philosophy "exercises its legislation."[6] Thereby, Kant does not aim at separating understanding from practical reason, for he does not contend that understanding is confined to the realm of appearances while practical reason extends beyond it to the noumena. Rather, he maintains that the *one and only* territory of the *one and only* human experience *is the same* for both faculties. This territory is experience viewed as the *sensible* world of appearances. Kant's point, however, is that this unique territory might be experienced in different ways by different faculties. Even though (practical) reason, unlike the understanding, gives the law only to itself as noumenon, it is only through and within experience that we can have access to knowledge of reason in its full determination and real activity. In this respect, Kant recognizes that practical reason's activity still belongs to the complex of all experience.

Kant raises the question of the kind of objects that we encounter in surveying the different regions of the map. "Concepts of experience" are located within the territory of nature that is defined, accordingly, as the "complex of all objects of the senses."[7] This territory, however, is for those concepts only *domicilium,* not domain, i.e., what juridically justifies the presence of concepts of experience on the territory of nature is their having residence therein, not a domain. With this suggestion Kant sheds light on the way in which laws operate in theoretical philosophy, thereby challenging the world of the first *Critique* with a new problem. Within the same territory of nature, we find not only a priori concepts of understanding but also a posteriori concepts of experience (*Erfahrungsbegriffe* and *empirische Begriffe*). Through its a priori concepts, the understanding legislates on "nature in general," establishing its domain therein.[8] Concepts of experience, on the contrary, do not directly legislate over nature. They are only "produced according to law," i.e., they are "lawful"[9] insofar as they can refer to objects in general on the ground of both understanding's a priori concepts and pure forms of sensible intuition. It follows that rules of theoretical knowledge, insofar as they regard concepts of experience and their objects, are empirical and contingent and do not guarantee objective (universal and necessary) cognition.[10] In other words, as we have seen in the previous chapter, from the universal laws of nature particular empirical laws do not follow analytically. This claim transforms the mechanical universe of the first *Critique* into a chaotic labyrinth. While the first *Critique* established the domain of understanding's legislation by inspecting the territory of theoretical cognition, it left the *domicilium* of the concepts of experience unexplored. It is this region, namely the labyrinth of nature's particular empirical laws, that Kant sets out to survey in the third *Critique.* The question is whether in the sphere of an experience apparently dominated by contingency—hence displaying the unsettling, disorienting figure of a labyrinth—an order and a peculiar type of lawfulness could still be detected that is not the order and lawfulness proper to the understanding. Accordingly, Kant also suggests a new and more articulate meaning for the notion of experience. "Experience" encompasses both the theoretical and the practical realm, both what belongs to a domain and what belongs to a *domicilium.* A parallel distinction is drawn with regard to practical reason. The *domain* of practical philosophy is constituted by reason's legislation through the concept of freedom, while its adjacent *domicilium* is represented by the sphere of its technical-practical use. Thus, while understanding and reason share one and "the same territory of experience,"[11] their respective legislations are radically separated and their *domicilia* intersect each other.

Kant suggests, on the one hand, that a transcendental inquiry is needed with regard to the two sensible *domicilia* of empirical concepts and of the technical-practical use of reason. Since neither understanding nor reason legislate therein, neither strict necessity and universality nor unconditioned and categorical validity can be attained. However, to the extent that both regions do belong to the common territory of human experience, they stand in need of a new transcendental investigation. On the other hand, the third *Critique* sets out to account for another, as yet unexplored region of this geography, the field of the supersensible. Accordingly, two crucial questions of the *Critique of Judgment* surface at this point. First, the redefinition of the complex domain of philosophy in general requires a new notion of experience as the territory on which that domain can successfully be established. Second, Kant holds on to the uniqueness of the territory of experience for the subject despite the new problems immediately revealed by the tension between that unique territory and the split of its two domains. The "abyss" separating theoretical and practical realms and the "field of the supersensible"[12] that constitutes the basis of nature are the new controversial regions that Kant's geography of the cognitive faculties now needs to accommodate. Since neither theoretical nor practical reason is able to navigate the new regions of this map, a third cognitive faculty and its peculiar "feeling," or sense for orientation, must be called into the picture. This new sense of orientation becomes indispensable both to circumvent the "abyss"—perhaps even to traverse it—and to approach the "supersensible" in a new form of experience.

The question of how two opposed and incompatible legislations are possible on one and the same territory occupies Kant again after the negative solution provided by the Transcendental Dialectic of the first *Critique.* There, Kant demonstrated that it is at least possible "to think without contradiction" that the two legislations along with their respective faculties coexist in one and the same subject.[13] In the third *Critique,* the radical separation of the two domains guarantees that the *principles* of understanding's and reason's respective legislations "do not interfere with each other." But Kant now recognizes that the "*effects*" of those legislations "in the sensible world" do conflict and limit each other all the time.[14] For reason's practical legislation is enacted—and thereby translated into the world of appearances—by the subject taken as "sensible being" (*Sinnenwesen*) determined through the moral law.[15] The territory of experience gains the shape of a "world"[16] in which freedom is realized and its effects manifested. Thus, our one and only territory is the "sensible world"; only in it is experience possible for us; it is on this common ground that reason's theoretical and practical legislations are exercised and concretely exhibit their different effects. And yet, having set both legislations on the same territory of the sensible world, Kant must save the results of the two previous *Critiques*. To this aim, he reinforces the reason that after all prevents the two domains from collapsing into one. The idea of the supersensible is called into the picture. What hinders such a merging is the impossibility of a theoretical access to the "supersensible."[17] In arguing for this impossibility, Kant implicitly sets both domains in relation to the same problem of the supersensible: paradoxically, that which separates the two domains also unites them (albeit in a different respect). Since concepts of nature need intuition in order to produce knowledge of objects—as *Gegenstände*—these can only be appearances and never things in themselves. The concept of freedom, on the other hand, does represent in its object—as *Objekt*—a thing-in-itself; yet lacking all intuition, this representation provides no theoretical cognition. Hence, in neither case is theoretical knowledge of objects (or even of the thinking subject, as claimed by rational psychology) possible as things in themselves. An object known as *Ding an sich* would be the "supersensible" (not only an object that is placed ontologically 'beyond' or 'above' the sensible world, but one whose theoretical cognition does not require the contribution of intuition). Kant admits that we must assume the supersensible as an "idea" in order to ground the possibility of the territory of experience on which both domains establish their legislation.[18] While the understanding's legislation must assume the supersensible as that which underlies the possibility of experience (as regulative idea), practical reason's legislation has the supersensible as its object (it gives practical reality to that idea). This different relation to the supersensible justifies the separation of the two domains by relocating them within the broader region of the new field of inquiry disclosed by the third *Critique*.

In this chapter I investigate the mediating and intermediary function that Kant assigns to the faculty of judgment and its peculiar new feeling of orientation at play between the sensible and the supersensible elements 'within' and 'without' the human being—between the sensible world of our experience and its supersensible "substrate." I contend that reflective judgment fulfills the function of connecting the two realms because its activity is thought under the transcendental condition of human embodiment. Transcendentally, reflection lends to reason's ideas (and particularly to the idea of freedom) a sensible body that can be concretely *felt,* for example, in the experience of the sublime or in the contemplation (and idealization) of the human figure. Conclusively, "taste" is revealed as "the capacity to judge of the way in which reason's ideas are made sensible."[19] The critique of aesthetic and teleological judgment articulates the different modalities in which the supersensible is rendered sensible in the world of living nature—

within and without ourselves. Thus, I investigate the act of *Versinnlichung* to which ideas are subject within the framework of Kant's transcendental philosophy. While ideas inevitably appear as disembodied to speculative reason, gaining objective reality only through the legislation of practical reason—a reality, however, that has exclusively moral validity[20]—in the space opened up by the third *Critique* ideas gain a new sensible body *within experience*. "Aesthetic ideas" are the "pendant" of reason's ideas.[21] Not only can their reality immediately be *felt* but the peculiar feeling produced in us by embodied ideas allows the human subject to gain a new insight into her place in the world—a world whose sensible and supersensible dimensions eventually come to a meeting point. Nature becomes a "scheme" for ideas.[22] Imagination transfigures nature to the point of producing yet "*another* nature from the material provided by the real one." Such an "other" nature fulfills our quest for a new type of experience to which our "ordinary" one on occasion yields.[23] Although for Kant any *Erweiterung* of theoretical cognition to the realm of ideas remains utterly forbidden, the feeling of the sublime discloses the act of violence that reason exerts over our sensibility so as to "expand it (*zu erweitern*) commensurately to reason's own domain." Thus, paradoxically, Kant suggests that it is our sensibility and never our understanding that, following reason's pressure, becomes able to stretch and expand to the *Abgrund* of the supersensible.[24] I discuss the relation between morality and reflective judgment—in both its aesthetic and teleological employment—with regard to the peculiar experience that the human being is finally able to gain of the idea of freedom once she becomes aware of herself as part of living nature. My argument presents Kant's moral theology as the final articulation of the topic of transcendental embodiment. Eventually, only the experience of ourselves as embodied living and moral beings brought forth by reflective judgment can lend (human) value to the results of both theoretical and practical reason's enterprises in this world.

Sensibility and the Field of the Supersensible

For our cognitive faculty, the supersensible is the region in relation to which the territory of experience gains a new qualification. Unlike the other regions of Kant's mental geography, this field is for us "unlimited" (it is itself the limit of the sensible world) and also "inaccessible" to our cognitive faculty.[25] The "immeasurable space of the supersensible," warned Kant a few years earlier in the 1786 essay "What Does It Mean to Orient Oneself in Thinking?," "is enveloped, for us, in an impenetrable night," whence reason's "own need for orientation" arises.[26] The field of the supersensible will never acquire the familiarity of a territory on which to build the edifice of a doctrine; neither understanding nor reason will ever establish on it a domain for theoretical knowledge. Yet this field is necessary to provide reason with a sense of orientation in its endeavors. Paradoxically, once we accept expanding the horizon of our world to a realm that can only be the object of a reflected—neither theoretical nor practical—experience, then that same inscrutable night of the supersensible from which the need for orientation first arose eventually allows us to gain a new sense of orientation in a transfigured, labyrinthine world. For reflection leads us to recognize that the supersensible is the ideal "place" from which, transcendentally, the territory of experience and its domains are laid out for us. It is the ideal focus from which the boundaries determining the territory of experience irradiate. The separation between the domain of nature and freedom is radical. Between them is an immense and immeasurable "abyss," which makes utterly impossible all "transition" from the realm of nature to the realm of freedom by means of theoretical reason.[27] We know that the *effects* of both legislations meet in the same sensible word, and that both legislations have to be rooted in the field of the supersensible in order to be possible. Yet the abyss that divides the two legislations makes them appear so far apart from each other as if they belonged to two different worlds.[28] Now, however, finally disposing of a map to orient ourselves in a universe whose horizon has suddenly expanded, we can *locate* for the first time the abyss that divides the two regions of our experience. Even though upon different occasions we have had a chance of sensing the presence of that gulf,[29] it is only at this point that we are able to track down the position of the abyss for the first time. With it, Kant marks the starting point of the inquiry of the third *Critique*. The abyss, which hitherto has only served to disorient us, does not lose its mysterious and inscrutable depths. But it now becomes the benchmark for a new type of experience reorienting the realm of our human experience in its entirety.

The separation between nature and freedom establishes an asymmetric relation that works differently if approached from the two banks of the abyss. Kant resolutely denies that the world of nature can exercise any influence on the world of freedom. For this would imply an extension of cognition to the supersensible. The Dialectic of the first *Critique* proves such an extension illusory; while the second *Critique,* by showing the way in which reason is practical, further denies the possibility of any "influence" of the world of nature upon reason. The opposite influence, however, is not only possible but is emphatically presented by Kant in the form of the (practical) necessity of an "ought to" (*soll*).[30] The concept of freedom *ought to* exercise an influence over the world of nature. Freedom must see its ends actualized in the sensible world, even though it cannot prescribe laws to the *Sinnenwelt* but only raise claim to nature's accordance with freedom's law. Kant's insistence on placing both domains on the same territory of experience and in locating the effects of their legislations within the same sensible world reveals here its *raison d'être*. In the framework of the third *Critique,* Kant's concern is not so much to underline the unique access that practical reason has to the supersensible but rather to stress its efficacy in the sensible realm of human experience. Kant carries this argument a step further, and suggests that freedom's efficacy in the sensible world would be impossible (and impossible to think of) were nature not constituted by its own laws so as to harmonize with the ends proper to freedom's law (even though the two legislations are thoroughly independent of each other). Thus, we arrive at the question that complements the one posed by the labyrinth of nature to the faculty of judgment: How does the world of nature appear if considered under the condition of the necessary efficacy or influence exercised on it by freedom? Given that freedom must see the purposes assigned by its law actualized in the world of nature, nature itself, at least as far as the "*form* of its lawfulness"[31] is concerned, must be thought of as compatible with the possibility for freedom to realize its purposes within it. This view opens a new perspective on our consideration of and relationship to nature. It discloses the possibility of thinking of and relating to yet "another nature"[32] than the one investigated by mechanical science. Even if the immense abyss that separates the sensible from the supersensible world makes any transition from nature to freedom impossible, its very presence between them compels us to think of nature as allowing in its form accordance with and attunement to (*Zusammenstimmung*) freedom's purposes. Thereby, the *reciprocal hindrance* that nature and freedom exercise over each other in their effects in the sensible world is complemented by the possibility of a *reciprocal harmony* between them. This argument is at the center of the Methodology of the critique of the teleological faculty of judgment.

The field of the supersensible constitutes both the *unitary ground* and the "*ground for the unity*" underlying nature and freedom. According to Kant's topology of the cognitive faculty, the "concept" of this unitary ground belongs neither to nature nor to freedom. It is rather the *Mittelglied* between theoretical and practical. Kant still maintains—and even stresses—the impossibility of a "transition" from one domain to the other: no bridge can be thrown over the abyss; the separation can only be reinforced. Yet the *Critique of Judgment* discloses as its own field of competence the possibility of another type of *Übergang*. Such a "transition" allows Kant to re-think the map of the cognitive faculties in an inclusive way so that the abyss becomes one of its regions. He suggests the possibility of a switch in the "way of thinking" (*Denkungsart*) and experiencing the gap between theoretical and practical, and with it, the supersensible. It is on the middle-ground thus instituted that the transition "from the way of thinking according to the principles of nature to the way of thinking according to the principles of freedom" can take place.[33] It is a new way—or an "extended" way—of thinking and experiencing the common ground underlying nature and freedom. The impossibility of gaining objective cognition of the supersensible reveals the practical reality of freedom. Yet, at least in its determinate and particular effects—namely, in our actions and in the feeling that the moral law produces in our conscience—freedom itself belongs to the sensible world as the only world of human experience. The possibility of locating the supersensible on the map of the cognitive faculties as a "field" in its own right and not, as was still the case in the first *Critique,* as that which lies *beyond* the "field of experience"; the possibility of seeing in the supersensible that which defines the furthest limits of experience and its ultimate ground; and finally the possibility of arguing that a "concept" of the supersensible is possible for us (although as neither a theoretical nor a practical concept legislating on a distinctive domain)—all these openings suggest that there is a "thought-way" or "way of thinking"[34] which, as it is not confined to any particular region of this mental geography, is itself the condition that allows us to construct such a geography in the first place. There is no "common although to us unknown root" to which, "perhaps," the different branches of human cognition go back as to their origin.[35] In the third *Critique,* Kant vigorously restates the claim that in the first *Critique* he played against Wolff's attempt to reduce all faculties of the soul to a metaphysical unity. The different realms of human experience maintain a distinctive, transcendental independency from each other. The possibility of a "point of unification of all our a priori faculties in the supersensible" remains theoretically unknown and necessarily unknowable. And yet it is possible to think the constitution of both the natural and the moral worlds in a unifying and unified way, thereby "bringing reason into harmony with itself."[36] This possibility is disclosed by the *Denkungsart,* by which the reflective faculty of judgment construes a new—and as yet unexplored—realm of human experience. Given the separation of the two worlds, the "ground for the unity"[37] of the supersensible, which underlies nature and is the practical object of freedom, can have only the critical force of a new way of thinking (not the force of a law). Such *Denkungsart* allows us, if not a transition between the two separate worlds of nature and freedom, at least a transition between two ways of thinking, living, and experiencing our human condition as beings that participate in both the sensible and the intelligible world. According to this reflected and reflecting *Denkungsart* the human being is, for the first time, constitutively thought of as an integral part of the world of nature. The condition of embodiment, the feeling of life, and the pure feelings of pleasure and displeasure are the distinctive, transcendental conditions that make an experience of our belonging to living nature possible. They complement the human being's moral destination by allowing for a representation of nature as related to the purposiveness that rests in the subject. The accordance between nature and freedom cannot be objectively known and does not need to be practically postulated. It is, instead, simply and directly *felt* in the moment in which we gain a reflected feeling of ourselves as living part of nature.

The asymmetry by which freedom ought to influence nature, while nature cannot exercise influence on freedom, is reflected in another asymmetry that Kant discovers between the sensible and the "supersensible in the subject." He contends that though we would find no evidence in nature of the "*determining grounds*" of freedom's causality, we might instead be able to detect the *effects* or "*consequences*" of freedom in the sensible world. Such an asymmetric relation is a necessary implication of the concept of "causality through freedom."[38] Freedom is granted an influence not on the *legislation* of nature as such, but on the *objects* of this legislation, one of which is the human subject as embodied moral agent. The efficacy of freedom's causality ought to be manifested in the sensible world according to its formal laws. It follows that, in the sensible world, besides the mechanical effects of nature's causality, there are effects that follow from the purely formal legislation of practical reason. Kant suggests that there might be cases in which *one and the same sensible effect,* while it should be known exclusively in terms of the transcendental laws of nature as mechanism, must *also and at the same time* be accounted for with regard to the sensible "consequences" of the supersensible legislation of reason, and hence, in the moral-practical perspective, must be explained as a sensible effect of the formal law of freedom—as its *embodiment* or *Versinnlichung,* as it were. This claim, however, is possible only by endorsing the perspective of the reflective faculty of judgment. For only this faculty can account for the way in which freedom is present in the world of appearances, i.e., for the ways in which the world of nature "speaks" to us, for the subject's moral worth, or for the ways in which the moral subject feels herself an integral part of the natural world.

Kant clarifies that, in the case of the supersensible, to be "cause" (*Ur-sache*) means only to be the "ground (*Grund*) that determines the causality of natural things to an effect (*Wirkung*) in conformity to their own natural laws, and yet, *at the same time, also* in accordance with the formal principle of the laws of reason."[39] Natural things are mechanistically determined according to their own natural laws, and yet "at the same time" they are "also" determined so as to be in accordance with the order of freedom. The ground of this peculiar *accordance, harmony, or congruence* is the supersensible. Thus, in the *Denkungsart* proper to reflective judgment the idea of purposive *Zusammen-* or *Ein-Stimmung* replaces the notion of "*influence*"[40] as a means to think of the relation between nature and freedom. Kant's apparently contradictory argument that claims, at the same time, the *impossible recipro-cal influence* of nature's and freedom's legislations on the one hand, and the *possibility of accordance* between them, on the other, is predicated upon his view of the human subject. The "subject" as "human being" (*Mensch*)[41] is a being that acts according to her sensible nature (as *Sinnenwesen* placed in the *Sinnenwelt*) and *also, and at the same time,* according to the supersensible nature in herself. *Mensch* is the middle-ground on which nature's and free-dom's paths intersect. The human being as natural being is a "natural cause" that works in a strictly mechanistic way; the "determination" of her free causality, however, even though it takes place in the world of appearance, "is grounded in the intelligible, which is thought of under freedom in a manner not otherwise explicable." This claim, valid initially for the human being, is eventually extended to nature as a whole. In the perspective of reflective judgment, nature is transfigured: nature as well can be said to have a "supersensible substrate."[42] Kant thereby raises the issue of the foundation of our human experience in the supersensible, and of the ways that we have of becoming aware of this foundation. For if we cannot explain or *know* this relation through understanding and reason, we may still *feel* it and *judge it in analogy* to what we can indeed know.

How, then, do we come to think of the *accordance* between the two legislations? Expressed in the conceptual terminology proper to the faculty of judgment, the "effect" following from the law of freedom is the "final purpose" or *Endzweck*. Freedom's effect *ought to* come to existence and be actualized in the sensible world. This final purpose is a moral demand. Its "condition of possibility is presupposed in nature," i.e., in the embodied human being as "subject."[43] We must assume that nature proceeds as if it were producing its forms technically, precisely because we are ourselves beings who belong to nature and who are able to act in a purposive way. Causality through freedom is the causality of the human being as moral agent. But free causality can take place in the sensible world only because the agent as sensible, embodied being belongs to nature. It follows that nature must be conceived so as to allow free causality to be realized within it; human sensibility must be thought of as allowing for a responsiveness to freedom's efficacy in the world. Thus, "with the concept of a *purposiveness* of nature, the faculty of judgment provides us with the concept that mediates between the concepts of nature and the concept of freedom."[44] Thereby, we effect a "transition" from the "lawfulness" of nature to that of freedom. Purposiveness is itself a peculiar form of lawfulness: it is the lawfulness of the contingent as such. More precisely, "aesthetic purposiveness is the lawfulness of the faculty of judgment in its freedom."[45]

Thereby Kant has not constructed a bridge over the abyss that divides nature from freedom. Instead, he has made transcendentally explicit the conditions under which alone we can think of the interplay between the two lawful orders. They work indeed as separate orders that fulfill, nonetheless, the demand of being enacted (differently constructed and experienced) by the same human subject on the same territory of experience. Reflective judgment structures their relationship in terms of "purposiveness" (or accordance), not in terms of reciprocal "influence." The concept of purposiveness enables us to recognize the "possibility of the final purpose"—a possibility that is denied both to understanding and to practical reason (which could only "postulate" the actualization of freedom in the world). Accordingly, we judge that the final purpose "can only become actual in nature and in accordance with its laws."[46]

Kant places the supersensible "*in* us as well as *outside* of us"[47]—namely, within the human subject and in the world of nature outside of the subject. He presents us with the three ways that our cognitive faculty has of approaching the supersensible: through understanding, the faculty of judgment, and reason.

The understanding's a priori legislation on nature is limited to nature as appearance. This same limitation, however, hints at something beyond appearances, namely to nature's "supersensible substrate." Supersensible things, i.e., things as noumena, mark the limit of cognition, thereby bringing it back to the conditions of sensibility.[48] Understanding cannot but leave the supersensible "entirely *indeterminate*"; for, in the perspective of the understanding and by means of its concepts nothing can be said or determined of the supersensible substrate of nature. It is the faculty of judgment that makes the supersensible *determinable* for the first time. By means of the a priori principle of nature's formal purposiveness, judgment allows us an experience of nature as system of *possible* particular empirical laws and forms, not as homogeneous mechanism governed by universal laws. This idea makes possible the "*determinability*" of the supersensible substrate, both in us and outside of us. Judgment does not determine the supersensible. It opens up an access for reflecting upon it and for determining it analogically. "*Determinability*" is a disposition that the supersensible gains through our *aesthetic reflective* faculty of judgment; it is judgment's own way of bridging the gap between sensible and supersensible; it is the open-ended task that involves our entire intellectual faculty by invoking the collaboration of understanding, imagination, reason, and intuition. Determinability is the analogical way that we have to think of the supersensible in us and outside of us *as if it were sensible for us.*

Only reason is able to practically determine the supersensible substrate through the moral law. This practical determination works precisely on the determinability disclosed by the faculty of judgment. Thereby, the "transition from the domain of the concept of nature to the domain of the concept of freedom" eventually takes place.[49] While any other way of making sense of the supersensible is forbidden to the understanding, except merely *thinking* of it in its complete indeterminateness, reflective judgment concretely makes sense of it through *analogy, imagination,* and *feeling.* There are things in nature and in us of which we can—and must—be able to talk meaningfully even though we cannot know (or determine) them. We must be able to talk and communicate meaningfully about them even before raising the question of whether we can know them at all, and even independently of this question and its answer. Through the faculty of judgment, the realm of the supersensible becomes accessible to us as a realm that does not lie beyond the sensible in an alleged transcendence but as a realm to which we are led by our experience of the sensible world—and, reflectively, of ourselves as part of this world. The supersensible is placed, as it were, "in us as well as outside of us."[50] Within the space opened by mere determinability, we can understand the special freedom or the "spontaneity"[51] that our cognitive faculties enjoy while at play in the act of reflection. Placed within this space, the supersensible in its determinability receives a non-conceptual, free determination by means of reflection.

The reflective faculty of judgment that functions as *Mittelglied* or as agent for the *Verknüpfung* between sensible and supersensible is specifically the *aesthetic* faculty of judgment. Kant recognizes that the concept of nature's formal purposiveness still belongs to the concepts of nature, although not as a constitutive principle but only as a *"regulative* principle of the cognitive faculty."[52] The idea of nature's formal purposiveness is a maxim for our reflection upon the whole of nature in its empirical manifold. Yet, in the case of the *aesthetic* faculty of judgment, Kant discovers the *constitutive status of the principle with regard to the feeling of pleasure and displeasure.* Thus it becomes clear why Kant insists on relating the cognitive faculties to the respective powers of the soul by means of each faculty's a priori principle. For, if the a priori principle of the faculty of judgment is not constitutive with regard to a realm of objects, it is indeed constitutive with regard to the corresponding power of the soul, namely, to the feeling of pleasure and displeasure. Our aesthetic judgment on certain specific and contingent products of nature and art, which prompts the concept of formal purposiveness (as harmony between the object's form and our cognitive faculties), is a constitutive principle for the feeling of pleasure and displeasure because this feeling is grounded a priori on that principle. The ground for the feeling of pleasure is the harmony or attunement of the cognitive faculties in the free play in which they spontaneously engage once they are set free of the strict conditions imposed by understanding's cognitive legislation, as well as by reason's practical order. In this respect, the "free play" of the cognitive faculties from which aesthetic pleasure arises is the *pendant* to the asset that the same faculties display in the cognitive situation. On the other hand, with regard to reason and the practical sphere, Kant contends that the freedom and "spontaneity" proper to the faculties at play in aesthetic reflection make the concept of purposiveness "suitable as mediation of the connection of the domain of nature with the domain of freedom in its consequences, and also promotes, at the same time, the receptivity of the *Gemüt* to moral feeling."[53] Aesthetic judgment is at work in the realm of the sensible, and yet through its constitutive principle of purposiveness, this faculty discovers, within the sensible, the traces of the supersensible—it discovers *within nature* the sensible consequences of freedom's final end. Aesthetic feeling is independent of moral feeling and yet, belonging to the same family of pure feelings, does prepare and facilitate our receptivity and responsiveness to morality. Aesthetic reflection allows us to experience a type of freedom different from (and yet related to) moral freedom. However, since moral freedom cannot be—properly speaking—experienced by us, the "spontaneity" in the "free play of our cognitive faculties" opens up to the only *experience* of freedom that we may have as sensible embodied beings. Through the free play of the faculties that produces aesthetic pleasure, we experience, by way of analogy, moral freedom in the sensible world and gain a premonition of our intelligible determination. This is the mediating function that Kant assigns to the aesthetic faculty of judgment.

The Human Body and Nature's "Animal Body": A Feeling of Affinity

As suggested above, the mediating function of reflective judgment is predicated on Kant's view of the human being as intermediary link between the sensible and supersensible world, between reflecting animals and pure disembodied spirits. Taste as the sense for beauty that provides immediate perception and awareness of one's being alive is the disposition unique to human beings as animal and yet also rational beings.[54] We have seen that while the *Gemüt* is, for Kant, the very principle of life, we can gain a qualified feeling of pleasure or displeasure for our current state, i.e., we can judge of the (aesthetic) *quality* of our life only by relating to (and reflecting on) our embodied condition.

> Life without the feeling of bodily organs would be the bare consciousness of [. . .] existence, but not the feeling of being well or unwell [. . .]. The *Gemüt* by itself alone is life itself (the very principle of life), and hindrance and furtherance must be sought outside it and yet in the human being, consequently in connection with its body.[55]

Now Kant maintains that of the supersensible substrate of nature we know nothing else but that it is placed "in us as well as outside of us."[56] Transcendentally, the condition that allows us this important placement is, once again, the human living body—i.e., that sort of 'in-between' that lies *outside* of the *Gemüt* but still *within* the human being, the intermediary that shares the mysterious, "inscrutable property"[57] of natural organisms and accompanies the agent's action in the sensible world. Curiously, when set in relation to ourselves, the supersensible substrate shares with the human body a similar position. The peculiar, embodied feeling of pleasure and displeasure that is a priori connected to our faculty of judgment is the heuristic principle that guides us in the investigation of nature's particular empirical forms and discloses the traces of the supersensible in the field of the sensible—in ourselves and outside of ourselves. For, on the one hand, it reveals that we are not simply machines but part of living nature, while on the other hand, this feeling hints at a receptivity (*Empfänglichkeit*)[58] to moral ideas that finds expression in our relation to the sublime in nature. This feeling is the guiding thread that eventually leads us out of the chaotic labyrinth of nature and allows us to form a representation of nature's systematic order.

To represent nature as the ordered totality of a "system" on the ground of reflective judgment's principle of formal purposiveness implies two things. First, in the *Critique of Pure Reason,* Kant already connects the representation of a "system" to the Platonic image of the "animal body" and its inner structure (*articulatio*) and growth.[59] Second, the idea of nature as system sees the human being included in the whole as its organic, immanent part. To be part of the system of nature (and to *feel* oneself part of it) has a completely different meaning (and is a completely different experience) than to be one of the many homogeneous elements that constitute nature's mechanism or to be its detached observer. Transcendentally, however, this difference can be brought to light and indicate a philosophical problem in its own right, only from the perspective of reflective judgment. It is only in the third *Critique* that the experience of being part of the system of living nature gains meaning as an independent, irreducible *human experience.* Given the reflective character of judgment, the issue is twofold: at stake is the problem of conceiving the peculiar structure of living beings in general; but the issue also involves the specific experience of feeling oneself an organic part of living nature.[60] These two points are intrinsically related as part of the same reflective movement. To judge nature as an organized system (as opposed to a mere mechanism or chaotic labyrinth) is to reflect upon ourselves as human embodied beings and upon the role and place that we occupy within the whole of nature. The problem that Kant addressed, still using the language of scholastic metaphysics, in his early letter to Moses Mendelssohn of 8 April 1766 here receives its final critical solution.

In that early letter (and then in the *Dreams of a Spirit-Seer*) the issue of the embodiment of consciousness is combined with the question, "how is the soul present in the world?"—namely, how is it present both "in material nature and in other entities closer to its own kind?" Now the question is: what is it in nature itself that makes us aware of our belonging to it as an organized system, that prompts a feeling for our being part of nature but also, at the same time, makes us feel the higher, supersensible sense or value of our moral destination and thereby hints at the supersensible substrate of nature? In other words: what is it in nature that forces us not to be content with the results brought forth by determinant judgment and requires the additional, specific exercise of reflective judgment? In the previous chapter we examined the way in which reflective judgment in its aesthetic function transcendentally indicates the specific place of the human being between animals and pure spirits. Now we have to investigate the relationship that the human being entertains with the whole of nature—with nature (and the supersensible basis of nature) in and outside of ourselves. A central question underlies the *Critique of Judgment* and accounts for its necessity as the conclusion of Kant's transcendental philosophy: who is the subject that pronounces reflective (aesthetic and teleological) judgments? What constitutes the "humanity" respectively invested in determinant and reflective judgment? In judging nature and natural objects and events mechanistically, the subject stakes only that sensible part of herself that responds to (because it is, at least in part, responsible for) the laws of mechanism, namely, space and time as pure forms of intuition and her sensible character. The subject pronouncing the judgment is the mechanist scientist whose individuality and subjectivity are absorbed in the generic universality of the 'I think' that grounds the objectivity of all cognitive judgments. Moreover, knowledge of our empirical self is knowledge of a mechanism that, as far as the universal laws of nature are concerned, is identical in all natural mechanisms. The Newtonian scientist is legislator over nature and its mechanical laws; as part of nature, however, she is no more than a machine, subject to those laws as all other natural objects and events are. In order to occupy the privileged position of legislator in the mechanist world of nature in general, the knowing subject must pay the price of being a generic "object in general," homogeneous with all other natural objects. This situation is overturned in the *Critique of Judgment*. The subject uttering reflective judgments stakes her own life and individuality in her judgment. She places herself within the object that she judges, becomes one with and attuned to it, and invests in the judgment her deepest, utterly irreducible subjectivity, namely that of a pure, disinterested feeling. The scientist who this time investigates nature—searching for signs of life and its organization, bringing a fundamental sensitivity to beauty to bear on her enterprise—is immersed in her object in an ongoing research-process that knows of no final objective truth and aims at no legislation over a field of objects. At stake in this inquiry is the humanity of the subject and the meaning of her worldly existence. This is the ultimate sense of judgment's reflection. By abandoning the privileged standpoint of the legislator, the subject meets within nature her irreducible subjectivity, a pure feeling that grounds reflective judgment.

The idea of life and the relation that our embodied *Lebensgefühl* enter-tains with the reflective faculty of judgment is the leading idea of Kant's inquiry in both the critique of aesthetic and the critique of teleological judgment. It is the same a priori principle proper to the transcendental structure of the human *Gemüt* that allows us to reflect upon ourselves, to become aware of our sensitivity to beauty, to tremble in front of the sublime, to understand what characterizes other natural living beings out-side of ourselves, and to appreciate our tendency to connect the aesthetic response to beauty and the sublime to moral ideas. For, *transcendentally,* all these acts are linked to our human *embodied* condition. Following Kant's suggestion in the discussion of the idea of "system" in the first *Critique,* to judge of the whole of nature as a system means to represent it as an "animal body"—as the *same* animal body that we are (and that characterizes us, as human beings, in opposition to pure rational spirits).[61] The cognitively im-penetrable property of nature's organization that lends it systematic form is found incarnated in our own body. Although the possibility of finding particular natural forms reflected in the design of our own body does not make the cognitive problem of defining life in nature any more accessible, this possibility allows Kant to pose the question in a radically new way. The condition, however, is to leave all pretension of cognition to the vain efforts of determinant judgment and its mechanical explanations. Mechanical sci-ence cannot explain life because it cannot *feel* it (as Diderot remarked: even the stone is alive, yet we cannot hear its cry). The critical investigation into the teleological faculty of judgment hinges upon the fundamental turn in our *Denkungsart* that makes it possible to relate our embodied condition to the heuristic construction of nature as an organized system of which we are not legislators or detached spectators but integral (and perhaps privi-leged) parts. For Kant, the structure of the system implies the organization of a manifold of parts into a whole so that the whole is not constituted by the cumulative addition (*coacervatio*) of parts brought together merely on the basis of their contingent "similarity" (*Ähnlichkeit*), with an external end in view. The system is instead the architectural organization of parts that constitute the whole on the ground of their fundamental "affinity" (*Verwandtschaft*) with the totality (i.e., the whole is *articulatio*). Systematic parts derive their necessity from a unifying idea from which they issue as if from an "inner purpose."[62] The relation of "affinity" between parts and whole is the mark of that inner purpose. Accordingly, we can conclude that the relation that binds us—human embodied beings—to nature's "animal body" and its organization is not simply an external and extrinsic "similarity" (to be observed). It is rather a deeper, more necessary *Verwandtschaft* (to be felt). This "affinity," which we find transcendentally incarnated in our living body, plays a crucial role in spelling out the activity of teleological judgment.

We shall now take stock of where we are, of what our human predicament is in the world of the third *Critique:* facing the realm of nature in its manifold contingent forms we stand in front of an alternative. Either we hold on to the universal laws of the understanding and to our position as nature's legislators, in which case nature still appears, in its generality, as a coherent mechanism; and yet, since no account can be given of its particular empirical forms (no explanation of life is possible), the mechanism yields to the unmanageable chaos of a labyrinth. Or we consent to give up the position of determinant judgment with regard to the explanation of nature's contingent forms, in which case only a way out of the labyrinth becomes a real possibility. Abandoning the perspective of determinant judgment we are able to think of nature as an organized system. In this system, however, we can no longer occupy the privileged position of legislators. Instead, we become one of the many empirical, contingent forms of nature. However, we also gain specificity against the uniformity of mere mechanism by becoming *living* parts of nature's organization. Now we stand in front of the thoroughly new task of reflecting on the sense and meaning of the new position that we occupy in the system of living nature. This implies a revisitation (and a fundamental extension) not only of Kant's epistemology but also of his moral philosophy. Transcendentally this new, extended field of experience is disclosed to us by our human embodiment. How does Kant articulate the form of transcendental embodiment in the second part of the *Critique of Judgment?*

Even though the teleological faculty of judgment does not present an original a priori principle of its own (as does the aesthetic faculty of judgment), it exercises its reflection on a determinate and peculiar sphere of objects. To identify this particular set of objects as the realm of organisms and living beings (natural products as natural purposes), Kant proceeds to a careful distinction of different kinds of objective purposiveness drawn with regard to the different objects to which these notions respectively apply. He considers two general categories of objects: products of art (geometrical figures and mechanical artifacts) and natural products. Only in the latter case does the teleological faculty of judgment display a characteristic use of the principle of purposiveness, distinct from merely practical purposiveness. Kant states the crucial difference between external and internal purposiveness by claiming that to judge "a thing to be a natural purpose on account of its internal form is quite different from considering the existence of that thing to be a purpose of nature."[63] While material external purposiveness should be banned from natural science, internal purposiveness merits all our attention. In addressing the issue of internal purposiveness, Kant shifts from the notion of *Zweckmäßigkeit* to the notion of *Zweck*—purposiveness becomes objective in the internal form of a specific type of objects. On this basis he considers, respectively, products of art and natural products. Moreover, he identifies organisms or organized beings as the peculiar kind of objects that the reflective faculty of judgment represents according to the notion of an objective internal purposiveness as "natural purposes." Kant's argument is guided by the question: is there a case in which the mechanistic explanation of nature must yield to the claim that something "is possible *only* as purpose"?[64] To contend that something is possible *only if considered as a purpose* means to claim that its cause does not lie in the mechanism of nature but is a faculty whose causality is determined by concepts. In order to meet such a case, a condition is required: it must be the case that the "form" of the object cannot have arisen according to mere natural laws. Since the object's form is utterly "contingent" with regard to those laws, the only way to explain its peculiar constitution is to resort to concepts of reason and to reason's own causality.[65] An object, whose form is possible only through reason, is an object that is possible only as purpose. Kant sees this explanation at work both in the case of artistic products and in regard to natural products. While in the first case appeal is made to reason's practical-technical causality, the second case requires the intervention of a specific teleological reflection upon nature. Such a reflection discloses the possibility of a coherent system of our experience of nature's empirical forms. This system, however, can only be established under the condition of our inclusion in it as human living beings—rational and yet also animal beings—i.e., under the condition of abandoning the pretension of being nature's legislators according to the reductionistic claim of mechanical science.[66]

The "affinity" with nature's "animal body" an affinity that we can feel in and live through our own body plays a crucial role in the argument that Kant offers in §65 *in lieu* of a transcendental deduction of the concept of "natural purpose."[67] The task is to show what kind of things in nature provides "objective reality" to the concept of *Zweck* when this is not a practical purpose but a "purpose *of nature*" (*Naturzweck*).[68] Kant's thesis is that natural products as natural purposes constitute the peculiar objective "territory" of teleological judgment. In judging these objects we reflect, at the same time, upon ourselves and our place in nature. The solution to the problem of displaying the realm of objects that instantiates or embodies the concept of natural purpose lies in the regulative idea that allows us to reflect upon the "peculiar character" and "inscrutable property"[69] that characterize organized beings. This idea serves us as regulative principle for judging the internal purposiveness of organized beings.[70] "An organized product of nature is one in which everything is a purpose and reciprocally also a means."[71] There are only two kinds of causality: the *nexus effectivus* or the descending connection of efficient or "real" causes proper to the understanding, in which no reciprocity or reversibility is allowed; and the *nexus finalis* of "ideal" causes or the connection according to reason's concept of a final cause, in which reciprocity is indeed allowed as in the practical-technical domain of intentional causality.[72] This connection displays both an ascending and a descending structure. The question is now: can the *nexus finalis* ever be applied to nature? That is, to a realm different from that of our intentional causality through reason—a realm in which no direct exhibition of the concept of a purpose but where only, at the most, an indirect (not a schematic but only a symbolic) exhibition can be carried through? Can we think of a different, non-practical (and non-cognitive) access to nature's organization and technique? In other words, how can organisms—precisely as organisms—become objects of our experience? While the answer to these questions is the crucial topic of Kant's critique of teleological judgment, special attention must be paid to the very need for raising these questions. For herein lies the properly transcendental character of the problem posed by the third *Critique*. Why do we feel a need for a special experience of living nature as such? Why aren't we satisfied with conceptualizing the world around us and ourselves in it in terms of mechanism?

The general question concerns the set of conditions required to define something as a natural purpose. In both a mechanical artifact and a natural product viewed as a purpose, it must be the case that the parts are possible only through their relation to the whole. For anything that is thought of as *Zweck* is thought of under "a concept or idea" that determines it a priori. This condition defines the artifact or work of art as the purpose of an external rational cause producing its work according to an idea. It follows that, in order to define the specificity of that which is possible "*only* as a *natural* purpose," without appealing to the external causality of concepts exercised by rational beings, a second condition must supplement the first.[73] The second requirement points to the problem of our *reflection upon* and *judgment of* things that are possible only as natural purposes; it does not concern the conditions of their objective existence or effectual production. Thereby it reveals the regulative character of the principle that guides our judging of the systematic unity of nature. This requirement is that "the parts of the thing combine into the unity of the whole because they are reciprocally cause and effect of their form." In this case, the purposiveness of the whole is constitutive of the disposition of its parts, i.e., it is intrinsic or immanent to it. The causality involved therein is no longer external; rather, the causality of the cause is, in this case, the same causality of the effect. The idea of the whole determines reciprocally the connection and form of the parts, yet not as a real "cause"—as in the case of the artifact—but as *Erkenntnisgrund,* namely, as the basis for our cognition of the whole as systematic unity of manifold parts (as *ratio cognoscendi*). Kant argues that in this case, a sort of combination of the two aforementioned types of causal connection (*nexus effectivus* and *nexus finalis*) takes place. "The connection of efficient causes is judged at the same time as causation through final causes."[74] Nature is judged as if it were producing its forms not mechanically but technically (architectonically, in the language of the first *Critique*) or organically. This formal definition of *internal* purposiveness accounts for the specificity of the structure of organized beings. In an organized being, each part or organ produces the other parts and is reciprocally produced by them; each part is there "*for*" the others and "*through*" them. The productive cause is internal to or immanent in the self-organizing whole and does not lie externally in a rational cause that acts according to concepts. An organized being differs from a mechanical artifact such as a watch, since in the living being parts produce other parts; the whole reproduces itself; and the whole produces the systematic unity of the parts. Contrary to a machine, the organized and self-organizing being has "formative force" not just "motive force."[75]

How and according to which principle should we reflect upon organized beings? In order to determine the transcendental status of the idea of nature's organization, Kant explores the possibilities offered by *analogy* and discusses three possible arguments by analogy: the first proposes an analogy between organized beings and art products, while the second and third propose an analogy with the always mysterious principle of life.

(1) With regard to the possibility of thinking of a natural purpose as an "analogue of art" Kant contends that while natural beauty can indeed be defined in analogy to art as it implies "reflection upon an *external* intuition," an organized being is not just an "analogue of art."[76] Since art implies the purposive activity of the artist as a rational cause *external* to its product, the analogy does not account for the *immanent* self-productive causality

of natural organisms. Nor does the analogy to art account for the formative force proper to the inner principle of life, since this principle does not
simply reproduce identical exemplars but rather often implies contingent
deviations "useful for self-preservation (*Selbsterhaltung*) as required by circumstances." Self-preservation is not simply reproduction of an "exemplar"
but implies—and sometimes even requires—variation.[77] Life organizes itself
in order to further itself; self-preservation is part of nature's organization,
is part of what constitutes an organism as a natural purpose that is never
taken in isolation but always in interaction with its environment. Hence,
a better—although still insufficient—attempt at understanding organized
beings may be to describe them as the "analogue of life."[78] In discussing this
analogy, Kant rules out two very different arguments as candidates for an
explanation of organisms. While he rejects the first argument outright, by
addressing the second he is led to his own solution of the problem.

(2) By proposing an analogy between natural purposes and life, the first
argument anticipates the one later discussed in the Dialectic and utterly
dismissed by Kant for its dogmatism. Trying to explain the constitution of
organisms by appealing to a metaphysical principle of life (the soul) only
leads us to an unsolvable antinomy of reason (and besides, it implies the
clear circularity of attempting an explanation of empirical life by resorting
to metaphysical life, which in turn is justified only by the occurrence of
empirical cases). How can dead matter ever become capable of organizing
itself in living forms? Either the peculiarity of the organized being remains
unexplained or its scientific explanation is seriously threatened by metaphysical hylozoism or the dualism separating body and soul, dead matter
and the principle of life.[79] Hence, with regard to this dogmatic argument,
Kant resolutely concludes that "strictly speaking [. . .] the organization of
nature has nothing analogous to any causality known to us."[80]

(3) However, in order to conclude that the only sustainable explanation
of organized beings is the one offered by teleological judgment, Kant needs
to confront yet another, apparently different argument that also resorts to
the analogy to life. This time the analogy to life is an analogy to *our own life*
and to *our own living body*. While Kant shares the original intuition of this
second argument, he needs to reject its pretension to a *constitutive* use of the
concept of natural purpose as contradictory with the very notion of a living
organized being. For Kant, our embodied state is a *transcendental* condition,
not an empirical fact or a metaphysical assumption. Kant's conclusion is
that only teleological judgment, which makes a *regulative* use of the concept
of natural purpose, is able to take the *transcendental* status of our embodied

condition into account and bring it to bear on the explanation of other organized natural beings outside of ourselves.

The reason why the analogy to art is rejected is the need to account for the *immanence* of the principle of organization proper to natural purposes—the immanence that distinctively separates natural purposes from products of practical-technical causality. Moreover, Kant contends that while "natural beauty" appears externally and is perceived in a reflection on "external intuition," whereby it can be conceived in analogy to art, that which makes certain things possible only as natural purposes resides in the "internal natural perfection" of organized beings. Being completely autonomous and self-contained, life is neither related to an external cause nor does it appear in an external form given to our sensible intuition. From this it follows that such a peculiar type of inner purposiveness cannot be known in analogy to any "physical natural power known to us." The inference from the natural power that produces beauty to an alleged natural power that produces organisms is not sound. To this extent, the connection between beauty and life cannot be further pursued. Living organisms are not just objectified beautiful natural forms. And yet this second argument could still attempt to save the analogy to life and get to its point by claiming that if one could think of a natural power known to us and immanent in nature which could be related to natural purposes, the flaw of the analogy to art could be corrected and a valid analogy to life could be instituted for our goal of knowing nature.

The turning point is reached with the parenthetical clause that is called in support of the argument, a clause which Kant seems to fully endorse. The claim that "we too belong to nature in the broadest sense"[81] could aptly function as the entry point to the problem of our analogical knowledge of organized beings. We too are organized beings, living beings, and we can gain a sense of this through our own body, i.e., by establishing an analogy to our own life; we too are, in this respect, agents who exercise "physical natural power."[82] To this extent, our causality can be considered, in a certain way, *internal* to nature itself. The way our human body is organized, the way it reproduces itself and strives for self-preservation is the way in which nature is technically at work within and through our own body. Once included in the whole of nature, our physical causality becomes, in a certain sense, nature's own causality. Indeed, Kant seems to support this line of argument by underscoring that the "human being is a member (*Glied*) of nature in its totality as system."[83] As members of nature's organization and through the activity of our own living body—so the argument would go—we could indeed be able to understand how nature works in producing organized beings. In other words, while the analogy to art can be dismissed on the ground that the artist is a force *external* to her product, the analogy to our own physical, bodily activity institutes the *immanence* that the understanding of nature's organization requires.

What is Kant's position toward this use of the argument by analogy, an argument which, in extending life in ourselves to life in other beings and eventually to the whole of nature, seems to echo the ancient parallel (or analogy, as it were) between microcosm and macrocosm? If the aim is to produce *cognition* of natural life processes, Kant rejects the argument outright: in this case, the analogy that goes from our own living body to life in other natural beings does not hold. The reason is, once again, Kant's rejection of *physiology* as valid method of inquiry. If the analogy to life in our own body were a viable option, then physiology would be the method to follow in order to gain knowledge of living nature. The point, however, is that physiology produces no specific *knowledge of life* as distinct from mechanism—neither in ourselves nor in other beings outside of ourselves (just as it produces no knowledge of the specificity of *aesthetic* feeling as opposed to mere empirical affections).[84] Following the physiological method, one inevitably falls yet again into Epicurus's dogmatic mechanicism: life is ultimately reduced to mechanism.[85]

And yet, there is a way in which the analogy with our living body does become the guiding heuristic thread that allows Kant to reflect on (though not know of) nature in its systematic organization and to build the further analogy to our own activity according to purposes. In the Critique of Aesthetic Judgment Kant has shown that we do indeed have an access to life—albeit not a dogmatic or metaphysical but a transcendental one— namely, through a peculiar *Lebensgefühl* and through the connected aesthetic feeling of pleasure and displeasure that we owe to our embodied condition. Accordingly, extending the argument of the Critique of Aesthetic Judgment one can contend, analogically, that there is indeed an "affinity" between life in nature and life in ourselves, i.e., in our own body. Such affinity is now the ground of the "remote analogy" that Kant establishes between nature's technique and "our own causality concerning purposes in general."[86] We can analogically relate nature's purposiveness in organized being to our own practical agency only because we have a feeling and a consciousness of our belonging to living nature. The transcendental condition of human embodiment functions as the mediating link between nature's technique and our human purposive causality. In other words, the transcendental

condition on which Kant's argument depends is that if we had no awareness through a specific embodied feeling of our membership in the whole
of living nature, we would not even be able to pose the problem of things
which are possible only as natural purposes. Nature would remain for us a
strict mechanism. Compared to hylozoism, Epicurus's position would be
the most consequent.

Thus, Kant's conclusive argument runs as follows: our embodied condition makes us *feel* our inclusion in the whole of living nature (we represent
nature to ourselves as a living body, not as a mechanism); following the
suggestion of the first *Critique,* we can indeed claim that our living body
has an "affinity" to nature's animal body; and since we do feel (or we have
a special sense for) our membership in nature's organization (we think of
ourselves as *Glieder* of nature's whole), we also feel the need to understand
the inexplicable and irreducible property that distinguishes organized beings from mechanical artifacts and also from mere beautiful natural forms.
Such understanding is ultimately a mode of human self-reflection. In this
understanding, however, the cognitive aims of determinant judgment must
be left aside. For it is only under this condition that we can gain a sense
of and feeling for our membership within nature. To be sure, the analogy goes both ways, thereby instituting a complete process of reflection.
We need to refer to our own causality according to purposes in order to
understand—reflectively and merely regulatively—nature's organization.
But we also need to grasp the peculiarity of the notion of natural purpose
in order to gain a sense of ourselves as living members of the system of
nature, to understand what it means for the human being to be a part or
member of nature's whole. This reflection is indeed the basis of the *regulative* use of the concept of natural purpose. Kant suggests that as soon as we
recognize the merely regulative value of the concept of natural purpose for
the use of reflective judgment, the horizon of our inquiry expands. We are
led to a meditation not only on living organisms as we ourselves are but
also on "their highest ground" (*Grund*). Such reflection does not aim at
"gaining knowledge either of nature or of that original ground (*Urgrund*)
of nature." We reflect, instead, only for the sake of our own practical efficacy in the world.[87] The *Urgrund* of nature is the ground of our own life
and of our practical (and specifically moral) activity within the system of
nature. Thereby, Kant points to the supersensible basis or the "supersensible determining ground" of nature beyond nature's "blind mechanism."
Although no knowledge of this ground or of the system of nature is possible, our reflection upon it satisfies a necessary need of practical reason in

analogy to which the notion of natural purpose is formulated. In this way, the supersensible becomes the "determining ground"[88] of our teleological judgments on nature's contingent forms. Thus, the concept of purposiveness employed by the teleological faculty of judgment eventually discloses its value as intermediary concept between the theoretical and the practical use of our faculties.

In the regulative use of the concept of natural purpose by teleological judgment, the "external intuition" which, upon reflection, we relate to our *Lebensgefühl* and thereby feel a peculiarly aesthetic pleasure, yields to a sort of "organic intuition." Transcendentally, organisms refer back to a specific, 'organic' way of judging of objects. 'Organic' designates a transcendental condition, not an ontological mode of being. In other words, the term 'organic' is predicated of objects only through our 'organic,' i.e., *embodied* way of reflecting upon them. This modality of judgment is *constitutively* embodied. "Organic intuition" is the basis of a necessarily embodied modality of judgment that, reflecting on living beings, allows us a non-cognitive access to the supersensible substrate of nature. Thus, in Kant's idea of organic— or teleological—judgment we find the definitive critical answer against *Schwärmerei,* namely, against the idea of a privileged, disembodied, or purely spiritual access to the supersensible (e.g., through intellectual intuition). In a *Reflection* written in the years 1776–1778 Kant opposes "organic intuition" to "spiritual intuition," their difference consisting in the fact that the former takes place "through the body"—"*Organisches oder geistiges Anschauen, jenes durch den Körper.*" "Our intuition is not mystical but physical; the physical is not pneumatological but organic."[89] In turn, what organic intuition allows us to intuit—or better, in the perspective of the third *Critique,* to judge—is not the realm of pure spirits but embodied life, i.e., living organisms or life itself (within and outside of ourselves). The supersensible is not the realm of pure spirits or disembodied souls. It is rather the supersensible basis of nature disclosed by our organic, embodied reflection on living beings. The supersensible is accessible to us only to the extent that it is itself (somehow) 'embodied' (*versinnlicht*) in nature.

Living Beings and Moral Beings

If on the basis of our embodied condition our human purposive efficacy in this world provides us with the "remote analogy" with which to think of nature's purposive organization, then we need to further address the issue of how our activity appears within the systematic order of nature. At this point, the problem of the transcendental distinction between man, animals, and pure rational beings encountered at the outset of the critique of aesthetic judgment re-proposes itself—this time within the critique of teleological judgment. The crucial issue of distinguishing the human being from animals as well as from pure spirits or disembodied rational beings occupies Kant in both parts of the *Critique of Judgment.* The dangers that arise from failing in this twofold distinction—in aesthetic and teleological reflection—are pneumatology and *Schwärmerei* on the one hand, and Burke's physiology and Epicurus's materialism on the other.

As the teleological consideration of nature as system leads us to meditate or reflect on ourselves as parts of its living organization, the moral value that we owe to practical reason (to the moral law in ourselves)[90] comes to the fore as an essential element of this reflection. What is the meaning that our moral destination displays once we think of ourselves and our existence as *Weltwesen*—as "beings of the world" that consequently and necessarily are "connected with other things in the world"?[91] What is our relation to a purpose—and to the idea and value of a "final purpose"—once our sensible and yet also moral existence in this world is taken into consideration? What, in other words, is the final mediation that reflective judgment is able to accomplish between sensibility and reason, nature and freedom? The point is that *reflection* on our human embodied condition adds a specific aspect to the self-representation that the human being obtains from pure practical reason.

Man is not only animal but also rational being. Human rationality is embodied rationality. It is the task of the *Critique of Judgment* to spell out the full transcendental meaning of such a condition. Kant is well aware that the simple fact of being endowed with rationality can hardly justify the higher value that the human being claims over and above animals.[92]

> Man is a being of needs (*ein bedürftiges Wesen*), so far as he belongs to the world of sense (*Sinnenwelt*), and to this extent his reason certainly has an inescapable responsibility from the side of sensibility to attend to sensibility's interest and to form practical maxims with a view to the happiness of this life and, when possible, a future life.[93]

Kant recognizes that since the human being is a finite, embodied being who is part of the world of nature, there is an inescapable "interest" proper to human sensibility and to the needs of "this life" that reason cannot ignore. And yet, to the extent that practical reason is only put to the service of human sensible life and its needs for survival and enjoyment, reason's function is not so different from animal instinct.[94] Practical rationality must indeed satisfy the minimal requirements of (biological) life: its function—just as animal instinct's function—is self-preservation. In this respect, human reason's practical-technical causality does not differ from nature's own causality in bringing forth its organization. That man "has reason does not in the least raise him in worth above (*erhebt*) mere animality (*Tierheit*) if reason serves only the purposes which, among animals, are taken care of by instinct." If reason is evaluated only for the purposive function that it shares with instinct, no privileged "value" can be assigned to beings endowed with reason over animals.

At this point, however, Kant's argument shifts perspective and endorses nature's own view in producing the human being as part of its organization. If it were the case that man's worth was the same as that of animals,

> reason would be only a specific way nature had made use of to equip him for the same purpose for which animals are qualified, without fitting him for any higher purpose. No doubt, as a result of this unique natural arrangement (*Naturanstalt*), he needs reason to consider at all times his weal and woe. But he has reason for yet a higher purpose, namely, to consider also what is in itself good or evil, which pure and sensuously disinterested reason alone can judge.[95]

Practical reason seems suspended between the aims of self-preservation and a "higher" moral purpose. As we will see, this is precisely the experience conveyed by the feeling of the sublime. However, the question of what reason's function (or purpose) is in human activity yields a different question: what is the purpose that nature has assigned to man's existence or to his life within nature, by endowing him with reason? Kant specifically addresses this question in the Methodology of the reflective faculty of judgment. He further articulates the central problem that occupies the entire *Critique of Judgment:* what does it mean for the human being to be a constitutive part of living nature? The teleological reflection that provides us with an understanding of the specificity of life in and outside of ourselves yields, at this point, to a moral teleology that makes us reflect on the responsibility connected to our position within the whole of nature.

Despite the closeness of human reason to animal instinct, we must recognize that reason speaks to us in a language that, when taken by itself and not influenced by sensibility, is radically different from the language of mere instinct. Kant argues that man "is not so completely animal as to be indifferent to everything that reason says on its own and to use it merely as a tool for satisfying his needs as a sensuous being (*Sinnenwesens*)."[96] It is up to man to decide whether reason should be subservient to the needs of life and mere enjoyment or fulfill its higher purpose. The *Critique of Practical Reason* demonstrates, on the one hand, how reason is practical, i.e., able to determine the will immediately through the moral law, while it shows, on the other hand, what it means for practical reason to become, subjectively, motive or *Triebfeder* for moral action. Unquestionably, what marks the radical difference between man and animal is the moral force of pure practical reason.[97] In the *Critique of Judgment,* Kant approaches the problem from the different perspective of the realization of morality in the world of nature (the idea of the "highest good in the world"), i.e., with regard to the issue of the purposive accordance between nature and freedom. How shall the world of nature, of which man is an organic part, be represented in order for the higher purpose of practical reason to be conceivable in it and, furthermore, in order for this purpose to be carried out within this world?[98] How shall we think of the organization of nature in order to discover in it the highest value of an *Endzweck,* or in order to recognize the higher worth attached to the life of certain beings?

As we have just seen, simple possession of reason does not by itself justify any higher value for the human being over irrational animals. The crucial difference hinges upon the idea of morality. Kant argues that man is not so completely animal as to be indifferent to the language of morality. This is the case not only because reason has the power of determining the will purely and immediately, without resorting to any further sensible motive or interest. Man is also not morally indifferent (or, as Kant puts it, "morally dead") because his sensibility entails a fundamental receptivity (*Empfänglichkeit*) to moral ideas. Transcendentally, the animal, sensible part of man already displays a peculiarly human component.[99] Morality is brought back not only to the intimations of pure practical reason, but is also inscribed within man's sensibility as a mode of his being (morally) *alive.* Human sensibility is purposively 'attuned to' moral ideas. Or, to put it differently, it belongs to the transcendental structure of human sensibility to connect in a fundamentally purposive way with the aims of practical reason. To this extent, human sensibility comes to reason's assistance as nature supports the higher purpose of reason. While the second *Critique* aims at isolating sensibility from reason, reflective judgment brings their purposive connection to the fore.

In Kant's construction of human sensibility, the idea of *Empfänglichkeit* —receptivity, sensitivity, or responsiveness—to moral values replaces the notion of moral "sense" (*Sinn*). Such receptivity indicates a fundamental difference between man and animals. In the later *Metaphysical Principles of the Doctrine of Virtue,* Kant presents an indirect argument in support of the idea of grounding the distinction between man and animal on moral feeling: if we eliminate human moral sensitivity we risk chaos in nature's own organization since the dividing line between humanity and animality is completely erased. As the crucial distinction between man and animal hinges upon the moral value of practical reason, mere possession of reason (to the extent that reason functions just like instinct) is less essential to differentiate humans from animals than is sensitivity to moral ideas, i.e., receptivity to the "sensation" (*Empfindung*) of moral feeling. "No human being" —Kant contends—"lacks moral feeling." For if it were the case that man were completely insensitive (constitutionally indifferent) to such feeling, if he were characterized by sheer *Unempfänglichkeit* for morality, then

> he would be morally dead; and (to speak the language of physicians) if the moral vital force could no longer stimulate this feeling, then humanity (*Menschheit*) would dissolve itself (to speak according to the laws of chemistry) into mere animality (*Tierheit*) and would be immediately and irreparably mixed with the mass of all other natural beings.[100]

To miss this fundamental aspect of human sensibility is not just detrimental to the possibility of our moral life (as it would bring about our moral death). In the perspective of the third *Critique,* since the human being is an organic part of nature, to ignore this aspect of sensibility undermines nature's inner systematic organization as well: humanity is irretrievably mixed and confused with animality.[101] Ultimately, it undermines the possibility for man to represent himself as "*Weltwesen* under moral laws"[102]—as a being placed in relation with other natural beings, a being whose life's purpose in this world is not merely happiness or enjoyment, yet, under the condition of becoming worthy of happiness, is indeed also happiness. At this point the crucial issue is the embodiment of moral ideas. What is the insight that reflective judgment—aesthetic and teleological—offers for it?

In the third moment of the judgment of taste, in presenting beauty as the form of purposiveness without purpose, Kant discusses the "ideal of beauty" which, based on *Darstellung* and not on concepts, is properly an "ideal of the imagination."[103] *Darstellung* or *exhibitio* is the general procedure that concretizes a concept in a corresponding intuition. In the space of the third *Critique* it takes place in two different ways: through imagination, as in art; or through nature's technic, as in organized bodies.[104] Kant's question regards the specific type of beauty that admits of an "ideal." Clearly, since only beauty "fixed" by a concept of objective purposiveness admits of an ideal, this cannot be the object of a pure judgment of taste but only of a partly intellectual one. *Darstellung* somehow still implies a concept. This leaves only one possibility: for the only being that "has in itself the purpose of its existence" (which can fix beauty, as it were) is *Mensch*. Once again, what singles out the human being is not simply reason—not just possession of rationality, and not rationality as opposed to sensibility, and also not generically what is non-animal in humans. *Mensch* is able to give itself its purposes through reason; but even when it takes its purposes from "outer perception" (as is the case for desires and material interests) it can still compare them with universal purposes of reason and then judge "*aesthetically*" of the harmony (or disharmony) of those externally given purposes with the universal ones. Aesthetically, purposes are thereby placed in a universal context. "*This* human being," Kant declares, "admits of an ideal of beauty."[105] It is a fundamental act of reflection that brings out Kant's point here: the aesthetic ideal of beauty is incarnated in the bodily "figure" of a being who can judge aesthetically of purposes (rational and sensible). There are two components to the ideal of beauty. The "*Normalidee*" provides the standard for judging man as belonging to a particular animal species, that is, for judging aesthetically of the way in which its bodily constitution fulfills the purposes of nature's technic. To be sure, all animals can be judged aesthetically according to their own ideal standard, and not only human beings: the human body is judged on the basis of its *inclusion* in the animal world as a particular type of animal. The standard idea takes its elements from experience although is not derived from it, and thereby offers a criterion for aesthetically judging the human animal body that is dependent on empirically varying conditions.[106] In this respect, in a "psychological explanation,"[107] Kant observes that the "Negro" or "the Chinese or the European" each have their own standard idea for judging physical beauty— or for building the "ideal body" of a species or race—which differ in the same way in which the standard idea of a beautiful horse differs from that of a dog ("of a certain breed," adds Kant).[108]

The second component of the ideal of beauty is the "*Vernunftidee*." This is the point where "humanity"—*Menschheit* this time rather than *Mensch*— reveals its distance from "animality." The rational idea makes the human bodily figure the incarnation of the rational idea of the purposes of humanity. The important difference between representation and embodiment of ideas is implied in Kant's apparently paradoxical explanation of the

Vernunftidee. He claims that "*insofar* as the purposes of humanity cannot be sensibly represented (*nicht sinnlich vorgestellt werden können*)," they are made into "the principle for judging of the human figure, through which, as their *effect* (*Wirkung*) in appearance, those purposes are revealed."[109] The idea of humanity in its ends cannot be sensibly represented. Yet, precisely *because* it cannot be sensibly represented, it is used by aesthetic judgment to attend to the human figure as sensible manifestation of the idea. This is the *embodiment* of the idea, which implies the aesthetic and reflective idealization of the human figure as ideal of beauty. Instead of being rendered sensible, and precisely insofar as it cannot be made sensible, the idea is used to judge the human body as "effect" of the purposes of humanity in the sensible world: the body is presented as if shaped or figured by moral ideas as their effect; the body thus reflected is the meeting point of the sensible and the intelligible. The ideal of beauty embodied in the human figure—and among all animals in the human figure alone—is an expression of morality. Here the human body is transfigured into a "*visible* expression of moral ideas."[110] While the latter, being invisible and unrepresentable in sensible form are considered as "inwardly" governing man, the former becomes the vehicle of their outward expression, the representative of their sensible efficacy in the world.[111] Thus, in the first division of the *Critique of Judgment* the difference between human body and animal body is established as a transcendental aesthetic difference brought forth by an aesthetic reflection which, based on the idea of morality, allows for the idealization of the human body in the "ideal of beauty." Only the human figure (in its humanity and not animality) embodies ideas.[112]

While this is the answer of aesthetic judgment, we need now ask: How does teleological judgment argue against the menacing confusion between man and animals, i.e., against the necessity of complementing their distinction based on practical reason with a distinction that underscores the purposefully moral bent of human sensibility, namely, receptivity or attunement to moral ideas? In the Methodology of teleological judgment, this point is addressed in the crucial transitions from physical to moral teleology on the one hand, and from moral teleology to moral theology on the other.[113] At stake is the only condition under which we can think of the value of an *Endzweck* within nature. More generally, at stake is the very representation of nature when the human being is thought of as an organic part of it. In presenting the task of human action in the world of nature as the task of a "*Weltwesen* under moral laws,"[114] Kant's idea of moral teleology provides the final reflective mediation between nature and freedom. As man is represented as a "being of the world," the moral destination that he owes to practical reason carries the necessity of being concretely realized within nature. And reciprocally, since man is part of the whole of nature, not only as living natural being (on which, transcendentally, is based the possibility of reflecting aesthetically on nature's beauty and teleologically on objects possible only as natural purposes) but also as moral being, the world must allow for the possibility of man's purposes to be successfully carried out within it.[115]

Kant prefaces the crucial transition from moral teleology to theology with a description of the "frame of mind" (Gemütsverfassung) of a subject reflecting on his place within nature. "Consider a human being at those moments when his Gemüt is attuned (Stimmung) to moral feeling (moralische Empfindung). If, surrounded by a beautiful nature, he finds himself calmly and serenely enjoying his existence, he will feel within him a need to be grateful for this to someone."[116] At this point, the feeling for one's life (one's Lebensgefühl) and the judgment that qualifies such a feeling of life (as enjoyment or feeling of pleasure) meet moral feeling. This connection characterizes man as Weltwesen. The question is whether and to what extent the point of intersection of our natural constitution and moral destination—of sensibility and reason—is responsible for shaping our human earthly life: in what sense does this point become the axis on which freedom's actualization in the natural world revolves? But Kant also asks in what sense a reflection on our worldly condition leads us outside the world of nature to the representation of a moral cause of the world. Ultimately, the general issue that Kant pursues regards a transcendental reflection upon the value of human life. By denying that the value of human life is provided by mere possession of reason, he also resolutely denies that its purpose and worth is "happiness" and material enjoyment (which is, once again, the position of Epicurus's materialist hedonism).[117] And yet, the condition of universal happiness once man is conceived of as earthly creature is not excluded from the idea of Endzweck but is, subjectively, integral to it.

What is it that Kant considers worthy of being characterized as "final purpose," and what is the source of the value that this final purpose communicates to everything that is judged as being in relation to it and as meaningful only in this relation? Kant's transcendental formulation of the question is to ask which faculty is responsible for attributing "value" to our "consideration of the world" and to our own life in it—a value that furthermore is unconditioned and "absolute."[118] Kant denies that the faculty in point can be the cognitive faculty, because our cognitive approach to the world has value only if value is somehow already presupposed. The fact that the world is known by us does not make it more valuable. The world is not there for someone to contemplate it.[119] But the source of value cannot be our feeling of pleasure, either. To defend this claim would be to state that the world has value only insofar as it satisfies the condition of human happiness. Yet Kant argues that in this case also, the value of human existence on earth must already be presupposed in order to maintain that man's happiness can indeed be a purpose of nature. It follows that only practical reason can be the faculty through which a finite rational being (but not necessarily a human being)[120] gives value to its own existence. Value is generated by a subject acting according to the law of freedom. Such value, however, must be made concretely sensible and actual within the world of nature since man, in addition to being a rational moral being, is also *Weltwesen*—an embodied natural creature interacting with other living beings.[121]

Kant argues that "we find in ourselves" and even more so "in the concept of a rational being in general endowed with freedom"[122] a moral teleology which, unlike physical teleology, does not need the assumption of an intelligent cause "outside of ourselves" to account for the inner lawfulness proper to the reference to a purpose. Directly portraying our place in the world of nature and the moral responsibility connected to it, such "moral teleology" prescribes the ways in which moral action ought to be realized in the world. Moral teleology concerns us insofar as we are "*Weltwesen*" and consequently are "beings connected with other things in the world." For man to be part of the world of nature means never to be isolated but always and necessarily to be part of the purposive connection of nature's living whole.[123] The moral laws that enjoin us to consider those other things in connection to which we stand "either as purposes or as objects for which we ourselves are the final purpose" refer to this same condition. First, moral teleology regards the "reference of our causality to purposes and even to a final purpose at which we must aim *in the world*"—namely, the way in which we ought to act within nature in order to uphold our moral membership in it. Second, it concerns the "*reciprocal relation* the world has with that moral purpose and with the external possibility of carrying it out"[124]—namely, the way in which our purposive causality in nature is, in turn and reciprocally, affected by nature's purposive constitution and determined in its very possibility by nature itself. At stake here is not so much the a priori principle of moral action (the issue settled by the second *Critique*) but first its concrete endorsement by an agent who must consider herself as a moral being both with regard to her rationality and with regard to her sensibility (as *Weltwesen*); and second, the actual realization of the moral law within a world that reflection must represent as purposively attuned to the demands of practical reason and thus favorably interacting with human moral agency.

Moral teleology raises a question at this point: do we need to go "beyond the world" in order to account for that "relation of nature to what is moral in us," in order to account for a representation of "nature as purposive also in relation to our inner moral legislation and to how we carry it out"?[125] What guarantees the teleological orientation of nature toward the possible realization of freedom and the highest good? These questions imply the "*progress* of reason" (and not just the "transition") from physical teleology to theology by means of moral teleology.[126] Kant's moral theology concerns the issue of the connection between reason and the realization of a moral order which is possible only according to ideas. To this problem Kant has provided an initial answer in the doctrine of the postulates of the second *Critique*. This doctrine is now confirmed and more precisely articulated from the different standpoint of the third *Critique*. Kant no longer attempts to disclose a possible access to the supersensible through reason's postulates. Rather, he investigates the possibility of *somehow* having an *experience* of the supersensible *within the sensible world*. This possibility is revealed by a concept of freedom thought anew on the basis of teleology.[127] If freedom discloses a supersensible dimension of the human being as noumenon, teleology addresses the aspect of the realization of this dimension within the sensible world of experience (its *Versinnlichung,* as it were), i.e., within the human being considered as *Weltwesen.* Thus, the human being as '*Weltwesen* under moral laws' becomes the actual embodiment of moral ideas, whereby one's self-reflection upon this condition opens up the possibility of an experience of the supersensible in ourselves. In this perspective, the difference that separates the human being from other animals displays its transcendental *raison d'être,* and the aesthetic reflection started with the "ideal of beauty" receives its teleological fulfillment. To deny the transcendental difference between man and animals precipitates nature's organization into chaos, into a vacuum from which not only morality but also purposeful organization is ultimately absent. If man differs from other animals or living creatures only empirically (or metaphysically), but not *transcendentally,* then we must conclude that the world lacks a final end and that man's life is ultimately purposeless and without value.

Kant argues that if we apply our teleological reflection to the order of nature asking for the "highest (absolutely unconditioned) purpose," we meet a "principle" (*Grundsatz*) to which we are compelled (*genötigt*) to give our assent. This principle claims that "if there is indeed to be a *final purpose* that reason has to indicate a priori, then it can only be the *human being* (any rational *Weltwesen*) *under moral laws*."[128] This claim is supported by an indirect argument that draws a new classification of beings within the order of nature. The argument complements the one discussed above regarding the necessary presence of moral feeling in man: to deny man's *Empfänglichkeit* or sensible responsiveness to morality, Kant warns in the Doctrine of Virtue of the *Metaphysics of Morals,* would dissolve "humanity" into mere "animality." The human body idealized through the idea of morality and thereby assumed as an "ideal of beauty" is aesthetic judgment's first answer to the problem. In the Methodology of teleological judgment, the amorphous "mass of all other natural beings"[129] directly threatens the purposeful organization of nature. Kant's argument discusses three different assets of the natural universe characterized by the value conferred upon it by the different type of beings populating it.

(1) He contends that "if the world consisted exclusively of lifeless beings, or if it included living beings that were, however, non-rational, the existence of this world would have no value whatever, because there would exist in it no being that had the slightest concept of a value."[130] While *life* is necessary to the constitution of a world that has value, it is not sufficient to it since living beings as such are not capable of forming a concept of value. A world of mere living beings would ultimately have no value at all— certainly no more value than the world of mere mechanisms. Rationality seems to be required in addition to life for the world to display value.[131]

(2) Yet, if the world were populated by rational beings whose rationality was used for evaluating natural things only with regard to their own survival or even well-being, i.e., if the world were populated by rational but non-moral beings, "then there would indeed be purposes in the world [. . .] but no final [. . .] purpose." For though *rationality* is indeed capable of judging values or forming a concept of value relative to one's self-preservation or well-being, it is still not enough to "produce that value originally on its own (in its freedom)." Rational beings can indeed act according to purposes; yet their life—and the life of the natural universe to which they belong—would "still always be purposeless."[132] In this case, as far as value is concerned, rationality would still work just like animal instinct.

(3) Only moral laws can prescribe to reason purposes that have value absolutely and unconditionally—which is precisely what defines the value of the *Endzweck.* It follows that it is only "the existence of such a reason," i.e.,

a reason which can produce value originally in its freedom—the existence, namely, of rational beings under moral laws—that guarantees the value of a final purpose of the world. Now as I have argued in the course of this study, such reason as human reason is indeed morally practical but is also fundamentally embodied: human sensibility, and with it the natural world in which man as *Weltwesen* participates, is purposefully attuned to such reason. Hence, Kant concludes that the final purpose is possible only with regard to man considered as a moral being that acts within the natural world. The final purpose is "the *highest good in the world* possible through freedom."[133]

At this juncture, the idea of happiness is brought back into the picture. Although the final purpose is formally and objectively unconditioned, for man as a finite and embodied rational being, it rests on the condition of happiness. "Hence, the highest physical good we can achieve in the world is happiness, and this is what we are to further as the final purpose as far as we can."[134] Subjectively, in terms of its achievement, the morality of the final purpose must be thought of as connected to the possibility of happiness. In the subjective perspective of a finite rational being, the harmony between nature and freedom translates into the possibility of becoming worthy of happiness as a consequence of following the moral law. Practical reason determines us a priori to "strive to the utmost to further the highest good in the world." The highest good consists in the "combination (*Verbindung*) of universal happiness" with the supreme condition of our being good, that we be moral in conformity with the moral law.[135] The idea of final purpose—universal happiness combined with the condition of being moral, i.e., worthy of happiness—is the purpose that practical reason sets for human life. Thereby, in the idea of "final purpose" Kant presents the intersection and interdependence between nature and morality. Man's practical final purpose is linked to the final purpose of the world. For if nature indeed has a final purpose, we have to conceive of it as being in harmony with our moral final purpose. With regard to the practical sphere, the idea of final purpose has a "subjectively constitutive" value and reality.[136] Its first component, i.e., the possibility of happiness, is empirically conditioned, while the second, i.e., morality, is a priori certain. The "connection" (*Verknüpfung*)[137] of these two requirements of the final purpose—the "physical possibility" of the realization of the good and the "practical necessity" of our worthiness of happiness—is possible only in the idea of God as the moral cause of the world. This is Kant's "moral proof" of God's existence.[138] Only reflective judgment as a mediating faculty can accomplish such a "connection."[139]

Human Mortality and the
Feeling of the Sublime

Kant insists that the validity of the moral law is completely independent from the proof of God's existence. Yet the idea of a moral cause of the world must replace natural causality if we want to hold on to the possibility that happiness could harmoniously accompany our compliance with moral laws.[140] Now it becomes clear that the privileged position that man occupies in the totality of nature is indeed a precarious one—it is supported by nothing but the mere force of reflection. Indeed, only the faculty of judgment reflecting upon the position of man within living nature can detect his superiority over animals. This, however, is only a *transcendental* superiority. Kant makes the point with the help of Spinoza. In trying to imagine how a righteous man like Spinoza—who deeply reveres the moral law and yet denies God's existence and an after-life—would experience the human condition within the world of nature, a new proximity between man and other animals comes to the fore. Such a righteous man as Spinoza would follow the moral law without material expectations, his exclusive intention being to bring about, unselfishly, "the good to which that sacred law directs all his forces." And yet, his efforts meet *in nature itself* a fundamental limit—a limit that proves so powerful as to undermine the very possibility of the moral goal that the agent sets for himself; a limit that ultimately transfigures the whole of nature by erasing all difference of value among its creatures. For although man "can expect that nature will now and then cooperate contingently with the purpose of his that he feels so obligated and impelled to achieve, he can never expect nature to harmonize with it (*Zusammenstimmung*) in a way governed by laws and permanent rules."[141] Nature's contingency becomes the main objection to the physical possibility that the moral law could be actualized in the world. Consequently, nature's contingency also becomes the main objection to the (physical) possibility of moral agency for a human being considered not only as a purely rational but also as a living, embodied member of nature—a *Weltwesen*.[142] If, on Kant's account, the human being as such cannot be insensitive to moral ideas, nature certainly is. There is no necessity for nature to cooperate with man's moral agency in the world, no necessity for nature to even appreciate the value of man's moral destination or to respect the dividing line between humanity and animality. For that dividing line is not a natural but a transcendental one. Nature treats human beings without regard for any morality or value. From nature's perspective humans have the same value as all other animals. Righteous and vicious men encounter the same destiny of disease and death as all other living creatures. Nature does not hesitate to dissolve "humanity" into mere "animality" or to irreparably mix it "with the mass of all other natural beings."[143] Hence, Kant concludes that with regard to the other righteous men he encounters, Spinoza would have to acknowledge that nature, which pays no attention to how worthy of happiness they are,

> will still subject them to all the evils of deprivation, disease, and untimely death, *just like all the other animals on earth.* And they will stay subjected to these evils always, until one vast tomb engulfs them one and all (honest or not, that makes no difference here) and hurls them, who managed to believe they were the final purpose of creation, back into the abyss of the purposeless chaos of matter from which they were taken.[144]

In spite of the loftiness of the thought, man—the alleged "final purpose" of creation—is still nothing more than a vulnerable, mortal being. In the face of the unavoidable fact of human mortality, nature's irony toward the final purpose functions as a reminder of the limits, but at the same time of the force of transcendental reflection. While unable to erase human vulnerability to physical disease and ultimately to death, such a reflection becomes, at this point, a moral necessity since it must come—at least subjectively—in support of practical reason. Due to nature's contingency and the inviolable limit of death, collaboration between human agency and nature is secured only within the perspective of teleological judgment. Nature *must* be seen as harmonizing with man's moral purpose in the world for this purpose to be considered as achievable (and hence as physically possible) in it. To this aim, however, a moral cause of the universe must be assumed as well.

Kant's dramatic description of the common destiny of death and disease that awaits, from nature's standpoint, humans as well as animals irrespective of their worth, entails another important suggestion. Given the transcendental constitution of the human subject investigated by Kant in the two parts of the *Critique of Judgment,* and taking a step backwards, we should now examine the peculiar feeling that the images of the "abyss," the "purposeless chaos of matter," and nature's life-threatening "vast tomb"[145] excite in the human *Gemüt.* Such abysses shatter the composed "ideal of beauty" that aesthetic judgment imposes on the human figure, and expose the weakness of man's alleged superiority over other living beings. Transcendentally, the conjunction of our embodied sensible participation in nature—i.e., our condition of mortality and physical vulnerability—and the idea of morality gives rise to yet another situation by which to measure the power of reflective judgment. In this perspective, we must now examine the feeling of the sublime. For this is a feeling of man's *Überlegenheit*[146]—indeed of human superiority—over nature; a feeling through which we experience, within nature, "the supersensible substrate of nature in ourselves as well as outside of ourselves."[147] The feeling of the sublime, however, entails at the same time a *constitutive* awareness of human physical fragility and vulnerability, the feeling of "our own physical *Ohnmacht*"[148] when confronted with nature's irresistible "*Macht*" and even violence. Moreover, the feeling of the sublime hints at nature's lack of purpose with regard to ourselves and at the inner purposefulness of the subject toward nature.[149] The idea of life and our peculiar feeling for it comes, once again, to the fore. The question is: is there something besides the moral law and its pure immediate determination of the will, is there something *within nature itself* that makes us *feel* or perceive, reflectively, the value of man over mere living nature and, at the same time, leads us to experience our living embodied condition as part of nature's organization? As we shall see, Kant's exploration of the feeling of the sublime as a *transcendentally embodied, reflected feeling* allows him an answer that is, somehow, affirmative and negative at the same time.

Leaving behind the tranquil beauty of natural forms (wherein the object looks indeed as if it had been "pre-arranged"[150] for our judgment), but also leaving behind the reassuring world of Kant's ethico-theology (leaving it, however, only in order to encounter it again from yet another route), the feeling of the sublime is directed to and stimulated by very different appearances of nature. Just as in the case of the consideration of nature that threatens the moral world-order, upheld by the righteous Spinoza, "it is rather in its chaos or in its wildest and most ruleless disarray and devastation, provided it displays magnitude and might, that nature most arouses our ideas of the sublime."[151] Kant's discussion of the sublime in the Analytic of the critique of aesthetic judgment reveals the transcendental power of reflection as a faculty proper to man considered as an embodied living being. At stake is the solution to the apparently simple problem arising from such a representation of the threatening, devastating, and thereby indeed "purposeless" (*zwecklosen*)—even "counter-purposive" (*zweckwidrig*)[152]—chaos of nature. Kant remarks, "Who would want to call sublime such things as shapeless mountain masses piled on one another in wild disarray, with their pyramids of ice, or the glooming raging sea?"[153] Who indeed? "The vast ocean heaved up by storms cannot be called sublime. The sight of it is horrible."[154]

Crucial to the judgment of the sublime is the relationship between the human subject and nature, i.e., the relationship between an awareness of what lies "in ourselves" and what is found "outside of ourselves."[155] In order to call that formless chaos sublime, the faculty of judgment must operate a twofold transfiguration. First, it must transfigure the menacing, chaotic appearance of nature itself so as to reveal its sublimity; and second, it must work on the self-representation that the human subject has of herself as part of nature in order to dissipate the sense of physical fragility and fear for one's life that man shares with all other animals so as to make room for another, distinctively human feeling than that which is dictated by the mere instinct of self-preservation. At stake is, once again, the issue of the embodiment of ideas—i.e., the possibility of an intersection or an encounter between nature and freedom, between sensibility and reason's ideas. This is, transcendentally, a problem of mediation or schematism[156] which is meant to avoid the impasses of both empiricism and mysticism.[157]

Unlike the case of natural beauty, and due to the overwhelming magnitude or irresistible power of nature's appearances, in our judgments of the sublime (the mathematical and dynamical sublime, respectively) the relation between the subject and nature is not purposive but counter-purposive. Beautiful natural forms can be judged as if they were pre-arranged with a special regard to our faculty of judgment—so well do they fit our mental faculties that they seem to welcome our contemplation of them. Those appearances of nature, on the contrary, whose apprehension arouses in us the feeling of the sublime seem "counter-purposive for our judgment, incommensurate with our power of exhibition, and as it were violent to our imagination." This tension between nature and the subject's cognitive powers clearly points to the fact that the natural object cannot in itself be sublime. Once again: there is nothing sublime in shapeless mountain masses arranged in wild disarray or in the glooming, raging sea. Such sights, Kant insists, are rather "horrible." "Indeed, how can we call something by a term of approval if we apprehend it as in itself counter-purposive," even as doing violence to our mental powers?[158] Moreover, while natural beauty concerns the "form of the object"—which lies in limitation—the sublime regards an object that is "formless" insofar as it is boundless (either mathematically or dynamically). Hence, in the case of the sublime, neither the object itself nor its mere form can be said to be purposive. Following its purposive arrangement, beauty directly carries a "feeling of the furthering of life"[159] and leads to a tranquil contemplation of nature.[160] The sublime, on the contrary, arises "through the feeling of a momentary inhibition of the vital forces followed immediately by an outpouring of them that is all the stronger."[161] In this latter case, our judgment of the object is connected to a "movement of the *Gemüt*."[162] Unlike the beautiful, the sublime sets the *Gemüt* in motion—and deeply shakes it. It follows that while beauty is immediately related to a peculiar feeling of pleasure, the sublime sets us in an apparently contradictory predicament. For "the liking (*Wohlgefallen*) for the sublime contains not so much a positive pleasure" but something that Kant calls "a negative pleasure," indeed a feeling of displeasure and uneasiness. To be sure, such a negative pleasure is also experienced under other names: it is a feeling of "admiration or respect" (*Bewunderung oder Achtung*).[163] But how can we possibly like a feeling of displeasure and call its object sublime? This is the transcendental turn that Kant gives to the previous question: "Who would want to call sublime such things as shapeless mountain masses piled on one another in wild disarray, with their pyramids of ice, or the glooming raging sea?"[164]

The contrast between the beautiful and the sublime in nature makes clear: (1) that one of the necessary conditions for our judgment of the sublime is that the subject be an embodied living creature that represents itself as part of nature. For the judgment is necessarily connected with an aesthetic feeling in the judging subject, which, in addition, produces an awareness of one's being alive as part of nature. "If we were mere pure intelligences," Kant contends, there would be no aesthetic representation of beauty or of sublimity for us.[165] In front of that which we call sublime, our *Lebensgefühl* is affected and our *Gemüt* set in motion, even violently shaken: movement and life are closely connected in this experience.[166] We feel violence exercised on our imagination as this faculty struggles in the impossible apprehension of a formless object which hints at the infinite (mathematical sublime). While directly confronted by the overwhelming powers of nature, which are even perceived as life-threatening, we feel our own physical impotence (dynamical sublime).[167] Moreover, Kant notices that in the case of the dynamical sublime, nature's *Macht* produces fear in us, and yet the judgment of the sublime requires that, although fearful, we must be secure—in a position in which our life is not directly threatened by nature's forces.[168] Thus, a physical distance between ourselves and the natural phenomena that confront us must be respected in order for them to be judged sublime. Such distance is dictated precisely by our physical vulnerability. And yet, despite this necessary sensible component of our judgment, as in the case of the beautiful, Kant's explanation of the sublime is a transcendental not a physiological or psychological one.[169] The embodied sensible component of the judgment of the sublime is a transcendental, not an empirical condition of our reflection on nature.[170]

The judgment of the dynamical sublime entails an act of self-reflection by which the human subject—and with it nature itself—is ultimately transfigured. Man now appears both as "*Naturwesen*," physically subject to nature's irresistible might, and as an individual representative of the higher worth of "*Menschheit*," which no external power can threaten or humiliate. In the feeling of the sublime the human subject experiences the possibility of a kind of "self-preservation (*Selbsterhaltung*) entirely different from the one which can be attacked and brought into danger by external nature."[171] Thus, Kant's transcendental reflection offers man two ways out of the contingent labyrinth of nature's chaos—a teleological and an aesthetic one. Lacking the life-saving resources of reflective judgment,[172] the righteous Spinoza is placed in front of nature's devastation—the spectacle of "threatening rocks," "volcanoes in all their violence of destruction," and "hurricanes with their track of devastation,"[173]—in a word, in front of the "vast tomb"[174] that mercilessly engulfs all living creatures alike. And thus placed, he sees the call of self-preservation erase both the physical possibility of his moral goal and the aesthetic possibility of judging nature to be sublime. The transcendental perspective of the judgment of the sublime, on the contrary, opens up the possibility of considering sublime the destructive might of nature not

> insofar as it excites fear, but because it calls up that power in us (which is not nature) of regarding as small the things about which we are solicitous (goods, health, and life), and of regarding its might (to which we are no doubt subjected in respect of these things) as nevertheless without any dominion over us.[175]

(2) Because the feeling of the sublime is not directly caused by the natural object outside of ourselves (as happens instead in sensation and perception), the contrast between the beautiful and the sublime brings to light that 'sublime' is not a character to be found in the natural object or even in its form. For, in this case, no purpose is detected in the object's form (the object lacks any form); hence no pleasure in it is produced but rather the opposite. We can conclude that the sublime requires a certain transcendental disposition of our sensibility and yet cannot itself be contained in a "sensible form." Thereby, the sublime reveals yet another mode of transcendental embodiment. While the judgment of the sublime requires, transcendentally, the embodiment of the judging subject, it concerns an

object that has a transcendentally peculiar status. The object that is judged sublime is not a natural given object but the embodied representative of reason's ideas in nature—the sublime is the embodiment of reason's ideas in the natural world. The judgment of the sublime expresses the fact that a natural object "is suitable for exhibiting a sublimity that can be found in the *Gemüt*." Paradoxically, however, the object *is* suitable for the exhibition of ideas only because it is *not* entirely suitable for it. This is precisely the paradox of the sublime. The sublime concerns only the reality of reason's ideas. As established in the first *Critique,* however, ideas can never be adequately exhibited in reality. And yet, they can be judged—and indeed concretely experienced or *felt*—as sublime only when they are embodied in particular natural forms. Kant's suggestion is that the very "inadequacy" (*Unangemessenheit*) between sensible form and ideas—an inadequacy that, instead, can be very well exhibited in sensibility[176]—arouses and calls to mind those ideas through the feeling of the sublime. Hence Kant's answer to the problem:

> The vast ocean heaved up by storms cannot be called sublime. The sight of it is horrible; and one must already have filled one's *Gemüt* with all sorts of ideas if such an intuition is to attune it (*gestimmt werden soll*) to a feeling that is itself sublime, inasmuch as the *Gemüt* is induced to abandon sensibility (*die Sinnlichkeit zu verlassen*) and to occupy itself with ideas containing a higher purposiveness.[177]

Thus, only the *feeling* that connects (or harmonizes) natural objects outside of ourselves with reason's ideas in ourselves, is properly sublime.[178] And thus the feeling of admiration and respect that connects the starry sky above us and the moral law within us, is sublime.[179] For the truly sublime is a *Geistesstimmung* or *Gemütstimmung,*[180] i.e., a special attunement or (transcendental) mode or disposition of the whole mind. In the case of the sublime, if nature itself does not purposefully gesture toward us (nature's *Wink* seems, rather, counter-purposive),[181] our mind should listen instead to the "voice (*Stimme*) of reason,"[182] and our feeling attune itself to it.

The feeling involved in the judgment of the sublime is a feeling of "respect" or reverence—*Achtung.* For Kant, this feeling is always related to reason's law (the law which prescribes the measure of an absolute totality in the case of the mathematical sublime; the moral law in the case of the dynamical sublime): "Respect is the feeling of our inability (*Unangemessenheit*) to attain an idea that has for us the force of law."[183] As was the case in the *Critique of Practical Reason,* the feeling of reverence or respect is a feeling of humiliation and hence displeasure and even pain. Yet this feeling is accompanied, at the same time, by the pleasure of discovering our higher supersensible determination as moral beings. The feeling of the sublime in nature is a feeling of displeasure at our imagination's insufficiency in the aesthetic estimation of magnitude, and, at the same time, a feeling of respect for our own supersensible (moral) determination. *Achtung* is a feeling of both pleasure and displeasure[184] in the consciousness of our striving toward ideas—which striving is a law for us. Thereby, in the motion of our *Gemüt,* the feeling of displeasure is represented as "purposive"[185] since our imagination's inability uncovers the consciousness of an unlimited ability provided by reason. Such *Zweckmäßigkeit* enables us to project our liking onto the natural object that we would otherwise dislike (or even abhor). Under these conditions, we call nature sublime.

An illusion—truly, a logical error—creates the appearance of sublimity in nature. Kant contends that it is a deceiving logical "subreption" (*Subreption*) that leads us "to put a reverence for the object in place of the reverence for the idea of the humanity in the subject."[186] The judgment of the sublime contains a subreption that attributes to the objects a dignity and value (purposiveness) that belong, instead, only to the subject. Even though in the case of the beautiful Kant stresses the seemingly analogous operation according to which, with regard to the universality of aesthetic judgment, we predicate beauty "as if it were a property of the object,"[187] in that case, properly, no subreption takes place. Since purposiveness belongs to the *form* of the beautiful object apprehended by the imagination (even though it is not objective purposiveness), no value is actually transferred from the subject to the object. It is only in the case of the sublime, where the object itself is perceived as lacking all form and as being even *"zweckwidrig,"* that purposiveness can be discovered only within the subject. To attribute purposiveness to the object would immediately imply a contradiction. Thus, the notion of the sublime indicates nothing purposive in nature itself; 'purposive' is only the "use we can make of our intuitions of nature so that we can feel a *purposiveness within ourselves* entirely independent of nature."[188] It is precisely the feeling of our independency from nature's forces that characterizes our experience of the dynamical sublime. This is an experience of freedom in the 'negative' sense of the will's independency from the mechanism of nature.[189]

In sum, in the transcendental perspective of Kant's aesthetic judgment, the structure of the sublime requires a twofold embodiment: on the one hand, the transcendental condition of human embodiment; on the other hand, the embodiment of reason's ideas in the natural world mediated by the peculiar aesthetic feeling of displeasure and pleasure. This twofold condition is necessary in order for the supersensible substrate within and without ourselves to be disclosed and finally (aesthetically) experienced. To be sure, this is Kant's most radical rebuttal of the disembodied dreams of all kinds of *Schwärmerei*. Far from requiring (physical or metaphysical) abstraction from sensibility, the supersensible can be attained only by reflecting on the transcendental condition of embodiment. In this reflection, the horizon of our sensibility is extended. Indeed, in the case of the mathematical sublime, the infinite (absolute magnitude) that our imagination ineffectually attempts to comprehend induces us to abandon the dimension of time as form of sensible intuition.[190] To this task, a "supersensible faculty in the human *Gemüt* is required,"[191] which brings forward the idea of noumenon. If such an idea allows no sensible intuition, it nonetheless grounds, as "substrate," a *Weltanschauung*—a world-intuition or intuition of the world as appearance—in which the infinite can be felt as somehow present. Thus, it is only through this idea that the "infinite *of the sensible world*" (*das Unendliche der Sinnenwelt*) can be intellectually grasped.[192] In the mathematical sublime we leave the world of sensible intuition for yet another form of sensibility that discloses an image of the world—or *Weltanschauung*—in which reason's ideas are embodied (or constitute the ground as substrate) and thereby aesthetically felt in their actual presence.[193] Correspondingly, in the dynamical sublime, reason lets sensibility—insofar as this is endowed with a necessary "receptivity (*Empfänglichkeit*) for reason's ideas"—"look outward toward the infinite which, for it, remains an abyss."[194]

Transcendental Embodiment

A Final Assessment

IN *LE TOUCHER—JEAN-LUC NANCY* (2000), DERRIDA EXAMINES
the reasons that led Nancy to his "altercations" with Descartes in *Logodae-dalus.* At issue is the relation between the mind (Psyche) and the body, and the alleged non-extension and non-spatiality of the mind which is complicated by the theory of the pineal gland. Derrida's digressive questioning interests me at this point. Why did Nancy choose to confront Descartes? Certainly, Descartes is the "inventor" of the modern "subject." However, "the word 'subject,' *sensu stricto,* is not Cartesian but Kantian."[1] Hence, why not a confrontation "with Kant, who paid more attention, no doubt, to any subjectivity of the subject than Descartes did"? The answer by way of a rhetorical question is apparently clear: "Is it because Kant is fundamentally mute, taken aback when confronted with the body, confronted with the union of the soul and the body?" This, argues Derrida, is what Nancy suggests in *Le discours de la syncope: Logodaedalus.* "Kant the philosopher,"

declares Nancy, "has *nothing* to say" about the flesh, about the connection between the body and thought.[2] Derrida is intrigued by Nancy's restriction of the claim, which otherwise rehearses a widespread interpretive position: "Kant the philosopher." Is there *another* Kant, asks Derrida, besides "Kant *the philosopher*"? Nancy seems to suggest that *this* Kant, Kant the transcendental philosopher, for whom the subject is utterly disembodied, "is distinct from another one, *a Kant without cover, yet to be discovered.*"[3]

This is the suggestion that Derrida sets out to follow. In so doing, what he discovers is Kant the anthropologist, who pays attention to a physiology of the senses in view of a *pragmatic* anthropology. He thereby corrects Nancy's appraisal of Kant. It is, however, hardly the discovery of a *new* Kant. Ultimately, Derrida seems to agree that Kant the transcendental philosopher has nothing to say about the body. There is, to be sure, yet another suggestion, besides Kant's *Anthropology*. It is the suggestion given by Freud (in what Derrida names "transcendental psychologizing," "transcendental psychoanalysis," or even "transcendental psychoanalytic aesthetics")[4] when Freud turns to Kant with the exclamation: *"Psyche ist ausgedehnt"* (preceded by the remark, *"Anstatt Kants a priori Bedingungen unseres psychischen Apparats"*).[5] Such a position, however, seems much closer to Swedenborg than to Kant. Are psychology or anthropology (in whichever way they are further qualified) a way out from Kant's transcendentalism and its alleged blindness to the body? Is Descartes a better interlocutor?

At the end of *Self and World* (1997), Quassim Cassam cites Kant's criticism of Descartes's view that self-consciousness reveals us to ourselves as immaterial objects. Kant's position is instrumental to Cassam's own thesis, which in turn entails a criticism of the view of self-consciousness and subjectivity arising from Kant's "transcendental idealism." Cassam argues that Kant is wrong in claiming that self-consciousness does not reveal us as physical objects in a world of objects (the "Exclusion Thesis"). He maintains instead that self-consciousness implies intuitive awareness of ourselves as physical and *embodied objects,* that is, as objects that are shaped, located in space, and solid.[6] Although Cassam develops a series of transcendental arguments in support of this position, his thesis often seems to call for a stronger metaphysical commitment. He wants to maintain Kant's transcendental methodology but to reject (with Strawson) his transcendental idealism.

From the brief and sketchy examples of Derrida and Cassam—philosophers who are as widely separated from each other as one could imagine—we obtain an interestingly common problematic constellation that pervades, as it were, contemporary philosophy in its many inflections. The reflection on sensibility, embodiment, and spatiality is essential to a theory of the subject (or, alternatively, to its deconstruction). Kant still confronts Descartes: although Kant's position seems more promising, he ultimately does not seem to lead much further than Descartes; the transcendental method remains a deciding factor. The examples can be multiplied—from the immediate post-Kantian tradition to Heidegger's influential reading of Kant, up to contemporary phenomenology and feminist philosophy—and yet other aspects of Kant's reflection and reception can be brought to the fore. However, at the center of the current discussion we would still find the same crucial problems and the more or less direct, more or less critical references to Kant. Much of the contemporary discussion is built around a rejection, correction, and re-formulation of Kantian themes.

But the real question remains: which Kant?

Concluding this work and looking back retrospectively, I want to answer Derrida's question. At the end of our itinerary through the *Critiques,* we have indeed 'discovered' another Kant, who is, however, still "Kant the philosopher"—even Kant the "*transcendental* philosopher." For this newly discovered Kant the subject is not disembodied and the body does not vanish or, alternatively, become the province of anthropology or psychology. When read in the new way I have proposed, the core thesis of transcendental idealism is the basis for the idea that self-consciousness reveals us to ourselves as fundamentally embodied subjects.

In this study, traveling a long path through Kant's three *Critiques* and guided by the concept of "transcendental embodiment" as *Leitfaden,* we have "discovered" a new Kant or a Kant "without cover"—the cover being the ever-changing one imposed by a long tradition of interpretations and appropriations starting at least with Fichte and Hegel. The concept of "transcendental embodiment" brings together two terms that are generally considered to be almost oxymoronic: the transcendental method and the problem of the body or, in contemporary terminology, the issue of embodiment. The Kant-*Bild* that has come out of the present volume still portrays "Kant the *transcendental philosopher.*" I have programmatically excluded his *Anthropology* and more generally his "applied philosophy," and have shown in what sense transcendental philosophy replaces traditional (rational and empirical) psychology and lays out the premises for Kant's view of the subject as *Mensch.* Nonetheless, precisely within the a priori formality of the transcendental framework, the subject at the center of Kant's inquiry has emerged as a necessarily *embodied subject.* From the beginning of our study, the crucial point concerned the type of body that transcendental philosophy assumes as constitutive of the human subject of experience—cognitive, moral, and aesthetic experience. What does it mean to view the body and its sensibility as *a priori formal conditions of experience* (before viewing them as objects thereof)? What, transcendentally, are the a priori forms displayed by the body? Overturning Cassam's thesis and somehow leaning toward Merleau-Ponty: what does it mean to view the body as *subject* of experience? Transcendental philosophy—and transcendental embodiment—navigates the difficult route separating metaphysics and empirical observation. It holds on to a transcendental construction of the "subject" of experience whereby the subject is neither dissolved, nor reduced to one of the many objects in the world, nor hypostatized to a metaphysical entity. The metaphysical soul is critically dissolved while the body is "idealized" and viewed through the a priori forms of sensibility. Transcendental idealism is a centerpiece of Kant's theory of the embodied subject—a subject he still thinks of in terms of mental faculties, though these faculties are no longer to be psychologically investigated.

It is now time to take stock of where our inquiry has left us.

The first aim of this study was exegetical. I wanted to offer a *complete* reconstruction of Kant's critical articulation of the problem of human sensibility in the three *Critiques*. Thereby I intended, first, to counter-balance the widespread tendency to view Kant as the philosopher of "pure reason" *alone*—a tendency that goes back at least to the young Hegel's *Auseinandersetzung* with critical philosophy. Second, I intended to counter-balance current interpretations that focus on Kant's "applied philosophy" while ignoring its transcendental foundation, or even use it to oppose the purity and formalism of his transcendental philosophy. Finally, I intended to react against the temptation to isolate specific appealing moments, themes, and figures of Kant's philosophy while rejecting the rest or ignoring the specific problematic contexts in which they are placed. Examples of this are the privileged position often granted to transcendental imagination (in the aftermath of Heidegger's influential interpretation), and the attention that the ideas of moral "respect" and the "sublime" continue to receive in the contemporary debate. My aim has been to show in what sense those moments and themes are stations of a complex itinerary in which Kant develops the transcendental aspects of human sensibility.

What is compelling in Kant's analysis, in my view, is his highly nuanced and sophisticated conception of human sensibility and his attempts to differentiate forms of sensibility with regard to specific spheres of human experience. The body reveals its transcendental forms in the specificity of human modes of experience and in conjunction with different intellectual activities. Ultimately, such a conception makes the clear-cut sensible/intelligible dichotomy difficult to maintain. Whether this consequence leads us away from Kant's transcendental philosophy or confirms us deeper in its method is a question I have left to further investigation. The exegetical narrative of the present volume opens onto yet another task, the topic of a future project: what is the relation between the body as condition of experience and the experienced body? How is the transition accomplished, with regard to the issue of embodiment, from transcendental philosophy or the *Critiques* to the *Metaphysics of Morals,* the *Anthropology,* Kant's essays on race, and the *Opus Postumum*?

The second aim of this book was methodological. I wanted to assess the force of *transcendental* philosophy for a comprehension and articulation of the issue of embodiment. While its root is ancient and its development modern, the problem of the body and the embodiment of the self have come to center stage in contemporary philosophical discussion—from philosophy of mind to feminist and race theory. My interest is first and foremost methodological: what is the methodological perspective that brings us closer to a *philosophical* understanding of the (human) body and our embodied experience? In its relation with the mind, in its closeness to and distance from animals, in its sexed, gendered, racial, cultural, linguistic reality and construction? Specifically, how far can the transcendental method inaugurated by Kant help us in answering these questions, or perhaps in better laying out the groundwork for thinking of these questions today? In probing the force of Kant's transcendental philosophy on the issue of embodiment my decision has been to trust Kant all the way before raising doubts or challenging his points. I had to follow him through all three *Critiques* and see how far the transcendental method could bring me. I considered this suspension of doubt necessary to lift the "cover" under which the new Kant could be discovered—the Kant who, contrary to what Nancy and Derrida suspected, indeed had something important to say about the body and still has something important to say to us today.

The final assessment on this point can be summarized as follows. Kant's complex theory of "transcendental embodiment" offers an indispensable tool for thinking of the *universal* dimension of our human embodied experience, i.e., an experience that does not rely exclusively on principles and values dictated by reason but is based also on *feelings* that are universal and universalizable, as well as on a common predicament of mortality, suffering, and vulnerability that characterizes the human condition on an a priori level. There is, I believe, a lot of interesting work to be pursued in this direction. I mention here only two projects to which the conclusions of this book have led me. First, the attempt to propose a philosophy of woman's body on a transcendental basis: what would it mean to consider sexual difference in a transcendental perspective? Second, the attempt to construe the concept of moral and political "solidarity" as a feeling that, similar to Kant's moral feeling of respect, has universal and necessary validity (hence is not an empirical "sympathy") and yet is indeed a *feeling*—not a command of reason (it is rather a consequence thereof).

But there are also limits to Kant's transcendental consideration of the body. In my view, with regard to the issue of embodiment, Kant's transcendental philosophy has to face a strong competing model, namely dialectic. Although any influence or suggestion arising from that model has been programmatically excluded from the present inquiry, the alternative "transcendental embodiment" *versus* "dialectic of the body" remains a hard one for me to decide. Ultimately, the main objection to Kant's position is the difficulty of integrating into a transcendental exploration of the body the dimensions of history, culture, and dynamic transformation and development that (Hegel's and Marx's) dialectic assumes to be constitutive. Methodologically, the alternative remains open and worthy of further exploration.

The third objective of the book was historical and historiographical. Here I have two points. As I observed in the introduction, scholarly accounts of the mind or soul/body problem in early modern philosophy generally leave out Kant. The problem reappears, deeply transformed, in German idealism as the notion of *Geist* and its relation to nature takes center stage. A gap seems to separate the modern tradition from the nineteenth century, and the transition is never investigated. Kant is strangely absent in this story. This book intends to fill this gap and offer a first contribution to the development of the mind/body problem in Kant's critical philosophy. The way in which I have brought the pre-critical writings to bear on the problems of the *Critiques* fulfills this aim in part. The results achieved on this front are significant. I have shown how the critique of metaphysics (of psychology in particular) and a new theory of space have allowed Kant to overcome the traditional dualism of body and soul. The transcendental subject is now an *embodied human subject*. Body and soul are transcendentally "transfigured" insofar as they provide a priori formal conditions of experience. However, a new dualism seems to replace the metaphysical one, namely, the separation of nature and freedom as irreducible spheres of human experience. Although such a dualism is no longer construed along the separation between body and soul, it cuts deeply through the human being. The third *Critique* offers Kant's final reflection on this topic and becomes a fundamental inspiration of German idealism—the starting point of a new conception of the body confronted, this time, with *Geist*.

Although indirectly, this study looks forward to the history of the reception of Kant's philosophy and to Kant's presence in contemporary philosophy. Or better: it looks at the presence or rather absence of a *certain* Kant in the contemporary debate—the Kant of transcendental embodiment, "Kant the philosopher" who 'has *something* to say about the body.' The present volume provides the groundwork for this future story to be told. My general suggestion is to view the history of post-Kantian philosophy—from German idealism up to the contemporary discussion—as a succession of reactions, corrections, integrations of Kant's transcendental view of the human being. This, I believe, is the case even when Kant is not named, even when the method assumed seems radically different from Kant's, and even when the topics taken on seem utterly foreign to the horizon of Kant's thought. In its reactions to and corrections of Kant, post-Kantian philosophy takes for granted a certain conception of Kantian philosophy—it imposes on it a certain "cover," a certain *Bild*. The central question is the following: how does our view of post-Kantian philosophy (of Hegel, for example, Merleau-Ponty or John Sallis) change when we discover that the topic of embodiment—albeit in its transcendental version—is indeed at the center of Kant's philosophy? What is presented as a correction of Kant is made possible only on the basis of an interpretation of Kant that leaves out precisely the thought that the later philosopher deems important and claims to "discover" for the first time. (For example, Merleu-Ponty's phenomenological view of the body as subject and not simply object of experience; Sallis's view of imagination as a "force" that leads us back to the elemental sense of the sensible against the split between sensible and intelligible.)

Major philosophical currents of nineteenth, twentieth, and twenty-first-century Continental philosophy refer critically to Kant to raise the need to integrate sensibility in philosophical discourse. Most of the time, at stake is a reaction *against* the alleged "purity" of Kantian reason (often invoked as the paradigm of masculine rationality and Eurocentric vision), which is voiced as the need to fill the gap left open by his philosophy. Indirectly, this book shows that such a reaction is made possible precisely by the Kantian gesture by which the body is freed from its (modern) empirical and materialist reduction to the complement of the soul, and put at the center of the transcendental discourse on subjectivity and rationality. In displaying a transcendental form, the body significantly complicates the split between the sensible and the intelligible that is generally considered Kant's distinctive brand of dualism. Hegel's concept of *Geist* and its dialectic realization in history are fundamentally indebted to Kant's "transcendental embodiment" even though they are presented as overcoming the formal subjectivism of the pure 'I think' (they are, to wit, its true *Aufhebung*). The point, however, is that because of Kant's *transcendental* approach, the body seems to remain "invisible" in his philosophy; it seems to lose its lived, existential materiality.

The real issue facing philosophy today is not to recuperate something that Kant has allegedly ignored or was unable to see—namely, our embodied experience—but to thematize it differently, through a different philosophical approach. The question, again, remains whether this newly discovered Kant—the Kant of "transcendental embodiment"—confirms us in the usefulness of transcendental philosophy or leads us away from it.

Notes

Introduction

1. See KrV B xvi.

2. See, for example, Fulda and Horstmann, eds. (1994).

3. See J. G. Herder's *Metakritik zur Kritik der reinen Vernunft* in Herder (1913), vol. 22; and his *Kalligone,* in vol. 21; also J. G. Hamann's *Aesthetica in nuce* in Hamann (1957), vol. 2. A typical example of the charge of rational "purity" in ethics is Max Weber's influential criticism of Kant's "ethics of pure conviction" (*Gesinnungsethik*) as developed in particular in his *Politik als Beruf* (1919). An interesting critical perspective on the issue is offered by Michel Henry in *L'essence de la manifestation* (1963).

4. With regard to Kant's practical philosophy Ricoeur already distinguishes the transcendental Kant from the Kant of the anthropology. See P. Guyer (1996), 335–393. R. Louden focuses exclusively on Kant's applied ("impure") practical philosophy: *Kant's Impure Ethics* (2000). Important is Susan M. Shell, *The Embodiment of Reason: Kant on Spirit, Generation, and Community* (1996): this work centers on Kant's political theory and issues of community, and does not address the specific transcendental problem posed by the issue of embodiment. N. Sherman (1997) claims that emotions are relevant to Kant's project as they constitute a moral anthropology; accordingly, she often manifests frustration with the apparently spare remarks on the topic offered by the second *Critique.* My work is placed in the aftermath of B. Herman's defense of Kant's moral philosophy against the traditional charges of rigorism, formalism, and rejection of human affectivity in the practical sphere (charges taken up by feminist interpretations of Kant): see her *The Practice of Moral Judgment* (1993). The interest in Kant's anthropology has been enhanced by the recent publication of vol. 25 of the *Akademie* edition, which is dedicated to Kant's lectures on anthropology before the 1798/1800 *Anthropology from a Pragmatic Point of View.*

5. See recent attacks on Kant in R. Bernasconi (2001, 2002); followed by D. F. Krell (2000), 103–134, 108–110. A more balanced account is in Hill and Boxill (2001), 448–471, 460, 468. For a feminist critique of Kant's gendered notion of personality, see R. M. Schott, *Cognition and Eros: A Critique of the Kantian Paradigm* (1988); the collective volume *Feminist Interpretations of Immanuel Kant,* ed. R. M. Schott (1997); C. Bat-

tersby, "Stages on Kant's Way: Aesthetics, Morality, and the Gendered Sublime" (1998); and S. Benhabib, "The Generalized and the Concrete Other: The Kohlberg-Gilligan Controversy and Feminist Theory" (1987). Benhabib attacks Kant's "disembodied and disembedded" noumenal agent in section 3 of her essay.

6. See the literature discussed in chaps. 5–6, below. If it is true, as Mills claims (1997, 70), that Kant's "philosophical work"—i.e., his critical oeuvre—"has to be read in conjunction" with the lectures on anthropology and physical geography, a previous understanding of (1) Kant's "philosophical work" and (2) its relation to his applied philosophy is required. In the present volume I aim precisely at providing such an understanding. See the important essay by Adrian M. Piper, "Xenophobia and Kantian Rationalism" (1993).

7. See R. M. Schott (1987), where she reduces Kant's complex theory of sensibility to space and time as forms of intuition. E. Casey (1997, ch. 10) analyzes the connection between human body and place established by Whitehead, Husserl, and Merleau-Ponty, and contrasts it to the view developed by Kant's transcendental philosophy, which is accused of "mentalism in the form of a pure intuitionism" (p. 203). I intend to refute this charge of mentalism.

8. KU §5, 15.

9. *Prolegomena* A, 207; AA IV, 375n.—my emphasis.

10. See for example KrV B 420–421.

11. Hoke Robinson raises this issue in the opening of "Kant on Embodiment" (1992, 329). The topic is at the center of Shell (1996); however, this excellent study does not relate to pre-Kantian developments of the problem, and does not address the issue of what constitutes Kant's transcendental perspective on it.

12. Merleau-Ponty's phenomenology of the body, Deleuze's genetic methodology, Foucault's genealogy are all attempts to overcome Kant's transcendentalism and yet maintain the perspective on the body disclosed by it. Heidegger's reading of Kant's idea of imagination can also be brought back to this picture.

13. In light of my reconstruction, Merleau-Ponty's notion of "corporeal intentionality," whereby the lived body gains its fundamental independence from the mind's intentionality (which for Brentano was instead the specific mark of psychical phenomena), directly inherits the core idea of Kant's transcendental view of the human body. For Merleau-Ponty's "corporeal intentionality" see J. N. Mohanty (1972), 139–143. This concept is central to A. Lingis's own phenomenology: see, for example, Lingis (1998), 31–34, 56–59; and Lingis (1996).

14. The expression is new in the literature. F. Kaulbach speaks of "*apriorische Leiblichkeit*" and "*apriorische Theorie der Leiblichkeit*" (1963, 473, 470–482). For the historical success of the strategy that I call "transcendental embodiment," see C. Taylor (1995, 21–22). In discussing the specifically transcendental form of Kant's arguments, Taylor claims that "the conception of the agent as embodied agency, which has developed out of modern phenomenology, as in the works of Heidegger and Merleau-Ponty, has been deployed and argued for in a way which is ultimately derived from the paradigm arguments of the first *Critique*."

15. *Metaphysik der Sitten*, AA VI, 205.

16. Kant criticizes both Burke's "observation" (which he adopted instead in the pre-critical *Observations on the Feeling of the Beautiful and Sublime*) and Burke's and Locke's "physiology" (respectively, EE§X, AA XX, 238; KU §29 All. Anm. 128ff.; see chaps. 7–9, below). For a discussion of the different approaches to the topic of the human

body in recent literature, see V. Schürmann (2003). The position I propose with the notion of transcendental embodiment comes close to Merleau-Ponty's phenomenology of the flesh and to more recent projects, such as Lingis's, which follow in its aftermath. Interestingly, however, Merleau-Ponty criticizes Kant for not having recognized the body as subject.

17. See Taylor (1995, 22): the claim that "our manner of being as subjects is in essential respects that of embodied agents" is a claim "about the *nature* of our experience and thought, and of all those functions that are ours qua subject, *rather than about the empirically necessary conditions of these functions*" (my emphasis). I contend that this is one of the central tenets of Kant's transcendental philosophy throughout the three *Critiques*.

18. In particular, I take transcendental embodiment to be broader than imagination although, in many respects, closely related to it. It is on this notion that, in the aftermath of Heidegger's interpretation of Kant, much of the recent continental literature has concentrated. See, for example, J. Sallis (2000b) and (1987); and J. Llewelyn (2000).

19. See for example Eze's attacks on Kant in "The Color of Reason: The Idea of 'Race' in Kant's Anthropology" (1995), which are based on a fundamental misunderstanding of the specifically *transcendental* dimension of Kant's philosophy—from which his allegedly racist race-theory is seen to be derived. (The pre-critical *Observations* do not show, as Eze claims, Kant's "theoretic transcendental philosophical position at work" if only because, chronologically, transcendental philosophy is still to come in Kant's development.) See the correct critique of Eze's position in Hill and Boxill (2001, 452–459, esp. 453). The same failure to address the specifically transcendental dimension of Kant's discourse in the third *Critique* (as opposed to the *Observations*) can be found in Battersby (1998).

20. KpV A 128 (AA V, 73).

21. As noticed above, the role played by Kant in the transition from Cartesian dualism to post-Kantian philosophy is ignored in the literature. See, for example, D. Welton's "Introduction: Foundations of a Theory of the Body," in Welton, ed. (1999). Welton discusses the Cartesian mind/body dualism, observes that the fundamental turn in the thematization of the human body takes place only with the rise of phenomenology in the twentieth century, concedes that indeed "there were forerunners in the nineteenth century" such as Hegel, Marx, Kierkegaard, Nietzsche (p. 3), but makes no mention of Kant. Casey (1997, ch. 10) does recognize the historical importance of Kant's pre-critical essay "On the Ultimate Ground of the Differentiation of Regions in Space"; however, he sees Kant as completely abandoning this position in his transcendental philosophy, which remains, for him, a model of pure "mentalism." The historical reconstruction is interesting in Merleau-Ponty (2003), although Kant's role in this story is the same.

22. See for example Feuerbach's claim in his Leibniz book with regard to the central point of the *Monadology* (§72): "*Allein Gott is vom Körper gänzlich befreit.*"

23. This is only a sample of some of the most interesting recent works: Sallis (2000b, 1987); Lingis (1998, 1996); and Lyotard (1994).

24. KpV A 289 (AA V, 161)—my emphasis.

25. *Was heißt sich im Denken Orientieren?* A 311.

26. See KrV B 562/A 534 and KpV A 51, 58 (AA V, 29, 33).

27. MS, AA VI, 406.

28. KU, EE§V, AA XX, 214, 215.

29. The last development of Kant's notion of sensation is in the *Opus Postumum,* where he finally attempts to provide a *transcendental* theory of sensation.

30. The topic is studied by Shell (1996, chaps. 8–9) particularly with regard to the problem of "generation" and the origin of life in the critique of teleological judgment. R. Makkreel underlines how little attention the topic of life in the third *Critique* has received (1990, ch. 5).

31. KU §49, 193.

I. Bodies in Space

1. See J. V. Buroker (1981), 53; G. Nerlich (1973), 338 (which is discussed in C. Hoefer (2000), though the issue of embodiment plays no role in Hoefer's article); D. Walford (2001); and G. Hatfield (1990).

2. KrV B 44/A 28.

3. AA II, 381,32: "the most common and clear example"; AA II, 382, 24–25: "the common example."

4. *Was heißt sich im Denken Orientieren?* A 307.

5. Here I take up the perspective outlined in C. Taylor (1995), 20–33, esp. 21–22.

6. *Was heißt?* A 307.

7. KrV B 42/A 26.

8. KrV B 43/A 28.

9. The issue of embodiment figures rarely in the discussions of incongruent counterparts. A brief mention of the problem is made in L. Scaravelli (1968), 312–313. The topic is discussed explicitly, yet too quickly, in R. Hoke Robinson (1981), 391–397; and with references to Husserl, Heidegger, and phenomenology in A. Ferrarin (2006), 23–30. Because of this limitation of the analysis, all the texts in which Kant presents the example of the incongruent counterparts are rarely considered together; while Kant's changing views on space is responsible for the fact that the important continuity between them is missed. The 1786 *Was heißt sich im Denken Orientieren?* is generally left out, as the argument there seems to have no reference to the issue of space. (Heidegger cites it in *Sein und Zeit* (1927), §23—a reference that is missed by Derrida in "La main de Heidegger (Geschlecht II)" (1987b), 438.) The most comprehensive source historically is H. Vaihinger (1892), vol. 2, 518–532. Bibliographical information is provided in Vaihinger (1892), Buroker (1981), and Walford (2001). In the vast literature, K. Reich's introduction to his edition of two pre-critical texts is important: see Reich (1975). Interestingly, on the contrary, the reception of Kant's theory of space in the phenomenological tradition (in Husserl and, in particular, Merleau-Ponty), even though critical of Kant's abstract formalism, reproduces the Kantian connection between space and embodiment in the opposition between geometrical space and "lived space."

10. KrV B 37/A 22.

11. See KrV B 42/A 26.

12. KrV B 1—my emphasis.

13. See, for example, KrV B 118/A 86.

14. *Prolegomena,* A 207, AA IV, 375n.

15. See, for example, *Dissertatio* §3: "*Sensualitas* est *receptivitas* subiecti, per quam possibile est, ut status ipsius repraesentativus obiecti alicuius praesentia certo modo *afficiatur*"—my emphasis. ("Sensibility is the receptivity of the subject by which it is possible for the subject's representative state to be affected in a certain way by the presence of some object.")

16. See, for example, KrV B 122/A 90: "appearances can certainly be given in intuition independently of functions of the understanding." The active aspect of sensibility is rarely recognized in the literature (but see B. Centi (2002), 43f., 45, who speaks of "spontaneity of receptivity"). It is, however, an important source of inspiration for recent philosophers such as Lyotard, Derrida, and Lingis. In these cases, however, Kant's theory is not explicitly indicated as a source. Here we encounter yet again the paradox that this book has begun to uncover: there is a fundamental aspect of Kant's philosophy (what I call "transcendental embodiment") that is "unseen" in the literature, is ignored by most critics of Kant's pure reason, and nonetheless remains the unacknowledged source of inspiration for the liveliest currents of twentieth and twenty-first-century philosophy. See Lyotard's discussion of the active character of Kant's "receptivity" with regard to intuition in (1988a), 61–65—the "active subject of sensibility." And see Derrida's interpretation of the Platonic *khora* and its implications for the idea of "receptivity" as "receiving"/"receptacle" in (1993a), 61–62—"What does to receive mean?"—which leads Derrida to "the relation [. . .] between the question of sense or of the sensible and that of receptivity in general." See Lingis's notion of "sensuality" as active force, even as expressive face in Levinas's aftermath, in Lingis (1994, 64–65). In *Kant und das Problem der Metaphysik,* Heidegger (1973) sees Kant's pure intuition as always and necessarily receptive and passive, and invests the transcendental imagination of all active function. J. Sallis interprets pure intuition as "a formal order-giving component within sensibility," almost paradoxically indicating an "inward" dimension of what otherwise is mere outwardness of the senses (1987, 12). I stress, on the contrary, the radical outward orientation of space as pure intuition and the fact that an activity properly belongs to such outwardness as such, even without presupposing an inward dimension. In *The Gathering of Reason* (2005, 26–27), in a Heideggerian vein, Sallis indicates the activity of pure intuition as a "gathering" of the fragmented manifold of sensation (but since gathering is reason's function, the specificity of intuition is thereby lost).

17. KrV B 29/A 15; B 74/A 50 and the "two original sources of the *Gemüt*." See Sallis (1987, 73–81) who takes up the Heideggerian theme of the "common root" of the two branches. For Kant's rejection and criticism of Leibniz's position, see KrV B 60ff./A 43–44.

18. For a discussion of the complex problem of "affection" in Kant and its relation to modern philosophy see Hoke Robinson (1992); and A. Ferrarin (1995), esp. 66–70. Heidegger maintains that for Kant time is the mode by which the subject *affects itself,* and thus gives a resistance to itself: "Kant faßt die Zeit als die reine *Selbstaffektion,* d.h. als dasjenige, was a priori, aus dem Selbst entspringend, dieses affiziert, es angeht und in diesem Angang a priori Widerstand und Bindung a priori bietet" (1977, 391, 89–93; and see also Heidegger (1973), 183–184).

19. See KrV B 102/A 68, in which space and time are "*conditions* of the receptivity of our *Gemüt,* under which alone it can be receptive of representations of objects" (my emphasis). For a discussion of the relation between human body and cognition in the Transcendental Aesthetic, see L. Falkenstein (1995), ch. 3.

20. KrV B 36/A 22.

21. KrV B 34–35/A 20.

22. See for example KrV B 72, B 51/A 35; *Dissertatio* §10.

23. KrV B 35–36/A 21n. See Sallis (1987, 12–16) commenting on the almost paradoxical character of the title.

24. To explain this hesitation we should recall that in 1787 Kant was about to start working on the third *Critique;* see my *Kant and the Unity of Reason* (2005), ch. 4.

25. See A. G. Baumgarten (1758); and M. Gregor (1984). Kant's relation to Baumgarten is further developed in my "Kant and Herder on Baumgarten *Aesthetica*" (2006). A comparison of the versions of this footnote in the two editions of the *Critique* is a *locus communis* in the literature: see Windelband's *Einletung zur Kritik der Urtheilskraft* at AA V, 512–527, esp. 514; J.-H. De Vleeschauwer (1939), ch. 3; P. Guyer (1997), 26–27; and L. Amoroso (1998).

26. The four arguments on space and time are found, respectively, in KrV B 38–40/A 23–25, and B 46–48/A 30–32. A fifth argument is dedicated to the discussion of the infinite character of time (KrV B 47–48/A 32). For the details of Kant's arguments see M. Baum (1992), who argues against Guyer (1987, 345ff.); see also Falkenstein (1995). Sallis aptly observes how Kant develops these arguments under the heading of "*Erörterung*" as "setting the concept of space in its place," as "putting space within a space to which it has in advance a proprietary relation" (1987, 13ff.). See an analogous claim in Lyotard (1988a): to deal with the given as given "is to situate it, to place it in a phrase universe" (p. 61)—an operation that links sensibility and situation, similar to what is described by Sallis and Lyotard, takes place in Transcendental Aesthetic §1.

27. KrV B 42/A 26 and KrV B 50/A 34 respectively (my emphasis). See Baum (1991).

28. See KrV §6 B 52/A 35ff. and §§7–8.

29. See Scaravelli (1968), 71–141. Sallis (1987, 76–81) considers Kant's account of sensibility in the Analytic (culminating in the thematization of imagination) a disruption of the parallelism Aesthetics/Analytic or pure intuition/pure thought as the two sources of knowledge. His focus on imagination depends, in turn, on the centrality of the problem of the "common root" of the faculties. (A discussion of Sallis's positions and of the development of Heidegger's views with regard to space and imagination can be found at Llewelyn (2000), 107–109.) I place my account of the problem of sensibility on a more original level. I suspect that once the complexity and richness of Kant's idea of *Sinnlichkeit* is understood, the issue of the 'two branches of knowledge' versus their 'common root' (and consequently the interpretive dominance of imagination) will have to be thought anew.

30. *Prolegomena* §36, A110, AA IV, 318.

31. KrV B 178/A 139.

32. KrV B 273/A 225.

33. KrV B 209/A 167–168. This explains why Kant could not address the a priori of sensation at the level of the 'isolated' sensibility of the Transcendental Aesthetic, which, in fact, contains only the two a priori forms of intuition—space and time. The "degree" is *synthesis*.

34. Kant uses the "degree" again in the Dialectic, in the Paralogisms chapter, against Mendelssohn's proof of the immortality of the soul (KrV B 414).

35. Respectively KrV B 41/A 26 and *Anthropologie* §15; time instead, as inner sense, is "where the human body is affected by the *Gemüt*."

36. Buroker (1981) explores the relation to Leibniz; while Reich (1975) draws attention to the importance of Kant's relation to Wolff, which underlies both the 1766 *Dreams of a Spirit-Seer* and the 1768 essay.

37. AA II, 382, 1–3; *Dissertatio* §15 C: the internal difference between the left and the right hand "makes it impossible for the boundaries of their extension to coincide" (*impossibile est, ut termini extensionis coincidant*). See *Prolegomena* §13, A58, AA IV, 286, for the glove example.

38. This means that if our body did not display the asymmetry of left and right we would not be able to ascertain the property of incongruence in other external

objects. Incongruence is not an empirical property that can be abstracted or inferred from the empirical constitution of objects such as snails, etc. Walford makes a similar point (2001, 428).

39. AA II, 381,14.

40. AA II, 377,27–378,4.

41. AA II, 377,26. In 1768 "absolute cosmic space" and "universal space" are synonymous; in 1770 Kant abandons the notion of "absolute cosmic space."

42. AA II, 381,14–17.

43. See AA II, 383,13–15.

44. AA II, 381,18–20. For the view of space (and the body) as "ground," this precritical discussion may be seen as the framework for Sallis's considerations with regard to the grounding of reason in sensibility at KrV B 89/A 5 (1987, 25), and for its "tunneling" as "going toward a ground" (1987, 16ff.).

45. Kant mentions the "*Realität*" of space explicitly in AA II, 378,11 and 383,28; 378,30 has "*Wirklichkeit*." In the first passage, the reality of space is so closely connected to its specific function as to be identical with it: space has its "proper reality as first principle of the possibility of the composition of matter." See Reich (1975, xi–xii) for Kant's relation to Euler in the discussion of the absolute reality of space (both Kant and Euler, against Newton and Clarke, reject the reality of an absolute empty space); and see also A. Laywine (1993).

46. AA II, 383,27–29. For a discussion of the nature of these "difficulties" see Scaravelli (1968), 333–335; and K. Rademeister (1947), esp. 149.

47. AA II, 383,19.

48. See J. Derrida (1997). Although Derrida claims that Plato's *khora,* as "irreducible to the sensible and the intelligible" (p. 10), is a philosophical "scandal" in the history of philosophy (p. 108: differing from Aristotle's matter, Descartes's space, and Kant's form of space), I think his interpretation of *khora* comes close in several respects to the transcendental meaning that I see Kant developing here. Derrida writes, for example, that *khora* "is a place without space, before space and time" (p. 91). See also Sallis (2000a).

49. In this conclusion, I agree—albeit for quite different reasons—with Buroker (1981) and Scaravelli (1968).

50. The task (AA II, 381,14–17): "Thus we want to demonstrate [. . .]." The premise (AA II, 378,31): "To this aim, I make the following premise." The claims: while the distinction between "position" and "region" is formulated in §1 and the demonstrative task is formulated in §5, the three claims of the "premise" are contained, respectively, in §§2, 3, and 4.

51. AA II, 378,34–379,1. The influence of Kant's idea that space is always and necessarily oriented can be traced up to Derrida's claim that "the space of writing" is "not an originally intelligible space" but is "sensible" "in the sense that Kant intended; *space irreducibly oriented* within which the left does not recover the right" (1976, 289–291, my emphasis). Derrida also brings to the fore the asymmetry owed to the human body. In *Sein und Zeit* (1927, compare 103–104 with the notion of *Gegend;* 211; and 413 with the notion of *Plätze*) oriented space is, for Heidegger, the point in which time seems to yield to space in its priority in human existence (see D. F. Krell (1997), 53–54). Orientation is crucial to Merleau-Ponty's *espace vécu* (1945, 281, 344); and on the basis of bodily orientation Lingis distinguishes the "field of perception" from geometrical space (1998, 31–34).

52. This is a seminal insight for an understanding of space that remains central for Husserl (1973), Merleau-Ponty (1945), and Derrida (1997). Heidegger's reflections on

the relation time-space from *Sein und Zeit* (1927) to the later *Bauen, Wohnen, Denken* (1951), *Die Frage nach dem Ding* (1962), and "Die Kunst und der Raum" (1983) go in the direction of a progressive re-evaluation of space over time. Krell (1997, 41–88) follows the development of Heidegger's position, tracing it back to the tension between Kant and Hegel and ultimately claiming that the turn toward a view close to what Krell calls "ecstatic spatiality" (p. 42) is indebted more to Hegel than to Kant. Curiously, however, Krell makes no mention of embodiment in discussing Heidegger or Kant. (KrV B 860–861, though, is commented on with regard to Arnheim. Kant's passage mentions the "animal body" and Krell is struck by the "strangeness" of this reference: why the animal and not the human body? See my discussion in ch. 9, below.) E. Casey (1993, 1997) offers an excellent reconstruction of the itinerary that goes from Kant to later continental developments.

53. AA II, 380, 27.

54. For an analysis of the peculiar nature of this feeling see ch. 5, below, with regard to the relation between feeling and practical reason; and ch. 8 for the aesthetic nature of feeling (pleasure and displeasure). In *Sein und Zeit* §23 Heidegger contests that the subjective "feeling" incarnated in the body is a sufficient condition for orientation in the "world." Citing Kant's 1786 essay, he maintains that "'through the mere feeling of a difference of the two sides of my body' I could never find myself in a world." Heidegger's point is that Kant's transcendental investigation misses the "existential constitution of the *In-der-Welt-sein*" (1927, 109). Heidegger's view overturns Kant's position: the most original condition for orientation does not lie within the subject but in the structure of being-in-the-world.

55. *Was heißt?* A 308—my emphasis.

56. See Scaravelli (1968), 328.

57. AA II, 379,22–24. Later on, in the *Dissertatio,* Kant realizes that not only the determination of the "region" but even that of the mere "position" rests on a relation to our sensibility. Only at this point does he realize that geometry depends entirely upon the intuitive relation to sensibility. Thereby the argument of the incongruent counterparts is fully generalized.

58. AA II, 378,34–35. Compare this position to the role played by the body's "postural schema" and its function as "dynamic Gestalt" for orientation in the world, in Lingis's project of a new phenomenological account of nature based on the human body (1998, 60–63); see also his "Intentionality and Corporeality" (1971) for a discussion of Husserl.

59. See the final section of this chapter, below.

60. For the body as "instrument " for the "comprehension" of the perceived world, see Merleau-Ponty (1945), 272.

61. The transition from two-dimensional to three-dimensional space is explicitly signaled in *Prolegomena* §13, A 57, AA IV, 285.

62. AA II, 380,28: It is of "such a great necessity." Kant's use of the notion of "feeling" is the same in *Was heißt?* A 307.

63. The need to avoid such a double account of the status of the body is probably one of the reasons why the mention of incongruence is left out of the strictly formal argument of the Transcendental Aesthetic.

64. AA II, 382,3.

65. See Scaravelli's discussion of Milhaud's criticism of Kant (1968, 326n.). Kant does not deny that an analytic description of incongruent objects is possible in purely

mathematical terms. He claims, however, that the analytic description presupposes precisely the intuition of the spatial property in question. See Milhaud, "La connaissance mathématique et l'idéalisme transcendental," in: *Revue Métaphysique* (1904), 394. The same misunderstanding can be found in Gauss (cit. Vaihinger (1892), 527). Both Scaravelli (1968, 314n.) and Hoke Robinson (1981, 395 n. 21) point out that it is a practice of modern textbook introductions to geometry to appeal to the intuitive, physical evidence of space's orientation before addressing the issue in purely mathematical terms. Hoke Robinson refers to "the direction a *right-hand* screw moves when turned *clockwise*," Scaravelli mentions the image of a human figure with open arms and legs and three lines that divide the body along the vertical, horizontal, and the opposite arm-leg vectors.

66. Respectively AA II, 382,24 and AA II, 383,27.

67. KrV B 333/A 277.

68. The Amphiboly was probably composed between 1768 and 1770.

69. *De mundi sensibilis,* §15 C.

70. For the claim that space is not a property of things in themselves see next chapter.

71. AA IV, 483,29–37—my emphasis. A wide variety of examples follow, as in the 1768 essay.

72. AA IV, 484,14.

73. AA IV, 484,5–9.

74. For this reason, this text is generally left out of the numerous analyses of the incongruent counterparts (see, for example, Buroker, Nehrlich, Scaravelli). Kant distinguishes here geographical, mathematical, and logical "orientation."

75. *Was heißt?* A 308–309.

76. *Prolegomena* §13, A 58, AA IV, 285,19–20.

77. *Prolegomena* §13, A 58, AA IV, 286,4–8.

78. *Prolegomena* §13, A 58, AA IV, 286,23–26.

79. *Prolegomena* §13, A 58, AA IV, 286,26–28—my emphasis.

80. See *Prolegomena* §13, A 58, AA IV, 286,34–35.

81. Referring to the *Prolegomena,* William James formulates a criticism of Kant's argument of incongruence that would rather apply to the essay on the "Regions in Space." James observes that Kant is right in "speaking of up and down, right and left" as bodily "sensations." He adds, however, that Kant is wrong "in invoking relation to extrinsic total space [. . .]. *Relation to our own body is enough*" (James (1950), vol. 2, 150–151n.). That the relation to our body is perfectly enough is precisely Kant's point in the *Prolegomena,* where our body is the representative of the unitary "entire space." This conclusion, however, was implicit—despite Kant's intention—in the 1768 essay, in which the argument of incongruent counterparts already replaced absolute space with our body.

82. KrV B44/A28.

2. Bodies and Souls

1. See Hoke Robinson (1992, 329). The topic is central to S. M. Shell (1996).

2. KrV B 37/A 22.

3. Thereby, I re-propose the crucial question that Patricia Kitcher addresses as preliminary question for the introduction of a Kantian "transcendental psychology."

"What is transcendental psychology the psychology of?" (Kitcher (1990), 21). It should be noted, however, that the title "transcendental psychology" is nowhere to be found in Kant's work as designating a specific branch of transcendental philosophy. In the continental tradition, Heidegger's first book on Kant plays a fundamental role in liberating Kant from the charge of psychologism (which even Husserl, who considers Kant the forerunner of his own transcendental investigation, raises in *Logische Untersuchungen* (1900) I, §28) by disclosing a metaphysical Kant finally assimilated to the phenomenological school. In an anti-psychological direction, P. Strawson (1966) firmly dissociates Kant's transcendental argumentation from all psychology. Recently, especially in the Anglo-American literature, "transcendental psychology" has been revived and has come to indicate, in particular, Kant's theory in the transcendental deduction. The expression is meant to characterize an allegedly Kantian psychology and to establish the relation between Kant and, alternatively, philosophy of mind or contemporary cognitive psychology. See Kitcher (1990), who attempts to link what she calls Kant's "transcendental psychology" to contemporary cognitive psychology; H. Hoppe (1983), who endorses the perspective of a phenomenological psychology; A. Brook (1994); R. Aquila (1989); and B. Longuenesse (1998), who distances herself from this debate by concentrating on Kant's doctrine of the *logical* forms of judgment.

4. Kitcher's view (1990, 22) seems to be that the object of transcendental psychology is the phenomenal self which makes it indeed to an empirical discipline, although she then underscores that its empirical character differs both from what Kant means under empirical psychology and from contemporary empirical studies. It is not clear, however, what the *transcendental* nature of such discipline would be. My claim is that Kant replaces the traditional discipline of psychology with (1) transcendental philosophy and (2) an anthropology resulting from the principles laid out by his transcendental philosophy. The reason for this systematic arrangement is precisely the impossibility of considering the body and the mind/soul as two (metaphysically or empirically) separated entities or substances. Their separation makes sense only from and in a transcendental perspective, which, however, is concerned precisely with the modalities of their *interaction* to produce our cognitive experience.

5. See KrV B 391, B 506n./A 479n., A 351, 361, 397, 567. See also the passage of the Doctrine of Method in which Kant suggests a new role for psychology in postcritical metaphysics (KrV B 873ff./A 845ff.); here, however, he separates "transcendental philosophy" from the "physiology of pure reason" to which rational psychology as "*rationale Erkenntnis*" of "*denkenden Natur*" now belongs. It is important to stress that this Kantian rational psychology—which is metaphysical and not transcendental—is based, unlike scholastic rational psychology, on the concept of a thinking being that is *given* in the "*empirical* inner representation: I think" (KrV B 876/A 848—my emphasis). For the relevance of the latter argument, see below, and ch. 3. Furthermore, as we will see, Kant labels Descartes's idealism "psychological," thereby referring to the possibility of suspending the existence of the outside world and still maintaining a sense of inner self (KrV B xxxix n.).

6. *Fortschritte der Metaphysik,* AA XX, 308. Kant starts this posthumously published work in 1793.

7. KU §89, 442, AA V, 441.

8. My position can be illustrated by Longuenesse's conclusion in her reconstruction of the Third Analogy of Experience. In asking "who" the subject of cognition is (which Kant indicates as "we"), she comments: "I suggest it is the empirical unity of

a consciousness whose states are associated with the states of a body it recognizes as its own, in a relation of spatial and dynamic community with other bodies in space" (1998, 392). What I call "embodied subject" is precisely such empirical unity of a consciousness whose states are associated with states of a body that can be claimed as its own. Only such a subject (not a disembodied pure substance or a mere disembodied logical unity of apperception) can, for Kant, do mathematical and physical science.

9. This seemingly blunt claim will be argued for throughout part 1.

10. Can Kant's transcendental logic be called "transcendental psychology"? A positive answer to this debated question (notably by Strawson and Kitcher) would require the previous understanding of what is meant by psychology. For it is certainly not what Kant refers to with this title. In the present discussion, I use the expression "transcendental psychology" in the strict sense in which Kant employs it in the first *Critique* (in both editions: see the occurrences listed above: KrV B 391, B 506n./A 479n., A 351, 361, 397, 567; and B 873ff./A 845ff.). I do not discuss the other much-debated issue of whether or not Kant's theory in the first *Critique* (his transcendental logic and deduction in particular), by entailing a "psychological" or "mentalist" dimension, is in any sense "psychologistic." (The debate on an alleged Kantian psychologism is started by J. Bona Meyer (1870); see more generally, B. Centi (2002), 35–43; V. Satura (1971); and historically, S. Poggi (1977).) For the different question of Kant's relation to psychology (to what *he* calls psychology) see G. Hatfield (1992), 213–214, 216; R. Makkreel (2002); T. Mischel (1967); K. Ameriks (2000), 234ff. for Kant's view of rational psychology; G. H. Bird (2000), with an important criticism of Strawson; and W. Waxman (1999), who claims that Kant's "pure psychology" is the successor of Hume's empirical psychology.

11. Obviously, the fact that the Transcendental Doctrine of Elements proceeds by successively "isolating" the elements of sensibility and those of understanding (KrV B 36/A 22; B 87/A 62) as well as Kant's fundamental claim that sensibility and understanding constitute two radically distinct sources of knowledge (KrV B 29/A 15; B 74/A 50 and the "two original sources of the *Gemüt*"), is no objection to my argument. For neither claim implies that knowledge is possible by considering one of those sources in its isolation.

12. See the passing remarks in Longuenesse (1998), 207n. 23 that confirm my suggestion. This is also the direction in which Merleau-Ponty develops his transcendental phenomenology of perception (against both empiricism and "intellectualism"—see 1945, 240ff.). Merleau-Ponty's assumption—that my argument reveals as indeed Kantian—is that a "perceiving mind is an incarnated mind" (Merleau-Ponty (1964b), 3). As intuition leads Kant to the a priori of the body, perception leads Merleau-Ponty to the topic of corporeality.

13. Marc-Wogau (1932, chaps. 1–3) claims that two conflicting ideas are at play in Kant's early writing, namely the (Wolffian) notion of space as consequence of the relations of substances, and the (Newtonian) notion of space as original dimension within which alone those relations can be manifested.

14. AA II, 382,3.

15. *Dreams,* AA II, 358,15. This important text is rarely analyzed in the literature. I have gained crucial insight on the relation between Wolff's psychology and the idea of space from Reich's "Kants Behandlung des Raumbegriffs in den 'Träume eines Geistersehers' und im 'Unterschied der Gegenden im Raum'" (1975, v–xvii). An excellent exposition of the *Dreams* can be found in ch. 5 of Shell (1996); A. Laywine (1993) is also

important; and see M. Heinz, "Herder's Review of Dreams of a Spirit-Seer (1766)" (2001).

16. An analogous argument leads Kant to reject the reality of absolute space in 1770.

17. For this connection, see Reich (1975) and Laywine (1993).

18. AA II, 368,10–11.

19. AA II, 371,10—my emphasis; KrV B 800/A 772.

20. AA II, 371,28–30; 370,22. In the conclusion of the *Dreams,* Kant provides an additional moral argument for the claim that a proof of the soul's immortality is not only impossible but also unnecessary. He opposes the notion that knowledge of the soul's immortality is necessary as a motive to virtuous action (AA II, 372,10–12).

21. AA II, 370,23–29.

22. AA II, 368,1.

23. AA X, 71–72.

24. AA X, 72.

25. The reference to Swedenborg is in this letter to Mendelssohn (AA X, 72).

26. See *Versuch den Begriff der negativen Größen in die weltweisheit einzuführen* (*Attempt to Introduce the Concept of Negative Magnitudes into Philosophy*), AA II, 168.

27. See Wolff (1740), §752.

28. C. Wolff (1736), §§591, 611n. "Space results from the possibility of coexistence." §611n. is quoted by Reich (1975, viii), who underlines how Wolff appeals here to Géraud de Cordemoy, the founder of Occasionalism, as the one who has seen the "truth" of the connection between the issue of space and that of the soul/body relation.

29. See Knutzen (1745), §§28, 26. See also B. Erdmann (1876), 83ff.; E. Watkins (1995b, 1995a); Laywine (1993), ch. 2; and Ameriks (2000), 85ff. Shell (1996, ch. 2) underscores the ethical and political implications of the concept of physical influence.

30. See *Gedanken,* §§5–6.

31. *Gedanken,* §6 (AA I, 20,37–21,1—my emphasis).

32. *Gedanken,* §6 (AA I, 21,2–3).

33. *Gedanken,* §9.

34. AA II, 320,7–8.

35. AA II, 321,19–22.

36. AA II, 323,5–9.

37. AA II, 323,33–34.

38. See, with exactly the same intent, KrV B 799–800/A 771–772.

39. Significantly, Merleau-Ponty's development of the notion of space follows the same Kantian trajectory, displaying space as the body's rootedness in the "world" (1945, 281ff.). In his account, this gesture discloses a new form of intentionality (or experiential reference to the world) that is not intentionality of consciousness but of the body. The same Kantian thread can be followed in Heidegger's thought. If one of his central aims is to dismantle the Cartesian mind-body dualism, this aim is expressed first and foremost in the idea of human existence as being-in-the-world (in contrast to traditional inner-outer dichotomies), as openness to "being" mediated by the human embodied, worldly, and temporal condition (though *Dasein* originally and linguistically entails spatial reference). Significantly, one finds this connection up to Heidegger's late *Zollikoner Seminare,* in which the idea of *Leib* or lived body is used to opposed the inheritance of Cartesian dualism in contemporary psychology reflected in the mechanistic notion of *Körper.* In claims such as "the body is the necessary, though

not sufficient condition for relations (to the world)" (1987b, 204, 207, 220, 232–235), we can trace Heidegger's transformation of Kant's transcendental view of embodiment in terms of the ontic-ontological difference (see F. Dallmayr (1993), 240–241).

40. AA II, 343,12–17—my emphasis.

41. AA II, 343,21–23.

42. *Was heißt sich im Denken Orientieren?* A 307.

43. Kant is anti-Cartesian specifically, here, in that he contends that the soul is not localized in any specific portion of the body.

44. AA II, 324,18–35. The parallels with Merleau-Ponty's *corps propre* and its specific spatiality are interesting. See, for example, Merleau-Ponty (1945), 114ff. See also Shell (1996), 114ff.

45. AA II, 344,5–7. Significantly, Kant uses the image of the *focus imaginarius* again in the *Critique of Pure Reason* with regard to the ideas of reason (KrV B 672/A 644). See next chapter.

46. AA II, 347,16–17.

47. AA II, 346,4–6.

48. AA II, 364,1–2.

49. AA II, 364.

50. See for example KrV B 49/A 33.

51. The itinerary to which "transcendental embodiment" leads me in the first *Critique* should strike as an alternative to the many readings inaugurated by Heidegger's first book on Kant: from the Transcendental Aesthetic I move to the Analytic of Principles and the Refutation, skipping the Transcendental Deduction and the Schematism. Transcendental embodiment replaces the transcendental imagination. Is this the Kant-reading to which "ecstatic spatiality" would lead? (See Krell (1997), ch. 2.) Significantly, in his *Die Frage nach dem Ding,* where the focus is no longer the theory of imagination or the schematism but the logical doctrine of the first *Critique,* Heidegger examines the Analytic of Principles (1987a, 174–189). See J. Llewelyn (2000), 110–112; and also Sallis's reading of the work of imagination in the Dialectic, in *The Gathering of Reason* (2005).

52. See L. Scaravelli (1968), 305–306, n. 10.

53. See Krell (1997), 42–88 for the imbalance of this relation in the development of Heidegger's thought (from *Sein und Zeit* §70 to "Die Kunst und der Raum") and for his oscillating confrontation with Kant and Hegel as well as, more generally, for the subordination of space to time in the Western philosophical tradition, to which Krell opposes the idea of "ecstatic spatiality."

54. *Dissertatio,* §15 Corollary.

55. KrV B 50/A 34 (my emphasis): this passage makes clear how time replaces the metaphysical "soul."

56. KrV B 42/A 26.

57. See KrV B 50/A 34 quoted above. The fact that in the Transcendental Aesthetic space is indeed thought as the form of the body's sensibility and receptivity, the fact namely that the bodily dimension of sensibility is constitutively integrated in Kant's presentation of space, explains why, in the first *Critique,* he does not need to mention the incongruent counterparts. That this text does not entail the argument of the incongruents has been considered surprising and puzzling by most interpreters.

58. This schematization distinguishes mechanistic causality from the "causality through freedom" belonging to practical philosophy.

59. AA II, 370,20–25.

60. KrV B 256/A 211.

61. KrV B 260/A 213. See by contrast Kant's account of the visions of the ghost-seer in terms of the illusory projection described by the optic notion of *focus imaginarius* (AA II, 344,5–7). See Longuenesse's discussion of the role played by our own body in the schematization of reciprocal action. Importantly, she refers back to §18 (B 140) and §19 (B 142) of the Deduction, claiming an association of the empirical unity of consciousness with the states of one's own body. Longuenesse rightly maintains that "our body appears to us as one substance among other substances, with which it is in a relation of dynamical community" (1998, 391–392). However, it seems to me that our body, in addition to being one substance among other substances, occupies a privileged "place" among them. For our eye, for example, is one of the extremes of the mediate community that we establish with other bodies by means of light; our body identifies the "place" in which we are located as the place that we can perceive as *ours*. It should also be noted that Kant's argument connects the possibility of locating our position to the capacity of "empirically changing place"—a movement that is immediately equated to the perception of change (B 260/A 213). Later phenomenology, from Merleau-Ponty to Lingis, will underline precisely the link between space, our body, and motricity.

62. Respectively KrV B 272/A 225 and KrV B 273/A 225.

63. KrV B 273/A 226—my emphasis.

64. Kant formulates his first argument against idealism in the *Nova Dilucidatio* (AA I, 411–412: against idealism, he concludes from the mind's internal changes to the existence of outer objects and, in particular, to the existence of *our own body*); he mentions the problem again in the 1770 *Dissertatio* (§11); in the first edition of the *Critique of Pure Reason*, the argument is significantly integrated into the "critique of the fourth paralogism of transcendental psychology" of the Dialectic (KrV A 370–371); in the 1783 *Prolegomena*, Kant re-visits the problem (§13, Remarks 2, 3: significantly, the argument against idealism is placed in two remarks to the section in which Kant discusses the incongruent counterparts and their necessary relation to the human body; see also §49, where the argument relates to the discussion of psychological ideas). In the 1787 preface to the first *Critique* Kant restates the formulation of the new Refutation of Idealism (KrV B xxxviii ff.). A series of later *Reflexionen* (the latest dating 1790) testifies of Kant's ongoing interest in the issue. Important is also the text *On Inner Sense*, found in the Saltykov-Shcedrin State Public Library, Leningrad and published for the first time in 1986 (by A. Gulyga, R. Brandt, and W. Strak in: *Voprosy Filosofii*, 4 (1986), 126–136; re-published in English translation in: *International Philosophical Quarterly*, 29, 3 (1989), 250–261, see also the essays by G. Zöller, Hoke Robinson, and M. Baum in the same issue). Historically, the addition of the Refutation in the 1787 *Critique* is explained by Kant's reaction to the attacks of the Garve-Feder review (*Göttingen gelehrte Anzeigen*, 1782). The review maintains that Kant's "transcendental idealism" is, in fact, a form of "subjective idealism." The *Prolegomena* are Kant's first answer to such criticism.

65. This premise is directly addressed in the argument against idealism of *Prolegomena* §13, Remarks 2–3.

66. Hoke Robinson (1981) relates the argument of the incongruent counterparts to the Refutation of Idealism. My suggestion, however, is that the argument of the Refutation needs, in addition, to take into account the itinerary of the *Dreams* which is, as I have shown, closely connected to the "Regions in Space." Hoke Robinson's is

one of the very few studies that link the Refutation to the issue of embodiment. (See also R. Hanna (2000), 167ff.; and Q. Cassam (1993).) The literature on the Refutation is vast. Here I limit myself to the following references: H. Vaihinger (1884); E. Förster (1985); M. Gram (1982); P. Guyer (1998a, 1983, 1987); M. Hymers (1991); R. Meerbote (1987); J. H. Tufts (1896); and J. Vogel (1993). In his reading of the Refutation in *Sein und Zeit* (1927, 204), Heidegger claims that Kant only apparently refutes Descartes's ontological claim; that he still maintains the ontic position of the "isolated subject"; and that time, not space, remains the ultimate springboard to infer the reality of the outer world. Although Heidegger recognizes that Kant may have proved the *"Zusammenvorhandensein von Physischem und Psychischem"*—of body and soul—his claim is that this "being given together" is ontologically and ontically entirely different from the structure of *In-der-Welt-Sein:* ultimately, the Refutation does not reach this structure and consequently does not overcome Descartes's dualism. In *Kant und das Problem der Metaphysik,* Heidegger recognizes that the Refutation overturns the relationship established by the Transcendental Aesthetic between space and time and wonders "whether *everything* in Kant's Critique would have to change because of this new emphasis on *outer* sense" (1973, 193; see also §§10, 35). I argue instead in favor of a continuity of views between the Aesthetic and the Refutation.

67. KrV B xxxix n. In *Prolegomena* §13, Remark 3 (AA IV, 293), Kant lays claim to the name of "transcendental idealism" against Descartes's "empirical" or "dreaming" idealism and Berkeley's *schwärmerisches* or "mystical idealism." To avoid further misunderstandings, Kant's corrects "transcendental" with "critical" idealism.

68. Kant points to the "ambiguity" of the expression "outside ourselves" in KrV A 373. For Kant's treatment of the topic in the Paralogisms see the following chapter.

69. KrV B 274.

70. KrV B 70–71, the section of the General Remarks to the Transcendental Aesthetic that explicitly alludes to Berkeley (III) is only in the second edition. For Kant's relation to Berkeley, see H. Allison (1993); C. Murray Turbayne (1969); and L. Falkenstein (1995).

71. KrV B 275. This is the double meaning of Kant's expression "ein Dasein *außer dem unsrige* durch unmittelbaren Erfahrung zu beweisen"—my emphasis.

72. In the footnote to the 1787 Preface, Kant refers to the new Refutation as the "only possible proof" against idealism (KrV B xxxix n.).

73. KrV B 274. The discussion is open in the literature as to whether or not Kant uses the Analogies of Experience in the proof of the Refutation. P. Strawson (1966, 126) and H. Allison (1983, 298) claim that the Refutation does rely on the Analogies; while J. Bennett (1966, 202–203) denies it. However, the important fact that the Refutation follows the Postulates and explicitly refers to their result goes completely unnoticed in the literature.

74. KrV B 275.

75. See the first remark of the Refutation, KrV B 276.

76. What exactly the "empirical [. . .] consciousness of my own existence" is becomes clear at the end of the proof.

77. KrV B xlii. *Prolegomena* §13, Remark 2 (AA IV, 288,35–289,1) insists on the claim that what is outside us is not representation but real object.

78. KrV B xxxix n.—my emphasis. The reference to the postulate, although unnoticed in the literature, is crucial to Kant's argument at this juncture. Kant talks of "perception" of something persisting, not simply of "representation" of something

persisting. This reference allows him to solve the problem to which Guyer refers (1998a, 313): why does time-determination require "anything other than an enduring self"?

79. KrV B 276/277—latter emphasis is mine. See Merleau-Ponty's cited claim that "a perceiving mind is an incarnated mind" (1964b, 3).

80. See KrV B 50/A 34.

81. KrV B xli.

82. KrV B 276.

83. KrV B 277. Kant's radical transformation of the Cartesian problem should be confronted with Husserl's and Heidegger's aporetic interpretations of the *cogito*—respectively phenomenological and metaphysical—in terms of intentionality and representation: see J. L. Marion's discussion in *Cartesian Questions* (1999, 97–102).

84. KrV B lx (my emphasis); B 278. On the other hand, Kant argues that even "outer imagination" is based on outer sense (see KrV B 266–267n.): if we did not have outer sense, and hence could not refer to real outer objects, we would not be able to imagine any content as placed outside ourselves. In this case, the "faculty of intuition" as such would be eliminated. *Reflexion* 5653 (AA XVIII, 308) explains that to reduce all intuition to inner intuition, i.e., time, would imply the elimination of all receptivity and, accordingly, of sensibility as such. The only "affection" possible would consequently be a sort of "self-affection," which, however, is impossible. See Marion's discussion of self-affection in the confrontation of Descartes and Kant (1999, 102–103).

85. Kant's final restatement in KrV B xl.

86. KrV B 277–278; B 291. For a discussion of the relation between time and space with regard to motion, see Guyer (1998a, 316–317). See *Nova Dilucidatio* for the use of motion to conclude from the mind's "internal change" to outside things that exist in mutual connection with our mind. Here Kant claims that "change of representations occurs in conformity with external motion" (AA I, 412,1).

87. AA IV, 483–484 (see previous chapter).

88. KrV B 291.

3. Disembodied Ideas

1. According to Max Wundt (1924, 162–164), Kant's reading of Plato dates back to 1769.

2. In a different (metaphysical) perspective, the theme of an essential "absence" disclosed by reason in the Dialectic is investigated by J. Sallis (2005, ch. 2).

3. See KrV B 277–278; B 399–400/A 341–342; and the discussion of the Refutation of Idealism in the previous chapter.

4. Respectively, *Dissertatio* §2, AA II, 391 and 392; see §§2, 28 for the adumbration of antinomy. (I make use, here and below, of the English translation of the *Dissertatio* in Beck (1986), but have modified the translation when necessary.) For the development of Kant's antinomies in relation to the *Dissertatio,* see N. Hinske (1970), 109–110.

5. I concentrate, in particular, on *Dissertatio* §2.

6. See the preface to the two editions of the *Critique of Pure Reason.*

7. See H. Heimsoeth (1965).

8. A. G. Baumgarten, *Metaphysica* (1757), the edition used by Kant: "mundus, quatenus sensitive repraesentatur, sensibilis [. . .], quatenus distincte cognoscitur, intelligibilis est."

9. *Dissertatio* §2, AA II, 329.

10. *Dreams,* AA II, 330—my emphasis.

11. *Dissertatio* §3, AA II, 392.

12. §3, AA II, 392—my emphasis.

13. *Reflexion* 4449, AA XVII, 555.

14. See the chapter "Von dem Grunde der Unterscheidung aller Gegenstände überhaupt" (KrV B294ff.).

15. *Dissertatio* §3, AA II, 392

16. §4, AA II, 392. For the difficulties in the translation of *sensualitas,* see Beck (1986), 188–189 n. 1.

17. §11, AA II, 397.

18. §11, AA II, 397.

19. §4, AA II, 393 Kant observes that "objects do not strike the senses through their form or configuration (*per formam seu speciem*)"—in other words, the "form" of sensible cognition is not, in turn, sensible. This will lead Kant to his later typical reasoning in terms of "conditions of possibility." But his notions of space and time in the *Dissertatio* could have been already brought back to that claim.

20. §4, AA II, 393—my emphasis.

21. §7, AA II, 394 (translation revised). In this connection we should recall Baumgarten's cited definition of *mundus sensibilis* and *mundus intelligibilis* in *Metaphysica* §869.

22. For the relation between this distinction and the *Critique of Pure Reason*'s distinction of "general logic" and "transcendental logic," see Beck's brief remarks in his introduction to *Kant's Latin Writings* (1986).

23. See §5, AA II, 393–394.

24. §3, AA II, 392.

25. *Reflexion* 6051, AA XVIII, 438—my emphasis.

26. *Dissertatio* §6, AA II, 394—my emphasis. This confirms what §5, AA II, 393 maintains in relation to sensible knowledge: *cognitiones sensitivae* "are called sensitive *on account of their origin (genesin),* not on account of any comparison as to identity and difference"—my emphasis.

27. §6, AA II, 394—my emphasis.

28. KrV B 1—my emphasis.

29. For a more general discussion of Kant's transformation of "innate" into "a priori" see G. Zoeller (1989).

30. §8, AA II, 395. Kant speaks of *actiones* of the intellect: §8, AA II, 395.

31. §7, AA II, 395.

32. §8, AA II, 395.

33. See *Dreams,* AA II, 367–368.

34. *Dissertatio* §9, AA II, 395–396—translation modified, my emphasis.

35. §7, AA II, 395.

36. *Dissertatio* §9, AA II, 396. For the role of the *Dissertatio* in the development of Kant's ethics, see J. Schmucker (1961).

37. *Dissertatio* §9, AA II, 396. See K. Reich (1964); see also A. Nuzzo (1995).

38. *Dissertatio* §9, AA II, 396n.

39. See Heimsoeth (1965), 352.

40. *Reflexion* 4447, AA XVII, 555.

41. *Dissertatio* §9, AA II, 396—my emphasis.

42. See KrV B 605: the representation of the *Inbegriff aller Realität* is not merely a concept which, in regard to its transcendental content, comprehends all predicates *under*

itself; it also contains them *within itself:* the "complete determination *(durchgängige Bestimmung)* of any and every thing *rests on the limitation of this total reality (auf der Einschränkung dieser All der Realität)"*—my emphasis; see B 606–607.

43. See KrV B 596 for the "ideal"; KrV B 38ff./A 23ff. for space as form of intuition.

44. *Dissertatio* §10, AA II, 396.

45. KrV B 9/A 5. The connection between intuition (sensibility) and reason by reference to Plato in this passage is discussed in J. Sallis (1987), 24–25. Sallis dwells on Kant's metaphors and on the shift from sensibility as "medium" to the need of finding a "ground upon which to take stand." My suggestion is that the body, transcendentally considered, functions for Kant both as medium and as (non-metaphysical) ground. There is indeed no tension in this shift.

46. See the polemic against *Schwärmerei* at the end of *Was heißt sich im Denken orientieren?* which deals precisely with the issue of "orientation" in all its forms—i.e., geographical, spatial, mathematical, and finally orientation in thought (see ch. 1, above). Sallis suggests that Kantian reason is deranged by imagination as a force that is "congenitally mad" (see the thesis of Sallis (1987) and (2005); see also J. Llewelyn (2000), 105–118). I think that starting from the pre-critical period Kant aims at saving reason from the madness of enthusiasm precisely by combating the metaphysical dualism of body and soul. It is certainly true that as long as metaphysics is reason's "peculiar fate" (KrV A vii) the risk of metaphysical derangement (or the dream of disembodied souls or ideas) remains. My claim, however, is that madness is not so much intrinsic to imagination as, rather, proper to any intellectual operation that pretends to abstract from the condition of embodiment.

47. *Dissertatio* §25, AA II, 413; *Reflexion* 4446, AA XVII, 556.

48. *Reflexion* 3917, AA XVII, 342. One should not be deceived by Kant's reference to *Vernunftideen* in this passage.

49. KrV B 596.

50. KrV B 597—my emphasis. See Reich (1964), 210; and Heimsoeth (1965), 352.

51. The expression *Metaphysik der Sitten* is already in Kant's letters of 1765. See for example Kant's letter to Lambert dated 2 September 1770.

52. Respectively, KrV B 371 and B 372.

53. *Dissertatio* §9, AA II, 396.

54. Reich (1964), 212. See Cicero's notion of the *vir bonus* in De officiis, book 3.

55. AA XX, 9: "Rousseaus Buch [i.e., the *Emile*] dient die Alten zu verbessern."

56. KrV B 397/A 339.

57. KrV B 805–806/A 777–778, B 691–692/A 663–664, B 697/A 669. This does not mean, however, that a different deduction of ideas can be provided. For the issue of "deduction," see D. Henrich (1989).

58. KrV B 672/A 644.

59. In KrV B 671/A 643 Kant insists that the issue regards the "use" of ideas not their ontological constitution. Deleuze famously positions his conception of ideas between Plato and Kant. See his interesting recognition of Kant's "problematization" of ideas beyond Plato and Platonism (1990, 53–54), and *Différence et répétition* for the view of ideas as "problems" (and individual objects as "solutions") and of the "problematic unity" of ideas (1968, ch. 4). Deleuze's view of ideas as problems is close to Kant's notion of *regulative* idea. For Deleuze, however, ideas do not belong to reason but are immanent within sensibility (remaining nonetheless supersensible). Deleuzian ideas are

constitutively embodied. See also Sallis (2005), 59: ideas are not inventions. For Sallis as well, Kantian ideas do not belong to reason alone: on his view, despite its apparent absence in the argument of the Dialectic, imagination plays a fundamental role in bringing forth reason's ideas.

60. *Dreams,* AA II, 344,5–7.

61. Significantly, Kant uses the image of the *focus imaginarius* in the *Critique of Pure Reason* with regard to the ideas of reason (KrV B 672/A 644).

62. KrV B 671/A 643; see also KU §27 for the sublime.

63. KrV B 673–674/A 645–646—my emphasis.

64. KrV B 371/A 315 n.

65. KrV B 358/A 301, for the opposition between *Kampfrichter* and *Gesetzgeber* see B 451–452/A 423–424; and KrV B 449/A 421. See B 439/A 465 for reason's "certainty" and "interest." In *The Gathering of Reason* Sallis discusses the inner "crisis" inherent in the Kantian project of "critique" in which reason is brought in front of a tribunal that is reason itself. Sallis questions the possibility for reason to open up within itself the "distance" necessary for constituting its own tribunal (2005, 2). The problem, however, is further complicated as the Dialectic shifts its metaphor from the tribunal to the legislation of reason.

66. KrV B 410; also B 426. For the present purposes, I restrict my analysis to this first step of the deduction of ideas. Also, I confine my consideration to the B version of the Paralogisms. A more detailed discussion of the problem can be found in A. Nuzzo (1995). See Sallis (2005), 63–96. For the different versions of the Paralogisms in the two editions of the *Critique,* see: the extensive study, K. Ameriks (2000)—where Ameriks also discusses the issue of embodiment in the Paralogisms (99ff.)—and his (1998); D. Sturma (1998); R. P. Horstmann (1993); P. Kitcher (1982b), and (1982a) which, with its attention to Hume and the first paralogism, complements my considerations in the present chapter. See also T. C. Powell (1990).

67. KrV B 409.

68. KrV B 561ff./A 533ff.

69. This argument is taken up again in the Canon of Pure Reason.

70. KrV B 400/A 342.

71. In the transcendental perspective, Kant explicitly replaces the "I" with "he" or "it" in order to point to the neutrality and impersonality of the "transcendental subject of thinking = x" (KrV B 404/A 346: "= A"). The difference between the claim, "I exist thinking," and the claim, "every thinking being exists," is the difference between an empirical and a metaphysical claim (B 420n., 422–423 with reference to Descartes). See W. Sellars (1970); and see also the historical connection that G. Zoeller (1992) draws between Kant and Lichtenberg in discussing the latter's claim equating "it thinks" to "it lightens." A more general account of the issue with regard to the transcendental deduction is in M. Baum (2002).

72. See KrV B 260/A 213 discussed in the previous chapter.

73. KrV B 409.

74. KrV B 405/A 347. In discussing Heidegger's and Husserl's reconstruction of the *cogito* in the aporetic terms of intentionality and representation, J.-L. Marion (1999, 97–103) indicates in Kant's radically anti-Cartesian position the alternative model: Kant disjoins "what Descartes intended in all rigor to conjoin" (p. 103). Kant's conclusion serves, as it were, as a sort of *reductio ad absurdum* of the intentional model of the I. All the *ego* can claim is an "empirical existence"; but since the "pure I" cannot be known,

the *ego* remains, on Marion's account, "alienated by itself from itself." The I is alienated because disjoined from its "primary status as origin" (102–103). My suggestion instead is that for Kant the I, as empirical I, is not alienated but simply embodied. That the finitude therein implied is "alienation" will be Fichte's and Hegel's later inference. It is not, however, Kant's position. Significantly, Kant's gesture of "disjoining" empirical and pure (or logical) I aims rather at *reconciling* the split of body and soul promoted by metaphysics.

75. KrV B 401–402/A 343–344.

76. KrV B 418.

77. KrV B 403/A 345. The topic of the soul as principle of life in matter and the idea of "animality" will be further discussed in part 3, with regard to the *Critique of Judgment*. For an interpretation of this Kantian passage with a focus on Hegel's treatment of the soul-body problem in the Psychology of the *Encyclopaedia*, see M. Wolff (1992, 125).

78. Respectively, KrV B 426 and B 428, 429—second emphasis is mine.

79. KrV B 431.

80. KrV B 420.

81. A faculty to which Kant immediately refers as a "marvelous faculty" (*bewunderungswürdiges Vermögen*): KrV B 431.

82. KrV B 430–431—my emphasis.

83. KrV B 420–421. See also *Preisschrift über die Fortschritte der Metaphysik,* AA XX, 309 where Kant claims that "all experience can occur only in life, i.e., when soul and body are still united"; to assume the contrary would mean to propose the impossible experiment of removing the soul from the body while one is still alive. This, Kant suggests, is the experiment that someone attempted "by standing before a mirror with closed eyes and, when asked what he was doing, replied: 'I just want to know what I look like when I sleep'." For the connection between embodiment and life, see Ameriks (2000), 99ff. See P. Strawson (1959), 115–116 for the conditions under which a disembodied pure consciousness can be thought: although Strawson logically allows for a disembodied individual existence, he concludes that "disembodied survival [. . .] may well seem unattractive. No doubt it is for this reason that the orthodox have wisely insisted on the resurrection of the body."

84. KrV B 421. Notice Kant's characterization of this "spiritualism" as *herumschwärmend* (KrV B 421). On Kant and psychology see the references at the beginning of the previous chapter.

85. See ch. 6 in particular.

86. See KrV B 422–423 n.

4. Bodies in Action

1. *Dreams,* AA II, 372–373.

2. AA II, 373.

3. See H. Heimsoeth (1966), who concentrates on the concept of freedom in the context of cosmology and hardly mentions its relation to psychology; Sadik J. Al-Azm (1972); and K. Kawamura (1996).

4. See, for example Kawamura (1996). Allison merely hints at the problem (1996a; 1996b, 36–37). See also K. Ameriks (2000), 194–196; and R. Pippin (1997).

5. See ch. 2, above. For the importance of the concept of *Welt* in the Dialectic with regard to the issue of embodiment (and the connection space-embodiment) as

sign of human finitude, see Heidegger's *Sein und Zeit* (1927), §§19–24, 23 in particular. The metaphysical concept of *mundus* is transformed in Heidegger's interpretation into the existential structure of *In-der-Welt-sein* (1927, 109) that Kant's transcendental perspective allegedly misses. For the antinomies as dealing with *Weltbegriffe,* see J. Sallis (2005), 97–98.

6. *Dissertatio* §1.

7. KrV B 425.

8. KrV B 426, 431.

9. KrV B 425, for the technical distinction to which Kant refers with the term "domain" see KU, E §II; for the close connection in which "experience," "existence," and "life" are defined in the present context see also B 420 where "experience" is "our existence in life."

10. KrV B 425. Recall the "noble constitution of the soul" in *Dreams,* AA II, 372–373.

11. KrV B 426—notice the expression: not idea *of* the world but world *in* the idea.

12. While in the *Dissertatio* the intelligible world can still be known by the understanding's "real use" (*usus realis*) independently of sensibility (§§5–6), starting from the *Reflections* of the second half of the 1770s the *mundus intelligibilis* is identified with the *mundus moralis* and all theoretical knowledge of it is in principle rejected (see *Reflexion* 4349).

13. KrV B 424: Kant speaks of principles "*des mit dem spekulativen verbundenen praktischen Vernunftgebrauchs.*"

14. KrV B 428ff., "General Remark Concerning the Transition from Rational Psychology to Cosmology."

15. KrV B 569/A 541.

16. See KrV B 157n. Kant rejects the possibility of designating the "act" of the "I think" as "*selbstätiges Wesen*" (see below). Analyzing the solution to the third antinomy, Adrian M. Piper makes a similar point by distinguishing a third-person perspective (that of the 'object') from a first-person perspective (that of the 'subject'), see Piper (1993), 202–203. The problem of the constitution of the moral subject (person) is, at the same time, Ricoeur's point of entry into Kant's moral philosophy and the issue that divides him from Kant (1992, 1–25). Ricoeur's distinction between the identity of the self as *idem* or *ipse* is construed following some of the important Kantian moves that we have been outlining. (*Idem* implies temporality instead of spatiality; *ipse* "implies no assertion concerning some unchanging core of the personality" (p. 2), which I take as a repetition/variation of Kant's argument against the metaphysical soul.) The argument of the present chapter counters Ricoeur's criticism according to which Kant gave exclusive attention to the *idem*-subject (sameness) against the *ipse*-subject (selfhood) at the price of missing the real subject of moral action. Importantly, the latter is, for Ricoeur, an embodied subject. (See Ricoeur's reference to Rembrandt's self-portrait as evidence that the body belongs to someone "capable of designating herself as the one whose body is hers." Ricoeur is indebted to Marcel for the notion of *corps propre* with which his opposition to Descartes's dualism is construed. No reference to Kant is made on this issue. See P. Anderson (1993).) My claim is that Kant is fully aware of the relation between selfhood and embodiment: the solution of the antinomy hinges precisely on this relation. The divergence between Kant and Ricoeur is methodological: transcendental versus narrative accounts of the moral self.

17. See KrV B 158 (§25)—the "*so wie . . .*" that puts the mere thought of myself and my thinking of external objects on the same plane.

18. KrV B 428–429.

19. KrV B 431; B 68 in the Transcendental Aesthetic, and B 157–158 in the Transcendental Deduction §25.

20. KrV B 431–432.

21. KrV B 430–431—my emphasis.

22. See KrV B 476/A 448 where both transitions (namely, from psychology to cosmology, and from the theoretical sphere to the practical issue of "imputability") are mentioned. For this passage and the notion of imputability as "original structure of a power of acting" recognized as "necessarily dialectical," see Ricoeur (1992), 103–105; (1995), 47–49.

23. KrV B 431.

24. Lingis's idea of an imperative in/of things that addresses our perception is indeed indebted to Levinas more than to Kant. Systematically, however, it can be seen as a development of the Kantian idea of receptivity to the moral imperative. See A. Lingis (1998), 63–68. See also Lyotard's notion of a "passivity without *pathos*, which is the opposite of either the controlled or the unconscious activity of the mind" (1988b, 19). Lyotard develops here a theme of the third *Critique* which is, however, already present in the connection we have been following so far. See also his idea of the spontaneity of prescription: "the Kantian argument is that prescriptive phrases [. . .] are themselves the cause of the acts they engender" (1988a, 119).

25. See KrV B 476/A 448. Kant rejects the view that the "transcendental idea of freedom" constitutes the empirical content of psychology. An historical reconstruction of the sources of Kant's notion of spontaneity in the Antinomies is in R. Finster (1982). More generally, see S. Rosen (2001).

26. See for example J. C. Gottsched (1734), vol. 1, §991; H. A. Meißner (1737); J. H. Zedler (1750), vol. 57, sp. 268–269.

27. G. W. Leibniz (1710), III, §290. See C. Wolff (1738), §933: "*Spontaneitas est principium sese ad agendum determinandi intrinsecum.*"

28. Wolff (1720), §518.

29. Wolff (1738), §941 for the definition of freedom, and §934 for the connection with sufficient reason.

30. A. G. Baumgarten (1757), §704.

31. For the notion of *Grundkraft* see C. A. Crusius (1745), §§70–78, §81; for a discussion of freedom and spontaneity, Crusius (1744), §§40–41.

32. J. N. Tetens (1777), see vol. 2, 21.

33. For Kant's relation to Crusius, see M. Wundt (1924); A. Marquardt (1885); S. Carboncini (1981), 182–239; Finster (1982).

34. *Nova dilucidatio*, AA I, 393: "*Determinare autem cum sit ita ponere, ut omne oppositum excludatur, denotat id, quod certo sufficit ad rem ita, non aliter, concipiendam.*"

35. AA I, 402: "*Spontaneitas est actio a principio interno profecta.*" See Wolff (1738), §933; (1720), §§511–521.

36. *Fortschritte der Metaphysik*, AA XX, 268,13.

37. KrV B 74–75/A 50–51, B 93/A 68. As middle and mediating function between understanding and sensibility, imagination here finds its place. While the theme of imagination has been stressed in the immediate post-Kantian tradition, it is Heidegger's first Kant book that has brought transcendental imagination to the foreground in

contemporary philosophy along with the thesis of the "common root" of our mental faculties and the primacy of time. (See for example J. Llewelyn (2000): imagination is "hypo-Critical" for "it is prior to the opposition of sensibility and understanding" (p. 8), and see his discussions of Heidegger and Sallis in chaps. 2 and 6. For a hermeneutic reading of Kantian imagination: R. Makkreel (1990), 20–42.) Departing from this tradition, the concept of "transcendental embodiment" intends to maintain the radical separation between sensibility and understanding and yet to show their 'collaborative' work in the transcendental perspective. This may be regarded as the gesture that, in giving sensibility (and space) more relevance, confines imagination to a lesser role. I suggest that imagination may have gained the central stage in the literature simply because Kant's concept of sensibility has not been sufficiently appreciated. My aim is indirectly confirmed by Sallis's philosophical project. He draws the imagination to the center but also significantly departs from Kant's transcendentalism. Sallis's longstanding attention to imagination (from his 1980 *The Gathering of Reason* to the 2000 *Force of Imagination*) can be seen as an itinerary that starts with Kant but leads, as it were, to a radically non-Kantian position. (A position which is difficult to define: rather Nietzschean or Heideggerian, or phenomenological, or even pre-Socratic.) Sallis's project is to free imagination from the distinction of intelligible and sensible and to think of it differently than in terms of the subject's faculties (see Sallis (2005), 175): imagination becomes a "force." Within Kant's transcendental perspective, instead, imagination cannot display the role that contemporary philosophy claims for it.

38. KrV B 93/A 68: the "function" on which concepts rest is here opposed to the "affection" on which sensible intuitions rest; B 151–152: "Ausübung der Spontaneität."

39. KrV B 103/A 77. For the following considerations see G. Gigliotti (1995), 258–259; on spontaneity as synthesis and the role of apperception, see Pippin (1997).

40. *Reflexion* 3586 (dated by Adickes at the end of the 1770s/beginning of the 1780s).

41. KrV B 152.

42. KrV B 130: "Verbindung (*conjunctio*)" is "Actus der Spontaneität der Vorstellungskraft"; B 131 "Verbindung" is "Actus" of the subject's "Selbsttätigkeit"; B 132, B 157n.

43. *Reflexion* 3586: "The *possibility* of action is the capacity [or faculty (*Vermögen*)]. The inner *sufficient ground* of action is force (*Kraft*)" (my emphasis). Sallis's conception of imagination as "force" (2000b) may be contrasted with this Kantian position.

44. KrV B 158.

45. See KrV B 68: the manifold is "given in the Gemüt *without spontaneity*"—my emphasis.

46. KrV B 158—my emphasis.

47. See B. Centi (2002), 51–52.

48. KrV B 102/A 77—my emphasis; see *Prolegomena* §8.

49. KrV B 132.

50. KrV 423n.—my emphasis.

51. KrV B 157n.: I can "call myself *Intelligenz*" but this is not properly a "determination" of myself.

52. KrV B 474/A 446. In the present discussion, my interest is focused on Kant's solution of the antinomy rather than on its formulation. The literature on the third antinomy is immense. Historical reconstructions can be found in: H. Heimsoeth (1966); N. Hinske (1972); S. Al-Azm (1972); and K. Kawamura (1996). Recent textual analyses

and bibliographical information in: L. Kreimendahl (1998); E. Watkins (1998); H. Allison (1998); and J. Sallis (2005), 97–124. For the early reception of Kant's argument, see A. Nuzzo (2001).

53. KrV B 473/A 445. It is precisely for this issue of absolute beginning that transcendental freedom is crucial to the cosmological antinomy regarding the possibility of a beginning or "origin of the world" (KrV B 476/A 448). In the remark to the thesis, Kant insists that the "absolute first beginning" at stake here is not an absolute beginning "in time but in causality" (B 478/A 450); a similar point is made in the antithesis by distinguishing what is "mathematically" and what is "dynamically" first (B 477/A 449). See Ricoeur's comment on this passage in (1992), 105; and see (1995), 47–57 for the importance of Kant's connection between the "beginning of the world" (cosmology) and the "beginning in the world" (freedom).

54. KrV B 475/A 447; also B 476/A 448.

55. KrV B 518/A 490 title.

56. See KrV B 519/A 491 and footnote.

57. Or, which is the same, if we assume that space and time are not transcendental forms of our sensibility but properties of things in themselves.

58. Wolff (1738), §933. See R. Goclenius's influential *Lexicon philosophicum* (1613), 1080–1081, s.v. *sponte*: "*Ignis per se ipse ac sua sponte movetur, consumptus sua sponte extinguitur.*"

59. *Reflexion* 4094, on Baumgarten (1757), §392. Here the idealist is opposed to the "egoist."

60. KrV B 521/A 493; also B 524/A 496. Notice that Kant does not say, 'since we cannot intuit this cause in space and time, we cannot know it as an object,' but the reverse: 'since we cannot know the non-sensible cause, we cannot intuit it as object.' For, we can still think of it as transcendental subject of action.

61. KrV B 522/A 493.

62. KrV B 521/A 493.

63. KrV B 560/A 532. The shift from the transcendental *object* to the transcendental *subject* corresponds to what Ricoeur indicates as the move from the "description of 'what'?" to the "ascription to a 'who'?" (1992, 106)—the latter indicating the subject as moral responsible agent.

64. KrV B 561/A 533—my emphasis in the latter passage.

65. KrV B 561/A 533: "*Es ist überhaupt merkwürdig, dass auf diese transzendentale Idee der Freiheit sich der praktische Begriff derselben gründe.*" See B 562/A 534; B 564–565/A 536–537 for the consequence of denying transcendental freedom.

66. See above for the "exercise" of thinking's spontaneity in the cognitive process.

67. Kant suggests that the solution of the third antinomy does not prove the "*reality* (*Wirklichkeit*) of freedom" but only its "*possibility*" (KrV B 585–586/A 557–558); it is the task of the *Critique of Practical Reason* to show that pure reason can be practical.

68. In any event, the human will is not purely "intellectual" (as the divine will would be): see for example *Reflexionen* 4226, 4227.

69. KrV B 562/A 534; B 830/A 802. The important difference between action and cognition, however, is that no a priori form of sensible affection can be detected in the *arbitrium brutum*.

70. See Wolff (1738), §933.

71. KrV B 562/A 534—my emphasis.

72. KrV B 561/A 532; B 563/A 535.

73. See KrV B 561/A 533.

74. *Reflexion* 5618; 5616 for *libertas hybrida*. Kant presents the human will as "indeterminate" (as opposed to the divine will which is always determinate). See, for example, *Reflexionen* 4226 and 4227: the human will is neither "entirely intellectual" nor "entirely sensible"; rather, it is "in part sensible and in part intellectual so that sensibility cannot render passive the *intellectuale*."

75. KrV B 569/A 541.

76. KrV B 562/A 534. In discussing Kant's idea of freedom as absolute spontaneity or new beginning, Arendt underscores the difficulty of thinking freedom at the same time as spontaneity and as worldly phenomenon (1961, 169; 1978, vol. 2, 146). However, Arendt's insistence on the groundless nature of freedom (1978, vol. 2, 196) points rather in the direction of Schelling's 1809 *Freiheitsschrift*. See the comparison Kant/Arendt/Sartre on the "abyss of freedom" in S. H. Watson (1997), 91ff. In Arendt's thought, Kant's spontaneity, mediated through Heidegger, influences her (ontological) idea of "natality" as condition of freedom. Natality is a radical new beginning that interrupts natural processes (see, for example, Arendt (2005), 113). For the relation between absolute spontaneity and "beginning *in* the world" see Ricoeur (1992), 105.

77. KrV B 522/A 494 to be read together with B 565/A 537.

78. Respectively, KrV B 566/A 538—my emphasis; and B 567/A 539. For a thorough discussion of the notion of "character" in connection with practical issues—which I address in the following two chapters—see F. Munzel (1999); H. Heimsoeth (1973); K. Coble (2003); H. Allison (1996b), ch. 2; and S. Landucci (1994), ch. 5. Kant's notion of "intelligible character" is critically appraised from a Levinasian perspective in C. Chalier (2002), 110–131. (Chalier, however, refers exclusively to the second *Critique;* this may explain why she does not consider "character" in the perspective of the antinomies of the first *Critique*. The background of her discussion is rather a theological one; see p. 114 of her volume for a theological definition of character.)

79. KrV B 431: "*bewunderungswürdiges Vermögen*."

80. KrV B 566/A 538. It is essential to Kant's theory of the sensible/intelligible character that this distinction as well as its being predicated of one and the same subject applies specifically (and exclusively) to the human being as a being whose will is *arbitrium sensitivum* and yet *liberum*. See Ricoeur's interesting interpretation of Kant's "character" (as effect of the intelligible cause within appearance or as the "union of thesis and antithesis" in a phenomenon typical of the practical field) as "initiative": "initiative [. . .] is an intervention of the agent of action in the course of the world, an intervention which effectively causes changes in the world" (1992, 109). See also in "The Initiative" (1991, 215), the Kantian reference to the two "characters" is replaced by the mediating function of the body; and "Explanation and Understanding" (1991, 137). Ricoeur's interest for the idea of character (in a perspective at once Aristotelian and Kantian) goes back to *Fallible Man* (1986).

81. KrV B 522/A 493.

82. KrV B 573/A 545; B 567/A 539; B 568/A 540 establishes a correlation ("*so wie wir überhaupt einen transcendentalen Gegenstand den Erscheinungen im Gedanke zum Grunde legen müssen*") between the thought of the transcendental subject and the idea of the subject's intelligible character.

83. KrV B 567/A 539—my emphasis. Thereby Kant suggests that the transcendental subject may be known mediatedly or indirectly. The question is: *how* does this knowledge take place? The issue is addressed in discussing the relation between sensible and intelligible character (see below).

84. KrV B 567/A 539.

85. KrV B 157n.: *Intelligenz*. Following Ricoeur's suggestion (1992, 106), the practical problem is a problem of "ascription" of action to a "who" (not of "description" of natural events or a "what"). Unlike "intelligence," "intelligible character" fulfills precisely this function.

86. KrV B 568/A 540.

87. See the definition in KrV B 566/A 538. For an interpretation of Kant's "intelligible character" in a non-noumenal sense (as *Denkungsart*), see Coble (2003), 66n16; and Munzel (1999), xvi.

88. KrV B 157n.

89. KrV B 569/A 541; B 582/A 554. For an analysis of this passage, see Adrian M. Piper (2001); for an interpretation of Kant's freedom as "relative first beginning" see Ricoeur (1992), 105–107. Further consequences of this dynamic view are examined by Coble (2003), who, however, does not take the passage of the first *Critique* into account and is primarily concerned with the text of the *Religion Within the Limits of Reason Alone*.

90. In the acting subject as "noumenon," "nothing happens, no transformation takes place that implies a dynamic time-determination" (KrV B569/A 541).

91. See KrV B 571/A 543, B 582/A 554.

92. KrV B 579–580/A 551–552.

93. KrV B 571/A 543.

94. KrV B 574/A 546: "Laß uns dieses auf Erfahrung anwenden."

95. KrV B 572–573/A 544–545.

96. KrV B 573/A 545.

97. KrV B 574/A 546.

98. See KrV B 567/A 539: the intelligible character can never be "immediately known" by us; and B 569/A 541 for the mediation (*vermittelst*) of the empirical character.

99. See KrV B 578/A 550. See chaps. 8 and 9, below, for Kant's rejection of observation and physiology, which he opposes to his transcendental investigation.

100. Kant's argument counters Wolff's idea of spontaneity as internal determination on all fronts. In *Psychologia empirica* (1738, §933 Remark), after having defined *spontaneitas* as "*principium sese ad agendum determinandi intrinsecum*" Wolff adds, referring to Aristotle, that such internal determination can be met in inanimate things as well as in brute animals.

101. KrV B 574–575/A 546–547. It is reason, not understanding, to serve Kant's argument. At stake in this difficult passage is the transition from speculative reason to practical reason. A similar appeal to the spontaneity of the cognitive faculties to ground practical freedom is in the last chapter of the *Grundlegung zur Metaphysik der Sitten;* see D. Henrich (1998).

102. KrV B 578/A 550.

103. KrV B 575/A 547.

104. The discussion of this claim in the *Critique of Practical Reason* occupies the next chapter. For Kant's caution in presenting this proposition in the first *Critique,* see KrV B 575/A 547: "That this reason has indeed causality, or *that we at least represent it to ourselves as having causality*" (my emphasis); B 576–577/A 548–549: "Now, let us take our stand, and *regard it at least as possible* for reason to have real causality with regard to appearances" (my emphasis); and B 579/A 551: "Given that one could say: reason has causality with regard to appearances [. . .]." See P. Guyer (1989).

105. KrV B 576/A 548—my emphasis. With regard, more directly, to the practical context, Lingis challenges the Kantian idea of a moral order of reason really distinct from the theoretical, claiming that ultimately Kant derives the order of the moral law from logic (1998, 207, 209).

106. AA XXIII, 43–50.

107. KrV B 577/A 549—my emphasis.

108. See KrV B 578/A 550.

109. Respectively, KrV B 569/A 541 (1), B 574/A 546 (2–3), B 579/A 551 (2–3), B 581/A 553 (4). See *Reflexion* 5612 for the schematization of intelligible actions in the world of appearances: herein Kant notices that the word *Erscheinung* "means already schema." I come back to these propositions in ch. 6, below. Lyotard (1988a, 127) elaborates on Kant's suggestion that sensible character is sign of the intelligible commenting: "causality through freedom gives *signs,* never ascertainable *effects*"; and elaborates: "As sign, the ethical phrase is without a sequel, and thus final"—thereby deepening, if possible, the separation between the cognitive and moral sphere proposed by Kant himself. In his 1980 work *The Gathering of Reason,* Sallis claims that reason requires imagination (and its schematism) to lend plausibility, reality, and efficacy to ideas: see Sallis (2005). Freydberg (2005) develops Sallis's argument with regard to the second *Critique.*

5. Pure Practical Reason and the Reason of Human Desire

1. KpV A 4 (AA V, 3); the concept of freedom is instead *"Stein des Anstosses"* or "stumbling block" for all empiricist account of ethics (KpV A 13; AA V, 7).

2. KpV A 9 (AA V, 6).

3. KrV B 567/A 539, discussed in the previous chapter.

4. See KrV B 562/A 534; KpV A 51, 58 (AA V, 29, 33).

5. KpV A 15 (AA V, 8)—my emphasis.

6. KpV A 9, 10n. (AA V, 6); KrV B 574ff./A 546ff., extensively discussed in the previous chapter.

7. The transcendental structure is the condition under which alone the issue of "human nature" can be raised. See, by contrast, the way in which Kant still argues in the early *Beobachtungen über das Gefühl des Schönen und Erhabenen* (1764): herein the notion of moral obligation and moral value is tied directly to the anthropological doctrine of the "temperaments." For an assessment of the development of Kant's theory with regard to the separation between anthropological and purely moral concerns, see J. Edwards (2000), 429–430. The separation between moral anthropology and transcendental philosophy continues to influence today's reading and appropriation of Kant's ethics (for example Ricoeur's appreciation of Kant's anthropology in the aftermath of Hegel's *Phenomenology* and Weil's reading of it—discussed in P. Anderson (1993), 9, 21–22).

8. Respectively *Groundwork,* XII (AA IV, 390)—my emphasis; and 59 (AA IV, 425)—emphasis in the original.

9. KpV A 10 (AA V, 6).

10. Nor, as should be clear by now, is it a metaphysical issue.

11. Consequently, is neither a racially characterized body nor a gendered body as many recent critiques of Kant's practical philosophy claim. See for example the attacks by R. Bernasconi (2001, 2002); C. Mills (1997), 69ff.; and E. C. Eze (1995). See the more balanced account by T. E. Hill, Jr., and B. Boxill (2001), 460, 468; for a feminist critique, see for example R. M. Schott (1988); and C. Battersby (1998). None of these essays con-

siders the specificity of the *transcendental* perspective proper to the second *Critique*. (The problem is present to Eze but he, however, is unable to draw the distinction between the pre-critical, non-transcendental *Observations* and the *Critiques*.) Extremely fruitful, instead, is the perspective of Adrian M. Piper (1993).

12. The criticism of Kant's pure ethics is a *locus communis* since Weber's attack on *Gesinnungsethik*'s otherworldly purity and detachment from the concrete scene of moral decision; in particular see his *Politik als Beruf* (1919). In the history of the interpretation of Kant's ethics this criticism has worked in different ways—from the charge of formalism to that of rigorism, and to the rejection of Kant's allegedly over-strict and impracticable moral standard. More recently, however, a defense of Kantian ethics has been persuasively attempted by O. O'Neill (1989) and B. Herman (1993, 1983), who show that Kant's requirement "from duty" operating as a higher order moral principle is compatible with a variety of feelings and emotions. My work in this part of the book follows their line of argument. See also P. Guyer, "Duty and Inclination" (1996, 335–393); A. Reath (1989); and K. Ameriks (1987). Further literature is discussed in the next chapter. The critique of pure ethics in Kant's scholarship is complemented by different philosophical attempts (ranging from the Heideggerian to the phenomenological tradition, from Arendt to Ricoeur and from Levinas to Lingis) to develop specific motives of Kantian ethics that are viewed as exceptions or even contradictions within Kant's transcendental theory. The ideas of personality, dignity, and respect as feeling, the schematism of practical reason and the notion of reason's temporality, are all examples of Kantian themes that contemporary philosophy often uses against Kant's formalism. My aim in these chapters is to show the fundamental coherence of Kant's ethics on the basis of its transcendental foundation. The reconstruction of Kant's moral theory in the light of the notion of transcendental embodiment proves not only that there is no tension between practical reason and the idea of respect or moral feeling, but that the latter owe their force only to the former.

13. KpV A 277 (AA V, 155).

14. *Groundwork*, XVI (AA IV, 392).

15. KpV A 269 (AA V, 151).

16. KpV A 277 (AA V, 155)—the second emphasis is mine. The connection between the topic of the second *Critique* and the left/right hand distinction is overlooked in the literature and may indeed seem surprising and hard to explain without the context of transcendental embodiment.

17. See KpV A 52–53 (AA V, 29).

18. See KpV A 55–56 (AA V, 31); A 56: "*Faktum der Verununft.*"

19. KpV A 56 (AA V, 31)—my emphasis: "sich für sich selbst uns aufdringt." In his Reflections of the 1770s, Kant still advocates a form of "internal intellectual intuition" as means through which freedom is disclosed to us (see *Reflexion* 4336, AA XVII, 509; *Reflexion* 6860, AA XIX, 183; *Reflexion* 5440, AA XVIII, 182). See in general J. Schmucker (1961); and specifically G. Mohr (1988), 294–295.

20. KpV A 277 (AA V, 155).

21. See KpV A 210 (AA V, 116). For a different way of drawing the limits of Kant's "moral space" see Lingis's following passage, which, maintaining the rationality/sensibility opposition that dominates the literature, empties such space of all sensibility: "The movement in Kant is from the fact of the moral imperative, the fact that our nature ought to become totally rational, to the constitution of the rationally ordered world, as the context or field for such a nature to operate" (1989, 39–40). On my ac-

count, the "moral space" is, on the contrary, the space of a practical form of transcendental embodiment that lends pure practical reason its phenomenical efficacy: the fact of morality and the constitution of the moral world take place in the same "space." The attention to reason's "spacings" is also in Sallis's *Spacings of Reason and Imagination in Texts of Kant, Fichte, Hegel* (1987, esp. chaps. 2–3). Unlike Sallis, however, my focus is neither textuality nor the metaphoric of space but the space that sensibility transcendentally offers to reason as condition for its activity. Moreover, my insistence on space intends to counter-balance the exclusive interest in time that the scholarship generally manifests with regard to practical reason. Finally, see J.-L. Nancy, *L'expérience de la liberté* (1988), ch. 13 for the interplay "space of freedom"/"free space" (with reference to Arendt and Heidegger). Despite the differences, I am sympathetic to the view that the space of freedom is the "general form" or "place" that *makes* individual events *happen*.

22. KpV A 56 (AA V, 31).

23. KrV B 425. See the important suggestion of KU E §II, in which Kant sketches his geography of the human mind. One of its components is the "*Gebiet (ditio)*"; see my *Kant and the Unity of Reason* (2005), 125–145.

24. KpV A 10 (AA V, 6).

25. *Was heißt sich im Denken Orientieren?* A311. For this work, see the historical perspectives on post-Kantian philosophy in B. Jensen (2003) and A. Philonenko (1983).

26. *Was heißt?* A309.

27. *Was heißt?* A306.

28. *Was heißt?* A307–308.

29. See Heidegger's reading of this passage in *Sein und Zeit* §23, and our comment in ch. 1, above.

30. *Was heißt?* A311. The contrast between light and darkness characterizes the problem of knowledge already in the *Dreams*. To these examples we can add the "half-light with which the dim torch of metaphysics reveals the realm of shades" (*Dreams*, AA II, 329). The pedagogical idea of forming the habit of orientation in the darkness of the night is in Rousseau's *Emile* (1939, 139).

31. The image of darkness and the task of walking through the darkness of the night is in a fundamental Enlightenment manifesto such as the article "Philosoph" (probably by César Chesnau Dumarsais) of Diderot's *Encyclopédie* (1765, see XII, 509) where the difference between the philosopher and the ordinary man is drawn in the following way: "Other men are carried away by their passions; their actions are not preceded by reflection; *they are men who walk in darkness*. A philosopher, on the other hand, even in moments of passion, acts only according to reflection; *he walks through the night, but he is preceded by a torch*" (my emphasis). Notice that it is a common human predicament to be condemned to night's darkness. The interplay of darkness and light characterizes an epistemological situation often encountered in the rationalist debate of the seventeenth century; see C. Wilson, "Discourses of Vision in Seventeenth-Century Metaphysics" (1997).

32. *Was heißt?* A309: "ganz und gar kein Objekt der Anschauung, *sondern bloß Raum für dieselbe* findet"—my emphasis.

33. *Was heißt?* A309.

34. *Was heißt?* A310—my emphasis: "das Gefühl des der Vernunft eigenen *Bedürfnisses*."

35. KpV A 257 (AA V, 142).

36. See KpV A 259 (AA V, 143) and *Was heißt?* A 311–313.

37. Kant distinguishes between the need that reason has, respectively, "in its theoretical" and "in its practical use": *Was heißt?* A315. An analogous distinction is in KpV A 255–256 (AA V, 141–142): the need of speculative reason leads to "hypotheses," that of pure practical reason leads to "postulates." Here I concentrate on the practical use of reason; as for reason's need in its theoretical use, Kant shows its nature in the Dialectic of the first *Critique.* For reason's "right": *Was heißt?* A310–311.

38. *Was heißt?* A316. Considering the legal origin of Kant's problem of "deduction" (as quest for the legitimacy of a certain use of concepts), and the impossibility of a deduction of reason's ideas in the first *Critique,* the vocabulary of "right" introduced in 1786 is no surprise. It rather confirms the argument that Kant fully pursues in the *Critique of Practical Reason* with the doctrine of the postulates. This doctrine offers the deduction that could not be provided for speculative reason.

39. The means of orientation must be searched "in reason alone" (*Was heißt?* A317).

40. See the cited KpV 257 (AA V, 142).

41. *Was heißt?* A322. See KpV A 259 (AA V, 143) and Kant's discussion with Wizenmann for the difference between "need of reason" and empirical need based on mere inclination and desire.

42. See for example *Metaphysical Principles of the Doctrine of Virtue,* Introduction, §XII, AA VI, 399.

43. *Was heißt?* A316 and n. (my emphasis); for the discussion of Kant's notion of "moral feeling," see below. The connection between moral law and feeling of respect in the second *Critique* is the topic of the next chapter.

44. KpV A 259 (AA V, 143).

45. KpV A 289 (AA V, 161)—my emphasis.

46. One could repeat, on another plane, the remark with which Kant, in the *Dreams,* compares the capacity of seeing the "invisible world" to the gift with which "Juno honored Tiresias: she first made him blind, so that she could grant him the gift of prophecy" (AA II, 341).

47. Hence the body's physical features of race or sex do not count as discriminating who is a moral agent. I have developed this argument in "Transcendental Bodies— Women's Bodies?" (forthcoming). The light that the moral space finally enjoys can be opposed to the illusionary "brightest light" that characterizes Swedenborg's visions (*Dreams,* AA II, 364).

48. Thereby I correct Mohr's exclusive insistence on Kant's concerns with the 'materialism without soul' (1988).

49. The subject of the *Critique of Judgment* faces a new peculiar problem of orientation, which regards, this time, the "labyrinth" of nature's particular laws. See my *Kant and the Unity of Reason* (2005), 162–205; and ch. 7, below.

50. For Kant even the general determination of the "sensible" and the "intelligible" world is predicated upon the position that things have with regard to ourselves, namely, respectively, to our sensibility and to our understanding, see AA XXVIII, 1268 (1784 lecture-course). This is, more generally, a crucial feature of Kant's transcendental perspective. In his phenomenological investigation, Lingis endorses a similar view, linking the force of the imperative to the sensibility incarnate in the "postural schema" of our body (1998, 67). Significantly, however, Lingis presents this view as a *correction* of Kant's transcendentalism—in my view it is, instead, a fundamental component of it.

51. KpV A 9–10 (AA V, 6).

52. Thus, my reconstruction of the constitution of moral space in the *Critique of Practical Reason* finds its exact confirmation in KU E §II. Herein Kant draws a "geography" of the human mind that attributes a legislation over the domain of a "world" only to the understanding and practical reason, not to the faculty of judgment. See Heidegger's critique of Kant in *Sein und Zeit* (1927), §23 (citing the dark room example): Kant is unable to "see" the existential structure of the *In-der-Welt-sein*, which on Heidegger's account, should be already given or presupposed for orientation to be possible.

53. KpV A 289 (AA V, 161)—my emphasis.

54. See also *Grundlegung*, AB 26, (AA IV, 407: actions are visible but their inner principles are invisible). In the *Phaedo* (79a, 80d, 81a,c) and *Gorgias* (493b4–5), Plato distinguishes the two kinds of existence (*eides*) of the visible and the invisible (*aiedes*) and classifies the body in the first and the soul in the second class. R. Brague notices the interesting combination that arises by using the adjective *aiedes* as epithet of *eidos* and renders it with "an invisible visage" (2002, 46). This expression, I suggest, can be used to characterize the embodied moral agent within the *transcendental* perspective of Kant's philosophy. Many are the suggestions that this distinction (not primarily Kantian) has produced in twentieth-century philosophy (see only M. Merleau-Ponty, *Le visible et l'invisible* (1964c), Notes de travail, 282–283).

55. See KrV B 420, 426 discussed at the end of ch. 3.

56. For the reference to "animality" see, again, KrV B 403/A 345 discussed in ch. 3.

57. KpV A 54 (AA V, 30). Following Sallis's suggestion, this is indeed a point where the "spacing" of the moral space imposes an order on textuality.

58. KpV A 53 (AA V, 30).

59. My claim regards the possibility of discovering a specific transcendental function for sensibility within Kant's ethics. To this extent, I address an issue that is different from—although connected to—the question of whether Kant's ethical rigorism simply discards emotion and desire or rather somehow takes emotion and desire into account. My suggestion is that to answer this problem the meaning of sensibility in Kant's transcendental philosophy should first be investigated. For Kant allows for both merely pathological feelings and a pure moral feeling. The secondary literature on this issue is not as extensive as the literature on all other aspects of Kant's moral philosophy, although recently it has begun to draw more attention. See, however, Guyer's "Duty and Inclination" in (1996). My present analysis is concerned with providing the theoretical justification for the claim that the "aesthetics" of the second *Critique* is constitutive of Kant's moral philosophy, and yet that this part *must follow* the derivation of the highest principle of morality. A closer examination of the issue of feeling and inclination and a discussion of the relevant literature is in the following chapter.

60. For Kant's polemic against Wolff's *reductio ad unum* of the faculties of the mind, see KU E§II with regard to the impossibility of a "transition" between sensible and intelligible world (also KrV B 29/A 15), and the formulation of EE§III, AA XX, 206,1–8 (Wolff's task of "bringing unity in this multiplicity of faculties is futile"). Wolff's reduction of all faculties to *vis repraesentativa* presupposes Leibniz's notion of substance as representative force. Kant rejects this position by claiming that force is not inherent to substance but to its accidents, so that a simple substance, as the soul, can very well have manifold accidents. Against dogmatic metaphysics, Kant does not hypostatize forces or faculties of the soul but sees them as "functions that are dynamically actualized"; see H. Mertens (1975), 65; and D. Henrich, "On the Unity of

Subjectivity" in (1994), 17–54, 20–27. Against Wolff, Kant refers to the most recent results of contemporary German aesthetics and psychology, which already claimed the impossibility of reducing feeling to the cognitive faculty. Rüdiger, Crusius, Sulzer, Tetens, and Mendelssohn must be mentioned in this connection. (The importance of Crusius is stressed in Henrich (1994); and H. Heimsoeth, "Metaphysik und Kritik bei Ch. A. Crusius" in (1956), 125–188.)

61. *Grundlegung,* AB xiii–xiv (AA IV, 391).

62. KpV A 3 (AA V, 3). Ricoeur sees in this question the epoch-making question of Kantian philosophy. He considers the concept of practical reason or the idea that reason is "practical" as "essentially surmountable, although unavoidable" (1991, 198).

63. KpV A 35 (AA V, 19).

64. This continuity is still claimed in 1786 when the *Allgemeine Literaturzeitung* (*ALZ,* Jena, 21 November 1786), announcing the second edition of the *Critique of Pure Reason,* anticipates that this edition would entail a "critique of pure practical reason" as well. Evidently, at some point during the year 1786, Kant realized that the two critiques had indeed opposite tasks (their "parallelism" is only illusory: KpV A3 (AA V, 3): "*scheint*").

65. See KrV B 561/A 533.

66. KpV A 53–54 (AA V, 30).

67. See KpV A 32; 96 (AA V, 16, 55).

68. KpV A 80–81 (AA V, 46). In both the published introduction and the *First Introduction* to the *Critique of Judgment,* Kant further develops his distinction (already in KrV B ix–x).

69. KpV A 36 (AA V, 20).

70. See S. Landucci (1993), 41. For a suggestion in this direction—although too brief and sketched only *en passant*—see J. Butler (1987), 3. See also M. Henry's distinction between sensibility and "affectivity" (feeling of respect) in his claim that rationality is grounded in affectivity (1963, 833). While I try to show that pure practical reason is not opposed to desire but is itself conjoined with a pure form of desire and affection (pure practical reason is effective in a transcendental body), the dichotomy between reason and desire is the basis of Ricoeur's rejection of the formalism of Kant's practical reason and of his leaning rather toward Aristotle and Hegel (1991, 198ff.).

71. KpV §3 Remark I.

72. KpV §3 Remark I A 42 (AA V, 24); A 41ff. (AA V, 23ff.).

73. KpV A 41 (AA V, 23).

74. See the previous chapter. For the distinction between determination and causation, see Piper (1993), 198: she renders the theoretical meaning of *Bestimmen* as "to specify" and "to instantiate."

75. KpV A 44–45 (AA V, 24–25).

76. KpV A 52–53 (AA V, 29).

77. KpV A 3 (AA V, 3): "Sie soll bloß dartun, *daß es reine praktische Vernunft gebe.*"

78. See D. Henrich (1960).

79. See KpV A 15 (AA V, 8), for the "*Beschaffenheit*" according to which the human being is "*wirklich.*"

80. KpV A 3 (AA V, 3). *Factum* has the same relation to *facere* that *Wirken* has to *Wirklichkeit.* In the practical sphere, the proof of the reality of a concept is provided by the action that produces it or makes it real.

81. KpV A 72 (AA V, 42). Among the many interpretations of and variations on the *Faktum der Vernunft* (ranging from Fichte's idea of moral consciousness to Heidegger's *Gewissen* in *Sein und Zeit*), see Ricoeur for whom the *Faktum* "bears witness to the practical status of the free will" (1991, 212–213). Lingis sees it as "an event in an immemorial, unrepresentable past," an absolute event that thought can only suffer (1998, 182); on his account, the imperative is a "fact" not received by sensibility/receptivity but by a spontaneity of the mind (1989, 38ff.). I am instead construing the imperative as related to a pure receptivity of the mind. For Levinas in *Totality and Infinity,* the core of ethical experience is the *visage d'autrui* taken indeed as a "fact" but as a fact of a different kind than the Kantian since it does not disclose but rather challenges the subject's autonomy. For a comparison between Kant and Levinas see C. Chalier (2002), 85–86 (who, however, interprets Kant's *Faktum* quite incorrectly as a mere abstraction from concrete cultural conditions); and S. Critchley (2000). In *Kant und das Problem der Metaphysik* (1973), §30 Heidegger brings both practical reason and moral consciousness back to their common "origin" in the transcendental imagination (there is, however, no textual evidence for this connection).

82. For the juridical meaning of the deduction in the first *Critique* see D. Henrich (1989—see also the other essays of the volume on the second and third *Critiques*) and (1969); J.-H. De Vleeschauwer (1937); M. Baum (1986); and P. Guyer (1987), part 2.

83. See KrV B xxviii–xxix: moral philosophy "introduces (*anführt*) original practical principles lying a priori in our reason as its *data*." It is precisely this critical introduction that first establishes moral principles as "data." In this sense, the a priori data of practical reason are already a *factum*.

84. KpV A 82 (AA V, 47).

85. KpV A 177 (AA V, 99)—my emphasis. My interpretation is here in agreement with Ricoeur's reading of the *Faktum* as "the attestation of 'who?' in the moral dimension," that is, of the accountable and responsible moral subject. See Ricoeur (1991), 212–213.

86. KpV A 177 (AA V, 99).

87. KpV A 15, 16n. (AA V, 9).

88. KpV A 31–32 (AA V, 16), see A 32: in the *Critique of Practical Reason* "we begin with principles and move on to concepts and from these, for the first time, *where possible,* to the senses"—my emphasis.

89. One must recall that, on Kant's account, orientation is provided by a special "feeling" for differences. In the literature, the claim is generally made that Kant variously excludes, represses, or condemns sensibility—this claim, however, is made without ever paying attention to the nuanced notion of sensibility at work in his analysis.

90. Respectively KpV A 73 (AA V, 42) and A 110 (AA V, 62): here Kant takes up again, albeit implicitly, his refutation of the argument of his opponent in relation to the *Groundwork*.

91. KpV A 73 (AA V, 42).

92. KpV A 182–183 (AA V, 101–102).

93. KpV A 170 (AA V, 94–95).

94. KpV A 169ff. (AA V, 94ff.).

95. KpV A 182 (AA V, 102).

96. KpV A 173 (AA V, 96).

97. KpV A 170–171 (AA V, 94–95).

98. KpV A 175 (AA V, 98).

99. KpV A 177 (AA V, 99)—my emphasis.

100. KpV A 175 (AA V, 98). The question of what it means that moral action is not in space and time is explored in Piper (2001). See Lyotard's endorsement of Kant's position that denies time-determination to moral action in *Le Différend* (1988a), 126: "There is no ethical diachrony." For a comparison between Kant and Levinas, see Chalier (2002), 112–117: she claims that Kant is unable to conceive of a "practical time" (p. 117); here, however, Kant's issue of time-determination is historicized and transformed into the problem of the past and memory. See also Ricoeur's distinction between "historical responsibility" and "moral responsibility" in discussing Kant's third antinomy (1992, 107).

101. KpV A 178 (AA V, 99).

102. KpV A 244–245 (AA V, 135–136) also A 125 (AA V, 70) for the "mysticism of practical reason."

103. KpV A 289 (AA V, 161). This means, among other things, that the moral agent is not identified naturally by visible properties of race or gender. Moral embodiment is indeed "blind" to such distinctions. On the basis of my argument, we can construe racism and sexual discrimination as cases of "moral misrecognition" in which the physical, material body is erroneously taken for the body of the moral agent or person. In such cases the body is indeed an object that we empirically see and acknowledge on the basis of its merely empirical features. This, I claim, is not the body of the moral agent that results from Kant's account. (See in a different context M. U. Walker (1998), 178.) Since the idea that the moral agent of Kant's pure ethics is an embodied agent is never recognized in the literature, such a claim has come to identify moral theories in explicit opposition to Kant. Ricoeur holds the view that the agent is always embodied (and endorses Strawson's position on this point—see Ricoeur (1992), 30–31). Levinas's idea of *visage d'autrui* is, on my view, not the opposite of Kant's formalism (as is claimed, for example, by Chalier (2002), 32, 38); its peculiar function in ethics is rather very close to what I call the practical form of "transcendental embodiment": it is the tangible sign of human dignity to which we owe respect. (A similar view can be found in A. Lingis (1994), 64–65: "sensuality" is "the active, expressive face.")

104. Here my argument runs counter to the idea of an "internalization" of the moral law and is rather after the different idea of an embodiment of the law, of its "incorporation" in the agent's *Bildung* of a different kind of sensibility or receptivity. Relevant for my discussion is J. Butler's discussion of Foucault: "Foucault and the Paradox of Bodily Inscriptions" (1989).

105. KpV A 3 (AA V, 3).

106. KpV A 128 (AA V, 72); A 126–127 (AA V, 72).

107. KpV A 129 (AA V, 73). Reath uses the expression "affective force" to deny that practical reason "affects" the will as passions and desire affect it (1989, 290). I completely agree with Reath's analysis. However, its limit is that he never discusses the peculiarity of the moral feeling as a feeling *produced by* the moral law and *following from* it (p. 288). The crucial question is: how does this a priori origin of the moral feeling set it apart from all pathological feelings? And my conclusion here is that even though practical reason's determination of the will is indeed not affection, its production of a distinctive moral feeling (what Reath calls the "affective aspect" of respect, p. 289) is indeed affection. To this extent, practical reason does exercise an "affective force" even though of a very peculiar kind. See next chapter for the development of this point. See also Henry's idea of "affectivity" in his interpretation of Kant's notion of respect (1963,

833), which is discussed in Llewelyn (2000), 153–169. Henry detects a circularity in the thought that the moral law affects us, as he thinks that rationality must already be determined by affectivity in order to be efficacious. See Lingis's idea that "sensibility, sensuality, and perception" are "not reactions to physical causality [. . .] nor free and spontaneous impositions of order on amorphous data, but *responses to directives*" (1998, 3 —my emphasis; also 182–184, 202–204). Significantly, Lingis presents this position as a correction of Kant.

108. KpV A 130 (AA V, 73).

109. KpV A 133 (AA V, 75)—my emphasis.

110. KpV A 134 (AA V, 75).

111. The distinction between "action" and "sensation" becomes crucial in the Dialectic of practical reason. Herein the antinomy arises as the effect of an "optical illusion" from the confusion between "what one does" and "what one feels" (KpV A 210—AA V, 116).

112. KpV A 134 (AA V, 76).

113. Respectively KpV A 135 (AA V, 76) and A 137–138 (AA V, 77).

114. KpV A 133 (AA V, 75).

115. See the concluding page of the second *Critique* discussed above—KpV A 289 (AA V, 161). One should recall, at this point, the question that Kant raises in the letter to Mendelssohn of 8 April 1766: "How is the soul present in the world?" That is, how is it present both "in material nature and in other entities closer to its own kind?" While in 1766 Kant is concerned with the soul's presence in the *Weltraum*—i.e., in "cosmic space"—the development of his critical philosophy shows that the question can be answered only with regard to reason's moral space.

116. KpV A 289 (AA V, 161)—my emphasis.

6. Freedom in the Body

1. KrV B 576–577/A 548; B 579/A 551.

2. See KpV A 3 (AA V, 3).

3. See KpV A 129 (AA V, 73).

4. See KpV A 4n. (AA V, 4).

5. It is the objection raised by Pistorius in his anonymous review of the *Groundwork* (*Allgemeine deutsche Bibliothek*, May 1786, LXVI, 2, 447ff.) and referred to by Kant in the preface to the second *Critique* (A 15n., AA V, 9); see S. Landucci (1994), 272–275.

6. For the distinction between determination and causation, see Adrian M. Piper (1993), 198 and footnote 20, where she warns not to conflate the two concepts—not even to think of the one in analogy with the other.

7. Respectively, KpV A 132 (AA V, 74): "*Wirkung*"; A 129 (AA V, 73): "*bewirkt*"; KrV B 581/A 553: "condition" and "*unmittelbare Wirkung*."

8. Such an interpretation goes back at least to Hegel. See the previous chapter for bibliographical references.

9. See KpV A 3 (AA V, 3).

10. For a thorough discussion of Kant's distinctions within the concept of moral philosophy and for the relation between pure and applied moral philosophy, see M. Gregor (1963); P. König (1994), 128ff.; and S. Sedgwick (1997), 83–84.

11. See N. Sherman (1997), 121. In general, see O. O'Neill (1989) and (1975—111 for feeling and moral decision); and B. Herman (1993, 1983). Herman has persuasively argued against the interpretation of the categorical imperative (the requirement "from

duty") as entailing an exclusion of emotions and passions; duty is, on her account, a "limiting condition" against which emotions must be always be checked. See M. W. Baron (1995), in particular part 2, and the chapter "Sympathy and Coldness in Kant's Ethics" that raises the question of whether Kant could allow that "someone lacking in fellow feeling and affection is morally deficient" (194ff.). Baron, however, focuses on the *Anthropology* and *Metaphysics of Morals,* not on the transcendental foundation of the second *Critique.* See P. Guyer (1996), in particular "Duty and Inclination," 335–393; and R. B. Louden (2000), which discusses exclusively Kant's applied ("impure") practical philosophy. While Louden insists on the importance of the "second part" of Kant's ethics, namely, its applied part, it is my contention that the "first part," namely, the critical and foundational transcendental part still needs to be investigated with regard to the role that embodiment and sensibility play in it. Susan M. Shell (1996) is centered on Kant's political theory and issues of community, and consequently does not address the theory of the second *Critique.* See also Sherman (1997): her general thesis is that emotions are relevant in Kant's project as they constitute the topic of a moral anthropology; accordingly, she often manifests frustration with the apparently spare remarks on the topic in the second *Critique.* Recently, and more generally on the topic of emotions, see M. Nussbaum (2001). Close to my perspective, even though with a focus on the *Anthropology,* is C. La Rocca (1999); but see all the essays in this volume. Interpretations and appropriations of Kant's moral philosophy in the phenomenological perspective (broadly construed) tend to draw the theme of respect and, in Heidegger's aftermath, the imagination to the center. The formality of Kant's argument, his conception of practical reason, and its separation from speculative reason are often 'corrected' with Levinas, Merleau-Ponty, etc. Interesting proposals arise, such as: A. Lingis (1998) and (1989), 38–41; J. Llewelyn (2000), ch. 9; B. Freydberg (2005), in Sallis's wake. See also J. Derrida, "Passions" (1993b), 16. These interpretations eventually abandon Kant's transcendentalism or alternatively find the work of imagination incompatible with *pure* practical reason, whereas I intend to maintain Kant's transcendental framework. My claim is that practical reason functions only to the extent that it is itself (that is, not with the imagination's help) transcendentally embodied. C. Chalier (2002) offers a paradigmatic example: she turns to Levinas because she sees no relation between Kant's purely formal imperative and our natural, sensible striving toward satisfaction. She opposes Kant's "alienating" principles (p. 32) to Levinas's epiphany of the face, which she ties to the core of our living humanity (p. 38). Yet on my reading, Levinas's face is a practical form of "transcendental embodiment" in Kant's sense.

12. See in particular O'Neill (1989) and Herman (1993), who show that Kant's requirement "from duty" operating as a higher order moral principle is compatible with a variety of feelings and emotions.

13. KrV B 80/A 56.

14. KrV B 84/A 556.

15. *Reflexion* 5611—my emphasis.

16. *Reflexion* 5612. Lingis draws, against Kant, the distinction between the "force" and the "form" of the imperative: for him "the force of the imperative remains exterior to the form" (1998, 181); to gain force the imperative needs to be schematized or imaginatively enacted. My view, instead, is that the form of the imperative *is* precisely its force of *Triebfeder.* Interestingly, Lingis enlarges Kant's imperative by putting it on "things" (and not just on reason): "The reality of things is not given in our perception but orders it as an imperative" (p. 63). A. Reath (1989, 290) denies that practical reason

can have "affective force," that is, that it can "affect" the will in a way similar to passions and desire. My claim is that even though practical reason's determination of the will is indeed not affection (I agree with Reath that reason does not determine the will by exerting a "quasi-mechanical" force) its production of a peculiar and distinctive moral feeling (what Reath calls the "affective aspect" of respect, p. 289) is indeed affection. To this extent, practical reason does exercise an "affective force" even though of a very peculiar kind. I do agree with Reath that reason's affective force is not directed to the will (moral motivation is not affection); however, interestingly, reason's affective force is exercised on our sensible nature, or, more precisely, on our (practical) receptivity. (See also my discussion of this point in the previous chapter; and see L. Herrera (2000).) The first reformulation of Kant's idea of moral *Triebfeder* is in Fichte's 1798 *Sittenlehre nach den Prinzipien der Wissenschaftslehre.*

17. *Reflexion* 5612; in KrV B 581/A 552 the empirical character is "sensible schema" of the intelligible.

18. See KpV A 15n. (AA V, 10) and *Metaphysik der Sitten* AB 1 (VI, 211).

19. *Reflexion* 6870.

20. Part 3 will take up this point with regard to the third *Critique.*

21. Kant's claims that respect for the moral law thwarts self-love and humiliates self-conceit provide an example of the way in which morality affects and re-shapes our inclinations.

22. I use the term in the etymological sense to which Kant refers in KrV B 35–36/A 20–21n.

23. KrV B 579/A 551 and B 581/A 553.

24. KpV A 159 (AA V, 89).

25. For a further analogy between the division of logic and morals into a pure and an applied part, see König (1994), 128–136. The importance of the "aesthetic of pure practical reason" within the second *Critique* is stressed by F. Calori (2003), 122–123.

26. KpV A 161 (AA V, 90).

27. KpV A 127 (AA V, 72).

28. *Reflexionen* 7042, 6865; MAT, AA VI, 400. The issue of the evaluative aspect of feeling/emotion is crucial to Sherman's attempt to put Aristotle in dialogue with Kant. However, in discussing the possibility of attributing an evaluative function to emotions in Kant, Sherman misses Kant's important distinction between theoretical and practical cognition, to which he alludes precisely by distinguishing between "*Sinn*" and "*Wahl.*" See Sherman (1997), 177–178.

29. Thereby Kant follows a procedure similar to the one employed in the Transcendental Aesthetic of the first *Critique:* KrV B 36/A 22.

30. For what follows see Guyer's "Duty and Inclination" (1996), 335–393. Although I agree with most of the points raised by Guyer, I disagree with his main thesis, namely the claim that the relation between feelings and reason belongs exclusively to Kant's "moral psychology." Along similar lines, Sherman argues that "Kant introduces emotions, not as part of the ground of morality but as part of moral anthropology, or what we would call moral psychology" (1997, 123, 129, 135). Although emotions do not ground morality, I show that they can indeed belong to the transcendental pure part of moral philosophy precisely because they entail an a priori form. This form, however, can be discovered only if feeling is considered as consequence of the moral law. This form, in turn, is the condition for Kant's development of the topic of emotion in his applied practical philosophy.

31. KpV A 161 (AA V, 90)—my emphasis.

32. KpV A 126 (AA V, 71).

33. KpV A 127 (AA V, 72).

34. *Groundwork*, 63–64 (AA IV, 427); see König (1994), 159–165.

35. For example, see H. S. Reimarus, *Triebe der Tiere* (1760); and Goethe: "meine Schuld ist es nicht, [. . .] wenn meine Triebe und meine Vernunft nicht völlig habe in Einstimmung bringen können" (1887, vol. 23, 197). For the spectrum of meanings, which covers both mechanistic and organicistic uses, see *Trieb* in J. Grimm and W. Grimm (1952), vol. 22; the *Revue Germanique Internationale* (2002) has, s.v. *Trieb: tendance, instinct, pulsion*. Fichte's 1798 *Das System der Sittenlehre nach den Prinzipien der Wissenschaftslehre* is the work that develops Kant's idea of *Trieb* into the centerpiece of a new ethical theory; see my "Theory of Ethics and Applied Ethics in Fichte: *Sittenlehre* or *Metaphysik der Sitten?*" (forthcoming in *Revue de Metaphysique et de Morale*).

36. See the conclusion of the argument in KpV A 135 (AA V, 76).

37. KpV A 57 (AA V, 32)—my emphasis.

38. KpV A 161 (AA V, 90). See the feeling of "*Zwang*" that accompanies the respect for the law: KpV A 164 (AA V, 92). Sherman correctly observes that the categorical imperative already implies a reference to the human will (1997, 130). This, however, is not an empirical or anthropological presupposition, and does not imply that the categorical imperative "is itself an anthropological construct." See the beginning of the previous chapter; and König's analysis of Kant's distinction between pure, human, and holy will (1994, 128ff).

39. KpV A 127 (AA V, 72).

40. KpV A 128 (AA V, 72)—my emphasis.

41. KpV A 127 (AA V, 72)—my emphasis.

42. KrV B 579/A 551. This is also the point, crucial to the *Critique of Practical Reason*, on which any further claim regarding a cultivation of our emotions in view of virtue rests (*Doctrine of Virtue*). The dependence of the argument of the *Doctrine of Virtue* on the last chapter of the Analytic of the second *Critique* is overlooked both by Guyer and Sherman in the studies cited.

43. KpV A 128 (AA V, 73)—my emphasis.

44. As must by now be clear, the a priori character of this relation is crucial to the very possibility of an "aesthetic" of practical reason. On Sherman's account, on the contrary, the meaning of the a priori of the feeling of respect is said to be "unclear" and plays no role in her analysis. Moreover, the failure to understand the a priori relation between respect and practical reason leads her to misinterpret the cognitive value of this feeling, which is 'cognitive' only in a practical, not in a theoretical sense (1997, 176–177), and to misunderstand the uniqueness of the feeling of respect (its being the "only case" of a feeling whose relation to practical reason can be known a priori), which becomes a sort of exemplarity (pp. 175, 181): respect is "*the* moral emotion." For the notion of *Achtung* see König (1994), 198–202; L. W. Beck (1960), 210–212; Reath (1989); and the works by Henry and Lingis discussed in the previous chapter. Derrida connects Kantian respect to the idea of "sacrificial offering" (sacrifice of sensibility and passion) and sees the "whole apparatus of the 'critical' distinctions of Kantianism" as functional to such offering. Against Kant, Derrida exclaims: "What I am looking for here, passion according to me, would be a concept of passion that would be non-'pathological'" (1993b, 16). My claim is that Kant's idea of respect designates precisely such a non-pathological passion. Llewelyn addresses the issue of the constitutive "wordliness" of

respect. Important for my argument is the claim that respect is a feeling inscribed in the context of a "wordliness that is both intelligible and sensible" (2000, 154–155). Freydberg (2005), ch. 3 claims that the moral feeling "is a pure feeling *generated spontaneously from reason by imagination*" (p. 86, my emphasis), adding in a note that follows Sallis's thesis in *The Gathering of Reason,* that "reason by itself generates nothing." My claim is instead that reason does generate the feeling of respect and that this is its peculiar practical activity. Although he considers respect a "stranger" among all other feelings because of its purity, Freydberg seems to place respect "among the play of all other feelings" (86–88, "sensuous intuition" is viewed as "feeling with the moral and pathological content abstracted entirely from it") thereby missing its peculiar character due to its arising directly from reason (purity is related to apriority).

45. Respectively, (1) KpV A 132 (AA V, 74); (2–3) A 129 (AA V, 73); (4) A 130 (AA V, 73).

46. See respectively KpV A 132 (AA V, 74,37), and A 129 (AA V, 73,5).

47. For the connection *Triebfeder/Bestimmungsgrund,* see the important formulation of the *Metaphysik der Sitten Vigilantius,* AA XXVII, 493: "Der Bestimmungsgrund der Willkür (*causa determinans arbitrium*) ist *causa impulsiva* zur Handlung, die Bewegursache"; *causa impulsiva* is then identified with the "Triebfeder des Gemüths zur Handlung." Relevant here is Kant's translation of *Triebfeder* with *causa impulsiva.*

48. In KpV A 134 (AA V, 75) "respect" is even called a "sensation" (*Empfindung*).

49. KpV A 133–134 (AA V, 75)—my emphasis. Llewelyn distinguishes between "the indirect effect of respect for the law upon feeling and direct effect of the law upon the will" (2000, 156). At stake is the relation between the objectivity of the law and affectivity.

50. KpV A 134 (AA V, 75)—second emphasis is mine. Despite its sensible character, this feeling as practical feeling is not subject to the condition of time in a strict theoretical sense: it is a consequence of the moral determination of the will, and yet is identical with the moral principle that (objectively) *determines* the will insofar as this principle also (subjectively) *affects* it. An extension of Kant's moral feeling to feeling in general (which follows from an extension of the imperative from reason to things in general) is offered by Lingis: "Feelings are not simply inert states of being passive with regard to something impressed; they are responses in the direction of inclination. Thought becomes practical by displacing the sensuous representations with the representation of law" (1998, 204).

51. See for example MAT, AA VI, 457, this is the central topic of Sherman (1997).

52. KpV A 135 (AA V, 76).

53. For the important developments of this point in the *Anthropology,* see La Rocca (1999), who rightly stresses the relation to the second *Critique* as integral to the argument of the *Anthropology.* La Rocca analyzes the intriguing passage of the *Anthropology* entitled: "Von der Freiheitsneigung als Leidenschaft" (AA VII, 268–269). For Kant there is not only a feeling for freedom but even a *passion* for it.

54. KpV A 129 (AA V, 73)—my emphasis.

55. KpV A 130 (AA V, 73)—my emphasis.

56. This point is raised by Guyer (1996), 362–365. While his interests, however, point to the "*psychology* of moral sentiment," my aim is to show how Kant legitimately claims the crucial topic of moral feeling as belonging to transcendental philosophy: it offers a peculiar a priori side constitutive of the idea of a "critique of practical reason."

57. *Reflexion* 7042; MAT, AA VI, 400.

58. *Reflexion* 6865.

59. *Relfexion* 6864—my emphasis.

60. See Guyer (1996), 360. Once again my point here is not that, for Kant, feeling cannot be the motive of action, but only a consequence (see the previous chapter). Here I am concerned with the other side of the problem: how can feeling be a consequence of moral determination? What kind of feeling is a consequence thereof? And how does this consequence manifest itself in the phenomenal life of the agent?

61. See KpV A 40 (AA V, 22) with reference to a "rational being's consciousness of the agreeableness of life which without interruption accompanies his whole existence." This sounds indeed like a Kantian appropriation and transformation of an Aristotelian claim; see the development of *eudaimonia* in *Nicomachean Ethics* I.

62. *Reflexion* 6870.

63. *Reflexion* 6871—last emphasis is mine.

64. We should also recall the thesis of the Transcendental Aesthetic on the uniqueness of space and time. Is such uniqueness an expression of reason's "gathering," as suggested by Sallis and Freydberg? See Freydberg (2005), 88–89.

65. *Reflexion* 6862; KU §1 for the notion of *Lebensgefühl* and the earlier *Reflexion* 824.

66. See KpV A 15n. (AA V, 10), also MS AB 1 (VI, 211). I return to this connection in part 3. See C. La Rocca (1999), 84–85; R. Makkreel (1990), 88ff.; and A. Nuzzo (2007).

67. KpV A 137 (AA V, 77).

68. KpV A 174 (AA V, 97).

69. KpV A 168 (AA V, 94).

70. KpV A 175 (AA V, 97)—my emphasis.

71. See chaps. 8 and 9, below, for Kant's argument against Epicurus's physiology in the *Critique of Judgment*.

72. And from this it is just another step to pick sex or race and attach to them a discriminatory significance: only those agents whose bodies look a certain way count as moral agents. Kant's transcendental construction of the embodied agent counters precisely this sort of conclusion.

73. KpV A 175 (AA V, 97–98)—my emphasis.

74. *Reflexion* 6864.

75. For this interpretation of the passage, see the indication of Guyer (1996), 363–364 (who refers to K. Ameriks (1987), 187). The indication is precious—although neither Guyer nor Ameriks spell it out. In my view, however, it must be integrated by the second point, which, along with the argument presented so far, is the condition for any further application in the *Doctrine of Virtue*. The fact that Guyer focuses exclusively on the first issue goes hand in hand with his conclusion that it is the task of psychology ("rather than metaphysics" or transcendental philosophy) to investigate the influence of the moral motive on human sensibility and its limits (1996, 365).

76. MAT, AA VI, 402 (my emphasis): there is a clear proximity to Aristotle's notion of virtue here. Guyer claims that only psychology can "discover" the truth that "adherence to the principle of beneficence eventually produces the feeling of love" (1996, 365–366). My argument has shown, on the contrary, that this "truth" is a direct consequence of the thesis of the Analytic, hence it is *not* a matter of psychology but is integral to the project of a pure practical philosophy.

77. Among the many passages (extensively discussed in chaps. 1 and 2, above), see the first definition of *Sinnlichkeit* in KrV B 33/A 19. See Heidegger's brief reading of Kant's idea of practical receptivity in *Kant und das Problem der Metaphysik* (1973, 143–146): he inverts the terms of Kant's problem by addressing the issue of a receptivity of the spontaneous nature of finite reason (p. 143, instead of the issue of the intellectual receptivity of our sensibility). It may be that, for him, in the unifying perspective of transcendental imagination the two issues ultimately converge.

78. See KrV B 178/A 139 where Kant calls "*Modifikation unserer Sinnlichkeit*" the way in which objects are given to us (in sensible intuition).

79. KpV A 40 (AA V, 22)—these characters of feeling play a crucial role in defining the specific sphere of the feeling of pleasure and displeasure in the third *Critique*.

80. KpV A 39–40 (AA V, 21–22)—my emphasis. For the final development of this argument in the *Critique of Judgment,* see ch. 8, below.

81. "*Ästhetische Vorbegriffe der Empfänglichkeit des Gemüts für Pflichtbegriffe überhaupt,*" MAT, VI, 399. In her translation of the *Doctrine of Virtue,* Gregor always renders 'aesthetic' with 'feeling,' thereby betraying the uneasiness with the use of the notion of 'aesthetic' in the practical sphere already confessed by Kant. Kant, however, does consistently make use of the term. Gregor's translation obscures both Kant's intention of constructing a parallel (and an analogy) with the 'aesthetic' of the first *Critique,* and the importance that Kant's reflection on the complex topic of 'aesthetic' in the practical sphere has for the development of the strictly aesthetic problematic of the third *Critique.*

82. See the conclusion of MAT §XII (AA VI, 399): "Consciousness" of these dispositions "is not of empirical origin; it can, instead, *only follow* from consciousness of the moral law, as the *effect* this has on the *Gemüt*" (my emphasis). See KpV A 145n. (AA V, 82): Kant claims that the "concept of respect for persons" just presented in its transcendental origin can be very useful "from the psychological point of view to our understanding of the human being" insofar as it is made clear that the concept is based on "the consciousness of a duty," i.e., has a *moral* origin.

83. MAT, AA VI, 399–400.

84. *Religion,* AA VI, 26.

85. *Religion,* AA VI, 27.

86. *Religion,* AA VI, 28.

87. Freydberg reads this chapter as regarding the construction of the object by the imagination (2005, ch. 2). My claim, instead, is that at issue is a problem of deliberation that involves reason and the will but neither a "construction" nor imagination (the latter is not Kant's language here).

88. KpV A 100 (AA V, 57).

89. KpV A 101 (AA V, 58)—my emphasis.

90. This issue is further addressed in the *Typik:* KpV A 119ff. (AA V, 67ff.) as the issue of the schematization of the law. Such schematization, however, is functional to the process of deliberation (not to a cognitive aim) and can be understood only once such process is clarified. For the schematism and its relation to the imagination in the second *Critique* see Freydberg (2005), 81–83; Lingis (1998), 184–188. The concern for freedom's realization in the world is central to Arendt: if freedom were merely noumenal it could not be political. On her view, however, only in the third *Critique* does freedom acquire a worldly side (in the beautiful as symbol of morality): hence the privilege of judgment over practical reason in her reading of Kant. See Arendt (2002).

91. I owe this suggestion to Piper (1993), 207.

92. KrV B 578/A 550.

93. KrV B 579/A 551 and n.

94. *Groundwork,* AB 26 (AA IV, 407)—my emphasis. See Piper (1993), 205—I have emended her translation.

95. KrV B 579/A 551 and n.

96. KrV B 581/A 553.

97. KpV A 289 (AA V, 162). See previous chapter.

98. KrV B 579–580/A 551–552—my emphasis (Kant underlines *vorhergehen* and *durch*).

99. KrV B 584/A 556.

100. See G. Mohr (1988), 308. The problem of personality and moral agency is outlined by Ricoeur in the same terms of "ascription" of actions (imputability); see (1992), chaps. 1 and 4; Ricoeur follows Strawson in viewing the concept of person and that of its physical body as "primitive concepts"; on this basis he attempts a "transcendental deduction of the notion of person" as embodied agent (1992, 31ff.).

101. See Levinas's question: "what precedes?" discussed by Chalier (2002), 119. For Levinas such a question, central to the problem of freedom, is a question of origin. Kant, on the contrary, left the issue of origin behind in the antinomies.

102. As Piper (1993, 207) aptly puts it: "The effect of reason on action cannot be merely to nudge it into existence causally as an occurrence."

103. This sensible condition is not "in reason" itself. See KrV B 569/A 541: "in" it, no action takes place.

104. See *Religion,* AA VI, 23–24, with regard to the "freedom of the will (*Willkür*)." Allison calls this stance the "Incorporation Thesis" (1996b, 40): "Freedom of the will is of a wholly unique nature in that no *Triebfeder* can determine it to an action *except insofar as the human being (Mensch) has incorporated it into its maxim* [. . .]. Only in this way can a *Triebfeder*—whatever it may be—coexist with the absolute spontaneity of the will (freedom)."

105. *Reflexion* 5612 (AA XVIII, 253)—my emphasis.

106. See MS AA VI, 213–214, 226. I agree here with Allison (1996b, 256 n. 49); see also his analysis of the distinction (pp. 229ff.).

107. MS VI, 213.

108. MS VI, 226.

109. KrV B 581/A 552—my emphasis.

110. See KrV B 584/A 556: "reason is present and one (*gegenwärtig und einerlei*) in all human actions under all circumstances of time."

111. KrV B 578/A 550.

112. KrV B 580/A 552.

113. In the following discussion, I concentrate on the *moral* aspect of the notion of person. Hence, I do not discuss the issue of personal identity, which Kant addresses in the first *Critique* (and for which, see my reconstruction of the paralogisms). The epistemological issue of personal identity occupies most of the contemporary debate. For the difference between Kant's view of personality and contemporary philosophy of mind, see Ricoeur (1992), 27–39; and L. Siep (1984), 63. For the juridical aspect of personality, see for example MS AA VI, 230 and Siep (1992), 81–115. See also H. Zeltner (1967). With attention to the metaphysical aspects of personality, see H. Heimsoeth (1956),

227–257. Although not specifically on the notion of person, O. O'Neill (1989, 69ff.) addresses the connection I have just discussed. For some contemporary perspectives, see the collective volumes: *Personale Identität*, ed. M. Quante (1999); and *The Identities of Persons*, ed. A. O. Rorty (1969)—in this volume see S. Shoemaker, "Embodiment and Behavior" (109–138) for the connection between person and embodiment. See also H. G. Frankfurt (1971) and M. Theunissen (1966).

114. *Religion*, VI, 26, 28. See the early *Reflexion* 4225: "The question whether or not freedom is possible is perhaps identical with the question whether or not the human being is a true person."

115. MS VI, 223.

116. See KpV A 135–136 (AA V, 76–77). Animals, Kant contends, can awaken "*Neigung*" or inclination, and even "love" (or fear), while phenomena of nature can produce "admiration"—but never respect. The intersubjective dimension opened up by the notion of personality is treated here only as a consequence drawn from the main thesis established in this chapter and concerning Kant's transcendental foundation of practical sensibility. For a thematic analysis of the idea of personality as implying connection with other persons: see Piper (1993, 209ff.) for the problem of recognition of others as persons; more generally, on the issue of community, see Shell (1996) and C. Van Kirk (1986). In contrasting Kant's moral theory to Levinas's, Chalier (2002) underscores on many occasions the theme of the "other's face" as ground of responsibility in Levinas. Although Kant's introduction of intersubjectivity via the concept of person is quite different from Levinas's, the distance between the two philosophers is, I believe, less than Chalier thinks.

117. KpV A 117 (AA V, 66); see also the division of external objects according to the categories of relation in Kant's account of private law (Siep (1984), 73). See also G. Schönrich (1986) and S. Bobzien (1988).

118. KpV A 177 (AA V, 99)—my emphasis.

119. See KrV B 403, 427; and B 421, 307 hinting at a practical use of the concept of person. For this thesis, see Mohr (1988), 304ff.

7. Aesthetics of the Body

1. A. G. Baumgarten (1993), §115.

2. A. G. Baumgarten (1779), §518: "Status animae, in quo perceptiones dominantes obscurae sunt, est regnum tenebrarum (das Reich des Finsterniß), in quo clarae regnant, regnum lucis (das Reich des Lichtes in der Seele)." See C. Wolff (1738), §§34ff. See also U. Franke (1972).

3. Baumgarten (1779), §511: "Hic animae fundus [. . .] a multis adhuc ignoretur, etiam philosophis."

4. The hierarchy of the soul's faculties gains importance with the diffusion of Tauler's works. See I. Degenhardt (1967) and C. Champollion (1963). For the developments of Eckhart's idea in the German tradition, see H. Adler (1988) and A. Saccon (2001).

5. See Baumgarten (1758), §80; (1779), §§511, 514.

6. Baumgarten (1758), §14.

7. Baumgarten (1993), §116; (1779), §502: "Psychologia principia theologiarum, aestheticae, logicae, practicarum scientiarum prima continens, cum ratione (scil. qua 'scientia praedicatorum animae generalium', §501) refertur ad metaphysicam."

8. Herder represents the contemporary alternative to Kant's transcendental aesthetics. Herder's proposal follows a physiological and historicist model. See A. Nuzzo (2006) and J. Zammito (2001).

9. The third *Critique* has been read by the immediate post-Kantian philosophers in this sense, although no consensus can be found on the interpretation of Kant's gesture as well as on the question of whether Kant's proposal was successful. The same perspective, albeit updated in light of new issues, is at the center of contemporary readings and appropriations of the third *Critique*. In both cases, this text seems to be the starting point of philosophies that ultimately abandon Kant's transcendentalism.

10. In the Leibnizian tradition, instead, sensibility and understanding, while differing only in degree and not in kind, are arranged according to a precise hierarchy of (cognitive) value. This explains, among other things, why the terminology of higher and lower faculties is not endorsed by transcendental philosophy. When Kant uses this terminology, he refers to the traditional doctrines.

11. KrV B 33/A 19.—See ch. 1, above.

12. KrV B 376–377/A 320.

13. KrV B 209/A 167–168.

14. KrV B 35/A 21—my emphasis.

15. See the discussion of this text and the literature quoted in ch. 1, above. Falkenstein's detailed commentary on the Transcendental Aesthetic (1995) dedicates almost no reflection to this footnote; Brandt's remarks in (1998) are brief as well; still brief, but useful and informative, is L. Amoroso (1998). Derrida (1976, 290ff.) radicalizes Husserl's critique of the Transcendental Aesthetic on the basis of the charge of purity and ideality of Kantian sensibility. He advocates a "new transcendental aesthetics" that could allow him to integrate the social space into the space of writing. But how does this "new transcendental aesthetics" relate to the Kantian move from the aesthetics of the first to the aesthetics of the third *Critique*?

16. See Kant's analogous claim in *Logik*, AA IX, 15. In the pre-critical period Kant embraces Baumgarten's view; see *Nachricht von der Einrichtung seiner Vorlesungen in dem Winterhalbenjahre von 1765/66*, AA III, 311.

17. One could suggest that Kant replaces Baumgarten's *gnoseologia inferior* with a sort of *gnoseologia transcendentalis*.

18. KrV B35—my emphasis.

19. Kant's early *Beobachtungen über das Gefühl des Schönen und Erhabenen* (1764) can be considered as a psychology of taste with moral and anthropological rather than cognitive aims.

20. KrV B 829/A 801; B 29/A 15.

21. The manuscript of the second *Critique* was finished in the summer 1787: note the chronological proximity to the footnote of the Transcendental Aesthetic discussed above. For the transition between the second and the third *Critique* construed in terms of imagination instead of feeling, see B. Freydberg (2005, 131–146). Freydberg, however, recognizes the difficulty of such an interpretation.

22. At this point, however, the necessity for this aesthetic to be *critical* is not yet sufficiently grounded. The further step is the claim that the feeling of pleasure and displeasure is not only utterly distinct from the principles of theoretical and practical reason but also displays an a priori principle of its own.

23. See, for example, KpV A 211 (AA V, 117).

24. See KpV A 213 (AA V, 117).

25. It is the important difference between the consciousnesses of "what one *does*" and the consciousness of "what one *feels/perceives* (*empfindet*)." This difference, Kant notices, is too often obfuscated by a sort of "optical illusion" (KpV A 210; AA V, 116).

26. KpV A 161, 211 (AA V, 90, 117); MS AA VI, 406.

27. See A. Bäumler (1967), 18ff.

28. C. Thomasius (1687). Thomasius' passage continues: "Le gout universel d'autrui, qui est la vrai méthode de choisir. Car il en est comme d'un festin, ou les viandes ne s'apprentent pas du gout des cuisiniers, mais à celuy du convivez." Bäumler argues that the birthplace of Kant's aesthetics is not "high in the library" but "far under in the kitchen"; see the group of *Reflexionen* quoted in Bäumler (1967), 265. Kant writes in *Reflexion* 2040: "*Malim convivis quam placuisse cocis,*" probably quoting Martial who, in turn, was also Gracian's source (AA XVI, 209).

29. As for Hume, Home, Burke, and Hutcheson.

30. As for Gottsched, Bodmer, and Breitinger.

31. Herein Kant is indebted both to Mendelssohn, who recognizes as a third faculty the "faculty of approving" (*das Billigen*), which is contemplation of beauty; and to Tetens, who sees in the *Gefühl* a third and autonomous faculty next to the cognitive and the practical.

32. Accordingly, I propose to substitute a distinction that regards the internal configuration of the sphere of sensibility—*Sinnlichkeit* is the sphere of materiality, givenness, passivity, etc., and yet there are areas within this sphere that show the character of formality, spontaneity, etc.—to Guyer's claim that Kant's pre-critical theory of taste (and to a certain extent the theory of the third *Critique*) is based upon a *confusion* between aesthetic *response,* i.e., our *pleasure* in the beautiful, and aesthetic *judgment,* i.e., the *claim to universal validity* inherent in a judgment of taste. (See Guyer (1997), 13–32.) On my view, while aesthetic pleasure represents the empirical side of sensibility, aesthetic judgment is related to one of its a priori components.

33. See Kant's letter to Herz dated 21 February 1772.

34. G. F. Meier (1752), §22 (AA XVI).

35. To be dated at 1769–1770.

36. See for example *Reflexion* 1794 (1769–1770), AA XVI, 118; *Reflexion* 1799 (1769–1775), AA XVI, 119.

37. *Reflexion* 1780 on Meier (1752), §22 (either 1764–1768 or 1769), AA XVI, 112.

38. See *Reflexion* 1794.

39. Among the many Reflections on this topic, see *Reflexion* 1795 (1769–1773/1775), AA XVI, 118.

40. *Reflexion* 1791 (1769–1770), AA XVI, 116.

41. *Reflexion* 1799.

42. *Reflexion* 696 (1770), AA XV, 309.

43. *Reflexion* 628 (1769), AA XV, 273.

44. Respectively, "*doctrin*": *Reflexion* 1821 (1771–1775), AA XVI, 128; "*theorie*": *Reflexion* 1585 (1760–1779), AA XVI, 26; "*Wissenschaft*": *Reflexion* 1588 (1772–1775), AA XVI, 27, *Reflexion* 622 (1769), AA XV, 269, and *Reflexion* 1892 (1776–1778), AA XVI, 150: "There is no science (*Wissenschaft*) of the beautiful, but only art (*Kunst*)" (emphasis is always mine).

45. *Reflexion* 1823 (1772–1775), AA XVI, 129.

46. *Reflexion* 1585—hence the title of Kant's 1764 work: *Observations on the Feeling of the Beautiful and Sublime.* The topic of "observation" (the "theme of spectatorship") is developed by Susan M. Shell (2001).

47. *Reflexion* 1588.

48. *Reflexion* 1851 (ca. 1771), AA XVI, 137; see also the interesting suggestion of *Reflexion* 875 (1776–1778), AA XV, 384: "All cases in which rules cannot be drawn from objective grounds but only from subjective ones: taste, feeling—belong to *anthropology.*"

49. *Reflexion* 646 (1769–1770), AA XV, 284.

50. *Reflexion* 1796 (1769–1770), AA XVI, 118–119.

51. The two aesthetics remain radically separated for Kant in the years of the *Dissertatio*—contrary to Dumouchel's claim (1997), who sees them as merging into each other. Kant's theory of space and time, however, does manifest an influence on the theory of taste, contrary to Guyer's claim (1997, 26).

52. *Reflexion* 646.

53. *Reflexion* 647 (1769–1770), AA XV, 284.

54. *Reflexion* 648 (1769–1770), AA XV, 284.

55. *Reflexion* 672 (1769–1770), AA XV, 298.

56. See D. Henrich (1992), 35: Kant's temptation to justify the universal validity of aesthetic form through the a priori forms of space and time still has an influence in the argument of §14 of the *Critique of Judgment.*

57. KpV A 285 (AA V, 159)—my emphasis.

58. See also KpV A 286 (AA V, 160): the "*anfängliche Empfindung von Schmerz*" that the student of morality experiences in the "second exercise."

59. KpV A 285 (AA V, 160).

60. KpV A 285–286 (AA V, 160)—my emphasis.

61. KpV A 285–286 (AA V, 160).

62. This is the indirect way in which Kant's broadened "transcendental aesthetics" complicated by the itinerary of the second *Critique* eventually discloses that "social space" that Derrida (1976, 290) sees missing in Kant.

63. KpV A 286 (AA V, 160).

64. Recall the lesson that the first *Critique* teaches to Plato's dove regarding the indispensable resistance of the air for flight (KrV B 8–9/A 5)—and notice that it is an animal there that is rendering Plato's position. See J. Sallis (1987), 24–25.

65. KpV A 289 (AA V, 161); 290 (AA V, 162): "*Bewunderung und Achtung*" and "*Erhabenheit*" of the object.

66. See the detailed discussion of this passage in ch. 5, above. This is the "space between earth and heavens" to which Sallis assigns Plato's dove in the first *Critique* (1987, 25); see also his placing of the "Greek philosopher" between "the sky above and the earth beneath" (2000b, 148), which leads Sallis to the question of nature.

67. KpV A 289–290 (AA V, 161–162)—my emphasis.

68. The latter is the object of Kant's pre-critical *Observations on the Feeling of the Beautiful and Sublime* (1764).

69. See EE§XI, AA XX, 247,7–8.

70. EE§VIII, AA XX, 221,26–34.

71. EE§VIII, AA XX, 222,2–6.

72. KrV B 376/A 320: "*Perzeption, die sich auf das Subjekt, als die Modifikation seines Zustandes bezieht.*"

73. EE§VIII, AA XX, 222,7–8.

74. EE§VIII, AA XX, 222,9–11.

75. EE§VIII, AA XX, 222,9–15—my emphasis; §XI, 247,6–8, in which "*Ästhetik*" means "*Sinnenlehre*" referring to Kant's own use of the term, and not "critique of taste" as in the footnote to Transcendental Aesthetic §1.

76. EE§VIII, AA XX, 222,22–29. While the mediating function of aesthetic judgment is generally recognized, the paradox or contradiction at the heart of this expression is not. De Man's suggestion (1996, 73) is interesting—that "aesthetic" expresses for Kant the "need for a phenomenalized, empirically manifest principle of cognition" linking critique and "ideology." On this view, however, the distance from cognition is not sufficiently marked. Here is also the similarity with and fundamental difference from imagination.

77. EE§VIII, AA XX, 223,4–14.

78. EE§VIII, AA XX, 223,15–16.

79. EE§VIII, AA XX, 222,6—my emphasis.

80. EE§VIII, AA XX, 222,9–11—my emphasis.

81. EE§VIII, AA XX, 223,23.

82. EE§VIII, AA XX, 223,16–22—my emphasis.

83. EE§VIII, AA XX, 223,23–24. See the further distinction in the text of EE (§VIII, AA XX, 224,12–27) between "*ästhetische(n) Sinnesurteile*" and "*ästhetische(n) Reflexionsurteile*" with regard to the *Bestimmungsgrund,* and the previously analyzed EE§VIII, AA XX, 222,27–29.

84. This notion can be viewed as the critical successor of—and critical solution to—the metaphysical problem of the *influxus physicus* (see ch. 2, above). While maintaining the separation between sensibility and rationality, the concept of "transcendental embodiment" remains within the framework of Kant's criticism and shows the complex and necessary interaction between the two. My project can be compared and contrasted to Sallis's idea of imagination as a "force" which overcomes all separation between sensibility and rationality and overcomes as well the notion of a subject (2000b).

85. KU §3; EE§VIII, AA XX, 224, 12–14: there is only one "sensation" that "can never become a concept of object, and this is the feeling of pleasure and displeasure."

86. Respectively, KU §§3, 4, 5.

87. See the end of KU §3.

8. Reflections of the Body, Reflections on the Body

1. KrV B 403/A 345.

2. See KrV A 355, and B 420–421: "*Erfahrung*" is "*unser Dasein im Leben.*"

3. KrV B 409: the claim that I could exist as mere thinking being amounts, for Kant, to the claim that I could exist "*ohne Mensch zu sein.*"

4. KrV B 421.

5. KrV B 403/A 345—my emphasis.

6. *Dreams,* AA II, 329–330.

7. AA II, 327.

8. AA II, 330.

9. AA II, 327n.

10. KrV B 425–426—my emphasis. Here it is the assumption of a purposiveness of nature that leads to a sort of analogical inference to moral teleology (man as *Endzweck*

of the universe) and to the validity of morality itself. The transcendental status of the concept of purposiveness is utterly unclear to Kant at this time. In the third *Critique,* on the contrary, the argument runs in the opposite direction: it is morality that supports teleology as ethico-teleology.

11. KrV B 421.

12. KU §72, 320; §42, 169–170.

13. KU §72, 320.

14. *Dreams,* AA II, 331.

15. AA II, 327n.—my emphasis.

16. KrV B 403/A 345—my emphasis.

17. See KrV B 403/A 345. The claim implies something like: all spirituality is also animal but not all animality is also spiritual.

18. See Susan M. Shell (1996), chaps. 8 and 9, with particular attention to the problem of "generation" and the origin of life in the critique of teleological judgment. Rudolf A. Makkreel (1990, ch. 5) underscores the scant attention the topic of life in the third *Critique* has received in the literature; for post-Kantian developments see Makkreel (1985), B. Zeldin (1980), and A. Nuzzo (2007).

19. Here I limit myself to a brief sketch of the problem. For a historical perspective: J. Roger (1963); E. Farber (1954); T. S. Hall (1969). For a contemporary perspective: F. Jacob (1970); and for an introductory study that ties the problem of animal life to aesthetic imagination M. Ferraris (1996), 54–55, 71–77, 80–95.

20. I. Prigogine and I. Stengers (1979), ch. 2, 137, 140, and ch. 3.

21. See Jacob (1970), chaps. 1–2.

22. D. Diderot (1964), 367. The metaphysical background of Diderot's position is the idea of the "chain of being"; see the classic study A. Lovejoy (1960).

23. Diderot, "Entretien entre d'Alembert et Diderot" (1964), 258, 276.

24. Diderot (1964), 311, 313. *Mutatis mutandis,* an analogous debate can be found in the contemporary discussion, see *Zoontologies: The Question of the Animal,* ed. C. Wolfe (2003—in particular A. Lingis, "Animal Body, Inhuman Face," 165–182); J. Derrida, "The Animal That Therefore I Am (More to Follow)" (2002); and see also the problem raised by Heidegger in *Sein und Zeit* (1927), §68, 346. In commenting on Heidegger's passage, Derrida (2002, 391) underscores the issue of knowing whether "the animal *has time*"; instead, in the same passage, I underscore the question of the sensibility *"in einem Nur-Lebenden."*

25. For a possible historical relation between Bayle and Kant, see D. A. Rees (1954) on the first *Critique;* J. Ferrari (1967, 1979); N. K. Smith (1941), 284ff., 325ff., 506ff.; and J. Delvolvé (1906). For the reception of Bayle in the German Enlightenment, see I. Dingel (1998) and G. Sauder (1975).

26. See P. Bayle (1697), "Rorarius," note K. As is clear from the second *Critique,* Kant opposes the distinction between a lower and higher faculty of desire based on the material versus more spiritual (or less material) stimulus that prompts our desire. He shifts the discussion to the a priori *Bestimmungsgrund* of practical reason. If the ground of the will's determination is desire, the determination is material, no matter what type of desire (higher or lower).

27. Bayle (1697), "Rorarius," note C.

28. This argument is taken up by the anonymous writer of the article "Ame de bêtes" of the *Encyclopédie.* See Diderot (1765); see also Voltaire's article "Bêtes" in his *Dictionnaire philosophique* (1961, 50–53).

29. Bayle (1697), "Rorarius," note K. This anti-teleological argument goes back to Celsus.

30. Bayle (1697), "Rorarius," note L.

31. See Gassendi's fifth objection to Descartes's *Meditationes,* and his *Syntagma philosophiae Epicuri* (1649); the presence of Epicurus in this debate is relevant to our discussion of Kant, see below. For the eighteenth-century British tradition see, for example, J. W. Yolton (1983), 153–184.

32. See KU §§72–73.

33. KrV B 876/A 848.

34. KrV B 877/A 849.

35. KU §89, 442.

36. Similarly, Makkreel (1990, 154–162) proposes to read the validity of aesthetic and teleological judgment in relation to the problem of orientation raised by Kant's earlier essay.

37. KU E§IV, xxvi.

38. KU E§IV, xxviii.

39. KU E§IV, xxvii; EE§VIII, 225,27ff.

40. KU E§II, xx, AA V, 176,14–15; §40; KrV B xi ff., where Kant uses *Denkungsart* to indicate the realm in which "revolution" in science takes place. Revolutions in science—including the revolution brought forth by the first *Critique*—are radical transformations of the *Denkart,* of the way in which science has been practiced up until that point. B xvi: "*Umänderung der Denkart.*" The term is relatively new in the German language. It starts being used in the second half of the eighteenth century; see J. Grimm and W. Grimm (1952), art. *Denkart, Denkungsart.*

41. EE§V, 214,5; EE §IV, AA XX, 209,17: the image of the "crude chaotic aggregate without the slightest trace of a system."

42. See the crucial passage in EE §II, AA XX, 203–204n. (the content, if not the wording of the passage, is maintained in KU §V): "The possibility of an experience in general is the possibility of empirical cognitions as synthetic judgments. Hence this possibility cannot be derived *analytically* from a mere comparison of perceptions [. . .]; for the connection of two different perceptions in the concept of an object (to yield a cognition of it) is a *synthesis,* and the only way in which this synthesis makes empirical cognition, i.e., experience possible is through principles [*Prinzipien*] of the synthetic unity of appearances, i.e., through principles [*Grundsätze*] by which they are brought under the categories. Now these empirical cognitions do form an *analytic unity of all experience according to that which they necessarily have in common (namely those transcendental laws of nature); but they do not form that synthetic unity of experience as a system that connects the empirical laws even according to that in which they differ (and where their diversity can be infinite)*" (my emphasis).

43. See EE§V, 214,5. Obstruction of the senses characterizes—both for Kant and Diderot—mechanist rationality. For Kant the understanding is dumb in front of nature's heterogeneity and multiplicity of forms; for Diderot it is deaf to the stone's cry: in both cases "insensitive," as it were, to life's peculiar manifestations. The developments of this debate in J. G. Herder's *Treatise on the Origin of Language* are interesting. In 1772, Herder insists precisely in the opposite direction: our human capacity for "hearing," "feeling," and our general sensitivity to the sounds of the world of objects and other living beings (e.g., the bleating of sheep) is the point of origin of human language.

44. See EE§V, 214,7–8.

45. KU §IV, xxvi.

46. For this claim, I follow Prigogine and Stengers (1979, 135, 144, 145). Interestingly, with regard to the first *Critique* these authors consider Kant as exclusively providing the philosophical justification for the paradigm of the "unique language" of all phenomena proper to Newtonian science. They do not seem to suspect that the problem they are presenting—the emergence of particular processes of organization out of the universal, undifferentiated context of the "system of the world"—is precisely Kant's problem in the *Critique of Judgment*. For the differentiation of languages in the animal world, see M. de Montaigne, "Apology for Raymond Sebond" (1957), vol. 2, ch. 12, 331; it is discussed in Derrida (2002), 375.

47. KU §V, xxxvi, AA V, 185.

48. EE §II, AA XX, 203,9–11. See KU §VIII, L for Kant's use of *orientieren*. The problem of reflective judgment therein expressed is reformulated by Lyotard in terms of "gaps" (1988b, 28–44): put in this way, the question of reflective judgment seems common to both aesthetics and politics (p. 28). See also Lyotard (1990). De Man recognizes the counter-tendency to systematicity at play in the aesthetic, anti-teleological "materialism" of the third *Critique* as a dismembering "not only of nature but of the body" (1996, 89; discussed in J. Butler (2001), 268–272). I think, however, that such dismembering is not the work of reflective judgment but rather of the mechanism that judgment contrasts (more below): the aesthetic vision of the human body is not devoid of purposiveness, as it is not a "pure" judgment of taste (see next chapter for the "ideal of beauty"). The issue of the unity *with nature* is a crucial concern in J. Sallis (2000b). While for Sallis imagination as force (not as faculty) is the vehicle for a new understanding of nature beyond the traditional separation of sensible/intelligible or mind/body, I show that for Kant a transcendental concept of the "body reflected" is key to a more fundamental relationship with living nature which is close to what Sallis advocates. Unity with nature is indeed possible in the transcendental framework.

49. The higher faculties are the *facultas attendendi et reflectendi* and the *ingenium;* see D. Henrich (1992), 39. Kant renders "*Reflectieren*" with "*Überlegen*," whereby he follows the terminology of the school: see, for example, C. Wolff (1739), §72 for "*Überdenken*." See also C. Hauser (1994). For the notion of "transcendental reflection" see KrV B 316ff./A 260ff. (I use "reflection" and "reflective faculty of judgment" interchangeably in the context of the third *Critique,* although they are technically distinguished by Kant.)

50. See KrV B 316/A 260.

51. EE §V, AA XX, 211,14–20.

52. *Reflexion* 403, AA XV, 162.

53. See EE §V, AA XX, 211,20–21.

54. *Reflexion* 403, AA XV, 162. See, however, Kant's early work *Die falsche Spitzfindigkeit der vier syllogistischen Figuren* (1762), AA II, 59–60, where he denies to animals the capacity of judgment on the ground that "it is something quite different to *distinguish* things from each other and to *know* the difference among things."

55. See KU §90, 448–449n.

56. For an account of reflection in the empiricist tradition, see J. Locke, *An Essay Concerning Human Understanding,* book 2, ch. 1, no. 4: as a typically human operation of the mind, reflection is, along with sensation, the source of ideas. For a brief historical discussion of the claim that reflection is proper to both humans and animals, see M. Ferraris (1996), 95. In "Animal Body, Inhuman Face" (2003, 169–170), Lingis seems to

propose a reflection in the opposite direction: it is only through animals (and animal emotions) that we discover our *human* emotions. Lingis's move complements (rather than opposes) the perspective I present here. To be successful (or simply possible), the exchange between humans and animals must presuppose an idea of reflection that is genuinely Kantian.

57. See E §V title.

58. KU §V, xxix–xxx.

59. KU §V, xxxiii, AA V, 184,3–4 (my emphasis); see also KU §VI, xxxviii.

60. KU §V, xxxiii, AA V, 183,34–184,2.

61. EE §VI, AA XX, 217,28.

62. See KU §70, 315.

63. KU §74, 329, AA 395,30–32; in this connection Kant discusses the lack of "objective reality" proper to the concept of real purpose: KU §74, 330, 331, AA V, 396–397; see also §91, 454, AA 467,4–9.

64. KU §V, xxxi, and KrV B 685ff./A 657ff. where the principles of "homogeneity, specification, and continuity" of nature's forms are mentioned. For the general topic raised herein, see Lovejoy (1960), 240–241. It is worth noticing that Lovejoy never mentions the *Critique of Judgment,* and refers only to the Appendix of the Transcendental Dialectic of the first *Critique.*

65. KU §V, xxxiv, AA V, 184,16–19.

66. See KU §42, 169, AA V, 300 for nature's *Wink;* §42, 170, 172, AA V, 301 for nature's figurative language. See M. Riedel (1996), 524; also *Reflexion* 748, AA XV, 328 (more in the next chapter). For the theme of the "response" see Derrida (2002), 378, 382–383, 388. While Derrida construes the response *of* nature and *of* animals as the radical alternative to the (human, subject-centered) response *to* nature and *to* animals, I see the two responses as mutually implying each other, and connected in the structure of reflective judgment.

67. Nature gives us a *Wink* in both parts of the third *Critique:* KU §42, 169, AA V, 300 for the critique of aesthetic judgment, and §72, 320 for the critique of teleological judgment.

68. KU §VI title.

69. See KU §VI, xxxviii.

70. KU §VI, xl, AA V, 187,35.

71. See the clause *"wenn es gelingt"* in KU §VI, xl, AA V, 188,1.

72. KU §VI, xxxvi, AA V, 185,23.

73. KU §VI, xl, AA V, 188,3.

74. Kant speaks of *"widerstreiten"* in KU §VI, xli, AA V, 188,10.

75. Transcendentally, the distinction between beautiful and sublime goes back to this inner duality of feeling.

76. KU §VI, xl; §62, 274. The reference to the heavens at the end of the second *Critique* and the connection of admiration with orientation must be added to the discussion of the sublime—such a reference is curiously missing in De Man (1996, 82–84), though he addresses a somehow similar set of issues.

77. See EE §VIII, AA XX, 230,8–231,2 for a transcendental definition of the "feeling of pleasure."

78. KU §VI, xxxix, AA V, 187,12–14.

79. KU §VI, xxxix, AA V, 187,14–15. Guyer objects that universal validity does not follow from apriority (1997, 64–65).

80. KU §VI, xxxix, AA V, 187,15–18.

81. See EE §VIII, AA XX, 230,8–231,2.

82. KU §89, 443.

83. KU §VII, xliii, AA V, 189—my emphasis. For the immediacy of the relation, see also Preface, VIII, AA V, 169, 22.

84. KU §VII, xlvi–xlvii, AA V, 191–192.

85. KU §VIII, xlviii, AA V, 192. It is important to stress Kant's wording: the aesthetic representation of purposiveness rests on the "immediate pleasure we feel from the form of the object in the mere reflection on that form" (xlix, AA V, 192,24–25). Kant does not simply say 'the pleasure we feel when we reflect on the form of the object.' Kant's wording implies here two acts: the reflection on the form and the feeling of pleasure in it. Pleasure is produced by the form of the object on which we reflect. To this extent, judgments of taste do engage into a relation to the object.

86. KU §VII, xliv, AA V, 189, 36–37/190, 2.

87. KU §VII, xlviii, AA V, 191, 7–10.

88. EE§XII, AA XX, 250, 1–2.

89. KU §49, 192.

90. KU §VIII, xlviii, AA V, 192, 17.

91. KU §VIII, xlix, AA V, 192, 22–23, 28–29.

92. See §61, 270, AA V, 361, 5–6.

93. See KU Preface, IX, AA V, 169, 35.

94. KU §VIII, l, AA V, 193, 19.

95. KU §VII, xlviii.

96. KpV A 39–40 (AA V, 21–22)—my emphasis.

97. In the *Anthropology from a Pragmatic Point of View* (§15, AA VII, 153), Kant draws a distinction between "inner sense (*sensus internus*)" and "interior sense (*sensus interior*)" or "*innwendiger Sinn*." The former is a mere faculty of perception, while the latter is "the feeling of pleasure and displeasure—that is, the *Empfänglichkeit* of the subject in being determined by certain representations, either to preserve or to reject the state of the representations." See Makkreel (1990), 94.

98. KU §1, 4; also §3, 9.

99. KU §1, 4—my emphasis.

100. In *Prolegomena* §46, A 136n., AA IV, 334 in discussing the psychological ideas of reason, Kant presents the representation of the transcendental I of apperception as "nothing more than the *feeling (Gefühl)* of an existence without the least concept" (my emphasis). This feeling has, necessarily, a non-cognitive value. In the 1798 *Streit der Fakultäten* (AA VII, 100), Kant argues that our health is not an object of self-knowledge but only of feeling. "One can *feel* oneself healthy (judging from the comfortable feeling of his life), but one can never *know* that one is healthy." The question here is whether this feeling of one's own health displays a transcendental validity or is only a matter of empirical, psychological awareness. My claim is that the third *Critique* grounds the transcendental space for this type of self-experience.

101. And we should remember, from the first *Critique*, that "transcendental reflection" as "transcendental *Überlegung*" is the ground of a "transcendental topic" (KrV B 316ff./A 260ff.). In the third *Critique*, we have finally reached the point where transcendental reflection indicates the "place" (*topos*) that reflection itself or the reflective faculty of judgment occupies in transcendental philosophy.

102. KU §1, 4: "sich dieser Vorstellung mit der Empfindung des Wohlgefallens bewusst zu sein." Importantly, what "affects" us is not the object, its materiality or existence, but its *representation*.

103. KU §1, 4. Lingis's notion of "sensuality" and its connection to the "elemental" of life (which, following Levinas is "enjoyment," identification with the sensuous medium) being neither passive (like sensation) nor active (in the sense of the intellectual) corresponds, in another perspective, to this Kantian moment. See Lingis (1998), 15–22; (1994), 107, 122ff. However, whereas Lingis underscores the *ethical* significance of sensuality, for Kant the *Lebensgefühl* grounds a specifically *aesthetic* experience. A view of nature in the sense of the "elemental" that moves away from Kant going back to the Greeks is offered by Sallis (2000b), ch. 6: elemental nature precedes the sensible and is responsible for the original "gathering" of the sensible.

104. *Reflexion* 4857, AA XVIII, 11—my emphasis. For the fundamental character of life, see *Reflexion* 6862, AA XIX, 183 (and Shell (1996), 229) in which Kant claims that "it all comes down to life; what enlivens (*belebt*) (or the feeling of the furtherance of life) is pleasant."

105. *Reflexion* 288, AA XV, 108: "Sense is either the absolute or the relative; through the latter we refer our sensations to an object, through the former to ourselves. The absolute sense is feeling."

106. *Religion*, AA VI, 26. The passage was quoted in part 2 with regard to the concept of personality.

107. See Makkreel's suggestion (1990, 105). Derrida (2002, 393) considers Kant as one of the many philosophers who—from Aristotle to Descartes to Lacan—are unable to thematize the issue of animal life in its exchange with the human. Indeed, what the third *Critique* presents from the outset is what Derrida says of this entire tradition, namely, the "auto-situation of man [. . .] with respect to what is living and with respect to animal life." In my view, however, this connection between (auto-)reflection and *Lebensgefühl* undermines the clear-cut animal/human distinction drawn by the understanding, thereby ushering in a position that is much closer to Derrida's "*animot*" than he may be willing to recognize (2002, 409, 415–416). I read Derrida's proposal as a necessary complication of Kant's suggestion in light of our contemporary predicament, rather than as a radical alternative to it. In her interpretation of the third *Critique,* Arendt (1982, 23–25, 29ff.) only hints at the issue of life in a comparison with the Greek ethical tradition: for her, however, life raises only *moral* issues. In contrast, I would argue that the "enlarged" mentality that judgment promotes and on which Arendt particularly insists as the merit of the third *Critique* is grounded in the transcendental, *aesthetic* dimension of the "feeling for life."

108. Or it relegates it to a "dream" (Diderot).

109. See *Reflexion* 4857, AA XVIII, 11 quoted above.

110. KU §1, 5.

111. See KU §2.

112. KpV A 286 (AA V, 160).

113. As mentioned above, the connection between Kant's idea of aesthetic judgment and the concept of life has been discussed only rarely in the secondary literature. Makkreel's study (1990, ch. 5) is certainly the most extensive one (see also R. Zuckert (2007, 179) for the "feeling for life"). However, the connection that Makkreel establishes leaves out of the "transcendental" discussion the issue of embodiment. This issue presents itself inevitably in the conclusions of Makkreel's reflections, bringing along

the other issue of the relation between animals and humans. The presence of the body raises a problem for Makkreel's interpretation, as does the proximity between animal and human life and the "basic" character that Kant recognizes in animal life and its bodily component, for the body seems to "compromise" the purity of aesthetic feeling (1990, 104–105). In addition, Makkreel's interpretation commits Kant to the dogmatic claim that the body is "lifeless" (pp. 98, 101). My aim, on the contrary, is to show that the transcendental presence of the body is the basis of Kant's idea of the aesthetic feeling for life (and thereby also of the activity of teleological judgment). This account allows me to solve the difficulties encountered by Makkreel's interpretation with regard to the relation between feeling of life and embodiment.

114. Maybe for animals and spirits the experience of beauty is not necessary.

115. Significantly, in the quoted final passage of the second *Critique* (see ch. 7, above), Kant's discussion of the attitude of the "observer of nature" toward his specimens, which he eventually comes to like after they have offended his senses, receives an important turn as it connects to the idea of life. For Kant, Leibniz's attitude becomes exemplary as an "observer of nature" in the moment in which he "spared an insect which he had carefully examined under the microscope, and replaced it on its leaf" (KpV A 286, AA V, 160). Herein, respect for life is certainly not a moral imperative. Its status, however, is still unclear in this passage.

116. See KpV A 15n. (AA V, 10) and MS AB 1 (VI, 211).

117. Respectively, *Reflexion* 6870 and *Reflexion* 6862, AA XIX, 183.

118. KU §3.

119. KU §2 title, see also the *"Bestimmungsgrund"* of §1, 4.

120. See KU §§2–3.

121. KU §2, 6.

122. I represent the object as purposive without a purpose (see the third moment of the judgment of taste, KU §§10–17).

123. See KU §9, 28; §54, 223–224.

124. KU §4, 10.

125. KU §4, 12.

126. See KU §5, 14, AA V, 209, 21–22.

127. KU §4, 13; §5, 14, AA V, 209, 21–22.

128. See KU §5 title; 15.

129. KU §5, 14.

130. *Reflexion* 6862, AA XIX, 183.

131. *Reflexion* 823, AA XV, 367; also *Reflexion* 824, AA XIX, 368, and the passage of *Religion* AA VI, 26, discussed above.

132. The issue of animal life, which appears as a disturbing problem for Makkreel's interpretation (1990, 104) is also problematic for Scaravelli, who cannot find any justification for Kant's mention of the relation between animals and humans in the third *Critique* except the unsatisfactory systematic one that since animals "found a place neither in the *Critique of Pure Reason* (for Kant considers them machines) nor in the *Critique of Practical Reason* (because he does not want to attribute them noumenical freedom and representation of the law), if there are animals they should be hosted in the *Critique of Judgment*" (1968, 412).

133. It can be, at the most, the topic of empirical psychology. See KpV A 39–40 (AA V, 21–22) discussed above.

134. KU §5, 15.

135. See F. Calori (2003), 148–149. Calori discusses the passage of KU §5 in the perspective of the second *Critique*'s concept of *Achtung* and discovers a contradiction with KpV A 135, AA V, 76, in which Kant denies a feeling of respect for the law to the highest being. The *Wohlgefallen* for the good, however, is not the same feeling as the respect for the moral law. In addition, Kant's argument in KU §5 concerns the respective *validity* of the pleasurable, the beautiful, and the good, not directly the feeling connected to them. This issue presupposes the important claim (which Calori follows throughout his essay) that in the practical sphere the feeling *follows* the pure a priori principle of practical reason's legislation (in the case of the pleasurable, instead, the validity of what is pleasurable is based on the feeling that the object produces). In the case of the good, at stake is not the question of who is the subject that has a feeling toward the good, but rather the question: for whom is the good a value in its own right?

136. KU §5, 15: the "*freies* Wohlgefallen" of the judgment of taste.

137. There is an appearance of circularity here, which is, however, necessary and grounded in the nature of the reflective faculty of judgment. Since judgment of taste has an a priori principle of its own, there is the need for a third *Critique;* yet, only in the transcendental perspective opened up by the third *Critique* can we actually *see* the independency of the principle of aesthetic judgment. The first proposition is demonstrated by Kant in the introduction of the *Critique of Judgment,* the second is established by the four moments of the judgment of taste.

138. See KrV B 421.

139. KU §5, 15. This claim complicates Kant's position in KrV B 574/A 546 in which the difference between man and "leblose(n), oder bloß tierischbelebte(n) Natur" is placed in man's possession of understanding and reason in addition to the mere receptivity of sensibility. The passage is the starting point of F. Nobbe (1995).

140. The move from the assessment of the man/animals difference in the first and second *Critique* (reason) to the third *Critique* (aesthetic feeling) also complicates the perspective in which Derrida places Kant in "The Animal That Therefore I Am" (2002, 396), which seems indeed to refer exclusively to the first *Critique*. With Bentham, Derrida shifts the question from asking whether animals *have reason* (which he takes as Kant's problem) to asking whether animals *can suffer.* Kant's view in the third *Critique,* however—centered on the issues of feeling and life, individuality and contingency, and based on reflection—moves much closer to Derrida's own concerns and to the set of issues he expresses with the neologism "*animot*" (2002, 409, 415–416). (See also Derrida (1976), 81–87 for the "name of man," namely, the issue of how man gives himself this name by delimiting himself from all non-human others: the animal, the natural world, the non-living, and the important complications that Derrida brings to the problem posed by Kant.) The difference at stake is, for Kant, only *trascendental* and can be detected only *transcendentally;* moreover, being based on the necessary recognition of man's own "animality," such difference does not exclude the animal from the human but rather specifies it in terms of experience.

141. As described in KU §1.

142. KU §5, 15.

143. See for example KU §87, 428 (see next chapter).

144. See KU §70, 315; §73, 324–325. For the reference to Epicurus, see *Reflexion* 823 discussed above. For Kant's historical sources, see P. Giordanetti (2001), 106–112; and P. Aubenque (1969), 293–303.

145. *Reflexion* 4851, AA XVIII, 8.

146. *Reflexion* 4867, AA XVIII, 15.

147. For example, *Reflexion* 4868, AA XVIII, 15; *Reflexion* 4894, AA XVIII, 21; also KrV B 882/A 854.

148. *Reflexion* 823, AA XV, 367; *Reflexion* 824, AA XIX, 368 and the passage of *Religion* AA VI, 26 discussed above.

149. *Reflexion* 4866, AA XVIII, 14; also *Reflexion* 4893; AA XVIII, 21.

150. KrV B167; for Kant's comparison of physical and intellectual generation see Shell (1996), 230ff.

151. KrV B 119/A 87; B 126–127/A 94–95.

152. KrV A IX.

153. *Reflexion* 4859, AA XVIII, 12.

154. See KpV A 158 (AA V, 88–89). Accordingly, on Kant's account, the idea of 'respect for life' must receive a specification with regard to the principle that produces that feeling of respect. What prompts a feeling of respect is, truly, "something entirely different than life," it is the moral law from which we gain a feeling for our "supersensible existence"—see KpV A 157–158 (AA V, 88).

155. MS, A IX, AA VI, 378.

156. KrV B 128. Unlike Locke, Epicurus is, in Kant's view, a more consistent empiricist who never leaves the territory of experience—see KrV B 882/A 854.

157. *Prolegomena* §21, A 86; §24, A 90.

158. See *Prolegomena* §24, A 90.

159. KrV B 873–874/A 845–846.

160. KU §29, 128, AA V, 277. The 1790 edition of the *Critique of Judgment* has "psychological" exposition; "psychological" is replaced by "physiological" in the 1793 edition. Kant quotes Burke's *Philosophical Enquiry into the Origin of our Ideas of the Sublime and the Beautiful* from Garve's free German translation of the fifth edition: *Philosophische Untersuchungen über den Ursprung unserer Ideen vom Erhabenen und Schönen* (Riga: Hartknoch, 1773). Historical details on the Kant-Burke relationship can be found in Giordanetti (2001), 130ff.; see also V. Ryan (2001).

161. KU §29, 129, AA V, 277.

162. For Kant's agreement with Epicurus, see, in addition, the passage at the beginning of KU §54, 222: Epicurus "may perhaps not have been wrong" in claiming that all gratification is at bottom bodily sensation.

163. KU §29, 129, AA V, 277–278. See also Makkreel (1990), 105. This passage raises problems for his thesis of the "mental nature of life" because it seems to re-propose the dualistic body/mind opposition. I argue that Kant's transcendental notion of embodiment programmatically defies this dualism.

164. See again KU §5, 15. This argument transcendentally poses the question of animal suffering that Derrida (2002, 396) instead excludes from Kant's investigation.

165. The lack of understanding of the complex nature of Kant's *transcendental* inquiry and, more properly, the assumption that the transcendental perspective is *per se* exclusive of the bodily component of human experience leads T. Baumeister to reduce Kant's aesthetic position to the psychological aesthetic of his contemporaries. Baumeister (1998, 170) underscores the importance of the presence of the body in Kant's theory, yet cannot make any other sense of it but a psychological one.

166. The explanation of this difference constitutes a problem for Makkreel (1990, 105–106).

167. See KU §29, 130, AA V, 278.

168. See KU §54, 222: in this claim Epicurus "only misunderstood himself."

169. KU §54, 222.

170. KU §73, 324.

9. Embodied Ideas

1. KU E§II. See G. Deleuze's *Kant's Critical Philosophy. The Doctrine of the Faculties* (1984) which is a reflection on Kant's criticism in terms of the topology of the faculties and their interrelations. Deleuze reads the third *Critique* under the poetic heading of Rimbaud's "disorder of all the senses," as the place in which the "unregulated exercise of all the faculties" is finally sanctioned (p. xi).

2. KU E§II, xvi, AA V, 174,12–15.

3. Kant argues, however, that the field is for us unlimited (see below).

4. KU E§II, xvii, AA V, 174,28–29. See H. Holzhey (1970), 247; for the claim that experience is for us territory, see 250–252.

5. KU E§II, xviii, AA V, 175,11.

6. KU E§II, xvii, AA V, 174,27; XVI, AA V, 174, 3–5.

7. KU E§II, xvi/xvii, AA V, 174,17–19. This definition parallels the one of the territory as "the complex of the objects of all possible experience" taken as mere appearances (xvii, 174,28–29).

8. See for example KrV B 165.

9. KU E§II, xvii, AA V, 174,20.

10. For example: KrV B 218ff./ A 176ff.; B 64/A 47, B 148–149.

11. KU E§II, xviii, AA V, 175,5–6.

12. KU E§II, xix.

13. KU E§II, xviii, 175,9–12. See Kant's conclusion in KrV B 586/A 558.

14. KU E§II, xviii, AA V, 175,6–16—my emphasis.

15. See KpV A 170ff., 178, AA V, 95ff., 99.

16. KU E§II, xvii, AA V, 174,28–29; KrV B 446–447/A 418–419 for the distinction between "nature" and "world."

17. KU E§II, xviii, AA V, 175,22.

18. KU E§II, xviii/xix, AA V, 175,23–24

19. KU §60, 263.

20. KU E§II, xix, AA V, 175,33.

21. KU §49, 193.

22. KU §29, 110.

23. KU §49, 193; AA V 314—my emphasis. See Deleuze (2004).

24. KU §29, 110.

25. KU E§II, xix, AA V, 175,26.

26. *Was heißt sich im Denken Orientieren?* A311. See ch. 5, above.

27. KU E§II, xix.

28. See KU E§II, xviii–xx.

29. In addition to *Was heißt?* see, for example, the discussion on "empirical" and "intelligible character" in the first *Critique,* and the "dream" recounted by Kant in the *Observations,* in which the abyss appears significantly as "immeasurable abyss of darkness" (AA II, 209–210; discussed by J. Sallis (1987, 82–84) as leading to the thematic of the sublime).

30. KU E§II, xix, AA V, 176.

31. KU E§II, xx, AA V, 176,8.

32. KU §49, 193.

33. KU E§II, xx, AA V, 176,10–15.

34. See KrV B xi ff.: "Revolution der Denkart"; B xvi: "Umänderung der Denkart." Intellectual revolutions are, for Kant, radical transformations of the *Denkart*—transformations in the way in which science has been practiced up until that point. *Denkungsart* designates both the methodological structure of inquiry and the general mode or way of proceeding in the inquiry. For Kant, as for the Enlightenment, it means, in general, *Weltanschauung* and indicates the rational approach to the world and to life proper to our common human understanding. KU §40 presents the "maxims of the common human understanding" as an important integration and explanation of the principles of the critique of taste. Such maxims directly regard our *Denkungsart*.

35. KrV B 29/A 15; Kant further develops this point in KU E§III, xxii AA V, 177,18–19. The passage from the first *Critique* is notoriously the starting point of Heidegger, *Kant und das Problem der Metaphysik* (1973); see D. Henrich, "On the Unity of Subjectivity" (1994, 17–54).

36. KU §57, 239, AA V, 341.

37. KU E§II, xx, AA V, 176,10.

38. KU E§IX, liv, AA V, 195,17–23.

39. KU E§IX, liv, AA V, 195,24–28—my emphasis.

40. KU, liii, AA V, 195,10; lv, AA V, 195,35.

41. KU E§IX, lv, AA V, 196,34. In E§IX first footnote, Kant responds to an objection still formulated in the vocabulary of "influence" between nature and freedom. To claim that nature sets obstacles to freedom's causality or that nature furthers freedom's efforts, means, according to the objection, assuming a possible "influence" of nature on freedom, which Kant instead denies. In other words, the contradiction is placed between Kant's attempt to maintain nature and freedom as completely separated, and his claim that freedom's—and only freedom's—causality has an import on nature's own causality. Kant clarifies that the vocabulary of "hindrances" to or "furthering" of freedom does not establish any relation between nature and freedom as such. It only describes a relationship among appearances, i.e., the relation between natural appearances and the appearance of freedom's effects in the sensible world.

42. KU E§IX, lv n., AA V, 196,33–37; lvi, AA V, 196,17–18.

43. "[E]xistieren *soll*": KU E§IX, lv, AA V, 196,1; also §II, xix, AA V, 176,4; "Subjekt[s] als Sinnenwesen[s]": KU E§IX, lv, AA V, 196,2–3; already KpV A74, AA V, 43.

44. KU E§IX, lv, AA V, 196,4–7.

45. "General Remark on the Exposition of Aesthetic Reflective Judgments," 119, AA V, 270,33–34.

46. KU E§IX, lv, AA V, 196,9–11. Notice that Kant does not ask how the actualization of the final purpose is possible; rather, he asks *how we can know* the possibility of the final purpose as actualized in accordance with nature's laws; he asks *how* we are able to recognize that possibility: *by means (durch) of which faculty and by means of which concept*.

47. KU E§IX, lvi, AA V, 196,17–18—my emphasis. Recall the moral law placed within ourselves and the starry sky above us at the end of the second *Critique*.

48. See the inference drawn in KrV B xxvi–xxvii with regard to the relation appearance/thing-in-itself.

49. KU E§IX, lvi, AA V, 196,12–22.

50. KU E§IX, lvi, AA V, 196,17–18.

51. KU E§IX, lvii, AA V, 197,10.

52. KU E§IX, lvii, AA V, 197,7–8.

53. KU E§IX, lvii, AA V, 197,10–15; also §60, 263.

54. See KU §5 discussed in the previous chapter.

55. KU §29, 129; see R. Makkreel (1990), 105.

56. KU E§IX, lvi, AA V, 196,17–18.

57. KU §65, 293, AA V, 374,34–35.

58. KU E§IX, lvii, AA V, 197,10–15; §60, 263; §29, 110.

59. KrV B 860/A 833.

60. The Analytic of the teleological faculty of judgment is dedicated to the first issue, while the Methodology, and more specifically Kant's ethico-theology, are dedicated to the second issue.

61. KrV B 860/A 833. See Krell's puzzled remark (1997, 49) on this occurrence of the animal body (instead of the human body): ultimately, Kant's point is to establish the analogy between animals and humans on the basis of their embodied condition. For the link between animal body and systematicity (and the unsettling function of the sublime), see P. De Man (1996), 88: the image of the animal body is here Platonic, not Aristotelian. The position that I am advocating—whereby the human subject because of her embodied condition is drawn within the system/body of nature as its active, living part—may be compared to Deleuze's reading of the third *Critique* in terms of the idea of "genesis" (1984, 52ff.). The problem of how and where the philosopher is placed with regard to nature—between "the sky above and the earth beneath," *within* nature and "engaging in a mimetic reflection of the order beheld above back into the human soul"—is Sallis's concern in (2000), 147–148. Significantly, Sallis goes back to the *Timaeus*.

62. KrV B 860/A 833. For a broader discussion, see A. Nuzzo (2003).

63. KU §67, 299, AA V, 378,12–14.

64. KU §64, 284, AA V, 369,33—my emphasis; also §65, 294, AA V, 275.

65. KU §64, 284–285, AA V, 370,1–13.

66. Thereby the claim of KU §5 can be repeated for the second half of the third *Critique*. Kant recalls the issue of the system of experience at the beginning of §61.

67. Although Kant denies that a deduction is required for the concept of natural purpose, the reference to "objective reality" (§65), and the mention of necessity and universality of the principle of reflective judgment (§66) allows me to designate the present step of the argument as the proof that takes the place of a deduction. See EE§XII, AA XX, 250 which still contemplates a "deduction" for teleological judgment as well. After the *First Introduction,* one of the differences between aesthetic and teleological judgment is precisely the need for a deduction of the principle that is met by the former but not by the latter.

68. KU §65, 295, AA V, 376,1–2.

69. Respectively KU §64 title, and §65, 293, AA V, 374,34–35.

70. This principle claims "universality and necessity" for nature's internal purposiveness, whereby it must rest on an a priori ground. Proof is provided in KU §66.

71. KU §66, 295–296, AA V, 376,11–13.

72. KU §65, 289–290, AA V, 372,23–373,2.

73. KU §65, 290–291, AA V, 373,7–17.

74. KU §65, 291, AA V, 373,17–34.

75. KU §65, 291–293, AA V, 373,35–374,26. A watch, Kant argues, does not produce other watches, does not replace missing parts, and does not heal itself. In other words, only organized beings are self-producing and self-regulating beings. For the historical significance of the watch analogy in teleology and for Hume's important criticism thereof, see J. D. McFarland (1970), ch. 3.

76. KU §65, 293, AA V, 374,28–29.

77. Herein is rather the proximity between nature and the genius (which is precisely a force of nature: KU §17, 59 n.): KU §46; §57, 242.

78. KU §65, 293, AA V, 374,31–34.

79. See KU §72 of the Dialectic.

80. KU §65, 293–294, AA V, 375,5–7.

81. KU §65, 294. By distinguishing two different arguments by analogy with life and in particular by spelling out the argument that proposes an analogy to *our own* life, I try to solve the textual problem presented by this passage. Since Kant has clearly and effectively rejected both the analogy to art and the metaphysical analogy to life, why does he need to repeat that natural things as natural purposes cannot be called organized beings by analogy with a physical natural power, "given, as it were, that we too belong to nature in the broadest sense"? To make the situation worse, this claim is explicitly contradicted by the conclusion of §65 that does indeed establish an analogy (albeit a "remote" one) with our activity. On my view, our inclusion within nature is crucial to Kant's formulation of the specific regulative standpoint of reflective judgment as analogical standpoint.

82. KU §65, 294.

83. KU §67, 303, AA V, 380.

84. See the General Remark to §29, 128ff. For Kant's critique of physiology see ch. 8, above.

85. See KU §73.

86. KU §65, 295, AA V, 375, 18–20.

87. KU §65, 295. See Susan M. Shell (1996), 239–240.

88. KU §67, 297.

89. *Reflexion* 4863, AA XVIII, 13; see Shell (1996), 229–230. "Organism [. . .] provides the basis for a sort of intuitive knowledge that (somehow), by virtue of its unification of mind and body, steers clear of fanaticism."

90. See KpV A 288 (AA V, 161).

91. KU §87, 419; see Kant's letter to Mendelssohn dated 8 April 1766.

92. To this extent I do believe that Kant occupies a special position in the history outlined by Derrida (2002, 396).

93. KpV A 108 (AA V, 61).

94. In *Groundwork* AB 4–5 Kant suggests that if self-preservation and happiness were the sole aims of practical reason, we would be better off following animal instinct.

95. KpV A 108 (AA V, 61–62); also MAT§11, AA VI, 434.

96. KpV A 108 (AA V, 61).

97. See MAT §11, AA VI, 434.

98. KU §87, 423. In KpV A 122 (AA V 69), Kant formulates the "rule of judgment under laws of pure practical reason" in the following way: "Ask yourself whether, if the action which you propose should take place as a law of nature *of which you yourself were a part,* you could regard it as possible through your will" (my emphasis). The starting point of the third *Critique* is precisely the transcendental investigation of our condition as parts of nature.

99. This will become a central idea in Marx's anthropology.

100. See MAT, AA VI, 400 on "Moral Feeling." See F. Calori (2003, 120–121), in which, however, the perspective is that of the second *Critique*.

101. See below, the discussion of KU §87.

102. KU §86, 415.

103. KU §17, 54.

104. KUE §VIII, xlix.

105. KU §17, 56—my emphasis. "*Dieser* Mensch" is the one indicated by the transcendental perspective.

106. See KU §17, 56: "The standard idea of the figure of an animal of a particular species must take its elements from experience"; and §17, 58: "This standard idea is not derived from proportions taken from experience."

107. KU §17, 57: notice how Kant steps out of the transcendental perspective and proceeds tentatively in his "psychological explanation."

108. KU §17, 58.

109. KU §17, 56—my emphasis.

110. KU §17, 60—my emphasis.

111. KU §17, 60. For a discussion of the related perspective on the body as site in which the law is incorporated, and for the difference between internalization and incorporation of the law (with regard to Foucault), see J. Butler (1989).

112. For the importance of Kant's ideal of beauty in the post-Kantian reception, see for example David F. Krell (2005), 162–163 (with regard to Schelling), 384; and De Man (1996), 88 (for a contrast between beautiful and sublime with regard to the human body).

113. In the critique of aesthetic judgment the same point is addressed by the idea of the sublime—see below.

114. KU §86, 415.

115. See KU E§§II, XIX, 176 discussed above.

116. KU §86 Anm., 416.

117. KU §83 n., 396.

118. KU §86, 411, AA V, 442,33.

119. The argument is further developed in the General Remark to Teleology, 471, AA V, 477,9–19.

120. KU §87, 419, AA V, 447,19–10.

121. Echoing the *Critique of Practical Reason,* Kant maintains that only through a "good will" does human existence gain an "absolute value" and only in relation to it can everything else in the world have a "final purpose," i.e., a meaning (§86, 412, AA V, 443,10–13). Thus, only the moral determination of the human being as final purpose of creation allows Kant to move beyond physical teleology (and the *impasse* of deism and "demonology": KU §86, 413). On the other hand, the claim that man is a moral sensible being in connection with living nature, setting on him a moral obligation with regard to nature can open a fruitful perspective within an environmental ethics.

122. KU §87, 419. The double specification, 'in ourselves' and 'in the concept of a rational free being in general', is important. Thereby, our reflective self-awareness is supported by a rational reflection on what is implied by the concept of a rational being endowed with freedom. Clearly, the self-awareness to which Kant refers cannot be an empirical or merely psychological condition (for no empirical introspection can properly produce a moral teleology). It is instead a reflective state induced by reflective judgment.

123. KU §87, 419. This is Kant's final critical answer to the metaphysical problem of the *commercium* (see chaps. 1–3, above).

124. KU §87, 419—my emphasis.

125. KU §87, 420.

126. KU §87, 420, AA 448, 13–15. God as "moral author of the world" is the necessary assumption that makes the actualization of the final purpose of morality *subjectively* possible, i.e., possible *for us* in our limited human capacity (§87, 429, AA V, 453, 4–5).

127. See KU §§88–89, 91.

128. KU §87, 421.

129. See MAT, AA VI, 400; Calori (2003), 120–121.

130. KU §87, 422.

131. Similarly, in KU §5 the condition of animal life is deemed necessary to feel pleasure but insufficient to define the specific kind of *aesthetic* pleasure.

132. KU §87, 422.

133. KU §87, 423. By confronting this passage with KrV B 574/A 546 we can measure the advanced position reached by Kant in 1790.

134. KU §87, 423–424.

135. KU §88, 429, AA 453,16–20. Ultimately, Kant's moral proof depends upon the impossibility of a transition from nature to freedom by means of mere concepts of nature. The proof rests on the notion of the purposive harmony between the world of nature and the moral order established by moral teleology. Since the legislation of nature's mechanism and that of freedom retain their radical independence, only the reference to a moral cause of the world allows us to conceive of the purposive accordance between them.

136. KU §88, 429, AA 453,12,16.

137. KU §87, 424: "*verknüpft.*"

138. KU §87 title.

139. See KU E§IX; KU §88 Anm., 439: "Vereinigung der Natur mit ihrem inneren Sittengesetze."

140. KU §87, 425.

141. KU §87, 427.

142. Thereby, we fall back to the conflict between the "effects" of nature and freedom in this world described in KU E§II, xviii.

143. See MAT, AA VI, 400.

144. KU §87, 428—my emphasis. See Shell (1996), 261. This passage is proof that Kant is well aware of the issue of animal suffering, impotence, and vulnerability raised by Derrida (in Bentham's aftermath). See Derrida (2002), 396.

145. KU §87, 428.

146. KU §28, 105.

147. KU E§IX, lvi.

148. KU §28, 105.

149. See KU E§EVII, xlviii.

150. KU §23, 76.

151. KU §23, 78.

152. Respectively, KU §87, 428 and §23, 76.

153. KU §26, 95.

154. KU §23, 76. See De Man's reading of Kant's descriptions of sublime nature as anti-teleological "formal materialism" (1996, 82–89).

155. KU §23, 78. While Lyotard, in his well-known reading of the sublime as *differend* of imagination and reason, insists that the sublime is the subject's feeling of *"etwas ganz anderes,* or *differend"* (1994, 9), I show that for Kant the sublime is the reflected feeling that the embodied subject has *of itself.* Moreover, while Lyotard tends to separate the sublime from teleological judgment (p. 8), I argue for their close connection on the basis of the common task of reflection. Finally, Lyotard sees in sublime feeling the experience of a *limit* and the stretching of thinking itself to the limit (p. 131); on my view, the sublime arises instead from our experience of ourselves as the *center* or as internal part of nature. (Sallis raises the question of whether the sublime assumes a form that can be "confined to a determinate site"; see (1987), 105.) I am closer to De Man, who brings Kant's account of the dynamic sublime back to the architectonic of the first *Critique*—i.e., to the passage that compares system to the animal body, thereby raising the following question: "One will want to know what becomes of this Aristotelian"—but I would rather say Platonic—"zoomorphic architectonic when it is being considered, in the third *Critique*'s passage on heaven and the ocean, in a non-teleological, aesthetic perspective" (1996, 88). This is exactly my question. In order to answer it, De Man follows an analogous route to the one I propose (we must look at our own body and at its membership in nature) but reaches an opposite conclusion (a non-teleological view of the body is the view of a "mutilated" body).

156. See KU §29, 110: nature becomes a "schema for the imagination"; also KpV A 120ff. (AA V, 68ff.) in which the natural law, considered only in its form, becomes a "type" (*Typus*) of the moral law, and the "nature of the sensible world" is considered as "type of an intelligible nature" (A 124, AAV, 70). This is a crucial point for Sallis (1987), 115–116.

157. See KpV A 126 (AA V, 70–71).

158. KU §23, 76.

159. KU §23, 75.

160. KU §24, 80.

161. KU §23, 75, AA V, 245.

162. KU §24, 80; §27, 98.

163. KU §23, 76. See Sallis (1987), 103ff.; De Man (1996), 84–85; and ch. 7, 217 above.

164. KU §26, 95.

165. KU §29 General Remark, 120, AA V, 271, 3–7.

166. See *Reflexion* 4786, AA XVII, 728: "Bewegung in transcendentalen Verstande ist Leben."

167. KU §28, 105.

168. KU §28, 102, 104.

169. See Kant's clear statement in KU §29, 112–113, and §29 General Remark, 128–129, extensively commented in the previous chapter.

170. Clearly, this first condition sets Kant's transcendental inquiry into the sublime apart from a metaphysical one, as Makkreel (1990, 79–80) rightly sees. Guyer (1997, 294ff.) stresses instead the metaphysical character of Kant's investigation.

171. KU §28, 104–105.

172. On beauty as life-saving see E. Scarry (1999), 24–25, 27, 32.

173. KU §28, 104.

174. KU §87, 428.

175. KU §28, 105.

176. KU §23, 76: "sich sinnlich darstellen läßt."

177. KU §23, 76.

178. See also KU §26, 95.

179. See KpV A 289 (AA V, 161) and ch. 5, above. Lyotard (1994, 127) argues instead for the "irresolvable" nature of the sublime with regard to moral feeling.

180. Respectively KU §25, 85, and §26, 94.

181. KU §42, 169; §72, 320.

182. KU §26, 91. For teleological judgment, see §88 Anm., 438; §86 Anm., 416.

183. KU §27, 96, AA V, 257,9–10.

184. KU §27, 97.

185. KU §27, 100, AA V, 259,13–17.

186. KU §27, 96, AA V, 257,22–23.

187. KU §6, 18, AA V, 211, 23–24; also §23, 73, AA V, 245,25–26.

188. KU §23, 78, AA V, 246,22–25.

189. This connection is explored in P. Guyer (1998b, 342–345).

190. See Makkreel (1990), 73ff. Lyotard (1994, 20) concludes from the atemporal nature of this feeling to the erasure of the subject in the sublime.

191. KU §26, 92, AA V, 254,36–37. The case of an absolute magnitude (or the infinite) brings to light the idea that while apprehension has no limit and may go on *ad infinitum,* reason requires that the imagination complete the comprehension in the single graspable unity of a totality of intuition—a task that the imagination is unable to perform (§26, 92, AA V, 254,21–23). The imagination's striving to comprehend the infinite in a totality dissociates it from understanding, thereby revealing the presence of a supersensible faculty proper to the human *Gemüt.*

192. KU §26, 92—my emphasis. Kant's expression, underscoring the existence of an infinite proper to the sensible world, is already remarkable here.

193. KU §26, 93.

194. KU §29, 110.

Transcendental Embodiment

1. J. Derrida (2005), 36–37.

2. J.-L. Nancy (1976), 145; Derrida (2005), 37.

3. Derrida (2005), 38—my emphasis.

4. Derrida (2005), 44.

5. Derrida (2005), 43–44.

6. See Q. Cassam (1997), 3, 6.

Bibliography

Primary Sources

Baumgarten, A. G. 1993. *Meditationes philosophicae de nonnullis ad poema pertinentibus*, ed. A. Lamarra and P. Pimpinella. Florence: Olschki.

———. 1779. *Metaphysica*. Halle: Hemmerde.

———. 1758. *Aesthetica*. Frankfurt an der Oder, 1750–1758.

———. 1757. *Metaphysica*. Halle.

Bayle, P. 1697. *Dictionnaire historique et critique*. Amsterdam: Reinier Leers.

Beck, L. W. (trans.) 1986. *Kant's Latin Writings*. New York: Peter Lang.

Burke, E. 1757. *Philosophical Enquiry into the Origin of our Ideas of the Sublime and the Beautiful*. London: James Dodsley.

Crusius, C. A. 1745. *Entwurf der nothwendigen Vernunft-Wahrheiten*. Leipzig: J. F. Gleditsch.

———. 1744. *Anweisung vernünftig zu leben*. Leipzig: J. F. Gleditsch.

Diderot, D. 1964a. "Entretien entre d'Alembert et Diderot." In *Oeuvres philosophiques*, ed. P. Vernière. Paris: Garnier.

———. 1964b. *Le rêve de D'Alembert*. In *Oeuvres philosophiques*, ed. P. Vernière. Paris: Garnier.

———. (ed.) 1765. *Encyclopédie, ou Dictionnaire raisonné des sciences, des arts et des métiers, par une société de gens de lettres. Mis en ordre à publié par M. Diderot*. Paris: Briasson, 1751–1765.

Garve, C. (trans.) 1773. *Philosophische Untersuchungen über den Ursprung unserer Ideen vom Erhabenen und Schönen*. Riga: Hartknoch.

Gassendi, P. 1649. *Syntagma philosophiae Epicuri*. London: Johannis Redmayne.

Goclenius, R. 1613. *Lexicon philosophicum*. Frankfurt: Typis Mathiae Beckeri.

Goethe, J. W. 1920. *Werke*. Weimar: Hermann Bohlau, 1887–1920.

Gottsched, J. C. 1734. *Erste Gründe der gesammten Weltweisheit*, 2 vols. Leipzig: Breitkopf, 1733–1734.

Hamann, J. G. 1957. *Sämtliche Werke*, 6 vols., ed. J. Nadler. Vienna: Herder, 1949–1957.

Heidegger, M. 2000. "Bauen, Wohnen, Denken." In *Gesamtausgabe*, vol. 7: *Vorträge und Aufsätze*. Frankfurt am Main: Vittorio Klostermann.

————. 1987a. *Die Frage nach dem Ding. Zu Kants Lehre von den transzendentalen Grundsätze.* Tübingen: Niemeyer.

————. 1987b. *Zollikoner Seminare: Protokolle, Gespräche, Briefe,* ed. Medard Boss. Frankfurt am Main: Klostermann.

————. 1983. *Die Kunst und der Raum.* Frankfurt am Main: Klostermann.

————. 1977. *Phänomenologische Interpretation von Kants Kritik der reinen Vernunft. Marburger Vorlesungen 1927–28.* Frankfurt am Main: Klostermann.

————. 1973. *Kant und das Problem der Metaphysik.* Frankfurt am Main: Klostermann.

————. 1927. *Sein und Zeit.* Tübingen: Niemeyer.

Herder, J. G. 1913. *Sämtliche Werke,* 33 vols., ed. B. Suphan. Berlin: Weidmann, 1877–1913.

Husserl, E. 1973. *Ding und Raum. Vorlesungen 1907.* In *Husserliana* XVI, ed. U. Claesges. The Hague: Nijhoff.

————. 1900. *Logische Untersuchungen. Erster Teil. Prolegomena zur reinen Logik.* Halle: Niemeyer.

James, W. 1950. *The Principles of Psychology.* 2 vols. New York: Dover.

Knutzen, M. 1745. *Systema causarum efficientium, seu commentatio philosophica de commercio mentis et corporis per influxum physicum explicando.* Leipzig: Langenhem.

————. 1744. *Philosophische Abhandlung von der immateriellen Natur der Seele.* Königsberg: J. H. Hartung.

Leibniz, G. W. 1710. *Essais de théodicée sur la bonté de dieu, la liberté de l'homme et l'origine du mal.* Amsterdam.

Locke, J. 1690. *An Essay Concerning Human Understanding.* London.

Meier, G. F. 1752. *Auszug aus der Vernunftlehre.* Halle: Gebauer.

Meißner, H. A. 1737. *Philosophisches Lexicon.* Bayreuth und Hof.

Merleau-Ponty, M. 2003. *Nature. Course Notes from the Collège de France,* comp. D. Séglard, trans. R. Vallier. Evanston: Northwestern University Press.

————. 1964a. *L'oeil et l'esprit.* Paris: Gallimard.

————. 1964b. *The Primacy of Perception,* ed. J. Edie. Evanston: Northwestern University Press.

————. 1964c. *Le visible et l'invisible.* Paris: Gallimard.

————. 1948. *Sens et non-sens.* Paris: Nagel.

————. 1945. *Phénoménologie de la perception.* Paris: Gallimard.

Montaigne, M. de. 1957. "Apology for Raymond Sebond." In *Essays,* 2 vols. Stanford: Stanford University Press.

Reimarus, H. S. 1760. *Allgemeine Betrachtungen über die Triebe der Tiere, hauptsächlich über ihre Kunsttriebe, zum Erkenntnis des Zusammenhanges der Welt, des Schöpfers und unser selbst.* Hamburg: J. C. Bohn.

Rousseau, J.-J. 1939. *Emile.* Paris: Garnier.

Tetens, J. N. 1777. *Philosophische Versuche über die menschliche Natur und ihre Entwicklung,* 2 vols. Leipzig: M. G. Weidmann Erbens & Reich.

Thomasius, C. 1687. *Welcher Gestalt man denen Frantzosen in gemeinem Leben und Wandel nachahmen solle? ein Collegium über Gratians Grund-Reguln, vernünftig, klug und artig zu leben.* In *Deutsche Literaturdenkmale,* vol. 51.

Voltaire. 1961. *Dictionnaire philosophique,* ed. J. Benda and R. Naves. Paris: Garnier.

Wolff, C. 1740. *Psychologia rationalis methodo scientifica pertractata.* Frankfurt/Leipzig: Officina libraria Rengeriana.

———. 1739. *Vernünfftige Gedanken von Gott, der Welt und der Seele der Menschen.* Frankfurt/Leipzig: Officina libraria Rengeriana.

———. 1738. *Psychologia empirica.* Frankfurt/Leipzig: Officina libraria Rengeriana.

———. 1736. *Philosophia prima sive ontologia.* Frankfurt/Leipzig: Officina libraria Rengeriana.

———. 1720. *Vernünfftige Gedancken von Gott, der Welt und die Seele des Menschen, auch allen Dingen überhaupt.* Halle, 1719–1720.

Zedler, J. H. 1750. *Grosses vollständiges Universal-Lexicon aller Wissenschaften und Künste.* Halle/Leipzig, 1742–1750.

Secondary Sources

Adler, H. 1988. "Fundus Animae—der Grund der Seele. Zur Gnoseologie des Dunklen in der Aufklärung." In *Deutsche Vierteljahrsschrift für Literatur und Geistesgeschichte* 62: 197–220.

Al-Azm, S. J. 1972. *The Origins of Kant's Arguments in the Antinomies.* Oxford: Clarendon.

Allison, H. 1998. "The Antinomy of Pure Reason, Section 9 (A515/B543–A567/B595)." In *Kritik der reinen Vernunft,* ed. G. Mohr and M. Willaschek. Berlin: Akademie Verlag. 465–490.

———. 1996a. "Kant's Refutation of Materialism." In *Idealism and Freedom: Essays in Kant's Theoretical and Practical Philosophy.* Cambridge: Cambridge University Press. 92–106.

———. 1996b. *Kant's Theory of Freedom.* Cambridge: Cambridge University Press.

———. 1993. "Kant's Critique of Berkeley." *Journal of the History of Philosophy* 11: 1, 43–63.

———. 1983. *Kant's Transcendental Idealism: An Interpretation and Defense.* New Haven: Yale University Press.

Ameriks, K. 2000. *Kant's Theory of Mind: An Analysis of the Paralogisms of Pure Reason.* Oxford: Clarendon.

———. 1998. "The Paralogisms of Pure Reason in the First Edition (A 338/B 396–A 347/B 406; A 348–380)." In *Kritik der reinen Vernunft,* ed. G. Mohr and M. Willaschek. Berlin: Akademie Verlag. 371–390.

———. 1987. "The Hegelian Critique of Kantian Morality." In *New Essays on Kant,* ed. B. den Ouden and M. Moen. New York: Peter Lang.

Amoroso, L. 1998. "Kant et le nom de l'Esthétique." In *Kants Ästhetik–Kant's Aesthetics–L'esthétique de Kant,* ed. H. Parret. Berlin/New York: De Gruyter. 701–705.

Anderson, P. S. 1993. *Ricoeur and Kant: Philosophy of the Will.* Atlanta: Scholars Press.

Aquila, R. 1989. *Matter and Mind: A Study of Kant's Transcendental Deduction.* Bloomington: Indiana University Press.

Arendt, H. 2005. *The Promise of Politics.* New York: Schocken.

———. 2002. *Denktagebuch. 1950 bis 1973.* Munich: Pieper.

———. 1982. *Lectures on Kant's Political Philosophy.* Chicago: University of Chicago Press.

———. 1979. *The Recovery of the Public World,* ed. M. Hill. New York: St. Martin's.

———. 1978. *The Life of the Mind,* 2 vols. London: Secker & Warburg.

———. 1961. *Between Past and Future.* London: Faber & Faber.

————. 1958. *The Human Condition: A Study of the Central Dilemmas Facing Modern Man*. Chicago: University of Chicago Press.

Aubenque, P. 1969. "Kant et l'épicureisme." In *Actes du VIII Congrés de l'Association G. Budé*. Paris: Editions de l'Association G. Budé. 293–303.

Baron, M. W. 1995. *Kantian Ethics Almost Without Apology*. Ithaca: Cornell University Press.

Battersby, C. 1998. "Stages on Kant's Way: Aesthetics, Morality, and the Gendered Sublime." In *Race, Class, Gender, and Sexuality*, ed. N. Zack, L. Shrage, and C. Sartwell. Oxford: Blackwell. 227–244.

Baum, M. 2002. "Logisches und personales Ich bei Kant." In *Probleme der Subjektivität in Geschichte und Gegenwart*, ed. D. H. Heidemann. Stuttgart: Frommann-Holzboog. 107–123.

————. 1992. "Kant on Pure Intuition." In *Minds, Ideas, and Objects: Essays on the Theory of Representation in Modern Philosophy*, ed. P. D. Cummins and G. Zöller. Atascadero, Calif.: Ridgeview. 303–316.

————. 1991. "Dinge an sich und Raum bei Kant." In *Akten der siebenten Internationalen Kant-Kongresses*. Bonn: Bouvier. 63–72.

————. 1986. *Deduktion und Beweis in Kants Transzendentalphilosophie. Untersuchungen zur "Kritik der reinen Vernunft."* Königstein: Hain.

Baumeister, T. 1998. "Kants Geschmackskritik zwischen Transzendentalphilosophie und Psychologie." In *Kants Ästhetik–Kant's Aesthetics–L'esthétique de Kant*, ed. H. Parret. Berlin/New York: De Gruyter. 158–175.

Bäumler, A. 1967. *Das Irrationalitätsproblem in der Ästhetik und Logik des 18. Jahrhunderts bis zur Kritik der Urteilskraft*. Tübingen: Niemeyer.

Beck, L. W. 1960. *A Commentary of Kant's Critique of Practical Reason*. Chicago: University of Chicago Press.

Benhabib, S. 1987. "The Generalized and the Concrete Other: The Kohlberg-Gilligan Controversy and Feminist Theory." In *Feminism as Critique: Essays on the Politics of Gender in Late Capitalist Societies*, ed. S. Benhabib and D. Cornell. Cambridge: Polity.

Bennett, J. 1966. *Kant's Analytic*. Cambridge: Cambridge University Press.'

Bernasconi, R. 2002. "Kant as an Unfamiliar Source of Racism." In *Philosophers on Race: Critical Essays*, ed. J. K. Ward and T. L. Lott. Malden: Blackwell.

————. 2001. "Who Invented the Concept of Race? Kant's Role in the Enlightenment Construction of Race." In *Race*, ed. R. Bernasconi. Oxford: Blackwell.

Bird, G. H. 2000. "The Paralogisms and Kant's Account of Psychology." In *Kant Studien* 91: 129–145.

Bobzien, S. 1988. "Die Kategorien der Freiheit bei Kant." In *Kant. Analysen—Probleme—Kritik*, ed. H. Oberer and G. Seel. Würzburg: Königshausen & Neumann. 193–220.

Bona Meyer, J. 1870. *Kants Psychologie. Dargestellt und erörtert*. Berlin: Hertz.

Bourdieu, P. 1984. *Distinction: A Social Critique of the Judgment of Taste*. Cambridge, Mass.: Harvard University Press.

Brague, R. 2002. "History of Philosophy as Freedom." *Epoché* 7, no. 1: 39–50.

Brandt, R. 1998. "Transzendentale Ästhetik §§1–3." In *Kritik der reinen Vernunft*, ed. G. Mohr and M. Willaschek. Berlin: Akademie Verlag. 81–106.

Brook, A. 1994. *Kant and the Mind*. Cambridge: Cambridge University Press.

Buroker, J. V. 1981. *Space and Incongruence: The Origin of Kant's Idealism*. Dordrecht/London: Riedel.

Butler, J. 2001. "How Can I Deny that These Hands and This Body Are Mine?" In *Material Events: Paul De Man and the Afterlife of Theory,* ed. T. Cohen, B. Cohen, J. Miller, and A. Warminski. Minneapolis: University of Minnesota Press. 254–273.

———. 1993. *Bodies that Matter: On the Discursive Limits of "Sex."* New York: Routledge.

———. 1989. "Foucault and the Paradox of Bodily Inscriptions." *The Journal of Philosophy* 86: 601–607.

———. 1987. *Subjects of Desire: Hegelian Reflections in Twentieth-Century France.* New York: Columbia University Press.

Calori, F. 2003. "L'arraissonnement. (Rationalité pratique et sensibilité chez Kant)." In *Kant. La rationalité pratique,* ed. M. Cohen-Halimi. Paris: Presses Universitaires de France. 119–172.

Carboncini, S. 1981. *Crisi della metafisica dogmatica e fondazione del concetto di libertà nella filosofia di Christian August Crusius.* Florence. Dissertation.

Casey, E. 1997. *The Fate of Place: A Philosophical History.* Berkeley: University of California Press.

———. 1993. *Getting Back into Place: Toward a Renewed Understanding of the Place-World.* Bloomington: Indiana University Press.

Cassam, Q. 1997. *Self and World.* Oxford: Clarendon.

———. 1993. "Inner Sense, Body Sense, and Kant's Refutation of Idealism." In *European Journal of Philosophy* 1: 111–127.

Cavell, S. 1976. "Aesthetic Problems of Modern Philosophy." In *Must We Mean What We Say?* Cambridge: Cambridge University Press. 73–96.

Centi, B. 2002. *Coscienza, etica e architettonica in Kant. Uno studio attraverso le Critiche.* Pisa/Rome: Istituti Editoriali e Poligrafici Internazionali.

Chalier, C. 2002. *What Ought I to Do? Morality in Kant and Levinas.* Ithaca: Cornell University Press.

———. 1998. *Pour une morale au-delà du savoir: Kant et Levinas.* Paris: Albin Michel.

Champollion, C. 1963. "La place des termes 'gemuete' et 'grunt' dans le vocabulaire de Tauler." In *La Mystique rhénane.* Paris: Presses Universitaires de France. 179–192.

Coble, K. 2003. "Kant's Dynamic Theory of Character." *Kantian Review* 7: 38–71.

Critchley, S. 2000. "On Alain Badiou." In *Theory and Event,* 3.

Dallmayr, F. 1993. "Heidegger and Freud." *Political Psychology* 14, no. 2: 235–253.

Danto, A. C. 1999a. *The Body/Body Problem: Selected Essays.* Berkeley: University of California Press.

———. 1999b. *Philosophizing Art: Selected Essays.* Berkeley: University of California Press.

———. 1994. *Embodied Meanings: Critical Essays and Aesthetic Meditations.* New York: Farrar Straus Giroux.

———. 1981. *The Transfiguration of the Commonplace: A Philosophy of Art.* Cambridge, Mass.: Harvard University Press.

Degenhardt, I. 1967. *Studien zum Wandel des Eckartsbildes.* Leiden: Brill.

Deleuze, G. 2004. "The Idea of Genesis in Kant's Aesthetics." In *Desert Islands.* New York: Columbia University Press. 56–71.

———. 1990. *Logique du sens.* Paris: Editions de Minuit.

———. 1984. *Kant's Critical Philosophy: The Doctrine of the Faculties.* Minneapolis: University of Minnesota Press.

————. 1968. *Différence et répétition*. Paris: Presses Universitaires de France.

Delvolvé, J. 1906. *Religion, critique et philosophie positive chez Pierre Bayle*. Paris: Alcan.

De Man, P. 1996. "Phenomenality and Materiality in Kant." In *Aesthetic Ideology*. Minneapolis: University of Minnesota Press. 70–90.

De Pascale, C. 1990. "Kant: la natura umana tra antropologia e criticismo." *Filosofia politica* 4, no. 2: 283–304.

Derrida, J. 2005. *On Touching—Jean-Luc Nancy*. Stanford: Stanford University Press.

————. 2003. "And Say the Animal Responded?" In *Zoontologies: The Question of the Animal*, ed. C. Wolfe. Minneapolis: University of Minnesota Press.

————. 2002. "The Animal That Therefore I Am (More to Follow)," trans. D. Wills. *Critical Inquiry* 28: 369–418.

————. 1997. *Chora L Works*, ed. J. Kipnis and T. Leeser. New York: Monacelli.

————. 1993a. *Khora*. Paris: Galilée.

————. 1993b. "Passions." In *On the Name*, ed. T. Dutoit. Stanford: Stanford University Press. 3–30.

————. 1987a. "Chora." In *Poikilia. Festschrift pour J.-P. Vernant*. Paris: École des Hautes Études.

————. 1987b. "La main de Heidegger (Geschlecht II)." In *Psyché: Inventions de l'autre*. Paris: Galilée. 415–451.

————. 1976. *Of Grammatology*, trans. G. C. Spivak. Baltimore/London: Johns Hopkins University Press.

De Vleeschauwer, J.-H. 1939. *L'évolution de la pensée kantienne*. Paris: Alcan.

————. 1937. *La déduction transcendentale dans l'oeuvre de Kant*, 3 vols. Antwerp/Paris: De Sikkel.

Dingel, I. 1998. "La traduction du *Dictionaire historique et critique* de Pierre Bayle en allemande et sa réception en Allemagne." In *Critique, savoir et érudition à la veille des Lumières. Le Dictionaire historique et critique de Pierre Bayle (1647–1706)*, ed. H. Bots. Amsterdam: APA-Holland University Press. 109–124.

Dumouchel, D. 1997. "L'ésthétique pre-critique de Kant, Genèse de la théorie du 'gout' et du beau." *Archives de Philosophie* 60: 59–86.

Edwards, J. 2000. **"Egoism and Formalism in the Development of Kant's Moral Philosophy."** *Kant Studien* 91: 411–431.

Erdmann, B. 1876. *Martin Knutzen und seine Zeit. Ein Beitrag zur Geschichte der wolffischen Schule und insbesondere zur Entwicklungsgeschichte Kants*. Leipzig: Voss.

Escoubas, E. 1988. "Kant ou la simplicité du sublime." In *Du sublime*, ed. J.-F. Courtine. Paris: Berlin.

Eze, E. C. 1995. "The Color of Reason: The Idea of 'Race' in Kant's Anthropology." In *Anthropology and the German Enlightenment*, ed. K. Faull. Lewisburg: Bucknell University Press.

Falkenstein, L. 1995. *Kant's Intuitionism. A Commentary on the Transcendental Aesthetic*. Toronto: University of Toronto Press.

Farber, E. 1954. "Forces and Substances of Life." *Osiris* 11: 422–437.

Ferrari, J. 1979. *Les Sources françaises de la philosophie de Kant*. Paris: Klincksieck.

————. 1967. "Le *Dictionnaire historique et critique* de Pierre Bayle et les deux premières antinomies kantiennes de la Raison pure." *Études philosophiques et littéraires* (Société Philosophique du Maroc) 1, no. 1: 24–33.

Ferrarin, A. 2006. "Lived Space, Geometric Space in Kant." In *Studi Kantiani* 19: 11–30.

————. 1995. "Kant's Productive Imagination and Its Alleged Antecedents." In *Graduate Faculty Philosophy Journal* 18, no. 1: 65–92.

Ferraris, M. 1996. *L'immaginazione*. Bologna: Il Mulino.

Ferraris, M., and P. Kobau. (eds.) 2001. *L'altra estetica*. Torino: Einaudi.

Finster, R. 1982. "**Spontaneität, Freiheit und unbedingte Kausalität bei Leibniz, Crusius und Kant.**" *Studia Leibnitiana* 14, no. 2: 266–277.

Förster, E. 1985. "Kant's Refutation of Idealism." In *Philosophy, Its History and Historiography*, ed. A. J. Holland. Dordrecht: Riedel. 295–311.

Franke, U. 1972. *Kunst als Erkenntnis. Die Rolle der Sinnlichkeit in der Aesthetik des Alexander Gottlieb Baumgarten*. Wiesbaden: Steiner.

Frankfurt, H. G. 1971. "Freedom of the Will and the Concept of a Person." *The Journal of Philosophy* 14, no. 1: 5–20.

Freydberg, B. 2005. *Imagination in Kant's Critique of Practical Reason*. Bloomington: Indiana University Press.

Fulda, H. F., and R. P. Horstmann. (eds.) 1994. *Vernunftbegriffe in der Moderne*. Stuttgart: Klett-Cotta.

Gigliotti, G. 1995. "'Vermögen' e 'Kraft'. Una rilettura del concetto di 'sintesi' nella *Critica della ragion pura* di Kant." *Rivista di storia della filosofia* 2: 255–275.

Giordanetti, P. 2001. *L'estetica fisiologica di Kant*. Milano: Mimesis.

Gram, M. 1982. "What Kant Really Did to Idealism." In *Essays on Kant's Critique of Pure Reason*, ed. J. N. Mohanty and R. W. Shahan. Norman: University of Oklahoma Press. 127–156.

Gregor, M. J. 1984. "Baumgarten's *Aesthetica*." *Review of Metaphysics* 37: 357–385.

————. 1963. *Laws of Freedom: A Study of Kant's Method of Applying the Categorical Imperative in the 'Metaphysik der Sitten'*. New York: Barnes & Noble.

Grimm, J., and W. Grimm. 1952. *Deutsches Wörterbuch*. Leipzig: von Hirzel.

Guyer, P. 1998a. "The Postulates of Empirical Thinking in General and the Refutation of Idealism (A 218/B 265–A 235/B 294)." In *Kritik der reinen Vernunft*, ed. G. Mohr and M. Willaschek. Berlin: Akademie Verlag. 297–324.

————. 1998b. "The Symbols of Freedom in Kant's Aesthetics." In *Kants Ästhetik–Kant's Aesthetics–L'esthétique de Kant*, ed. H. Parret. Berlin/New York: De Gruyter. 338–355.

————. 1997. *Kant and the Claims of Taste*. Cambridge: Cambridge University Press.

————. 1996. *Kant and the Experience of Freedom: Essays in Aesthetics and Morality*. Cambridge: Cambridge University Press.

————. 1989. "The Unity of Reason: Pure Reason as Practical Reason in Kant's Early Conception of the Transcendental Dialectic." *The Monist* 72: 139–167.

————. 1987. *Kant and the Claims of Knowledge*. Cambridge: Cambridge University Press.

————. 1983. "Kant's Intention in the Refutation of Idealism." *Philosophical Review* 92: 329–383.

Hall, T. S. 1969. *Ideas of Life and Matter: Studies in the History of General Physiology 600 B.C.–1900 A.D.*, 2 vols. Chicago: University of Chicago Press.

Hanna, R. 2000. "The Inner and the Outer: Kant's 'Refutation' Reconstructed." *Ratio* 13, no. 2: 146–174.

Hatfield, G. 1992. "Empirical, Rational, and Transcendental Psychology. Psychology as Science and as Philosophy." In *The Cambridge Companion to Kant*, ed. P. Guyer. Cambridge: Cambridge University Press. 200–227.

———. 1990. *The Natural and the Normative: Theories of Spatial Perception from Kant to Helmholtz.* Cambridge, Mass.: MIT Press.

Hauser, C. 1994. *Selbstbewußtsein und personale Identität. Positionen und Aporien ihrer vorkantischen Geschichte. Locke, Leibniz, Hume, Tetens.* Stuttgart: Frommann-Holzboog.

Heidemann, I. 1958. *Spontaneität und Zeitlichkeit. Ein Problem der Kritik der reinen Vernunft.* Cologne: Kölner Universitäts verlag.

Heimsoeth, H. 1973. "Freiheit und Charakter. Nach den Kant-Reflexionen Nr. 5611 bis 5620." In *Kant. Zur Deutung seiner Theorie von Erkennen und Handeln,* ed. G. Prauss. Cologne: Kiepenhauer & Witsch.

———. 1966. "Zum kosmotheologischen Ursprung der Kantischen Freiheitsantinomie." *Kant Studien* 56: 206–229.

———. 1965. "Kant und Plato." *Kant Studien* 56: 349–372.

———. 1956. *Studien zur Philosophie Immanuel Kants: Metaphysische Ursprünge und ontologische Grundlagen.* Cologne: Kölner Universitätsverlag.

Heinz, M. 2001. "Herder's Review of *Dreams of a Spirit-Seer* (1766)." In *New Essays on the Precritical Kant,* ed. T. Rockmore. Amherst, New York: Humanity. 110–128.

Henrich, D. 1998. "The Deduction of the Moral Law." In *Kant's Groundwork of the Metaphysics of Morals: Critical Essays,* ed. P. Guyer. Lanham, Md.: Rowman & Littlefield. 303–341.

———. 1994. *The Unity of Reason: Essays on Kant's Philosophy.* Cambridge, Mass.: Harvard University Press.

———. 1992. "Kant's Explanation of Aesthetic Judgment." In *Aesthetic Judgment and the Moral Image of the World: Studies in Kant.* Stanford: Stanford University Press. 29–56.

———. 1989. "Kant's Notion of a Deduction and the Methodological Background of the First Critique." In *Kant's Transcendental Deductions,* ed. E. Förster. Stanford: Stanford University Press. 29–47.

———. 1969. "The Proof-Structure of Kant's Transcendental Deduction." *Review of Metaphysics* 22: 640–659.

———. 1960. "Der Begriff der sittlichen Einsicht und Kants Lehre vom Faktum der Vernunft." In *Die Gegenwart der Griechen im neueren Denken. Festschrift f. H.G. Gadamer.* Tübingen: Mohr. 77–115.

Henry, M. 1973. *The Essence of Manifestation,* trans. G. Etzkorn. The Hague: Nijhoff.

———. 1963. *L'Essence de la manifestation.* Paris: Presses Universitaires de France.

Herman, B. 1996. "Making Room for Character." In *Aristotle, Kant, and the Stoics. Rethinking Happiness and Duty,* ed. S. Engstrom and J. Whiting. Cambridge: Cambridge University Press. 102–141.

———. 1993. *The Practice of Moral Judgment.* Cambridge, Mass.: Harvard University Press.

———. 1983. "Integrity and Impartiality." *The Monist* 66, no. 2: 233–250.

Herrera, L. 2000. "Kant on the Moral Triebfeder." *Kant Studien* 91: 395–410.

Hill, T. E., Jr., and B. Boxill. 2001. "Kant and Race." In *Race and Racism,* ed. B. Boxill. Oxford: Oxford University Press. 448–471.

Hinske, N. 1972. "Kants Begriff der Antithetik und seine Herkunft aus der protestantischen Kontroversetheologie des 17. und 18. Jahrhunderts." In *Archiv für Begriffsgeschichte* 16: 48–59.

———. 1970. *Kants Weg zur Transzendentalphilosophie. Der dreizigjährige Kant.* Stuttgart/Berlin: Kohlhammer.

————. 1966. "Kants Idee der Anthropologie." In *Die Frage nach dem Menschen*, ed. H. Rombach. Freiburg: Alber. 410–427.

Hoefer, C. 2000. "Kant's Hands and Earman's Pions: Chirality Arguments for Substantival Space." *International Studies in the Philosophy of Science* 14, no. 3: 237–256.

Hoke Robinson, R. 1992. "Kant on Embodiment." In *Minds, Ideas, and Objects: Essays on the Theory of Representation in Modern Philosophy*, ed. P. D. Cummins and G. Zoeller. Atascadero, Calif.: Ridgeview. 329–340.

————. 1981. "Incongruent Counterparts and the Refutation of Idealism." *Kant Studien* 72, no. 4: 391–397.

Holzhey, H. 1970. *Kants Erfahrungsbegriff.* Basel/Stuttgart: Schwabe.

Hoppe, H. 1983. *Synthesis bei Kant.* Berlin: De Gruyter.

Horstmann, R. P. 1993. "Kants Paralogismen." *Kant Studien* 83: 408–425.

Hymers, M. 1991. "The Role of the Refutation of Idealism." *Southern Journal of Philosophy* 29: 51–67.

Jacob, F. 1970. *La logique du vivant. Une histoire de l'hérédité.* Paris: Gallimard.

Jensen, B. 2003. *Was heißt sich orientieren? Von der Krise der Aufklärung zur Orientierung der Vernunft nach Kant.* Munich: Fink.

Kaulbach, F. 1963. "Leibbewußtsein und Welterfahrung beim frühen und späten Kant." *Kant Studien* 4: 464–491.

Kawamura, K. 1996. *Spontaneität und Willkür. Der Freiheitsbegriff in Kants Antinomienlehre und seine historischen Wurzeln.* Stuttgart: Frommann-Holzboog. 124–128.

Kitcher, P. 1990. *Kant's Transcendental Psychology.* Oxford: Oxford University Press.

————. 1982a. "Kant on Self-Identity." *Philosophical Review* 91: 41–72.

————. 1982b. "Kant's Paralogisms." *Philosophical Review* 91: 515–547.

König, P. 1994. *Autonomie und Autokratie. Über Kants Metaphysik der Sitten.* Berlin: De Gruyter.

Kreimendahl, L. 1998. "Die Antinomie der reinen Vernunft 1. und 2. Abschnitt (A405/B432–A461–B489)." In *Kritik der reinen Vernunft*, ed. G. Mohr and M. Willaschek. Berlin: Akademie Verlag. 413–446.

Krell, D. F. 2005. *The Tragic Absolute: German Idealism and the Languishing of God.* Bloomington: Indiana University Press.

————. 2000. "The Bodies of Black Folk: From Kant and Hegel to Du Bois and Baldwin." *boundary 2* 27, no. 3: 103–134.

————. 1997. *Archeticture: Ecstasies of Space, Time, and the Human Body.* Albany: SUNY Press.

Landucci, S. 1994. *Sull'etica di Kant.* Milan: Guerini.

————. 1993. *La "Critica della ragion pratica" di Kant. Introduzione alla lettura.* Rome: La Nuova Italia Scientifica.

La Rocca, C. 1999. "La prima voce. Libertà come passione nell'antropologia kantiana." In *Etica y Antropología: un dilema kantiano*, ed. R. R. Aramayo and F. Oncina. Granada: Editorial Comares. 69–90.

Laywine, A. 1993. *Kant's Early Metaphysics and the Origins of the Critical Philosophy.* North American Kant Society Studies, vol. 3. Atascadero, Calif.: Ridgeview.

Lingis, A. 2005. *Body Transformations: Evolutions and Atavisms in Culture.* New York: Routledge.

————. 2003. "Animal Body, Inhuman Face." In *Zoontologies: The Question of the Animal*, ed. C. Wolfe. Minneapolis: University of Minnesota Press.

————. 1998. *The Imperative.* Bloomington: Indiana University Press.

————. 1996. *Sensation: Intelligibility in Sensibility.* Atlantic Highlands, N.J.: Humanities Press.

————. 1994. *The Community of Those Who Have Nothing in Common.* Bloomington: Indiana University Press.

————. 1989. *Deathbound Subjectivity.* Bloomington: Indiana University Press.

————. 1971. "Intentionality and Corporeality." *Analecta Husserliana* 1: 75–90.

Llewelyn, J. 2000. *The HypoCritical Imagination: Between Kant and Levinas.* London/New York: Routledge.

Longuenesse, B. 1998. *Kant and the Capacity to Judge. Sensibility and Discursivity in the Critique of Pure Reason.* Princeton: Princeton University Press.

Louden, R. B. 2000. *Kant's Impure Ethics: From Rational Beings to Human Beings.* Oxford: Oxford University Press.

Lovejoy, A. 1960. *The Great Chain of Being: A Study of the History of an Idea.* New York: Harper.

Lyotard, J.-F. 1994. *Lessons on the Analytic of the Sublime: Kant's Critique of Judgment, §§23–29,* trans. E. Rottenberg. Stanford: Stanford University Press.

————. 1990. "La réflexion dans l'esthétique kantienne." *Revue Internationale de Philosophie* 175, no. 4: 507–551.

————. 1988a. *Le Différend: Phrases in Dispute.* Minneapolis: University of Minnesota Press.

————. 1988b. *Peregrinations: Law, Form, Event.* New York: Columbia University Press.

Makkreel, R. 2002. "Kant on the Scientific Status of Psychology, Anthropology, and History." In *Kant and the Sciences,* ed. E. Watkins. Oxford: Oxford University Press. 185–201.

————. 1990. *Imagination and Interpretation in Kant: The Hermeneutical Import of the Critique of Judgment.* Chicago: University of Chicago Press.

————. 1985. "The Feeling of Life: Some Kantian Sources of Life-Philosophy." *Dilthey-Jahrbuch für Philosophie und Geschichte der Geisteswissenschaften* 3: 83–104.

Marc-Wogau, K. 1938. *Vier Studien zu Kants Kritik der Urteilskraft.* Uppsala/Leipzig: Lundequistska/Harrassowitz. 44–213.

————. 1932. *Untersuchungen zur Raumlehre Kants.* Lund: Hakan Ohlssons Buchdruckerei.

Marion, J.-L. 2001. *The Idol and Distance: Five Studies.* New York: Fordham University Press.

————. 1999. *Cartesian Questions.* Chicago: University of Chicago Press.

Marquardt, A. 1885. *Kant und Crusius. Ein Beitrag zum richtigen Verständnis der crusianischen Philosophie.* Kiel: Verlag Lipsius & Tischer.

McFarland, J. D. 1970. *Kant's Concept of Teleology.* Edinburgh: University of Edinburgh Press.

Meerbote, R. 1987. "Kant's Refutation of Problematic Material Idealism." In *New Essays on Kant,* ed. B. den Ouden. New York: Peter Lang. 112–138.

Mertens, H. 1975. *Kommentar zur Erste Einleitung in Kants Kritik der Urteilskraft.* Munich: Berchmans Verlag.

Mills, C. 1997. *The Racial Contract.* Ithaca/London: Cornell University Press.

Mischel, T. 1967. "Kant and the Possibility of a Science of Psychology." *The Monist* 51: 599–622.

Mohanty, J. N. 1972. *The Concept of Intentionality.* St. Louis: W. H. Green.

Mohr, G. 1988. "Personne, personalité et liberté dans la *Critique de la raison pratique.*" *Revue Internationale de Philosophie* 166, no. 3: 289–319.

Munzel, F. 1999. *Kant's Conception of Moral Character: The Critical 'Link' of Morality, Anthropology, and Reflective Judgment.* Chicago: University of Chicago Press.

Murray Turbayne, C. 1969. "Kant's Relation to Berkeley." In *Kant Studies Today,* ed. L. W. Beck. LaSalle: Open Court. 88–116.

Nancy, J.-L. 1988. *L'expérience de la liberté.* Paris: Galilée.

———. 1976. *Le Discours de la syncope. 1. Logodaedalus.* Paris: Flammarion.

Nerlich, G. 1973. "Hands, Knees, and Absolute Space." *The Journal of Philosophy* 70, no. 12: 337–351.

Nobbe, F. 1995. *Kants Frage nach dem Menschen. Die Kritik der ästehtischen Urteilskraft als transzendentale Anthropologie.* Berlin/New York: Lang.

Nussbaum, M. 2001. *Upheavals of Thought: The Intelligence of Emotions.* Cambridge: Cambridge University Press.

Nuzzo, A. 2007. "*Leben* and *Leib* in Kant and Hegel." In *Das Leben Denken,* vol. 2: *Hegel Jahrbuch.* 97–101.

———. 2006. "Kant and Herder on Baumgarten's *Aesthetica.*" *Journal of the History of Philosophy* 44, no. 4: 577–597.

———. 2005. *Kant and the Unity of Reason.* West Lafayette, Ind.: Purdue University Press.

———. 2003. *System.* Bielefeld: Transcript Verlag.

———. 2001. "Transformations of Freedom in the Jena Kant-Reception (1785–1794)." *The Owl of Minerva* 32, no. 2: 135–167.

———. 1995. "'Idee' bei Kant und Hegel." In *Das Recht der Vernunft. Kant und Hegel über Denken, Erkennen und Handeln,* ed. P. König, C. Fricke, and T. Petersen. Stuttgart: Frommann-Holzboog. 81–120.

O'Neill, O. 1989. *Constructions of Reason.* Cambridge: Cambridge University Press.

———. 1975. *Acting on Principle, an Essay on Kantian Ethics.* New York: Columbia University Press.

Parret, H. (ed.) 1998. *Kants Ästhetik–Kant's Aesthetics–L'esthétique de Kant.* Berlin/New York: De Gruyter.

Philonenko, A. 1983. "Introduction." In *Emmanuel Kant, Qu'est-ce que s'orienter dans la pensée,* ed. A. Philonenko. Paris: Vrin. 15–74.

Piper, A. M. 2001. "Kants intelligibler Standpunkt zum Handeln." In *Systematische Ethik mit Kant,* ed. H. U. Baumgarten and C. Held. Freiburg/Munich: Alber. 162–190.

———. 1993. "Xenophobia and Kantian Rationalism." *The Philosophical Forum* 24, nos. 1–3: 188–232.

Pippin, R. 1997. "Kant on the Spontaneity of the Mind." In *Idealism and Modernism: Hegelian Variations.* Cambridge: Cambridge University Press. 29–56.

Poggi, S. 1977. *I sistemi dell'esperienza: psicologia, logica e teoria della scienza da Kant a Wundt.* Bologna: Il Mulino.

Powell, T. C. 1990. *Kant's Theory of Self-Consciousness.* Oxford: Clarendon.

Prauss, G. 1990. *Die Welt und wir,* 2 vols. Stuttgart: Metzler.

Prigogine, I., and I. Stengers. 1979. *La nouvelle alliance. Métamorphose de la science.* Paris: Gallimard.

Quante, M. (ed.) 1999. *Personale Identität.* Paderborn: Schönig.

Rademeister, K. 1947. "Über den Unterschied der Gegenden im Raum." *Zeitschrift für philosophiche Forschung* 2: 131–151.

Reath, A. 1989. "Kant's Theory of Moral Sensibility: Respect for the Moral Law and the Influence of Inclination." *Kant Studien* 80: 284–302.

Rees, D. A. 1954. "Kant, Bayle, and Indifferentism." *The Philosophical Review* 63, 4: 592–595.

Reich, K. 1975. "Kants Behandlung des Raumbegriffs in den 'Träume eines Geistersehers' und im 'Unterschied der Gegenden im Raum'." In I. Kant, *Träume eines Geistersehers,* ed. K. Reich. Hamburg: Meiner.

———. 1964. "Die Tugend in der Idee. Zur Genese von Kants Ideenlehre." In *Argumentationen. Festschrift f. Josef König,* ed. H. Delius and G. Patzig. Göttingen: Vandenhoeck & Ruprecht. 208–215.

Ricoeur, P. 1995. *Le Juste.* Paris: Esprit.

———. 1992. *Oneself as Another.* Chicago: University of Chicago Press.

———. 1991. *From Text to Action. Essays in Hermeneutics II.* Evanston: Northwestern University Press.

———. 1986. *Fallible Man,* trans. C. A. Kelbley. New York: Fordham University Press.

Riedel, M. 1996. "Sensibilität für die Natur. Zum Verhältnis von Geschmacksurteil und Interpretation in Kants Philosophie des Schönen." In *Kant in der Diskussion der Moderne,* ed. G. Schönrich and Y. Kato. Frankfurt am Main: Suhrkamp. 506–525.

Roger, J. 1963. *Les sciences de la vie dans la pensée francaise du XVIIIe siècle.* Paris: Armand Colin.

Rorty, A. O. (ed.) 1969. *The Identities of Persons.* Berkeley: University of California Press.

Rosen, S. 2001. "Is Thinking Spontaneous?" In *Kant's Legacy: Essays in Honor of Lewis White Beck,* ed. P. Cicovacki. Rochester: University of Rochester Press. 3–23.

Ryan, V. 2001. "The Physiological Sublime: Burke's Critique of Reason." *Journal of the History of Ideas* 62, no. 2: 265–279.

Saccon, A. 2001. "L'anima tra fondo e sostanza." In *L'altra estetica,* ed. M. Ferraris and P. Kobau. Torino: Einaudi. 111–124.

Sallis, J. 2005. *The Gathering of Reason,* 2d ed. Albany: SUNY Press.

———. 2000a. *Chorology: On Plato's Timaeus.* Bloomington: Indiana University Press.

———. 2000b. *Force of Imagination: The Sense of the Elemental.* Bloomington: Indiana University Press.

———. 1987. *Spacings of Reason and Imagination in Texts of Kant, Fichte, Hegel.* Chicago: University of Chicago Press.

Satura, V. 1971. *Kants Erkenntnispsychologie in den Nachschriften seiner Vorlesungen über empirische Psychologie.* Bonn: Bouvier.

Sauder, G. 1975. "Bayle-Rezeption in der deutschen Aufklärung." In *Deutsche Vierteljahresschrift für Literaturwissenschaft und Geistesgeschichte* (Special issue): 83–104.

Scaravelli, L. 1968. *Scritti kantiani.* Florence: La Nuova Italia.

Scarry, E. 1999. *On Beauty and Being Just.* Princeton/Oxford: Princeton University Press.

Schmucker, J. 1961. *Die Ursprünge der Ethik Kants in seinen vorkritischen Schriften und Reflexionen.* Königstein: Hain.

Schönrich, G. 1986. "Die Kategorien der Freiheit als handlungstheoretische Elementarbegriffe." In *Handlungstheorie und Transzendentalphilosophie,* ed. G. Prauss. Frankfurt am Main: Vittorio Klostermann. 246–270.

Schott, R. M. 1996. "The Gender of Enlightenment." In *What Is Enlightenment? Eigh-teenth-Century Answers and Twentieth-Century Questions,* ed. J. Schmidt. Berkeley: University of California Press.

———. 1988. *Cognition and Eros: A Critique of the Kantian Paradigm.* Boston: Beacon.

———. 1987. "Kant's Treatment of Sensibility." In *New Essays on Kant,* ed. B. den Ouden and M. Moen. New York: Lang. 213–244.

Schott, R. M. (ed.) 1997. *Feminist Interpretations of Immanuel Kant.* University Park: University of Pennsylvania Press.

Schürmann, V. 2003. "Die Bedeutung der Körper. Literatur zur Körper-Debatte—eine Auswahl in systematischer Absicht." *Allgemeine Zeitschrift f. Philosophie* 1: 50–69.

Sedgwick, S. 1997. "Can Kant's Ethics Survive the Feminist Critique?" In *Feminist Interpretations of Immanuel Kant,* ed. R. M. Schott. University Park: University of Pennsylvania Press. 77–100.

Sellars, W. 1970. "'. . . this I or he or it (the thing) which thinks . . .' Immanuel Kant, *Critique of Pure Reason* (A 346/B 404)." In *Proceedings of the American Philosophical Association* 44: 5–31.

Serequeberhan, T. 1996. "Eurocentrism in Philosophy: The Case of Immanuel Kant." *Philosophical Forum* 27: 333–356.

Shell, S. M. 2001. "Kant as Spectator: Notes on *Observations on the Feeling of the Beautiful and Sublime.*" In *New Essays in the Precritical Kant,* ed. T. Rockmore. Amherst, New York: Humanity. 66–85.

———. 1996. *The Embodiment of Reason: Kant on Spirit, Generation, and Community.* Chicago: University of Chicago Press.

Sherman, N. 1997. *Making a Necessity of Virtue: Aristotle and Kant on Virtue.* Cambridge: Cambridge University Press.

———. 1995. "Reasons and Feelings in Kantian Morality." *Philosophy and Phenomenological Research* 55: 369–377.

———. 1990. "The Place of Emotions in Kantian Morality." In *Identity, Character, and Morality,* ed. O. Flanagan and A. O. Rorty. Cambridge, Mass.: MIT Press. 158–170.

Siep, L. 1992. *Personbegriff und praktische Philosophie bei Locke, Kant und Hegel.* In *Praktische Philosophie im deutschen Idealismus.* Frankfurt am Main: Suhrkamp.

———. 1984. "Person and Law in Kant and Hegel." *Graduate Faculty Philosophy Journal* 10, no. 1: 63–85.

Silverman, H., and G. Aylesworth. (eds.) 1990. *The Textual Sublime.* Albany: SUNY Press.

Smith, N. K. 1941. *The Philosophy of David Hume.* London: Macmillan.

Strawson, P. 1966. *The Bounds of Sense: An Essay on Kant's Critique of Pure Reason.* London: Methuen.

———. 1959. *Individuals: An Essay in Descriptive Metaphysics.* London: Methuen.

Sturma, D. 1998."Die Paralogismen der reinen Vernunft in der zweiten Auflage (B 406–432; A 381–405)." In *Kritik der reinen Vernunft,* ed. G. Mohr and M. Willaschek. Berlin: Akademie Verlag. 391–412.

Taylor, C. 1995. "The Validity of Transcendental Arguments." In *Philosophical Arguments.* Cambridge, Mass.: Harvard University Press. 20–33.

Theunissen, M. 1966. "Skeptische Betrachtungen über den anthropologischen Personbegriff." In *Die Frage nach dem Menschen, Festschrift f. M. Müller.* Freiburg: Alber. 461–490.

Tonelli, G. 1959. "Von den verschiedenen Bedeutungen des Wortes Zweckmässigkeit in der Kritik der Urteilskraft." *Kant Studien* 49, no. 2: 154–166.

Trieb, tendance, instinct. Revue Germanique Internationale, no. 18. 2002. Paris: Presses Universitaires de France.

Tufts, J. H. 1896. "Refutation of Idealism in the *Lose Blätter*." *Philosophical Review* 5: 51–58.

Vaihinger, H. 1892. *Kommentar zu Kants Kritik der reinen Vernunft*, 2 vols. Stuttgart: Spemann, 1881–1892.

————. 1884. "Zu Kants Widerlegung des Idealismus." In *Strassburger Abhandlungen zur Philosophie. Festschrift für E. Zeller.* Tübingen: Mohr.

Van Kirk, C. 1986. "Kant on the Problem of Other Minds." *Kant Studien* 77: 41–58.

Vogel, J. 1993. "The Problem of Self-Knowledge in Kant's Refutation of Idealism: Two Recent Views." *Philosophy and Phenomenological Research* 53: 875–887.

Walford, D. 2001. "Towards an Interpretation of Kant's 1768 *Gegenden im Raume* Essay." *Kant Studien* 92: 407–439.

Walker, M. U. 1998. *Moral Understandings: A Feminist Study in Ethics.* New York: Routledge.

Watkins, E. 1998. "The Antinomy of Pure Reason, Sections 3–8 (A462/B490–A515/B543)." In *Kritik der reinen Vernunft,* ed. G. Mohr and M. Willaschek. Berlin: Akademie Verlag. 447–464.

————. 1995a. "The Development of Physical Influx in Early Eighteenth-Century Germany: Gottsched, Knutzen, and Crusius." *Review of Metaphysics* 49: 295–339.

————. 1995b. "Kant's Doctrine of Physical Influx." *Archiv für Geschichte der Philosophie* 77: 285–324.

Watson, S. 1997. *Tradition(s): Refiguring Community and Virtue in Classical German Thought.* Bloomington: Indiana University Press.

Waxman, W. 1999. "Kant's Psychologism I." *Kantian Review* 3: 41–63.

Weber, M. 1919. *Politik als Beruf.* Munich/Leipzig: Dunker & Humblot.

Welton, D. (ed.) 1999. *The Body.* Oxford: Blackwell.

Wiggins, D. 1980. "Deliberation and Practical Reason." In *Essays in Aristotle's Ethics,* ed. A. O. Rorty. Berkeley/Los Angeles: University of California Press. 221–240.

Wilson, C. 1997. "Discourses of Vision in Seventeenth-Century Metaphysics." In *Sites of Vision: The Discursive Construction of Sight in the History of Philosophy,* ed. D. M. Levin. Cambridge, Mass.: MIT Press. 117–138.

Wilson, H. L. 2006. *Kant's Pragmatic Anthropology.* Albany: SUNY Press.

Wolfe, C. (ed.) 2003. *Zoontologies: The Question of the Animal.* Minneapolis: University of Minnesota Press.

Wolff, M. 1992. *Das Körper-Seele-Problem, Kommentar zu Hegel, Enzyklopädie (1830), §389.* Frankfurt am Main: Vittorio Klostermann.

Wundt, M. 1924. *Kant als Metaphysiker.* Stuttgart: Enke.

Yolton, J. W. 1983. *Thinking Matter: Materialism in Eighteenth-Century Britain.* Minneapolis: University of Minnesota Press.

Young, I. M. 2003. "Lived Body vs. Gender: Reflections on Social Structure and Subjectivity." In *The Philosophy of the Body,* ed. M. Proudfoot. Oxford: Blackwell. 94–111.

————. 1990. *Throwing Like a Girl and Other Essays in Feminist Philosophy and Social Theory.* Bloomington: Indiana University Press.

Zammito, J. 2001. *Kant, Herder, and the Birth of Anthropology.* Chicago: University of Chicago Press.

Zeldin, B. 1980. "Pleasure, Life, and Mother-Wit." In *Freedom and the Critical Undertaking: Essays in Kant's Later Critique.* Ann Arbor: University Microfilms International. 116–139.

Zeltner, H. 1967. "Kants Begriff der Person." In *Tradition und Kritik, Festschrift f. R. Zocher.* Stuttgart: Frommann-Holzboog. 331–350.

Zoeller, G. 1992. "Lichtenberg and Kant on the Subject of Thinking." *Journal of the History of Philosophy* 30, no. 3: 417–441.

———. 1989. "From Innate to A Priori. Kant's Radical Transformation of a Cartesian-Leibnizian Legacy." *The Monist* 72: 222–235.

Zuckert, R. 2007. *Kant on Beauty and Biology: An Interpretation of the Critique of Judgment.* Cambridge: Cambridge University Press.

Index

Llewelyn, J., 325n18, 328n29, 335n51, 340n46,
	345n37, 357n107, 358n11, 360n44, 361n49
Lichtenberg, G. C., 341n71
life, 15–16, 74, 89–91, 120, 137–139, 149,
	165, 172, 174–175, 183, 217, 227–233, 237,
	240, 246, 261–262, 282, 284–287, 290–292,
	295–296, 298, 301, 304–305, 308–311, 326,
	342, 362, 370–371, 375–378, 380, 382, 385;
	after-life, 17, 95–96, 100, 105, 118, 165,
	192–193, 254, 295, 306; animal/human,
	251–254, 256–261, 306–307, 375–379, 381;
	experience of/in, 16–17, 228, 230–231,
	234, 238–239, 251–254, 259–261, 283, 288;
	lifeless, 377; present, 99–100, 226–228,
	234, 295–296, 369; principle of, 232, 261,
	282–283, 289–290; respect for, 376, 378. See
	also feeling, of life
Lingis, A., 13, 324n13, 325nn16,23, 327n16,
	329n51, 330n58, 336n61, 349n105,
	350nn12,21, 352n50, 355n81, 356n103,
	357n107, 358nn11,16, 360n44, 361n50,
	363n90, 370n24, 372n56, 375n103
living being, 227–234, 237, 249, 252–254, 283,
	285–287, 291–295, 301, 304, 306–307, 326,
	371, 372n56, 375–376. See also organism
Locke, J., 76, 231, 262–263, 267, 324n16,
	372n56, 378n156
Longuenesse, B., 332nn3,8, 336n61
Louden, R. B., 323n4, 358n11
Lovejoy, A., 370n22, 373n64
Lyotard, J.-F., 13, 325n23, 327n16, 328n26,
	344n24, 349n109, 356n100, 372n48,
	385n155, 386nn179,190

Makkreel, R. A., 326n30, 333n10, 345n37,
	362n66, 370n18, 371n36, 374n97,
	375nn107,113, 376n113, 378nn163,166,
	381n55, 385n170, 386n190
Marc-Wogau, K., 333n13
Marcel, G., 343n16
Marion, J.-L., 338nn83,84, 341n74
Marquard, A., 344n33
Martial, 367n28
Marx, K., 12, 320, 325n21, 383n99
materialism, 6, 47, 49, 90–91, 137, 227,
	230–231, 233–235, 240, 259, 295, 301, 352,
	372, 384
McFarland, J. D., 382n75
Meerbote, R., 337n66
Meier, G. F., 210, 367nn34,37
Meißner, H. A, 344n26
Mendelssohn, M., 52, 99, 131, 283, 328n34,
	334n25, 354n60, 357n115, 367n31, 382n91

Merleau-Ponty, M., 12–13, 318, 321,
	324nn7,12–14, 325nn16,21, 326n9,
	329nn51,52, 330n60, 333n12, 334n39,
	335n44, 336n61, 338n79, 353n54,
	358n11
Mertens, H., 353n60
metaphysics, metaphysical, 7, 12–13, 17, 24,
	28, 33–34, 45–53, 59, 61, 69–70, 72–80,
	85, 134, 199, 229, 232–234, 237–238,
	241, 259–260, 290, 292, 316, 318, 320,
	332, 338, 342, 351, 362, 365, 385; of mor-
	als, 80, 83, 125, 142. See also cosmology;
	psychology
Milhaud, G., 330n65
Mills, C., 324n6, 349n11
Mischel, T., 324n13
Mohanty, J. N., 324n13
Mohr, G., 350n19, 352n48, 364n100, 365n119
Montaigne, M. de, 372n46
mortality, 261, 306–312, 319
motive, 11, 16, 141–148, 150, 157, 166–167,
	176, 179, 186, 189, 263, 359; empirical, 131,
	144, 151, 158–159, 169, 177, 184, 263, 297,
	362; pure, 129–131, 145, 158, 177. See also
	determination, ground of; Triebfeder
Munzel, F., 347n78, 348n87
Murray Turbayne, C., 337n70

Nancy, J.-L., 315–316, 319, 351n21, 386n2
natural products, 247, 286–291
nature, 61, 101, 118, 120, 123, 131, 140, 151,
	161, 179, 183, 187, 190, 215–217, 227, 229,
	235, 237, 245, 252, 262, 271–289, 292–293,
	295, 297, 305–314, 320–321, 373, 375–376,
	379–382, 385; "elemental," 375; in gen-
	eral, 236–237, 240, 264, 270, 284; living,
	230, 235–237, 241, 245, 261, 272–273, 277,
	283, 286, 288–295, 302, 306–308, 372, 383;
	in material sense, 31–32; organic, 199,
	283, 288–296 (see also organism); power
	of (Macht), 308–311; purposive order of,
	216–217, 219, 302–308, 381; system of,
	237–240, 242, 283–289, 291–295, 298–299,
	371–372, 381, 384. See also cause; human,
	nature; life; purpose, Naturzweck; super-
	sensible; world
need, Bedürfnis, 133–135, 137–138, 240–244,
	274, 288, 293, 351–352; being of need, 295
Nerlich, G., 326n1, 331n74
Newton, I., 35, 231, 237, 329n45
Nietzsche, F., 12, 325n21
Nobbe, F., 377n139
Nussbaum, M. C., 358n11

Swedenborg, E., 53, 56, 58, 64, 68, 73, 82, 84, 89, 166, 252, 316, 334n25, 352n47
symbol, symbolic, 288, 363
system, 237–240, 242, 283, 285, 287–289, 291, 371–372, 381, 385. *See also* nature

taste, *Geschmack,* 15, 29–30, 174, 200, 203–204, 206, 208–214, 219–220, 225, 243, 246–247, 257, 272, 282, 366, 368–369, 380; judgment of, *Geschmacksurteil,* 245–247, 250, 254–256, 266–267, 299, 366, 372, 374, 376–377 (*see also* faculty of judgment, aesthetic)
Tauler, J., 365n4
Taylor, C., 324n14, 326n5
technical, technique, 239, 245, 267, 270–271, 279, 288–289, 291–292; nature's, 298–299; technical-practical, 287–288, 296
teleology, teleological, 245, 247, 370, 380; anti-teleological, 371–372, 384–385; moral, 296, 300–303, 369–370, 383–386; physical, 300–303, 383. *See also* faculty of judgment, teleological
temperaments, 349
Tetens, J. N., 106, 344n32, 354n60, 367n31
theology, moral/ethico-, 235, 273, 300–301, 305–306, 308, 381
Theunissen, M., 365n113
thing in itself, *Ding an sich,* 31, 33, 41–43, 62, 64–65, 78, 89, 113, 124, 153, 176, 272, 346, 380
Thomasius, C., 208–209, 367n28
time, 12–15, 25, 31–32, 48, 59–62, 66–68, 76, 85, 110, 113–114, 118–119, 124, 149–154, 163, 176, 178–179, 184–185, 187–192, 203–204, 225, 252, 284, 314, 324, 327–330, 335–339, 345, 346, 356, 361, 364, 368, 370. *See also* sense, inner; space
Tiresias, 352n46
transcendental, 1–4, 7–11, 17, 30, 38, 56, 61, 91, 110–115, 125–126, 140, 142, 148, 155, 158, 160, 162–164, 175, 177, 181–185, 199–201, 204, 206, 213–215, 218–219, 229–230, 233, 235, 239–240, 247–252, 254, 256–257, 265–268, 270–272, 274–275, 279, 282–283, 285–286, 289–290, 292–293, 297, 300, 306–311, 323–324, 341, 343, 348–353, 358–359, 362–363, 365, 370, 372–373, 374–375, 377, 383–385; principle, 239–240, 243–244, 248, 257, 259. *See also* embodiment; freedom; idealism; philosophy
transition, *Übergang,* 274–277, 279–280, 303, 353

Triebfeder, elater animi, drive, 11, 155, 157, 160–173, 181–185, 297, 358–361, 364; moral law/reason as, 164–110, 167–173, 175, 189–190, 214, 239
Tufts, J. H., 337n66

understanding, *Verstand,* 2–3, 16, 27–28, 31–32, 35, 43, 48–49, 58, 61–63, 70, 88, 90–91, 97–98, 107–110, 119–120, 142, 146, 202–204, 209–210, 216, 220–222, 235–240, 243, 245, 247, 249, 252, 256, 262–265, 267, 269–274, 279–281, 288, 327, 344–345, 348, 366, 371, 375, 377, 380, 386; *intellectus,* 77–78, 339; intuitive, 108. *See also* concepts; spontaneity, of thinking/understanding

Vaihinger, H., 326n9, 331n65, 337n66
value, 301–302, 304, 306–308, 377, 383
Van Kirk, C., 365n116
visible. *See* body, physical/'visible'
Vogel, J., 337n66
Voltaire, F.-M. A., 96, 370n28

Wagner, F., 106
Walford, D., 326n9, 329n38
Walker, M. U., 356n103
Watkins, E., 334n29, 345n52
Watson, S. H., 347n76
Waxman, W., 333n10
Weber, M., 323n3, 350n12
Weil, E., 349n7
Welton, D., 325n21
Weltwesen, 297–298, 300–306. *See also* human, being (*Mensch*)
Whitehead, A. N., 324n7
will, 11, 13, 15, 51–52, 105–106, 113–118, 121–122, 131, 142–151, 153–155, 159–161, 164, 166–170, 176–181, 183–193, 222, 257, 263, 308, 313, 361, 363–364, 370, 383; holy, 14–15, 115, 125, 142, 149, 155, 164–166, 168, 171–172, 207, 217, 297, 346–347, 356, 360; human, 168–169, 171–172, 207, 346–347, 360; rational, 14, 167–169; *Wille/Willkür,* 166, 190–191, 361. *See also* arbitrium; deliberation; determination
Wilson, C., 351n31
Windelband, W., 328n25
Wizenmann, T., 352n41
Wolff, C., 28, 32, 48, 53–56, 59, 69, 73, 77, 79–80, 89, 98, 105–107, 111, 114, 125, 142, 145, 160, 197–198, 206, 276, 328n36, 333n15, 334nn27,28, 344nn27–29,35,

ANGELICA NUZZO

is Professor of Philosophy at the Graduate Center and Brooklyn College (City University of New York). She has received a Mellon Fellowship at the Center for the Humanities, CUNY, Graduate Center (2007–2008), an Alexander von Humboldt Fellowship (2005–2006), and been a Fellow at the Radcliffe Institute for Advanced Studies at Harvard (2000–2001). Among her publications are *Kant and the Unity of Reason* (2005), two volumes on Hegel (*Logica e sistema,* 1992; *Rappresentazione e concetto nella logica della Filosofia del diritto,* 1990), and the monograph *System* (2003). Her numerous essays on German Idealism, modern philosophy, and theory of translation appear in such journals as the *Journal of the History of Philosophy, Metaphilosophy, Journal of Philosophy and Social Criticism, Hegel Studien,* and *Fichte Studien.*

Printed and bound by CPI Group (UK) Ltd, Croydon, CR0 4YY

09/06/2025

14685944-0001